# Visual Attention

*Edited by Richard D. Wright*

D0017475

Vancouver Studies in Cognitive Science is a series of volumes in cognitive science. The volumes will appear annually and cover topics relevant to the nature of the higher cognitive faculties as they appear in cognitive systems, either human or machine. These will include such topics as natural language processing, modularity, the language faculty, perception, logical reasoning, scientific reasoning, and social interaction. The topics and authors are to be drawn from philosophy, linguistics, artificial intelligence, and psychology. Each volume will contain original articles by scholars from two or more of these disciplines. The core of the volumes will be articles and comments on these articles to be delivered at a conference held in Vancouver. The volumes will be supplemented by articles especially solicited for each volume, and will undergo peer review. The volumes should be of interest to those in philosophy working in philosophy of mind and philosophy of language; to those in linguistics in psycholinguistics, syntax, language acquisition and semantics; to those in psychology in psycholinguistics, cognition, perception, and learning; and to those in computer science in artificial intelligence, computer vision, robotics, natural language processing, and scientific reasoning.

## Vancouver Studies in Cognitive Science

*Forthcoming volumes*

Volume 9    *Colour Perception: Philosophical, Psychological,*
*Artistic, and Computational Perspectives*
Editor, Brian Funt
School of Computing Science
Simon Fraser University

Volume 10   *Metarepresentations: A Multidisciplinary Perspective*
Editor, Dan Sperber
CNRS and
CREA, Ecole Polytechnique, Paris

# Visual Attention

edited by Richard D. Wright

*New York   Oxford*
OXFORD UNIVERSITY PRESS
1998

# Oxford University Press

Oxford  New York
Athens  Auckland  Bangkok  Bogotá  Buenos Aires  Calcutta
Cape Town  Chennai  Dar es Salaam  Delhi  Florence  Hong Kong  Istanbul
Karachi  Kuala Lumpur  Madrid  Melbourne  Mexico City  Mumbai  Nairobi
Paris  São Paulo  Singapore  Taipei  Tokyo  Toronto  Warsaw

and associated companies in
Berlin  Ibadan

## Copyright 1998 by Oxford University Press, Inc.

Published by Oxford University Press, Inc.,
198 Madison Avenue, New York, NY 10016

Oxford is a registered trademark of Oxford University Press

**Library of Congress Cataloging-in-Publication Data**
Visual attention / edited by Richard D. Wright.
     p.   cm. -- (Vancouver studies in cognitive science: v. 8)
     Includes bibliographical references.
     ISBN 0-19-512692-0 (alk. paper).  -- ISBN 0-19-512693-9 (pbk.: alk. paper)
     1. Visual perception.   I. Wright, Richard D., 1956–  .  II. Series.
BF241.V55   1998
152.14--dc21                                        98-28395
                                                        CIP

Printing 9 8 7 6 5 4 3 2 1

Printed in Canada
on acid-free paper

# Acknowledgments

This project was supported by grants from the Social Science and Humanities Research Council of Canada, and the Publications Committee and Office of the Vice-President Academic of Simon Fraser University. Thanks are due to Steven Davis, Lindsey Thomas Martin and Eleanor O'Donnell of Simon Fraser University for putting the book together, and to Christian Richard of the University of British Columbia for creating many of its figures. Thanks also to Lawrence Ward of the University of British Columbia for his moral support throughout the project. And most of all, a special thanks to the following people for taking the time to carefully review the chapters in this book.

*Roger Blackman*, Simon Fraser University

*Darlene Brodeur*, Acadia University

*Thomas Carr*, Michigan State University

*Patrick Cavanagh*, Harvard University

*Kyle Cave*, Vanderbilt University

*Howard Egeth*, Johns Hopkins University

*John Findlay*, University of Durham

*Charles Folk*, Villanova University

*Steven Hillyard*, University of California, San Diego

*Bruce Hood*, Massachusetts Institute of Technology

*Keith Humphrey*, University of Western Ontario

*Glynn Humphreys*, University of Birmingham

*Martin Jüttner*, University of Munich

*Chris Koch*, George Fox College

*Steven Luck*, University of Iowa

*Colin MacLeod*, University of Toronto

*Maritta Maltio-Laine*, University of Helsinki

*Michael Masson*, University of Victoria

*Bruce Milliken*, McMaster University

*Vito Modigliani*, Simon Fraser University

*Todd Mondor*, Mount Allison University

*Hermann Müller*, Birkbeck College, University of London

*Michael Posner*, University of Oregon

*Robert Rafal*, University of California, Davis

*David Robinson*, National Eye Institute, Maryland

*Charles Spence*, University of Cambridge

*Lew Stelmach*, CRC, Ottawa

*Anne Treisman*, Princeton University

*Jan van Gisbergen*, University of Nijmegen

*Michael von Grünau*, Concordia University

*Lawrence Ward*, University of British Columbia

*Robert Ward*, University of Wales

*Steven Yantis*, Johns Hopkins University

# Contents

# Contributors

*Nancy J. Beach*, Department of Psychology
  University of Iowa

*Brian J. Compton*, Department of Psychology
  University of Illinois

*Burkhart Fischer*, Department of Biophysics,
  University of Freiburg

*Gina Gerardi*, Department of Psychology
  University of Oregon

*Narly Golestani*, Department of Psychology
  McGill University

*Gary Hatfield*, Department of Philosophy,
  University of Pennsylvania

*Glyn W. Humphreys*, Department of Psychology
  University of Birmingham

*David LaBerge*, Department of Cognitive Sciences
  University of California, Irvine

*Gordon D. Logan*, Department of Psychology,
  University of Illinois

*Steven J. Luck*, Department of Psychology,
  University of Iowa

*Arien Mack*, Department of Psychology,
  New School for Social Research

*John J. McDonald*, Department of Psychology
  University of British Columbia

*Hermann J. Müller*, Department of Psychology,
  Birkbeck College, University of London

*Andrew C. Olsen*, School of Psychology
  University of Birmingham

*John Palmer*, Department of Psychology,
  University of Washington

*Michael I. Posner*, Department of Psychology,
   University of Oregon

*Zenon Pylyshyn*, Center for Cognitive Science,
   Rutgers University

*Christian M. Richard*, Department of Psychology
   Simon Fraser University

*Irvin Rock*, Department of Psychology
   University of California, Berkeley

*Mary K. Rothbart*, Department of Psychology
   University of Oregon

*Kimron Shapiro*, Department of Psychology,
   University of Wales, Bangor

*Kathleen Terry*, Department of
   University of Wales, Bangor

*Steven P. Tipper*, Department of Psychology,
   University of Wales, Bangor

*Lisa Thomas-Thrapp*, Department of Psychology
   University of Oregon

*Anne Treisman*, Department of Psychology,
   Princeton University

*Lawrence M. Ward*, Department of Psychology,
   University of British Columbia

*Bruce Weaver*, Department of Psychology
   University of Wales, Bangor

*Richard D. Wright*, Department of Psychology,
   Simon Fraser University

*Steven Yantis*, Department of Psychology,
   Johns Hopkins University

# Visual Attention

# 1

## Attention in Early Scientific Psychology

### Gary Hatfield

Attention is a salient feature of human mentality, at least in its conscious manifestations. Yet attention became a central topic in psychology only recently by comparison with such areas as sensory perception, imagination, or memory. Descriptions of the chief characteristics of attention were built up from classical antiquity to the seventeenth century. But attention first became a chapter heading in standard psychology textbooks during the 1730s.

This chronology has an air of paradox about it because it dates the entrance of attention into psychology prior to the commonly accepted dates for the origin of psychology itself. The origin of natural scientific psychology is now typically dated to 1879, or to sometime in the two preceding decades. This dating reflects a certain perspective on "natural scientific psychology" that equates it with the experimental psychology of Wundt and Titchener. If one takes a broader perspective, permitting the definitions of the terms "natural science" and "psychology" to vary across the historical past (according to their interpretation by past thinkers), then natural scientific psychology has a much longer history than is suggested by Ebbinghaus's celebrated phrase contrasting a "short history" with a "long past" (1908, p. 1).

It is from the perspective of this longer history that attention achieves chapter status in psychology textbooks only recently. Part 1 sets this entrance, by sketching the historical contexts in which psychology has been considered to be a natural science. Part 2 traces the construction of phenomenological descriptions of attention, and then compares selected theoretical and empirical developments in the study of attention over three time slices: mid-eighteenth century, turn of the nineteenth century, and late twentieth century. We shall find significant descriptive, theoretical, and empirical continuity when these developments are considered in the large. This continuity is open to several interpretations, including the view that attention research shows long-term convergence because it is conditioned by the basic structure of attention as a natural phenomenon. The less optimistic view would hold that theory making in at least this area of psychology has been remarkably conservative when considered under large-grain resolution, consisting in the reshuffling of a few core ideas.

## Attention and the Origin of Psychology as a Natural Science

The historical development of psychology as a natural science has not been treated adequately in contemporary histories of psychology. From the time of Boring (1929, 1950), such histories primarily have served the function of providing a strong identity for the discipline of experimental psychology. Boring and his followers (e.g., Schultz & Schultz, 1987) have thus celebrated "foundings" and "founders," rather than explicitly posing and thoroughly investigating the question of whether scientific psychology should be seen as deriving primarily from the experimental psychology of Wundt and Titchener.

### From Psyche to Mind

If psychology is considered in its root meaning, as the "science of the soul" (*logon peri tes psyches*), then it has been an autonomous discipline from the time of Aristotle's treatise *De Anima*. In Aristotelian terms, the literal meaning of the word psychology is the science of the soul (*psyche*), which was considered to be a vital or animating principle, and hence to possess the so-called vegetative powers such as nutrition and growth. When psychology is so understood, the study of the soul's cognitive powers, including sense, imagination, memory, and intellect, is a subdiscipline of it. Within this Aristotelian subdiscipline, the emphasis was on providing a taxonomy of the cognitive powers, and of characterizing the physical or qualitative relation between object properties and sensory states that represent those properties. Study of the soul itself fell under the umbrella discipline of physics, considered as the science of nature in general, but this fact carried no materialistic or reductionistic implications. Paradoxically, from our point of view, quantitative investigations of vision, including discussions of the perception of size and distance, were carried out in the distinct discipline of optics, which did not fall under physics and whose subject matter was understood to be the complete "theory of vision" (Hatfield, 1995).

In the course of the seventeenth century, the dominant Aristotelian conception of the soul was replaced, primarily, by Cartesian dualism. Descartes effectively equated soul with mind. He consequently redrew the line between body and soul, so that the functions of the vegetative soul were assigned to purely material processes, the sensory functions were attributed to mind and body conjointly, and purely cognitive (and volitional) functions were assigned to the mind alone (Hatfield, 1992). Although this turn toward dualism is well known, less well known is that Descartes and his dualistic followers considered the immaterial mind to be a part of nature (Hatfield, 1994). In particular, the influential Cartesians Le Grand (1694) and Regis (1691) explicitly placed the study of mental operations, including sense, imagination, and memory, under the rubric of "physics" (again conceived as the science of nature in general). The notorious Cartesian interest in clear and distinct perception elicited several analyses of the phenomenology of cognition, and featured the role of attention in the act of judgment, especially in cases of allegedly self-evident cognition (Berlyne, 1974).

## Attention in the Independent Discipline of Psychology

During the eighteenth century "psychology," understood as the science of the mind, was founded as an independent discipline. Professorships in psychology were established, textbooks were published, journals were started. As it happens, none of the chief practitioners of this new science of mind were materialists or reductionists: they were either dualists or were agnostic on ontology, adopting a position sometimes described as "empirical dualism" (Schmid, 1796). They sought "laws of the mind" by analogy with Newton's laws of motion. Among the proposed laws, the most widely accepted were the famous laws of association (such as the associative law of simultaneity, or that of resemblance). Other explicitly stated laws pertained to memory: Christian Wolff, who apparently coined the word "psychometrics" (1738, §522, p. 403), proposed that "goodness of memory" can be estimated by such quantitative factors as: the temporal latency of response to a memory demand, the number of tries it takes to retrieve an item from memory, and the number of acts it takes to fix an item in memory (1738, §191, p. 131); however, none of these tests were operationalized in his textbook. Wolff (1740) also formulated several generalizations concerning attention. One described an inverse relation between the intensity of attention and the extent of the cognitive material that can be brought under it: the greater the attention, the smaller the part of the visual field to which it extends (§360). Another contended that, with equally distributed attention, that part of a whole which otherwise is cognized most clearly will come to the fore (§367). A third suggested that conscious attention serves the process of combining spatial representations and temporal processes into spatially and temporally ordered wholes (§§380–5). Several of these generalizations concerning memory and attention are formulated as proportions, but they were not accompanied by quantitative data to support this relation.

Wolff's discussions of attention mark its introduction into psychology as a major topic. Comparison of the standard chapter headings from textbooks treating psychological topics supports this claim. In

Table 1, a summary of main topics from the seventeenth-century works in the Aristotelian and Cartesian traditions is compared with a summary derived from surveying standard textbooks from around the end of the nineteenth century (Ebbinghaus, 1911; James, 1890; Ladd, 1895; Wundt, 1874). Many of the topic areas are identical or closely equivalent: the external senses, the physiology of nervous processes, the control of bodily motion, higher cognition, and appetite and will. But within one area there was considerable change. Authors in the Aristotelian tradition, and immediate subsequent authors as well, recognized "internal senses" in addition to the traditional five "external senses." The "internal senses" included memory and imagination, as well as other cognitive powers or capacities. Nineteenth-century works continue to have chapters on memory and on imagination, but they contain two new chapters in comparison with the seventeenth century: chapters on association and on attention. The latter topics received only scattered treatment in the seventeenth century, in connection with other headings, including the senses, reasoning, and judgment. Wolff (1738) has a chapter on "attention and reflection," and his (1740) has one on "attention and intellect." Other works soon appeared with separate sections on attention, including Bonnet (1755, chap. 38) and Abel (1786/1985, pp. 81–106).

| *On Soul or Mind* (seventeenth century) | *Psychology* (1874–1911) |
| --- | --- |
| External Senses | External Senses |
| Neural Structures and Processes | Neural Structures and Processes |
| Internal Senses:<br>  Memory and Imagination | Memory and Imagination<br>Attention<br>Laws of Association |
| Higher Cognition:<br>  Judgment and Reasoning<br>  Bodily Motion<br>  Appetite and Will | Higher Cognition:<br>  Judgment and Reasoning<br>  Bodily Motion<br>  Appetite and Will |

*Table 1. Standard Psychological Topics in Textbooks.* Comparison of standard topics in textbooks treating psychological topics in the seventeenth century and in the period 1874–1911. Attention and Laws of Association appear in the latter but not the former. Category labels signify topical areas that may be named otherwise in the original textbook. Only the main common areas are shown.

Any adequate explanation of the increased attention to attention in the eighteenth century would have to trace the discussion forward from seventeenth-century treatises on logic and mind. It is already known that impetus was given to the investigation of both attention itself and the empirical conditions in which it is exercised by the Cartesian doctrine that knowledge consists in clear and distinct ideas (Berlyne, 1974). Clarity and distinctness, as understood in this tradition, are phenomenal characteristics. One recognizes clarity and distinctness, and even increases it, by paying attention to one's ideas. Descartes (1642) brought clarity and distinctness to the forefront of his own analyses of knowledge and cognition. The authors of the Port Royal *Logic* drew upon this analysis (Arnauld & Nicole, 1683, II.19., pp. 343, 363; VI.6, p. 422), and Malebranche (1980, I.18, VI.1.2–VI.2.1; pp. 79–81, 411–439) extended it greatly.

Careful study of the origin of attention as a topic in psychology would require a fuller examination of the development of psychology itself. At present, we have little knowledge of the development of either the theoretical or experimental side of psychology prior to the latter part of the nineteenth century. This means that we are lacking a good assessment of the relative roles of theory and experiment in the early development of psychology as an empirically based science. Although it is no doubt true that new experimental techniques were introduced to psychology in the latter half of the nineteenth century, it is also true that the extant theoretical formulations show significant continuity with the early nineteenth and even the eighteenth centuries. Part 2 considers both empirical and theoretical continuity in the history of the psychology of attention.

## History of Research and Thinking on Attention

Titchener (1908) credits the new "experimental psychology" with three achievements, the third being "the discovery of attention": "What I mean by the 'discovery' of attention is the explicit formulation of the problem; the recognition of its separate status and fundamental importance; the realisation that the doctrine of attention is the nerve of the whole psychological system, and that as men judge of it, so shall they be judged before the tribunal of psychology" (1908, p. 173). Titchener's claim about the "discovery" of attention becomes less interesting if we focus on the rhetorical excesses of the third point, that "discovery" implies bringing attention to the centre of the "whole psychological system." If we just consider the first two points, Titchener's claim is clearly false: attention was noticed and discussed in the ancient and medieval worlds, and, as we have seen, had been introduced into the discipline of psychology by the 1730s. These developments can conveniently be traced under the rubrics of *phenomenological* descriptions of attention, *theoretical* analyses, and *empirical* investigations.

## Phenomenological Descriptions of Attention

Neumann (1971) surveys the introduction of various descriptive or phenomenological characteristics of attention across the span of Greek, Roman, and European thought. His remarkable results, summarized in Table 2, indicate that the primary attributes of attention had been recorded by the seventeenth century. We need not endorse his taxonomy of attention fully; although it provides a reasonably comprehensive description of the conscious manifestations of attention, his taxonomy also mixes the nonphenomenal category of "effector sensitivity" with descriptive categories, and it fails to note phenomenal reports of involuntary shifts of attention as a descriptive category (an added item in Table 2). Nor should we suppose that in every case Neumann is correct in identifying the "first" mention of each of these aspects (often he is not). His findings provide a listing of early descriptions of the main conscious or phenomenal manifestations of attention, showing that the main features had been recorded by the seventeenth century, at the latest. We shall consider these attributes one by one.

| Descriptive Aspect | Neumann | Hatfield |
|---|---|---|
| Narrowing | Aristotle | Aristotle |
| Active Directing | Lucretius | Lucretius |
| Involuntary Shifts | ——— | Augustine |
| Clarity | Buridan | Aristotle/Lucretius |
| Fixation over Time | Descartes | Descartes |
| Effector Sensitivity | Descartes | Lucretius |
| Motivational Aspect | Leibniz | Augustine |

*Table 2. Phenomenological Descriptions of Attention.* Early occurrences of phenomenological descriptions of various aspects of attention as reported by Neumann (1971) and found by Hatfield in the present study. Neumann does not include Involuntary Shifts as a category of phenomenological description. Neumann's original German terms are provided in the discussion.

*Narrowing (Engeaspekt)*    This first aspect of attention attributes to it a narrow scope, such that stimuli are in competition to be perceived.

Neumann attributes this observation to Aristotle, who did not speak explicitly of attention, but who raised the following question about sense perception: "assuming, as is natural, that of two movements the stronger always tends to extrude the weaker, is it possible or not that one should be able to perceive two objects simultaneously in the same individual time?" (1984, chap. 7, 447a11–14). That Aristotle had in mind the phenomena of attention is made clear when he continues: "The above assumption explains why persons do not perceive what is brought before their eyes, if they are at the time deep in thought, or in a fright, or listening to some loud noise." Aristotle accepts the assumption that the stronger sensory stimulus does indeed tend to extrude the weaker, but he does not conclude that therefore two objects cannot be perceived simultaneously. For, he observes, we can perceive white and sweet at the same time (449a11–19). He seems to have held, however, that only one object is perceived at one time by the same sense (e.g., vision). But in this case, the presence of weaker stimuli affects the distinctness with which the stronger one is perceived: "If, then, the greater movement tends to expel the less, it necessarily follows that, when they occur, this greater should itself too be less distinctly perceptible than if it were alone" (447a22–24). In any event, Aristotle fixed the question of whether there can be a single perceptual response to simultaneous stimuli, and hence of the scope of sensory awareness, in the literature of psychology for subsequent millennia.

*Active Directing (Taetigkeitsaspekt)*    Neumann attributes to Lucretius, in the first century B.C., the observation that human cognizers actively direct attention. Lucretius made two related points regarding the phenomenology of the mind's activity in sense perception. First, he observed that things are not seen sharply, "save those for which the mind has prepared itself" (1965/1967, IV.803–804). Thus, "do you not see that our eyes, when they begin to look at something that is tenuous, make themselves intent (*contendere*) and ready, and that, unless they do this, it is not possible for us to see clearly (*cernere acute*)?" (IV.808–810). Intentness and readiness, clearly activities of mind and not simply external orientings of the sense organs, result in some things being seen rather than, or more clearly than, others. But, second, the mind can alter its perception of things already at hand by directing its perception: "Even in things that are plainly visible you can note that if you do not direct the mind (*advertas animum*), the things are, so to speak, far removed and remote for the whole time" (IV.811–813). Consequently, Lucretius calls for "attentive (*attenta*) ears and mind" when he gives a long explanation (VI.920). In both of the cases described, the mind (*animus*) actively directs (*advertere*) its perceiving toward objects of perception, whether these objects are merely anticipated (first case), or are present at the time. This "active directing" clearly implies the *voluntary* preparation of or direction of the mind in attending to objects of perception, and in the anticipatory case, is an early description of a *priming effect* (Johnston & Dark, 1987), though Lucretius did not use either of the italicized terms.

Though Aristotle did not use cognates for "attention" and Lucretius did so rarely, several cognate terms were entrenched in Latin vocabulary by the middle of the first century B.C. These included *attentio* and related words, *intentio*, straining or directing the mind toward something or concentrating the mind on something, and *animadversio*, turning the mind toward, noticing something (Glare, 1982, pp. 132–133, 200, 938). In the middle of the first century B.C., Cicero used these words regularly in his writings, including his work on oration, in which he, for example, opined that "with verse equal attention (*attendere*) is given to the beginning and middle and end of a line" (Cicero, trans. 1968, III.192). The Greek word for attention, *prosektikon*, apparently became common as the name of a faculty only with the writings of John Philoponus in the sixth century A.D. (see Hamilton, 1895, p. 945).

*Involuntary Shifts*    Neumann credits Augustine of Hippo (A.D. 354–430) with fixing terms cognate with "attention" (*attentio, intentio*) into the technical vocabulary used to analyze cognition. In a work on music, Augustine discusses the role of attention or alertness in perception generally (1969, VI.5.9), and in the perception of musical phrases (VI.8.20–21). He describes the functioning of attention in religious experience (1991/1992), including cases in which attention is to be voluntarily directed (1991/1992, III.11.19, X.40.65), and he recognizes that attention can be drawn involuntarily. Augustine describes not only cases in which one is drawn toward objects of sensory pleasure, but also those in which objects of cognitive interest "tug at" one's attention (1991/1992, X.35.56). Augustine thus described involuntary shifts in attention (without using the term "involuntary"), implicitly contrasting them with cases of voluntary control.

*Clarity (Klarheitsaspekt)*    Neumann credits Jean Buridan (14th c.) with the observation that simultaneous apprehension of more than one object decreases the clarity with which any of them is represented. Passages quoted above show that a relation between attention and clarity had been suggested earlier by Aristotle and Lucretius. Buridan (1518) presented a more varied description of this relation, using the terms "perfection" and "distinctness" to describe the dimension of perceptual cognition affected by stimulus plurality. Where Aristotle observed that the simultaneous presence of several objects reduces the clarity with which the "strongest" alone is perceived, and where Lucretius noted that attention or mental preparedness can increase clarity of perception, Buridan remarked that the relation between distinctness and plurality varies. For a single object that is very large and wide, a lesser part of it is clearly visible though the whole is not, because it extends beyond of the field of view. But for a middle-sized object near at hand, the whole may well be more clearly perceived than its many parts. And in some cases, though we perceive the presence of many objects, we perceive them less clearly than if only one of them were present (Buridan, 1518, qu. 21, fol. 39v).

*Fixation (Fixierungsaspekt)* In the seventeenth century, Descartes (1596–1650) described more fully the *Taetigkeitsaspekt* of attention by clearly distinguishing between the voluntary fixation of attention and involuntary shifts. As had Augustine, Descartes noted that attention may be involuntarily drawn to things. He described cases in which attention is drawn to what is novel, a phenomenon he attributed to the emotion of wonder: "Wonder is a sudden surprise of the soul which brings it to consider with attention the objects that seem to it unusual and extraordinary" (1985, §70). In such cases, attention is not under voluntary control, but is simply drawn to the novel thing. The mind can, all the same, choose to stay fixed on one object: "when we want to fix our attention for some time on some particular object," this volition causes physiological changes that maintain the relevant physiological state of the brain (§43), and that "serve to keep the sense organs fixed in the same orientation so that they will continue to maintain the impression in the way in which they formed it" (§70). We can also voluntarily fix our attention on mental contents in order better to remember something (§75). Finally, the mind or soul can avoid noticing some new things by fixing attention on others: "The soul can prevent itself from hearing a slight noise or feeling a slight pain by attending very closely to some other thing, but it cannot in the same way prevent itself from hearing thunder or feeling fire that burns the hand" (§46). Descartes here posits a balance between the power of fixation and the strength of involuntary changes in attention. He indicates that within limits we can retain our fixation, but that these limits can be surpassed by loud stimuli, and presumably by strikingly novel stimuli. Malebranche added that it is functionally appropriate that sensory materials should attract our attention, because "the senses represent objects as present," and "it is fitting that of several good or evils proposed to the soul, those present should affect and occupy it more than absent ones, because the soul must decide quickly what it should do about them" (Malebranche,

1980, I.18, pp. 79–80). The positions of Descartes and Malebranche pre-suppose a limited span of consciousness (*Engeaspekt*), the contents of which are subject to alteration by voluntary or involuntary shifts in attention (see also Locke, 1975, II.19.3).

Later authors, including Wolff (1738, §237) and Stewart (1793, p. 113), describe cases in which a cognizer can track one phenomenon, such as a conversation, while ignoring other sensory objects. Stewart argues that the ability to switch at will between two present conversations implies that the untracked conversation must be represented:

> When two persons are speaking to us at once, we can attend to either of them at pleasure, without being much disturbed by the other. If we attempt to listen to both, we can understand neither. The fact seems to be, that when we attend constantly to one of the speakers, the words spoken by the other make no impression on the memory, in consequence of our not attending to them; and affect us as little as if they had not been uttered. This power, however, of the mind to attend to either speaker at pleasure, supposes that it is, at one and the same time, conscious of the sensations which both produce (Stewart, 1793, p. 113).

Stewart's suggestion that the unattended conversation is still present in consciousness, though unnoticed, is related to the more recent distinction between automatic and controlled processing in relation to selective attention (Johnston & Dark, 1987). Stewart (1793, chap. 2) discusses a version of the latter distinction at great length in connection with the role of attention in memory fixation, and in connection with the conscious, voluntary control of cognitive or motor tasks that later become habitual or automatic (though he counsels against use of the latter term).

The ability to track either of two conversations implies the ability to shift attention without an accompanying change in the orientation or direction of the body or sense organs. Such a possibility was implied by earlier descriptions, from Aristotle on, of cases in which a person does not notice what is in front of him or her: in those cases, a person might attend to first one sequence of thoughts and then another, or switch from internal reverie to attend to a sound, while the gaze remains fixed (and blank). Wolff (1738, §256) provides the first explicit notice I have found of the ability to shift visual attention among the parts of a fixed perceptual representation without changing the total representation. He describes perceiving a whole tree (presumably in one glance, standing at some distance), and then shifting attention from leaves to branches to trunk; or perceiving a single leaf, and shifting attention from its shape to its colour. It is not clear from these descriptions that Wolff envisaged a genuine decoupling of attention from the axis of vision, and he elsewhere maintained that the two are strongly coupled (1740, §§358–364).

*Effector Sensitivity (Effektorischer Aspekt)*   The effectoric aspect attributes to attention the power of making it "easier" for the sense organs (or effectors) to receive an impression. There are two factors here that should be kept distinct. Originally, some thinkers observed that one can prepare to perceive an expected object, through mental concentration and by pointing mobile sense organs, such as the eyes, in the proper direction. Although Neumann credits this observation to Descartes, it can be found much earlier in Lucretius's remark about intentness and readiness, quoted above. A second effectoric aspect arises with the hypothesis that attention can affect the sensitivity of the sensory receptors or nerves themselves. Strictly speaking, this is not merely a phenomenal-descriptive aspect of attention, because it posits hypothetical physiological changes in sensory receptors or nerves to explain how attention affects sensory acuteness (otherwise, the *Effektorischer Aspekt* would not differ from the *Klarheitsaspekt*). This hypothesis about effector sensitivity is not found in the passage Neumann cites from Descartes (§70) nor elsewhere in Descartes's works; Descartes simply claims that fixation of attention can keep the sense organs steadily pointed at a target object.

Specific mention of heightened sensitivity in the sensory nerves is found in the eighteenth-century work of Charles Bonnet (1720–1793), a Swiss naturalist. Bonnet (1769) described a situation in which he was paying attention to one object among several, each of which he assumed to be simultaneously affecting the sense organs with equal force: "Induced by some motive to give my attention to one of these objects, I fix my eyes on it. The perception of that object immediately becomes more lively: the perceptions of the neighboring objects become weaker. Soon I discover particularities in that object that previously escaped me. To the extent my attention increases, the impressions of the object become stronger and augment. Finally, all this increases to such a point that I am scarcely affected except by that object" (1769, §138).[1] Bonnet goes on to explain that the liveliness of a sense perception is expected to vary in direct proportion with the "movement" or activation of sensory nerves, and since in this case each of several objects is assumed to affect the nerves with the same force, the increased liveliness of the perception of the target object must be due to an increase in the activation of the relevant nerves resulting from the influence of the mind in accordance with the fixation of attention (ibid., §§139–141). He also produced a physiological explanation, involving the redirection of limited neurophysiological resources, for the reciprocal relation he described between the strengthened perception of the target object and the weakened perception of neighboring objects (ibid., §142).

*Motivational Aspect (Motivationalen Aspekt)*   Neumann credits Leibniz (1646–1716) with having introduced motivational factors to the description of attention, citing a passage in which Leibniz observes that "we exercise attention on objects which we pick out in preference to others" (Leibniz, 1981, II.19.1). Indication that one object can be picked out in preference to others through attention is found earlier in Augustine's mention of the voluntary direction of attention, and in Descartes's discussion of fixation, and perhaps implicitly in Lucretius's discussion of mental preparedness.

*Overview*   Some sense of how comprehensively these descriptions cover the domain may be gained by comparing them with a survey of the chief "processes" of attention (Parasuraman & Davies, 1984) or "manifestations" of attention (LaBerge, 1995) described in recent reviews. Parasuraman and Davies found that attention researchers had described three chief processes in attention: *selective, intensive*, and *alerting and sustaining* (1984, pp. xii-xiii). To a first approximation, their selective process corresponds to the Active Directing category, intensive to the combined Narrowing and Clarity categories, and alerting and sustaining to a combination of Involuntary Shifts, Effector Sensitivity, and Fixation. LaBerge (1995, pp. 12–13) lists *selective, preparatory*, and *maintenance* manifestations of attention, which correspond respectively to the Narrowing and Active Directing, Effector Sensitivity, and Fixation categories.

## Theoretical Analyses of Attention
The phenomenal descriptions of attention in the previous section are comparatively theory-free: they impose a descriptive vocabulary on the phenomena of attention, by classifying attentional acts as voluntary or involuntary, by relating attention to limitations on the momentary scope of sensory awareness, and by relating attention to phenomenal clarity and distinctness. Terms such as "voluntary" or "phenomenal clarity" are not, of course, theory neutral. Still, the descriptive vocabulary used in the previous section, save for the invocation of Effector Sensitivity and related hypothetical physiological mechanisms, does not engage in the theoretical activity of positing explanatory mechanisms or structures to account for the observed attentional phenomena. Moreover, the instances in which these descriptive categories were used arose in a variety of intellectual contexts, which only sometimes,

as with Wolff and Bonnet, involved a systematic examination of the attentional capacities of the human mind.

On occasion, the ancients and early moderns did discuss theoretical frameworks for understanding attention. John Philoponus provides an early discussion of the concept of attention itself, considered as a lynchpin for all cognition. In his commentary on Aristotle's *De Anima*, III.2, he favorably reviews the following position, attributed to "recent interpreters" of Aristotle:

> The attention, they say, assists in all that goes on in man. It is that which pro-nounces *I understand, I think, I opine, I resent, I desire.* The attentive function of the rational soul, in fact, pervades in all the powers without exception – the rational, the irrational, the vegetative. If then, they proceed, the attentive fac-ulty be thus thorough-going, why not let it accompany the sensations and pronounce of them, *I see, I hear,* etc.? for to do this is the peculiar office of what is recognisant of the several energies. If, therefore, it be the attention which pronounces this, attention will be the power which takes note of the energies of sense. For it behoves that what takes note of all should itself be indivisible and *one*; seeing also at the same time that the subject of all these operations, *Man*, is one. For, if this faculty took cognisance of these objects, that faculty of those others, it would be, as he himself [Aristotle] elsewhere says, as if you perceived that, I this. That, therefore, must be one to which the attentive function pertains; for this function is conversant with the faculties – both the cognitive and the vital. In so far as it is conversant with the cogni-tive energies it is called Attention (as translated in Hamilton, 1895, p. 942).

Attention is assigned the function of unifying human consciousness, by "taking cognisance" of the materials provided by the various senses. Attention is not here described as selecting, but rather as unit-ing and hence delimiting the momentary cognitive contents of any in-dividual cognizer. Although Philoponus assigned theoretical centrality to attention in the analysis of cognition, extended theoretical analysis of attention apparently did not soon become common. From consider-ing sources from antiquity through the seventeenth century, I have found that attention received the kind of hit-and-miss notice chroni-cled in the sequence of phenomenal-descriptive observations. Such theoretical analysis as did occur arose primarily in the contexts of ap-plying terms and concepts developed elsewhere to the description of attention, of drawing variously phenomenally based distinctions, such as that between involuntary and voluntary attention, or of discussing the function of attention.

With the development of psychology as an independent science in the eighteenth century, attention came under more systematic theoretical and empirical scrutiny. In Wolff's psychology textbooks from the 1730s, attention was defined as the "faculty of bringing it about that in a perception compounded from parts, one part has greater clarity than the others" (1738, §237). What theoretical order Wolff brought to attention came in his chosen dimensions of empirical analysis. Having chosen cognitive clarity as the primary effect of attention, he set about to analyze the conditions under which clarity occurs. He found that attention to merely imagined representations is impeded by simultaneous sensory stimulation (§238), that attention to such representations is more easily conserved when fewer things act on the external senses (§240), that it is easier to attend to one image than to several (§241). He distinguished several dimensions in which attention admits of degree. These include *intensity* (not his term): attention is greater if it is harder to distract (§243); *longevity*: attention may last for longer or shorter periods (§244); *extension*: one may be able to pay attention to one or to several objects at once (§245); *voluntary control*: attention may be more or less subject to voluntary control (§246), and so on. In his *Psychologia Rationalis*, Wolff continued the same sort of analysis, now focusing largely on the relation between the direction of the visual axis and the focus of attention, describing the movement of the eyes in relation to voluntary attention and involuntary shifts of attention (§§358–365). He speculated on the physiological conditions accompanying and affecting attention (§§374–378), and he formulated the generalizations about attention mentioned in Part 1.

After Wolff, the literature on attention in the eighteenth century virtually exploded. This large literature has been the subject of a monograph by Braunschweiger (1899), which remains useful. Braunschweiger divided the theoretical dimensions of this literature into several categories. He distinguished *sensory* and *intellectual* dimensions of the literature of attention: attention can select among external objects available for perception, but it can also direct "inner" cognitive states such as imagination and memory, or "inner" cognitive processes such as self-reflection or self-observation (1899, pp. 25–31). In connection with this discussion, thinkers took various stances on the essence of attention itself (pp. 31–36), treating it either as a causal-explanatory factor in its own right, or as a phenomenon needing to be explained. Some treated attention as a *faculty* (i.e., as a mechanism that exists even when it is not in use), others as *mental effort* (i.e., as an activity of mind that exists only in its exercise), others as a *state of mind* (i.e., as a quality of sensations or perceptions, such as clarity). In the first two cases, attention is the result of causal agency; in the latter, it is an attribute of experience.

Braunschweiger (1899) analyzed several other eighteenth-century discussions. These included: degrees of attention, which extended

Wolff's treatment; the stimulus to involuntary attention and the control exercised in voluntary attention; the physiological correlate of attention; the effects of attention, from sensory acuity to memory and higher cognition; the means of improving attention; and limitations on or hindrances to attention. Throughout Braunschweiger's analysis, the primary theoretical results are manifested in taxonomies of the dimensions of variation in and conditions on the exercise of attention.

The main dimensions of theoretical variation attributed by Parasuraman and Davies (1984) and Johnston and Dark (1987) to late twentieth-century theories can be located within eighteenth-century discussions. Parasuraman and Davies found three main theoretical tendencies at work: the view of attention as a selective mechanism, the analysis of attention in terms of processing resource allocation, and the distinction between automatic and attentional processing. Wolff (1738) defined attention as a selectional process operating over degrees of clarity, though subject to both voluntary and involuntary control. As we have seen, Bonnet (1769, §142) explained the reciprocal relation between strengthened representation of a target object and weakened representation of neighbouring objects by postulating that limited neurophysiological resources must be allocated, with consequences for subsequent perceptual representation. Finally, the distinction between processes that are under the control of voluntary attention and those that occur without even being noticed was commonplace in eighteenth-century psychology, partly as a result of the postulation of unnoticed and hence automatic inferential processes to explain size and distance perception (forerunners of unconscious inference, on which see Hatfield 1990, chs. 2, 4, 5). Stewart reviews this distinction in the eighteenth-century literature (1793, chap. 2). Johnston and Dark (1987, pp. 66–70, citing James, 1890) divide twentieth-century theories into those that see attention as a cause, as opposed to those that see it merely as an effect. In Braunschweiger's (1899) terms, the faculty and mental effort positions correspond to the former classification, the state of mind position to the latter.

## Empirical Investigations of Attention

It would be arbitrary to seek a firm dividing line between phenomenal descriptions of aspects of attention and empirical investigations proper. To suppose that the latter must involve experiment would only push the problem back one step, as the concept of experimentation has itself undergone considerable development since the rise of modern science. If we adopted too stringent an attitude toward experiment – say, restricting it to the standards of mid-twentieth-century journals of experimental psychology – we would be faced with the paradoxical result that much of Helmholtz's and Wundt's work on visual perception, as indeed much of Newton's work in optics, does not count as experiment. Consequently, here I will focus the discussion of empirical investigations on those empirical claims from the eighteenth century that are presented as part of a systematic scientific treatment of attention. My principal primary sources will be Wolff's (1738, 1740), Bonnet's (1755), and Abel's (1786/1985) eighteenth-century textbook treatments of attention and its empirical laws. As a standard of comparison with traditional experimental psychology, I return to Titchener's (1908) review of the results of the "new psychology" of the late nineteenth century, which will, to fix referents, be coordinated with the recent reviews of Johnston and Dark (1987), Kinchla (1992), and LaBerge (1995).

Titchener organized his review of the experimental psychology of attention around seven empirical "laws," or general (though not strictly universal) "statements of the behaviour of conscious contents given in the state of attention" (1908, p. 211). The first law states that "*clearness is an attribute of sensation*, which, within certain limits, may be varied independently of other concurrent attributes" (ibid.). Titchener takes this independence to be well confirmed for most attributes, though he cites considerable controversy with respect to intensity, finally concluding that clearness can vary independently of intensity (loud and soft sounds can be equally clear), but that clearness can affect intensity (an attended, and hence "clear" sensation may seem to differ less than stimulus intensity would suggest from an unattended, hence unclear, sensation produced by a tone of greater intensity). Earlier, Wolff held that we can voluntarily shift attention and hence affect the clarity of perceptions that otherwise would not be clear (1738, §§236–237). Bonnet, as quoted above, states a relationship between attention and the "liveliness" of perceptions, with their other qualities presumed to remain the same, and Abel (1786/1985, §195) maintains that attention can be varied at will to affect the clarity of sensory representations. Clarity is only rarely mentioned in recent discussions of attention (e.g., LaBerge, 1995, p. 27). The related notion of accuracy in perceptual judgment, usually not stated in phenomenal-descriptive terms, remains central (LaBerge, 1995, p. 9).

Titchener's second law is the *law of two levels*, which accepts that "increased clearness of any one part-contents of consciousness implies the decreased clearness of all the rest," and asserts that only two "levels or degrees of clearness may coexist in the same consciousness" (1908, p. 220). Titchener reviews several opinions, including those that posit three or four levels of clearness, and sides with those that posit only two: focal attention, and what is outside it. (He confounds figure/ground reversal with clarity of representation in arguing for his position: 1908, pp. 228–229.) Eighteenth-century opinion was divided on this question. Wolff did not address it directly, but *de facto* he spoke only of the focus of attention (which in vision may be larger or smaller, inversely with the degree of attention) and what is outside it (1740, §360), though in other contexts he allowed that attention may be divided among several objects, without stating whether each target has equal clarity (1738, §245). Bonnet asserted an "infinity" of degrees of attention (1755, pp. 130–131). In an example from vision, he described these degrees as falling off continuously from the centre of the visual field to the boundary of peripheral vision. Abel observed that attention can be directed on one object, or it can divided among several, presumably in different degrees as the ideas themselves are livelier or more pleasant (1786/1985, §§213, 237–241; see also Schmid 1796, pp. 324–325). Recent spotlight metaphors suggest a two-level division (Johnston & Dark, 1986, pp. 50–56), though LaBerge interpets the zoom-lens metaphor as permitting a gradation (1995, p. 27). The conception of attention as a processing resource that can be allocated to one or more spatial positions in differing amounts is consistent with multiple levels of attention (Kinchla, 1992, pp. 712–713).

Titchener gives two laws in the third instance, both pertaining to the temporal relations of attention (1908, pp. 242–247). The *law of accommodation* concerns the relation between cuing and reaction time: it takes a certain period (1 to 1.5 sec) to focus attention once cued; reaction time improves with cuing. The *law of inertia* states that it is more pleasing, or easier, to hold attention on one object than to shift it. Eighteenth-century literature does not contain reaction-time results, and so has no correlate to the first of these laws. As for the ease or difficulty of shifting attention, Wolff (1738, §§246–247) observed that in some instances attention tends to wander, and the problem is keeping it in place, and Abel (1786/1985, §214) listed a number of conditions that affect the duration of attention.

Titchener's fourth is the *law of prior entry,* according to which "the stimulus for which we are predisposed requires less time than a like stimulus, for which we are unprepared, to produce its full conscious effect" (1908, p. 251). Although observation of the connection between attention and mental preparedness goes back at least to Lucretius, the eighteenth century made no advances here that I have found. In recent literature, the correlate to Titchener's *accommodation* and *prior entry* is the *priming effect,* which has been studied extensively (Johnston & Dark, 1987, pp. 46–47; Kinchla, 1992, pp. 724–733), along with the notion of attention as *preparatory* to perception (LaBerge, 1995, pp. 12–13).

Titchener's fifth is the *law of limited range,* which says that for brief (tachistoscopic) exposures of objects within the scope of clear vision, "a practiced observer is able to cognise from four to six of them 'by a single act of attention'" (1908, pp. 260–261). In the eighteenth century, this question was not posed in connection with tachistoscopic presentation. The earlier question concerned the number of objects that can be held in clear consciousness, apperceived, or attended to, at one time. Opinions were divided. Krueger held that through attention the understanding is able to make just one of its representations clearer at a time (1756, pp. 228–229). Bonnet tested the question by seeing how many objects he could imagine at one time. He reported: "I find considerable variety in this connection, but in general the number is only five or six. I attempt, for example, to represent to myself a figure with five or six sides, or simply to represent five or six points; I see that I imagine five distinctly: I have difficulty going to six. It is perhaps true that regularity in the position of these lines or points greatly relieves the imagination, and helps it to go higher" (1755, p. 132).

The task of determining how many items can be cognized clearly at one time was pursued with relative continuity over a period of two hundred years. In the 1830s the Scottish philosopher and psychologist William Hamilton proposed the following experiment to answer the question: "If you throw a handful of marbles on the floor, you will find it difficult to view at once more than six, or seven at most, without confusion; but if you group them into twos, or threes, or fives, you can comprehend as many groups as you can units ... You may perform the experiment also by an act of imagination" (1859, p. 177). Hamilton controlled for time by fixing the onset of the task and operating under instructions that the number of marbles must be taken in "at once," that is, in one cognitive act. Later in the century, Jevons (1871) performed a similar experiment by throwing various quantities of black beans into a shallow round paper box and estimating their number as soon as they came to rest. His results, originally reported in *Nature*, are shown in Table 3. He concludes that since a 5% error rate was obtained when the number of beans reached five, the proper figure for the limit of correct numerical estimation by a "single act of mental attention" is four. In the middle of the twentieth century, Kaufman, Lord, Reese, and Volkmann (1949) studied the discrimination of visual number using dots projected on a large screen, varying the instructions for speed and accuracy. They found no errors for two, three, or four dots. For both accuracy and speed instructions, error began at five dots; the errors were fewer for accuracy instructions and reaction time longer. Kaufman et al. (1949) also reported reaction times from a similar experiment by Saltzman and Garner (1948), which showed that the times increase monotonically as the number of stimuli is increased from two to 10. Following Saltzman and Garner, they concluded that there is no such thing as a single "span of apprehension" or capacity of momentary cognition. Hence, they did not present their findings as bearing on attention, but they focused instead on the judgment of numerousness itself, and coined the term *subitizing* for cases in which number is determined "suddenly" (1949, p. 520). This literature about subitizing is not commonly included in current discussions of attention. However, a correlate of Titchener's fifth law, and of the question posed by Bonnet, Hamilton, and Jevons, occurs in recent literature through comparisons of attention to a bottleneck (LaBerge, 1995, p. 34).

| | | Actual Numbers | | | | | | | | | | | | |
|---|---|---|---|---|---|---|---|---|---|---|---|---|---|---|
| | | 3 | 4 | 5 | 6 | 7 | 8 | 9 | 10 | 11 | 12 | 13 | 14 | 15 |
| | 3 | 23 | | | | | | | | | | | | |
| | 4 | | 65 | | | | | | | | | | | |
| | 5 | | | 102 | 7 | | | | | | | | | |
| | 6 | | | 4 | 120 | 18 | | | | | | | | |
| | 7 | | | 1 | 20 | 113 | 30 | 2 | | | | | | |
| | 8 | | | | | 25 | 76 | 24 | 6 | 1 | | | | |
| Estimated Numbers | 9 | | | | | | 28 | 76 | 37 | 11 | 1 | | | |
| | 10 | | | | | | 1 | 18 | 46 | 19 | 4 | | | |
| | 11 | | | | | | | 2 | 16 | 26 | 17 | 7 | 2 | |
| | 12 | | | | | | | | 2 | 12 | 19 | 11 | 3 | 2 |
| | 13 | | | | | | | | | | 3 | 6 | 3 | 1 |
| | 14 | | | | | | | | | | 1 | 1 | 4 | 6 |
| | 15 | | | | | | | | | | | 1 | 2 | 2 |
| Totals | | 23 | 65 | 107 | 147 | 156 | 135 | 122 | 107 | 69 | 45 | 26 | 14 | 11 |

*Table* 3. Data showing W. Stanley Jevons's estimates of the number of black beans thrown into a white paper box at the moment at which the beans come to rest, in comparison to the actual number of beans thrown. Adapted from Jevons (1871).

Titchener's sixth is the *law of temporal instability*, which says that attention is unstable in itself. Titchener cites Wundt (1874) to the effect that attention is constantly broken, from moment to moment (Titchener 1908, p. 263). However, Titchener himself considered the estimate of two to three minutes for the self-limiting duration of focused attention to be conservative (p. 268). Wolff (1738, §244) noted that the ability to hold attention fixed varies from individual to individual, without giving a temporal estimate. Recent empirical work discusses this topic under the rubric of *sustained attention*, or the *duration of attention*

(LaBerge, 1995, pp. 35–38); these findings suggest a duration on the order of hundreds of milliseconds.

Seventh and finally, Titchener expresses the wish that there were a law for measuring the *degree of clearness* or the degree of attention. Finding no single measure extant, he discusses several candidates, including the effect of distractors on some measure of performance (such as errors in a well-practised sensory discrimination task). Other proposed measures of "attentional degree" or "attentional capacity" include measures of simultaneous range of attention (cf. law five), the effect of attention on sensory discrimination (cf. law four), the effect of attention on the formation of associations, and finally its effect on reaction time (1908, pp. 279–280). In the eighteenth century, Wolff discussed several measures of degree of attention, including ease of distraction, capacity, and duration (1738, §§243–245). Contemporary work assesses various dimensions of attention through sophisticated measures of performance characteristics such as reaction time and performance error (Kinchla, 1992).

These comparisons suggest that there is both continuity and divergence across the past 250 years of attention research: continuity at the global levels of theoretical conceptions and main dimensions of analysis, discontinuity in the development of sophisticated instrumentation for testing reaction time (late nineteenth century) and sophisticated approaches to measuring the fine-grained spatial and temporal characteristics of attention-based and unattended processing (twentieth century). As elsewhere in psychology, current work on attention tends to be fragmented: there are traditions of work on attention as a selective mechanism (which might be early or late, voluntary or involuntary), as allocation of processing resources, and as something to be contrasted with automatic processing. Within these theoretical traditions, elaborate flow-chart models are being developed and tested. New empirical questions have arisen concerning the extent to which semantic (as opposed to simple physical) dimensions of stimuli are processed outside the focus of attention. New neural imaging techniques now make it possible to track the neurophysiology of attention more closely than before. At the same time, the questions that were at the centre of discussions in the eighteenth century and earlier, the cognitive function of attention, are less frequently posed, and the functioning of attention in higher cognition is less frequently discussed. As many authors have observed, "attention" now defines a complex field of research that may or may not be unified by a single underlying process or set of phenomena. It is less common now for a single author to attempt a systematic taxonomy of all the phenomena of attention. There is richness of results and of microtheory, but theoretical unification remains elusive.

## Concluding Remarks

Examination of the early history of attention reveals that the chief phenomenal descriptive aspects of attention had been recorded by the seventeenth century. The main theoretical positions were formulated by the end of the eighteenth century, and the primary areas of experimental investigation by the end of the nineteenth. Experimental technique has been much refined, and new instruments make possible fine-grained analyses of the psychophysics of attention. These permit formulation of sophisticated questions about the temporal course, spatial distribution, and content-related characteristics of attentional processing.

Titchener's claim that research on attention was born with the "new" experimental psychology of the late nineteenth century is false. His claim in fact differs markedly from the attitude of William James, who is now cited more prominently than Titchener on attention. James referred freely to eighteenth-century works, including those of Wolff and Stewart (James, 1890, chap. 11). The extent to which the theoretical context set by eighteenth-century psychology conditioned and controlled the psychology of Wundt, Titchener, and indeed James, and thereby set the context for twentieth-century psychology, is at present unknown. This state of ignorance has largely resulted from the misbelief that scientific psychology is itself only slightly more than 100 years old. For the case of attention, I hope to have shown that that contention is at least 150 years off the mark.

## Note

1 Unless otherwise indicated, all translations are the author's.

## References

Abel, J.F. (1786/1985). *Einleitung in die Seelenlehre*. Stuttgart. Reprint, Hildesheim and New York: Olms. Cited by section number.

Aristotle (1984). *Sense and* sensibilia. Translated by J.I. Beare. In J. Barnes (Ed.), *Complete Works of Aristotle* (2 vols.). Princeton: Bollingen. Cited by chapter, page, and line numbers.

Arnauld, A., & Nicole, P. (1683). *Logique, ou L'Art de penser* (5th ed.). Paris: Guillaume Desprez.

Augustine of Hippo (1969). *De musica*. Edited and translated into Italian by G. Marzi. Florence: Sansoni. Cited by book, chapter, and section number.

Augustine of Hippo (1991). *Confessions*. Translated by H. Chadwick. Oxford: Oxford University Press. Cited by book, chapter, and section number.

Augustine of Hippo (1992). *Confessions*. Edited by J. O'Donnell. Oxford: Oxford University Press.

Berlyne, D.E. (1974). Attention. In E.C. Carterette & M.P. Friedman (Eds.), *Handbook of perception, Volume 1: Historical and philosophical roots of perception* (pp. 123–147). New York: Academic Press.

Bonnet, C. (1755). *Essai de psychologie.* London.

Bonnet, C. (1769). *Essai analytique sur les facultés de l'ame* (2nd ed., 2 vols.). Copenhagen: Philibert. Cited by section number.

Boring, E.G. (1929). *A history of experimental psychology.* New York: Century.

Boring, E.G. (1950). *A history of experimental psychology* (2nd ed.). New York: Appleton-Century-Crofts.

Braunschweiger D. (1899). *Die Lehre von der Aufmerksamkeit in der Psychologie des 18. Jahrhundert.* Leipzig: Haacke.

Buridan, J. (1518). *In librum Aristotelis De sensu & sensato.* In G. Lockert (Ed.), *Questiones et decisiones.* Paris: Ascensius & Resch. Cited by question and folio number.

Cicero (1968). *De oratione, Book III.* Translated by H. Rackham. Loeb series. Cambridge, MA: Harvard University Press. Cited by book and passage number.

Descartes, R. (1642). *Meditationes de prima philosophia* (2nd ed.). Amsterdam: Elsevier.

Descartes, R. (1985). Passions of the soul. In *Philosophical Writings of Descartes* (Vol. 1, pp. 325–404). Translated by J. Cottingham, R. Stoothoff, & D. Murdoch. Cambridge: Cambridge University Press. Cited by section number.

Ebbinghaus, H. (1908). *Abriss der Psychologie.* Leipzig: Veit & Co.

Ebbinghaus, H. (1911). *Psychology: An elementary textbook.* Translated by M. Meyer. Boston: Heath & Co.

Glare, P.G.W. (1968). *Oxford Latin dictionary* (8 vols.). Combined edition. Oxford: Clarendon Press.

Hatfield, G. (1990). *The natural and the normative: Theories of spatial perception from Kant to Helmholtz.* Cambridge, MA: MIT Press/Bradford Books.

Hatfield, G. (1992). Descartes' physiology and its relation to his psychology. In J. Cottingham (Ed.), *Cambridge Companion to Descartes* (pp. 335–370). Cambridge: Cambridge University Press.

Hatfield, G. (1994). Psychology as a natural science in the eighteenth century. *Revue de Synthèse, 115,* 375–391.

Hatfield, G. (1995). Remaking the science of mind: Psychology as a natural science. In C. Fox, R. Porter, & R. Wokler (Eds.), *Inventing Human Science* (pp. 184–231). Berkeley: University of California Press.

Hamilton, W. (1859). *Lectures on metaphysics.*

Hamilton, W. (1895). Notes and supplementary dissertations. In W. Hamilton (Ed.), *Works of Thomas Reid* (8th ed.). Edinburgh: James Thin.

James, W. (1890). *Principles of psychology* (2 vols.). New York: Henry Holt.

Jevons, W.S. (1871). Power of numerical discrimination. *Nature, 3,* 281–282.

Johnston, W.A., & Dark, V.J. (1987). Selective attention. *Annual Review of Psychology, 37,* 43–75.

Kaufman, E.L., Lord, M.W., Reese, T.W., & Volkmann, J. (1949). The discrimination of visual number. *American Journal of Psychology, 62,* 498–525.

Kinchla, R.A. (1992). Attention. *Annual Review of Psychology, 43,* 711–742.

Krueger, J.G. (1756). *Versuch einer Experimental-Seelenlehre.* Halle and Helmstaedt: Hermann Hemmerde.

LaBerge, D. (1995). *Attentional processing: The brain's art of mindfulness*. Cambridge, MA: Harvard University Press.

Ladd, G.T. (1895). *Psychology: Descriptive and explanatory.* New York: Charles Scribner's Sons.

Le Grand, Antoine (1694). *An entire body of philosophy, according to the principles of the famous Renate des Cartes*. Translated by R. Blome. London: Samuel Roycroft & Richard Blome.

Leibniz, G.W. (1981). *New essays on human understanding*. Translated and edited by P. Remnant & J. Bennett. Cambridge: Cambridge University Press. Cited by book, chapter, section.

Locke, J. (1975). *An essay concerning human understanding*. Edited by P.H. Nidditch. Oxford: Clarendon Press. Cited by book, chapter, and section number.

Lucretius (1965). *On nature*. Translated by R.M. Geer. Indianapolis: Bobbs-Merrill. Cited by book and line number.

Lucretius (1967). *De rerum natura* (revised ed.). Oxford: Clarendon Press.

Malebranche, N. (1980). *Search after truth*. Translated by T.M. Lennon & P.J. Olscamp. Columbus: Ohio State University Press. Cited by book and chapter.

Neumann, O. (1971). Aufmerksamkeit. In J. Ritter (Ed.), *Historisches Woerterbuch der Philosophie* (new ed., Vol. 1, cols. 635–645). Darmstadt: Wissenschaftliche Buchgesellschaft.

Parasuraman, R., & Davies, D.R. (1984). Preface. In R. Parasuraman & D.R. Davies (Eds.), *Varieties of attention* (pp. xi-xvi). Orlando: Academic Press.

Régis, P.-S. (1691). *Système de philosophie* (7 vols.). Lyon: Anisson, Posuel & Rigaud.

Saltzman, I.J., & Garner, W. (1948). Reaction time as a measure of span of attention. *Journal of Psychology, 25*, 227–241.

Schmid, C.C.E. (1796). *Empirische Psychologie* (2nd ed.). Jena: Croeker.

Schultz, D.P., & Schultz, S.E. (1987). *A history of modern psychology* (4th ed.). San Diego: Harcourt Brace Jovanovich.

Stewart, D. (1793). *Elements of the philosophy of the human mind*. Philadelphia: William Young.

Titchener, E.B. (1908). *Lectures on the elementary psychology of feeling and attention*. New York: Macmillan.

Wolff, C. (1738). *Psychologia empirica*. Frankfurt & Leipzig: Officina Libraria Rengeriana. Cited by section number.

Wolff, C. (1740). *Psychologia rationalis*. Frankfurt & Leipzig: Officina Libraria Rengeriana. Cited by section number.

Wundt, W. (1874). *Grundzuege der physiologischen Psychologie*. Leipzig: Wilhelm Engelmann.

# 2

# *The Perception of Features and Objects*

## Anne Treisman

This paper describes some recent research exploring the visual perception of features and objects, and the role of attention in creating the integrated and organized representations that we consciously experience. Some years ago, I summarized a set of findings from experiments on visual search, texture segregation, and the perception of brief, masked displays (Treisman & Gelade, 1980). The results seemed to fit together coherently: search for feature-defined targets is parallel, but search for a conjunction of features seems to require attention. Texture segregation is easy when based on simple features, but difficult or impossible when the boundaries are defined only by conjunctions. Cuing attention in advance helps us to identify a conjunction much more than it helps with any of its features. When attention is overloaded, illusory conjunctions are formed, and so on. These findings fit nicely together to support what I labelled *feature integration theory* (see Treisman, 1988, p. 202). The claims were that simple features are registered in parallel across the visual field, in a number of specialized subsystems. Information from the resulting feature maps is localized and recombined to specify objects through the use of focused attention, scanning serially through a master-map of locations and giving access to the features currently occupying the attended location. These are then integrated to form a representation of the object in that location.

But of course simple stories never stay that way. We can either complicate and stretch them to fit new discoveries, or we can scrap them. People usually start with the first alternative before moving to the second, and I am no exception. In this paper, I will select a few of the more interesting developments, and see whether I can update this picture so that it will accommodate them without bursting at the seams. I will try to group the new findings and ideas under five main headings, as follows: (1) features; (2) divided attention vs. inattention vs. pre-attention; (3) the coding of locations and conjunctions; (4) object files and object selection; (5) selection for action.

## Features

Back in 1980, features were the colours, orientations, and shapes on my ink-drawn tachistoscope cards. That saved me some difficult decisions about whether they consisted of the features of the 2-D image as coded by retinal receptors, or the features of real-world, 3-D objects. I have always insisted that this is an empirical question, to be answered by converging operations designed to diagnose the functional features in the visual dictionary. Functional features are defined, in terms of the theory, as properties for which we have evolved or acquired separate sets of detectors responding in parallel across the visual scene. The detectors need not be individual neurons; they could be groups or hierarchies of cells so long as they respond directly to their particular properties without attentional control and without (much) crosstalk from other functional detectors.

Among the behavioural diagnostics I suggested were: pop-out in search, the ability to mediate texture segregation, and the possibility of recombination in illusory conjunctions. For the features I tried out, these operations did converge quite well. But many questions remained unanswered. I will briefly describe some recent findings and their implications.

The first concerned the coding of separable features within dimensions – for example, different colours or different orientations. When I drew my picture of the mind, I put in three feature maps for each dimension, mainly because drawing 50 was beyond my artistic abilities. But I now like the idea that the visual system uses "coarse coding" (Hinton, 1981), representing different values on each dimension by ratios of activity in just a few separate populations of detectors (e.g., red, green, blue and yellow; or vertical, horizontal, left and right diagonal). If this is correct, it suggests that attention should be needed not only to integrate features across dimensions (e.g., colour with orientation) but also to integrate them within dimensions (blue and red to make purple; vertical and diagonal to make a more steeply tilted orientation). I should then predict serial search for these new, within-dimension conjunctions, and a risk of illusory conjunctions when attention cannot be focused on each item in turn. Figure 1(a) shows a display I used both in a search task and in a test for illusory conjunctions when it was flashed briefly and masked (Treisman, 1991a). The target is a purple bar tilted 27° left among pink vertical bars and blue bars tilted 63° left. In both cases, I compared performance with a target with standard values (blue vertical among purple and turquoise tilted bars, with similarity relations matched; Figure 1[b]). The standard target should be less dependent on conjoining two coarse-coded values. In fact, the non-

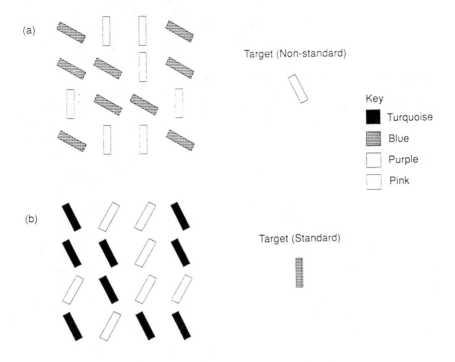

*Figure* 1. Examples of displays used to test search for targets defined either (a) by "non-standard" colours and orientations, which may be coded as conjunctions of coarsely coded features within the dimensions of colour and orientation, or (b) by "standard" colours and orientations, which may have their own specialized feature maps.

standard "conjunction" target gave much steeper search functions (Figure 2) and far more illusory conjunctions than the standard targets (26% compared to 6%). So maybe the few discrete examples of feature maps in my figure are not, after all, a caricature, but a serious proposal.

The second discovery was made in a study with Cavanagh and Arguin (Cavanagh, Arguin, & Treisman, 1990). Our results seem to require a feature hierarchy as well as parallel feature modules. We distinguished surface-defining features from shape-defining features. Shape is characterized by the spatial layout of discontinuities in any one surface feature (or more). For example, we can create a horizontal bar (Figure 3) whose boundaries are defined by changes in brightness, colour, stereoscopic depth, texture, or direction of motion. We showed that simple *shape*-defining features like orientation and size could be detected in parallel within at least five different *surface*-defining media – luminance, colour, relative motion, texture and stereoscopic depth. The displays contained bars differing in orientation or dots differing in size, where the elements were defined by discontinuities in each of

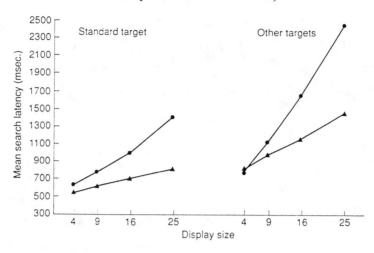

*Figure* 2. Search latencies in search for a "standard" target or for "nonstandard" targets.

these five media. When the differences in size or orientation were sufficiently discriminable, they gave flat search functions in every case. Interestingly, we found that some of the same coding principles apply within all these media: in particular, each showed a search asymmetry between the standard feature (vertical) and the deviating feature (tilted). Luminance and colour are first-order features defining points whose spatial, temporal or interocular relations in turn can define second-order discontinuities. Thus we have a hierarchy of possible shape-

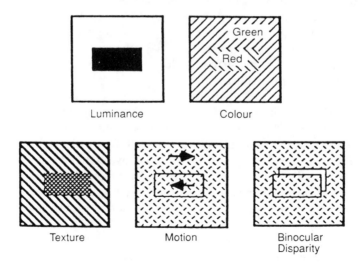

*Figure* 3. Rectangles defined by discontinuities in various surface-defining media.

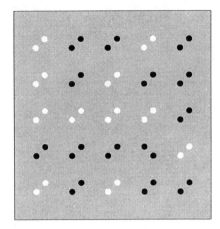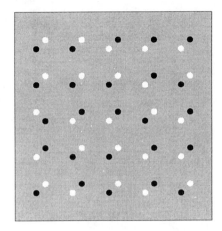

Figure 4. Examples of displays testing search for a dot pair tilted left among dot pairs tilted right, where the direction of contrast within pairs is (a) the same, and (b) different. (Note that the grey shown here is lighter than the one actually used, which was about equally different from the white and the black dots.)

defining media, with features of shape coded either separately within each, or perhaps in some subsequent pooled representation.

Finding constraints on perception is as important as finding capacities. My students and I have recently found examples of media which do not create directly detectable features. Kathy O'Connell and I defined orientations by the virtual lines connecting pairs of dots (Figure 4). When both dots in a pair share the same direction of contrast (both dark on a light background or the reverse, as in the display on the left), a unique orientation pops out of a display just as it does for lines, bars, or edges. However, if each dot pair consists of one black and one white dot on an intermediate grey background (as in the display on the right of Figure 4), search is slow and apparently serial (O'Connell & Treisman, in preparation).

Similarly, we can create apparent motion by presenting dots successively in different locations. If the spatial and temporal separation are small enough to activate the short-range motion system, a vertically oscillating set of dots will pop out of a horizontally oscillating background (Ivry & Cohen, 1990). But, Horowitz and I showed that if successive dots within an oscillating sequence alternate in contrast relative to a grey background, so that if one is black the next is white and vice versa (Figure 5, right displays), again search becomes serial rather than parallel (Horowitz & Treisman, 1994). We found that detecting long-range motion, when the dots are separated by at least three dot widths, requires attention, whether the dots share the same direction of contrast or whether they alternate in direction of contrast across successive locations.

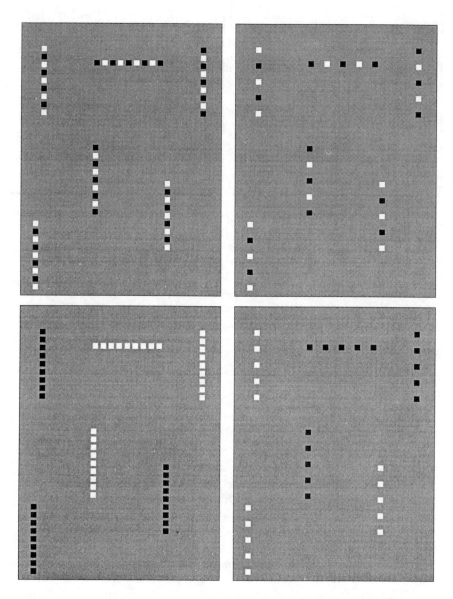

*Figure* 5. Displays testing search for a vertically oscillating target among horizontally oscillating targets, where the stimuli in each set either share the same direction of contrast or alternate in contrast. The figure shows all the dots simultaneously, but in the actual displays they were presented sequentially, giving an impression of motion. The upper displays show short-range motion and the lower displays show long-range motion.

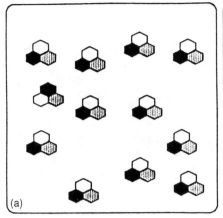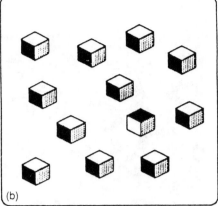

*Figure* 6. Displays used by Enns and Rensink (1990) to demonstrate pop-out in search for targets defined by the direction of lighting (b), but not for target patterns of matched complexity that cannot be interpreted as 3-D figures (a).

These studies are consistent with the idea that there may be two separate luminance media (darker and lighter contrast), each supporting parallel processing. When elements defined in separate media must be combined to generate either apparent motion or the orientation of a virtual line, we have a conjunction problem, and focused attention is required.

The third set of feature findings are the recent discoveries of 3-D properties that also pop out. Enns (1990; Enns & Rensink, 1990) used geometric stimuli suggesting cubes that differed either in their 3-D orientation or in the apparent direction of illumination (Figure 6, right display). Although from the point of view of the retinal image, these are relatively complex conjunctions of lines and luminance, the unique cube could be detected in parallel, whereas the corresponding target in the flat display on the left in Figure 6 could not. Similarly, Ramachandran (1988) showed good parallel segregation based on differences in shape from shading, with a group of convex eggs standing out clearly from a background of egg-shaped hollows. Only the spatial pattern of shading defined the target.

This research suggests that the features that determine grouping and pop-out are features that specify 3-D objects in the real world rather than features of the retinal image. Certainly, the location map in my model must represent real-world locations rather than retinal ones, since subjects make eye and head movements in scanning displays. Broadbent and Broadbent (1990) have also shown that viewing distance has little effect on the interference from flanking distractors, suggesting that attention operates on real rather than retinal separation. Even the earliest stages of visual system seem to have evolved to represent the real world around us, detecting the particular combinations and correlations of physical dimensions that specify object properties, such as convexity, transparency and occlusion, as well as surface colour, depth and motion. Some may be directly sensed: for example, Lehky and Sejnowski (1988) suggest that simple cells in V1 are actually specialized to sense shape from shading, and not line or bar orientations. However, 3-D properties can often be *interpreted* only for a particular setting of parameters (e.g., light from above, a tilted surface, forward motion of the observer). So some combination of information is required before the elementary features yield a veridical description of the scene. Why would these stimuli not count as conjunctions requiring focused attention?

## Divided Attention vs. Preattention vs. Inattention

A possible solution depends on a distinction between divided attention and preattention. In my earlier papers, I followed Neisser (1967) in attributing feature pop-out and texture segregation to "*pre*attentive processing." However, in applying the distinction to explain performance, I now prefer to contrast divided attention with focused attention (Treisman & Gormican, 1988). Preattentive processing cannot directly affect responses or experience; it is an inferred stage of early vision, which I attribute to the separate feature modules. Before any conscious visual experience is possible, some form of attention is required, since information from the different feature maps must be combined. We can never be aware of a free-floating orientation, colour, or shape. What varies across tasks is how broadly or narrowly focused the attention window is. Thus I assume a dichotomy between preattentive and attentive processing levels, and a continuum between divided and focused attention, as the size of the attention window narrows down or spreads wide. Texture segregation, visual pop-out and detection of global alignment and shape (e.g., Donnelly, Humphreys, & Riddoch, 1991) are done with a broad setting of the attention window, integrating feature maps at a global level. Accurate localization and conjoining of features for individual objects require narrowly focused attention. Note, however, that when the distractors are homogeneous and arranged in a regular array like a circle or a grid, even a conjunction target is sometimes detectable as a break in alignment or a gap in the global shape or texture.

When we set the parameters for interpreting a particular 3-D scene, (or a 2-D representation of 3-D objects, as in the experiments of Ramachandran, 1988, and those of Enns & Rensink, 1990), the setting is normally a global one, applied to the scene as a whole. Divided attention allows an overall assessment of global features like illumination, surface orientation, or optic flow. Ramachandran (1988) showed that the visual system adopts a unique setting to specify the source of light (the normal assumption being light from above). This implies that brightly lit surfaces are facing upwards, and any discrepant surface in an otherwise homogeneous array of elements can be interpreted as a concavity. A prediction is that 3-D features would no longer pop out in a heterogeneous array to which no global interpretation can apply. Epstein, Babler, & Bounds (1992) have in fact shown that with heterogeneous arrays of real 3-D objects, attention is needed to see real shape by combining projected shape and slant in depth, even though separately both projected shape and slant are detected in parallel.

The distinction between preattention and divided attention is also relevant in interpreting the results of texture segregation experiments. I claimed in an early paper that segregation occurs preattentively within separate modules (Treisman, 1982). Callaghan (1984) showed, however, that there may be interference in judging one kind of boundary when another varies orthogonally. The reason, I believe, is that we cannot consciously access the representations created within any individual feature module, so preattentive segregation is not directly reflected in phenomenal segregation. If separate boundaries are defined within the dimensions of colour and orientation, they will be combined with divided attention to form a global representation of the display, and we will normally see both. In Figure 7, we clearly see four subdivisions created by two different boundaries, even though at the preattentive level the two boundaries could still be quite independently registered. What we cannot do is see global boundaries that are defined by separate conjunctions of local elements, for example blue Vs and red Os among blue Os and red Vs (Treisman & Gelade, 1980). We cannot simultaneously *focus* attention on each local element and *divide* attention to see the global boundaries defined by the local conjunctions.

In addition to preattention and divided attention, a third fate may lie in store for sensory stimuli: they may be *un*attended when attention is narrowly focused elsewhere. In this case, even global feature boundaries should no longer be available, if they emerge only when attention is divided over the scene. For the same reason, pop-out might no longer occur for a unique feature embedded among contrasting distractors. Some recent findings by Rock and his colleagues (Rock, Linnett, Grant, & Mack, 1991; Rock & Mack, 1991) are consistent with the predictions. They asked what information is available about truly unattended stimuli. Their subjects focused attention on

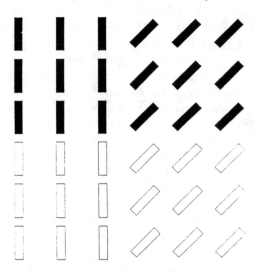

*Figure 7*. Example of a display in which we see two boundaries, one defined by colour and one defined by orientation.

the lines of a plus to judge their relative length. When on the fourth trial an unexpected stimulus showed up in one quadrant, on the very first trial on which it appeared, about one quarter of the subjects were completely blind to it. The majority, however, could report its presence, the quadrant in which it appeared and its colour, but not its shape, even when the alternatives were simple and highly discriminable; nor could they segregate textures by orientation or group elements by any Gestalt principles of organization. The results contrast with those obtained with divided attention in some of the predicted respects.

To review our discussion of features, preattention and divided attention, the new ideas I have outlined include the hypothesis of coarse coding within dimensions; a hierarchical ordering of surface-defining media, each supporting a similar coding of features of shape; separate representations for figures defined by darker and by lighter contrast, with focused attention required to combine across representations; the idea that feature coding remains parallel and global up to the level that defines surfaces in a 3-D (or perhaps a 2.5-D) world; and finally a distinction between *pre*attention (inaccessible to awareness and to the control of behaviour), *in*attention (that reflects whatever results of preattentive processing can still be retrieved once attention is redirected), and *divided* attention (that integrates the preattentive, feature-defined boundaries and allows conscious access to global properties of the display).

## Coding of Feature Locations and Conjunctions

Next, I will update the ideas that I have previously put forward on the coding of feature locations and conjunctions. In my early papers, I reported strong attentional constraints on the localization of features and on the coding of conjunctions. I have not altogether changed my mind, but again new findings have led me to elaborate my account.

I will start with feature localization. Gelade and I reported that feature targets could be identified substantially better than chance even when they were wrongly localized, whereas identification of conjunction targets was at chance (Treisman & Gelade, 1980). Johnston and Pashler (1990) correctly pointed out a possible guessing artefact in our experiment: since only two targets were used, subjects might sensibly guess the less discriminable of the two on trials in which they did not see the more discriminable. As a result, accuracy would be above chance on identification, but the subject would have no information about location. Johnston and Pashler (1990) repeated our experiment with better matched features and more discriminable locations, and found little or no evidence that feature identities were available independently of their locations. Note, however, that their criterion for accurate localization was very crude; in effect, they counted the location correct if the subject placed the target in the correct half of the display. My theory would allow this degree of accuracy if subjects simply focused attention in advance on either half of the display, randomly selected. They could then locate the side that contained the target feature by noting whether it was inside or outside the window of attention.

I ran another version of the same experiment, using 12 possible feature targets instead of two, to minimize the guessing artefact (Figure 8). I found identification that was substantially above chance (0.35, where chance was 0.08) when subjects made adjacent location errors, and slightly but significantly above chance (0.15) when they picked some more distant location. They were also well above chance in locating the target feature when they got its identity wrong (0.39, where chance was 0.125), but only when the distractors were homogeneous. Perhaps subjects can detect a discontinuity in the location map without knowing *what* defined it, as well as detecting the presence of a unique feature without always knowing *where* it was. There does seem to be a dissociation between what and where, even if it is less extreme than Gelade and I initially believed.

Do these results mean that features are preattentively bound to coarsely defined locations, as suggested by Cohen and Ivry (1989)? Or could it be the case that without attention, features are truly "free-floating," but that subjects can rapidly zoom attention in on the approximate area before the sensory information is lost? "Free-floating" was a

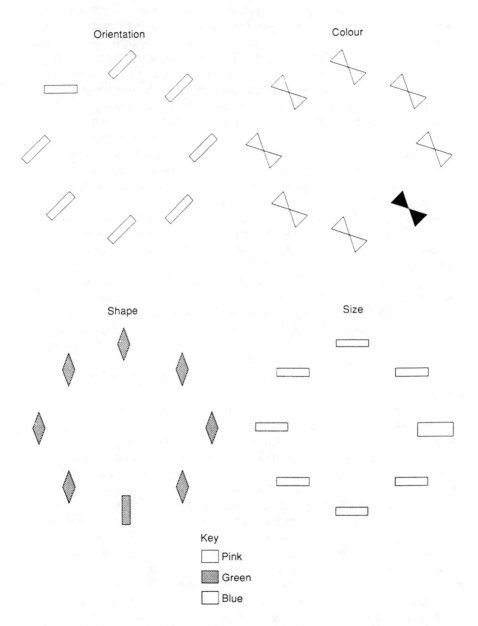

*Figure* 8. Examples of displays used to test the dependency between identification and localization of feature targets. There were twelve possible targets, (diamond, rectangle, hourglass; pink, blue, green; small, medium, large; vertical, tilted, horizontal), shown against a homogeneous set of randomFree-lance editor, compositor, designer and production co-ordinator

term I used in my early papers, which has since caused me some re-
grets! When I used the expression, I was referring to information that
we can consciously access, not to the information implicitly available
in the preattentive code. As implied by the term feature maps, I assumed that feature locations are implicitly coded, but suggested that
they are accessed, or made explicit, only through focused attention.
The more narrowly focused, the more precise the localization will be
for features within the attention window. To test the attentional versus
the coarse feature localization accounts, it would be interesting to compare a condition where attention is initially divided across the display
with a condition where attention is narrowly focused elsewhere, on the
stimuli for a primary task presented to one side or other of the display.
We are currently trying to run such a condition.

Next, let us look at the coding of conjunctions. Quite a few studies
now have shown fast or parallel search for conjunction targets (Duncan & Humphreys, 1989; Humphreys, Quinlan, & Riddoch, 1989;
McLeod, Driver, & Crisp, 1988; Nakayama & Silverman, 1986; Steinman, 1987; Treisman, 1988; Treisman & Sato, 1990; Wolfe, Cave, & Franzel, 1989). These studies fall into two separate categories, which I believe should be distinguished because they deal with two different
kinds of conjunctions: (1) spatially integral conjunctions of properties
like colour and orientation – for example, a bar that is red and vertical;
(2) spatial arrangements of parts of shapes – for example, a T among
Ls, each comprising one vertical and one horizontal line but in different relative locations.

I will discuss first the results with conjunctions of properties. Experiments showing parallel processing have in common the use of highly
discriminable properties to define the conjunctions. Nakayama (1990),
Wolfe et al. (1989), and Treisman (1988) all suggested similar accounts –
that separate grouping by highly distinctive features might allow selective access to their intersection. For example, if we can selectively shut
out anything that is coloured green and also anything that is vertically
oriented, a red horizontal target will emerge from a background of
green horizontal and red vertical distractors without any need to conjoin its features. Within my framework, I suggested that the mechanism
for achieving this may be through inhibitory connections from the feature maps to the master map of locations (Figure 9). Notice that the
same inhibitory feature control could also play a role in enhancing
figures against ground – a more generally useful task, if one wants to
supply evolutionary motivation.

In conjunction search, the efficient use of this strategy depends on
prior information about either the features of the target (inhibit anything that is neither red nor horizontal) or the features of the distrac-

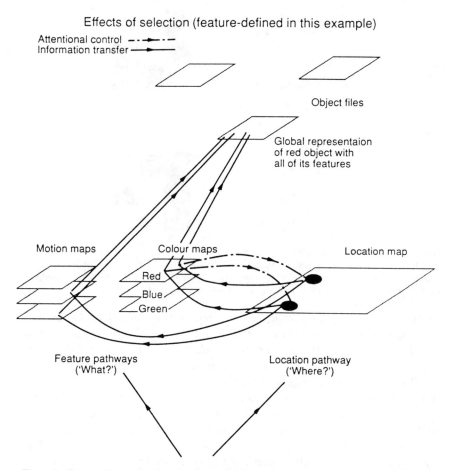

*Figure* 9. Figure illustrating the idea that attention might select locations containing particular features, by inhibitory (or excitatory) links from particular feature maps to the master map of locations.

tors (inhibit anything that is green or vertical). When all we have is information about distractor *conjunctions*, this strategy should fail. Sato and I gave subjects two sessions of practice at shutting out two predefined conjunction distractors, for example, large pink right-diagonal distractors and small green left-diagonal distractors (Treisman & Sato, 1990). We found that, despite learning these two fixed distractor types, our subjects were unable to achieve pop-out for the six targets defined by other conjunctions of the same simple features. In another experiment, we compared separate measures of grouping salience and of search rates, using the same conjunction displays. In separate experiments, subjects both matched the global shape of the boundaries

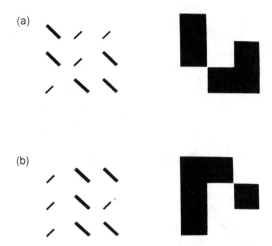

*Figure* 10. Examples of displays used to test the correlation between a same-different matching task (comparing a solid figure with the outline of cells containing one set of distractors) and the search rate for conjunction targets defined in the same displays. From Treisman & Sato (1990).; reprinted with permission of the A.P.A.

dividing one set of distractors from the other (Figure 10), and searched for a conjunction target. The correlation between the two tasks across six different conjunction targets was 0.92, supporting the idea that segregation mediates conjunction pop-out for known targets.

What about conjunctions of parts? Unlike integral dimensions, two parts of the same object cannot share exactly the same location. Feature-controlled inhibition of locations may therefore be ineffective and a different account may be needed for cases where these conjunctions seem to pop out (e.g., Humphreys et al., 1989). I have two different suggestions, each of which may play a role in explaining performance. I will give one now and save one for later, after I have laid a little more groundwork.

The first point to note is that what counts as a separable part is an empirical question, not something that can be decided a priori. Conjunctions of parts often give rise to new emergent features, which may themselves be directly detectable. One example is the closure generated when three lines form a triangle rather than an arrow (Pomerantz, Sager, & Stoever, 1977; Treisman & Paterson, 1984). Parallel detection of conjunctions with emergent features is not a problem for my theory, except that it makes it hard to disprove. We can argue that if search looks parallel, an emergent feature must be present, and if an emergent feature is present, search will be parallel. The way out of this circularity is to find converging evidence for "featurehood" of the particular property in question. For example, Treisman and Paterson (1984) showed that closure could give texture segregation and migrate to generate illusory conjunctions with other features, as well as mediating parallel search. Unless other tests for featurehood have been tried and failed, I think it is difficult to prove that conjunctions as such are detected in parallel.

Let me recall the main developments in the localizing and conjoining story. I think I still want to hold on to my basic premise, claiming that when other strategies are ruled out, focused attention is required both to locate and to conjoin. However, I and others (Nakayama, 1990; Treisman, 1988; Wolfe et al., 1989) have proposed a second form of attentional selection, controlled not by an externally directed window of attention but by selective inhibition or activation from one or more separable feature maps. This allows selection of a subset of elements that are spatially intermingled with others rather than grouped in a single spatial window. Coarse coding of features may explain why conjunction pop-out depends on highly discriminable features. If inhibition is controlled by separate feature maps, it may only be possible to select between stimuli that have non-overlapping representations.

The new model also differs from my earlier ones in showing parallel access to the shared location map and to the feature maps, making it consistent with the notion of separate parallel pathways coding "what" and "where" (first proposed by Schneider, 1969, in relation to cortical vs. midbrain systems, and more recently by Ungerleider & Mishkin, 1982, in relation to separate dorsal and ventral cortical pathways). Having drawn both sequential orders in different papers, one with the feature modules preceding the location map and one in which they followed it, I now suggest a two-way interaction, allowing either direction of control. When we are given location information in advance (e.g., a spatial cue to where the target will appear), we use the attention window to restrict which features we select. When we have advance information about the relevant features, we use inhibitory control from the appropriate feature maps. When we have neither, we choose an appropriate scale for the attention window, and scan serially through locations.

One additional point on the nature of attentional control: throughout this discussion, I have used the notion of inhibitory control and the analogy of a window of attention rather than the analogy of a spotlight (Treisman & Sato, 1990). On this view, the problem for perception is one of suppressing all *but* the correct picture of the scene, not one of building up a single correct picture. This idea resembles the filtering model of attention that Broadbent originally proposed (1958), and it echoes William James's idea (1890) that attention is like a sculptor carving one statue selected from the many latent within a single block of stone. Within the feature integration domain, the implication is that without attentional control, all possible conjunctions of the features currently present would be formed rather than none of them. The choice of this interpretation is at present somewhat arbitrary, but it fits at least with the most relevant piece of physiological evidence – the finding by Moran and Desimone (1985) that attention narrows the receptive field of cells receiving the critical stimuli. Other physiological instantiations are of course possible – for example, the recent proposal by Eckhorn et al. (1988) that feature binding depends on synchronized oscillations in the visual cortex. If firing rates can be synchronized only for one set of units at a time, for example, and the synchronized units control further processing, the effect would be equivalent to gating all other activity at whatever level this bottleneck occurs.

## Object Files and Object Selection

So far, I have proposed two attentional strategies provided by the interaction between feature modules and the location map. We may need a third. In the past few years, a debate has been brewing between location-based and object-based theories of attention. I have been firmly on both sides since 1983, when Treisman, Kahneman and Burkell described attentional effects that could not be attributed to spatial selection and that seemed to reflect the selection of perceptual objects. We gave subjects a divided attention task (Figure 11) – to read a word as quickly as possible and to locate the gap in a rectangular frame (Treisman, Kahneman, & Burkell, 1983). We found that they did better when the frame surrounded the word than when the word was outside the frame, even though the spatial separation of the gap and the word was exactly the same in both cases. It seems that attending to the word made subjects select the whole perceptual object. This included the frame when it was around the word, but not when it was separate (cf. a similar experiment by Duncan, 1984).

Our idea was that information about any particular object in the field is collected within an episodic representation that includes all its current arbitrary properties, as they appear in its present location at the present time. We used the analogy of an object file that specifies the current state of a particular object, and updates it if necessary when the object moves or changes. When attention is focused on a single element in the display, the object file represents that single element. When attention is divided more broadly, the object file creates a global representation with the emergent features that characterize the overall structure of the elements as a group.

An experiment by Pylyshyn and Storm (1988) gives perhaps the most dramatic evidence of object-based selection (although Pylyshyn

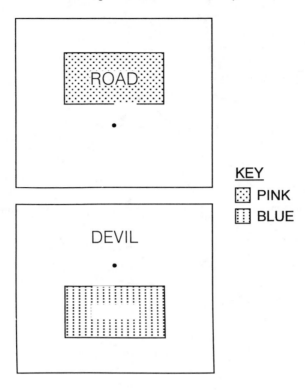

Figure 11. Examples of displays used to test the effect of perceptual objects on the ease of dividing attention between reading a word and locating a gap in a rectangle. The distances from fixation are matched in the two displays, but subjects were faster to read the word and more accurate in locating the gap in (a) than in (b).

himself offers a different account). Their task would, in our terms, depend on object files in their purest form. Imagine eight identical white dots on a screen. Four randomly selected dots flash for a second, telling you that you are responsible for those, and that you should ignore the others. Then all eight start to move in random directions quite fast, their pathways intermingling. After a few seconds, one of the eight dots flashes again, and you must say whether it was one of your dots or not. The only thing that distinguishes your four dots from the others is their past history of movement through space and time. Yet subjects can do the task – not perfectly – but well above chance.

How could this task be explained within my perceptual framework? Pylyshyn argued that spatial attention could not be used because it is generally assumed to be unitary, like a single window or spotlight. The dots were moving too fast and too unpredictably to allow a switching account in which the attention window repeatedly cycles from one dot

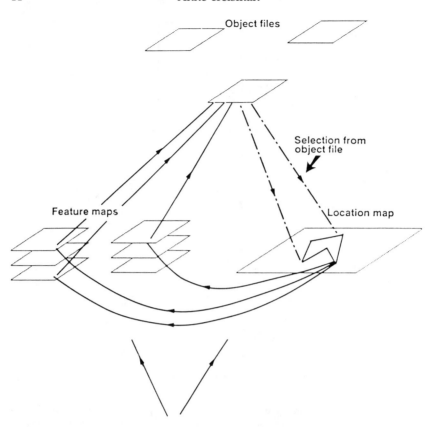

*Figure* 12. Figure illustrating the idea that attention could select the locations currently containing a particular object, through links between a currently active object file and the master map of locations.

to the next. However, Meg Wilson and I have shown that attention *is* needed to track the dots accurately. When we gave subjects a concurrent task of monitoring the colour and texture of a border around the moving dots, they did much worse on both tasks.

The second attention mechanism I proposed – control from one or more feature maps – would be ruled out because the target dots are identical to the non-targets in all their features. That leaves a third possible selection mechanism – control from one or more object files, since these are the structures that individuate objects and maintain their identity through change and motion. Perhaps attention can be controlled through object files acting back onto the master map (Figure 12) to select constantly changing locations together with the features they contain (Treisman, 1991b; see also Humphreys, Riddoch, & Müller, in preparation, for similar ideas).

There is some evidence that a single global object file may be used in this task, rather than a separate one for each target dot. When one does the task, one has the impression that one is watching the vertices of a single polygon deforming in time. Yantis (1991) showed that dot trajectories that collapse the polygon tend also to destroy the ability to track the relevant dots. When the target dots flash at the beginning of a trial, subjects may set up an object file containing the global shape implied by virtual lines joining the positions of the target dots. They also select those dot locations in the master map by downward control from the object file. When the dots start to move, subjects update the deforming shape that the dots define for as long as they can maintain the object file. If the global shape collapses when dot trajectories cross, they may lose the representation and, as a result, may lose track of some or all the target dots. (Yantis, 1991, offers a similar account in somewhat different language.)

The idea that an object file can exert attentional control may also help to explain certain cases of conjunction pop-out. Earlier in this paper, I deferred a suggestion about the coding of conjunctions of parts, to which I will now return. It applies only to within-object conjunctions that share the same parts in different spatial arrangements (for example Ts among inverted Ts) and not to between-object conjunctions, which recombine parts from two separate objects. Within-object conjunctions are often tested with homogeneous distractors, whereas displays testing between-object conjunctions must contain at least two different distractor types. There may be something special about the coding of identical elements. Duncan and Humphreys (1989) attribute the advantage of homogeneous displays to the strength of grouping by similarity. But for conjunction displays this presupposes that all stimuli are identified automatically, and that attention limits arise only postperceptually, (as, indeed, Duncan and Humphreys, 1991, believe).

If one thinks, as I do, that there are also perceptual limits, the conjunction homogeneity effect needs some other explanation. Perhaps we can use object-based selection in another way, as follows. Suppose that initially a single random element in a homogeneous conjunction display is identified with focused attention, setting up an object file for its parts and their spatial relations. This token is then used as a template to suppress matching objects across the whole display in parallel, allowing detection of any single discrepant object against the homogeneous background. Because attention is needed to maintain an object file, spatially parallel suppression is possible only for one template at a time. If the distractors are not identical, (e.g., if a set of distractor Ts are presented in varied orientations), a unique item no longer pops out. Nor does a between-object conjunction, because its distractors are necessarily of two different kinds.

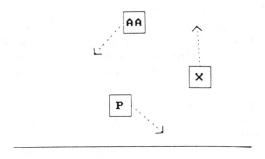

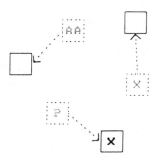

*Figure* 13. Examples of displays used to test the role of attention in creating object files. The pair of identical letters represent a single letter flashed on and off to attract attention. Between Time 1 and Time 2 the frames moved empty to their new locations.

To summarize so far: object perception and attention, as I interpret them, depend on a three-way interaction – among the feature maps, the location map and a current object file. Different tasks lead to different control strategies, picking one of these subsystems to select information from the other two. Notice that for object-based selection we necessarily have an attentional cycle. I have claimed that attention is needed to set up an object file, but once set up, the object can maintain attention to the location or locations that it currently occupies.

## The Role of Attention in Setting Up Object Files

What evidence do we actually have that attention is needed to set up an object file, beyond the evidence about conjoining features? Kahneman and I looked at this question in the context of a priming paradigm with moving objects. We tried several different experiments, of which I will describe two. In the first, we manipulated attention with a peripheral cue that is likely to call attention (Figure 13). We presented three frames, then exposed a letter briefly in each, flashing one of the three letters off and on again, in order to attract attention to it. The frames then moved empty to three new locations. Finally a single letter appeared in one of the three frames, and the subject named it as quickly as possible. The letter sometimes matched one of the earlier three and sometimes did not. The question was whether the priming benefit would be object-specific, and if so, whether this would be the case only for the attended (double-flashed) letter, as it should be if attention is required to integrate the letter with its frame. This is indeed what we found. When the final letter matched the flashed letter, priming was much stronger if the final letter appeared in the same frame as the prime. When it matched one of the two *un*attended letters, significant priming did occur, but it was no longer object-specific.

In the second experiment, we presented only one preview letter in one of the three frames, and now found almost no object-specificity. Why not? Our suggestion is that, with no competing letters present, there is no need to focus attention down to the letter in its local frame. Instead, attention is divided over the display as a whole. The three frames are entered into a global object file that rotates and expands, and the single letter moves freely within that global object. It is always identified, since there are no competing letters, and it is always retrieved and matched to the target, whether it is in the same frame or in a different one. The phenomenology here is that the initial letter seems to skip from its early frame to the final one if it appears in a different frame in the final display.

To test this rather ad hoc account, we tried anchoring the target letter to its own frame by presenting neutral stimuli (asterisks) in each of the other two frames of the first display (Figure 14). This should have led subjects to focus attention and to individuate the single letter within its own particular frame, which in turn should have increased the tendency to match within rather than across frames. Sure enough, the anchoring asterisks had the predicted effect. The preview benefit was now twice as large when the target letter appeared in the same frame as it was when it appeared in a different frame. Thus the pattern of results is consistent with the idea that attention is involved in establishing object files and integrating information within them.

## Object Files and the Control of Action

So far, I have not said much about the age-old debate on early vs. late selection (which began about the time I first became a graduate student). Would the three selection strategies – location-based, feature-based and object-based selection – count as early or late selection? I think all three constitute possible early selection mechanisms, but the level of selection will depend on whether the perceptual load is high

**Time 1**

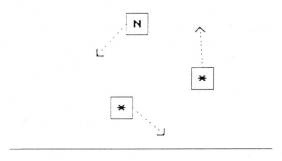

**Time 2**

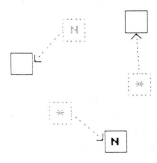

*Figure* 14. Example of displays used to test the effect of asterisks in the first field in inducing object specificity of priming.

or low, and in particular whether it poses a conjunction problem. My belief is that early selection occurs only when the perceptual load would otherwise create interference within the perceptual analyzers. Some years ago, I suggested that the nervous system may be "forced to use whatever discriminative systems it has available, *unless* these are already fully occupied . . . so that we tend to use our perceptual capacity to the full on whatever sense data reach the receptors" (Treisman, 1969, p. 296). Recently Nilli Lavie (1995) has confirmed in several different experiments that interference from irrelevant distractors in an Eriksen task varies inversely with the load imposed by processing the target.

Perceptual overload is, however, not the only reason for attentional selection. In most situations, we must also select what to respond to and how to respond. Early selectionists have always been early-plus-late selectionists. The elegant findings reported by Rizzolatti and Berti (1990) have shown how attention and perception are tailored to the type of overt behaviour they are supporting. When the perceptual load

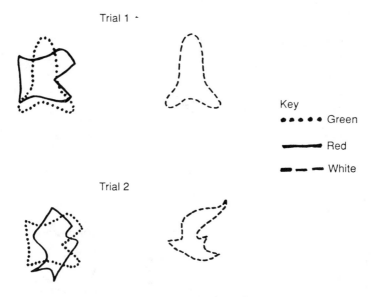

Figure 15. Example of displays used to test the role of object tokens in the negative priming paradigm. Subjects were slower to decide whether the green shape in the second display matched the white shape when it also matched the unattended red shape on the preceding trial. This was the case even on the very first pair of trials in which a new shape was presented.

is low, and especially when conflicting responses are evoked, selection for action will be the only form of selection, and it may well show different properties from those of early selection.

A clear example of late selection is the negative priming paradigm devised, under another name, by Greenwald (1972) and further explored by Neill (1977) and by Tipper and his colleagues (e.g., Allport, Tipper, & Chmiel, 1985; Tipper, 1985; Tipper & Driver, 1988). Typically, only two letters or pictures are presented, and a naming response is required, where the naming response would normally be equally strongly evoked by the relevant and by the irrelevant item. In this paradigm, the single unattended letter or picture is clearly identified on at least some proportion of trials, since it becomes harder to select on the following trial. Neumann and DeSchepper (1992), however, found a steep reduction in negative priming as the number of irrelevant letters increased from one to two or three, consistent with a switch to early selection when the load is increased.

DeSchepper and I (1996) used overlapped nonsense shapes (like those used by Rock & Gutman, 1981), to test whether inhibition in negative priming tasks is attached to temporary object files, created on the fly, or whether it is better thought of as affecting nodes in a permanent recognition network of object types. We asked subjects to make a same-

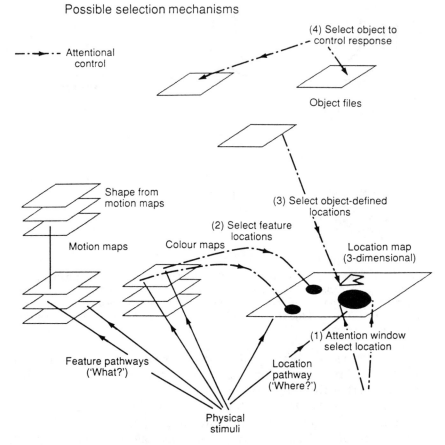

Possible selection mechanisms

*Figure* 16.   Figure illustrating the four different forms of attentional selection, mediated by interactions between the location map, the feature maps, an object file and a late selection stage determining which object file should control the response.

different judgment, comparing the green shape in an overlapped pair with a single white one to the right, ignoring the red shape in the overlapped pair (Figure 15). We found that negative priming was actually strongest on the very first trial on which a new shape was presented. Since the subjects had never seen that shape before, they must have created a new object file for the irrelevant shape as well as for the relevant shape, and the inhibition must have been attached to the representation within that object file, irrespective of whether the response was the same as that on the previous trial or different from it. The inhibition therefore depends neither on the existence of a pre-established identity or label, nor on a shared response.

So, to complete my revised picture of the perceptual system, I now add a late selection stage to the other three forms of attentional selection (Figure 16). In tasks like the negative priming paradigm, the suggestion is that attention determines which identified object file should currently control the choice of response. When the perceptual load is low, it may be the only form of attentional selection. However, when the load is high, I still believe in early selection, just as I did many years ago when I first read *Perception and Communication* (Broadbent, 1958).

## Acknowledgments

This article was reprinted by permission of Oxford University Press with slight changes from *Attention: Selection, Awareness and Control: A Tribute to Donald Broadbent*, edited by Alan Baddeley & Lawrence Weiskrantz (Oxford: Clarendon, 1993), pp. 5–35. This research was supported by the U.S. Air Force Office of Scientific Research and Office of Naval Research, Grant No. 90–0370. The manuscript is submitted for publication with the understanding that the U.S. Government is authorized to reproduce and distribute reprints for government purposes, notwithstanding any copyright notation thereon. Preparation of this chapter was also supported by the Russell Sage Foundation. I am grateful to Daniel Kahneman and Beena Khurana for helpful comments and to Marcia Grabowecky, Ephram Cohen and Beena Khurana for help in preparing the figures.

## References

Allport, D.A., Tipper, S.P., & Chmiel, N.R.J. (1985). Perceptual integration and postcategorical filtering. In M.I. Posner & O.S.M. Marin (Eds.), *Attention & Performance, Vol. XI* (pp. 107–132). Hillsdale, NJ: Erlbaum.

Broadbent, D.E. (1958). *Perception and communication.* London: Pergamon Press.

Broadbent, D.E., & Broadbent, M.H.P. (1990). Human attention: The exclusion of distracting information as a function of real and apparent separation of relevant and irrelevant events. *Proceedings of the Royal Society, London, Series B, 242,* 11–16.

Callaghan, T.C. (1984). Dimensional interaction of hue and brightness in preattentive field segregation. *Perception & Psychophysics, 36,* 25–34.

Cavanagh, P., Arguin, M., & Treisman, A. (1990). Effect of surface medium on visual search for orientation and size features. *Journal of Experimental Psychology: Human Perception & Performance, 16,* 479–491.

Cohen, A., & Ivry, R. (1989). Illusory conjunctions inside and outside the focus of attention. *Journal of Experimental Psychology: Human perception & Performance, 15,* 650–663.

DeSchepper, B., & Treisman, A. (1996). Visual memory for novel shapes: Implicit coding without attention. *Journal of Experimental Psychology: Learning, Memory, and Cognition, 22,* 27–47.

Donnelly, N., Humphreys, G.W., & Riddoch, M.J. (1991). Parallel computation of primitive shape descriptions. *Journal of Experimental Psychology: Human Perception & Performance, 17*, 561– 570.

Duncan, J. (1984). Selective attention and the organization of visual information. *Journal of Experimental Psychology: General, 113*, 501–517.

Duncan, J., & Humphreys, G. (1989). Visual search and stimulus similarity. *Psychological Review, 96*, 433–458.

Eckhorn, R., Bauer, R., Jordan, W., Brosch, M., Kruse, W., Munk, M., & Reitboeck, H.J. (1988). Coherent oscillations: A mechanism of feature linking in the visual cortex? *Biological Cybernetics, 60*, 121–130.

Enns, J.T. (1990). Three dimensional features that pop out in visual search. In D. Brogan (Ed.), *Visual search* (pp. 37–45). London: Taylor & Francis.

Enns, J.T., & Rensink, R.A. (1990). Influence of scene-based properties on visual search. *Science, 247*, 721–723.

Epstein, W., & Babler, T. (in press). Searching for shape in 3-D space. *Perception & Psychophysics.*

Greenwald, A.G. (1972). Evidence of both perceptual filtering and response suppression for rejected messages in selective attention. *Journal of Experimental Psychology, 4*, 58–67.

Hinton, G.E. (1981). Shape representation in parallel systems. In A. Drinan (Ed.), *Proceedings of the 7th International Joint Conference on Artificial Intelligence* (1981, Vancouver, B.C., Canada) (pp. 1088–1096) . Los Altos, CA: William Kaufmann.

Horowitz, T., & Treisman, A. (1994). Attention and apparent motion. Spatial Visions, 8, 193–219

Humphreys, G.W., Quinlan, P.T., & Riddoch, M.J. (1989). Grouping processes in visual search: Effects of single- and combined-feature targets. *Journal of Experimental Psychology: Human Perception & Performance, 118*, 258–279.

Humphreys, G.W., Riddoch, J., & Müller, H. (in preparation). Where, what and why: On the interaction between ventral object vision and dorsal space vision in humans.

Ivry, R.B., & Cohen, A. (1990). Dissociation of short- and long-range apparent motion in visual search. *Journal of Experimental Psychology: Human Perception & Performance, 16*, 317–331.

James, W. (1890). *The principles of psychology.* New York: Dover.

Johnston, J.C., & Pashler, H. (1990). Close binding of identity and location in visual feature perception. *Journal of Experimental Psychology: Human Perception & Performance, 16*, 843–856.

Kahneman, D., Treisman, A., & Gibbs, B. (1992). The reviewing of object files: Object-specific integration of information. *Cognitive Psychology, 24*, 175–219.

Lavie, N. (in press). Perceptual load as a necessary condition for selective attention. *Journal of Experimental Psychology: Human Perception & Performance.*

Lehky, S.R., & Sejnowski, T.J. (1988). Network model of shape-from-shading: Neural function arises from both receptive and projective fields. *Nature, 333*, 452–454.

McLeod, P., Driver, J., & Crisp, J. (1988). Visual search for a conjunction of movement and form is parallel. *Nature, 332*, 154–155.

Moran, J., & Desimone, R. (1985). Selective attention gates visual processing in the extrastriate cortex. *Science, 229,* 782–784.

Nakayama, K. (1990). The iconic bottleneck and the tenuous link between early visual processing and perception. In C. Blakemore (Ed.), *Vision: Coding and efficiency.* Cambridge University Press.

Nakayama, K., & Silverman, G.H. (1986). Serial and parallel encoding of visual feature conjunctions. *Investigative Opthalmology & Visual Science, 27,* (Suppl. 182).

Neill, W.T. (1977). Inhibitory and facilitatory processes in selective attention. *Journal of Experimental Psychology: Human Perception and Performance, 3,* 444–50.

Neisser, U. (1967). *Cognitive psychology.* New York: Appleton Century Crofts.

Neumann, E., & De Schepper, B. (1992). An inhibition-based fan effect: Evidence for an active suppression mechanism in selective attention. *Canadian Journal of Psychology, 46,* 1–40.

Pomerantz, J., Sager, L., & Stoever, R.G. (1977). Perception of wholes and their component parts: Some configural superiority effects. *Journal of Experimental Psychology: Human Perception & Performance, 3,* 422–435.

Pylyshyn, Z.W., & Storm, R.W. (1988). Tracking multiple independent targets: Evidence for a parallel tracking mechanism. *Spatial Vision, 3,* 179–197.

Ramachandran, V.S. (1988). Perceiving shape from shading. *Scientific American, 259,* 76–83.

Rizzolatti, G., & Berti, A. (1990). Neglect as a neural representation deficit. *Revue Neurologique, 146,* 626–634.

Rock, I., & Gutman, D. (1981). The effect of inattention on form perception. *Journal of Experimental Psychology: Human Perception & Performance, 7,* 275–285.

Rock, I., Linnett, C.M., Grant, P., & Mack, A. (1991). Results of a new method for investigating inattention in visual perception. *Cognitive Psychology, 24,* 502–534.

Rock, I., & Mack, A. (1991). Attention and perceptual organization. In S. Ballesteros (Ed.) *Cognitive approaches to human perception.* Hillsdale, NJ: Erlbaum.

Schneider, G.E. (1969). Two visual systems: Brain mechanism for localization and discrimination are dissociated by tectal and cortical lesions. *Science, 163,* 895–902.

Steinman, S.B. (1987). Serial and parallel search in pattern vision. *Perception, 16,* 389–398.

Tipper, S.P. (1985). The negative priming effect: Inhibitory effect of ignored primes. *Quarterly Journal of Experimental Psychology, 37A,* 571–590.

Tipper, S.P., & Driver, J. (1988). Negative priming between pictures and words in a selective attention task: Evidence for semantic processing of ignored stimuli. *Memory & Cognition, 16,* 64–70.

Treisman, A. (1969). Strategies and models of selective attention. *Psychological Review, 76,* 282–299.

Treisman, A. (1982). Perceptual grouping and attention in visual search for features and for objects. *Journal of Experimental Psychology: Human Perception and Performance, 8,* 194–214.

Treisman, A. (1988). Features and objects: The fourteenth Bartlett memorial lecture. *Quarterly Journal of Experimental Psychology, 40A,* 201–237.

Treisman, A. (1991a). Search, similarity, and integration of features between and within dimensions. *Journal of Experimental Psychology: Human Perception & Performance, 17*, 652–676.

Treisman, A. (1991b). Representing visual objects. In D. Meyer and S. Kornblum (Eds.), *Attention & Performance, Vol. XIV*. Hillsdale, NJ: Erlbaum.

Treisman, A., & Gelade, G. (1980). A feature-integration theory of attention. *Cognitive Psychology, 12*, 97–136.

Treisman, A., & Gormican, S. (1988). Feature analysis in early vision: Evidence from search asymmetries. *Psychological Review, 95*, 15–48.

Treisman, A., Kahneman, D., & Burkell, J. (1983). Perceptual objects and the cost of filtering. *Perception & Psychophysics, 33*, 527–532.

Treisman, A., & Paterson, R. (1984). Emergent features, attention, and object perception. *Journal of Experimental Psychology: Human Perception & Performance, 12*, 3–17.

Treisman, A., & Sato, S. (1990). Conjunction search revisited. *Journal of Experimental Psychology: Human Perception & Performance, 16*, 459–478.

Treisman, A., & Schmidt, H. (1982). Illusory conjunctions in the perception of objects. *Cognitive Psychology, 14*, 107–141.

Ungerleider, L.G., & Mishkin, M. (1982). Two cortical visual systems. In D.J. Ingle, M.A. Goodale, & R.J.W. Mansfield (Eds.), *Analysis of visual behavior* (pp. 549–586). Cambridge, MA: MIT Press.

Wolfe, J.M., Cave, K.R., & Franzel, S.L. (1989). Guided search: An alternative to the feature integration model for visual search. *Journal of Experimental Psychology: Human Perception & Performance, 15*, 419–433.

Yantis, S. (1991). Multielement visual tracking: Attention and perceptual organization. *Cognitive Psychology, 24*, 295–340.

# 3

# Inattentional Blindness: Perception without Attention

## Arien Mack and Irvin Rock

This chapter summarizes a body of research done over the last five years in both the perception laboratory at the New School for Social Research in New York and in Irvin Rock's laboratory at the University of California, Berkeley. The majority of the research to be described here concerns a phenomenon we have named *Inattentional Blindness* (IB), which literally forced itself on our attention while we were studying perception under conditions of inattention.

We begin by briefly summarizing some of the research that caused us to pay attention to IB in the first place. This research project began as an attempt to determine: (1) whether grouping by Gestalt principles of organization occurred without attention, which most investigators have assumed to be the case (e.g., Treisman, 1982), and (2) whether the features which others have found to pop out when searched for in otherwise homogeneous arrays also were perceived under conditions of inattention. Because pop-out has been taken as an indicator of preattentive processing (e.g., Treisman & Gelade, 1980), we conjectured that most people, if asked, would assume that these features, too, would be perceived without attention.

Our original research was motivated by our doubts about both these widely held assumptions, namely that grouping and pop-out occurred without attention. However, for the sake of brevity, we will not rehearse the reasons for these doubts here since they are detailed elsewhere (Mack, Tang, Tuma, Kahn, & Rock, 1992; Rock, Linnett, Grant, & Mack, 1992).[1] Instead, we turn directly to the method devised to explore the general question of what is perceived without attention, which, with several variations, served as our experimental method for all the research.

## A New Method

Various methods have been used to study perception without attention. The most frequently used engages subjects in two tasks. One is a distraction task and the other is a search for a predefined target element. The distraction task is meant to divert the subjects' attention away from the test stimulus so that any perception of the test stimulus is assumed to be independent of attention. However, because the subjects in these experiments know that the test stimulus may appear, and if it does, that they are to report it, some attention inevitably will be directed to it, and consequently the method fails to adequately eliminate attention. This procedure is more correctly described as one entailing divided attention. The other widely used procedure for investigating preattentive perceptual processing is one in which subjects search for a target within an array of a varying number of nontarget or distractor elements. If the amount of time it takes subjects to report the target is unaffected by an increase in the number of distractor elements, the search is assumed to be parallel and therefore independent of attention (e.g., Treisman & Gelade, 1980). However, this also cannot be correct since here too the subjects are searching for the target and therefore, by definition, attending to it. Thus, neither procedure succeeds in adequately eliminating attention.

Since no completely adequate method was available, we had to construct a new one. This method had to guarantee that the observer would neither be expecting nor looking for the object of interest, hereafter referred to as the critical stimulus but, at the same time, would be looking in the general area in which it was to be presented. We initially thought it might be necessary to engage the subject's attention in some other task, although we recently have found this not to be necessary.[2] An example of the method is illustrated in Figure 1. Observers were asked to report the longer arm of a briefly presented cross that was either centred at fixation or in the parafovea within 2.3° of fixation. Unless otherwise indicated, the cross is present on the computer screen for 200 ms, and is immediately followed by a pattern mask that covers the entire display area for 500 ms. The appearance of the cross is preceded by a fixation mark at the centre of the screen, which remains visible for 1500 ms. On the third or fourth of these trials, the critical stimulus is presented without warning along with the cross. If the cross is centred at fixation, the critical stimulus appears in one or more quadrants of the cross (see Figure 1a) and is therefore parafoveal. Conversely, if the cross is centred in the parafovea (see Figure 1b), the critical stimulus is presented at fixation. The mask again appears and remains present on the screen for 500 ms. This is the critical inattention trial. On this trial, immediately after the subjects have reported the longer arm of the cross, they are asked whether they had seen anything that had not been present on previous trials. The answer to this question provides the crucial data about what is seen without attention, since the critical stimulus is neither anticipated nor searched for by the subjects on this

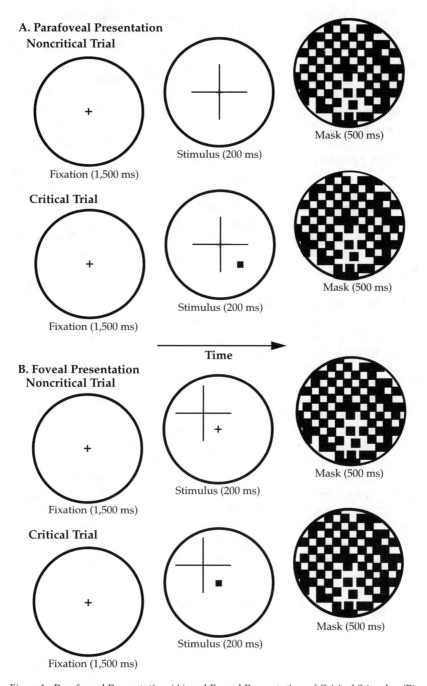

*Figure* 1.  Parafoveal Presentation (A) and Foveal Presentation of Critical Stimulus (B)

trial. If subjects report seeing something else, they are asked to identify it or to select it from an array of between four and six possible objects. In many experiments, they were asked to do so even if they reported having seen nothing other than the cross.

Since this method permits only one true, critical inattention trial per subject (on subsequent trials the subject is likely to be expecting the critical stimulus to appear), all of the experiments necessarily involved large numbers of subjects. The trials that followed the critical inattention trial therefore served different purposes. In the laboratory of New School for Social Research there were two more triads of trials, with the critical stimulus appearing with the cross on the last trial of each triad, that is, on the sixth and ninth trials. The three trials following the critical inattention trial were explicit divided attention trials in which, before these trials began, subjects were asked to report the longer arm of the cross and anything else that was present on the screen. The results from the sixth trial indicated whether both tasks, namely, reporting the longer arm of the cross *and* detecting and identifying the critical stimulus, could be done, given the exposure conditions. The final set of three trials in the New School laboratory were full attention control trials in which the subjects were instructed to ignore the cross and only report anything else present on the screen. The data from the last of these trials, the ninth trial, indicated whether the critical stimulus could be perceived with full attention, and provided the baseline against which the results from the critical inattention trial were evaluated.

In the Berkeley laboratory, the critical inattention trial was preceded by three rather than two trials, in which only the cross appeared. There were then an additional four trials on the third and fourth, of which the critical stimulus was presented along with the cross. The third of these trials was considered an implicit divided attention trial, since the subjects were no longer naïve with respect to the critical stimulus and were very likely expecting it. The fourth of these trials was the full attention control trial in which the subject's only task was to report anything that appeared on the screen other than the cross. Table 1 summarizes the procedures followed in the New School and Berkeley laboratories (a check on the consequences of these differences indicated that they did not affect the results).

## Early Results

In the experiments that investigated texture segregation and Gestalt grouping without attention, the critical stimulus was either a standard texture segregation or grouping pattern that filled the four quadrants of the cross (see Figure 2). The cross was centred at fixation. Neither texture segregation based on a vertical horizontal difference in the orien-

| New School | Berkeley |
| --- | --- |
| **Attention Trials: report distraction task only** | |
| (1) Distraction task | (1) Distraction task |
| **Inattention Trials** | |
| (2) Distraction task | (2) Distraction task |
| (3) *Distraction task and critical stimuli* | (3) Distraction task |
| | (4) *Distraction task and critical stimuli* |
| **Divided Attention Trials** | |
| Explicit | Implicit |
| (1) Distraction task | (1) Distraction task |
| (2) Distraction task | (2) Distraction task |
| (3) *Distraction task and critical stimuli* | (3) *Distraction task and critical stimuli* |
| **Full Attention Trials: ignore distraction task** | |
| (1) Distraction task | (1) *Distraction task and critical stimuli* |
| (2) Distraction task | |
| (3) *Distraction task and critical stimuli* | |

*Table* 1. Summary of procedures at the New School and Berkeley laboratories.

tation of the texture elements, nor grouping by proximity, similarity of lightness, or common fate were perceived in the inattention condition, but each was perceived in the full attention control condition (see Mack et al., 1992, for a full description of these experiments and their results).

We began this research with the assumption that something had to be perceived without attention, because attention has to have an object to which it could be directed. Therefore, that object had to pre-exist, and the next question followed directly from this assumption. If grouping is not perceived without attention, what is?[3] To answer this question, we explored the perception of a set of features under conditions of inattention we thought might be likely candidates. The features selected were location, motion, colour, numerosity, and shape. Except for numerosity, these particular stimulus attributes had been found to pop

**A. Segregation by Texture**

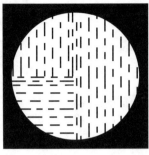
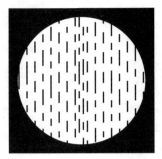

Heterogeneous                          Homogeneous

**B. Segregation by Grouping**

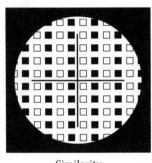
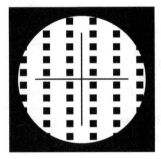

Similarity                              Proximity

*Figure* 2. Segregation by texture (A) and by grouping (B)

out, and therefore were assumed by other investigators to be processed in parallel and presumably without attention. They therefore seemed like appropriate candidates for perception without attention. In each case, the critical stimulus was presented within a quadrant of the cross that was centred at fixation (see Figure 1).

We found that location, motion, colour, and numerosity were perceived without attention about 75% of the time in the inattention condition. Shape, however, was an exception. Simple geometric shapes were also detected about 75% of the time, but they were not correctly identified at better than chance rates (a detailed account of this research, except that involving a moving critical stimulus, can be found in Rock et al., 1992). Our initial interpretation of these results, which we subsequently were led to discard, was that, with the exception of shape, these stimuli were perceived without the engagement of attention. Table 2 summarizes the results of this research and the research on grouping.

| Critical Stimulus (CS) | CS Retinal Location | |
| --- | --- | --- |
| | Foveal | Parafoveal |
| Spot | | perceived |
| Apparent motion | | perceived |
| Colour | | perceived |
| Location | | perceived |
| Shape | not perceived | not perceived |
| Texture figures | not perceived | not perceived |
| Grouping by similarity | not perceived | not perceived |
| Grouping by motion | not perceived | not perceived |
| Grouping by proximity | not perceived | not perceived |

*Table* 2: Summary of Prior Findings

An aspect of these results, and the one that ultimately led us to reject this original interpretation, gradually forced itself upon our attention. This was the fact that in every experiment involving one or a very few individual stimulus elements, an average of about 25% of the observers consistently failed to see anything other than the cross on the critical inattention trial. That is, in answer to the question, "Did you see anything on the screen that had not been present previously?," about 25% of the observers always answered "No." Moreover, these subjects were unable to pick out the critical stimulus from the array of alternatives when asked to guess. In contrast, virtually no observers ever failed to see what was there on the full attention trial.[4] The consistency of this result made it difficult to ignore, and before long it became clear that it was a highly predictable phenomenon.

Because this *sighted blindness*, this failure to detect the presence of a completely visible stimulus (e.g., a red square or a moving bar) within 2° of fixation seemed to be caused by the fact that subjects were not attending to the stimulus, we named this phenomenon, *inattentional blindness*, and it soon became the major focus of our research. From the start, the phenomenon of IB suggested that there might be no conscious perception without attention.

This changed focus to IB raised a new set of research questions. (1) Could the frequency of IB be increased by manipulating attention? (2)

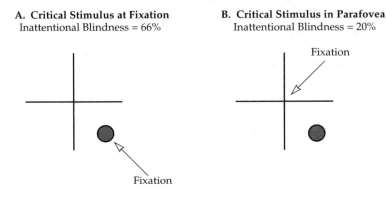

*Figure* 3. Critical stimulus and inattentional blindness

If nothing is perceived without attention, what, if any, sorts of objects capture attention? (3) What is the fate of stimuli that are not perceived under conditions of inattention? (4) Do these unseen stimuli simply drop out at some early stage of processing or are they processed more fully?

## Inattentional Blindness at Fixation

The one finding that, more than any other, confirmed our conviction that IB was a robust and important phenomenon was that, if the critical stimulus was presented at fixation and the cross was centred in one of the four parafoveal locations previously occupied by the critical stimulus (i.e., if the locations of the cross and critical stimulus are transposed), IB increases dramatically (see Figure 3). For example, a coloured spot that is seen about 75% of the time when it is presented parafoveally in a quadrant of the cross, is seen only 35% of the time or less if it presented at fixation and if the cross is located in the parafovea.

We originally switched the position of the cross and the critical stimulus in order to rule out the possibility that the consistent failure of approximately 25% of the subjects to perceive the critical stimulus under conditions of inattention when it was located about 2° from fixation, was due to its parafoveal location.[6] It seemed intuitively reasonable to believe that fixation is privileged with respect to attention, and so we thought that placing the critical stimulus at fixation and centering the cross 2° away from fixation in one of the positions previously occupied by the critical stimulus might completely eliminate IB. We never suspected that it would have exactly the opposite effect. In transposing the position of the critical stimulus and the cross, we believed that any failure to detect or identify the critical stimulus when it appeared at fixation in the inattention condition had to be entirely a function of inattention.

The reasonable expectation, of course, was that this change would eliminate IB, for how could an observer fail to detect a suprathreshold stimulus presented for 200 ms at fixation? Moreover, even though it is well known that, with effort, attention can be separated from fixation, it nevertheless seemed likely that some residue of attention might remain attached to fixation, which was another reason we expected no IB. (To our knowledge there has been no research on the question of whether attention can be entirely withdrawn from fixation.)

The opposite of what we anticipated occurred. The amount of IB more than doubled. When the critical stimulus was, for example, a solid black or outline shape identical to those that had served as critical stimuli earlier, 60% to 80% of the subjects failed to detect it in the inattention condition when it was placed at fixation. (Subjects, of course, invariably detected and identified it in the full attention, control condition.) Between 60% and 80% of the subjects reported over and over again in separate experiments that they had not seen anything other than the cross on the critical trial when the critical stimulus was presented at fixation. This result, far more than the original results from which the discovery of IB emerged, illuminated the causal connection between perceiving and attending. The hypothesis that without attention there is no perception seemed strongly supported by the sharp increase in IB at fixation.

### Exploration of IB at Fixation

In order to attempt to explain why IB was so much greater at fixation than in the parafovea, we speculated that attention might be actively inhibited from operating at fixation when subjects had a task that required that they attend elsewhere. In other words, if we assume that attention is normally focused on objects at fixation, then when a visual task requires attending to an object placed at some distance from fixation, attention to objects at fixation might have to be actively inhibited. Were this so, it would explain why IB is so much greater when the inattention stimulus is present at fixation. In the original procedure in which the cross was centred at fixation and the critical stimulus appeared unexpectedly in a parafoveal location, subjects had no reason to inhibit their attention from any particular region. Thus, IB was less.

This speculation about the inhibition of attention was verified in a series of experiments. In one series of these experiments, it was possible to create as much IB for a parafoveal stimulus as was obtained with a stimulus at fixation. In these experiments, the cross was again centred at fixation and the critical stimulus was again presented in a quadrant of the cross. But now on the trials prior to the critical trial, a small black square was also present in each of the four quadrants of the cross. These squares were located in each of the positions in which the critical stimulus could appear. On the critical trial, the critical stimulus replaced one of these squares. So if the critical stimulus was a red square, it appeared in the place of one of the black squares. As usual, the subjects were not asked about anything other than the longer arm of the cross until immediately after the critical trial.

We thought of these experiments as a way of trying to induce the inhibition of attention to particular spatial locations. Since the four squares were always present with the cross and were irrelevant to the subject's task to report its longer arm, it seemed possible that the subject might *tacitly* learn *not to pay attention to these locations*. That is, they may have learned to inhibit attention from them, just as we presumed they did with the region at fixation in the experiments in which the centre of the cross was in the parafovea. Were this to be the case, there should be a significant increase in the frequency of IB for the critical stimulus, the red square in the illustration described above, compared to the frequency of IB for the same stimulus in the same location when nothing but the cross appeared on trials prior to the critical one. This was precisely the outcome. The frequency of IB under these conditions was now as great as the IB for the same stimulus presented at fixation, and much greater than the IB obtained when nothing appeared with the cross on trials prior to the critical one (see Figure 4).

These results and others like them provided support for the proposed account of the sharp increase in IB for a critical stimulus located at fixation when the object of attention was elsewhere. They also support the more general hypothesis that, under the appropriate conditions, subjects may tacitly learn to inhibit attention from particular spatial locations which then leads to a significant increase in IB.

### IB and the Area of Attentional Focus

If IB results from the failure of a stimulus to attract attention, then it also might follow that attention might be easier to capture if the critical stimulus were located *within*, rather than *outside* the zone to which attention is directed. We assumed that the zone of attention was defined by the area occupied by the distraction stimulus which, on the inattention trials, was the object of the subject's attention. When the subjects are attending to the cross task, the assumed zone of attention is considered to be the circular area, the diameter of which is determined by the longer arm of the cross. To determine whether this was so, we manipulated the size of the hypothetical zone of attention and looked at the effect this had on the frequency of IB. We reasoned that decreasing the area of attentional focus should lead to an increase in IB for a critical

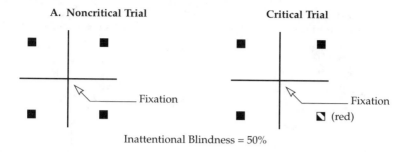

Inattentional Blindness = 50%

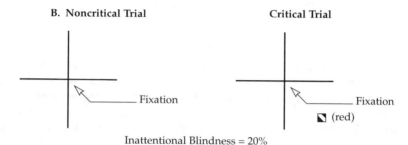

Inattentional Blindness = 20%

*Figure* 4. Inhibition of Attention. Noncritical and critical trials with Inattentional Blindness (IB) indicated.

stimulus outside this zone relative to the amount of IB for the same stimulus in the same position but within the attentional zone. This hypothesis was supported by several experiments.

In one set of experiments, the size of the cross was sharply reduced from one with an approximately 4° longer arm to one with only a 0.6° longer arm. On the assumption that the diameter of the zone of attention is defined by the longer arm of the cross, this change sharply reduces it. When this small cross was centred at fixation and the critical stimulus (e.g., a red square) was present in one of the four parafoveal positions around fixation, which, of course, were no longer in quadrants of the cross but *outside* it at the same distance from fixation), there was a highly significant increase in the frequency of IB relative to that obtained with the standard large cross (see Figure 5).

This finding not only reinforced the intimate connection between attention and perception but provided a new explanation for the lower incidence of IB (25%) in the original experiments in which there was only one critical stimulus element (or a few of them) present in a quadrant of the cross. Given the fact that the critical stimulus in these original experiments fell within the area to which attention was paid, namely within the area defined by the virtual circle whose diameter was the longer line of the cross, it was more likely to benefit from the

**Large Cross: Critical**
**Stimulus inside Zone**

**Small Cross: Critical**
**Stimulus outside Zone**

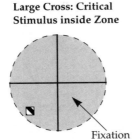

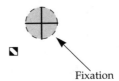

Fixation

Fixation

Inattentional Blindness = 20%

Inattentional Blindness = 66%

*Figure* 5. Zone of Attention with Inattentional Blindness indicated

attention to the cross and thus to capture attention. Consequently, it was more likely to be seen. This explanation now replaced the original explanation of these early results which we had thought meant that, because motion, colour, location, and numerosity were stimulus attributes that were perceived about 75% of the time, they were perceived without attention.

Other manipulations produced similar results. For example, in one set of experiments, the distraction stimulus was transformed to a rectangle with the same dimensions as the standard crosses, and was placed either immediately to the right or left of fixation. The task was to judge which side of the rectangle was longer. On the critical trial, the critical stimulus appeared either *within* the rectangle or at the same distance from fixation but *outside* the rectangle. Thus, if the rectangle was to the right of fixation, the critical stimulus appeared either about 2° to the right of fixation, which placed it *inside* the rectangle, or 2° to the left of fixation, which placed it *outside* the rectangle (see Figure 6). As predicted, IB was much greater for a critical stimulus (e.g., a moving square) that appeared outside the rectangle than for the same stimulus located *inside* the rectangle.

In short, when the inattention stimulus falls *outside* the area to which attention is paid, it is much less likely to capture attention and be seen. Moreover, if for whatever reason, attention is also withdrawn (inhibited) from the region where the critical stimulus is displayed (e.g., the area at and around fixation), this too will decrease the likelihood that the critical stimulus will not be seen. With both factors operating, IB may be almost 100 percent.

## IB and Salient Stimuli

The accumulating and compelling evidence of IB and its relation to attention engendered a question about whether or not there might be

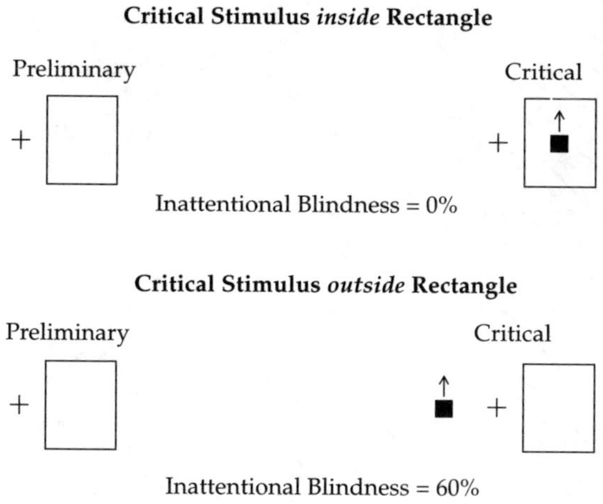

**Critical Stimulus *inside* Rectangle**

Inattentional Blindness = 0%

**Critical Stimulus *outside* Rectangle**

Inattentional Blindness = 60%

*Figure* 6. Zone of Attention Experiments, with Inattentional Blindness (IB) indicated.

some visual stimuli that would capture attention under conditions in which most other stimuli went undetected. If perception requires attention, and attention, when otherwise engaged, must be captured before perception can occur, then it seems highly likely that only a stimulus that is in some sense, important, would be a candidate for such capture. Because one's own name seemed like such a stimulus, it seemed a reasonable place to begin – particularly since it is one of the very few stimuli most likely to be heard when it is presented to the un-attended ear in a selective listening experiment. We wondered whether there was a visual analogue to this effect. Would one's own name be seen when presented under conditions of inattention?

Somewhat surprisingly, given the visual complexity of this stimulus and the fact that even a brightly coloured spot or moving bar was not likely to be seen under these conditions, we found that one's own name is, in fact, both detected and identified. Our observers almost invari-ably saw their own names under conditions of inattention when they were presented at fixation and when attention was directed to the cross that was centred in the parafovea, the condition that produced the most frequent IB with other stimuli. Under exactly the same condi-tions, a highly familiar word like "house" or "time" or someone else's name yielded strong IB when it served as the critical stimulus in the in-attention condition (see Figure 7). This continued to be true even when the cross distraction task was replaced by a lexical decision task that significantly narrowed the zone of attention to the area in which the word or non-word was presented (see Figure 8). The lexical distraction task entailed reporting whether or not a lexical stimulus, which was

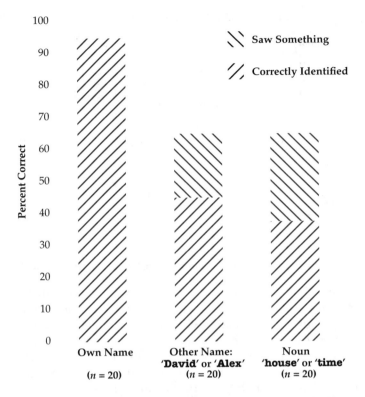

*Figure 7.* Frequency of Inattentional Blindness with lexical stimuli. Chi-square Analysis. Inattentional Blindness (IB): identifying own name versus another name (and noun) $x^2$ = 5.6, $p < .02$; identifying own name versus noun $x^2 = 18.02$, $p < .001$; identifying own name versus another name $x^2 = 11.9$, $p < .001$.

presented in one of the four locations around fixation where the centre of the cross might appear, was a word.

Even more surprising than the name effect was the finding that observers are largely blind to a stimulus that is letter-for-letter identical to their name, with the exception that the first vowel is replaced by another vowel.[6] For example, if the subject's name was "Jack," it was changed to "Jeck." This apparently trivial alteration had far from trivial perceptual consequences. While someone named "Jack" both detects and identifies "Jack" under conditions of inattention, a subject with that name not only will fail to identify but will also fail to detect the presence of "Jeck."[7] Of course, subjects presented with these versions of their name did perceive it on the full attention control trial, although there was a clear tendency to commit a proofreader's error and report seeing one's own name rather than the altered version that actually had been present. This finding suggested that a critical stimulus

**Noncritical Trial: No critical stimulus**

Fixation

\+

**Havc**

**Critical Trial: Own name and Inattentional Blindness**

Fixation

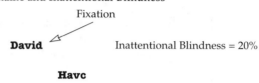

**David**          Inattentional Blindness = 20%

**Havc**

**Critical Trial: Noun and Inattentional Blindness**

Fixation

**Time**          Inattentional Blindness = 60%

**Havc**

*Figure* 8. Lexical Decision Task and Inattentional Blindness

presented under conditions of inattention might be processed to a deep level of analysis even when it is not consciously perceived.

We found several other stimuli that also appear to capture attention under conditions of inattention. Like one's own name, these stimuli also could be characterized as having high signal value as well as being very familiar. For example, we found that a cartoon-like happy face is very likely to be perceived when presented at fixation under conditions of inattention. And, just as a mildly doctored version of one's name is not likely to be seen, so, too, a scrambled or sad version of the happy face is detected far less frequently. Presenting these modified stimuli under exactly the same conditions produces frequent IB (see Figure 9).

Since happy faces and one's own name are both potentially important stimuli and highly familiar, it seemed relevant to determine whether or not familiarity alone played a role in decreasing the likelihood of IB. To this end, we compared the frequency of IB obtained when the critical stimulus was a highly familiar but relatively meaningless word with the IB for a structurally similar, more meaningful but far less frequently appearing word. The words selected were

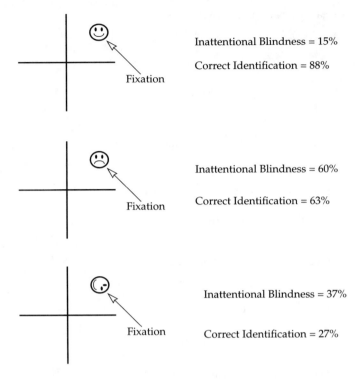

*Figure* 9. Inattentional Blindness with Face-like Icons. A: Happy Face. B: Sad Face. C: Scrambled Face

"The," which is the most frequently appearing word in the English language but carries little meaning; and the structurally similar word "Tie," which, while more meaningful, appears far less frequently. This comparison yielded no clear evidence of the role of familiarity in the capture of attention: although "The" was seen somewhat more frequently than "Tie" under conditions of inattention, this difference was not significant. Moreover, when we compared the frequency of IB for "The" with that for a happy face or one's own name, we found a significant difference in favour of names and happy faces, indicating that meaningfulness plays a significant role in the capture of attention that is independent of familiarity.

## Deep Processing

The discovery that there are complex stimuli, such as names and faces, that are able to overcome the inhibition of attention at fixation, suggested that stimuli which suffer IB might be undergoing deep processing. If a happy face or one's name are perceived while a scrambled or sad face and slightly altered name are not,[7] then it seems reasonable to consider that the bottleneck or filter that is responsible for limiting the contents of conscious perception might be located at a late stage of processing, perhaps even after semantic processing has occurred.[8] If this were not the case, it becomes difficult to explain why "Jack" is seen but "Jeck" goes undetected, or why a happy face is seen and a sad or scrambled one is detected so much less frequently.

Were this true, it would rule out an explanation of our results in terms of an early selection theory of selective attention because, according to this theory, the reason one's own name, for example, is likely to be seen under conditions of inattention is that gross features of stimuli do pass through this low-level or early filter that operates on the unattended input, and these features are sufficient for the recognition of highly familiar stimuli that have very low recognition thresholds (Broadbent, 1958; Treisman, 1969). In other words, according to an early selection theory of attention, one's own name is perceived even if not attended to, because global features are sufficient for its recognition.

The fact that a slightly altered version of one's name, which would seem to leave its global features intact, produces frequent IB therefore makes this account unlikely. If global characteristics of highly familiar stimuli that pass through a low-level filter are sufficient for its perception, then it would seem to follow that the sad face or the slightly modified name would be detected even if misidentified under conditions of inattention. It is for these reasons that we believe our results are more consistent with a late-selection model of attention (Deutch & Deutch, 1963, 1967; Logan, 1988; Norman, 1968) which accounts for the perception of stimuli such as one's own name with the assumption that all sensory input is processed to a deep level and that attentional selection occurs at the highest level of information processing.

We believe that a version of a late selection theory provides the most plausible explanation of our findings – namely, that all retinal input is subjected to deep processing, and only those stimuli to which attention is either voluntarily directed or which capture attention at a late stage of processing are perceived. On this account, it makes some sense that attention might only be captured by an important stimulus but not by a modified version of it. It is as if attention provides the key that unlocks the gate dividing unconscious perception (which, according to our working hypothesis, entails deep processing) from conscious perception. Without this attentional key, there simply is no awareness of the stimulus.[9]

## Evidence from Priming Studies

The late-selection hypothesis that even unattended stimuli are processed to a deep level, which we think is suggested by most of our results, received additional support from priming experiments. These
experiments were designed to determine whether stimuli to which
subjects were inattentionally blind or which they failed to correctly
identify, nevertheless were tacitly perceived and encoded. The evidence sought was that these undetected or misidentified stimuli de-
monstrably influenced a subject's performance on a subsequent task –
in other words, evidence of priming was sought. The typical method
used for studying priming entails measuring reaction time. We could
not do this, since our method limited us to a single inattention trial. Instead, we used a stem-completion method (Roediger, Stadler, Welden,
& Riegler, 1992). A five-letter word served as the critical stimulus and
was presented at fixation on the inattention, the divided, and the full
attention trials. In each of the three triads of trials, the words that were
selected as critical stimuli met the standard conditions for priming
stimuli in stem-completion tasks. That is, they were among the least
frequently appearing of the group of at least 10 words that completed
a particular three-letter stem. The words chosen as primes were: Flake,
Grace, Short, Chart, and Prize.[10] One of these words were presented at
fixation on the critical trial. In contrast to our other experiment, however, subjects were told at the outset that they were participating in two
different experiments that would be run successively with no break between them. The first experiment used our standard methodology and,
as usual, subjects were asked to report the longer line of the cross that
was centred in one of the four possible positions around fixation. The
subjects were told at the same time that as soon as this experiment was
completed, the next one would begin with the appearance of three letters at the centre of the computer display screen. When these letters appeared, they were to report the first two English words they could
think of that completed this word stem. They were given an example
to be sure they understood what was meant. On the critical trial, immediately following the report of line length, subjects were asked, as
usual, if they had seen anything else and, if so, what it was. As soon as
they had answered this question, the stem appeared on the screen. For
example, if "Flake" was the critical stimulus, the three-letter stem "Fla"
appeared on the computer screen. The same procedure was followed
in the divided and full attention conditions, with the exception that a
different five-letter word served as the critical stimulus in the divided
attention condition.

We reasoned that if subjects who failed to detect the presence of the
critical stimulus or who failed to identify it correctly, and reported it as

one of their stem-completion words significantly more often than control subjects who had not previously been exposed to it, this would be evidence of the encoding and unconscious perception of the critical stimulus. The results of these experiments yielded significant evidence of priming. One hundred and eighty-five subjects were tested in the main experiment. Of these, 63% demonstrated IB to the critical stimulus and, of these IB subjects, 36% gave the critical stimulus as one of their two stem-completion words. Of the 185 subjects who reported they had seen something else on the critical trial but misidentified the critical stimulus, 26% gave the critical stimulus as one of their stem completions. In contrast, of the 100 subjects tested in the control condition, only 3% offered the critical stimulus as one of their two stem-completion words.[11] Almost all of the subjects saw and correctly identified the critical stimulus in the full attention trial, and almost every one of these subjects gave it as one of their two stem-completion words. These results added significant support to our speculation that unattended and unperceived stimuli are processed to a high level where they either capture or fail to capture attention, and are consequently either consciously perceived or go undetected.

## Conclusion

The centrality of attention to perception is, of course, not limited to vision, and we do not believe that the phenomenon of Inattentional Blindness is a peculiarly visual phenomenon, although, of course, other sensory modalities would exhibit their own versions of inattentional insensitivity. In fact, we believe that inattentional insensitivity, that is, a failure to perceive as a result of inattention, is a pervasive characteristic of all our sensory systems. The visual variety, as it turns out in retrospect, is familiar to almost everyone. Everyone has, we think, had the experience of looking without seeing. During these moments, even though our eyes are open and the various objects before us are imaged on our retinas, we seem to perceive little or nothing. These moments of sighted blindness seem to occur during moments of deep absorption and, if they occur while driving, they can be alarming. Moreover, there is a correlative experience that underlines the relation between perception and attention – namely, that of hearing or seeing something that in fact is not there but which we are eagerly awaiting, an experience described eloquently by William James.

A phenomenon similar to that which we have called IB seems, at least anecdotally, to occur with the experience of pain. There are reports of the complete unawareness of the pain of a severe wound under conditions of great danger, for example when soldiers report being unaware of a wound inflicted while in battle. These reports may be an example of the same phenomenon, that is, of inattentional insensitivity. Here, when attention is absorbed by the desperate need to find safety, the pain of even severe wounds may simply not be felt. Recently in the New School laboratory, we have begun to look at inattentional insensitivity to tactile stimulation, and have had no difficulty in finding it. Similarly, but less surprising, we also have been able to demonstrate auditory deafness. So in the end, we have been driven by our data to conclude that attention is essential for conscious perception. Without it, we simply do not perceive.

## Acknowledgments

The research assistants at the New School for Social Research were Teresa Hartmann, Sarah Hahn, Jack Hoppenstand, Jonathan Katz, and Willann Stone. The research assistants at the University of California, Berkeley laboratory were Diane Beck, Quinn Hume, Harris Ingle, Christopher Linnett, and Tony Ro. Arien Mack can be reached via e-mail at: mackarie@newschool.edu

## Notes

1 Briefly stated, our doubts about the early achievement of grouping in the information processing stream were based on evidence that grouping by proximity (Rock & Brosgole, 1964) and by similarity of lightness (Rock, Nijhawan, Palmer, & Tudor, 1992) were not a function of retinal proximity or retinal similarity but rather depended on constancy operations. Since these entail later stages of postretinal processing, they are more likely to engage attention. In the case of pop-out, our doubts were based on the fact that investigations of this phenomenon require the subjects to search for the target, and therefore seem to depend on the active engagement of attention.

2 We recently have been able to elicit robust IB when the subjects have no competing task but simply do not expect the critical stimulus. This indicates that an attention absorbing distraction task is not necessary for IB, although IB is more frequent when subjects are given a distraction task.

3 The results of our research ultimately led us to reject this assumption.

4 In both the texture segregation and grouping experiments, subjects were always aware that a pattern containing multiple elements was present on the screen on the critical trial in the inattention condition, even though they failed to perceive the grouping. We attribute this to the fact, confirmed by subsequent research, that large stimuli or a stimulus pattern that covers a significant portion of the field normally will capture attention when presented under conditions of inattention.

5 Even though almost all subjects were able to detect and identify the critical stimulus with full attention, it seemed possible that there might be a decrease in functional acuity in the parafovea caused by inattention. If this were the case, we reasoned that placing the critical stimulus at fixation should either eliminate or markedly reduce IB.

6  If the subject's name began with a vowel, then the second vowel in the subject's name was changed.

7  The reader is asked to bear in mind that it is not that these slightly modified stimuli are incorrectly identified, but rather that their very presence is not detected.

8  None of the data we have obtained provides unequivocal evidence of semantic processing of stimuli to which subjects are inattentionally blind.

9  We are in the process of investigating the role of pure stimulus factors in the capture of attention under conditions of inattention, and have already found that the size of the stimulus is a factor in determining the frequency of IB. A stimulus larger than about 1.5° is significantly less likely to elicit IB than the same stimulus when it is about 0.6°. It is not yet clear, however, whether it is the perceived or retinal size of this stimulus which is producing this effect. Should it turn out to be retinal size, this would suggest the need for a revision in the theory sketched out above, which places the capture of attention at a deep level of processing. If pure proximal stimulus factors play a role in the capture of attention, which seems intuitively likely, then it may be that the processing level at which attention is engaged, is determined by the nature of the input.

10  These words were chosen on the basis of a widely cited word-frequency analysis (Francis & Kucera, 1982).

11  The control subjects were simply asked to complete one of the stems from the main experiment with the first two English words that came to mind. These subjects were obtained by stopping people in the halls of the New School and asking them to complete one of the three-letter stems from our main experiment with the first two English words that came to mind. Each control subject was shown only one stem.

# References

Broadbent, D. (1958). *Perception and communication*. London: Pergamon Press.

Deutch, J., & Deutch, D. (1963). Attention: Some theoretical considerations. *Psychological Review, 70*, 80–90.

Deutch, J., & Deutch, D. (1967). Comments on "Selective Attention": Perception or response? *Quarterly Journal of Experimental Psychology, 19*, 362–363.

Francis, W., & Kucera, H. (1982). *Frequency analysis of English usage: Lexicon and grammar*. Boston: Houghton Mifflin

Logan, G. (1988). Toward an instance theory of automatization. *Psychological Review, 95*, 492–527.

Mack, A., Tang, B., Tuma, T., Kahn, S., & Rock, I. (1992). Perceptual organization and attention. *Cognitive Psychology, 24*, 475–501.

Norman, D. (1968). Towards a theory of memory and attention. *Psychological Review, 75*, 522–536.

Rock, I., & Brosgole, L. (1964). Grouping based on phenomenal proximity. *Journal of Experimental Psychology, 67*, 531–538.

Rock, I., Linnett, C., Grant, P., & Mack, A. (1992). Perception without attention: Results of a new method. *Cognitive Psychology, 24*, 502–534.

Rock, I., Nijhawan, R., Palmer, S., & Tudor, L. (1992). Grouping based on phenomenal similarity of achromatic color. *Perception, 21,* 779–789.

Roediger III, H., Stadler, M., Welden, M., & Riegler, G. (1992). Direct comparison of two implicit memory tests: Word fragment and word stem completion. *Journal of Experimental Psychology: General, 18,* 1251–1269.

Treisman, A. (1967). Strategies and models of selective attention. *Psychological Review, 76,* 282–299.

Treisman, A. (1969). Strategies and models of selective attention. *Psychological Review, 76,* 282–299.

Treisman, A. (1982). Perceptual grouping and attention in visual search for features and for objects. *Journal of Experimental Psychology: Human Perception & Performance, 8,* 194–214.

Treisman, A., & Gelade, G. (1980). A feature integration theory of attention. *Cognitive Psychology, 12,* 97–136.

# 4

## The Medium of Attention: Location-Based, Object-Centred, or Scene-Based?

### Steven P. Tipper and Bruce Weaver

There are two questions one can ask about selective attention. The first, and perhaps more basic question, concerns what functions it serves: Why does attention exist? The second question is more specific, and asks what the actual mechanisms of attention are. However, one's approach to answering the second question is entirely determined by how one answers the first. That is, until we understand what we are studying, there is little chance of making progress. This point has been made many times before, perhaps most forcefully by Marr (1982). He argued for the computational level of analysis, where the functions subserved by a system in an animal's normal environment are clearly defined.

Throughout the recent history of investigations of attention, the answer to the first question has been that attention's main function is to facilitate perceptual processes. For example, in Broadbent's (1958) filter theory, perception only analyzed the low-level physical properties of visual stimuli, such as colour, size, motion, and so forth. For higher levels of internal representation to be achieved, attention had to be directed towards the perceptual representations of a particular object. Thus, objects were only recognized when they received attentional processing.

More recently, Treisman (1988) has also argued that one of attention's main functions is to facilitate perceptual processes. In this case, attention is required to integrate the various perceptual properties that are analyzed separately in different neural structures, such as motion in MT and colour in V4. Only when attention is directed towards an object is a complete and coherent internal representation achieved. Unattended objects are only represented in terms of free-floating features.

However, when considering the initial question about what functions attention evolved to serve in an animal's normal environment, a different view emerges. It is necessary to consider both behavioural goals and the environment in which the goals are to be achieved. It can be argued that there are massive constraints in the real world that facilitate automatic perceptual processes – that is, invariant properties of objects that can be detected by perceptual systems to guide action

77

(Gibson, 1979). Furthermore, the animal has well-established internal representations of its environment. Some of these may be hard-wired. For example, objects quickly approaching the face will have a damaging effect on the perceiver and so should be avoided (Bower, 1971; Bower, Broughton, & Moore, 1970). Other representations may be more specific and learned, such as the layout of a particular bedroom. In these situations it appears that perceptual analysis of many objects can be achieved in parallel. Multiple objects, indeed the entire scene (such as that of a bedroom) can be represented very quickly, independently of the focus of attention (see Houghton & Tipper, 1994, for further discussion).

It is important to note that such an analysis does not dispute the view that attention can play a role in perceptual processes. We have argued previously that attention can be very flexible (Tipper, Weaver, & Houghton, 1994). It can have access to a range of internal representations, depending upon task demands. Thus, it is not surprising that in the somewhat artificial experimental situations sometimes studied, where the context is unfamiliar to the observer, and many unrelated stimuli can be presented (e.g., words unrelated to each other), attention is required to aid perception. However, our concern is with understanding how attention functions in more ecologically valid real-world settings. We suggest that in very familiar environments, the main function of attention is to link perception with action. It should be noted that the experiments to be described are not in real-world settings, as we feel that the highly controlled experimental procedures developed by cognitive psychologists are necessary to observe the elusive and often transparent mechanisms of perceptual-motor processes. However, these experiments do contain simple, highly constrained properties that become familiar to subjects, hence facilitating automatic processing.

Most organisms regularly confront environments that contain many objects that afford competing actions (Gibson, 1979). However, it is often critical, for the achievement of behavioural goals, that action be directed to only one object at any point in time. We propose that attention is the mechanism that selects particular internal representations of the environment to guide action.

With these ideas concerning the functions of attention in mind, issues concerning the mechanisms of attention can be engaged. For example, the dominant position concerning selection has been that it is achieved purely by excitation processes. The main analogy is that of a spotlight moving across an internal representation of space. When an object is within the beam of the spotlight, its internal representations receive further processing, and the object is selected (e.g., Broadbent,

1982; Eriksen & Eriksen, 1974). Such a view of selection is clearly influenced by a particular view concerning the functions of attention. That is, if attention is necessary for perceptual analysis, then it follows that the main selection mechanism will be one of furthering the perceptual processing of the target.

However, if one assumes that very elaborate representations of the world can be achieved independently of the focus of attention, and that the main function of attention is to direct action towards particular objects, then different ideas concerning the mechanisms of selection can be considered. For example, if a number of objects can be represented in parallel to a deep level, where they evoke conflicting responses, then a single excitation mechanism will not be sufficient to achieve the remarkably efficient selection observed (see Houghton & Tipper, 1994 for more detailed discussion of this issue). Rather, active inhibition directed towards the representations of the distracting objects will probably be required.

Over the past decade, inhibitory effects of attention have garnered considerable interest. Quite independently of debates over their precise cause, research on several such empirical phenomena has contributed greatly to our understanding of the forms of internal representation accessed by attention. In this chapter, we describe recent research from our laboratory that uses inhibitory phenomena of attention to answer the question: What is the medium of attention?

As discussed above, this issue is critically determined by how one views the functions of attention. When attention was considered to be necessary for perceptual processes to achieve deeper levels of internal representation, it was believed that attention acted like a spotlight moving over a spatial map. Thus, an internal representation of space, or a spatial map, was assumed to be the medium over which attention moved. The attentional beam was not affected by objects in the world, it simply moved from one place to another. Any objects within the beam of the spotlight received further processing.

We do not dispute that attention can have access to such a spatial frame of reference in some circumstances. However, we wish to emphasize the flexibility of attention. Attention is not rigidly and inflexibly limited to only low-level perceptual representations via a spatial map. Rather, attention is highly flexible. Thus, in the context of familiar environments, where rich, elaborate perceptual representations are achieved in parallel, and where the main goal of attention is to select objects for action via inhibitory mechanisms, it is likely that attention has access to object-based internal representations. That is, we direct action towards objects, and thus the selection mechanisms manipulate such object-based representations.

The idea according to which the medium of attention can be object-based rather than merely spatial has gradually gained support over the last decade. Initial ideas of Duncan (1984) and Kahneman and Treisman (1984) have been corroborated by other researchers, (e.g., Baylis & Driver, 1993; Egly, Driver, & Rafal, 1994; Harms & Bundesen, 1983; Kramer & Jacobson, 1991). In this chapter, we review some of the experiments from our laboratory that have also found support for a flexible attention system that can gain access to different forms of internal representation. This evidence comes from three main research areas: Negative Priming (NP), Inhibition of Return (IOR), and Visual Neglect (VN). This variety of research approaches provides strong converging evidence for the existence of object-based mechanisms of selective attention.

## Negative Priming

One approach to observing the inhibition associated with ignored objects is to use a priming procedure. The logic underlying this procedure is as follows. If the internal representations of an irrelevant object are encoded to a deep level, and they conflict with those of the target object for the control of action, then inhibition of these competing internal representations will aid selection. The inhibition associated with the distractor can be detected by observing the processing of an object that requires those inhibited representations shortly after the act of selection.

For example, in experiments such as that shown in Figure 1A, subjects are required to report the location of the target O and ignore the distractor X (e.g., Tipper, Brehaut & Driver, 1990). To direct action to the target, action towards the distractor's location must be inhibited. Therefore, when a subsequent target appears in the inhibited location shortly afterwards (the Ignored Repetition [IR] condition), any residual inhibition will be observed in longer reaction times to respond to the new target. This NP effect was first observed in 1966 in a Stroop colour naming task (see Dalrymple-Alford & Budayr, 1966), subsequently was replicated by Neill (1977), and has now been observed in many different experimental procedures in many laboratories around the world (see Neill, Valdez, & Terry, 1995 for review).[1]

As described above, the negative priming effect provides some evidence for an inhibitory mechanism of selective attention. That is, action can be directed towards targets because of inhibition associated with the competing internal representations of distractors. But what kinds of representations are inhibited? If the medium of attention is a spatial map of the environment, then it is likely that the spatial locus of the distracting object is inhibited. Processing of the subsequent probe target is impaired (in the IR condition) because that target appears in an inhibited location on the spatial map.

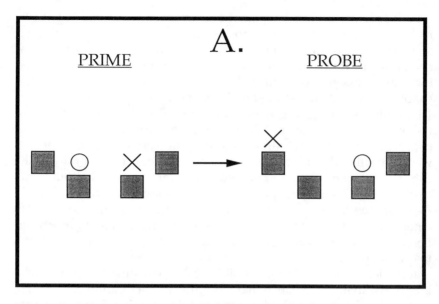

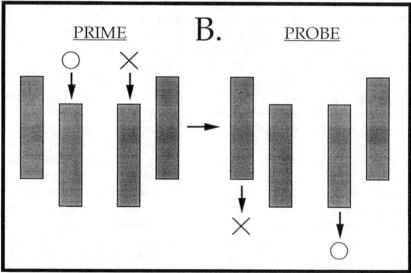

*Figure* 1. Panel (A): Subjects were required to press one of four keys to report the locus of the target O in the prime display. Shortly afterwards, a probe display was presented, and again subjects had to report the locus of the target O. This figure represents the Ignored Repetition (IR) condition, where the probe target appears in the location recently occupied by the prime distractor. This situation was compared with the control condition, where the probe target appeared in a location that was empty in the previous prime display. Panel (B): This represents an IR condition, where the target probe O emerges from the occluding column behind which the prime distractor disappeared.

Subsequent work, however, has shown that this account is not correct – or at least not adequate to account for all negative priming effects. We now know that inhibition is not always tied to a particular spatial locus. Rather, it can be associated with dynamic object-based internal representations, such that it moves with an object through space. This was demonstrated in the experiment represented in Figure 1B. In this task, the prime display was presented at the top of the computer screen. The target and distractor moved down the screen, disappearing behind the occluding columns. The subjects' task, as before, was to localize the target with a key press response. Importantly, the subsequent probe objects appeared to emerge from the bottom of occluding columns as they moved down the screen. Again subjects had to report the locus of the target O. In the IR trials, the probe target emerged from the bottom of the same column that had occluded the ignored prime object at the top of the screen. Thus, there were over 4° between the prime and probe.

A model proposing that the inhibitory mechanisms of attention have access to a spatial map, such that inhibition is of a location on the map, would predict no negative priming in this situation, because the ignored prime and target probe are in completely different spatial loci. In contrast, a model arguing that inhibition is associated with the object that competes for the control of action would predict that negative priming will still be observed. That is, the inhibited ignored object moves behind the occluding surface and reappears as the target requiring a response. In support of such object-based models, very robust negative priming was observed in this experiment.[2]

Data demonstrating that mechanisms such as inhibition can be associated with dynamic object-based representations help to explain the remarkable perceptual-motor performance shown by many mammals. Often the most important objects with which an animal interacts are animate. Interactions between members of a species, and interactions with prey and predators determine the very survival of the species. It is clear, for example, that a lioness pursuing antelope prey must continuously direct action towards the target object. Other prey within range must not be allowed to evoke conflicting attack responses. These distractors are also in motion, and thus inhibition of a particular location at one moment will not aid selection when the distractor moves into an uninhibited location a moment later. Evolution must have selected attentional mechanisms that can cope with such enormously complex perceptual-motor interactions. The next example also demonstrates the need for the evolution of object-based attention mechanisms.

## Inhibition of Return

Aside from selecting targets for action from among competing distractors, mechanisms of attention must also initially find the target. This is a very fundamental task undertaken by attention. Just as a human may search an office for a mislaid pen, so a chimpanzee may search the forest for food. It is crucial that attention not keep returning to recently examined loci. Such perseveration would have disastrous consequences, probably resulting in the starvation of the animal.

Posner and Cohen (1984; see also Maylor, 1985; Rafal, Calabrasi, Brennan, & Sciolto, 1989, for other examples) have proposed that inhibitory mechanisms aid efficient search. They have argued that after attention has been directed to a particular location, inhibition prevents attention from returning to that location. These models provide good examples of attention having access to internal spatial maps. They specifically state that attention is inhibited from returning to a particular spatial location, as opposed to, for example, a particular location on the retina (e.g., Maylor & Hockey, 1985).

Evidence for such inhibition of return has been gained from very simple and elegant experimental procedures. Figure 2A represents a typical task. Three boxes are presented on a computer screen (A1). One of the peripheral boxes brightens for 100 ms (A2). This sudden increase in illumination automatically orients attention to that location via subcortical mechanisms in the superior colliculus of the mid-brain (see below for details). The central box then brightens, drawing attention away from the peripheral location and back to the centre of the display (A3). Shortly afterwards, a target (in this example the target is a small white box) is presented (A4), and subjects simply press a key as quickly as possible upon seeing it. The target is presented (with equal probability) in either the cued or uncued peripheral box. The important observation is that with stimulus onset asynchronies greater than 300 ms, detection of the target is substantially slower when it appears in the recently cued box. This provides support for the idea that attention is inhibited from returning to a location recently examined.

Such a spatial inhibition mechanism will function efficiently when searching for static objects – and, indeed, below we will demonstrate further support for the notion of a spatial inhibition mechanism. However, as discussed, some of the most important objects with which animals interact are mobile. Consider the following examples. A chimpanzee may have to search for its offspring among a group moving through the forest; or a lioness may have to search a herd of moving antelope for the individual most likely to result in a successful kill (e.g., young, old, or injured). Again, in such interactions with

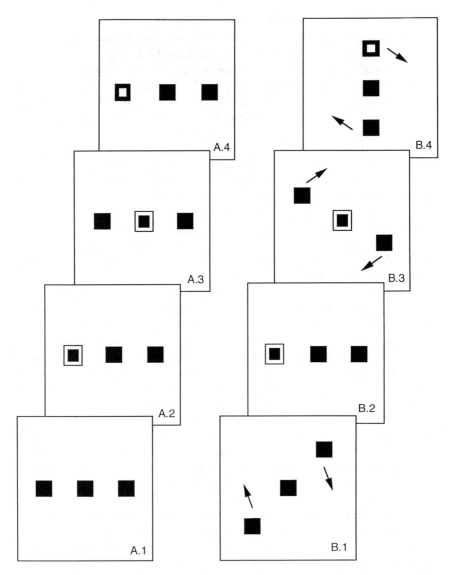

*Figure* 2. Panel (A): The procedure developed by Posner & Cohen (1984). This is an example of a cued trial (A2), where the target appears in the location that was cued (A4). Panel (B): The procedure developed by Tipper, Driver, & Weaver (1991). This example shows a cued trial (B2), where the target appears in the object that was cued after it has rotated 90° away from the spatial location of the cue (B4).

the environment, an object-based search mechanism must have evolved. Otherwise, search would be seriously impaired as attention returned to objects previously examined as they moved from the inhibited location.

Figure 2B demonstrates an experiment that attempted to show that IOR could be object-based in some circumstances. The procedure was similar to that described in Figure 2A. However, after cueing, the objects moved away from the initially cued location. In this situation, the cued and uncued objects are equidistant from the cued location at the time of target detection. Therefore, a model proposing that inhibition is spatially based predicts no differences between cued and uncued objects. In contrast, a model proposing that inhibition can be object-based predicts that inhibition will move with the cued object. This object-based model was supported by subsequent research. Reaction time to detect the target in the cued object was longer than that for the uncued object (see Abrams & Dobkin, 1994; Tipper, Driver, & Weaver, 1991; Tipper, Weaver, Jerreat, & Burak, 1994).

When we initially discovered this object-based IOR, we suggested it was the only mechanism (Tipper et al., 1991). That is, location-based inhibition was felt to be redundant. However, our subsequent work has shown that in fact both object-based and location-based IOR can exist simultaneously (Tipper et al., 1994). For example, Figure 3 represents experiments by Tipper and Weaver. Three boxes are presented. After cueing (panel A), the boxes move. This experiment replicates the object-based inhibition, where RTs are impaired to detect the target in the cued box. However, it also allows a test for inhibition remaining in the spatial locus that was cued. That is, one of the objects moves into the spatial locus of the peripheral cue. We find that RTs are longer in this box as well, relative to the control box that shares neither location nor object with the cue.

Another important point worth stressing here is that this is one of the first demonstrations of a pure spatial IOR effect (see also Experiments four and five from Tipper et al., 1994). That is, in virtually all other research arguing for spatial IOR, there is a confound with object-based effects. The cue and target both appear in a static object that is present throughout the trial (see Figure 2A for an example). The IOR effects observed in such experiments are very robust and often quite large (e.g., about 40 ms). This may be because such experiments measure the additive effects of both object-based and location-based IOR. In the experiment described in Figure 3 where such a confound is removed, location-based effects are often much smaller (15–20 ms). Furthermore, the sum of the separate object-based and location-based IOR effects in the three-box experiments produces an overall IOR of approximately 40 ms.

In a recent pilot study, Jordan and Tipper directly examined whether the relatively large IOR effects observed when static boxes were cued was due to the combined effects of location-based and object-based IOR. This study simply compared IOR when an object was presented at the cued location, with conditions in which no object was presented. We attempted to hold constant the physical features present in the

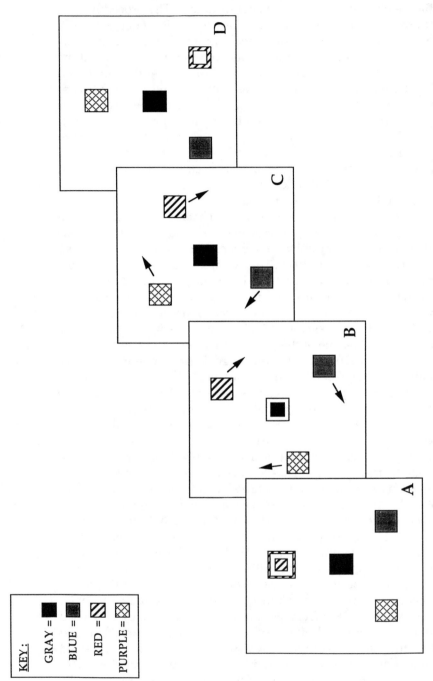

KEY :

GRAY = ■
BLUE = ■
RED = ▨
PURPLE = ▨

*Figure* 3. The procedure developed by Tipper & Weaver (in preparation). In this example the red box is cued (A). Then the objects rotate for 120° (B & C). Finally the target is presented in one of the boxes. In this example the target is in the cued red object (D). Targets appearing in the cued location would be presented in the purple box, and those in the uncued control condition would be presented in the blue box.

86

object and no object conditions, which could cause metacontrast masking effects for example. To this end Kanisza square figures were utilized. For the condition where no object was visible, the "pac-man" figures were reoriented.

In Figure 4, the cues and target could appear in the white squares (to left and right) or objectless locations (above and below). Of course, the alternative layout, in which the Kanisza squares were above and below fixation, was also examined. The example presented in Figure 4 shows an objectless location cued condition (panel c), in which no object is visible. The target is presented in the right square (panel d), so this is an example of one of the uncued trials. The results of this preliminary study are clear. IOR is almost twice as great when the visible white square object is cued (41 ms) than when the empty location is cued (23 ms). This latter pure location-based result is similar in magnitude to the location effect of the three-box experiment shown in Figure 3. It needs to be stressed, however, that this data is from an intial pilot study, and much further research is necessary.

## Dissociations between Location-based and Object-based IOR

An obvious issue to consider, now that both location-based and object-based IOR have been demonstrated in the same experimental preparation, is whether they possess the same properties. A series of studies have in fact shown that these two frames of reference can be dissociated with particular experimental procedures. Examples of such dissociations follow.

First, as we have seen with the three-box experiment described above (Figure 3), location-based IOR can be associated with an empty featureless part of the environment (computer screen). That is, after cueing, the box moved from the cued location, which remained empty until the arrival of the next box. Thus, the inhibition was unaffected by the departure and arrival of objects, remaining attached to a particular location. In sharp contrast, the inhibition associated with the object is only applied if the object is visible when attention is oriented to it at the time of cueing. Consider Figure 5A. In this task there are four boxes presented on the computer screen; two are red and remain static, and two are blue and can move. In this situation, the smaller blue boxes move behind the static red boxes at the time of cueing. Subsequently they re-emerge and move to a new location where a target is presented. In this procedure, no object-based IOR is observed.

In contrast, consider the similar situation represented in Figure 5B. In this case, the now larger moving blue boxes are visible at the time of cueing, occluding the static red boxes. After such cueing, object-based

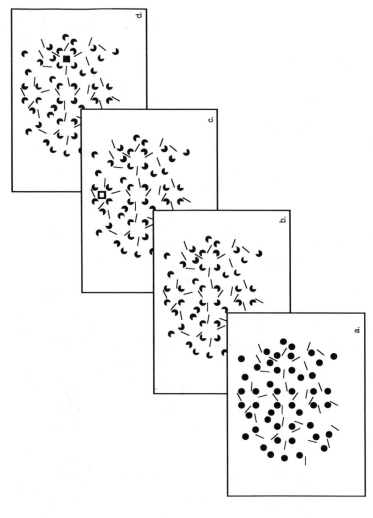

*Figure 4.* Panel (a) shows the initial display presented for 1500 ms. Panel (b) shows the removal of the circle slices to reveal the pac-man figures throughout the display. This is experienced as the sudden onset of the display. Panel (c) represents the cue. In this example, the empty objectless location above fixation is cued. Panel (d) shows the target for detection in the right side square. Hence this is an example of one of the uncued trials.

IOR is observed when the objects move to a new location and the target is presented. Such results support the notion that the inhibition is associated with a specific object. Even though the spatial locus of the cue is constant in Figures 5A and 5B, only when attention is directed to the visible blue object is inhibition associated with the object (see Tipper et al., 1994, for details).

The second dissociation between object-based and location-based IOR was discovered by Abrams and Dobkin (1994). They demonstrated that the location-based effect is associated with inhibition of the oculomotor system that controls saccades, as well as with perceptual systems that detect the onset of the target. Thus, IOR is observed at the cued location in two kinds of task. In one, no target is presented at the cued location, but eye movements to that location, determined by a central arrow cue pointing in a particular direction, are impaired. In the second task, detection of a target, via a key press, is impaired when it is presented in the cued location. In contrast, the object-based system is only associated with inhibition of the latter perceptual detection system. Thus, saccades are inhibited from moving to the location originally cued, but the saccade inhibition is not updated as the object moves.

The third dissociation between these two frames of reference has been observed recently by Tipper and Weaver. They observed that location-based and object-based IOR effects can be dissociated by manipulating the stimulus-onset-asynchrony (SOA) from initial cue to target. They examined location-based and object-based IOR at SOAs of 598 ms, 1054 ms, and 3560 ms. The location-based effects at these SOAs were −18 ms, −15 ms, and −24 ms, respectively. As these numbers suggest, the location-based effect did not interact with SOA. But a different pattern emerged for the object-based effects. Here, the three effects (in the same order) were −31 ms, −15 ms, and −1 ms. In this case, the interaction with SOA was highly reliable. Furthermore, the interaction was significant even when only the two shorter SOAs (598 ms and 1054 ms) were compared. Thus, it would appear that location-based IOR is relatively long-lasting, whereas object-based IOR decays fairly quickly.

This contrast in the stability of IOR across time makes some sense when one considers various properties of real-world environments. Inhibition associated with a spatial location may well be relatively stable if nothing is changing. In contrast, mobile animate objects always have the potential of drastically changing their meaning to a perceiver, and hence stable long-term inhibition of such objects may impair performance. For instance, consider an antelope monitoring a pride of lions as they move across the savannah. Attention moves from one lion to another, and inhibition probably prevents attention from returning immediately to an animal just examined. However, because each lion's

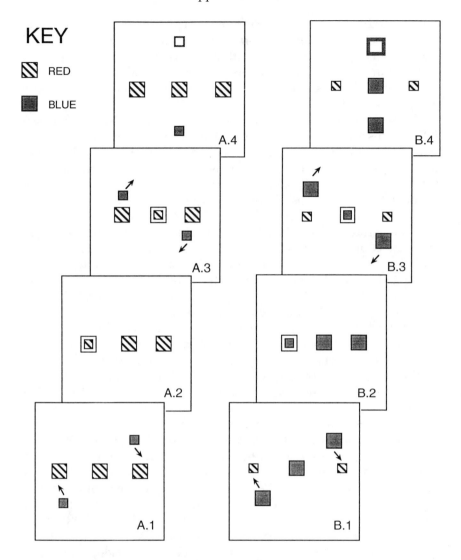

*Figure* 5. Panel A: The smaller moving blue boxes are occluded by the larger red static boxes at the time of cueing (A2). After offset of the peripheral cue, the blue boxes emerge from behind the red boxes and move for a further 90°, at which point a target can be presented (A4). In this example the target appears in the object that was occluded by the cued red object. Panel B: The larger moving blue boxes occlude the smaller red boxes at the time of cueing (B2) In this example, the target appears in the cued blue object (B4).

behavioural state can change qualitatively at any time, as when beginning to move towards the antelope, it may not be wise to maintain inhibition over long periods of time.

Having discovered that both object and spatial frames of reference can be associated with inhibition, and that these two frames can be dissociated, we speculated about whether they were subserved by different neural structures. Rafal and his colleagues have forcefully argued that location-based IOR is mediated by the superior colliculus (e.g., Posner, Rafal, Choate, & Vaughan, 1985). There are now three pieces of evidence that support this proposal. First, there are asymmetric pathways projecting to the superior colliculus from the retina, where greater inputs arise from the temporal hemifield. Such an asymmetry is not observed in retinal projections to the cortex. In line with the asymmetrical projections to the superior colliculus, if stimuli are presented monocularly, IOR is larger when cues are presented to the temporal hemifield. Second, patients with Progressive Supranuclear Palsy have damage to the superior colliculus, and they are the only known clinical population who fail to demonstrate IOR. And third, visual processing in the newborn human infant is mediated almost exclusively by subcortical structures such as the superior colliculus. Interestingly, IOR has been observed in infants as young as one day old (Valenza, Simion, & Umilta, 1994).

In contrast, we argued that object-based IOR is too sophisticated for subcortical structures (Tipper et al., 1994). Although neurons in the superior colliculus respond to moving stimuli, they are not efficient at encoding speed and direction of motion. In fact, the superior colliculus is dependent on cortical systems such as MT for analysis of moving stimuli (Goldberg & Wurtz, 1972; Gross, 1991; Schiller, 1972). Furthermore, it has been shown that lesions to the cortex destroy the ability to encode the motion of a moving object, and to direct action towards it (e.g., Ingle, 1977; Ingle, Cheal, & Dizio, 1979).

We suggested therefore that the object-based IOR is subserved by later evolving cortical systems. Recent work with Bob Rafal and his colleagues has provided some support for this idea (Tipper, Rafal, Reuter-Lorenz, Starrveldt, Ro, Egly, & Weaver, in press). In a split-brain patient with a complete lesion of the corpus callosum, each cortical hemisphere is isolated from the other, in that there are no direct links between homologous regions of cortex. We predicted that if inhibition were associated with an object, and this inhibition was subserved by cortical structures requiring direct corpus callosum connections, it would move with the object as long as the object remained in the same visual field, and hence in the same cortex. (See Figure 6, panel A1 to A5 for examples of such trials.) On the other hand, if the cued object moved into the other visual field, and hence to the cortex that did not have knowledge of the inhibition, as represented in panels B1 to B5 of Figure 6, then no IOR should be observed.

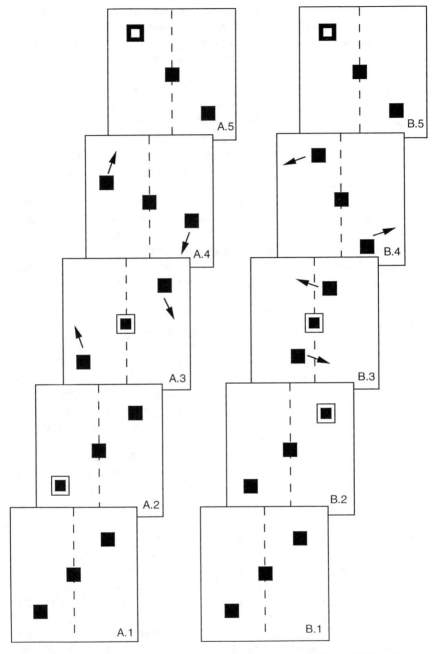

*Figure* 6. Panel A: The cued object rotates 90° in the same visual hemifield, so that on cued trials the cue (A2) and target (A5) are presented to the same cortical hemisphere. Panel B: The cued object crosses the midline from one visual hemifield to the other, such that the cue (B2) and target (B5) are presented to different cortical hemispheres.

This result is precisely what was observed in two split-brain patients. In contrast, control subjects demonstrated IOR whether the object remained within the visual fields or moved between them. A further result was completely unexpected: not only did we fail to see object-based IOR in split-brain patients when the objects crossed the midline, but in fact we observed facilitation effects. This result suggests that there is a residual excitation associated with the cued object, and that it is subserved by subcortical structures (because it crosses the midline). This excitation is usually invisible because the object-based inhibition dominates.

In summary, these studies have reported dissociations between location-based and object-based IOR. The studies have also provided some evidence that dissociations may be mediated by different neural structures. However, other experimental manipulations can affect both forms of IOR equally. For example, changing the speed of moving objects, to be discussed more fully below, disrupts both location-based and object-based IOR. Similarly, both inhibition mechanisms appear to be utilized less as subjects have increasing experience with the task.

Thus, in a study in which subjects participated in the three-box experiment described above, three times a day for four days (Tipper, Weaver, & Watson, in preparation), even though the usual IOR effects were observed on the first day, by the end of the fourth day IOR effects were drastically reduced in both frames of reference. We speculate either that inhibition mechanisms are used sparingly, and that when subjects have had extensive experience with a task, other attentional mechanisms may become dominant; or more simply, that subjects habituate to the cue over hundreds of trials, and hence attention is less strongly captured by the cue.

### Object-Centred and Scene-Based Frames of Reference

The distinction has been made between location-based and object-based representations. Whereas some traditional notions of attention pay heed only to location-based representations, the research described to this point makes clear that the medium of attention is often that of an object-based representation. Our most recent work has begun to ask more precise questions about the object-based representations involved in IOR (Tipper & Weaver, unpublished). We make the contrast between scene-based internal representations and object-centred representations. Scene-based representations describe the spatial locations of separate objects in a scene. Importantly, these objects are independent, such that the spatial locus of one is separate from and independent of that of others. For example, two people could be three feet or three miles apart. The location of one object is completely independent of the location of the other.

Object-centred descriptions are quite different. These are much more similar to the spatial frames described above. In this case, the components within an object are represented within a spatial structural description (Biederman, 1987). The locations within an object are not independent. Take as an example a triangle. Even though the triangle is an object that can move through space, each corner is constrained relative to the other corners. That is, they have a static invariant spatial relationship.

In the three-box experiment described above and represented in Figure 3, questions concerning the object-based representation remain. Although we have considered this IOR to be scene-based, where each box is independent of the others, this need not be the case. In these studies, the boxes move in a very constrained manner, maintaining the same speed and spatial relationship between each other. Therefore, it may be that they are encoded in object-centred co-ordinates, where each box is represented as a corner of one large triangle (see also Gibson & Egeth, 1994, for evidence that IOR can be associated with one part of an object).

To investigate these alternatives, we have taken two approaches. The more obvious was to disrupt the coherence of the three boxes by giving each one a different pattern of movement. For example, one box maintained a constant speed throughout its motion; another started slowly and then accelerated; and the third started quickly and then slowed down. If inhibition has access to a scene-based description, where each box is represented as a separate and independent object, then changing the speed of motion of each box should not disrupt IOR. On the other hand, if the boxes are represented as parts of one coherent object, because of the constant speed and spatial relationships between each box, then changing speed should disrupt this object-centred effect. Importantly, such a manipulation of object speed of motion should not affect the location-based IOR, which is associated with an empty, featureless part of the scene.

Because we believed that attention was gaining access to scene-based representations in our normal procedure, we expected to see the usual pattern of results emerge from this experiment. To our surprise, however, there was no reliable object-based IOR effect. At first blush, this might suggest that the object-based effect in our normal procedure (i.e., all boxes moving at the same speed) is really an object-centred effect. However, two other results from this experiment suggest that this conclusion is incorrect. First, it should be noted that both location-based and object-based IOR effects were much smaller in this experiment than in comparable experiments with all boxes moving at a constant speed. Second, there was a significant main effect of speed: subjects responded most quickly to the box that accelerated at the end, and responded most slowly to the one that slowed down. This pair of findings suggests that both location-based and object-based IOR really are attentional phenomena (see Reuter-Lorenz, Jha, & Rosenquist, in press); and that both effects were smaller than usual because they were disrupted when attention was captured by the accelerating object.

It is clear that accelerating animate objects have great biological significance. Such stimulation could signal the sudden attack of a predator, for example. Like the looming effect observed in infants (Bower et al., 1970), detection of sudden increases of object speed may be hard-wired, due to pressures of natural selection. Therefore, there are clear biological reasons why acceleration of an object could veto all previous inhibition, and automatically capture attention. Similar asymmetries of motion have been observed by Ivry and Cohen (1992). They showed that fast-moving targets pop out from slower distractors, but not vice versa.

The alternative approach for investigating scene-based versus object-centred frames of reference was to join the three boxes together with lines, to create a rotating triangle (see Figure 7). The logic here is to explicitly create an object-centred representation and contrast it with results obtained when the objects are not explicitly connected. The results from this latter study suggest that in our original experiments, in which the boxes were unattached, attention was gaining access to scene-based representations. The main evidence for this is the fact that subjects detect the target significantly more quickly when the three boxes are explicitly connected than when they are not (Tipper & Weaver, unpublished).

We interpret this latter finding in light of the work of Duncan (1984) and others (Baylis & Driver, 1992; Kramer & Jacobson, 1991). Their findings suggest that attention can be shifted more easily (and more quickly) within an object than between objects. In the case of our experiments, subjects are slower overall to detect the target when the three boxes are not connected. This suggests to us that those three boxes are perceived as three separate objects when they are not explicitly connected, and hence movement of attention among these separate objects is slower than movement within an object. It should also be noted, however, that despite this difference in overall response time, we did observe similar IOR effects in both procedures, although they tended to be smaller when the three objects were explicitly connected. We conclude from this that IOR can have access to location-based, scene-based, and object-centred representations depending on task demands (see also Abrams & Dobkin, 1994; Gibson & Egeth, 1994).

In summary, these studies of IOR have clearly demonstrated that the effects are not simply determined by inhibition of a location on some internal representation of a spatial map (location-based). Rather, the

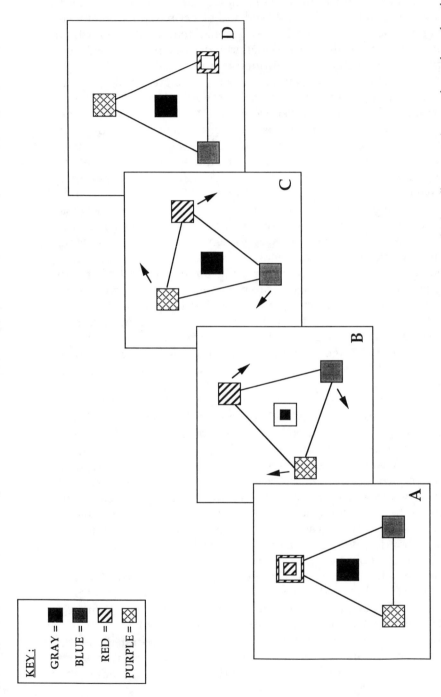

*Figure 7.* The three boxes are connected by black lines, and subjects perceive a rotating triangle. Overall response times are lower than when the boxes are not connected (see Figure 3).

inhibition can be associated with objects. Other researchers have come to similar conclusions (e.g., Abrams & Dobkin, 1994; Gibson & Egeth, 1994), and other laboratories have confirmed these specific object-based IOR effects (Rafal and Ro; Buck & Behrmann, personal communication, January 1995; McDowd, personal communication April, 1995; Lupianez, personal communication, March 1995). We now turn to a quite different research approach to provide further converging evidence that attention has access to object-based internal representations.

## Visual Neglect

The neurological disorder called unilateral or hemispatial neglect is characterized by the patients' failure to respond or orient to stimuli on the side contralateral to a brain lesion. Neglect occurs most frequently after lesions to the right hemisphere, and is especially associated with lesions to the right parietal lobe, although other lesion sites in the midbrain and frontal lobes can also result in neglect. The failure to respond to stimuli contralateral to the lesion is generally interpreted as a failure in the distribution of attention to that side of space (e.g., Bisiach, 1993; Halligan & Marshall, 1993). However, in light of the research reviewed above, the frame of reference in which neglect can be observed needs further examination.

The phenomenon usually appears to be a neglect of some internal representation of space. That is, there is some difficulty in terms of moving the spotlight of attention from the right to the left side of space. However, it could be that visual neglect, like inhibitory mechanisms of attention, is also associated with object-based frames of reference.

This idea was tested in the following experiment by Behrmann and Tipper (1994; see also Driver & Halligan, 1991). Initially a barbell stimulus (e.g., a blue circle to the left and a red circle to the right connected by a black bar) was presented to the subject for one second. A target was then presented in either the left or right circle on two-thirds of the trials. The subjects' task was simply to depress a key as soon as the target was detected. In control subjects, it makes no difference whether the target is presented to the left or right. In contrast, patients with lesions to the right parietal lobe have severe difficulties detecting the target when it is presented in the circle on the left side of space. This situation is depicted in Figure 8A.

In a separate block of trials, we employed the logic used in the IOR experiments described above. That is, to dissociate location-based frames of reference from object-based frames of reference, we rotated the barbell through 180° (see Figure 8B). The logic of the experiment was as follows. If neglect was in fact associated with the left side of the object rather than simply with the left side of some spatial map when

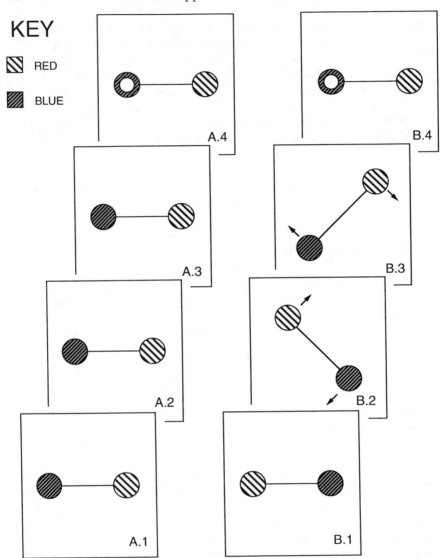

*Figure* 8. Panel A: A barbell stimulus, containing a blue circle and a red circle connected by a black line, was presented to subjects for 2.7 seconds. Then on two thirds of the trials a target was presented in one of the circles (A4). Panel B: The barbell was presented without motion for 1 second (B1). It then slowly rotated for 1.7 seconds over a distance of 180° (B2 & B3). Finally, in two-thirds of the trials, a target was presented for rapid detection (B4).

the object rotates, the left side may take its neglect with it. This process would produce a dramatic change in the neglect observed. Basically neglect should be observed on the right side of space because the neglected left side of the barbell has moved to the right. Similarly, neglect to the left side of space should be reduced when detecting the target on the original right side of the barbell. Panel C of Figure 9 represents this object-centred situation.

On the other hand, if neglect is simply spatial, then detection should be worse when the target is presented to the left side of space independently of object motion (see panel A in Figure 9). Of course the third possibility is that neglect is present in both frames of reference simultaneously (see panel D in Figure 9). A precedent for this latter idea has been found in the studies of IOR reviewed above. Recall that Tipper et al. (1994) demonstrated that both location-based and object-based IOR could be observed simultaneously. If both frames of neglect were active, then detection on the left may be improved by the movement of the right side of an object into that area; and similarly, detection on the right would be impaired by movement of the neglected left side of the object into that area. However, there may still be an overall neglect of the left side of space, depending on the relative strengths of these location-based and object-based effects.

The initial results reported by Behrmann and Tipper (1994) were quite clear. Neglect appeared to be only object-based. That is, there was a complete reversal of neglect from the left to the right side of space when the barbell rotated by 180°. However, subsequent work has shown that the original result does not generalize to all neglect patients (Tipper & Behrmann, 1996). In these new studies, we found that in some patients, neglect appeared to be acting in both location-based and object-based frames. Showing that both frames of reference could be simultaneously active is very similar to the IOR research described above.

Therefore, in further studies we directly tested the idea that both location-based and object-based neglect could be observed simultaneously (Behrmann & Tipper, unpublished). In these experiments, the rotating barbell was again presented, but in addition, static grey boxes were also present (see Figure 10). Throughout the experiment, although the barbell could rotate, the boxes never moved.

Considerations of ecological situations motivated this research. Everyday environments are complex, but also highly constrained. Multiple objects are encountered, but these have quite specific properties. One of the main contrasts is between animate and inanimate objects. An environment could contain objects that never move, such as furniture, and those that often move, such as people or pets. Thus, when simultaneously encountering static and mobile objects, such as depicted in the experimental situation of Figure 10, are both mobile objects and their static backgrounds or contexts simultaneously represented? If they are, then this would lead us to predict that neglect may be shown simultaneously in both forms of representation.

## A.LOCATION-BASED NEGLECT

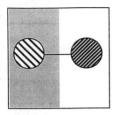 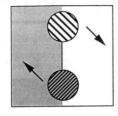 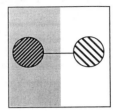

## B.SCENE-BASED NEGLECT

 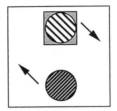 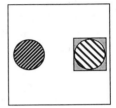

## C.OBJECT-CENTRED NEGLECT

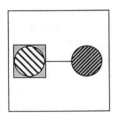 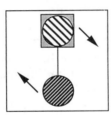 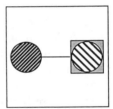

## D.LOCATION-BASED AND OBJECT-CENTRED NEGLECT

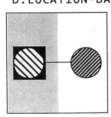 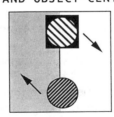 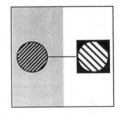

*Figure* 9. The possible frames of reference mediating neglect. The shading signifies the different forms of neglect that have been hypothesized. Panel A represents location-based neglect, where the left side of space is neglected. Panel B depicts scene-based neglect, where objects that appear initially on the left side of space are neglected, even if they subsequently move to the right side of space. Panel C shows object-centred neglect, where the left-hand side of an object (in its initial orientation) is neglected. Panel D represents the possibility of neglect occurring concurrently in both location-based and object-centred coordinates.

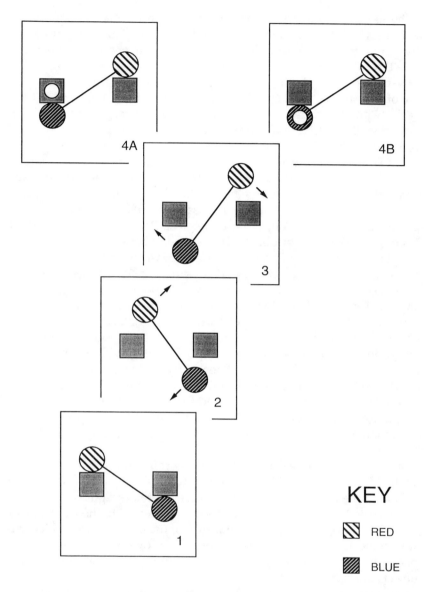

*Figure* 10. In this experiment, two static grey boxes and a rotating barbell are simultaneously presented. Panel 1 is the starting display, the barbell then slowly rotates (panels
2 and 3), finally the target is presented in one of the two boxes or ends of the barbell. In
this example, the target is presented in the left box (4A), and detection is impaired relative to the right box. In panel 4B, the target is presented on the left side (right side of the
barbell). In this situation, target detection is facilitated relative to the barbell on the right
side of space (left side of object). As can be seen, the targets shown in panels 4A and 4B
are on the same side of space, and are close together. Yet performance is poor in 4A and
relatively good in 4B.

The experimental predictions were as follows. Because the boxes never move, detection of the target in the left box will be impaired relative to target detection in the right box. In sharp contrast, when the barbell rotates, detection of targets on the left side of space (right side of the object) will be better than detection on the right side of space (left side of the object). In the preliminary analysis of five neglect subjects, precisely this pattern of results was obtained. The remarkable thing about this data is that quite different target detection performance was observed for stimuli that are very close together on the same side of space. Thus, in Figure 10, detection of the target in the left square is slow (panel 4A), whereas detection of the target in the left side of space in the adjacent right side of the barbell is relatively fast (panel 4B).

Like the IOR research already discussed, we also investigated more specifically the form of object-based neglect. Recall that in the work of Tipper and Weaver (unpublished) described above, we distinguished between object-centred and scene-based IOR. The former describes locations within an object (e.g., the corners of a triangle), whereas the latter describes a representation of separate independent objects. The question Tipper and Behrmann posed was quite simple: was the movement of neglect we had observed previously, determined by object-centred or scene-based frames of reference? The experiment compared the original barbell condition (panel C, Figure 9) with a condition in which the two circles were not connected by the black bar (panel B, Figure 9). Neglect again appeared to rotate with the moving object, but only when the two circles were joined to produce the barbell, and one complete object was perceived. Indeed, when the two circles were separate, there was some evidence that left spatial neglect was even larger than usual.

One final point is worth making concerning these barbell experiments. Many readers will immediately think that eye movements are mediating the transfer of neglect from the left to the right side of space as the barbell rotates. That is, if attention is directed to the right side of the barbell, subjects may fixate that side of the object. As the object rotates, subjects may track the right side as it moves into the left side of space. Therefore, detection of the target on the left side is faster because subjects are fixating that location.

Three pieces of evidence, however, suggest that this explanation is unlikely. First, if subjects were fixating the barbell on the left side of space at the end of the rotation, detection of the target in the spatially adjacent square should also be facilitated relative to detection of targets in the square on the right (see Figure 10). As discussed, this pattern is not observed. Second, a strategy of tracking objects from the right to the left side of space suggests that this should also happen when two separate objects are present (scene-based). This does not happen because detection is worse for target in the final left position for disconnected displays. Finally, and most directly, Tipper and Behrmann (1996) monitored eye movements in one patient, and there was no evidence for the large tracking eye movements necessary to follow the right side of the barbell into the left side of space.

In summary, therefore, these studies of neglect have reinforced our previous conclusions. They show that attention can have access to object-based representations, and that we need to consider carefully the different kinds of object-based representations (i.e., scene-based or object-centred). Furthermore, this work supports previous findings from studies of IOR. That is, both spatial-based and object-based frames can influence behaviour simultaneously in some situations.

## Conclusions

This article has reviewed some of the research we have undertaken in recent years. The aim of this work has been to guide our investigations by considering the functions that attention evolved to serve. It is necessary to consider what attention may be doing when we interact with our normal environments. We believe that considerations of ecological validity (Gibson, 1979) are worthwhile, because there is always the possibility that theories developed from the sometimes artificial experiments undertaken in the laboratory may not generalize to performance in more normal environments.

From such a viewpoint, we propose that the typical role of attention is not necessarily to facilitate perceptual processes, although it can do so in some situations. Rather, attention is necessary to achieve particular behavioural goals via selection of specific internal representations of individual objects from the complex internal representation of a scene. Such a view suggests that the medium of attention is not simply space. If attention is selecting information to guide action, then it is probably manipulating object-based representations, because our actions are typically directed towards objects.

To convincingly demonstrate that attention is indeed gaining access to object-based internal representations, converging evidence from a variety of sources is necessary. Hence the variety of approaches adopted here. In each area of research it has been revealed that the mechanisms of attention, such as inhibition, do not act only on a representation of a spatial map. On the contrary, inhibition can be associated with an object as it moves through space. As we continue to investigate how attention manipulates various forms of internal representation, further issues arise. Is it the case that some frames of reference, such as space, have priority over others? How do behavioural goals influence which frames of reference are active? Answers to such questions will increase our knowledge of attention.

## Acknowledgments

The research described in this chapter was supported by the Natural Science and Engineering Research Council (NSERC) of Canada, and the Higher Education Funding Council of Wales (HEFCW). Steve Tipper may be contacted via e-mail at S.TIPPER@bangor.ac.uk.

## Notes

1 Park and Kanwisher (1994) have suggested that this sort of negative priming effect is caused by mismatching information between the prime and probe, rather than by inhibition. The ignored prime is an X and the subsequent probe target is an O. When the probe target appears in the same location as the ignored prime, two identities are associated with the same location. This conflict, which does not occur in the baseline control condition, necessitates updating the object file record (Kahneman, Treisman, & Gibbs, 1992), which takes time. Hence the longer reaction times (RTs) in the ignored repetition condition. However, we have demonstrated in numerous experiments that negative priming can be observed consistently when there is no such mismatching information between prime and probe. That is, robust negative priming is obtained when the ignored prime and subsequent probe are exactly the same object (see e.g., Milliken, Tipper, & Weaver, 1994; Tipper, Weaver, & Milliken, 1995).

2 Other results have also shown that inhibition is not simply associated with the location occupied by a distractor. Tipper (1985) originally showed negative priming effects when the target and distractor (line drawings) were superimposed on the same spatial location. Furthermore, Tipper and Driver (1988) demonstrated that inhibition could be associated with abstract semantic properties of distracting objects.

## References

Abrams, R.A., & Dobkin, R.S. (1994). Inhibition of return: Effects of attentional cuing on eye movement latencies. *Journal of Experimental Psychology: Human Perception & Performance, 20*, 467–477.

Baylis, G.C., & Driver, J. (1993). Visual attention and objects: Evidence for hierarchical coding of locations. *Journal of Experimental Psychology: Human Perception & Performance, 19*, 451–470.

Behrmann, M., & Tipper, S.P. (1994). Object based attentional mechanisms: Evidence from patients with unilateral neglect. In L. Umilta & M. Moscovitch (Eds.), *Attention & Performance Vol. 14* (pp. 351–375). Hillsdale, NJ: Erlbaum.

Bisiach, E. (1993). Mental representation in unilateral neglect and related disorders. *Quarterly Journal of Experimental Psychology, 46A*, 435–446.

Biederman, I. (1987). Recognition-by-components: A theory of human image understanding. *Psychological Review, 94*, 115–147.

Bower, T.G.R. (1971). The object in the world of the infant. *Scientific American, 225*, 30–38.

Bower, T.G.R., Broughton, J.M., & Moore, M.K. (1970). Infant responses to approaching objects: An indicator of response to distal variables. *Perception & Psychophysics, 9*, 193–196.

Broadbent D.E. (1958). *Perception and communication.* London: Pergamon Press.

Broadbent, D.E. (1982). Task combination and selective intake of information. *Acta Psychologica, 50,* 253–290.

Dalrymple-Alford, E.C., & Budayr, B. (1966). Examination of some aspects of the Stroop colour-word test. *Perceptual & Motor Skills, 23,* 1211–1214.

Driver, J., & Halligan, P.W. (1991). Can visual neglect operate in object-centred co-ordinates? An affirmative single-case study. *Cognitive Neuropsychology, 8,* 475–496.

Duncan, J. (1984). Selective attention and the organization of visual information. *Journal of Experimental Psychology: General, 113,* 501–517.

Egly, R., Driver, J., & Rafal, R.D. (1994). Shifting visual attention between objects and locations: Evidence from normal and parietal lesion subjects. *Journal of Experimental Psychology: General, 123,* 161–177.

Eriksen, B.A., & Eriksen, C.W. (1974). Effects of noise letters upon the identification of a target letter in a non-search task. *Perception & Psychophysics, 16,* 143–149.

Gibson, J.J. (1979). *The ecological approach to visual perception.* Boston, MA: Houghton Mifflin.

Gibson, B., & Egeth, H. (1994). Inhibition of return to object-based and environment-based locations. *Perception & Psychophysics, 55,* 323–339.

Goldberg, M.E., & Wurtz, R.H. (1972). Activity of superior colliculus cells in behaving monkey I. Visual receptive fields of single neurons. *Journal of Neurophysiology, 35,* 542–559.

Gross, C.G. (1991. Contribution of striate cortex and the superior colliculus to visual function in area MT, the superior temporal polysensory area and inferior temporal cortex. *Neuropsychology, 2,* 211–228.

Halligan, P.W., & Marshall, J.C. (1993). The history and clinical presentation of neglect. In I.H. Robertson & J.C. Marshall (Eds.), *Unilateral neglect: Clinical and experimental studies* (pp. 3–25). Hove, UK: Erlbaum.

Harms, L., & Bundesen, C. (1983). Color segregation and selective attention in a nonsearch task. *Perception & Psychophysics, 33,* 11–19.

Houghton, G., & Tipper, S.P. (1994). A model of inhibitory mechanisms in selective attention. In D. Dagenbach & T. Carr (Eds.), *Inhibitory mechanisms of attention, memory, and language* (pp. 53–112). Orlando, FL: Academic Press.

Ingle, D. (1977). Role of the visual cortex in anticipatory orientation towards moving targets by the gerbil. *Society for Neuroscience Abstracts, 3,* 68(b).

Ingle, D., Cheal, M., & Dizio, P. (1979). Cine analysis of visual orientation and pursuit by the Mongolian gerbil. *Journal of Comparative & Physiological Psychology, 93,* 919–928.

Ivry, R.B., & Cohen, A. (1992). Asymmetry in visual search for targets defined by differences in movement speed. *Journal of Experimental Psychology: Human Perception & Performance, 18,* 1045–1057.

Jordan, H.B., & Tipper, S.P. (1997). University of Wales, Bangor (unpublished).

Kahneman, D., & Treisman, A. (1984). Changing views of attention and automaticity. In R. Parasuraman & R. Davies (Eds.), *Varieties of attention* (pp. 29–61). San Diego, CA: Academic Press.

Kahneman, D., Treisman, A., & Gibbs, B.J. (1992). The reviewing of object files: Object-specific integration of information. *Cognitive Psychology, 24,* 175–219.

Kramer, A.F., & Jacobson, A. (1991). Perceptual organization and focused attention: The role of objects and proximity in visual processing. *Perception & Psychophysics, 50,* 267–284.

Marr, D. (1982). *Vision.* New York: Freeman.

Maylor, E.A. (1985). Facilitatory and inhibitory components of orienting in visual space. In M.I. Posner & O.S.M. Marin (Eds.), *Attention & Performance Vol. 11* (pp. 189–204). Hillsdale, NJ: Erlbaum.

Maylor, E.A., & Hockey, R. (1985). Inhibitory component of externally controlled covert orienting in visual space. *Journal of Experimental Psychology: Human Perception & Performance, 11,* 777–787.

Milliken, B., Tipper, S.P., & Weaver, B. (1994). Negative priming in a spatial localization task: Feature mismatching and distractor inhibition. *Journal of Experimental Psychology: Human Perception & Performance, 20,* 624–646.

Neill, W.T. (1977). Inhibition and facilitation processes in selective attention. *Journal of Experimental Psychology: Human Perception & Performance, 3,* 444–450.

Neill, W.T., Valdes, L.A., & Terry, K. (1995). Selective attention and inhibitory control of cognition. In F.N. Dempster & C.J. Brainerd (Eds.), *New Perspectives on interference and inhibition in cognition* (pp. 207–263). San Diego, CA: Academic Press.

Park, J., & Kanwisher, N. (1994). Negative priming for spatial locations: Identity mismatching, not distractor inhibition. *Journal of Experimental Psychology: Human Perception & Performance, 20,* 613–623.

Posner, M.I., & Cohen, Y. (1984). Components of visual orienting. In H. Bouma & D.G. Bouwhuis (Eds.), *Attention & Performance Vol. 10* (pp. 531–554). Hillsdale, NJ: Erlbaum.

Posner, M.I., Rafal, R.D., Choate, L.S., & Vaughn, J. (1985). Inhibition of return: Neural basis and function. *Journal of Cognitive Neuropsychology, 2,* 211–228.

Rafal, R.D. (1992). Visually guided behavior in progressive supranuclear palsy. In I. Litvan & Y. Agid (Eds.), *Progressive supranuclear palsy: Clinical and research approaches.* Oxford: Oxford University Press.

Rafal, R.D., Calabrasi, P.A., Brennan, C.W., & Sciolto, T.K. (1989). Saccade preparation inhibits re-orienting to recently attended locations. *Journal of Experimental Psychology: Human Perception & Performance, 15,* 673–685.

Reuter-Lorenz, P.A., Jha, A.P., & Rosenquist, J.N. (in press). What is inhibited in inhibition of return? *Journal of Experimental Psychology: Human Perception & Performance.*

Schiller, P.H. (1972). The role of the monkey superior colliculus in eye movement and vision. *Investigations in Ophthalmology and Visual Science, 11,* 451–460.

Tipper, S.P. (1985). The negative priming effect: Inhibitory priming with to be ignored objects. *The Quarterly Journal of Experimental Psychology, 37A,* 571–590.

Tipper, S.P., & Behrmann, M. (1996). Object-centred not scene-based visual neglect. *Journal of Experimental Psychology: Human Perception & Performance, 22,* 1261–1278.

Tipper, S.P., Brehaut, J.C., & Driver, J. (1990). Selection of moving and static objects for the control of spatially directed action. *Journal of Experimental Psychology: Human Perception and Performance, 16,* 492–504.

Tipper, S.P., & Driver, J., (1988). Negative priming between pictures and words in a selective attention task: Evidence for semantic processing of ignored stimuli. *Memory and Cognition, 16,* 64–70.

Tipper, S.P., Driver, J., & Weaver, B. (1991). Object-centred inhibition of return of visual attention. *Quarterly Journal of Experimental Psychology, 43A,* 289–298.

Tipper, S.P., & Milliken, B. (1996). Distinguishing between inhibition and episodic retrieval based accounts of negative priming. In A.F. Kramer, M. Coles, & G.D. Logan (Eds.), *Convergent operations in the study of visual selective attention* (pp 337–364). Washington, D.C.:American Psychological Association.

Tipper, S.P., Rafal, R.D., Reuter-Lorenz, P., Starrveldt, Y., Ro, T., Egly, R., & Weaver, B. (in press). Object-based facilitation and inhibition from visual orienting in the human split-brain. *Journal of Experimental Psychology: Human Perception & Performance.*

Tipper, S.P., & Weaver, B., (1996). University of Wales, Bangor (unpublished).

Tipper, S.P., Weaver, B., & Houghton, G. (1994). Behavioral goals determine inhibitory mechanisms of selective attention. *Quarterly Journal of Experimental Psychology, 47A,* 809–840.

Tipper, S.P., Weaver, B., Jerreat, L.M., & Burak, A.L. (1994). Object-based and environment-based inhibition of return of visual attention. *Journal of Experimental Psychology: Human Perception & Performance, 20,* 478–499.

Tipper, S.P., Weaver, B., & Milliken, B. (1995). Spatial negative priming without mismatching: A reply to Park and Kanwisher. *Journal of Experimental Psychology: Human Perception & Performance, 21,* 1220–1229.

Tipper, S.P., Weaver, B., & Watson (1996). University of Wales, Bangor (unpublished).

Treisman, A.M. (1988). Features and objects. *Quarterly Journal of Experimental Psychology, 40A,* 201–237.

Valenza, E., Simion, F., & Umilta, C. (1994). Inhibition of return in newborn infants. *Infant Behavior and Development, 17,* 293–302.

# 5

## *Attention and Automaticity*

### Gordon D. Logan and Brian J. Compton

Attention and automaticity are intimately related. In everyday life, attention determines what is focal, and automatic processing determines the background. Like well-choreographed dancers, attention leads and automatic processing follows. Shifts in attention bring new input to bear on the cognitive system, some of which is processed deliberately and with effort but most of which is processed automatically. Shifts in attention are driven by goals and purposes, so what is processed automatically is determined by an interaction between goals and purposes and the external environment.

The relation between attention and automaticity is as intimate in theory as it is in everyday life. However, many theorists suggest the dance is an illusion. From a distance, or from a large enough time scale, attention and automaticity may move together gracefully, but up close – at the millisecond level – they are independent and often oppose each other. From this perspective, attention and automaticity are opposites; automatic processing is processing without attention (e.g., Jacoby, 1991; LaBerge & Samuels, 1974; Posner & Snyder, 1975; Schneider, 1985; Shiffrin & Schneider, 1977). According to these theories, automatic processing takes the lead, marching to the beat of its own drummer, the stimulus. Attention can oppose automatic processing or "go with the flow," but in either case stimulus-driven automatic processing is dominant. It is the major force to which attention must adjust. From this perspective, the dance apparent in everyday life is more of a struggle, with attention continually adjusting to compensate for the perturbations produced by automatic processing.

The instance theory of automaticity (Logan, 1988b, 1990, 1992b) takes a perspective that is more consistent with intuitions from everyday life. According to the instance theory, automatic processing is processing governed by memory retrieval, in which the stimulus retrieves an appropriate response from memory. However, the stimuli that drive automatic processing are filtered by attention. Attention forms the retrieval cues that elicit automatic responses from memory. Thus, automatic processing is a consequence of attention. From this perspective, mental life is a dance; attention leads and automaticity follows.

In this chapter, we review some recent evidence on the interaction between attention and automaticity from the perspective of the instance theory of automaticity. Our purpose is not to contrast the instance theory with the others because that has been done often enough in the past (e.g., Logan, 1988a, 1988b, 1989, 1991; Logan & Klapp, 1991). Rather, our purpose is to show how attention takes the lead, both in determining what is learned during the acquisition of automaticity and what is retrieved during the expression of automaticity in skilled performance.

Our review focuses on the effects of visual spatial attention, to make contact with the current literature. Visual spatial attention has been a dominant paradigm for the last 15 years, and great advances have been made during that period. However, much of the literature addresses immediate performance and says little about learning or the aspects of the history of the person that enable immediate performance. It is as if attention dances by itself. Our intention is to point out the partner in the dance by showing how automatic processing is an integral part of visual spatial attention.

## Attention and Automaticity in the Instance Theory

The instance theory of automaticity rests on three main assumptions: *obligatory encoding*, which says that attention to an object or event is sufficient to cause it to be encoded into memory; *obligatory retrieval*, which says that attention to an object or event is sufficient to cause things associated with it to be retrieved from memory; and *instance representation*, which says that each encounter with an object or event is encoded, stored, and retrieved separately even if the same thing is encountered on different occasions (Logan, 1988b, 1990).

These assumptions account for the acquisition of automaticity and the expression of automaticity in skilled performance. The theory assumes that initial performance is supported by a general algorithm that is sufficient to produce solutions to the problems posed by the task without prior experience. Automatization involves a transition from algorithm-based performance to memory-based performance. The obligatory encoding assumption says that a task-relevant knowledge base builds up with repeated exposure to a task. The more experience with the task, the larger the knowledge base. The obligatory retrieval assumption says that whatever knowledge is relevant to the current task will become available at retrieval time. The larger the task-relevant knowledge base, the "stronger" the "response" from memory. With sufficient practice on the task, memory may become strong enough and reliable enough to support performance by itself, without the assistance of the general algorithm that supported novice performance. The instance representation assumption is important for the quantitative predictions of the theory (Logan, 1988b, 1992b) and for certain qualitative predictions, which we will address as we review the experiments.

Several important points embedded in this brief description are worth closer examination. First, the instance theory is a theory of memory retrieval and not a theory of the algorithms that can support initial performance. The theory claims that all automatic processing is essentially the same; it is processing based on single-step, direct-access memory retrieval. However, no one would assert that all of the algorithms that can be replaced by this one-step memory retrieval are essentially the same. They can vary in many ways that are constrained by task demands but arbitrary with respect to memory retrieval. They are as hard to characterize in general as the programs written in a particular programming language, such as FORTRAN or Pascal. The most that can be said in general is that programs must begin and end and do something in between. Thus, the instance theory is not a theory of the algorithm. However, in practice, the instance theory is intended to interface with a theory of the particular algorithm that is used for a specific application. In this chapter, for example, we will consider algorithms for visual search, enumeration, and lexical processing. The theory of the algorithm specifies the steps that the person must go through in order to compute a solution, and each of those steps will be attended and therefore encoded into memory, according to the obligatory encoding assumption. The steps of the algorithm also provide opportunities to retrieve past solutions from memory, according to the obligatory retrieval assumption. Thus, the theory of the algorithm – which is separate from the instance theory – interacts with the instance theory in determining what is learned and what is expressed in skilled performance.

Second, the obligatory encoding assumption says that the knowledge base that builds up with practice depends on how the person attends to the task-relevant materials. Different attention to the same materials will lead to different memory traces. The ability to perform automatically is not a necessary consequence of obligatory encoding. It depends as well on the consistency of attention and the consistency of the environment. If the environment changes or if the way the person attends to the environment changes sufficiently, the knowledge base will grow in a different way than if the environment and attention stay the same. A consistent environment (Schneider & Fisk, 1982) and consistent attention (Logan, 1990) are jointly necessary for the development of automaticity.

Third, the obligatory retrieval assumption says that whatever was associated with the current focus of attention will be retrieved. That in itself does not necessitate automatic processing. For processing to be automatic (i.e., based on memory retrieval), the things that are retrieved from memory must be sufficient to provide a solution to the problem posed by the current task. Consistency is important because it provides an opportunity to express what was learned in the past. If the environment was inconsistent, the same object of attention may retrieve conflicting solutions, in which case the person should abandon memory retrieval and run the algorithm to produce a solution. If attention was inconsistent, the same object may retrieve inconsistent solutions, so that the person cannot rely on memory to produce a coherent response. Again, it would be better to ignore memory and rely on the algorithm.

The important point, for the purposes of this chapter, is the central role of attention in the acquisition and expression of automaticity. Attention constructs the representations that are encoded into memory, and attention constructs the retrieval cues that pull solutions from memory. Attention is the interface between memory and the external world, and as such, it exerts strong constraints on automaticity. This point of view, referred to as the *attention hypothesis*, makes predictions about the effects of attention in training and transfer. The following review of the literature focuses on tests of the attention hypothesis in tasks that involve visual spatial attention.

## Automatic Processing and Preattentive Processing

It is just as important to be clear about what we are not discussing as it is to be clear about what we are discussing. We are not talking about preattentive processing. Preattentive processing bears a strong resemblance to what we construe as automatic processing, but it is different in important respects (for a full discussion, see Logan, 1992a; also see Treisman, Vieira, & Hayes, 1992). Preattentive processing is like automatic processing in that it is obligatory, parallel, and independent of attention. However, preattentive processing precedes attention, whereas automatic processing follows it. Preattentive processing parses the display into objects or regions among which attention may choose. Preattentive processing is logically prior to attention because it provides the informational basis for selection. By contrast, automatic processing is based on memory retrieval, and attention forms the cues that drive the retrieval process (from the perspective of the instance theory). Thus, automatic processing is logically subsequent to attention and therefore different from preattentive processing.

Preattentive processing and automatic processing are different from a computational perspective. Preattentive processing is accomplished by local parallel processes (Ullman, 1984). That is, preattentive computations are performed separately, redundantly, and simultaneously all over the visual field. Computations that require spatial indexing and computations that require interactions between sources of information in arbitrarily different regions of the visual field cannot be done preattentively (Ullman, 1984). By contrast, automatic processing is accomplished by single-step, direct-access memory retrieval. Computations requiring information that is not readily available in memory or computations requiring integration of information from separate acts of retrieval cannot be done automatically. Thus, preattentive and automatic processing are different. The class of computations that can be done by local parallel processing is very different from the class of computations that can be done by single-step, direct-access memory retrieval.

Preattentive processing and automatic processing are also different in terms of the variables that affect them. Perceptual salience is critically important for preattentive processing (Cave & Wolfe, 1990; Treisman & Gelade, 1980; Treisman & Gormican, 1988; Wolfe, 1994). Uniform or similar perceptual characteristics are parsed into common regions, whereas distinct or dissimilar perceptual characteristics are parsed into separate regions. Learning appears to have little effect on preattentive processing (Treisman et al., 1992). By contrast, learning is critically important for automatic processing. Automatic processing develops with learning, and the consistency of discrimination, interpretation, and stimulus-to-response mapping seems to be the critical variable (Schneider & Fisk, 1982). Acquisition of automaticity does not appear to depend on perceptual salience, because automatic processing can be produced by training subjects on stimuli divided into arbitrary classes (Shiffrin & Schneider, 1977).

The confusion between preattentive processing and automatic processing may stem from the polysemy of the word "automatic." The word is used in two different senses. On the one hand, it is used as a shorthand way of describing processes that are fast, parallel, obligatory, and effortless: both preattentive processes and acquired automatic processes fit that description. On the other hand, automaticity is used to describe a mode of processing that is acquired through training in a consistent task environment, or in terms of the instance theory, a mode of processing that depends on single-step, direct-access memory retrieval. For the purposes of this chapter, at least, we would like to use the latter meaning for the term "automatic" (also see Logan, 1992a).

## Varieties of Attention

The dance between attention and automaticity may also be considered to be like a masquerade ball, with attention appearing in many guises. William James (1890) said "everyone knows what attention is" but he did not say that everyone had a different opinion. Regarding the varieties of attention, Treisman (1969) provided an insightful analysis that has been a useful heuristic in our studies of the interactions between attention and automaticity. Treisman (1969) focuses on the concept of an *analyser*, which is a specialized processor that performs some computation. Given an input, it produces an output. Treisman suggested that attention involved the selective application of analysers to problems faced by the processing system. The configuration of analysers constituted a strategy that was implemented by the attentional system. She distinguished four ways in which analysers could be deployed selectively, which amounted to four kinds of selective attention.

*Input Selection* The first strategic choice facing the attention system is which input should be selected for analysis. Input selection involves choosing among alternative inputs. In visual spatial attention, input selection amounts to choosing one (or more) object(s) from a set of alternatives for analysis and ignoring the rest, where "ignoring" means not analyzing. Studies of visual spatial attention have focused primarily on input selection, ignoring other varieties of attention.

*Analyser Selection* Once an input is selected, the next choice facing the attention system is which analyses to perform on the input. Analyser selection involves choosing among alternative analysers. The same input can be processed in many ways.

*Target Selection* Once an input is analyzed, the attention system can choose among courses of action, depending on the outcome of the analysis. In visual search, for example, the system stops searching and generates a "target present" response if the analyser determines that the current input is a target, and it continues selecting and analyzing other inputs if the analyser determines that the current input is not a target. Target selection is also involved in filtering, in which some results of analysis lead to further processing and others lead to selection of alternative inputs (Broadbent, 1971; Treisman, Kahneman, & Burkell, 1983). Filtering is involved in cueing paradigms, in which subjects report, for example, the identity of the green letter. Inputs are analyzed for colour, and target selection (or filtering) involves processing the identity of the item if it is green or selecting another item to analyze for colour if the current item is not green.

*Output Selection* Output selection involves choosing the most highly activated response. It is the "latest" form of selection, invoked after all relevant analyses have been performed on all possible inputs (cf. Deutsch & Deutsch, 1963). It is also related to *response selection*, in which a specific course of action is chosen as a result of prior analyses.

## Varieties of Attention and Automaticity

Over the years, we have conducted several studies of the attention hypothesis in our laboratory, investigating the interaction between automaticity and each of the varieties of attention described by Treisman (1969). In most cases, we focused on the effects of attention on encoding; in some cases, we dealt with the effects at retrieval as well. The remainder of this review will be organized according to Treisman's (1969) distinctions, beginning with input selection and proceeding through the system to output selection.

## Input Selection at Encoding and Retrieval

According to the instance theory, attention drives both the acquisition of automaticity and the expression of automaticity in skilled performance. The object at the current focus of attention is encoded into memory, supporting the acquisition of automaticity. The object at the current focus of attention acts as a retrieval cue, pulling related traces from memory to support the expression of automaticity in current performance. This view has implications for objects inside and outside the current focus of attention: objects inside the focus will be learned, whereas objects outside will not be learned, and objects inside the focus will act as retrieval cues, whereas objects outside will not.[1] Over the past few years, several experiments conducted in our laboratory have tested these predictions.

### *Input Selection at Encoding: Category Search*

Logan and Etherton (1994) tested the importance of spatial attention at encoding. They had subjects perform a *category search* task, in which subjects examined two-word displays to see if one of the words was a member of a target category (e.g., metals). The main questions were (1) whether subjects would learn co-occurrences of specific targets and distractors, and (2) whether that learning would be modulated by spatial attention to targets and distractors. Logan and Etherton (1994) were interested in the learning of co-occurrences to test the instance representation assumption of the instance theory. That assumption interprets instances as representations of co-occurrences (Barsalou, 1990), so evidence that subjects learned co-occurrences would be evidence that automatization was based on instance representations.

Each experiment involved a training phase and a transfer phase. In the training phase, a particular distractor was paired consistently with a particular target. Thus, whenever STEEL appeared, it appeared with CANADA. In the transfer phase, the words were re-paired, so that STEEL now appeared with FRANCE and CANADA appeared with COPPER. If subjects had learned the co-occurrences of targets and distractors during training, their performance should have been disrupted when the pairings changed at transfer. They should take longer to respond to STEEL-FRANCE in transfer than they took to respond to STEEL-CANADA at the end of training. The main dependent measure was cost in reaction time, which was the difference in mean reaction time between the transfer phase and the last training block.

Logan and Etherton (1994) manipulated spatial attention by cueing the position of the target (by colouring it green) or withholding the cue. When the target's position was cued (*focused attention*), subjects could restrict their attention to the target and ignore the distractor. Under these conditions, subjects should not learn about the distractor or the co-occurrence of specific distractors and specific targets, so there should be no cost when targets and distractors are re-paired at transfer. By contrast, when the target's position was not cued (*divided attention*), subjects would have to inspect both words to decide whether a display contained a target. Under those conditions, subjects should learn about the distractor and they should learn the co-occurrence of specific distractors and targets. There should be a substantial cost at transfer when targets and distractors are re-paired.

Logan and Etherton (1994) conducted two experiments with focused attention and two experiments with divided attention. One experiment in each pair involved a single sessions' practice before transfer, in which each target and distractor was presented 16 times. The other experiment in each pair involved four session's practice before transfer, in which each target and distractor was presented 64 times. The results were the same regardless of the level of practice. There was little cost of changing pairing in focused attention (4 ms in the single-session experiment and 13 ms in the multi-session experiment) and substantial cost of changing pairing in divided attention (95 ms in the single-session experiment and 103 ms in the multi-session experiment).

These results confirm the hypothesis that spatial attention determines what is learned during automatization. Divided-attention subjects paid attention to both targets and distractors and so learned the co-occurrences between them. Focused-attention subjects paid attention to targets and ignored distractors, and so did not learn target-distractor co-occurrences.

## Input Selection at Retrieval: Category Search

Boronat and Logan (1997) extended Logan and Etherton's (1994) results to encompass both encoding and retrieval. Boronat and Logan replicated Logan and Etherton's experiments using four groups of subjects, manipulating attention (focused vs. divided) factorially in training and in transfer. One group of subjects had focused attention in training and transfer and another group had divided attention in training and transfer, like Logan and Etherton's (1994) subjects. However, the third group had focused attention at training but divided attention at transfer and the fourth group had divided attention at training and focused attention at transfer.

Boronat and Logan (1997) compared transfer costs between groups to evaluate the effects of attention on encoding and retrieval. They assessed encoding effects by comparing training conditions while holding transfer conditions constant. This involved comparing subjects who had focused attention in training and divided attention at transfer with subjects who had divided attention in training and divided attention at transfer. The cost of changing pairing at transfer was small in the former group (25 ms) and large in the latter (66 ms). This suggests that attention determined what was encoded during training, and is consistent with Logan and Etherton (1994).

Boronat and Logan (1995) assessed retrieval effects in a similar manner, by comparing transfer conditions while holding training conditions constant. This involved comparing subjects who had divided attention in training and focused attention in transfer with subjects who had divided attention in training and divided attention in transfer. The cost of changing pairing at transfer was small in the former group (6 ms) but large in the latter group (66 ms). This suggests that attention determined what was retrieved as well as what was encoded. Logan and Etherton's (1994) research suggests that subjects trained in divided attention would likely have encoded the co-occurrence of specific targets and distractors, but focusing attention at retrieval apparently screened out information from the distractor. Only the target contributed to the retrieval cue, so associations between targets and distractors were not retrieved.

### Input Selection at Encoding: Enumeration

Lassaline and Logan (1993) studied automatization in an *enumeration* or *counting* task. Subjects were presented with a display containing several dots and were asked to report their numerosity. This is a difficult task when there are more than four or five dots in the display. Reaction time is slow and increases linearly with the number of dots in the display with a slope on the order of 300 to 400 ms per dot (Kaufman, Lord, Reese, & Volkmann, 1949; Mandler & Shebo, 1982; Trick & Pylyshyn, 1994). However, Lassaline and Logan (1993) found that when the same dot patterns were presented repeatedly for 12 sessions (192 presentations per pattern), the slope diminished from an initial value of 324 ms/dot to an asymptote of 17 ms/dot. They interpreted this reduction in slope as evidence of a transition from counting the dots in the pattern to using the pattern as a retrieval cue to retrieve its numerosity from memory – automatization. To test this interpretation, they transferred subjects to a new set of patterns on session 13 and found that the slope increased to 233 ms/dot, indicating that much of the learning was item-specific, as the instance theory suggests.

Compton (1994) adapted the counting task to examine the effects of input selection at encoding. He presented subjects with two sets of randomly intermixed dots, one red and one green, and had them count one set and ignore the other. Within each display, the pattern of red dots remained the same over training, and the pattern of green dots remained the same as well. Thus, either the pattern of red dots or the pattern of green dots or both patterns could become associated with the required numerosity response (cf. Logan & Etherton, 1994). Subjects were trained for four sessions, with 32 repetitions of each pattern in each session. The training data showed the same reduction in the slope of the function relating reaction time to numerosity that was observed by Lassaline and Logan (1993), indicating the development of automaticity with practice.

Compton (1994) tested the effects of input selection at encoding by manipulating the patterns in a transfer session. Subjects saw four kinds of displays: *old-old, new-new, old-new,* and *new-old.* In old-old displays, both the attended and the unattended patterns were the same as they were in training. In new-new displays, both the attended and unattended patterns were different from the ones in training. The contrast between these conditions addressed the item-specificity of the learning: if learning were item-specific, as the instance theory suggests, there should be a large difference between old-old and new-new patterns (cf. Lassaline & Logan, 1993). The data showed a large difference. Old-old slopes increased slightly from the last training session, but new-new slopes were close to the magnitude of slopes in the first training session.

In old-new displays, the attended pattern was the same as in training, but the unattended pattern changed. Thus, if subjects had counted red dots and ignored green ones in training, the red dots would have remained the same and the green dots would have changed. If selective attention during training led subjects to encode only the positions of the attended (red) dots, then performance in the old-new condition should be much the same as performance in the old-old condition. The data showed that the slope in the old-new condition was slightly (but not significantly) smaller than the slope in the old-old condition.

In new-old displays, the attended pattern was changed and the unattended pattern remained the same. In the previous example, the positions of the red dots would have changed while the green dots remained the same. If selective attention during training led subjects to encode the positions of the attended (red) dots and not the unattended (green) ones, then performance in the new-old condition should be much the same as performance in the new-new condition, because in both cases, the attended dots are different from the ones seen in training. The data showed that the slope in the new-old condition was slightly (but significantly) smaller than the slope in the new-new condition.

The importance of selective attention at encoding can also be assessed by comparing performance on old-new and new-old displays. Attention aside, there is the same amount of change in the two display types. Half of the dots changed position in both old-new and new-old displays. If selective attention during training had no effect on encoding, then there should be no difference in performance between old-new and new-old displays because the amount of change between training and transfer is the same. However, if selective attention during training led subjects to encode the positions of the attended dots and not the positions of the unattended dots, then the old-new displays should lead to better performance than the new-old displays because the attended portion of the display would not be different from what was experienced during training. The data showed a large (and highly significant) difference favoring old-new over new-old displays.

Together, the contrasts between old-old and old-new, new-old and new-new, and old-new and new-old patterns suggest that attention had strong effects on encoding in the enumeration task. Subjects learned to associate numerosities with the patterns they attended but not with the patterns they ignored. Strictly speaking, the data do not distinguish between the effects of attention at encoding and the effects of attention at retrieval. It is possible that the positions of both attended and unattended dots were encoded but attention at retrieval time filtered out the unattended dots. An experiment like the one conducted by Boronat and Logan (1997) would be necessary to separate encoding and retrieval effects convincingly. However, Boronat and Logan (1997) did show that attention affected both encoding and retrieval, so it is reasonable to conclude that Compton's (1994) results were due to attention at encoding.

## Analyser Selection at Encoding and Retrieval

According to the instance theory, performance is automatic when traces retrieved from memory can be used to justify the responses required for the current task (Logan, 1990). This idea places great emphasis on analyser selection. The kinds of analyses performed on stimuli at encoding – determined by analyser selection – determines the contents of the traces and therefore determines the utility of the traces for various transfer tasks. Transfer should occur between tasks that are similar but not identical, because the interpretations given in one task context may be retrieved and used to justify responses in the other. More generally, transfer should occur between tasks that are compatible. Compatibility is hard to specify generically – it requires a detailed task analysis applied to specific cases – but in essence, it means that the traces laid down in one task context can be used to support performance in another. By contrast, there should be little transfer between tasks that are orthogonal or incompatible, because traces acquired in one task context may be useless or confusing when retrieved in the other. We conducted several studies that examined analyser selection in encoding and retrieval.

## Lexical Processing

Logan (1988b, 1990) investigated analyser selection by presenting subjects with the same stimuli and manipulating the analyses they performed on them and the interpretations they gave them. The stimuli were words (e.g., BRAT), pronounceable nonwords (e.g., BLAT), and unpronounceable nonwords (e.g., BLJT). There were two main tasks subjects performed on the stimuli. *Lexical decisions* required subjects to decide whether the stimulus was a word or a nonword, discriminating words on the one hand from pronounceable and unpronounceable nonwords on the other. *Pronounceability decisions* required subjects to decide whether the stimulus was pronounceable or not, discriminating words and pronounceable nonwords on the one hand from unpronounceable nonwords on the other.

According to the instance theory, automaticity should develop if the traces acquired on one occasion can be used to justify responses on another. Consistent analyses should lead to automaticity because prior lexical decisions can justify current lexical decisions, and prior pronounceability decisions can justify current pronounceability decisions. However, inconsistent analyses should not lead to automaticity because prior pronounceability decisions do not justify current lexical decisions, and prior lexical decisions do not justify current pronounceability decisions.

The results confirmed the instance theory's predictions. Logan (1990) investigated transfer from lexical decisions to pronounceability decisions, training subjects on lexical decisions and transferring them to pronounceability decisions, and found little transfer. Logan (1988b, 1990) compared training with consistent decisions, in which subjects made lexical decisions about the same stimuli repeatedly or pronounceability decisions about the same stimuli repeatedly, with inconsistent decisions, in which subjects alternated between lexical and pronounceability decisions. He found more learning – greater automaticity – when decisions were consistent than when they were inconsistent.

Logan (1988b) showed that the effects of consistent versus inconsistent decisions on automaticity were likely a retrieval phenomenon. The poorer performance with inconsistent decisions could have resulted from poorer encoding or less effective retrieval. To distinguish between these alternatives, Logan (1988b) transferred subjects to a *frequency judgment* task that required them to estimate the frequency with which they had seen the stimuli about which they had made consistent or inconsistent decisions. If subjects had encoded the stimuli less well when they made inconsistent decisions on them, they should have been less sensitive to their frequency of occurrence. There should have been fewer traces available for them to use to justify responses in the frequency judgment task. However, if they had encoded stimuli just as well under both encoding conditions but were less able to make use of inconsistent-decision stimuli at retrieval time in one decision task or the other, then they should have been be equally sensitive to their frequency of occurrence in the frequency judgment task. Traces acquired during lexical decision may not support pronounceability decisions, but they should be just as effective as traces acquired under pronounceability decisions at supporting frequency judgments. The data were consistent with the retrieval hypothesis, showing that subjects were equally sensitive to the frequency with which consistent- and inconsistent-decision stimuli were presented.

## Enumeration

Lassaline and Logan (1993) investigated the effects of analyser selection on automatization by examining the encoding of irrelevant stimulus dimensions. According to the instance theory, only the dimensions relevant to the selected analyses should be encoded. Irrelevant dimensions should not be analyzed and therefore should not be encoded. The research strategy was to hold constant during training stimulus dimensions that were irrelevant to the enumeration task, and then to change them at transfer. The transfer condition involved the same enumeration task performed on three kinds of displays: *old-old* displays that retained the old spatial pattern of to-be-enumerated elements and the old values of the irrelevant dimension, *old-new* displays that retained the old spatial pattern of elements but changed the irrelevant dimension, and *new-new* displays that changed the spatial pattern of elements. If subjects encoded only the relevant dimensions of the displays – the spatial pattern of the elements – then performance should be equivalent for old-old displays and old-new displays. If subjects encoded irrelevant as well as relevant dimensions, then old-new patterns should be worse than old-old patterns but better than new-new patterns because old-new patterns are intermediate in similarity to the training stimuli.

*Element identity*   The first experiment examined the identity of the elements that made up the spatial patterns. There were five patterns from each of six numerosities (six to 11 elements) and one pattern in each numerosity was made from one of five letters (A, E, I, O, and U). Thus, letter identity did not predict numerosity. Subjects were trained for one session in which each pattern was repeated 16 times, or for four sessions in which each pattern was repeated 64 times. The transfer block (in the single-session experiment) or session (in the multi-session experiment) involved three types of patterns: (a) old-old patterns, in which the patterns experienced in training were presented again, made from the same letters they were made from in training, (b) old-new patterns, in which patterns experienced in training were made from different letters than in training (e.g., a pattern made from A's was now made from E's), and (c) new-new patterns, in which novel patterns not experienced during training were made from the five letters.

The results were the same in the two experiments. The slope of the function relating reaction time to numerosity decreased with practice during the training blocks. At transfer, performance on old-old displays was about the same as on the last transfer session, and performance on new-new displays was much worse, suggesting the item-specific learning predicted by the instance theory. The slopes for the old-new displays were slightly (but not significantly) steeper than the slopes for old-old displays but much shallower (and significantly shallower) than the slopes for new-new displays. Either letter identity was not encoded in the instances that supported automatic enumeration or it was encoded but not retrieved. Further experimentation will be required to address that possibility.

*Colour*   The second set of experiments examined the effects of irrelevant colour. The displays contained one to 11 asterisks, half of which (approximately) were coloured red and half of which were coloured green. Unlike Compton's (1994) experiment, colour was irrelevant to the enumeration task because subjects had to count all of the elements in the display whether they were red or green. Again, there were two experiments, one single-session experiment and one multi-session experiment, and the assignment of colours to asterisks was held constant over practice.

Transfer involved three types of displays. Old-old displays used the same spatial patterns of asterisks and the same assignment of colours to asterisks. Old-new displays used the same spatial pattern but assigned colour differently, randomly choosing to change or maintain the colour of each asterisk. New-new displays presented novel configurations of red and green elements. Again, the results were the same in the long and short versions of the experiment.

The slope of the function relating reaction time to numerosity decreased over training, as before. At transfer, the slope for old-old items was about the same as the slope in the last training session and much shallower than the slope for new-new items. The slope for old-new items was slightly (but not significantly) steeper than the slope for old-old items and substantially (and significantly) shallower than the slope for new-new items. Again, irrelevant colour was either not encoded in the instance that supported automatic enumeration or it was encoded but not retrieved. Further experimentation will be required to address that possibility.

*Spatial configuration*    In a final pair of experiments, Lassaline and Logan (1993) manipulated the orientation of the spatial pattern at transfer, figuring that the spatial relations between individual elements would be preserved but the appearance of the pattern as a whole would be much different (cf. Rock, 1973). Lassaline and Logan thought that the whole pattern was associated with the numerosity response, so this change might be relevant to memory retrieval and might have a considerable effect on transfer performance.

The experimental design was the same as before. Subjects trained for one or four sessions, and then transferred to old-old displays (in which elements were in the same spatial relations and the display was in the same orientation), old-new displays (in which elements were in the same spatial relations as in training but the display was rotated 180°), and new-new displays (in which novel patterns were presented). The results were the same in the short and long versions of the experiment.

The slope of the function relating reaction time to numerosity decreased over practice. At transfer, the slope for old-old patterns was the same as in the last transfer block and much shallower than the slope for new-new patterns. The slope for old-new patterns was quite steep. It was much steeper (and significantly steeper) than the slope for old-old patterns and almost as steep as (but not significantly shallower than) the slope for new-new patterns. Apparently, the orientation of the pattern was not irrelevant and therefore was encoded in the memory trace that supported automatic enumeration.

## Target Selection at Encoding and Retrieval

In filtering tasks, the relevant stimulus is selected on the basis of one dimension, and the relevant response is selected on the basis of another. In Logan and Etherton's (1994) focused attention experiments, for example, subjects selected the green word from a two-word display and reported whether it was a member of the target category. It is clear that subjects encode and retrieve the information that they use to justify the response they select (Boronat & Logan, 19957; Logan & Etherton, 1994). Logan, Taylor, and Etherton (1996) asked whether subjects also encode and retrieve the information that they use to select the target.

Their experiments involved a variation of the cueing procedure used by Logan and Etherton (1994). Whereas Logan and Etherton (1994) always cued the target by colouring it green, Logan et al. (1996) cued the target by colouring it red or green. Thus, the target was distinguished from the distractor by being coloured instead of white. A given target appeared in the same colour consistently throughout training, with half of the targets appearing in red and half appearing in green. At transfer, target colour was changed to see whether it had been encoded in the memory trace that supported automatic performance.

Changing colour at transfer produced a negligible cost: 4 ms for target-present displays and -6 ms for target-absent displays. These data might be taken to suggest that colour was neither encoded nor retrieved (cf. Lassaline & Logan, 1993). However, Logan et al. (1996) conducted another experiment in which the transfer task involved explicit recognition of the colour change, and found that subjects were above chance at discriminating same-colour displays from changed-colour displays. That experiment suggested that colour was encoded. The former experiment, which used the category search task in training and transfer, suggested that although colour might have been encoded, it was not retrieved to support automatic performance.

These data are important because they support a distinction between encoding and retrieval in the acquisition and expression of automaticity. They can be understood in terms of the demands of the retrieval task: automatic performance emphasizes speed and ease of access. According to the instance theory, automatic responses are generated by a race between the various traces available in memory, and performance is determined by the first trace to finish. colour traces or traces that included colour may have been retrieved too slowly to win the race, so colour was not among the attributes that supported automatic performance. By contrast, the recognition memory test places less emphasis on speed and ease of access, so slow, hard-to-retrieve colour traces appeared to have had an impact on performance.

## Output Selection at Encoding and Retrieval

Are the physical responses that the subject executes encoded in the memory trace that supports automatic performance? Shiffrin and Schneider's (1977) theory and Schneider's (1985) theory suggest they are, but the suggestion may stem more from convenience of expression than theoretical necessity. In both studies, they argued that stimuli were associated with "responses" but did not draw a sharp distinction between the physical responses that subjects execute and the response categories that are mapped onto physical responses. They talked as if subjects' fingers would twitch when they saw a highly automatized stimulus, but they likely did not mean it.

According to the instance theory, memory retrieval is an obligatory consequence of attention, but overt responding is not. The theory assumes that the person can decide whether to base overt responses on memory retrieval or on the algorithm (thus inhibiting responses retrieved from memory, if need be; for a full discussion, see Logan, 1989). Several experiments have addressed the role of output selection in automaticity.

### Physical Responses Are Not Necessarily Automatic

Three sets of data suggest that the physical response is not an important part of the memory trace that supports automatic performance. First, Shiffrin and Schneider (1977, Experiment 3) trained subjects in a visual search task in which two sets of stimuli were consistently distinguished from each other. Targets were drawn from one set on some trials and from the other set on other trials, so responses could not be associated consistently with particular stimuli. However, the distinction between sets was maintained because members of a set were never targets and distractors on the same trial. Under these conditions, performance improved substantially with training, and the effect of processing load diminished and disappeared, which is characteristic of automaticity.

Second, Fisk and Schneider (1984) trained subjects in a visual search task in which two sets of items were also consistently distinguished from each other. Targets were always drawn from one set and distractors were always drawn from the other. However, the responses that subjects used to report "target present" and "target absent" alternated throughout practice so that particular stimuli were not associated consistently with particular physical responses. Nevertheless, automaticity developed just as effectively as it did when stimuli were associated consistently with physical responses.

Third, Logan (1990) trained subjects on a lexical decision task in which they responded with "word" by pressing one key and "nonword" by pressing another, pressing the same keys for each alternative consistently throughout practice. At transfer, the response mapping changed so that the key that had been pressed for "word" was now supposed to be pressed for "nonword" and the key that had been pressed for "nonword" was now to be pressed for "word." There was no cost of changing mapping. In a second experiment, Logan (1990) compared changing the assignment of response categories ("word" vs. "nonword") to response keys (left vs. right) between blocks throughout practice with holding it constant, and found the same development of automaticity in both conditions. These data, together with Shiffrin and Schneider's (1977) and Fisk and Schneider's (1984), suggest that the physical response is not an important part of the memory trace that supports automatic performance.

## Physical Responses May Be Included in the Memory Trace

Logan, Taylor and Etherton (1996) found evidence that responses may be included in the memory traces that support automatic performance under some conditions. They conducted category search experiments in which subjects examined two-word displays to determine whether one of the words was a member of a target category (e.g., vegetables). The potential target was always coloured red or green; the distractor was always coloured white. Their initial experiments (reviewed above) suggested that target colour may have been included in the memory trace but was not retrieved to support automatic performance. Puzzled by these results, they sought conditions in which target colour would be important.

They conducted a series of experiments in which subjects had to report the colour of the target explicitly if the display contained a target. There were three response keys. One key was to be pressed if the coloured word was not a member of the target category. The second key was to be pressed if the coloured word was a member of the target category and it was coloured red. The third key was to be pressed if the coloured word was a target coloured green. Subjects trained under these conditions were able to recognize changed colours in an explicit recognition task well above chance. Moreover, subjects trained under these conditions showed a substantial (83 ms) cost when colours changed at transfer, when target colour had to be reported both in training and in transfer. This suggests that colour was encoded in the trace and retrieved to support automatic performance.

In a subsequent experiment, subjects were required to report target colour in training but not in transfer. The cost of changing colour at transfer was negligible (0 ms). In the next experiment, subjects were required to report target colour in transfer but not in training. The cost of changing colour at transfer was also negligible (13 ms). The first result suggests that if colour is in the trace, it need not be retrieved at transfer unless the task explicitly requires colour report. The second result suggests that colour is not encoded in the trace (very strongly) unless colour report is explicitly required in training.

What about responses? The one condition that showed substantial costs of changing colour at transfer – colour report in both training and transfer – involved switching the mapping between targets and responses. Subjects had to press different keys for the same target words. For example, if SPINACH appeared in red in training and green at transfer, subjects would have had to press one key to report SPINACH as a target in training and the other key to report it as a target in transfer. It is possible that targets were associated with physical responses, and that the cost of transfer was due to incompatibility between the required response and the response that was encoded during training.

Logan et al. (1996) conducted two further experiments to test this possibility. Subjects reported colour at training and transfer in both experiments, but the keys they used to report colour changed between training and transfer. In one experiment, subjects pressed completely new keys at transfer. Reaction times were slower in transfer than in the last training block (by 44 ms), but there was no difference between same- and different-colour stimuli at transfer (4 ms). These results are consistent with the hypothesis that subjects associated targets with physical responses. However, they are also consistent with the hypothesis that subjects formed three-way associations between targets, colours, and responses. The other experiment was conducted to distinguish between these alternatives.

In the other experiment, subjects switched keys at transfer, pressing the key they had formerly pressed to report "red" to report "green," and pressing the key they had formerly pressed to report "green" to report "red." If associations between targets and responses were responsible for the transfer costs, then subjects should have been faster, at transfer, to report differently coloured targets than to report identically coloured targets because they would require the same physical response they required in training. The transfer data showed a small (15 ms) advantage for differently coloured targets that was not significant, so associations between targets and responses were unlikely to underlie the transfer cost. However, reaction times in the transfer block were substantially longer than reaction times in the last training block (by 59 ms), which suggests that three-way associations between targets, colours, and responses were responsible for the transfer cost.

These experiments suggest that the physical response may sometimes be part of the memory trace that supports automatic performance, but when it is, it is bound together with other attributes, like colour and category membership. From a broader perspective, we might expect the response to be part of the memory trace in tasks that emphasize motor performance. However, output selection may have little impact on automaticity in tasks that emphasize cognition more than motor performance.

## Discussion

The experiments reviewed in this chapter suggest that automaticity does dance with attention, and that it has many partners. The acquisition and expression of automaticity are influenced by each of the four varieties of attention distinguished by Treisman (1969): input selection, analyser selection, target selection, and output selection. In each case, attention determines what is encoded in the memory trace during acquisition, and it determines what is retrieved from memory and expressed in skilled performance. This intricate interaction between attention and automaticity is very different from the picture painted by traditional views of automaticity, in which attention and automaticity are construed as independent or opposite processes (e.g., Jacoby, 1991; LaBerge & Samuels, 1974; Posner & Snyder, 1975; Schneider, 1985; Shiffrin & Schneider, 1977). However, the interaction is consistent with the instance theory of automaticity, which relates attention and automaticity in its fundamental assumptions (i.e., obligatory encoding and retrieval). Many of the effects were predicted a priori by the theory, and their confirmation provides support for the theory.

The intricate relation between attention and automaticity has implications for studies of visual spatial attention, which largely ignore the effects of learning and the history of the person performing the task. The encoding effects suggest that subjects will learn what they attend to, and the retrieval effects suggest that the things they learn can have an impact on subsequent performance. Thus, performance may be less stable than researchers might wish it to be, changing over the course of the experiment. Fortunately, the abundant research on automaticity suggests, on the one hand, that the changes should be predictable, and on the other hand, that the changes can be avoided or minimized by choosing an appropriate experimental design (e.g., one that incorporates varied mapping; Shiffrin & Schneider, 1977).

An important direction for future research is to understand how experience and learning contribute to the factors that govern the direction of attention. Determinants of the spatial direction of attention have been an important topic of research throughout the last decade, though the research has focused primarily on exogenous factors that pull attention involuntarily. Sudden onsets and perceptual discrepancies are good examples of stimuli that attract attention "automatically"

(Wolfe, 1994; Yantis, 1996). Very little research has been conducted on the voluntary direction of attention (but see Logan, 1995). We suggest a third area of investigation, that of studying the effects of learning on the direction of attention (the *schooling of attention*; see Czerwinski, Lightfoot, & Shiffrin, 1992; Treisman et al., 1992).

Learning to direct attention may be an important component of expertise. Experts typically do better than novices on tasks that involve perceiving stimuli that are relevant to their expertise (Charness, 1983; Chase & Simon, 1973; Simon, 1980). These benefits are usually explained in terms of the size of the experts' task-relevant knowledge base: experts have many patterns in long-term memory that match task-relevant displays (Chase & Simon, 1973; Simon, 1980). However, we suggest that some of the knowledge may be used for directing attention to the important parts of the displays. Experts may do better than novices because they are more likely to attend to relevant information and ignore irrelevant information. Novices, not knowing where to look, may attend to irrelevant information as often as relevant information. Further research will be necessary to assess the validity of this hypothesis.

Compton (1996) has begun to investigate the schooling of attention by studying shifts in the direction of attention over the course of automatization. His studies address the *retrieval strategy hypothesis*, which says that people will learn to pay attention to stimulus attributes (and locations) that contain information that predicts appropriate responses to the task at hand. Compton (1996) argues that the initial algorithm forces people to pay attention to certain attributes (*algorithm-relevant attributes*), and encourages them to pay attention to attributes that are not directly relevant but correlated with attributes they would attend to in the course of executing the algorithm (*algorithm-irrelevant attributes*). The priority of attending to algorithm-irrelevant attributes changes with practice, depending on their perceptual salience, the consistency with which they predict task-relevant responses, and the frequency with which they occur. Attributes that are salient, predictive, and frequent will increase in priority over training, and at some point, the person will choose to attend to those attributes to retrieve an appropriate response instead of computing one algorithmically.

Compton (1996) is addressing the retrieval strategy hypothesis in the context of an enumeration task, but the hypothesis has relevance well beyond enumeration. In principle, it can apply to any of the tasks commonly used to study visual spatial attention and to the broad range of tasks that are used to study other aspects of attention. The key idea is that learning not only affects how people respond to tasks, which was the original focus of research on automaticity, but it also affects the way they attend to the environment. We suspect (and hope) that learning what to attend to may be as rich and important an area of investigation as learning how to respond.

## Acknowledgments

This research was supported by Grant No. SBR 91–09856 and Grant No. SBR 94–10406 to Gordon Logan from the National Science Foundation. We are grateful to Connie Boronat, Tom Carr, Danny Gopher, Colin Mac-Leod, and Stan Taylor for comments on the manuscript. Gordon D. Logan may be contacted via electronic mail at glogan@s.psych.uiuc.edu.

## Note

1  We cannot distinguish between a strong version of the attention hypothesis, which says that attention is necessary for learning and that nothing unattended will be learned, from a weak version, which says that attention facilitates learning so that unattended things can be learned but not as well as attended things. It is virtually impossible to rule out the possibility that subjects will not pay some attention sometime to things that the experimenter designates as unattended (see Hollender, 1986, and commentary), so evidence that unattended things were learned is ambiguous. Advocates of a strong attention hypothesis would argue that subjects paid some attention to the nominally unattended things, whereas advocates of a weak attention hypothesis would interpret the same data as evidence for learning without attention.

## References

Barsalou, L.W. (1990). On the indistinguishability of exemplar memory and abstraction in category representation. In T.K. Srull & R.S. Wyer (Eds.), *Advances in social cognition* (Vol. 3, pp. 61–88). Hillsdale, NJ: Erlbaum.

Boronat, C.F., & Logan, G.D. (1997, May). *Does attention operate at encoding, retrieval, or both?* Paper presented at the annual meeting of the Midwestern Psychological Association, Chicago, IL.

Broadbent, D.E. (1971). *Decision and stress.* London: Academic Press.

Cave, K.R., & Wolfe, J.M. (1990). Modeling the role of parallel processing in visual search. *Cognitive Psychology, 22,* 225–271.

Charness, N. (1983). Age, skill, and bridge bidding: A chronometric analysis. *Journal of Verbal Learning & Verbal Behavior, 22,* 406–416.

Chase, W.G., & Simon, H.A. (1973). Perception in chess. *Cognitive Psychology, 4,* 55–81.

Compton, B.J. (1994). *Selective attention and automatization in an enumeration task.* Unpublished manuscript, University of Illinois.

Compton, B.J. (1996). *Retrieval strategies in memory-based automaticity.* Unpublished Ph.D. thesis, Department of Psychology, University of Illinois.

Czerwinski, M., Lightfoot, N., & Shiffrin, R.M. (1992). Automatization and training in visual search. *American Journal of Psychology, 105,* 271–315.

Deutsch, J.A., & Deutsch, D. (1963). Attention: Some theoretical considerations. *Psychological Review, 70,* 80–90.

Fisk, A.D., & Schneider, W. (1984). Consistent attending versus consistent responding in visual search: Task versus component consistency in automatic processing development. *Bulletin of the Psychonomic Society, 22,* 330–332.

Hollender, D. (1986). Semantic activation without conscious identification in dichotic listening, parafoveal vision, and visual masking. *Behavioral & Brain Sciences, 9,* 1–23.

Jacoby, L.L. (1991). A process-dissociation framework: Separating automatic from intentional uses of memory. *Journal of Memory & Language, 30,* 513–541.

James, W. (1890). *Principles of psychology.* New York: Holt.

Kaufman, E.L., Lord, M.W., Reese, T.W., & Volkmann, J. (1949). The discrimination of visual number. *American Journal of Psychology, 62,* 498–525.

LaBerge, D., & Samuels, S.J. (1974). Toward a theory of automatic information processing in reading. *Cognitive Psychology, 6,* 293–323.

Lassaline, M.E., & Logan, G.D. (1993). Memory-based automaticity in the discrimination of visual numerosity. *Journal of Experimental Psychology: Learning, Memory & Cognition, 19,* 561–581.

Logan, G.D. (1988a). Automaticity, resources and memory: Theoretical controversies and practical implications. *Human Factors, 30,* 583–598.

Logan, G.D. (1988b). Toward an instance theory of automatization. *Psychological Review, 95,* 492–527.

Logan, G.D. (1989). Automaticity and cognitive control. In J.S. Uleman & J.A. Bargh (Eds.), *Unintended thought: Limits of awareness, intention, and control* (pp. 52–74). New York: Guilford.

Logan, G.D. (1990). Repetition priming and automaticity: Common underlying mechanisms? *Cognitive Psychology, 22,* 1–35.

Logan, G.D. (1991). Automaticity and memory. In W. Hockley & S. Lewandowsky (Eds.), *Relating theory and data: Essays on human memory in honor of Bennet B. Murdock* (pp. 347–366). Hillsdale, NJ: Erlbaum.

Logan, G.D. (1992a). Attention and preattention in theories of automaticity. *American Journal of Psychology, 105,* 317–339.

Logan, G.D. (1992b). Shapes of reaction-time distributions and shapes of learning curves: A test of the instance theory of automaticity. *Journal of Experimental Psychology: Learning, Memory & Cognition, 18,* 883–914.

Logan, G.D. (1995). Linguistic and conceptual control of visual spatial attention. *Cognitive Psychology, 28,* 103–174.

Logan, G.D., & Etherton, J.L. (1994). What is learned during automatization? The role of attention in constructing an instance. *Journal of Experimental Psychology: Learning, Memory & Cognition, 20,* 1022–1050.

Logan, G.D., & Klapp, S.T. (1991). Automatizing alphabet arithmetic: I. Is extended practice necessary to produce automaticity? *Journal of Experimental Psychology: Learning, Memory & Cognition, 17,* 179–195.

Logan, G.D., Taylor, S.E., & Etherton, J.L. (1996). Attention in the acquisition and expression of automaticity. *Journal of Experimental Psychology: Learning, Memory & Cognition.*

Mandler, G., & Shebo, B.J. (1982). Subitizing: An analysis of its component processes. *Journal of Experimental Psychology: General, 111*, 1–22.

Posner, M.I. & Snyder, C.R.R. (1975). Attention and cognitive control. In R.L. Solso (Ed.), *Information processing and cognition: The Loyola symposium* (pp. 55–85). Hillsdale, NJ: Erlbaum.

Rock, I. (1973). *Orientation and form.* San Diego, CA: Academic Press.

Schneider, W. (1985). Toward a model of attention and the development of automatic processing. In M.I. Posner & O.S.M. Marin (Eds.), *Attention & Performance*, 11 VI (pp. 475–492). Hillsdale, NJ: Erlbaum.

Schneider, W., & Fisk, A.D. (1982). Degree of consistent training: Improvements in search performance and automatic process development. *Perception & Psychophysics, 31*, 160–168.

Shiffrin, R.M., & Schneider, W. (1977). Controlled and automatic human information processing: II. Perceptual learning, automatic attending, and a general theory. *Psychological Review, 84*, 127–190.

Simon, H.A. (1980). Models of competence in solving physics problems. *Cognitive Science, 4*, 317–345.

Treisman, A. (1969). Strategies and models of selective attention. *Psychological Review, 76*, 282–299.

Treisman, A., & Gelade, G. (1980). A feature-integration theory of attention. *Cognitive Psychology, 12*, 97–136.

Treisman, A., & Gormican, S. (1988). Feature analysis in early vision: Evidence from search asymmetries. *Psychological Review, 95*, 14–48.

Treisman, A., Kahneman, D., & Burkell, J. (1983). Perceptual objects and the cost of filtering. *Perception & Psychophysics, 33*, 527–532.

Treisman, A., Vieira, A., & Hayes, A. (1992). Automaticity and preattentive processing. *American Journal of Psychology, 105*, 341–362.

Trick, L.M., & Pylyshyn, Z.W. (1994). Why are small and large numbers enumerated differently? A limited-capacity preattentive stage in vision. *Psychological Review, 101*, 80–102.

Ullman, S. (1984). Visual routines. *Cognition, 18*, 97–159.

Wolfe, J.M. (1994). Guided search 2.0: A revised model of visual search. *Psychonomic Bulletin and Review, 1*, 202–238.

Yantis, S. (1996). Attentional capture in vision. In A.F. Kramer, M.G. H. Coles, & G.D. Logan (Eds.), *Converging operations in the study of visual selective attention.* Washington, DC: American Psychological Association.

# 6

# *The Control of Visual Attention*

## Richard D. Wright and Lawrence M. Ward

> But [attention's] towering growth would appear to have been achieved at the price of calling down upon its builders the curse of Babel, "to confound their language that they may not understand one another's speech." For the word "attention" quickly came to be associated . . . with a diversity of meanings that have the appearance of being more chaotic even than those of the term "intelligence." (Spearman, 1937, p. 133)

Attention is a foundational concept in cognitive psychology. Many researchers have credited it with a central role in the "cognitive revolution" of the 1950s and 1960s (e.g., Broadbent, 1958; Egeth, 1992; Neisser, 1967). It is, however, a concept with a stormy history, as the above quotation indicates, and there was little agreement until recently about how it should be defined. Spearman (1937) chronicled many proposed definitions including clearness, vivacity or intensity of percepts or concepts, an attitude of mind, a definite process or special stage in a process, the relative proportion of activated traces to all memory traces, some form of energy or desire involving will or effort, and the sensation of exertion of will. Since 1937, definitions or metaphors such as a filter (Broadbent, 1958), a skill (Neisser, 1976), a selective attenuator (Treisman, 1964), a resource (Kahneman, 1973), a "spotlight beam" within which processing is enhanced (Posner, 1980), a "zoom lens" (Eriksen & Yeh, 1985), a "glue" that binds features together (Treisman & Gelade, 1980), and a decoupler of modules from public communication channels (Navon, 1989), among others, have added to the confusion. Moreover, a number of different aspects of attention (e.g., capacity, selectivity, control, relation to consciousness, relation to arousal) have been engaged by specific paradigms and emphasized by particular writers (e.g., Solso, 1991). Recently, however, some definite progress has been made in understanding how attention to locations and/or objects in visual space is controlled. This research has been carried out within several closely related experimental paradigms including those that allow conclusions to be made about physiological mechanisms. It has emphasized the way in which shifts of attention in visual space can be evoked by stimuli and by goals, and how these shifts are related to the control of eye movements. Although there are no final answers yet, the body of data amassed so far has several clear implications for our understanding of attention control processes. It also suggests integrative models and further research. We summarize some of these implications and propose one possible integrative model that has interesting implications for how we understand attention more generally.

Shifts of visual attention are changes in the spatial location to which we attend. They usually accompany eye movements but can also occur independently of eye fixation. For example, suppose you are sitting in a restaurant having dinner with a friend. While your eyes are fixed on your companion's face and you are listening intently to what is being said, your attention may stray to the interesting person at the next table. Your eyes have not moved but for a moment you are not attending to the object of your gaze. Two of the primary goals of contemporary research on this phenomenon are to determine when attention shifts are under voluntary control and when they are more reflexive, and to examine the nature of the relationship between attention shifts and eye movements.

More than a century ago, Helmholtz conducted an experiment to test his ability to shift visual attention independently of eye fixation (see Warren & Warren, 1968). He fixed his eyes on an illuminated pinhole in the centre of a dark field of large printed letters and, on each trial, illuminated the display with an electric spark. The illumination did not last long enough for an eye movement to be made away from the fixation point while the display was visible, and Helmholtz was unable to perceive all of the letters or even all of those near the fixation point. By deciding in advance of the illumination which part of the display to attend to, however, he was able to recognize single groups of letters in the attended region. Moreover, he was able to voluntarily shift his attention to different regions of the display while maintaining eye fixation on the central, illuminated pinhole. This experiment is often cited as the first scientific demonstration of the independence of visual attention shifts and eye fixation.

James (1890) stated that when we selectively attend to an object, the mind "takes possession" of it even though other objects are present that the mind also could have taken possession of (cf., LaBerge, 1990a). He described "paying attention" in terms of resources that have their greatest concentration at the focal point and a decreasing concentration as a function of increasing distance from the focal point. James also proposed that there are two domains of attention – the *immediate sensory domain* and the *voluntary intellectual domain*. The first involved, in his terms, the accommodation or adjustment of sensory organs. The second domain involved anticipatory preparation from within the cognitive centres concerned with the object attended to. This proposal foreshadows one of the central aspects of more recent investigations – the distinction between voluntary and involuntary attentional processes. Titchener (1910), among others, studied involuntary processes after observing that abrupt flashes in the visual periphery appear to draw attention to their locations. Thus, contemporary research on the control of attentional processes was anticipated in proposals made 100 years or more ago.

Despite the pioneering efforts of Helmholtz and James, studies conducted long after their proposals produced very little supporting evidence (e.g., Grindley & Townsend, 1968; Mertens, 1956; Mowrer, 1941). In fact, it was not until the 1970s and the advent of location cueing experiments that significant empirical evidence began to accumulate to substantiate the claim that visual attention *can* be aligned independently of eye fixation.

## Location Cueing and Shifts of Visual Attention

Visual attention is often described in terms of a focal point that is aligned with different locations in space as we inspect our visual world. These attentional alignments can also be initiated in response to cues about the probable locations of impending targets that interest us. Many location cueing experiments have been conducted to study the "beneficial" effect of a valid cue and the "negative" effect of an invalid cue on target detection and identification responses (e.g., Posner, Nissen, & Ogden, 1978; Posner & Snyder, 1975; Posner, Snyder, & Davidson, 1980). Typically (e.g., 70% of trials), the location information conveyed by a cue is a valid indicator of where the target will appear on that trial (see Figure 1). And, in the remaining cases (e.g., 30% of trials), cue information is either invalid or neutral. Like valid and invalid cues, neutral cues provide a temporal warning signal about the impending target's onset. But they are referred to as "neutral" because they are supposed to provide no information about target location. Their purpose is to serve as a baseline measure for a cost-benefit analysis of location cueing effects. That is, the mean response times or accuracies for trials involving valid and invalid cues are compared to the same measures for trials involving neutral cues. The "valid vs. neutral comparison" provides a measure of the *benefit* of valid cueing, and the "invalid vs. neutral comparison" provides a measure of the *cost* of invalid cueing (see Figure 1).

While cost-benefit analysis has played an important role in the study of attentional processes, there has also been a growing awareness of its limitations in recent years (see e.g., Jonides & Mack, 1984; Wright,

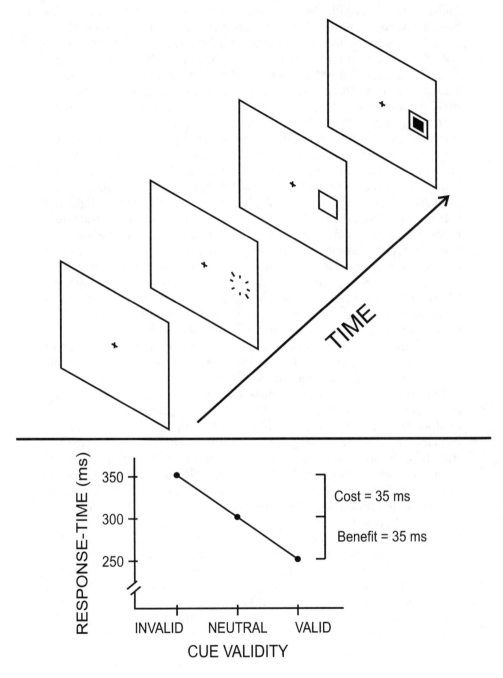

*Figure* 1: Pattern of data obtained by Posner et al. (1978) indicating the response-time cost and benefit of invalid and valid location cueing.

Richard, & McDonald, 1995). The main concern is about the neutral cue baseline measure, and particularly when examining the effects of direct location cues (those that appear at or near the locations of targets). More specifically, neutral cues are difficult to present in a truly location-non-specific manner. Several strategies have been adopted to compensate for this including foregoing neutral cueing and using only a "valid vs. invalid comparison" to get what amounts to a "cue effectiveness" measure (Wright & Richard, 1996). Without the neutral baseline, however, it is unclear whether or not this comparison reflects costs or benefits. That is, without a neutral baseline, there is no way of knowing the relative effectiveness of valid vs. invalid cues. Another strategy is to minimize the degree to which the neutral cue has a specific position by, for example, presenting a uniform flash of the entire display background (Mackeben & Nakayama, 1993). Selecting an appropriate neutral cue is more straightforward when examining the effects of symbolic location cues. All types of symbolic cues are usually presented in the central location, and therefore do not convey potential target locations on the basis of their physical position. For a detailed discussion of this issue, see Wright et al. (1995). In this chapter and many other articles in the literature, references to response facilitation and inhibition due to location cueing are usually based on some form of cost-benefit analysis.

There are two main types of location cues. *Symbolic cues* (e.g., arrows or digits) can be used to initiate an attention shift by virtue of symbolic information about the probable location of the target. They are also called central cues, in part, because they are usually presented at the centre of the display (Posner, 1978). *Direct cues* (e.g., outline boxes, bars, or dots) initiate attention shifts merely by appearing at or near the probable location of the target, as in Figure 1. They are also called peripheral cues, in part, because they (and targets) are usually presented at noncentral locations within the display (Posner, 1978). While the terms *central* and *peripheral* refer to the location of the cue in the visual field or on the retina, location does not fully indicate the fundamental difference between the two types of cues. That is, central cues do not have to be presented in the centre of the stimulus display to be effective, and peripheral cues remain effective even when presented centrally (e.g., Eriksen & Colgate, 1971). For this reason, other pairs of terms such as "push vs. pull cue" and "information vs. stimulus cue" are also found in the attention shift literature. The primary difference between them is that the direct type of cue summons attention to the location of its onset without the need for interpretation of cue meaning. On the other hand, the symbolic type of cue does require some initial interpretation of cue meaning before attention can be shifted to the cued location (e.g., Remington, 1980).

Shifts of attention initiated by symbolic vs. direct cues have been referred to as "intrinsic vs. extrinsic" (Milner, 1974), "endogenous vs. exogenous" (Posner, 1978), and "voluntary vs. involuntary" (Jonides, 1981; Luria, 1973; Müller & Rabbitt, 1989). The latter pair of terms is common because shifts initiated by a symbolic cue can be voluntarily suppressed while shifts initiated by a direct cue can be difficult to suppress (e.g., Jonides, 1981, 1983; Müller & Rabbitt, 1989). When an observer chooses to use a symbolic cue to aim an attention shift, the target's probable location is incorporated into a *computational goal* for carrying out the task (i.e., use the cue information to shift attention to the expected target location). Therefore, in this chapter, we use the more general term, *goal-driven* control, when referring to the initiation of endogenous, voluntary, and intrinsic attention shifts.

While shifts of attention triggered by direct cues can be difficult to suppress, there are some situations in which a direct cue onset will *not* result in a reflexive shift of attention to its location. Yantis and his colleagues found that while abrupt-onset visual stimuli can trigger attention shifts to their locations, observers can also override such shifts if they are actively focusing their attention elsewhere when the abrupt-onset stimuli appear (e.g., Yantis & Jonides, 1990). In other words, an attention shift is not a mandatory consequence of a direct cue onset. Without this capacity to suppress attention shifts to stimuli that suddenly appear in our visual field, we would be distracted by many irrelevant visual events. And our performance of any task requiring sustained attention and vigilance would be disrupted. Therefore, the effect of direct cue onsets is not entirely involuntary. In this chapter, we use the more general term, *stimulus-driven* control, when referring to the initiation of exogenous, involuntary, and extrinsic attention shifts.

Several studies have been conducted to test the claim that direct cues "capture" attention more readily than symbolic cues do. One of these studies involved a comparison of direct cue and symbolic cue effectiveness when subjects performed a target-identification task and a concurrent memory-load task (Jonides, 1981). Symbolic cue effectiveness was diminished by increases in memory load but direct cue effectiveness was not. It was concluded that attention shifts were initiated more automatically by the direct cues than by the symbolic cues because the latter required attentional resources that were also needed to perform the competing memory load task. Direct cue effectiveness, on the other hand, appeared to be independent of the need for attentional resources (cf. Schneider, Dumais, & Shiffrin, 1984). Also, explicit instructions to *ignore* the location cues decreased the effectiveness of symbolic cues more than that of direct cues (Jonides, 1981). Furthermore, decreasing cue validity (e.g., valid cue on 20% as opposed to 80% of trials as in the previous experiments) also decreased the effectiveness of symbolic cues more than that of direct cues (Jonides, 1981; Kröse & Julesz, 1989; Müller & Humphreys, 1991). Presumably, this is because subjects do not voluntarily use low validity cues. These results therefore imply that direct cue effects are more reflexive than symbolic cue effects.

Claims about the "automaticity" of direct cue effectiveness should be qualified. This effectiveness appears to depend on the nature of the cue's onset and on the current state of the observer's attentional focus. Location cues can have either an *abrupt-onset* or a *gradual-onset* (see e.g., Todd & Van Gelder, 1979; Yantis & Jonides, 1984, 1990). Abrupt-onset stimuli appear suddenly in the visual field and can be targets (e.g., letters, flashes of light) or cues (e.g., bar markers, arrows, brightened boxes). Gradual-onset stimuli (cues or targets) emerge less suddenly, either because they are revealed by the removal of camouflage elements or because they are "turned on" so slowly that luminance changes over time are below "onset thresholds" (see Figure 2).[1] The results of several experiments indicate that targets with abrupt onsets capture attention more effectively than those with gradual onsets (e.g., Yantis & Jonides, 1984). In some cases, however, when search is initiated by a symbolic cue, the time to respond to abrupt-onset targets does not differ from that to respond to gradual-onset targets (Yantis & Jonides, 1990). This finding suggests that the attention-capturing effectiveness of an abrupt-onset stimulus appears to be attenuated if an observer is, at the same time, actively focusing on a symbolic cue at another location (see also, Folk, Remington, & Johnston, 1992). Thus, an abrupt-onset stimulus can initiate an attention shift to its location in a stimulus-driven manner, but the shift may not occur if attention is actively focused or engaged elsewhere.

Differences in direct cue and symbolic cue effectiveness as a function of cue-target-onset-asynchrony (CTOA) are another indication that the former elicit stimulus-driven shifts and the latter elicit goal-driven shifts. In particular, valid direct cues appear to be maximally effective when the CTOA is approximately 100 ms, but this effectiveness begins to attenuate with further CTOA increases (e.g., Müller & Findlay, 1988; Shepard & Müller, 1989).[2] On the other hand, the effectiveness of symbolic cues appears to increase gradually as the CTOA is increased from 0 to 300 ms, and effectiveness appears to be sustained at a maximum level with further CTOA increases (e.g., Müller & Findlay, 1988; Shepard & Müller, 1989). In some cases, the effectiveness of direct cues can be sustained at slightly lower than the maximum level with CTOAs larger than 100 ms (Cheal & Lyon, 1991). Presumably, the occurrence of a sustained direct cue effect at CTOAs larger than 100 ms depends on whether this cue also functions as a symbolic cue after the initial reflexive effects of cue onset subside.[3]

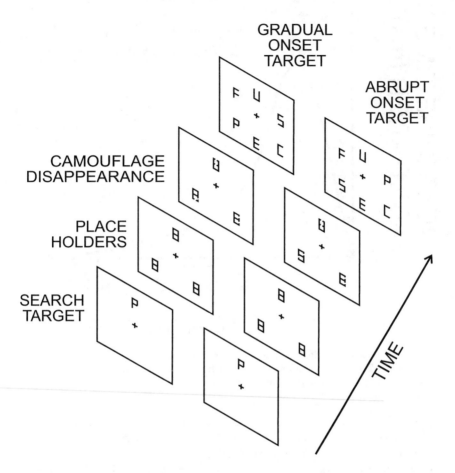

*Figure* 2: Abrupt-onset and gradual-onset presentations of the target P. The stimulus sequence on the left involves the gradual removal of irrelevant camouflage lines from a stimulus that is already present. The stimulus sequence on the right involves the abrupt appearance of a stimulus in a previously blank location.

The transient nature of direct cue effectiveness is also evident when studying the interference caused by irrelevant abrupt-onset stimuli. In particular, if an irrelevant abrupt-onset stimulus is presented *less* than 100 ms after cue onset, a stimulus-driven shift will still be triggered by the relevant direct cue. If an irrelevant abrupt-onset stimulus is presented *more* than 100 ms after the relevant direct cue, however, the former can disrupt the shift of attention and cause it to be made instead to the irrelevant stimulus location (Müller & Rabbitt, 1989). Thus, direct cueing appears to be resistant to interference for only about 100 ms.

In general, stimulus-driven attention shifts appear to be triggered rapidly by abrupt-onset direct cues, and the transient nature of direct-

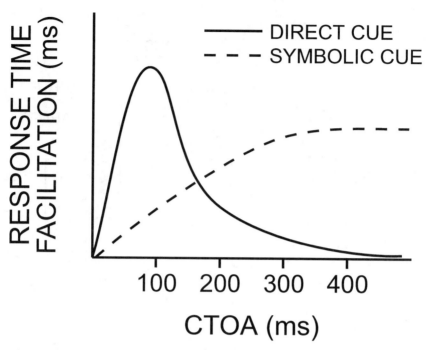

*Figure* 3: Typical data indicating the time-course of response-time facilitation produced by direct and symbolic locations cues as a function of cue-target-onset-asynchrony (CTOA). The dashed line represents direct cueing effectiveness and the solid line represents symbolic cueing effectiveness.

cue effectiveness is indicated by a decline in response-time facilitation when CTOAs are increased beyond 100 ms. Goal-driven shifts, on the other hand, appear to be initiated less rapidly, and the time required to focus attention on a symbolic cue and interpret it (and perhaps to disengage attention after the interpretation) may account for reports that symbolic cues require CTOAs of 300 ms or more to be maximally effective. The difference in the time course of effectiveness of the two types of cues is summarized in Figure 3.

Questions have also been raised about whether the costs and benefits of location cueing reflect changes in perceptual processing or whether they arise from changes in an observer's criterion for reporting the presence or identity of stimuli (Lappin & Uttal, 1976; Shaw, 1983). Researchers have attempted to determine whether faster response times for targets presented on valid cue trials (benefits) arise from greater perceptual sensitivity at the target location or from a more liberal decision criterion, and whether slower response times for targets presented on invalid cue trials (costs) arise from lesser sensitivity at the target location or from a more conservative criterion. Signal detection theory provides a way to measure perceptual sensitivity ($d'$) independently of the decision criterion ($\beta$) and is usually used to differentiate between these two possibilities (e.g., Green & Swets, 1966/1974). Although the results of early experiments using this approach were equivocal, more recent data indicate that location cueing does affect perceptual processing (e.g., Bonnel, Possamai, & Schmidt, 1987; Downing, 1988; Müller, 1994; Müller & Humphreys, 1991; Possamai & Bonnel, 1991). That is, perceptual sensitivity to targets appearing at cued locations is greater than that to targets at uncued locations. Moreover, the greatest change in perceptual sensitivity at cued locations appears to follow the onset of direct cues as opposed to symbolic cues (Müller, 1994).

## Visual Attention Shift Models

Several models have been proposed to account for attention shifts. One of these is the analog spotlight model. According to some theorists, analog mechanisms shift from one state to another by traversing the set of intermediate states (e.g., Shepard, 1975). Advocates of analog attention shifts claim that as the focal point is "moved" from one location to another, it also traverses the intermediate spatial locations like a metaphorical spotlight (see Figure 4). The validity of analog spotlight models has been tested by studying how costs or benefits of location cueing vary with the distance between the cue and the target. These studies are based on the assumption that as this distance is increased, more time will be required to "redirect" an analog spotlight of attention from an invalid cue location to the target location. Some studies indicate that increases in invalid-cue/target distance lead to *linear* increases in response time, which is consistent with the notion of a constant velocity spotlight (e.g., Shulman, Remington, & McLean, 1979; Tsal, 1983). Other researchers, however, have found nonlinear increases in response time with increasing invalid-cue/target distance, which implies that analog spotlight velocity is either variable or perhaps constant but defined relative to distance in visual angle units scaled by visual receptive field size (e.g., Downing & Pinker, 1985). Still others have found that costs or benefits did not vary with invalid-cue/target distance, which implies that if the attention shift involves an analog spotlight, its velocity is proportional to the distance it moves (e.g., Remington & Pierce, 1984). Critiques of this research have implicated other possible reasons for the constant-velocity results (e.g., Eriksen & Murphy, 1987; Yantis, 1988). Although analog attention shift models are appealingly simple, a lack of unequivocal empirical support has limited their usefulness.

An alternative explanation of the proportional-velocity results is that shifts of an attentional focal point are discrete. That is, during an

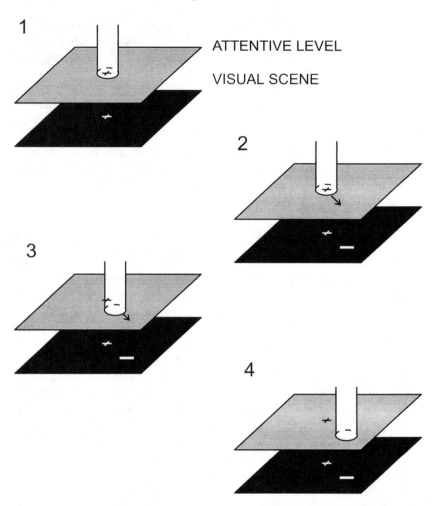

ATTENTIVE LEVEL

VISUAL SCENE

*Figure* 4: Analog spotlight account of a visual attention shift from the centre of a display to the location of the horizontal line stimulus. The black surface is the stimulus display, and the grey surface is a mental representation of it. The spotlight is said to be analog because it remains "turned on" when shifted.

attention shift, the beam is "turned off" and does not traverse the intermediate locations between the initial point and the destination (see Figure 5). A pure discrete spotlight model requires that costs and benefits be unaffected by changes in invalid-cue/target distance. In other words, the time required to turn off the spotlight at the initial point and turn it back on again at the destination should not be a function of the distance between the two locations. Evidence supporting such a model has been obtained, for example, in a series of studies in-

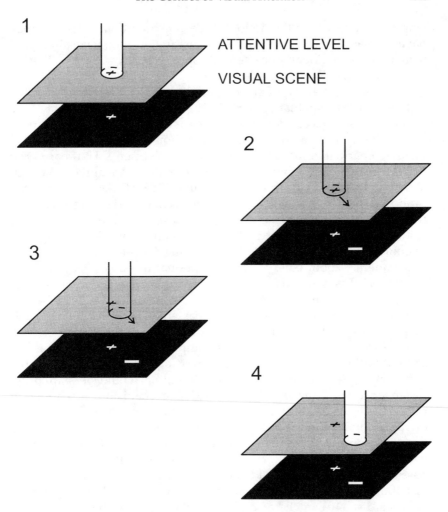

*Figure* 5: Discrete spotlight account of a visual attention shift from the centre of a display to the location of the horizontal line stimulus. The spotlight is said to be discrete because it is "turned off" during a shift and then "turned on" again at the destination.

volving multiple simultaneous direct cues (Eriksen & Webb, 1989; Eriksen, Webb, & Fournier, 1990). The main finding was that differences in the distances between these cues did not affect the time required to identify targets at the cued locations. While subjects appeared to check the cued locations serially, the time required to do so was independent of the distance between the locations. Other results have also suggested that, in some cases, attention shift time is independent of shift distance (Kwak, Dagenbach, & Egeth, 1991; Sagi & Julesz, 1985; Skelton & Eriksen, 1976). Thus, there is considerable empirical support for the notion of discrete attention shifts and they have been assumed to occur by many researchers who have attempted to associate attentional processes with specific brain areas (e.g., Posner, Petersen, Fox, & Raichle, 1988).

One of the limitations of analog and discrete spotlight models is the lack of a mechanism that systematically varies the spatial extent of the beam. This is a concern because there is evidence that attentional focus that can range from a broad extent throughout the visual field to a fine focus at a particular location of interest (e.g., Eriksen & Hoffman, 1974; Eriksen & Yeh, 1985; Jonides, 1980; LaBerge, 1983; Ward, 1985). Eriksen and his colleagues (e.g., Eriksen & St. James, 1986; Eriksen & Yeh, 1985) proposed that the attentional focal point is characterized by a distribution of attention resources. They also proposed that the distribution of resources and the spatial extent of focused attention have a reciprocal relationship like that between the resolving power and spatial extent of a camera's zoom lens. That is, attentional resources become more concentrated as the spatial extent of attentional focus is decreased. Furthermore, when attention is shifted, it is was said to be defocused at one location (an increase in the spatial extent of attentional focus) and then refocused at another location (a decrease in the spatial extent). Most descriptions of focusing models imply that they are analog in the sense that the attentional focus remains "turned on" when its spatial extent changes. Figure 6 shows how attention would be shifted between locations in the visual field if such a mechanism was required to traverse intermediate states of focus (i.e., narrow to broader to broadest at the old location and then broadest to less broad to narrow at the new location). Other researchers have suggested that an attentional zoom lens may have only two states – a broad, diffuse focus encompassing the entire visual field and a narrow focus (perhaps 1° to 2° of visual angle) on a specific location – and therefore that focusing involves a discrete switch between these states (called the "Law of Two Levels" in the early twentieth century and adopted by some contemporary researchers, e.g., Jonides, 1980). Still others have argued that adjustments of the zoom lens are discrete while not making specific claims about the number of different states of focal resolution (e.g., Shepard & Müller, 1989, p. 152). In general, the distinction between analog and discrete mechanisms can be understood as attention remaining "turned on" or engaged during shifts from one spatial locus to another in the analog case versus attention being "turned off" or disengaged during shifts in the discrete case.

To summarize the points made in this section, stimulus-driven attention shifts appear to be initiated rapidly in response to the *transient* effect of abrupt-onset direct cues, but only if attention is not actively

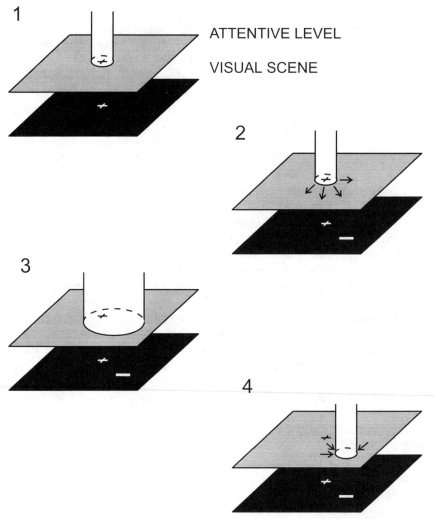

*Figure* 6:  Analog zoom lens account of a visual attention shift from the centre of a display to the location of the horizontal line stimulus. The zoom lens is shifted by increasing in spatial extent and decreasing again around the destination.

engaged elsewhere. Goal-driven attention shifts made in response to symbolic cues appear to be initiated voluntarily and less rapidly, and only after interpretation of cue meaning. Most evidence indicates that stimulus-driven shifts are discrete as opposed to analog.

## Preattentive and Attentive Visual Processing

Neisser (1964) was among the first of the researchers in the modern era to make a distinction between preattentive and attentive visual processes. Much of this work was based on the study of visual search in controlled laboratory experiments. Observers in these experiments typically searched for a target letter surrounded by distractor letters in order to make a Target Present or Target Absent response as quickly as possible. If the target was sufficiently different from the distractors in such a way that it stood out, responses were rapid. For example, if the target letter was roundish (e.g., O or Q) and the distractors were angular (e.g., M, N, Z, X, W), then the target's location was often immediately apparent. Rapid detection of the target's presence soon came to be known as "pop out." If the target was similar to the distractors (e.g., both were angular), then search was slower, effortful, and required more time as the number of items in the search set was increased. This "set-size effect" occurred, in other words, if the target did not stand out from the distractors by virtue of a unique feature, but virtually no set-size effect occurred if the target had a unique feature not possessed by the distractor items. This was taken as evidence for two separate stages of visual processing. More specifically, Neisser (1964) suggested that a positive relationship between the number of search set items and Target Present or Target Absent response time implies that items are being serially inspected to determine whether or not they are the target. Conversely, when the response time was virtually independent of the number of search set items, as is the case when the target stands out by virtue of possessing a unique feature, a preattentive stage of processing was thought to be mediating target detection. The preattentive/attentive distinction has shaped much of the thinking about visual search processes since Neisser's (1964) proposal.

Treisman and Gelade (1980) developed an explanation of these results that builds on the preattentive/attentive proposal outlined by Neisser (1964). They suggested that, at the preattentive analysis stage, feature information (e.g., colour, orientation, motion) is analyzed in parallel throughout the visual scene by separate feature analysis modules. The presence of a unique-feature target (e.g., one with a unique colour) was said to be immediately apparent because the target is the only one of its type detected by the relevant feature module. On the other hand, the presence of a conjunction target (e.g., one with a unique shape/colour combination) was said to require attention because comparisons had to be made across feature modules to determine the feature combination of objects at particular locations. Conjunction-target search could involve, for example, checking the information in the colour module and then the shape module to find out the colour/shape combination of, say, the third object from the left in a stimulus display. Thus, in Treisman and Gelade's (1980) terms, attention would be required to "glue" these features together (integrate them) to form a perceptual object. They called this proposal the *feature-integration theory*. When a scene is inspected in a serial manner to locate a conjunction target, attention was therefore said to glue features together to determine whether or not each object's combination matched that of the target.

Feature-integration theory can be described with a map-based model. In Figure 7, each of a number of *feature maps* are connected indirectly through common inputs to a *master map of locations*. And each feature map corresponds to a different dimension (e.g. colour, orientation, motion). When a unique-feature target pops out, it is registered within the feature map in question (e.g., the target is the only red object in the display) and the observer immediately detects its presence. When this type of target is located, the feature map sends a signal that causes focused attention to be aligned with the corresponding location of the red object in the master map of locations. When a conjunction target is located, as in Figure 8, focused attention is aligned in a serial manner with each of a number of locations in the master map. And, at each master map location, information about features at the corresponding location within each feature map is accessed. In this way, according to Treisman and Gelade (1980), feature integration occurs. One property of the feature-integration process is that focused attention can only be positioned at one location at a time within the location map and, therefore, only one set of object features can be integrated at a time. The spotlight metaphor is sometimes used to describe movements of focused attention from one location to another within the master map of locations.

The effects of location cueing on visual search efficiency have been studied to test the claim that conjunction-target search involves serial attentive processing while unique-feature-target search occurs on the basis of preattentive analysis. It was expected that the presentation of a location cue at the impending target's location immediately prior to the onset of the search display (within 100 ms) would have a greater effect on conjunction-target search times than on feature-target search times. The results of several experiments confirmed this prediction (e.g., Nakayama & Mackeben, 1989; Treisman & Gelade, 1980). The presentation of a location cue did little to increase the speed of the already rapid feature-target search. This is further evidence that the detection of a unique-feature target is mediated primarily by preattentive processes because facilitating the alignment of focused attention had no effect on the operations involved. On the other hand, the facilitative effects of location cueing on conjunction-target search times indicates that serial alignments of the attentional focal point are involved.

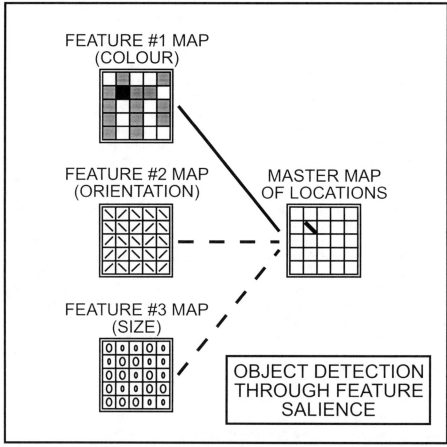

*Figure* 7: A simplified map-based account of feature integration theory. In this case, the larger white "upper-left/lower-right" bar pops out of the display because its unique colour triggers activation in the colour map. See Treisman and Gormican (1988) for a detailed description of the theory.

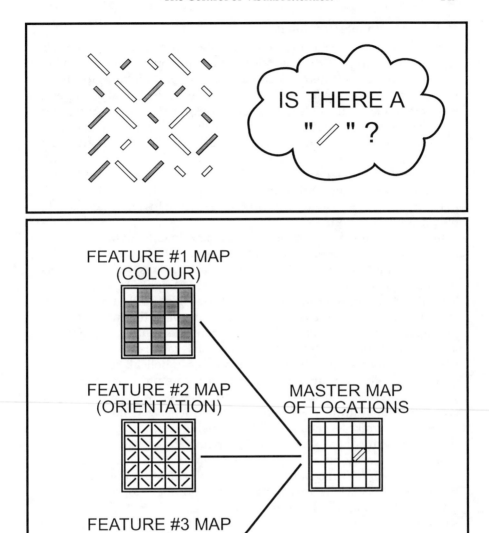

*Figure* 8: Another simplified account of feature integration theory. In this case, the larger black "upper-right/lower-left" bar does not pop out and must be serially searched for because it has no unique feature within any of the feature maps.

## Preattentive Location Encoding

Several researchers have attempted to determine whether attention is confined to a single focal point or can be simultaneously divided between a number of different locations. Although some disagree, there is a general consensus in the literature that the attentional focal point is unitary and nondivisible (e.g., Posner, 1980). This claim is supported by the results of experiments in which two symbolic cues are presented simultaneously and observers must try to direct their attention to both cued locations at the same time in anticipation of the impending target (e.g., Kiefer & Siple, 1987; McCormick & Klein, 1990). The data are a compelling indication that we are unable to do so and still perform visual tasks with the same efficiency as when attending to only a single location.[4]

In contrast, the results of more recent experiments involving the simultaneous presentation of two or more direct location cues have indicated that single and multiple cueing can facilitate responses to targets presented at cued locations (e.g., Richard, Wright, & Ward, 1996; Wright, 1994; Wright & Richard, 1996; Wright, Richard, & McDonald, 1995, 1996). Perhaps, the critical difference between the two sets of experiments could be *cue type*. When more than one location was symbolically cued at the same time, average response facilitation across trials was weaker than when a single location was symbolically cued. On the other hand, when simultaneous direct cues were presented in our experiments, average response facilitation across trials was roughly equivalent on multiple cue trials (Wright & Richard, 1996).

Are these symbolic cueing and direct cueing results in conflict about the indivisibility of the attentional focal point? In other words, must attention necessarily be divided between two or more locations at the same time in order to account for the multiple direct cueing results? We have argued elsewhere that the answer is no; they do not refute the unitary attentional focal point proposal (e.g., Wright, 1994; Wright & Richard, 1996; Wright, Richard, & McDonald, 1996). In particular, we suggested that a direct location cue appears to affect responses in two ways: (1) its abrupt onset appears to trigger nonattentional sensory processes that facilitate responses, and (2) it enables the attentional focal point to be aligned with its location, thereby allowing attentional processes to facilitate responses. Thus, simultaneous multiple direct cues may trigger sensory-driven (nonattentional) operations that facilitate responses to targets subsequently presented at their locations. This argument has been shaped, in part, by the model proposed by LaBerge and Brown (1989). In short, the symbolic multiple cueing data may reflect alignments of an attentional focal point that is constrained to a single location at any given time. But the results of our direct multiple cueing experiments may reflect the encoding of one or more locations in a *preattentive* manner that is not spatially constrained to a single location in the same way that the attentional focal point is. And, we argue, preattentive encoding of these direct cued locations could have been responsible for roughly equal response facilitation on single vs. multiple cue trials. The key point is that the preattentive encoding of direct cue locations we proposed would have no implications for arguments about the unitary nature of the attentional focal point.

Like many others, we assume that a single attentional focal point can be directed from one location in the visual field to another in a voluntary manner (e.g., in response to the interpretation of symbolic location cues). This is a purely attentive operation. But it is also the case that the visual system must encode locations on the basis of sensory operations that occur prior to the "arrival" of the attentional focal point. If this were not true, then how else could a direct location cue provide a signal to the attentional focal point about where it should go? If location encoding were only possible after some form of attentional processing, then direct cues could not function as triggers for guiding focused attention to their location. Therefore, a processing event that can trigger attentional processing (e.g., location encoding) does not require attentional processing for its own initiation. The spatial locations of such events (e.g., direct cue onsets) must undergo some degree of encoding that is independent of attention. Unlike purely attentive processing, there are fewer spatial constraints on preattentive sensory processing (e.g., Marr, 1982; Neisser, 1964; Treisman & Gelade, 1980). Because our visual system must be capable of encoding locations on the basis of sensory operations, and because these operations are not spatially constrained in the same sense that attentive operations are, preattentive location encoding is possible at more than one location at the same time.

## Spatial Indexing and Preattentive Localization

The notion of preattentive location encoding has been implicit in many proposals that are not part of the mainstream attention literature (e.g., Dawson, 1991; Pylyshyn, 1989; Ullman, 1984). They sometimes hold that preattentive operations can be mediated by some form of *spatial indexing* mechanism. In simple terms, indexing is the process by which location information is made available to other visual operations.

The results of several experiments indicate that an index appears to remain "attached" or assigned to objects as they move. As seen in Figure 9, observers in one type of study were shown a number of identical objects (e.g., 10) and asked to keep track of a subset of them. Surprisingly, they could usually track at least four at the same time as the objects moved randomly and independently (Pylyshyn & Storm, 1988;

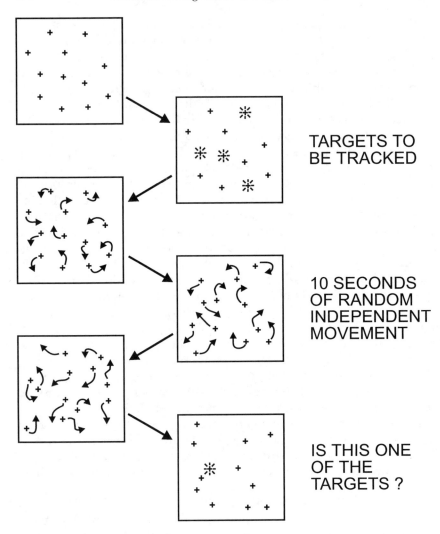

*Figure 9*: Example of the multiple-target tracking task.

Yantis, 1992). Of particular interest is that the high velocity of the objects seemed to preclude the possibility that a serial "scanning and encoding" procedure was used. Instead, tracking appeared to involve a parallel procedure whereby processing was simultaneously directed to each of the four target locations.

Many attention researchers were aware of this finding for several years before it began to influence their work. Part of the reason for this slow acceptance is that high-speed multiple target tracking is difficult to explain in terms of attentional operations. When an observer is asked to visually track a subset of moving objects, attention seems to be required. On the other hand, the data indicate that tracking several moving objects in parallel is unlikely to be the result of rapid shifts of a single attentional focal point. Therefore, if these data are valid, it is tempting to conclude that the focal point is divisible into multiple attentional foci. In terms of the spotlight metaphor, this is referred to as "splitting the beam of attention." As we have pointed out, however, there is compelling evidence that a single attentional focal point is aligned with different locations in visual space in a serial manner. So if one tried to explain the tracking data in terms of purely attentional processing, the result would be an account that is inconsistent with the current consensus about the unitary nature of the attentional focal point.

Another possible explanation is that while observers must pay attention when performing a tracking task, the maintenance of individual target locations is not due to alignments of focused attention. Perhaps the first clear description of target location encoding that is independent of attention was Ullman's (1984) proposal about *intermediate-level* visual processing. Intermediate-level processing, like low-level sensory processing, is said to be rapid, sometimes parallel, and not always completely available to conscious awareness. On the other hand, it can be influenced and controlled in a goal-driven manner in accordance with the perceptual task that the observer intends to perform (see Figure 10 and Wright & Richard, this volume).[5]

In the case of multiple target tracking, maintenance of target locations by intermediate-level processes would be rapid and parallel. But the initiation of these processes and the selection of the subset of objects to be tracked would be under the observer's control. This is consistent with Ullman's (1984) claim that the intermediate level shares some properties with low-level sensory operations and some properties with high-level cognitive operations. When tracking a subset of four targets, attention is required to control the operation of an intermediate-level tracking procedure; but the encoding of each tracked target's location at any given time is due to a sequence of intermediate-level procedures rather than a series of rapid alignments of a single attentional focal point.

Pylyshyn (1989, this volume) developed an intermediate-level account of high-speed multiple target tracking that was based on a preattentive location-encoding mechanism. In particular, a limited number of indexes (approximately four) were said to be allocated to different objects, and this allocation could be maintained independently of attention as the objects moved. He called these indexes FINSTs for Fingers of INSTantiation. The location information provided by FINSTs is said to be crude. Their primary role when tracking

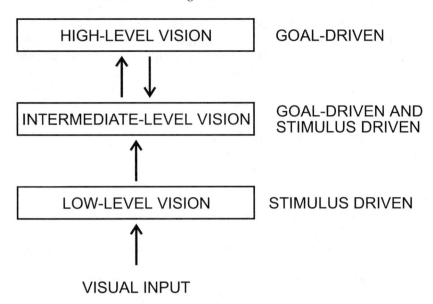

*Figure* 10:  Three levels of visual processing. The intermediate level can be influenced in a goal-driven and a stimulus-driven manner.

targets is simply to stay "glued" to the moving object. If, at some point, the observer is required to verify that a particular object is a target, he can respond on the basis of whether or not the object is indexed. Thus, Pylyshyn's proposal addresses the preattentive maintenance of continually changing location information.

It has also been suggested that a form of spatial indexing is involved in preattentive encoding of objects that suddenly appear in the visual field. Recall that when attention is actively focused or engaged at a particular location, an abrupt onset of an irrelevant stimulus in the visual periphery will *not* "distract" the observer and cause attention to be disengaged and captured at the irrelevant stimulus location (Yantis & Jonides, 1990). But abrupt-onset stimuli appear to maintain some level of enhanced processing at their locations for a brief period of time despite engagement of the attentional focal point elsewhere. And if attention is disengaged within this brief period, a stimulus-driven shift may still be triggered to the location of one of these stimuli (Yantis & Johnson, 1990; Yantis & Jones, 1991). On the basis of their finding that as many as four abrupt-onset stimuli can do this, Yantis and Johnson (1990) proposed that such stimuli generate *interrupt signals* like those sent from peripheral devices to the central processing unit of a computer. If actively focused or engaged attention blocks these signals, they can be temporarily stored in a hierarchical queue or buffer while attention is engaged. In other words, their locations remain preattentively indexed even while the attentional focal point is unavailable. Müller and Humphreys (1991) developed a similar proposal. Note that, according to these researchers, the maximum number of location interrupt signals generated and temporarily stored in the buffer (four or five) is the same as the number of spatial indexes Pylyshyn and Storm (1988) thought to be available for tracking multiple moving objects.

In our opinion, the primary role of a spatial index is to convey location information. One common misunderstanding about index allocation is the extent to which this operation is thought to cause processing facilitation or inhibition. We suggest that an index serves only to provide subsequent operations with information about its location, and allocation does not facilitate or inhibit subsequent processing there. It is simply a marker for encoding and keeping track of a relevant location. This was Pylyshyn's (1989) motivation for describing spatial indexes as "fingers" that point to locations while attention is elsewhere.

Some of the properties of spatial indexes include the following: (1) there seem to be about four of them; (2) they can remain allocated to objects in a dynamic manner as indicated by the performance of multiple target tracking tasks; (3) they can be allocated in a stimulus-driven manner to the locations of abrupt-onset stimuli and other visual transients, and in a goal-driven manner in accordance with the perceiver's computational goal (e.g., track four objects as they move); (4) signals from indexed locations may be stored in a queue and objects at these locations will be given "attentional priority" in the event that attention becomes disengaged and available for further processing; and (5) indexes are merely markers and do not themselves cause facilitation or inhibition of processing as a result of their allocation at a particular location (see also, Pylyshyn, this volume).

### The Activity Distribution Model

The spotlight and zoom lens models described in the previous section were proposed as metaphors of the attentional focal point. They do not, however, describe the sensory-driven events that trigger its alignment with different locations. It is implied that attention is somehow captured by the appearance of a direct location cue or is somehow guided to a symbolically cued location in a voluntary manner. But no account is given of the processes that control alignments of the attentional focal point.

In the 1980s, David LaBerge and his colleagues developed a model to account for goal-driven and stimulus-driven control of attentional alignments (e.g., LaBerge & Brown, 1989). They proposed that preattentive sensory operations lead to the accumulation of "activity distributions" within representations of the visual field. This is quite a different proposal than its predecessors. In particular, when the analog spotlight metaphor is used to describe a shift of visual attention, this alignment involves a movement component. In contrast, when an activity distribution model is used to describe the shift, no movement occurs. Instead, neural activity is dynamically distributed throughout a representation of the visual field (see Figure 11) and, as visual events occur, activity in neighbouring regions can accumulate to form a number of activation peaks at different locations. When a sufficient amount of activation accumulates at a particular location (e.g., a cued location), a channel of focused attention will open up there.

Advocates of activity distribution models claim that response facilitation produced by valid location cueing is a consequence of a "head start" in the accumulation of activation at the impending target's location. Similarly, they claim that differences in response facilitation produced by differences in the time between cue and target onset arise from differences in the amount of activation that accumulates at the cued location before target onset. At the optimal delay between cue and target onset, the greatest amount of activation is present at the cued location prior to the target's appearance there. Note that these activity distributions are not accumulations of attentional resources and therefore should not be confused with attentional gradient models (e.g., Downing & Pinker, 1985). As seen in Figure 11, neural activation occurs at a preattentive level, and stimulus-driven alignments of focused attention at a particular location are the result of this activation.

The stimulus-driven components of the model initiate the accumulation of neural activation at the represented locations of abrupt-onset stimuli and other visual transients. The goal-driven components determine, in accordance with the observer's computational goals, the chosen represented location at which neural activation accumulates. When either the stimulus-driven or goal-driven accumulation of activation is great enough, a channel of focused attention is opened at that location. Attention, then, is described in a "positive" way as depending on the buildup of activation at the attended site. Note that attention has also been described by others in a "negative" way in terms of buildup of inhibition at unattended sites (e.g., Treisman & Gormican, 1988). This implies that some kind of filter or mask allows only the attended location to be processed because this is the only location with an absence of inhibition. The positive vs. negative distinction is sometimes referred to as "amplification" vs. "filtering" (e.g., Martindale, 1991). There is empirical evidence in favour of both views and LaBerge (1995, this volume; LaBerge & Brown, 1989) proposed that they play complementary roles in attentional alignment and focusing.

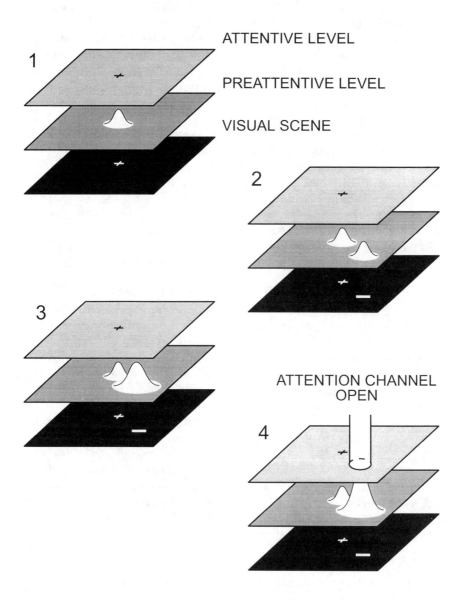

ATTENTIVE LEVEL

PREATTENTIVE LEVEL

VISUAL SCENE

ATTENTION CHANNEL
OPEN

*Figure* 11: A simplified version of LaBerge and Brown's (1989) activity distribution model. The black surface is the stimulus display, and the grey surface is an intermediate-level representation of it within which activity distributions accumulate. The upper surface is a higher-level representation within which a channel of focused attention can be opened if the accumulation of activity at a particular location exceeds a threshold level. The peaked distributions are a form of preattentive location encoding.

Spatial indexing can also be accounted for by the model because several stimulus onsets can occur at the same time and lead to the accumulation of multiple activity distributions independently of the channel of focused attention. This is tantamount to preattentive location encoding. Response facilitation is said to occur when a target is presented at a location at which there has already been some prior accumulation of neural activation. As seen in Figure 11, this can occur at several locations at the same time. LaBerge and Brown (1989) did not intend their model to fully account for the complex nature of attentional alignments. But theirs was one of the first formal models to suggest how a single indivisible attentional focal point could be aligned in a serial manner with different locations while, at the same time, locations could be encoded preattentively in a parallel sensory-driven manner. In our terms, the model is a possible account of how the destinations of attention shifts are indexed by preattentive localization operations. As discussed in the next section, preattentive destination indexing may play the same role in the initiation of saccadic eye movements.

## Visual Attention and Eye Movements

While we are able to shift visual attention independently of eye fixation, there are some situations (e.g., performance of laboratory attention tasks) in which this seems unnatural and effortful. Visual analysis is more efficient if, instead, we pay attention to objects on which our eyes are fixated. Moreover, the locations of attentional focus and eye fixation correspond so frequently that many researchers feel that there must be a close relationship between them.

Consider the *orienting reflex* that occurs in most large animals, including humans, to sudden sounds, lights, movements, and other abrupt changes in the perceptual field (see Rohrbaugh, 1984, for a review). This could be a saccade in the direction of an orienting stimulus that results in the foveation of that stimulus and a finer analysis of its object properties. Foveation is an integral part of this reflex, which also includes postural adjustments, and possibly head and body motion toward the stimulus. It is plausible that a mechanism for attentional orienting evolved along with that controlling foveation and the other orienting responses involved in this reflex, several of which are often taken as indicating attending (decreased heart rate, pupil dilation, pause in breathing). Furthermore, the foveating saccades would be nonfunctional if attentional focus were independent of them, since the necessary higher-level processing of the orienting stimulus for meaning would be less likely. Thus, a close relationship between human eye movements and attention shifts may, in part, be a consequence of the evolution of the orienting reflex in our ancestors.

Several researchers have studied this relationship but its details have not been easy to uncover (e.g., Groner & Groner, 1989; Henderson, 1992; Klein, 1980; Posner, 1980; Remington, 1980; Shepard, Findlay, & Hockey, 1986). Experiments conducted to determine whether or not attention precedes a saccadic eye movement to its destination have led to some disagreement. One position is that attention shifts always precede saccades to their destination, and it is implied by some researchers that attention plays a role in eye movement programming (e.g., it may serve as an "advance scout" that relays some form of location information to the saccade mechanism). The opposite position is that while attention shifts and saccades often have a common destination, they are mediated by functionally independent systems and therefore attentional operations are not necessary for saccadic operations and vice versa. Of course not every researcher supports one or the other of these two extreme positions, but it is helpful for reader to know what the positions are when attempting to understand the current debate about the relationship between attention shifts and eye movements.

Saccades can be programmed and executed either in a reflexive (stimulus-driven) manner in response to the abrupt onset of a visual stimulus or in a voluntary (goal-driven) manner (e.g., Abrams & Jonides, 1988; Findlay, 1981; Fischer & Weber, 1993; Klein, 1978; Posner, Crippen, Cohen, & Rafal, 1986; Shepard et al., 1986; Todd & Van Gelder, 1979). Readers who are familiar with the eye movement literature may notice that what we call stimulus-driven saccades are sometimes referred to by eye movement researchers as "goal-directed" (e.g., Fischer & Breitmeyer, 1987; Fischer & Weber, 1993). Their use of the term goal-directed is meant to convey that the observer has a basic goal of allowing a saccade to be made to the location of a cue or target. We use the terms stimulus-driven and goal-driven in a way that is consistent with our description of the control of attention shifts. That is, stimulus-driven saccades are triggered by abrupt-onset stimuli whereas goal-driven saccades are voluntarily initiated on the basis of the observer's computational goals (e.g., on the basis of a symbolic location cue's meaning).

Figure 12 shows three models of the possible relationship between attention shifts and eye movements. The first is a unitary-system model. To our knowledge, there is little support for the unitary-system model in a literal sense, but it serves as a useful comparison for the other two models. The second is an "independent-systems" model. Attention and oculomotor operations are carried out independently and share no functional components. The third model is a hybrid of the other two. Some attentional processes are independent of those involved in programming oculomotor movements that adjust eye position. But both

## UNITARY SYSTEM MODEL

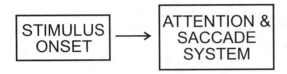

## INDEPENDENT SYSTEMS MODEL

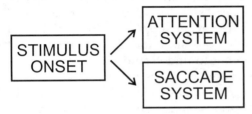

## DESTINATION INDEXING MODEL

*Figure* 12: Three models of the relationship between the attention and saccadic eye movement systems. The upper panel is the unitary system model, the middle panel is the independent systems model, and the lower panel is a hybrid of the other two but with a common destination indexing (preattentive localization) mechanism.

the attentional and saccadic components share a common mechanism that encodes the location of alignment destinations. This is the model we favour. And it has the general structure of the more detailed *destination indexing* model we introduce in the next section.

One proposal that many researchers assume comes close to a claim that eye movements and attention shifts are carried out by the same system is the *premotor theory* of Rizzolatti, Riggio, Dascola, and Umilta (1987). This idea was put forward to explain an attention shift phenomenon sometimes called the "meridian effect." It occurs when detection response times for invalid-cued targets are inhibited to a greater extent when the cue and target are presented in opposite hemifields (i.e., on opposite sides of the central point in the display) as opposed to in the same hemifield. Rizzolatti et al. (1987) reasoned that detection of same hemifield invalid-cued targets was faster than that of opposite hemifield invalid-cued targets because the attention shift required recalibration for direction in the latter case. They suggested an association of attention with the oculomotor system because a "direction recalibration effect" is known to occur when making successive saccades in different directions. For example, if a saccade is made to a cued location on the right side of the display and then a second saccade is made to a target even further to the right, the latency of the second one will be faster than if the target was in the opposite direction on the left side of the display. More specifically, if the direction component of a saccade must be reprogrammed, this increases the time required before the next saccade can be executed. Therefore, Rizzolatti et al. (1987) reasoned that the meridian effect indicates that, like saccades, changing the direction of two successive attention shifts increases the time required to execute the second shift. On this basis, they concluded that the same calibration procedure is used to program saccades and attention shifts. Taken to the extreme, some researchers have interpreted the proposal of Rizzolatti and colleagues to mean that a single system mediates oculomotor and attentional processes as shown in Figure 12.

One attempt to test this proposal involved a series of direct location-cueing experiments (Crawford & Müller, 1993). The results indicated that attention shift and saccade response-time patterns were qualitatively different. This implies that the operations in the two cases are not identical. But, in fairness to Rizzolatti et al. (1987), it clearly was not their intention to propose that eye movements and visual attention shifts are executed in exactly the same manner. In fact, it would be surprising to find a great degree of similarity between the time-course of these operations because saccade execution involves oculomotor muscle programming and activation that is not required for attention shift execution. Their intended claim seems, instead, to be that calibration of saccades and attention shifts involves a similar procedure.

A counterproposal to premotor theory is the independent-systems model in Figure 12. It yields several predictions including (1) completely independent mechanisms for calibrating saccade and attention shift trajectories, and (2) the eventual discovery of separate brain mechanisms for oculomotor processing and for attentional processing. Based on recent findings, however, it appears that these predictions are too extreme and that oculomotor and attentional processing share common mechanisms.

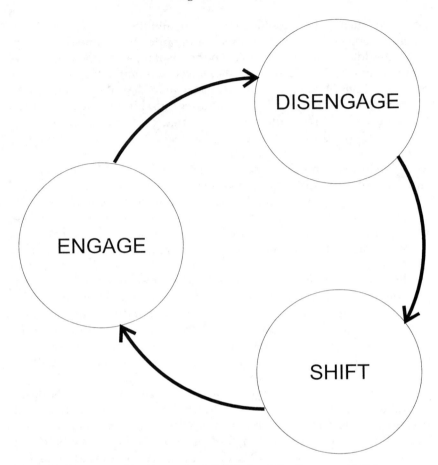

*Figure* 13: The proposal by Posner et al. (1988) about the disengage/shift/engage sequence of attentional alignment.

## Attentional Disengagement and Saccades

Posner et al. (1988) proposed an attention shift model that is similar, in some ways, to a discrete spotlight mechanism (see Figure 5). It involves a sequence in which (1) attention is disengaged before the shift occurs, (2) remains disengaged throughout the shift, and (3) is re-engaged at the shift destination (see Figure 13). This is consistent with reports that attention shifts and saccades will not be triggered by abrupt-onset stimuli if attention is actively engaged at another location (Sparks & Mays, 1983; Yantis & Jonides, 1990).

Saccadic eye movements, like some shifts of visual attention, are discrete. This begs the question "do saccades also undergo the same attentional disengage/shift/engage sequence when they are executed?"

Some researchers have argued that this is not necessarily the case (e.g., Kingstone & Klein, 1993). In their view, disengagement and re-engagement as described by Posner et al. (1988) are attentional operations that have no role in oculomotor processing. But perhaps the relationship between attention and oculomotor systems is closer than this. In particular, there is some evidence that, if attention is in a disengaged state, saccades (Fischer & Weber, 1993) and attention shifts (Mackeben & Nakayama, 1993) can be executed faster than when attention is initially engaged. This implies that both discrete attention shifts and saccades are characterized by the attentional disengage/shift/engage sequence.

Fischer and his colleagues examined the effect of prior attentional engagement on saccade latencies (Fischer, this volume; Fischer & Breitmeyer, 1987; Fischer & Ramsperger, 1984, 1986; Fischer & Weber, 1993). One motivation for doing so was to examine an earlier finding called the *gap effect* (named after the temporal "gap" between fixation point offset and target onset; Saslow, 1967). The time required to initiate a saccade to the location of an abrupt-onset target is about 220 ms when a central fixation point remains visible, but is reduced to about 150 ms when the fixation point disappears shortly before the target's onset. Using a similar procedure, Fischer and others found that when subjects were instructed to fixate their attention on a central point before a peripheral target's onset, saccade latencies were approximately 220 ms. When the fixation point disappeared 200 ms before target onset, however, the latencies of some saccades were closer to 100 ms (e.g., Fendrich, Hughes, & Reuter-Lorenz, 1991; Fischer & Breitmeyer, 1987; Fischer & Ramsperger, 1984, 1986; Fischer & Weber, 1993; Jüttner & Wolf, 1992; Mayfrank, Mobashery, Kimmig, & Fischer, 1986; Reuter-Lorenz, Hughes, & Fendrich, 1991). These are often referred to as *express saccades* because of their relatively short latency.

Fischer and Ramsperger (1984) proposed that if attention is not actively focused when an eye movement target is presented, the latency of the saccade will be reduced. In other words, attentional disengagement was thought to be a precursor to saccade execution and, if an observer's attention is already disengaged prior to saccade preparation, latencies would be shorter (see Figure 14). Thus, express saccades were said to occur because the disappearance of the central point caused attentional disengagement prior to saccade preparation, thereby eliminating one of the steps in the saccade initiation process (see Fischer, this volume; Fischer & Weber, 1993; Munoz & Guitton, 1989).

Saccades to the locations of abrupt-onset targets are called *prosaccades* while those in the opposite direction are called *antisaccades*. If there is a 200 ms gap between fixation cross offset and target onset, express saccades will occur in a prosaccade condition but apparently never in an anti-

# THE DISENGAGE/SHIFT/ENGAGE SEQUENCE

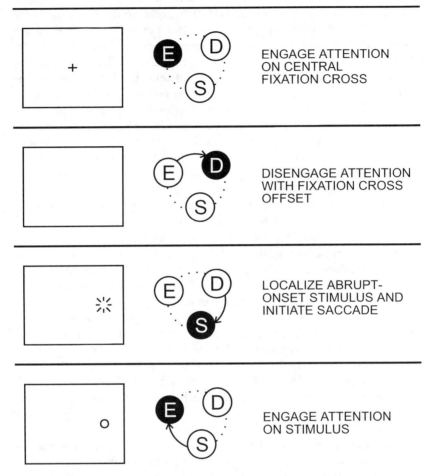

*Figure* 14: The disengage/shift/engage sequence that may occur when observers make express saccades while performing the gap task.

saccade condition (Fischer & Weber, 1992; Reuter-Lorenz, Hughes, & Fendrich, 1991). Presumably, observers can make express prosaccades because, from a state of attentional disengagement, they can allow the saccade target to elicit the saccade directly in a stimulus-driven manner. They are unable to make express antisaccades, however, because they appear to engage attention at the site of the target when it appears (i.e., the target serves as a symbolic cue) and then initiate a goal-driven saccade in the opposite direction. The absence of express antisaccades is another indication that attention is disengaged prior to express saccade execution.

A key property of express saccades is that they are subject to goal-driven and stimulus-driven influences. More specifically, express saccades do not occur if attention is actively focused at any location, including the saccade destination, prior to saccade preparation (Mayfrank et al., 1986). Observers can "override" the occurrence of express saccades, despite the fixation point's offset, simply by engaging their attention in a goal-driven manner. On the other hand, with practice, observers can learn to make express saccades despite the continued presence of the central fixation point or any other object in the direction of gaze (Fischer & Brietmeyer, 1987). They "enable" their occurrence by disengaging attention in a goal-driven manner. But goal-driven control is not necessary for express saccades. Even unpracticed observers who do not voluntarily engage or disengage attention show express saccades as a consequence of the fixation point's offset. Thus, while the frequency of express saccades can be influenced in a goal-driven manner, they are triggered in a stimulus-driven manner as a consequence of a sensory event.

When it was first proposed, the express saccade generated considerable debate among attention researchers (see e.g., Fischer & Weber, 1993). One initial concern was that only a few laboratories had successfully and consistently found them. Another was about whether they constituted a separate and qualitatively different population of saccades with a latency of roughly 100 ms or instead were part of a continuum with latencies ranging from 100 to 160 ms. With the growing number of replications, however, these concerns are subsiding. The debate about express saccades now seems to centre around the role that attention plays in their execution. For example, there is evidence that stimulus offsets lead to rapid saccades, even when these offsets are unattended (Kingstone & Klein, 1993). On this basis, it was suggested that the operations involved in preparing the express saccade must not be attentional. More specifically, the rationale of this suggestion was that if an observer does not pay attention to a particular sensory event, then any subsequent operations triggered by that event cannot be attentional. When applied to express saccades, the reasoning is that an unattended stimulus offset will not trigger attentional disengagement or any other attentional operation. And therefore, so the argument goes, attentional operations do not play a role in the express saccades.

One concern with this reasoning is that the extent to which a particular process is attentional is *not* determined by the nature of the event that triggers it. Recall the earlier discussion about how direct cue onsets guide attention shifts to their locations without requiring prior attentional processing. These onsets are sensory events that trigger attentional events without attention playing a role in the triggering process.

Similarly, stimulus offsets, whether attended to or not, are sensory events. We suggest that the extent to which these sensory events are attended to has no bearing on whether attentional operations play a role in express saccades.

## Physiology of Attentional and Oculomotor Processes

Some researchers have suggested that disengagement before eye movements is qualitatively different than disengagement before visual attention shifts (e.g., Klein & Taylor, 1994, p. 134). The latter is said to be an *attentional* operation while the former is said to be an *oculomotor* operation. This leads to an expectation that they should be carried out by separate brain areas. It is becoming apparent, however, that many neural structures play a common role in both attentional and saccadic operations (see e.g., Rafal & Robertson, 1995). Thus, while the independent-systems model implies that attention and eye-movement mechanisms should be physiologically independent, there is now considerable evidence to the contrary.

Some of the brain areas that play a role in both attentional and saccadic operations are the midbrain/collicular structures, the thalamus, the posterior parietal cortex, and the frontal eye fields. Locating and directing saccadic eye movements and attention toward an abrupt-onset stimulus is predominantly under the control of midbrain and superior colliculus (e.g., Wurtz & Albano, 1980). Some neurons in the superior colliculus become very active prior to and during regular saccades, express saccades, and attention shifts (Goldberg & Wurtz, 1972; Rohrer & Sparks, 1986; Wurtz & Mohler, 1976) and electrical stimulation of these neurons will also trigger saccades (Sparks & Mays, 1983). Furthermore, express saccades do not occur if the superior colliculus is damaged (Munoz & Wurtz, 1992; Schiller, Sandell, & Maunsell, 1987), and are not elicited as easily by electrical stimulation of this area when attention is engaged (Sparks & Mays, 1983). It has been suggested that the superior colliculus mediates saccade programming by determining the vector between initial and final eye positions within a map of visual space (Munoz, Pelisson, & Guitton, 1991). There is a general consensus that the primary roles of the superior colliculus are to (1) select the locations of abrupt-onset stimuli and visual transients (Albano, Mishkin, Westbrook, & Wurtz, 1982) and (2) initiate rapid stimulus-driven saccades and attention shifts to these locations (Sparks & Mays, 1980; Wurtz & Albano, 1980).

The posterior parietal cortex is another brain area associated with the control of eye movements and attention shifts (e.g., Petersen, Corbetta, Miezin, & Shulman, 1994). Like the superior colliculus, neural activity in the posterior parietal cortex increases prior to and during saccades and attention shifts in monkeys (Andersen, Essick, & Siegel, 1985; Bush-nell, Goldberg, & Robinson, 1981; Mountcastle, 1978; Robinson, Gold-berg, & Stanton, 1978; Wurtz, Goldberg, & Robinson, 1980) and humans (Posner, Walker, Friedrich, & Rafal, 1984, 1987). Damage to the posterior parietal cortex can cause an impairment of eye movements called ocu-lomotor apraxia (Allison, Hurwitz, White, & Wilmot, 1969) and can in-crease saccade and attention shift latencies in monkeys (Lynch & McLaren, 1989) and humans (Posner et al., 1984, 1987; Sundqvist, 1979).

The frontal eye fields also contain neurons that are active prior to and during saccades as well as neurons that are active after saccade ex-ecution (Goldberg & Bushnell, 1981). Some researchers (e.g., Breitm-eyer, 1986) have suggested that sustained postsaccadic activity of these neurons may counteract the suppression of visual processing during saccades (cf. Grimes, 1995) so that this suppression does not carry over into the next fixation interval. And the frontal eye fields appear to exert goal-driven control over saccadic eye movements and perhaps atten-tion shifts (e.g., Dassonville, Shlag, & Schlag-Rey, 1992; Guitton, Buch-tel, & Douglas, 1985; Henik, Rafal, & Rhodes, 1994; Schiller, True, & Conway, 1979).

The frontal eye field neurons may work in conjunction with the pulvinar nucleus of the thalamus to mediate attentional filtering. Stud-ies of the thalamus indicate that neural activity in the pulvinar in-creases when humans perform attentional filtering tasks (LaBerge, 1995; LaBerge & Buchsbaum, 1990; Petersen, Robinson, & Morris, 1987) and that this type of performance is impaired as a result of pulvinar damage (Rafal & Posner, 1987). Moreover, the same performance defi-cits occur when monkey pulvinar functioning is impaired by chemical injections (Petersen, Robinson, & Keys, 1985; see also, LaBerge, 1990b). Thus, the pulvinar appears to be involved in focusing or engaging at-tention. LaBerge (this volume) has since developed a detailed proposal about the role of the thalamus in attentional processing.

Posner et al. (1988) associated the disengage/shift/engage model in Figure 13 with different brain areas, and proposed that the superior colliculus, posterior parietal cortex, and pulvinar work together as a network to mediate attention shifts. Recent data support this proposal. In particular, the posterior parietal cortex appears to work with the pulvinar to engage and maintain visual fixation and attentional focus, and to work with the superior colliculus to control the initiation of at-tention shifts and saccades from one location to another. An important but often overlooked point is that the posterior parietal cortex contains many different neurons including some that are involved in disengage-ment and some that are involved in maintaining engagement (Mount-castle, 1978). Thus, damage to posterior parietal cortex in humans can disrupt the capacity to disengage attention from an object (e.g., Rafal & Robertson, 1995). But it can also disrupt the capacity to focus attention on a new object (Cohen & Rafal, 1991). Furthermore, some neurons in the monkey posterior parietal cortex are active prior to saccade execution and do not require the presence of a stimulus for their activation (Duhamel, Colby, & Goldberg, 1992). This presaccadic activation could be related to attentional disengagement. In contrast, neighbouring "visual fixation" neurons are active while attention is engaged or focused on a stationary stimulus (Lynch, 1980; Mountcastle, 1978), and express saccades are inhibited when this type of neuron is electrically stimulated (Shibutani, Sakata, & Hyvaerinen, 1986). These results indicate that the posterior parietal cortex is involved in both the maintenance of engaged attention and the disengagement of attention prior to stimulus-driven saccades and attention shifts.

Unlike saccades, smooth pursuit eye movements are not discrete. And, in some cases, focusing attention can even facilitate their execution. Smooth pursuit tracking performance, for example, has been shown to improve when observers focus their attention on a moving target in order to read changing letters or numbers (Shagass, Roemer, & Amadeo, 1976), press a button when the centre of the moving target fills (Iacono & Lykken, 1979), or notice a target colour change (Levin, Lipton, & Holzman, 1981). Moreover, deficits in tracking performance common in schizophrenic patients (Holzman, 1985; Holzman, Proctor, & Hughes, 1973) are attenuated if these patients are required to analyze the target for some type of detail as it moves (Van Gelder, Anderson, Herman, Lebedov, & Tsui, 1990). This suggests that attention remains engaged during smooth pursuit eye movements and that tracking performance deficits are due to attentional disengagement from the target. Therefore, there appears to be a great degree of interdependence between oculomotor and attentional processes.

## Destination Indexing

A common experimental procedure is to require a stimulus-driven saccade to the peripheral location of a direct cue. Then, shortly after the cue's onset, a target is presented at the cued location. The purpose is to examine the effects of saccade preparation and execution triggered by the cue's onset on target detection and identification responses. There is a concensus that responses to targets presented at the location of a direct cue are facilitated before, during, and after a stimulus-driven saccade's execution to that destination (Posner, 1980; Remington, 1980). There is less agreement about whether the same pattern of response facilitation occurs when saccades are goal-driven. But the results of one experiment indicated that if a goal-driven eye movement is made in the same direction as the location of the target to be detected, its preparation will facilitate response times even when the CTOAs are as short as 70 ms (Shepard et al., 1986). At intervals of this duration, saccade preparation is underway but execution requires more time (regular saccade latency is about 220 ms). Therefore, there may be some aspect of saccade *preparation*, even when goal-driven, that facilitates target detection at the saccade destination.

One interpretation of these data is that the attentional focal point precedes the eye movement to its destination. This could explain why responses were facilitated even when targets were presented prior to the saccade. But the eyes are stationary only about 25% of the time and, during some portion of this interval, attention may not even be actively engaged (Fischer & Weber, 1993). Therefore, only a short period of time is actually spent both foveating and focusing attention at a particular location. If the attentional focal point is aligned with each new saccade destination as a sort of "advance scout" (perhaps to send back more precise spatial coordinate information to assist in the saccade trajectory calibration), then this raises questions about how we attend to foveated objects when, as suggested, attention is usually "one step ahead" at the next location to be foveated. It is unlikely that the attentional focal point is split into two "beams" – one for the currently foveated location and one for the next location to be foveated. And if attention is directed to new saccade destinations well before the saccades are executed, this limits the time we spend attending to the locations that are foveated.

One plausible alternative is that, when preparing a saccade, a *spatial index* is allocated to the saccade destination to preattentively encode this location. And focused attention, relieved of the scouting role, can remain at the foveated location to enable analysis of the fixated object in more detail. Note that if indexing is part of saccade preparation, it will occur even if this preparation is followed by suppression of the saccade. This accounts for a visual search finding called *inhibition-of-return* (IOR) that is produced by saccades and attention shifts (Harman, Posner, Rothbart, & Thomas-Thrapp, 1994; Posner & Cohen, 1984; Rafal, Egly, & Rhodes, 1994; Tipper & Weaver, this volume; Wright & Richard, this volume). In particular, stimulus-driven attention shifts can produce IOR in the absence of eye movements, but goal-driven shifts only produce IOR if goal-driven saccades are also made (Posner & Cohen, 1984; Posner, Rafal, Choate, & Vaughan, 1985). An important exception to this is when observers make a goal-driven attention shift but merely prepare an accompanying goal-driven saccade without actually making it (Rafal, Calabresi, Brennan, & Sciolto, 1989). The resulting IOR suggests that saccade preparation is sufficient for indexing the saccade destination. And, as mentioned previously, indexing could mediate attention shifts triggered by direct location cueing (e.g., Wright, 1994; Wright & Richard, 1996). We suggest that the same is true of externally triggered saccades, and that a common *destination-indexing mechanism* initiates both stimulus-driven attention shifts and saccades. This is consistent with the third model in Figure 12 and with the model we describe in the next section.

## Cognitive Architecture of Stimulus-Driven Attention Shifts

One of the first brain areas to be studied in detail to determine its role in attentional processing was the reticular activating system (RAS). This research was not a great catalyst to the study of attentional physiology, however, because the RAS findings were difficult to interpret. They implied only that the role of the physiological mechanism underlying attentional processing is to somehow increase our general arousal level. Psychologists began to study the physiology of attention more seriously in the 1980s following a series of findings that separate areas within the cortex appear to be specialized for the processing of colour, form, and motion (e.g., Livingston & Hubel, 1987). Recall that feature-integration theory is based on the assumption that feature information is processed in separate anatomical maps and that focused attention is required at a particular location within a master location map in order for these features to be correctly conjoined to form a perceptual object. Thus, it now seems clear that attentional processing is not a consequence of the operation of a single brain area like the RAS. Instead, it is the product of a network of different brain areas working together cooperatively as suggested by Posner et al. (1988).

The model of Posner et al. (1988), positing a sequence of disengage, shift, engage, can be re-conceptualized so that processing within each module operates on a simple $5 \times 5$ spatial map. In Figure 15, the upper left map in each set corresponds to the DISENGAGE module, the lower map corresponds to the ENGAGE module, and the middle right map corresponds to the SHIFT module. A chain of events is shown that begins with attention in an engaged state at the centre location within the ENGAGE and DISENGAGE maps. Note, too, that the DISENGAGE module inhibits the SHIFT module (as signified by the line with the closed circle that connects them). In the second event, attention is disengaged and the DISENGAGE module no longer inhibits the SHIFT module. In the third event, a stimulus appears at a location within the SHIFT module map. And finally in the fourth event, the SHIFT module activates the ENGAGE module and begins the process of attentional engagement at the location of the new stimulus. The sequence can begin again but this time with attention focused at the new location on the right side of the ENGAGE and DISENGAGE maps.

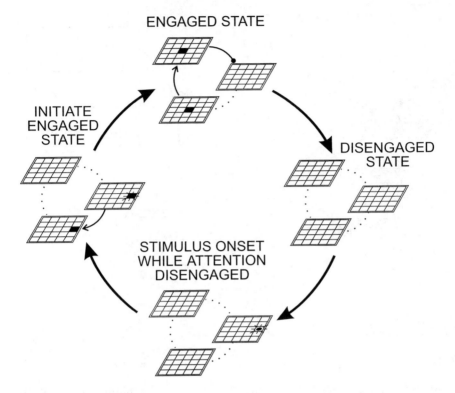

*Figure* 15: An example of the chain of events associated with the disengage/shift/engage sequence, beginning at the top and moving clockwise. An old stimulus in the centre of the display disappears, and then a new stimulus appears on the right side of the display.

A map-based model has also been used to describe feature integration (Treisman & Gelade, 1980). As shown in Figure 8, information from feature maps is combined within a master map at the location on which attention is focused. These feature maps are very likely located in specialized regions of visual cortex (Treisman & Gormican, 1988). We suggest that the master map in the feature-integration model is similar in function to the DISENGAGE module map in Figure 15. Thus, the two models can be combined as in Figure 16 on the basis of a common master/DISENGAGE map. By doing so, a framework is in place for describing how features are integrated to form objects and how the attentional focal point can be shifted from one location to another within the master map, and particularly in response to an abrupt-onset location cue.

We suggested in the previous section that attention shifts and saccadic eye movements share the same destination indexing operation. In Figure 16, this is carried out by the SHIFT module within the superior colliculus. Stimulus onsets are detected by this module and their

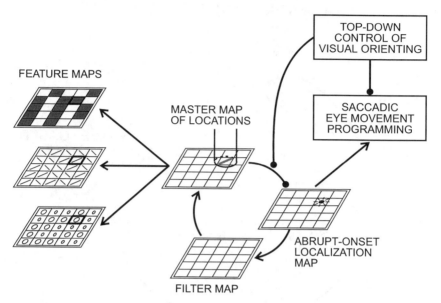

*Figure* 16: Combining the map-based feature-integration model with the map-based disengage/shift/engage model. The common representation is the master/disengage map. Saccade programming is carried out by the motor cortex module, and goal-driven control of model operations is the result of input from the frontal cortex module.

locations are encoded within its map and made available for attention shift and saccade programming. The latter is shown as occurring within the motor cortex as opposed to within the disengage/shift/engage attention network.

A more specific description of the processing involved when stimulus-driven attention shifts are executed is shown in Figure 17. We call this the *destination-indexing* (DI) system. When one or more abrupt-onset stimuli are presented, the superior colliculus automatically encodes their locations as potential destinations for stimulus-driven saccades and attention shifts, and allocates as many as four indexes (one per stimulus) to their locations. If, at this time, attentive fixation is actively maintained at a particular location (via the frontal lobes), the posterior parietal cortex will inhibit a stimulus-driven shift or saccade. The ability of the stimuli to attract attention persists for a while until it attenuates or until attention is disengaged (see e.g., Müller & Humphreys, 1991; Yantis & Johnson, 1990). Some superior colliculus neurons provide a sustained signal about the locations of stimuli and are thus possibly involved in temporarily "storing" this information (Mays & Sparks, 1980; Peck, Schlag-Rey, & Schlag, 1980). If or when attention is disengaged, the superior colliculus initiates a shift/saccade to the in-

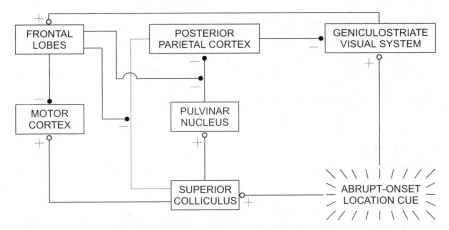

*Figure* 17: The Destination Indexing model's simplified account of the initiation of stimulus-driven saccadic eye movements and stimulus-driven attention shifts.

dexed stimulus location with the highest priority. After the execution of an attention shift (and a saccade if it is not suppressed) to the indexed location, attention may be re-engaged and actively maintained at this new location through the coordinated actions of the pulvinar and the posterior parietal cortex.

The DI system operates on the assumption that stimulus-driven attention shifts and saccades are triggered by abrupt-onset stimuli but can be temporarily suppressed if attention is currently engaged (Yantis & Jonides, 1990). A key property of the model is that stimulus-driven saccade destination indexing is *not* under voluntary control. Therefore, even if the execution of such a saccade is suppressed, its initial preparation will still be carried out, and this includes selecting the highest priority indexed location as the saccade destination (cf. Yantis & Johnson, 1990). Similarly, the execution of a stimulus-driven attention shift, unless inhibited by attentional engagement, is not under voluntary control. And, even if the shift is inhibited, destination indexing will still occur.

The DI system is similar in some ways to Treisman and Gormican's (1988) proposal in which the processing of unattended locations in visual space is inhibited while attention is focused at a particular location. More specifically, they suggested that "paying attention" occurs when the inhibitory links between the master map and the corresponding locations in the feature maps (e.g., colour, shape, movement, depth) are themselves inhibited. This allows features at the selected location within each feature map to be integrated into a perceptual object (e.g., "a stationary red sphere"). Further integrative processing of the features of all objects at locations not being attended to, however, continues to be inhibited in these feature maps.

Inhibition between modules also occurs in the DI system. As shown in Figure 17, we postulate an inhibitory link from the pulvinar to the posterior parietal cortex and another inhibitory link from the posterior parietal cortex to the superior colliculus. Both links are themselves temporarily inhibited by the frontal lobe when attention is disengaged. When the superior colliculus is freed from inhibition by the posterior parietal cortex in this manner, it can initiate a shift/saccade to the highest priority indexed location. As a result, the corresponding location is facilitated in a map of visual space in the pulvinar which, in turn, releases from inhibition the corresponding location in the posterior parietal cortex map. This produces a release from inhibition by the posterior parietal cortex of the corresponding locations in the feature maps of the geniculostriate system. This amounts to a shift of attention to the indexed location followed by re-engagement at that location when inhibitory links are re-activated (i.e., links from the pulvinar to the posterior parietal cortex and from the posterior parietal cortex to the superior colliculus). At the same time, the superior colliculus also initiates a stimulus-driven saccade to this location unless eye movements are voluntarily suppressed as a result of motor cortex inhibition by the frontal lobes. Thus, when attention is disengaged, selection of an indexed location by the superior colliculus results in a stimulus-driven release from inhibition at the corresponding locations within the feature maps of the geniculostriate system.

Note that the DI system in intended to be a *functional* model, and we emphasize that structural implications should be made with care. For example, long-range inhibitory connections between brain areas may occur only indirectly through the combined action of long-range excitatory pathways to neurons that have short-range inhibitory connections to other neurons in target areas.

The DI model does not describe the processes involved in calibrating attention shift and saccade trajectories, and it does not make explicit the differences between oculomotor muscle programming and attentional alignment operations. In addition, the model does not account for analog attention shifts. Instead it provides a general description of the spatial localization operations involved in selecting shift/saccade destinations and in triggering shifts and saccades to these locations.

## Concluding Remarks

This chapter began with a quote by Spearman (1937) about various attempts to characterize attention over years. For quite some time after Spearman's observation, there was a good deal of mystery about the nature of attentional processing. We have argued elsewhere that methodological differences across empirical studies in the literature may have added to this mystery (Wright & Ward, 1994).

In recent years, however, some of the pieces of the puzzle have started to fall into place. Attentional processing appears to be mediated not by a single brain area, but by a network of areas that work cooperatively. Some carry out preattentive analyses of visual feature information, and researchers soon realized that the existence of specialized visual areas must require a master area to integrate their inputs. Treisman and Gelade's (1980) model had a great impact on the field because it developed the notion of location-based feature integration and because it framed the description of attention in terms of spatial maps. Soon after, Posner et al. (1988) concluded, on the basis of considerable physiological evidence, that a network of mechanisms using a disengage/shift/engage sequence appears to align the attentional focal point within a representation of the visual field. When both are described in terms of spatial maps as in Figure 16, the proposals of Treisman and Gelade (1980) and of Posner et al. (1988) are complementary – one describes the alignment of a unitary attentional focal point and the other accounts for the integration of feature information that occurs when this alignment is made with a particular destination. LaBerge (1995, this volume; LaBerge & Brown, 1989) has since proposed a model of stimulus-driven and goal-driven control of these alignments, and Fischer and his colleagues (e.g., Fischer this volume; Fischer & Weber, 1993) elaborated on a possible link between the parietal/collicular interactions involved in attentional disengagement and the collicular/motor-cortex interactions involved in saccadic eye movement programming. Several other researchers, including Pylyshyn (1989, this volume), Yantis (1992; Yantis & Johnson, 1990), and Tipper, Driver and Weaver (1991), developed proposals about visual analyses that involve preattentive encoding of objects and their locations.

When these proposals are taken together, a picture starts to emerge. There appears to be a network of different mechanisms that work together to preattentively encode the destination of visual orienting, to align the attentional focal point and sometimes the eyes with this destination, to selectively attend to a relevant object at the destination, and to integrate the features of that object once attention is engaged.

## Acknowledgments

This project was supported by Natural Sciences and Engineering Research Council of Canada Grants 133551 awarded to RDW and A9958 awarded to LMW. We are grateful to David LaBerge for his thoughtful advice, and to Christian Richard for his many helpful comments and for preparing the figures. Address correspondence to Richard Wright, Department of Psychology, Simon Fraser University, Burnaby, B.C., Canada, V5A 1S6 (e-mail: rwright@arts.sfu.ca)

## Notes

1  In typical experiments, all cues (symbolic and direct) and targets are abrupt-onset stimuli. This fact is often overlooked. We have omitted the "abrupt-onset" designation whenever all cues, targets, and other stimuli have an abrupt onset, or whenever the distinction is not important (e.g., when a statement applies to both abrupt-onset and gradual-onset stimuli).

2  The results of visual search experiments also indicate that direct cues are maximally effective at short CTOAs (Nakayama & Mackeben, 1989). When the location of a conjunction target (a target defined by a unique conjunction of the features shared by the distractor items in the search set) was indicated by a direct cue, search accuracy was maximal when the CTOA was 50 ms, but declined when the CTOA was increased to 200 ms.

3  Other evidence that, at longer CTOAs, direct cues can also function as symbolic cues was obtained with a rapid-serial-visual-presentation (RSVP) task (Weichselgartner & Sperling, 1987). A "stream" of numbers was presented at a single display location, one every 80 to 100 ms. When subjects were required to report the first four numbers after direct cue onset, those presented 0 to 100 ms after the cue were reported accurately, effortlessly, and without practice. On the other hand, the next reported numbers were not presented until 300 to 400 ms after the cue, and these reports were effortful, dependent on practice, expectations, the cue's signal-to-noise ratio, and the probability of occurrence of the numbers presented. In other words, reports of the numbers presented 0 to 100 ms after the cue were indicative of the reflexive processes initiated by direct cues at short CTOAs. In contrast, reports of numbers presented 300 to 400 ms after the cue were indicative of the voluntary, effortful processes initiated by symbolic cues at longer CTOAs.

4  Another type of double-cue experiment has also been cited as evidence that attention is directed first to one location and then to the next, rather than being divided between both locations at the same time (Eriksen & Yeh, 1985). It should be noted, however, that each trial involved only a single cue that served as both a direct and a symbolic cue. Therefore, the results of this type of experiment could be due to the different time courses of stimulus-driven and goal-driven attention shifts. As mentioned in the previous section, the effectiveness of symbolic cues at initiating voluntary attention shifts does not appear to be maximal until the CTOA approaches 300 ms (e.g., Cheal & Lyon, 1991; Müller & Findlay, 1988; Shepard & Müller, 1989). Therefore, at the 150 ms CTOA used in this experiment, attention was probably "pulled" to the direct cue location first before being voluntarily shifted to the symbolically cued location. Conclusions about attending to multiple locations that are based on experiments involving symbolic and direct cueing by the same stimulus should therefore be treated with caution. At shorter CTOAs, the results may indicate only that stimulus-driven attention shifts will take precedence over goal-driven shifts.

5  Intermediate-level processing may also be responsible for the automatization
   of visual search. In particular, both feature targets and highly practiced conjunction targets pop out during visual search. A series of experiments was
   therefore carried out to determine whether or not the automatized search processes mediating conjunction-target search are the same as those mediating
   unique-feature target search (Treisman, Vieira, & Hayes, 1992). In general, automatized search was found to be more task-specific and target-location-specific than feature-target search. For example, the possession of a unique feature enabled a target to pop out from distractors during single-target search
   and the same feature enabled a boundary around a group of these targets to
   pop out in a texture-segregation task. Conversely, while a conjunction-feature
   target popped out during single-target search, after extensive practice, the resulting automatization *did not* enable a boundary around a group of these targets to pop out when the texture-segregation task was then performed. This
   suggests that the pop-out of unique-feature targets is mediated by processes
   that are more primitive than the ones mediating the automatized popout of
   conjunction-feature targets. Preattentive analysis of feature information appears to be the result of low-level sensory operations, while automaticity may
   arise from improved efficiency of intermediate-level operations that become
   rapid with practice (see also Wright & Richard, this volume).

## References

Abrams, R.A., & Jonides, J. (1988). Programming saccadic eye movements. *Journal of Experimental Psychology: Human Perception & Performance, 14*, 428–443.

Albano, J.E., Mishkin, M., Westbrook, J.E., & Wurtz, R.H. (1982). Visuomotor deficits following ablation of monkey superior colliculus. *Journal of Neurophysiology, 48*, 338–351.

Allison, R.S., Hurwitz, L.J., White, J.G., & Wilmot, T.J. (1969). A follow-up study of a patient with Balint's syndrome. *Neuropsychologia, 7*, 319–333.

Andersen, R.A., Essick, G.K., & Seigel, R.M. (1985). Encoding of spatial location by posterior parietal neurons. *Science, 230*, 456–458.

Bonnel, A.M., Possamai, C., & Schmitt, M. (1987). Early modulation of visual input: A study of attentional strategies. *Quarterly Journal of Experimental Psychology, 39*, 757–776.

Breitmeyer, B.G. (1986). Eye movements and visual pattern perception. In E.C. Schwab & H.C. Nusbaum (Eds.), *Pattern recognition by humans and machines, Vol. 2.* Toronto: Academic Press.

Broadbent, D.E. (1958). *Perception and communication.* New York: Pergamon Press.

Bushnell, M.C., Goldberg, M.E., & Robinson, D.L. (1981). Behavioral enhancement of visual responses in monkey cerebral cortex. I. Modulation in posterior parietal cortex related to selective visual attention. *Journal of Neurophysiology, 46*, 755–772.

Cheal, M., & Lyon, D.R. (1991). Central and peripheral precueing of forced-choice discrimination. *Quarterly Journal of Experimental Psychology, 43A*, 859–880.

Cohen, A., & Rafal, R.D. (1991). Attention and feature integration: Illusory conjunctions in a patient with a parietal lobe lesion. *Psychological Science, 2,* 106–110.

Crawford, T.J., & Müller, H.J. (1993). Spatial and temporal effects of spatial attention on human saccadic eye movements. *Vision Research, 32,* 293–304.

Dassonville, P., Schlag, J., & Schlag-Rey, M. (1992). The frontal eye field provides the goal of saccadic eye movement. *Experimental Brain Research, 89,* 300–310.

Dawson, M.R.W. (1991). The how and why of what went where in apparent motion: Modeling solutions to the motion correspondence problem. *Psychological Review, 98,* 569–603.

Downing, C.J. (1988). Expectancy and visual-spatial attention: Effects on perceptual quality. *Journal of Experimental Psychology: Human Perception & Performance, 14,* 188–202.

Downing, C.J., & Pinker, S. (1985). The spatial structure of visual attention. In M.I. Posner & O.S.M. Marin (Eds.), *Attention & Performance, Vol. 11.* Hillsdale, N.J.: Erlbaum.

Duhamel, J-R, Colby, C.L., & Goldberg, M.E. (1992). The updating of the representation of visual space in parietal cortex by intended eye movements. *Science, 255,* 90–92.

Egeth, H.E. (1992). Dichotic listening: Long–lived echoes of Broadbent's early studies. *Journal of Experimental Psychology: General, 121,* 124.

Eriksen, C.W., & Colgate, R.L. (1971). Selective attention and serial processing in briefly presented visual displays. *Perception & Psychophysics, 10,* 321–326.

Eriksen, C.W., & Hoffman, J.E. (1974). Selective attention: Noise suppression or signal enhancement? *Bulletin of the Psychonomic Society, 4,* 587–589.

Eriksen, C.W., & Murphy, T.D. (1987). Movement of attentional focus across the visual field: A critical look at the evidence. *Perception & Psychophysics, 42,* 299–305.

Eriksen, C.W., & St. James, J.D. (1986). Visual attention within and around the field of focal attention: A zoom lens model. *Perception & Psychophysics, 40,* 225–240.

Eriksen, C.W., & Webb, J. (1989). Shifting of attentional focus within and about a visual display. *Perception & Psychophysics, 42,* 175–183.

Eriksen, C.W., Webb, J.M., & Fournier, L.R. (1990). How much processing do nonattended stimuli receive? Apparently very little, but... *Perception & Psychophysics, 47,* 477–488.

Eriksen, C.W., & Yeh, Y. (1985). Allocation of attention in the visual field. *Journal of Experimental Psychology: Human Perception & Performance, 11,* 583–597.

Fendrich, R., Hughes, H.C., & Reuter-Lorenz, P.A. (1991). Fixation-point offsets reduce the latency of saccades to acoustic targets. *Perception & Psychophysics, 50,* 383–387.

Findlay, J.M. (1981). Spatial and temporal factors in the predictive generation of saccadic eye movements. *Vision Research, 21,* 347–354.

Fischer, B., & Breitmeyer, B. (1987). Mechanisms of visual attention revealed by saccadic eye movements. *Neuropsychologia, 25,* 73–83.

Fischer, B., & Ramsperger, E. (1984). Human express-saccades: Extremely short reaction times of goal directed eye movements. *Experimental Brain Research, 57,* 191–195.

Fischer, B., & Ramsperger, E. (1986). Human express-saccades: Effects of daily practice and randomization. *Experimental Brain Research, 64,* 569–578.

Fischer, B., & Weber, H. (1992). Characteristics of "anti" saccades in man. *Experimental Brain Research, 89,* 415–424.

Fischer, B., & Weber, H. (1993). Express saccades and visual attention. *Behavioral & Brain Sciences, 16,* 553–610.

Folk, C.L., Remington, R.W., & Johnston, J.C. (1992). Involuntary covert orienting is contingent on attentional control settings. *Journal of Experimental Psychology: Human Perception & Performance, 18,* 1030–1044.

Grimes, J. (1995). On the failure to detect changes in scenes across saccades. In K. Akins (Ed.), *Perception.* New York, NY: Oxford University Press.

Goldberg, M.E., & Bushnell, M.C. (1981). Behavioral enhancement of visual responses in monkey cerebral cortex. II. Modulation in frontal eye fields specifically related to saccades. *Journal of Neurophysiology, 46,* 773–787.

Goldberg, M.E., & Wurtz, R.H. (1972). Activity of superior colliculus in behaving monkey. II. Effect of attention on neuronal responses. *Journal of Neurophysiology, 35,* 560–574.

Green, D.M., & Swets, J.A. (1966/1974). *Signal detection theory and psychophysics.* Reprint: New York: Krieger.

Grindley, C.G., & Townsend, V. (1968). Voluntary attention in peripheral vision and its effects on acuity and differential thresholds. *Quarterly Journal of Experimental Psychology, 20,* 11–19.

Groner, R., & Groner, M.T. (1989). Attention and eye movement control: An overview. *European Archives of Psychiatry & Neurological Sciences, 239,* 9–16.

Guitton, D., Buchtel, H.A., & Douglas, R.M. (1985). Frontal lobe lesions in man cause difficulties in suppressing reflexive glances and in generating goal-directed saccades. *Experimental Brain Research, 58,* 455–472.

Harman, C., Posner, M.I., Rothbart, M.K., & Thomas-Thrapp, L. (1994). Development of orienting to locations and objects in human infants. *Canadian Journal of Experimental Psychology, 48,* 301–318.

Henderson, J.M. (1992). Visual attention and eye movement control during reading and picture viewing. In K. Rayner (Ed.), *Eye movements and visual cognition: Scene perception and reading.* New York: Springer-Verlag.

Henik, A., Rafal, R., & Rhodes, D. (1994). Endogenously generated and visually guided saccades after lesions of the human frontal eye fields. *Journal of Cognitive Neuroscience, 6,* 400–411.

Holzman, P.S. (1985). Eye movement dysfunctions and psychoses. *International Review of Neurobiology, 27,* 179–205.

Holzman, P.S., Proctor, L.R., & Hughes, D.N. (1973). Eye tracking patterns in schizophrenia. *Science, 181,* 179–181.

Iacono, W.G., & Lykken, D.T. (1979). Electrooculographic recording and scoring of smooth pursuit and saccadic eye tracking: A parametric study using monozygotic twins. *Psychophysiology, 16,* 94–107.

James, W. (1890). *Principles of psychology,* Volumes 1 & 2. New York: Holt.

Jonides, J. (1980). Towards a model of the mind's eye's movement. *Canadian Journal of Psychology, 34*, 103–112.

Jonides, J. (1981). Voluntary versus automatic control over the mind's eye's movement. In J.B. Long & A.D. Baddeley (Eds.), *Attention & Performance, Vol. 9*. Hillsdale, NJ: Erlbaum.

Jonides, J. (1983). Further towards a model of the mind's eye's movement. *Bulletin of the Psychonomic Society, 21*, 247–250.

Jonides, J., & Mack, R. (1984). On the cost and benefit of cost and benefit. *Psychological Bulletin, 96*, 29–44.

Jüttner, M., & Wolf, W. (1992). Occurrence of human express saccades depends on stimulus uncertainty and stimulus sequence. *Experimental Brain Research, 89*, 678–681.

Kahneman, D. (1973). *Attention and effort*. Englewood Cliffs, NJ: Prentice Hall.

Kiefer, R.J., & Siple, P. (1987). Spatial constraints on the voluntary control of attention across visual space. *Canadian Journal of Psychology, 41*, 474–489.

Kingstone, A., & Klein, R.M. (1993). Visual offsets facilitate saccade latency: Does pre-disengagement of visuo-spatial attention mediate this gap effect? *Journal of Experimental Psychology: Human Perception & Performance, 19*, 1251–1265.

Klein, R. (1978). Chronometric analysis of saccadic eye movements: Reflexive and cognitive control. In D. Landers & R. Christina (Eds.), *Psychology of motor behavior and sport*. Champaign, IL: Human Kinetics.

Klein, R. (1980). Does ocular motor readiness mediate cognitive control of visual attention? In R.S. Nickerson (Ed.), *Attention & Performance, Vol. 8*. Hillsdale, NJ: Erlbaum.

Klein, R.M., & Taylor, T.L. (1994). Categories of cognitive inhibition with reference to attention. In D. Dagenbach & T. Carr (Eds.), *Inhibitory processes in attention, memory, and language*. Orlando, FL: Academic Press.

Kröse, B.J.A., & Julesz, B. (1989). The control and speed of shifts of attention. *Vision Research, 29*, 1607–1619.

Kwak, H., Dagenbach, D., & Egeth, H. (1991). Further evidence for a time-independent shift of the focus of attention. *Perception & Psychophysics, 49*, 473–480.

LaBerge, D. (1983). Spatial extent of attention to letters and words. *Journal of Experimental Psychology: Human Perception & Performance, 9*, 371–379.

LaBerge, D. (1990a). Attention. *Psychological Science, 1*, 156–162.

LaBerge, D. (1990b). Thalamic and cortical mechanisms of attention suggested by recent positron emission tomographic experiments. *Journal of Cognitive Neuroscience, 2*, 358–372.

LaBerge, D. (1995). *Attentional processing*. Cambridge, MA: Harvard University Press.

LaBerge, D., & Brown, V. (1989). Theory of attentional operations in shape identification. *Psychological Review, 96*, 101–124.

LaBerge, D., & Buchsbaum, M.S. (1990). Positron emission tomographic measurements of pulvinar activity during an attention task. *Journal of Neuroscience, 10*, 613–619.

Lappin, J.S., & Uttal, W.R. (1976). Does prior knowledge facilitate the detection of visual targets in random noise? *Perception & Psychophysics, 20*, 367–374.

Levin, S., Lipton, R.B., & Holzman, P.S. (1981). Pursuit eye movements in psychopathology: Effects of target characteristics. *Biological Psychiatry, 16,* 255–267.

Livingston, M.S., & Hubel, D.H. (1987). Psychophysical evidence for separate channels for the perception of form, color, movement, and depth. *Journal of Neuroscience, 7,* 3416–3468.

Luria, A.R. (1973). *The working brain.* New York: Penguin.

Lynch, J.C. (1980). The functional organization of the posterior parietal association cortex. *Behavioral & Brain Sciences, 2,* 485–499.

Lynch, J.C., & McLaren, J.W. (1989). Deficits of visual attention and saccadic eye movements after lesions of parietoocciptal cortex in monkeys. *Journal of Neurophysiology, 61,* 74–90.

Mackeben, M., & Nakayama, K. (1993). Express attentional shifts. *Vision Research, 33,* 85–90.

Marr, D. (1982). *Vision.* New York, NY: Freeman.

Martindale, C. (1991). *Cognitive psychology: A neural network approach.* Pacific Grove, CA: Brooks/Cole.

Mayfrank, L., Mobashery, M., Kimmig, H., & Fischer, B. (1986). The role of fixation and visual attention on the occurrence of express saccades in man. *European Journal of Psychiatry & Neurological Science, 235,* 269–275.

Mays, L.E., & Sparks, D.L. (1980). Dissociation of visual and saccade-related responses in superior colliculus neurons. *Journal of Neurophysiology, 43,* 207–232.

McCormick, P.A., & Klein, R. (1990). The spatial distribution of attention during covert visual orienting. *Acta Psychologica, 75,* 225–242.

Mertens, J.J. (1956). Influence of knowledge of target location upon the probability of observations of peripherally observable test flashes. *Journal of the Optical Society of America, 46,* 1069–1070.

Milner, P. (1974). A model for visual shape recognition. *Psychological Review, 81,* 521–535.

Mountcastle, V.B. (1978). Brain mechanisms for directed attention. *Journal of the Royal Society of Medicine, 71,* 14–28.

Mowrer, O.H. (1941). Preparatory set (expectancy): Further evidence for its "central" locus. *Journal of Experimental Psychology, 28,* 116–133.

Müller, H.J. (1994). Qualitative differences in response bias from spatial cueing. *Canadian Journal of Experimental Psychology, 48,* 218–241.

Müller, H.J., & Findlay, J.M. (1988). The effect of visual attention on peripheral discrimination thresholds in single and multiple element displays. *Acta Psychologica, 69,* 129–155.

Müller, H.J., & Humphreys, G.W. (1991). Luminance-increment detection: Capacity-limited or not? *Journal of Experimental Psychology: Human Perception & Performance, 17,* 107–124.

Müller, H.J., & Rabbitt, P.M.A. (1989). Reflexive and voluntary orienting of visual attention: Time course activation and resistance to interruption. *Journal of Experimental Psychology: Human Perception & Performance, 15,* 315–330.

Munoz, D.P., & Guitton, D. (1989). Fixation and orientation control by the tecto-reticulo-spinal system in the cat whose head is unrestrained. *Revue Neurologique, 145,* 567–579.

Munoz, D.P., Pelisson, D., & Guitton, D. (1991). Movement of neural activity on the superior colliculus motor map during gaze shifts. *Science, 251,* 1358–1360.

Munoz, D.P., & Wurtz, R.H. (1992). Role of the rostral superior colliculus in active visual fixation and execution of express saccades. *Journal of Neurophysiology, 67,* 1000–1002.

Nakayama, K., & Mackeben, M. (1989). Sustained and transient components of focal visual attention. *Vision Research, 11,* 1631–1647.

Navon, D. (1989). The importance of being visible: On the role of attention in a mind viewed as an anarchic intelligence system. I. Basic tenets. *European Journal of Psychology, 1,* 191–213.

Neisser, U. (1964). Visual search. *Scientific American, 210,* 94–102

Neisser, U. (1967). *Cognitive psychology.* New York: Appleton, Century, Crofts.

Neisser, U. (1976). *Cognition and reality.* San Francisco: W.H. Freeman.

Peck, C.K., Schlag-Rey, M., & Schlag, J. (1980). Visuo-oculomotor properties of cells in the superior colliculus of the alert cat. *Journal of Comparative Neurology, 194,* 97–116.

Petersen, S.E, Corbetta, M., Miezin, F.M., & Shulman, G.L. (1994). PET studies of parietal involvement in spatial attention: Comparison of different task types. *Canadian Journal of Experimental Psychology, 48,* 319–338.

Petersen, S.E., Robinson, D.L., & Keys, J. (1985). Pulvinar nuclei of the behaving rhesus monkey: Visual responses and their modulation. *Journal of Neurophysiology, 54,* 867–886.

Petersen, S.E., Robinson, D.L., & Morris, J.D. (1987). Contributions of the pulvinar to visual spatial attention. *Neuropsychologia, 25,* 97–105.

Posner, M.I. (1978). *Chronometric explorations of mind.* Hillsdale, NJ: Erlbaum.

Posner, M.I. (1980). Orienting of attention. *Quarterly Journal of Experimental Psychology, 32,* 3–25.

Posner, M.I., & Cohen, Y. (1984). Components of visual attention. In H. Bouma & D.G. Bouhuis (Eds.), *Attention & Performance, Vol. 10.* Hillsdale, NJ: Erlbaum.

Posner, M.I., Cohen, Y., & Rafal, R.D. (1982). Neural systems control of spatial orienting. *Philosophical Transactions of the Royal Society of London, B298,* 187–198.

Posner, M.I., Crippen, P.J., Cohen, A., & Rafal, R. (1986, November). *Speed of covert orienting of attention and express saccades.* Paper presented at the annual meeting of the Psychonomic Society, New Orleans.

Posner, M.I., Nissen, M.J., & Ogden, W.C. (1978). Attended and unattended processing modes: The role of set for spatial location. In H.L. Pick & I.J. Saltzman (Eds.), *Modes of perceiving and processing information.* Hillsdale, NJ: Erlbaum.

Posner, M.I., Petersen, S.E., Fox, P.T., & Raichle, M.E. (1988). Localization of cognitive operations in the human brain. *Science, 240,* 1627–1631.

Posner, M.I., Rafal, R.D., Choate, L., & Vaughan, J. (1985). Inhibition of return: Neural basis and function. *Cognitive Neuropsychology, 2,* 211–218.

Posner, M.I., & Snyder, C.R.R. (1975). Facilitation and inhibition in the processing of signals. In P.M.A. Rabbitt & S. Dornic (Eds.), *Attention & Performance, Vol. 5.* Hillsdale, N.J.: Erlbaum.

Posner, M.I., Snyder, C.R.R., & Davidson, B.J. (1980). Attention and the detection of signals. *Journal of Experimental Psychology: General, 109,* 160–174.

Posner, M.I., Walker, J.A., Friedrich, F.J., & Rafal, R.D. (1984). Effects of parietal injury on covert orienting of attention. *Journal of Neuroscience, 4,* 1863–1874.

Posner, M.I., Walker, J.A., Friedrich, F.J., & Rafal, R.D. (1987). How do the parietal lobes direct covert attention? *Neuropsychologia, 25,* 135–146.

Possamai, C., & Bonnel, A.M. (1991). Early modulation of visual input: Constant versus varied cueing. *Bulletin of the Psychonomic Society, 29,* 323–326.

Pylyshyn, Z. (1989). The role of location indexes in spatial perception: A sketch of the FINST spatial-index model. *Cognition, 32,* 65–97.

Pylyshyn, Z., & Storm, R.W. (1988). Tracking multiple independent targets: Evidence for a parallel tracking mechanism. *Spatial Vision, 3,* 179–197.

Rafal, R.D., Calabresi, P.A., Brennan, C.W., & Sciolto, T.K. (1989). Saccade preparation inhibits reorienting to recently attended locations. *Journal of Experimental Psychology: Human Perception & Performance, 15,* 673–685.

Rafal, R.D., Egly, R., & Rhodes, D. (1994). Effects of inhibition of return on voluntary and visually guided saccades. *Canadian Journal of Experimental Psychology, 48,* 284–300.

Rafal, R.D., & Posner, M.I. (1987). Deficits in human visual spatial attention following thalamic lesions. *Proceedings of the National Academy of Science of the USA, 84,* 7349–7353.

Rafal, R.D., & Robertson, L. (1995). The neurology of attention. In M. Gazzaniga (Ed.), *The cognitive neurosciences.* Cambridge, MA: MIT Press.

Remington, R. (1980). Attention and saccadic eye movements. *Journal of Experimental Psychology: Human Perception & Performance, 6,* 726–744.

Remington, R., & Pierce, L. (1984). Moving attention: Evidence for time-invariant shifts of visual selective attention. *Perception & Psychophysics, 35,* 393–399.

Reuter-Lorenz, P.A., & Fendrich, R. (1992). Oculomotor readiness and covert orienting: Differences between central and peripheral precues. *Perception & Psychophysics, 52,* 336–344.

Reuter-Lorenz, P.A., Hughes, H.C., & Fendrich, R. (1991). The reduction of saccadic latency by prior offset of the fixation point: An analysis of the gap effect. *Perception & Psychophysics, 49,* 167–175.

Richard, C.M., Wright, R.D., & Ward, L.M. (1996). *Separate sensory-driven and goal-driven effects of cue onsets in visual space.* Paper presented at the annual meeting of the Canadian Society for Brain, Behaviour, and Cognitive Science, Montreal, Quebec.

Rizzolatti, G., Riggio, L., Dascola, I., & Umilta, C. (1987). Reorienting attention across the horizontal and vertical meridians: Evidence in favour of a premotor theory of attention. *Neuropsychologia, 25,* 31–40.

Robinson, D.L., Goldberg, M.E., & Stanton, G.B. (1978). Parietal association cortex in the primate: Sensory mechanisms and behavioral modulations. *Journal of Neurophysiology, 41,* 910–932.

Rohrbaugh, J.W. (1984). The orienting reflex: Performance and central nervous system manifestations. In R. Parasuramen & D.R. Davies (Eds.), *Varieties of attention.* Orlando, FL: Academic Press.

Rohrer, W.H., & Sparks, D.L. (1986). Role of the superior colliculus in the initiation of express saccades. *Investigative Ophthalmology & Visual Science, 271,* 156.

Sagi, D., & Julesz, B. (1985). Fast noninertial shifts of attention. *Spatial Vision, 1,* 141–149.

Saslow, M.G. (1967). Effects of components of displacement-step stimuli upon latency of saccadic eye movement. *Journal of the Optical Society of America, 57,* 1024–1029.

Schiller, P.H., Sandell, J.H., & Maunsell, J.H.R. (1987). The effect of frontal eye field and superior colliculus lesions on saccadic latencies in the rhesus monkey. *Journal of Neurophysiology, 57,* 1033–1049.

Schiller, P.H., True, S.D., & Conway, J.L. (1979). Effects of frontal eye field and superior colliculus ablations on eye movements. *Science, 206,* 590–592.

Schneider, W., Dumais, S.T., & Shiffrin, R.M. (1984). Automatic and controlled processing and attention. In R. Parasuraman & D.R. Davies (Eds.), *Varieties of attention.* Orlando, FL: Academic Press.

Shagass, C., Roemer, R., & Amadeo, M. (1976). Eye tracking performance and engagement of attention. *Archives of General Psychiatry, 33,* 121–125.

Shaw, M.L. (1983). Division of attention among spatial locations: A fundamental difference between detection of letters and detection of luminance increments. In H. Bouma & D.G. Bouwhuis (Eds.), *Attention & Performance, Vol. 10.* Hillsdale, NJ: Erlbaum.

Shepard, M., & Müller, H.J. (1989). Movement versus focusing of visual attention. *Perception & Psychophysics, 46,* 146–154.

Shepard, M., Findlay, J.M., & Hockey, R.J. (1986). The relationship between eye movements and spatial attention. *Quarterly Journal of Experimental Psychology, 38A,* 475–491.

Shepard, R.N. (1975). Form, formation, and transformations of internal representations. In R.L. Solso (Ed.), *Information processing and cognition: The Loyola symposium.* Hillsdale, NJ: Erlbaum.

Shibutani, H., Sakata, H., & Hyvaerinen, J. (1986). Saccade and blinking evoked by microstimulation of the posterior parietal association cortex of the monkey. *Experimental Brain Research, 55,* 1–8.

Shulman, G.L., Remington, R.W., & McLean, J.P. (1979). Moving attention through visual space. *Journal of Experimental Psychology: Human Perception & Performance, 5,* 522–526.

Skelton, J.M., & Eriksen, C.W. (1976). Spatial characteristics of selective attention in letter matching. *Bulletin of the Psychonomic Society, 7,* 136–138.

Solso, R.L. (1991). *Cognitive psychology.* Boston, MA: Allyn & Bacon.

Sparks, D.L., & Mays, L.E. (1980). Movement fields of saccade-related burst neurons in the monkey superior colliculus. *Brain Research, 190,* 39–50.

Sparks, D.L., & Mays, L.E. (1983). Spatial localization of saccade targets: I. Compensation for stimulus-induced perturbations in eye position. *Journal of Neurophysiology, 49,* 45–63.

Spearman, C. (1937). *Psychology down the ages.* London: Macmillan.

Sundqvist, A. (1979). Saccadic reaction time in parietal lobe dysfunction. *Lancet, 1,* 870.

Tipper, S., Driver, J., & Weaver, B. (1991). Object-centred inhibition of return of visual attention. *Quarterly Journal of Experimental Psychology, 43*(A), 289–298.

Titchener, E.B. (1910). *A textbook of psychology.* New York: Macmillan.

Todd, J.T., & Van Gelder, P. (1979). Implications of a transient-sustained dichotomy for the measurement of human performance. *Journal of Experimental Psychology: Human Perception & Performance, 5*, 625–638.

Treisman, A. (1964). Selective attention in man. *British Medical Journal, 20*, 12–16.

Treisman, A., & Gelade, G. (1980). A feature integration theory of attention. *Cognitive Psychology, 12*, 97–136.

Treisman, A., & Gormican, S. (1988). Feature analysis in early vision: Evidence from search asymmetries. *Psychological Review, 95*, 15–48.

Treisman, A, Vieira, A., & Hayes, A. (1992). Automaticity and preattentive processing. *American Journal of Psychology, 105*, 341– 362.

Tsal, Y. (1983). Movements of attention across the visual field. *Journal of Experimental Psychology: Human Perception & Performance, 9*, 523–530.

Ullman, S. (1984). Visual routines. *Cognition, 18*, 97–159.

Van Gelder, P., Anderson, S., Herman, E., Lebedev, S., & Tsui, W.H. (1990). Saccades in pursuit eye tracking reflect motor attention processes. *Comprehensive Psychiatry, 31*, 253–260.

Ward, L.M. (1985). Covert focusing of the attentional gaze. *Canadian Journal of Psychology, 39*, 546–563.

Ward, L.M. (1994). Supramodal and modality-specific mechanisms for stimulus-driven shifts of auditory and visual attention. *Canadian Journal of Experimental Psychology, 48*, 242–259.

Warren, R.M., & Warren, R.P. (1968). *Helmholtz on perception: Its physiology and development.* New York: Wiley.

Weichselgartner, E., & Sperling, G. (1987). Dynamics of automatic and controlled visual attention. *Science, 238*, 778–780.

Wright, R.D. (1994). Shifts of visual attention to multiple simultaneous location cues. *Canadian Journal of Experimental Psychology, 48*, 205–217.

Wright, R.D., & Richard, C.M. (1993). *Inhibition-of-return of visual attention to multiple location cues.* Paper presented at the annual meeting of the Psychonomic Society, Washington, D.C.

Wright, R.D., & Richard, C.M. (1994). *Inhibition-of-return to successively and sequentially cued locations.* Paper presented at the annual meeting of the Psychonomic Society, St. Louis, Missouri.

Wright, R.D., & Richard, C.M. (1996). *The effects of simultaneous location cueing at multiple locations in visual space.* Manuscript in preparation.

Wright, R.D., Richard, C.M., & McDonald, J.J. (1995). Neutral location cues and cost/benefit analysis of visual attention shifts. *Canadian Journal of Experimental Psychology, 49*, 540–548.

Wright, R.D., Richard, C.M., & McDonald, J.J. (1996). *Simultaneous sensory-driven effects of cue-onset at multiple locations in visual space.* Paper presented at the annual meeting of the Canadian Society for Brain, Behaviour, and Cognitive Science, Montreal, Quebec.

Wright, R.D., & Ward, L.M. (1993). Indexing and the control of express saccades. *Behavioral & Brain Sciences, 16*, 494–495.

Wright, R.D., & Ward, L.M. (1994). Shifts of visual attention: An historical and methodological overview. *Canadian Journal of Experimental Psychology, 48*, 151–166.

Wurtz, R.H., & Albano, J.E. (1980). Visual-motor function of the primate superior colliculus. *Annual Review of Neuroscience, 3*, 189–226.

Wurtz, R.H., Goldberg, M.E., & Robinson, D.L. (1980). Behavioral modulation of visual responses in the monkey: Stimulus selection for attention and movement. *Progress in Psychobiology and Physiological Psychology, 9*, 43–83.

Wurtz, R.H., & Mohler, C.W. (1976). Organization of monkey superior colliculus: Enhanced visual response of superficial layer cells. *Journal of Neurophysiology, 39*, 745–765.

Yantis, S. (1988). On analog movements of visual attention. *Perception & Psychophysics, 43*, 203–206.

Yantis, S. (1992). Multielement visual tracking: Attention and perceptual organization. *Cognitive Psychology, 24*, 295–340.

Yantis, S., & Johnson, D.N. (1990). Mechanisms of attentional priority. *Journal of Experimental Psychology: Human Perception & Performance, 16*, 812–825.

Yantis, S., & Jones, E. (1991). Mechanisms of attentional selection: Temporally modulated priority tags. *Perception & Psychophysics, 50*, 166–178.

Yantis, S., & Jonides, J. (1984). Abrupt visual onsets and selective attention: Evidence from visual search. *Journal of Experimental Psychology: Human Perception & Performance, 10*, 601–621.

Yantis, S., & Jonides, J. (1990). Abrupt visual onsets and selective attention: Voluntary versus automatic allocation. *Journal Experimental Psychology: Human Perception & Performance, 16*, 121–134.

# 7

# Objects, Attention and Perceptual Experience

## Steven Yantis

Visual perception is the process of constructing an internal representation of the local environment, based on patterns of light reflected from objects and surfaces in the scene. It is convenient to categorize the operations that contribute to visual perception according to the relative influence of bottom-up information (e.g., properties of the stimulus) and top-down information (e.g., memory and expectation) upon their normal functioning (and keep in mind that these groupings are by no means well defined or universally recognized). Early vision refers to the functioning of the retina and early cortical areas in response to patterns of light and dark that vary over space and time. Much is known about the neural basis for early vision from neurophysiological and psychophysical investigations, although much still remains to be learned. High-level vision is concerned with complex operations such as object and face recognition, mental imagery, and other forms of visual cognition; these operations interact heavily with memory and knowledge. Most of the evidence for high-level vision comes from behavioural studies of normal human observers or from the analysis of patterns of impairment in brain-damaged patients.

Between early and high-level vision is intermediate or middle-level vision. Among the operations at this level of the visual system are the processes of perceptual organization and attention. Perceptual organization refers to those operations responsible for joining together image fragments that are created by partial occlusion of one object by another (Kellman & Shipley, 1991). For example, the image of a tree situated behind a chain-link fence is highly fragmented, yet the tree is experienced as complete and spatially continuous. Visual attention refers to those perceptual operations responsible for selecting important or task-relevant objects for further detailed visual processing such as identification. Selection is required to minimize interference or crosstalk among different identification operations (see Tsotsos, 1990, for a detailed discussion).

My goal in this chapter is to discuss the crucial interaction between the middle-vision operations of perceptual organization and attention. Perceptual organization mechanisms create object representations from the fragmented early visual image; visual attention selects one or more of these for delivery to high-level mechanisms. To illustrate the interaction between perceptual organization and attention, I will discuss the phenomenon of stimulus-driven attentional capture, which has been a focus of research in my laboratory for some years (Yantis, 1993). Although we did not start with this idea in mind, it has become clear that attentional capture provides a revealing context in which to examine the interaction between organization and attention.

## Visual Salience and Attentional Capture

To start, one might ask what it is about certain visual events that captures attention. An initial introspective answer is this: salient things capture attention. Of course, this definition begs the question. To avoid circularity, salience can be defined in terms of the stimulus; for example, one could borrow from Duncan and Humphreys (1989) and define a salient stimulus as one that differs substantially from its background in some perceptual dimension and whose background is roughly homogeneous in that dimension (e.g., a red element in a background of blue elements). Of course, whether any given physical difference is psychologically important will usually have to be assessed psychophysically.

It is widely assumed that attention is captured by such salient stimuli, and it is easy to see why. There are scores of reports of efficient visual search performance (i.e., rapid and accurate target detection) when the target stimuli were salient according to this definition. However, although salient stimuli are efficiently detected in visual search, they cannot be said to capture attention on that basis alone. Consider the design of a typical "feature search" experiment. The subject is instructed to search for a target stimulus that differs from the nontarget stimuli in some dimension (e.g., the target is red and the nontargets are blue). Such a stimulus will be referred to as a *feature singleton* or simply a singleton (after Pashler, 1988). The task might be to detect the presence of the red singleton (which is present on half the trials), or it might require the subject to identify the shape or some other attribute of the red singleton (which is present on all trials). As stated earlier, such experiments routinely show extremely efficient performance (e.g., as indexed by the absence of a substantial display-size effect in visual search), and it is usually concluded that the singleton captured attention.

However, in these and most other experiments yielding evidence that is taken to demonstrate attentional capture by a feature singleton, the singleton itself was the target of search; in other words, the task required subjects to adopt a state of attentional readiness in which they actively searched for that singleton. This means that there is some (possibly substantial) contribution of top-down strategic control in the deployment of attention, which seriously undermines the conclusion that the singleton captured attention in a purely stimulus-driven fashion.

In order to assess whether a stimulus captures attention in a stimulus-driven fashion, one must devise a task in which the stimulus under investigation is not relevant to the subject's task. If such an irrelevant singleton still influences the deployment of attention, then one can conclude the singleton captured attention in a stimulus-driven fashion.

Yantis and Egeth (1994; see also Jonides & Yantis, 1988) recently reported the results from a series of experiments that were designed to assess whether truly irrelevant feature singletons can be said to capture attention. In these experiments, subjects were required to search for a vertically oriented bar (0.6° visual angle in length and 0.15° in width) in a background of tilted bars (30° left and right of vertical with equal probability). The target was present on half the trials. There were three, six, or nine elements in each display. Subjects pressed one button if the vertical target was present, and another button if it was absent.

In the baseline version of the task (Experiment 1), the bars were all red and stationary. Response time increased linearly with display size, and the slope for Target Present trials was approximately half that for Target Absent trials. This pattern suggest that this task requires an effortful, attentionally demanding (possibly serial) visual search.

In order to assess the extent to which a to-be-ignored colour singleton captures attention, it was first necessary to establish that the singleton yields efficient visual search (i.e., that it pops out) when it is the target of search (and therefore relevant). In Experiment 2, one of the bars in each display was coloured blue (and the remaining bars were red, as before). When the target (a vertical bar) was present, it was always the blue element; subjects were informed of this perfect contingency, and they were encouraged to exploit it to minimize response time. A reasonable strategy here is to direct attention to the blue element, determine whether it is vertical or not, and respond accordingly; the red elements should be ignored. Keep in mind that it was not enough to detect the presence of the blue stimulus (there was a blue singleton in every trial); once the blue element was localized, it was necessary to determine whether it had the target orientation (i.e., vertical orientation), which presumably required an act of attention (as suggested by the steep slopes obtained in Experiment 1). The blue target singleton in a background of red nontargets could be used very efficiently to deploy attention: response times did not increase with display size. This result ensured that these red and blue stimuli were sufficiently different from one another in colour that a blue singleton could reasonably be called salient, according to the definition offered at the start of this section. We were now in a position to determine whether this salient colour single-ton captures attention when it is *not* relevant to the visual search task.

Experiment 3 was run with a new group of naïve subjects to elimi-nate the possibility that previous experience with the contingencies in Experiment 2 would influence subjects' attentional strategies in Exper-iment 3 (and new groups of subjects were recruited for all of the sub-sequent experiments reported). As in Experiment 2, a blue singleton was present on every trial. In Experiment 3, however, the position of the target, when it was present, was uncorrelated with the position of the blue singleton. In particular, the target corresponded to the blue bar on $1/n$ of the trials, where $n$ is display size (three, six, or nine). In this case, subjects could not completely ignore the blue singleton (because it was sometimes the target), but there was no incentive to deliberately direct attention toward it, either. Optimally, subjects should simply ig-nore colour in this task.

That is just what they did. Mean response time when the target hap-pened to correspond to the blue singleton (a rare event) was no faster than when the target corresponded to one of the red elements. If the blue singleton captured attention in a purely stimulus-driven fashion, response times in the target-singleton condition should have been sub-stantially faster than in the target-nonsingleton condition, and should have produced a near-zero slope as in Experiment 2. Clearly, this did not happen.

Jonides and Yantis (1988) and Hillstrom and Yantis (1994) reported experimental results that corroborate those of Yantis and Egeth (1994). In each case, subjects could direct attention to a colour, motion, or brightness singleton efficiently when the task made it was sensible to do so, but they could and did completely ignore that same singleton when that strategy was called for. Folk and Annett (1994) asked whether the failure to observe capture by a salient colour singleton might be due to the relative sparsity of the common feature in the dis-plays used by Jonides and Yantis (1988). They performed an experi-ment similar to the colour condition of Jonides and Yantis, but with various densities of randomly arranged dots of the same colour as the common letter colour, so that the colour contrast near the uniquely co-loured element was increased. This did not increase the extent to which that element captured attention.

It has been shown that to-be-ignored feature singletons can capture attention in certain special situations. For example, Theeuwes (1992) has shown that the presence of a to-be-ignored colour singleton slows search for a shape singleton, suggesting that the colour singleton captured attention in a stimulus-driven fashion. However, this sort of attentional capture only occurs when the subject is actively searching for a target which is itself a singleton. Bacon and Egeth (1994) recently showed that when searching for a singleton target, observers often strategically enter what they call *singleton detection mode*. In this case, the deployment of attention is controlled by a feature difference detector that directs attention to the location in the visual field containing the highest local feature contrast, regardless of the dimension in which that contrast occurs. In some sense, attentional capture under these conditions is a strategic choice. When the task is changed so that singleton detection mode is no longer an effective strategy for search, then Bacon and Egeth (1994) found that irrelevant singletons do not capture attention. Thus, a deliberate goal-driven state of attentional readiness seems to be required even for the sort of attentional capture documented by Theeuwes (1992) to occur.

The story is not completely without complication. Some reports suggest that even irrelevant feature singletons can influence visual search performance. For example, Todd and Kramer (1994) found that in visual search with large display sizes (up to 25), responses to singleton targets are slightly faster than those to nonsingleton targets, even when the position of the singleton is uncorrelated with the position of the target. Why this occurs remains to be seen. It is possible that with large displays, requiring a second or more for each response, subjects choose to direct attention to the unpredictive colour or luminance singleton earlier than would be expected if it were truly being ignored. However, even in this case, the colour singleton does not capture attention in the sense that it is the first element identified in search. If this were the case, one would expect the search function in the singleton target conditions to be flat with display size, and it was not.

These experiments help clarify the attentional mechanisms at work when a feature singleton is the target of search. The absence of a display-size effect, which is often taken as reflecting stimulus-driven attentional capture, must be interpreted with caution. In many instances, an explicit incentive to deliberately attend to feature singletons is present, and this implicates top-down attentional strategies in the deployment of attention. The bottom-up, nonstrategic aspects of attentional control can be assessed only by eliminating task demands that encourage top-down control.

## New Objects Capture Attention

The experiments reviewed in the last section suggest that visual salience alone is not sufficient to capture attention in a purely bottom-up fashion. One might then ask, if things like motion and colour singletons do not capture attention, then what does? I have argued that there is one visual event that does seem to capture attention even when it is irrelevant to the observer's task, and that is abrupt visual onset. We have examined this hypothesis using visual search tasks that are similar to the ones described earlier.

Consider an experiment in which one element had an abrupt onset and no other element did (e.g., Yantis & Jonides, 1984). The top of Figure 1 shows what a typical trial looked like. Each trial was preceded by the appearance of a target letter (not shown) for which the subject was to search during that trial. The trial itself began with a display of figure-8 placeholders for 1 second, followed by a display of letters. A no-onset letter is one that is present in the placeholder display but camouflaged by irrelevant line segments before the appearance of the search display; the camouflaging segments are removed at search display onset. An abrupt onset stimulus is one that appears in a previously blank display location at the same time the no-onset letters are revealed.

In our experiment, exactly one of the elements in each trial had an abrupt onset, and the rest were no-onsets. When the target was present, it was the onset element on $1/n$ of the trials (where $n$ is the display size), and it was a no-onset element on the remaining trials. The position of the onset stimulus thus provided no information about the position of the target, and so there was no incentive for subjects to deliberately attend to it.

As illustrated in the bottom panel of Figure 1, when the target was the single element with an abrupt onset, the time to find it did not increase significantly with the number of elements in the display. When the target was one of the no-onset elements, reaction time did increase significantly with display size. This pattern suggests the following interpretation. On each trial, attention is automatically captured by the abrupt onset element. The conclusion that this is a manifestation of stimulus-driven attentional capture is based on the absence of any incentive for subjects to deliberately attend to the onset stimulus. If the onset element is the target, a positive response is made immediately, and the trial ends. Response time on trials in which the target happens to be the abrupt-onset element will therefore be constant (it will depend on the time required to shift attention to the onset element and identify it as the target), and it will not depend on how many other elements there are in the display. If the target is not the onset element, then search will continue until the target is found or the display is exhaustively searched. The display size function for the Target Present, no-onset condition is roughly half that for the Target Absent condition; this pattern suggests that the search was attentionally demanding, and it is consistent with (but does not demand) the conclusion that search

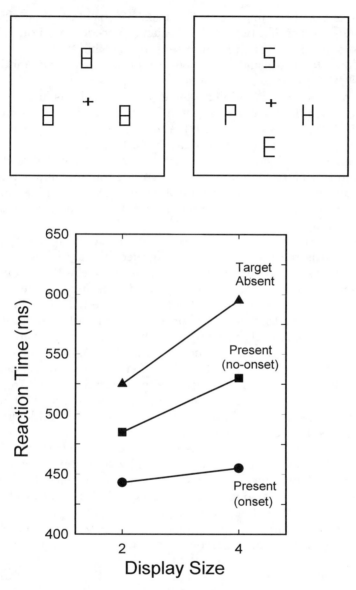

*Figure* 1. Top: Typical trial in Yantis and Jonides (1984). A display consisting of figure-8 placeholders is present for 1,000 ms, followed by the appearance of the search display. One letter in the search display appears in a previously blank location; the remaining letters are revealed by removing two segments from a placeholder. Bottom: Data from Yantis and Jonides (1984). Response time is plotted as a function of display size for Target Absent, Target Present (no-onset) and Target Present (onset) conditions. (From Yantis & Jonides, 1984, p. 607, top and p. 608, bottom. Adapted with permission from the American Psychological Association.)

is serial and self-terminating in this task.[1] We have considered, and ruled out, the possibility that the elements preceded by figure-eight placeholders suffer from a form of sensory masking that delays their availability to the visual system (see Gibson, 1996, and Yantis & Jonides, 1996, for an exchange of views on this issue).

Several additional experiments have corroborated this finding, and led to very similar conclusions (e.g., Jonides & Yantis, 1988; Yantis & Johnson, 1990; Yantis & Jones, 1991; Yantis & Jonides, 1990). The data reveal that abrupt visual onsets capture attention in visual search. However, this conclusion, together with the fact (reviewed above) that other highly salient attributes – such as unique colours, unique brightnesses, and motion – do not capture attention leaves us with a puzzle. If not mere salience, what features of abrupt visual onsets cause them to capture attention?

There are at least two possible answers to this question. The first answer, which is the position initially adopted by Yantis and Jonides (1984), is that some low-level visual mechanism detects the luminance increment exhibited by abrupt onsets and directs attention automatically to that region of the visual field. This is referred to as the *luminance-increment explanation*. It is consistent with earlier suggestions about the role of neural mechanisms in the visual system that are responsive to high temporal frequencies and thus signal change over time (e.g., the magnocellular stream; see Lennie, Trevarthen, Van Essen, & Wässle, 1990). For example, Breitmeyer and Ganz (1976) suggested that transient visual channels might function to direct attention to regions of the visual field that exhibit rapid change. Todd and Van Gelder (1979) further pursued this idea.

Another possible account, termed the *new-object explanation*, places the locus of attentional capture more centrally. According to this view, when a new object appears in the visual field, a new perceptual representation must be created for it. The visual system is predisposed to attend to new perceptual object representations because they are often behaviourally significant. The appearance of a new perceptual object may require an immediate response, and survival may depend on its speed and accuracy. It therefore is reasonable to suppose that there is a very efficient mechanism, one that does not depend on strategic thought processes but that operates essentially automatically, to direct attention to the new perceptual object.

With this possible account of attentional capture by abrupt visual onsets, we approach the core idea of this chapter, which concerns the interaction between perceptual organization and attention. Perceptual organization mechanisms are responsible for the creation of perceptual object representations – attentional capture by the appearance of new perceptual objects provides a way to probe this mechanism. In the remainder of this section, I will review evidence for the new-object account for attentional capture by abrupt visual onsets, and in subsequent sections I will describe several more experiments that exploit this mechanism to further illuminate the interaction between perceptual organization and attention.

How can we test the luminance-increment and the new-object explanations for attentional capture by abrupt onsets? In all of our previous experiments, either of these explanations could account for the data: in each case, the abrupt onset stimuli were new objects that exhibited a luminance increment.

To find an answer, Yantis and Hillstrom (1994) carried out a series of experiments in which the two factors were unconfounded. We used visual search tasks in which the shapes of the stimulus letters were defined by contrast with their background, not in luminance (in fact, their mean luminance was equal to the background), but in relative motion, binocular disparity (perceived as depth), or texture. For example, the depth-defined stimuli were random-dot stereograms with the letter-shapes appearing to float in front of the background field. If the field was viewed with only one eye, it appeared to be a uniform array of randomly positioned dots. In this way, it was possible to present a new perceptual object in a previously blank location without an accompanying luminance increment.

On each trial of the experiment, we first showed a set of equiluminant figure-eight placeholders for two seconds. Then we showed an array of letters also rendered via relative motion, binocular disparity, or texture contrast. As always, the no-onset letters were revealed by removing a subset of the camouflaging line segments in the figure-8 placeholders. The onset element appeared in a previously blank location. In this sense, the displays were similar to those depicted in Figure 1. The key factor was that the new object was not accompanied by a change in mean luminance.[2] If the luminance-increment explanation for capture by abrupt onsets is correct, then no attentional capture should result, because no location exhibited a luminance increment. However, if the new-object account is the correct one, then capture by the new object should be observed. Remember that attentional capture is manifested by a relatively flat display-size function when the target happens to be the new object, and a relatively steep function when the target is one of the old elements.

Figure 2 shows the results from the texture version of this study. The data strongly support the new-object account. Attention was captured by the new object even though that object did not exhibit a luminance increment. The results were the same for the disparity and relative-

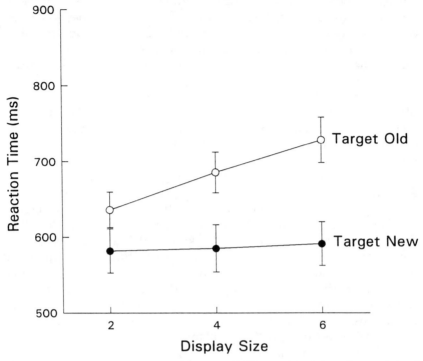

*Figure* 2. Results from Experiment 1 of Yantis and Hillstrom (1994). Stimuli were defined
by discontinuities in texture and were equiluminant with the background. The display-
size effect is absent when the target appeared in a previously blank location even without
a luminance increment, supporting the new-object hypothesis. (From Yantis & Hillstrom,
1994, p. 99. Adapted with permission from the American Psychological Association.)

motion experiments; in each case, when the target happened to be the
new object, reaction time was nearly unaffected by display size, but
when the target was one of the old elements, there was a strong effect
of display size.

Another source of evidence for the claim that new objects capture attention comes from the study by Hillstrom and Yantis (1994), mentioned above. Hillstrom and Yantis found that element motion failed to
capture attention in visual search when motion was known to be irrelevant to the task. We sought evidence that motion might capture attention when it serves to segment the moving element from a stationary
background. We offered an analogy to a moth, whose mottled wings
resemble the lichen-covered bark in its environmental niche. So long as
the moth remains motionless, it is camouflaged and therefore invisible
to predators. At the moment its wings begin to move, their shape is immediately manifest (due to the motion contrast thereby created), and

an object that was previously invisible (and therefore perceptually nonexistent) appears. The idea was that object segmentation via motion could capture attention.

We obtained evidence for just this sort of mechanism with an experiment in which one stimulus element in a large rectilinear configuration of stationary elements captured attention when it moved and was thereby segregated from the rest of the configuration (Hillstrom & Yantis, 1994). The conclusion was that motion per se does not capture attention, but that motion can capture attention by virtue of its ability to segment an object from its background, causing the creation of a new perceptual object representation.

The claim that new perceptual objects capture attention in a purely stimulus-driven fashion has not gone unchallenged. For example, Folk, Remington, and Johnston (1992) have argued that all instances of attentional capture, including those involving abrupt visual onset, entail a state of attentional readiness, called an attentional control setting, for the feature in question. This debate has not yet been fully resolved (for further discussion, see Yantis, 1993, and Folk, Remington, & Johnston, 1993).

The experiments reviewed in this section suggest that there is something special or important about the appearance of a new perceptual object in the visual field. What might that be? I have already provided an intuitive answer to this question: new perceptual objects are likely to have behavioural significance, so efficient visual selection of such objects has survival value. But there may be a more fundamental reason for these findings.

To fix ideas, recall that the world consists of coherent surfaces that bound objects, but because of the geometry of 3-D space and its projection onto the 2-D retina, the initial visual signal – the retinal image – is fragmented in both space and time. Figure 3A illustrates spatial fragmentation: image regions are not explicitly labelled as belonging to one or another object, yet we effortlessly experience spatially separate regions (e.g., regions 1 and 2) as belonging to the same surface. Figures 3A and 3B illustrate temporal fragmentation: for example, as an observer moves through the environment, an 'object may be temporarily occluded by an intervening surface, yet the representations of the object before and after occlusion are experienced as a single, continuously present object. Therefore, one of the first operations to be performed by a visual system is to organize the fragmented retinal image into a representation that recovers the coherence and continuity of the surfaces and objects around us. The principles of perceptual organization first described by the Gestalt psychologists 70 or 80 years ago (e.g., Koffka, 1935; Wertheimer, 1912) state what aspects of the image might be useful in doing this (e.g., common fate, collinearity). A recent resurgence of interest in this issue has led to further insights about the organization problem (e.g., Kellman & Shipley, 1991, 1992; Nakayama, He, & Shimojo, 1995; Palmer & Rock, 1994).

The discussion in the paragraph above leads to the conclusion that a critical attribute of any perceptual object is spatiotemporal continuity. The human visual system has evolved to recover the continuity of the visual world, despite retinal image fragmentation. Of course, spatiotemporal discontinuity does occur, for example, when an object first appears in the field of view or disappears permanently from the field of view, and these events are of special importance to our perceptual systems. I will argue, with the results from two related sets of experiments, that the reason the abrupt appearance of a new perceptual object captures attention is that it represents one of these forms of discontinuity, and such events are perceptually crucial for the construction of perceptual representations of a scene.

## Continuity and Interruption in Motion
## Perception and Attention

The appearance of a new object in a previously blank location is an extreme form of spatiotemporal discontinuity, and the evidence reviewed in the last section suggests that this is something to which the visual attention system is especially attuned. One might ask whether there are degrees of discontinuity that might be reflected in the attentional response of the system. For example, could it be that stimuli that are only slightly discontinuous (e.g., stimuli that flicker off only briefly) are less likely to capture attention than stimuli that appear in a previously blank location? More importantly, are there other manifestations of this sensitivity to *degrees of discontinuity* in visual perception? Yantis and Gibson (1994) set out to answer this question.

We began by employing a visual search paradigm that is a variant of the one used by Yantis and Jonides (1984, depicted in Figure 1). Figure 4A shows a typical trial. The display started with a set of figure-8 placeholders arranged in a circle about fixation. After 1 second, the figure 8s all changed into letters. In this sense, all the stimuli in this experiment were no-onset letters. However, one of the figure 8s disappeared (i.e., exhibited a temporal gap) for varying lengths of time (the *gap duration*) immediately before the appearance of the letters. The gap duration ranged from 0 ms (in which case, of course, there was no gap at all) to 1,000 ms (in which case, one location began as a blank and a letter appeared there after 1 second; this amounts to the onset condition of Figure 1). At issue was the form of the visual search function (a) when the target did and did not appear in the gap location (gap vs.

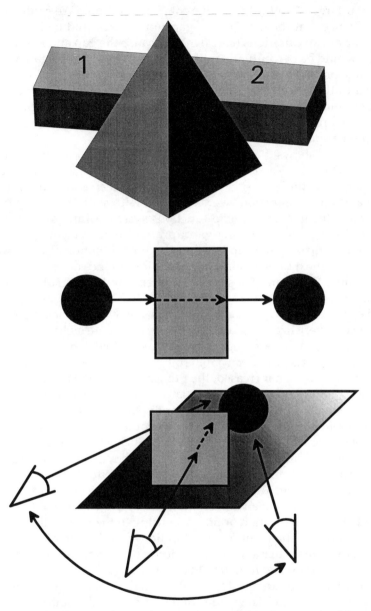

*Figure* 3. Spatial and temporal image fragmentation. a: Although regions 1 and 2 are spatially separated by intervening regions, they are perceived as part of the same scenic surface. b: When the circle passes behind an occluding surface, its reappearance is perceived as a continuation of the circle that earlier disappeared behind the occluder. c: As the observer moves through the environment, intervening surfaces temporarily occlude objects, but their continuity is nevertheless maintained.

no-gap targets) and (b) for different gap durations. We could predict in advance that the gap and no-gap functions would be identical for very brief gap durations (e.g., 0 ms), because the gap and no-gap locations would be perceptually indistinguishable (and, for a gap duration of 0 ms, physically indistinguishable). We also could predict that long gap durations (e.g., 1,000 ms) would yield flat search functions for gap targets and steep functions for no-gap targets (the standard distinction between onset and no-onset stimuli as in Figure 1). At issue was what would happen for intermediate gap durations.

Figure 4B shows the results. Each panel plots the data from a different gap duration. As predicted, flat search functions were obtained for gap targets at the longest gap durations, and steep and nearly identical gap and no-gap functions were obtained with short gap durations. In between, the gap and no-gap functions systematically diverged. This pattern suggests that as the gap duration increased, the probability that the element in the gap location captured attention also increased.

In the context of our claims about the importance of new objects and continuity, Yantis and Gibson (1994) interpreted this result as follows. Short gap durations were easily discounted by the visual system as flicker rather than as discontinuity; thus a letter appearing after a brief gap was experienced as a continuation of the figure eight preceding the gap. Because these letter representations were "old," they enjoyed no attentional advantage over any of the other letters in the display. However, as the gap duration increased, the probability that the perceptual object representation could span the gap, and thus maintain its continuity over time, systematically declined. A letter appearing after a very long gap was therefore experienced as a new perceptual object, not as a continuation of the figure eight preceding the gap. Such letters would capture attention according to the principle that new objects capture attention.

In order to quantify the extent to which the letter in the gap location captured attention, Yantis and Gibson (1994) fit a very simple mixture model to the data. On any given trial, attention was assumed to be captured by the gap location or not. According to the model, there exists a probability, $p$, dependent on gap duration, that the letter in the gap location captured attention. The magnitude of $p$ ranged from 0.0 to 1.0 as gap durations ranged from 0 to 1,000 ms. The gap and no-gap functions are predicted to be identical for $p = 0.0$, and the gap function is predicted to be flat for $p = 1.0$. The values of $p$ that best fit the obtained RT data grew from .17 to .95 as the gap duration increased from 33 to 1,000 ms.

To corroborate the conclusion that the time-course of attentional capture in the gap task is a manifestation of perceived spatiotemporal continuity, Yantis and Gibson (1994) performed a companion experiment in which the effect of perceived spatiotemporal continuity in apparent-

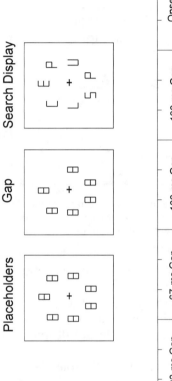

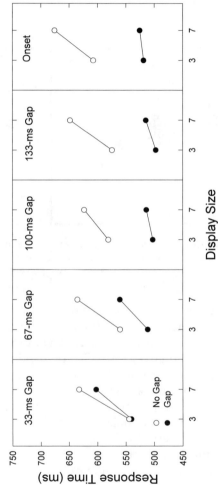

*Figure 4.* Stimulus displays and results from Experiment 1 of Yantis and Gibson (1994). Top: An array of figure-8 placeholders appears for 1,000 ms, at which time each figure 8 turns into a letter. At various moments in time before the letters appear, one of the figure 8s disappears briefly. Bottom: Each panel depicts mean response time for gap targets (filled symbols) and no-gap targets (open symbols) and for display sizes three and seven. (From Yantis & Gibson, 1994, p. 190, top and p. 193, bottom. Adapted with permission from the Canadian Psychological Association.)

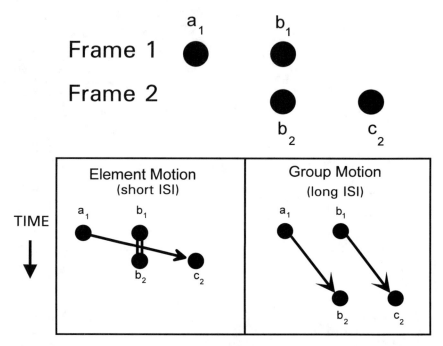

*Figure 5.* Ternus display. Top: Elements appear in locations *a* and *b* during Frame 1, which lasted 200 ms in the experiments summarized here. After a variable blank interval, elements appear in locations *b* and *c*. Bottom: Two percepts that are reported by observers who view the Ternus display.

motion perception was measured. Although visual motion perception seems quite distinct from attentional capture in visual search, motion perception depends on the perceived continuity of visual objects as they change position over time. The perception of apparent motion is paradoxical because it entails the perception of continuity despite a physically discontinuous stimulus.

An apparent motion display that dramatically reveals the role of spatiotemporal continuity in object perception is the Ternus display, first described by Josef Ternus (1926 / 1939). Figure 5 illustrates a typical sequence of frames in the Ternus display. The display consists of two elements (e.g., disks) presented side by side. Three locations are defined (labeled *a*, *b*, and *c* in Figure 5) that are equally spaced on the horizontal meridian. In Frame 1, the two elements are presented in locations *a* and *b*. The elements are removed, and after a blank interstimulus interval (or ISI), Frame 2 is displayed. In Frame 2, the elements appear in locations *b* and *c*. After another blank ISI, Frame 1 may be repeated, followed by Frame 2, and so on for *n* cycles (where a cycle consists of the sequence Frame 1-ISI-Frame 2-ISI, and $n \geq 2$; in our experiments, $n = 4$).

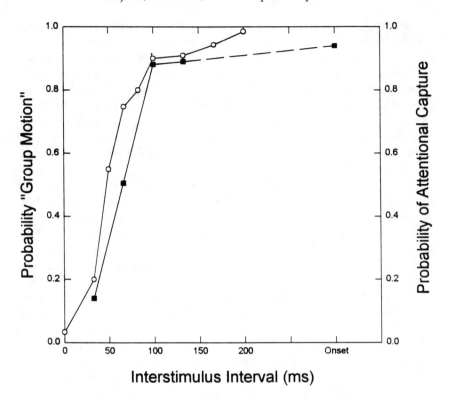

*Figure* 6. Results from Experiment 1 of Yantis and Gibson (1994). The filled symbols depict the probability of attentional capture in the visual search task shown in Figure 4 as a function of gap duration; the open symbols show the probability that subjects reported "group motion" percepts as a function of the blank interval between frames. (From Yantis & Gibson, 1994, p. 192. Adapted with permission from the Canadian Psychological Association.)

All other things being equal, observers typically perceive *element motion* at very short ISIs and *group motion* at long ISIs. In element motion, the object in location *b* appears to remain in place, and the other element appears to hop back and forth from location *a* to location *c* and back again. In group motion, the two elements appear to be connected and to move together back and forth as a group. Yantis and Gibson (1994) obtained performance data from subjects viewing a version of the Ternus display that matched as closely as possible the conditions of the visual search experiment described earlier (e.g., the stimuli in the Ternus task were figure-8 characters). The results were similar to results obtained in many previous studies: the probability of seeing group motion was near zero for very short ISIs, and it gradually increased to near unity for ISIs of 100 ms or more (Figure 6, solid function and left axis).

One may interpret the time-course of apparent-motion perception in the Ternus display as follows (for this discussion, refer to Figure 5). The dominant motion correspondence assignments in the Ternus display are the ones observed in group motion, because these are the shortest motion trajectories available. However, when the ISI is short (e.g., in the extreme case when the ISI is zero), the element in location $b$ is perceived as a single stable object spanning both Frames 1 and 2. In this case, the correspondence $b_1 - b_2$ is assigned because of the strong spatiotemporal continuity of the element in location $b$. Once element $b_2$ is assigned to a correspondence match with $b_1$, it is no longer available for matching with $a_1$; instead, $a_1$ must be matched with $c_2$, and this is the assignment yielding element motion. The duration of the ISI between frames determines whether element or group motion is perceived by influencing whether the element in location $b$ is perceived as a single continuous object or not. In other words, the time-course of apparent motion perception in the Ternus display can be viewed as reflecting the extent to which an object's identity can persist across a temporal gap. The data obtained by Yantis and Gibson (1994) suggest that perceptual objects persist across a gap with a maximum duration of approximately 100 ms.

Yantis and Gibson compared the time-course of group motion and element motion in the Ternus display with the time-course of attentional capture obtained in the gap experiment in visual search (Figure 6, solid and dashed functions, respectively). The functions obtained in these two quite different tasks were remarkably similar. We concluded that the two tasks are manifestations of the same underlying mechanism: perceived spatiotemporal continuity and the lack thereof.

These experiments reveal how the perception of continuity – or discontinuity – may contribute to a range of perceptual experience that spans (at least) the perception of motion and the deployment of attention. This finding suggests that perceptual organization (in this case, over time) operates at a stage of perception before motion is computed or attention can serve its selective function.

## Perceived Continuity under Occlusion

Finally, let me turn to some recent experiments that provide further evidence about the role of perceived continuity in vision. These experiments involve a form of amodal perception, in which an object that is physically absent can have clear perceptual effects. A simple example of amodal completion, first discussed as such by Michotte, Thinès, and Crabbé (1964/1991), is shown in Figure 7. Partly occluded objects are perceptually completed effortlessly by most observers, yielding a coherent representation of the surface structure of the scene.

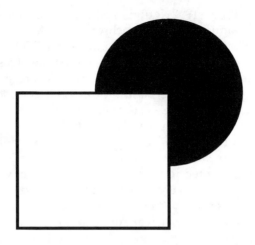

*Figure 7.* If this scene is viewed as a mosaic, the black region may be seen as a segmented disk ("Pacman"). Typically, however, observers will report that the black region is a complete disk that is partly occluded by the square, which is in front.

There is a great deal of evidence that amodal completion as depicted in Figure 7 is an early, precognitive form of perceptual organization. A study by Sekuler and Palmer (1992) illustrates one source of this evidence. In their study, subjects viewed pairs of geometric forms (circles and/or segmented circles), and judged whether or not they were identical in shape. On *same* trials, they saw a pair of circles or a pair of segmented circles ("Pacmen"); in *different* trials, they saw one circle and one segmented circle. For present purposes, I will focus only on responses to the *same* trials.

At various points in time preceding the appearance of the target pair of forms, a prime stimulus was presented. The prime could consist of a circle, a segmented circle, or a more complex configuration such as that shown in Figure 7. It is known that *same-different* judgments are facilitated (e.g., speeded) when the forms to be judged are preceded by an identical priming form. Based on this principle, Sekuler and Palmer (1992) expected faster *same* judgments when a pair of circle targets was preceded by a circle prime and when a pair of segmented circle targets was preceded by a segmented circle prime. Of greatest interest were the response times to circle and segmented circle target pairs when preceded by a partly occluded circle prime (Figure 7). If the Figure 7 stimulus is seen as a mosaic, then it should yield faster *same* judgments for segmented circle target pairs; if, instead, the partly occluded circle is completed behind the occluding square, then the complete circle target pairs should be matched faster.

Sekuler and Palmer (1992) found that the mosaic interpretation dominated for short stimulus-onset asynchronies (SOAs), whereas the completed circle interpretation dominated at longer SOAs. This suggests that perceptual completion takes place over time. This result nicely complements results from other sources that also attest to the precognitive, probably preattentive, nature of amodal completion in space (e.g., Enns & Rensink, in press; He & Nakayama, 1992, 1994; Kellman & Shipley, 1992; Shimojo & Nakayama, 1990).

Although completion of objects across space is certainly a major task of perceptual organization, it is important to remember that the retinal image is also fragmented in time. As the observer moves through the environment, nearby objects may temporarily occlude objects and surfaces that are farther away (Figure 3C). However, when temporarily occluded objects reappear, they are not experienced as new; instead, a representation of those objects persists during the occlusion interval, which serves to correctly maintain the spatiotemporal continuity of objects and surfaces in the scene.

Therefore, one might predict that there exists a phenomenon in the temporal domain that complements amodal completion in the spatial domain. I have termed that phenomenon *amodal integration*. Amodal integration refers to the perception of continuity of an object that is completely but briefly occluded.[3]

Yantis (1995) reported evidence for amodal integration by recording observers' judgments of motion in a variant of the Ternus display. As I stated earlier, one may interpret the time-course of group and element motion perception in the Ternus display as reflecting the time-course of perceived continuity and discontinuity. Specifically, when subjects report element motion, they are reporting that element $b$ appears to be continuous in time; when they report group motion, they are reporting that the element in location $b$ is not continuous in time – the perceived motion correspondences are $a_1 \rightarrow b_2$ and $b_1 \rightarrow c_2$ (see Figure 5).

Data from the Ternus task suggest that subjects actually experience the middle element as continuously present (i.e., they report a motion correspondence of $b_1 - b_2$) even at some short intervals when element $b$ is physically absent for a small but nonzero duration. This is sometimes explained by assuming that what persists is an iconic representation of the object, a brief visual trace of the element after its physical disappearance (e.g., Breitmeyer & Ritter, 1986a, 1986b). The data reported by Yantis (1995) suggests that this is not the only factor contributing to perceived spatiotemporal contiguity in the Ternus display.

Subjects viewed two versions of the standard Ternus display. One version was similar to the standard Ternus display. The second version differed in that an occluding surface appeared over the middle position during the ISI (Figure 8). The occluding surface was termed a

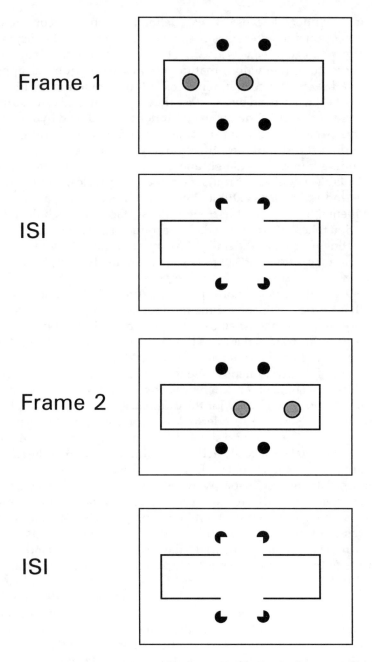

*Figure* 8. Occluded Ternus display used by Yantis (1995). The display was similar to the one shown in Figure 8, except that a virtual surface appeared over the middle location during the blank interstimulus interval. (From Yantis, 1995, p. 183. Adapted with permission from the American Psychological Society.)

"virtual occluder" because it was defined by illusory contours induced by segmented disks positioned above and below the display itself. A virtual occluder was used instead of a real occluder to avoid possible contour interactions that might have arisen from the appearance and disappearance of luminance contours or motion conflict that would have been caused by a surface that moved up and down during the course of the trial. The virtual occluder was induced by removing segments from the inducing disks above and below the outline box surrounding the stimuli and by removing a short segment from the surrounding frame immediately above and below the middle location. The display was viewed through stereoscopic goggles, and the frame and the inducing disks exhibited crossed binocular disparity, which made them appear to float in front of the surface on which the apparent-motion tokens were situated. This produced a vivid occluding surface floating in front of the middle apparent motion element.

In this first experiment, subjects were more likely to report element motion when the virtual occluder was present than when it was absent at all SOAs but the very shortest ones (Figure 9A). This outcome suggests that the occluder caused the representation of the object appearing in location *b* to persist across greater temporal gaps between successive stimulus frames than was possible without the occluder; this is a form of what I have termed amodal integration.

Although this experiment is suggestive, its design leaves open the possibility that some other difference between the occluder and no-occluder conditions accounted for the difference in the functions plotted in Figure 9A. Therefore I undertook a second experiment that more closely equated the two conditions. In this new experiment, every trial included a virtual surface located at the middle location of the display. On half the trials, the virtual surface was induced by elements exhibiting crossed binocular disparity when viewed through stereoscopic goggles, yielding a surface that floated in front of the apparent motion elements; this surface could therefore support occlusion. This condition was the same as the occluder condition of the previous experiment. On the other half of the trials, the virtual surface was induced by elements with uncrossed disparity; in this case, the virtual surface appeared to be floating *behind* the apparent-motion tokens, and such a surface could not support occlusion. The two displays differed only in the polarity of the binocular disparity of the inducing elements (crossed in the front-occluder condition, uncrossed in the rear-occluder condition), and so the only factor that could explain differences in behavior emerging from the two conditions is the 3-D layout of the virtual surface and its ability to occlude one of the display locations.

The results of this experiment are shown in Figure 9B: subjects were more likely to report element motion when the virtual surface was in

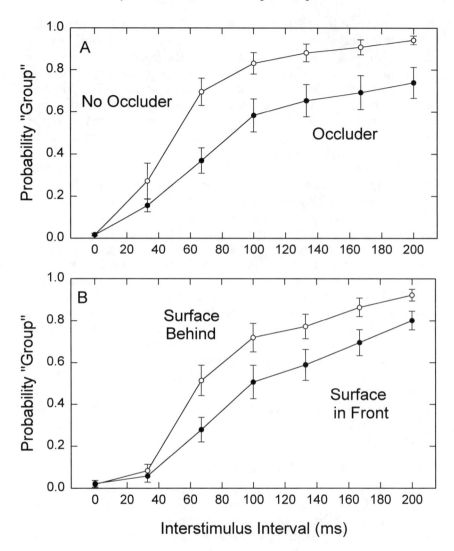

*Figure* 9. Results from Yantis (1995). A: Experiment 1. B: Experiment 2. (From Yantis, 1995, p. 184, A and p. 185, B. Adapted with permission from the American Psychological Society.)

front (supporting occlusion) than when it was behind (no occlusion). This result provides corroboration for the results of the previous experiment: when a perceptual object is momentarily occluded, a representation of that object is more likely to persist during the occlusion, which in turn yields perceived continuity of that object through time.

As stated earlier, Breitmeyer and Ritter (1986a, 1986b) suggested that variation in group and element reports in the Ternus display may be due to variation in visible persistence, and they provided compelling evidence for this claim by showing that factors known to influence the duration of visible persistence also affect the position of the psychometric function in the Ternus display in predictable ways. However, such an account cannot explain the results in Figure 9. The difference between the front and rear-occluder displays was too minor to have had any effect on the duration of visible persistence, at least as conventionally conceived. Instead, the data implicate amodal integration of an occluded visual object.

Sigman and Rock (1974) reported data from an apparent-motion task that anticipates in some respects those reported by Yantis (1995).[4] In their experiments, subjects viewed a display in which elements in two adjacent locations alternately appeared and disappeared (so that element 1 was present during frame 1, followed by element 2 during frame 2, followed by element 1, and so forth). This version of the display produced strong apparent motion between elements 1 and 2, as expected. Sigman and Rock then introduced an occluding surface that appeared over the location of the element that had just disappeared. Thus at any given moment, there was an element in one location and an occluding surface in the other location. Subjects reported that no apparent motion was perceived, presumably because they experienced the element in the occluded location as persisting in time behind the occluder.

Together, these experiments suggest that the visual system will go to great lengths to make sense of the retinal image in terms of the perceived surface layout. Perception is constructive and not merely literal: it goes beyond the spatiotemporally fragmented retinal image to construct a veridical representation of reality.

## Concluding Remarks

I have described a variety of experiments in support of the following claims. First, I have shown that visual salience is not sufficient to capture attention in a purely bottom-up fashion, and that theories of attentional capture that assign to visual salience a critical explanatory role are bound to meet resistance from empirical observation.

Second, I reviewed evidence that the appearance of a new perceptual object does capture attention in a bottom-up fashion – that is, even when such objects are known to be uninformative and irrelevant to search. The appearance of a new object in the visual field obviously has behavioural significance, and the visual system has evolved to be sensitive to such events and to automatically deploy attention in response to them. This finding provides a tool for studying the mechanisms responsible for the creation of perceptual representations, and is a natural way to examine the interaction between perceptual organization and attention.

Third, I showed that performance in two seemingly disparate visual tasks can be characterized as manifestations of a single underlying visual mechanism. The visual system is faced with the problem of parsing the visual input stream into objects that are continuous in time. To the extent that one object is disrupted for a significant period of time, a new perceptual representation will be required upon its reappearance. The creation of a new perceptual object representation plays a causal role both in capturing attention and in assigning correspondence matches in apparent motion perception.

Finally, I introduced the idea that amodal integration of momentarily occluded visual objects can occur through time just as amodal completion of partly occluded visual objects can occur across space. Amodal completion and amodal integration are two ways that perceptual organization mechanisms recover spatiotemporal coherence and continuity from fragmented image data.

These studies begin to provide some insights into the interaction between the middle-vision operations of perceptual organization and attention: organizational mechanisms determine what the objects are that attention can select. That our visual systems are acutely attuned to perceptual coherence and discontinuity should not be surprising. Visual systems evolved, after all, to provide us with information about significant events in the local environment, and the appearance, continuity, and disappearance of objects are defining aspects of the physical world. Further explication of this interaction remains an important challenge for further research.

## Acknowledgments

Preparation of this chapter, and much of the research described in it, was supported by National Institute of Mental Health grant R01-MH43924 and by Air Force Office of Scientific Research grant 92-J-0186 to S. Yantis. Steven Yantis can be reached via e-mail at yantis@jhu.edu.

## Notes

1 Yantis and Johnson (1990) considered the possibility that the pattern of response times in this task reflect a parallel, capacity-limited search in which perceptual sampling rate may vary from one element to the next, and the onset element enjoys a substantially greater sampling rate than do the no- onset elements. This model is difficult to distinguish from a serial self-terminating search model.

2 In order to create a shape defined by binocular disparity, it was necessary to move some of the dots in the stimulus location containing the new object. To eliminate this local motion signal, which could potentially contribute to attentional capture, dot locations were moved throughout the display at the moment the new object appeared.

3 Amodal integration is similar in some respects to what Michotte et al. (1964/ 1991) referred to as "tunneling." Tunneling can occur when subjects view displays in which a moving object (call it object 1) passes behind an occluding surface, and object 2 emerges from the other side. If object 1 is experienced as being the same as object 2, then tunneling is said to have occurred.

4 A discussion with Irvin Rock in the spring of 1993 inspired the experiments described in Yantis (1995), and I gratefully acknowledge his contribution to the work.

# References

Bacon, W.F., & Egeth, H.E. (1994). Overriding stimulus-driven attentional capture. *Perception & Psychophysics, 55*, 485–496.

Breitmeyer, B.G., & Ganz, L. (1976). Implications of sustained and transient channels for theories of visual pattern masking, saccadic suppression, and information processing. *Psychological Review, 83*, 1–36.

Breitmeyer, B.G., & Ritter, A. (1986a). The role of visual pattern persistence in bistable stroboscopic motion. *Vision Research, 26*, 1801–1806.

Breitmeyer, B.G., & Ritter, A. (1986b). Visual persistence and the effect of eccentric viewing, element size, and frame duration on bistable stroboscopic motion percepts. *Perception & Psychophysics, 39*, 275–280.

Duncan, J., & Humphreys, G.W. (1989). Visual search and stimulus similarity. *Psychological Review, 96*, 433–458.

Enns, J.T., & Rensink, R.A. (in press). An object completion process in early vision. In A.G. Gale (Ed.), *Visual Search III*. London: Taylor & Francis.

Folk, C.L., & Annett, S. (1994). Do locally defined feature discontinuities capture attention? *Perception & Psychophysics, 56*, 277–287.

Folk, C.L, Remington, R.W., & Johnston, J.C. (1992). Involuntary convert orienting is contingent on attentional control settings. *Journal of Experimental Psychology: Human Perception & Performance, 18*, 1030–1044.

Folk, C.L, Remington, R.W., & Johnston, J.C. (1993). Contingent attentional capture: A reply to Yantis (1993). *Journal of Experimental Psychology: Human Perception & Performance, 19*, 682–685.

Gibson, B.S. (1996). Visual quality and attentional capture: A challenge to the special role of abrupt onsets. *Journal of Experimental Psychology: Human Perception & Performance, 22*, 1496–1504.

He, Z.J., & Nakayama, K. (1992). Surfaces versus features in visual search. *Nature, 359*, 231–233.

He, Z.J., & Nakayama, K. (1994). Perceived surface shape not features determines correspondence strength in apparent motion. *Vision Research, 34*, 2125–2135.

Hillstrom, A.P., & Yantis, S. (1994). Visual motion and attentional capture. *Perception & Psychophysics, 55*, 399–411.

Jonides, J., & Yantis, S. (1988). Uniqueness of abrupt visual onset in capturing attention. *Perception & Psychophysics, 43*, 346–354.

Kellman, P.J., & Shipley, T.F. (1991). A theory of visual interpolation in object perception. *Cognitive Psychology, 23*, 141–221.

Kellman, P.J., & Shipley, T.F. (1992). Perceiving objects across gaps in space and time. *Current Directions in Psychological Science, 1*, 193–199.

Koffka, K. (1935). *Principles of Gestalt psychology*. New York: Harcourt Brace.

Lennie, P., Trevarthen, C., Van Essen, D., & Wässle, H. (1990). Parallel processing of visual information. In L. Spillmann and J.S. Werner (Eds.), *Visual perception: The neurophysiological foundations* (pp. 103–128). San Diego, CA: Academic Press.

Michotte, A., Thinès, G., & Crabbé, G. (1964/1991). Amodal completion of perceptual structures (E. Miles & T.R. Miles, Trans.). In G. Thinès, A. Costall, & G. Butterworth (Eds.), *Michotte's experimental phenomenology of perception* (pp. 140–167). Hillsdale, NJ: Erlbaum.

Nakayama, K., He, Z.J., & Shimojo, S. (1995). Visual surface representation: A critical link between lower-level and higher-level vision. In S.M. Kosslyn and D.N. Osherson (Eds.), *Invitation to cognitive science* (pp. 1–70). Cambridge, MA: MIT Press.

Palmer, S., & Rock, I. (1994). Rethinking perceptual organization: The role of uniform connectedness. *Psychonomic Bulletin & Review, 1*, 29–55.

Pashler, H. (1988). Cross-dimensional interaction and texture segregation. *Perception & Psychophysics, 43*, 307–318.

Sekuler, A.B., & Palmer, S.E (1992). Perception of partly occluded objects: A microgenetic analysis. *Journal of Experimental Psychology: General, 121*, 95–111.

Shimojo, S., & Nakayama, K. (1990). Amodal representation of occluded surfaces: Role of invisible stimuli in apparent motion correspondence. *Perception, 19*, 285–299.

Sigman, E., & Rock, I. (1974). Stroboscopic movement based on perceptual intelligence. *Perception, 3*, 9–28.

Ternus, J. (1926/1939). The problem of phenomenal identity. In W.D. Ellis (Ed. and Trans.), *A source book of Gestalt psychology* (pp. 149–160). New York: Harcourt Brace.

Theeuwes, J. (1992). Perceptual selectivity for color and form. *Perception & Psychophysics, 51*, 599–606.

Todd, S., & Kramer, A.F. (1994). Attentional misguidance in visual search. *Perception & Psychophysics, 56*, 198–210.

Todd, J.T., & Van Gelder, P. (1979). Implications of a transient-sustained dichotomy for the measurement of human performance. *Journal of Experimental Psychology: Human Perception & Performance, 5*, 625–638.

Tsotsos, J. (1990). Analyzing vision at the complexity level. *Behavioral & Brain Sciences, 13*, 423–445.

Wertheimer, M. (1912). Experimentelle Studien über das Sehen von Bewegung. *Zeitschrift für Psychologie, 61*, 161–265.

Yantis, S. (1993). Stimulus-driven attentional capture. *Current Directions in Psychological Science, 2*, 156–161.

Yantis, S. (1993). Stimulus-driven attentional capture and attentional control settings. *Journal of Experimental Psychology: Human Perception & Performance, 19*, 676–681.

Yantis, S. (1995). Perceived continuity of occluded visual objects. *Psychological Science, 6*, 182–186.

Yantis, S., & Egeth, H.E. (1994). Visual salience and stimulus-driven attentional capture. *Investigative Ophthalmology & Visual Science, 35*, 1619.

Yantis, S., & Gibson, B.S. (1994). Object continuity in motion perception and attention. Special Issue on Visual Attention, *Canadian Journal of Experimental Psychology, 48,* 182–204.

Yantis, S., & Hillstrom, A.P. (1994). Stimulus-driven attentional capture: Evidence from equiluminant visual objects. *Journal of Experimental Psychology: Human Perception & Performance, 20,* 95–107.

Yantis, S., & Johnson, D.N. (1990). Mechanisms of attentional priority. *Journal of Experimental Psychology: Human Perception and Performance, 16,* 812–825.

Yantis, S., & Jones, E. (1991). Mechanisms of attentional selection: Temporally modulated priority tags. *Perception & Psychophysics, 50,* 166–178.

Yantis, S., & Jonides, J. (1984). Abrupt visual onsets and selective attention: Evidence from visual search. *Journal of Experimental Psychology: Human Perception & Performance, 10,* 601–621.

Yantis, S., & Jonides, J. (1990). Abrupt visual onsets and selective attention: Voluntary versus automatic allocation. *Journal of Experimental Psychology: Human Perception & Performance, 16,* 121–134.

Yantis, S., & Jonides, J. (1996). Attentional capture by abrupt onsets: New perceptual objects or visual masking. *Journal of Experimental Psychology: Human Perception & Performance, 22,* 1505–1513.

# 8

## Visual Indexes in Spatial Vision and Imagery

### Zenon Pylyshyn

It is a truism that the visual system does some things in parallel and some things serially. The eye moves in rapid saccades several times each second. The centre of the fovea is the centre of our gaze and provides a focus of attention. In addition, attention can also move independently of eye movements. Many people (e.g., Posner, 1980) have shown that a region of most efficient processing can be scanned across the visual field at about 100 degrees / second when the eye is fixated (published estimates run from 30 to 250 deg / sec). Much research has been done on this "covert attention movement." The assumption has generally been made that such focal attention is confined to a contiguous region, possibly expandable in size, that must be scanned over the display from place to place.

There are two good reasons why the visual system should have such a locus of maximum resource allocation. The first is that the visual system has a limited information capacity at some level so some selection must occur. Various people (e.g., Tsotsos et al., 1995) have argued for the importance of a serial component in visual processing simply from computational complexity considerations. The second reason is that there may be patterns that, in principle, require serial scanning for their evaluation, as suggested by the Perceptron Theorems of Minsky and Papert (1969). Such a process of serial evaluation of patterns is referred to by Ullman as a "visual routine" (Ullman, 1984).

Notice that a serial process that scans the display cannot by itself execute a visual routine. For example, it is not possible to determine, by scanning alone, whether a set of points is collinear or whether a given point is inside a closed curve. That is because the process has to be told which objects are being referred to. The process also has to have a way to determine which objects it has already visited and which objects to visit next. Like the Sesame Street lessons in counting, a critical part of the process is remembering which items have already been counted!

A number of people, including Ullman (1984) and Yantis and Jonides (1984), have referred to this process of keeping track of objects as "marking." While the metaphor of marking objects is tempting, it is also misleading since we cannot literally mark the display. This terminology suggests, instead, that we have a geostable (or allostable) icon somewhere in our heads where we can place a marker. As I have argued elsewhere (Pylyshyn, 1981), there are many reasons to refrain from hypothesizing such a metrical iconic display in the head. Consequently, over the past decade we have developed an alternative view of how places in the visual field are marked or, to use our terminology, "indexed." In the remainder of this paper, I will briefly summarize the theory of indexes (sometimes referred to, for purely historical reasons, as FINST indexes) and will sketch a variety of empirical evidence to support the general idea (for a more detailed exposition, see Pylyshyn, 1989, 1994a; Pylyshyn et al., 1994). This theory is programmatic, however, and incomplete in many important respects. This is why we are continuing our research on it. On the other hand, it is hard to see how this growing body of evidence can be assessed without a theory of indexes or something like it.

## A Theory of Visual Indexes

According to the theory, an early, preattentive stage in visual perception involves a resource-limited mechanism for individuating a small number (four to six) of visual tokens. We follow the precedent set by Treisman (1988) and others, and refer to these visual tokens as "objects" in order to emphasize that what are indexed are temporally enduring entities identified in terms of their historical continuity.

Individuating is more primitive than encoding either the properties of the objects of their location in the visual field. Individuating implies that the objects are selected or distinguished from one another as discrete entities with a historical continuity. Once individuated, each object maintains its identity over time and continues to be identified as the "same" object despite changes in its location and possibly other properties as well. Objects are individuated by being indexed in the same sense that a book in a library or a data structure in a computer might be indexed: the index serves as a mechanism by which subsequent operations can access the object. A small number of objects is selected (presumably by virtue of possessing certain salient properties) and indexed in order to make possible the following further functions.

(1) Subsequent stages of the visual system have the capacity to reference the indexed objects – say, for purposes of determining their individual and relational properties. By hypothesis, only indexed objects can be bound to arguments of visual routines and consequently evaluated or otherwise operated on. (2) An index remains attached to its object as the object changes its retinal location or other properties, allow-

ing the object to be tracked *qua* individual object. (3) Indexed objects can be interrogated (or "strobed") without the necessity of first locating them through some form of search. Consequently, once they have been indexed, any set of objects can be separated functionally from the rest of the display without reference to their properties or locations. (4) Motor programs, like visual routines, also require that their arguments be bound. Consequently, only indexed objects can be the targets of such visually controlled motor actions as eye movements or ballistic reaching.

As a result of having assigned indexes to salient visual objects, the cognitive system can, in effect tag objects in the scene, and attach stored information to these objects. By linking stored information with indexes that point to the objects in the scene to which this information refers, the visual system can use access memory and visually present information with equal ease. And it can use one to locate the other. In this way the scene can be thought of as an extension of memory. It can be interrogated for such things as the relative location of remembered objects and for other properties of the scene that have not yet been "noticed" or encoded. As others have noted, this provides a way to reduce the load on internal visual storage (Ballard, Hayhoe, Pook, & Rao, in press; O'Regan, 1992). Even more important, it may no longer be necessary for the perceptual representation itself to have metrical or pictorial properties (as assumed by Kosslyn, 1994) since these can be extracted from the scene as needed. Rather, the percept can be an incrementally evolving schema, with the following additional feature: by maintaining links to actual objects in the scene, indexes help to "situate" or "embody" vision. This allows the cognitive system to carry out a variety of operations on the scene, including scanning the scene and operating on it using what Ballard et al. (in press) call a "deictic strategy." This strategy minimizes memory load when the cognitive system is operating on a display. The strategy relies on indexes to get back to where the information is located at the time it is actually needed for the task (in the Ballard et al. case, this is the task of copying a layout of colored boxes).

## *How Does Indexing Differ from Focal Attention?*

Since indexes and focal attention both provide a way to allocate processing resources to an object in the visual field, questions arise about how they differ. These are the main points of difference, according to the theory.

First, several indexes can be assigned and are available in parallel. This does not mean that they will necessarily be accessed in parallel – only that they are simultaneously available for further processing.

Moreover, whether or not they remain assigned indefinitely without being reactivated by being visited by focal attention is not known, though there is reason to believe that maintenance of indexes is not automatic and preattentive.

Second, according to the current assumptions of the theory of visual indexing, indexes can be assigned in one of two ways. One is autonomously, by the occurrence of a visual event such as the onset of a new object in the visual field (but perhaps also by other transients such as luminance changes). The other is by a deliberate cognitive act of assignment of an index to an object currently under scrutiny by focal attention. Unitary focal attention, by contrast, can be assigned either by scanning the display along a continuous path or by skipping to an object that has already been indexed.

Third, indexes are object-based. Therefore, they stick with the object to which they are assigned as the object moves. This is what is meant by individuating an object: the continuity of the object over time is automatically maintained by the index, as is its distinctiveness from other objects.

Fourth, indexes provide for a direct access to the indexed object, so these objects do not have to be searched for and located first. Consequently, the relative distance between objects does not matter: a nearby object can be accessed just as quickly as one that is removed from the one currently being processed.

### Summary: Why Do We Need Indexes?

We have already suggested some general reasons for our having hypothesized a mechanism for assigning and maintaining visual indexes. Here we summarize the arguments presented in more detail elsewhere (Pylyshyn, 1985; Pylyshyn et al. 1994).

We need indexes in order control where to move focal attention. Unitary focal attention need not be scanned around at random. It is usually directed to loci of interest or relevance to the task at hand. Consequently, there must be some way to specify where such focal attention should move.

We need indexes to execute visual routines such as those that compute whether an item is inside a closed curve or whether $n$ objects are collinear. By hypothesis, whenever we evaluate an $n$-place visual predicate we must first bind all $n$ of its arguments to appropriate visual objects. Indexes provide just such a variable-binding mechanism.

We need to situate vision in the world so we can act on the basis of what we see. The problem here is apparent when we note that one can point to or reach for objects without feedback as to where our hand is in relation to the object (Merton, 1961). This means that there must be a cross-modality binding of places: the visual system must have a way to inform the motor system – which necessarily operates in a different coordinate system – where things are. Although this problem is far from solved, the role of indexes seems essential unless one is prepared to hypothesize a common global 3D coordinate frame to represent locations, which is far too strong a requirement.

Recently, a great deal of evidence has been uncovered showing that our visual memory is much more limited that our phenomenology suggests. We retain very little detailed information from one fixation to another unless we have reason to notice particular features because they are relevant to our task. It appears, rather, that we typically use the world itself as a continuing source of information about the visual scene. This, however, requires a way to merge information in memory with information in the scene. Indexes are such a mechanism, since they provide a way to keep track of preattentively salient places so that memory information can be bound to them.

Finally, we need indexes in order to avoid assuming a 2D metrical display in the head. Mental displays have often been hypothesized precisely in order to account for such things as visual stability and the ability to superimpose visual information in memory on visual information in the scene (see Kosslyn, 1994, but see the review in Pylyshyn, 1994b). We shall argue that these abilities can be accounted for to a large extent without the highly undesirable assumption that there is a 2D display in the brain.

## Empirical Support for Indexes

The idea of a simple indexing mechanism has turned out to provide a rich source of empirical predictions. It also has far-reaching implications for explaining a wide range of phenomena. The following is a sample of some of our recent findings, summarized here to illustrate the range of empirical phenomena that can be handled by this simple theoretical apparatus. Many additional lines of investigation have also been conducted in our laboratory and elsewhere, but are not reported here. These include parametric investigations of multiple-object tracking (Mckeever, 1991; Sears, in press), studies relating indexing to multi-locus inhibition-of-return as well as to attentional enhancement (Sears, 1995; Wright, 1994; Wright & Richard, in press), studies relating indexing to such visual routines as those for detecting the inside-outside relation and collinearity (as suggested in Pylyshyn, 1989), applications to the explanation of apparent motion (Dawson & Pylyshyn, 1989), as well as preliminary studies of spatial indexing in the auditory modality. The question of how the indexing mechanism might be implemented, both computationally and neurophysiologically, also continues to be a major research pursuit (Acton, 1993; Acton & Eagleson, 1993; Eagleson & Pylyshyn, 1991).

## Multiple Precuing of Locations
## in Search Tasks

Search tasks provide a nice demonstration of the use of indexes to control which items are examined or queried in visual search tasks. In a series of studies, Jacquie Burkell and I showed that sudden-onset location cues could be used to control search so that only the precued locations are visited during the course of the search (Burkell & Pylyshyn, 1996). This is what we would expect if onset cues draw indexes and indexes can be used to determine where to carry out processing. In these studies, a number of placeholders (12 to 24) consisting of black Xs, appeared on the screen for some period of time (at least one second). Then an additional three to five placeholders (the late-onset items) were displayed. After 100 ms, one of the segments of each X disappeared and the remaining segment changed color, producing a display of right-oblique and left-oblique lines in either green or red. The entire display had exemplars of all four combinations of color and orientation. The subject's task was to say whether the display contained a pre-specified item type (say, a right-oblique green line). In most studies there was only one of these targets in the display. As expected, the target was detected more rapidly when it was at a location precued by a late-onset cue. There were, however, two additional findings that are even more relevant to the indexing theory. These depend on the fact that we manipulated the nature of the precued subset in certain ways, to be explained below.

It is well known that when subjects try to find a target that differs from all nontargets by a single feature (e.g., it is the only red line or the only right-oblique line in the display), then they are not only faster overall at locating the target, but the search rate is also very fast (i.e., response time increases very little as the number of nontargets is increased – about 10 to 15 ms per item). This is called a "simple feature" search. By contrast, when the target differs from some nontargets by one feature and from other nontargets by another feature, so that what makes the target distinctive is the combination of two or more features, then it takes longer to locate the target, and the search rate is also slower (it takes additional time for each added nontarget in the display – about 40 to 60 ms in our case). This is called a "conjunction feature" search. As mentioned above, the displays in the present experiments typically contained all four types of items, so the displays were always of the conjunction-feature type. However, the subset that was precued by late-onset placeholders could be either a simple- or a conjunction-feature search set. So the critical question here is whether the feature type of the subset is the determining factor in the search. We found clear evidence that it is. Here are the two most relevant findings.

First, when the precued subset consisted of elements that differed from the target by a single feature, search had the same pattern as with simple-feature searches. That is, we observed shorter response time and faster search rate. However, when the precued subset consisted of some nontargets that differed from the target in one of the features and some nontargets that differed in the other feature, then search rate was much slower. This suggests that the precued subset was being selected and separated from the rest of the display. It provides evidence that indexes, assigned to sudden-onset placeholders, can be used to control which items are visited in a visual search task.

Second, even more relevant to the indexing thesis was the additional finding that when we systematically increased the distance between precued items (or their dispersion) there was *no* decrease in search rate. It seems that the spatial dispersion of the items does not affect the time it takes to examine them, even when the examination appears to be serial (e.g., the time increases linearly as the number of nontargets increases). This is precisely what one would expect if, as we predict, the cued items are indexed and indexes can be used to access the items without spatial scanning.

## Parallel Tracking of Multiple Targets

One basic assumption of the theory is that a small number of "sticky" index pointers can be assigned preattentively to primitive visual objects and will continue to be assigned to the same object as the object moves on the retina. This hypothesis has been tested directly using a multiple-target tracking paradigm.

In these studies, subjects were shown a screen containing 12 to 24 simple identical objects (plus signs, figure-8s) that moved in unpredictable ways without colliding (because of a simulated barrier or a linear or distance-squared "force field" between them, depending on the study). A subset of these objects was briefly rendered distinct by flashing them on and off a few times. The subjects' task was to keep track of this subset of points. At some later time in the experiment an object was flashed on the screen. The subjects' task was to indicate whether the flash occurred on one of the tracked objects or one of the others (or in some cases, on neither).

The initial Pylyshyn and Storm (1988) studies showed clearly that subjects can indeed track up to five independently moving identical objects. The parameters of these experiments were such that tracking could not have been accomplished using a serial strategy in which attention is scanned to each point in turn, updating its stored location each time it is visited, until the probe event occurs. Recently, a large number of additional studies in our laboratory (McKeever, 1991; Sears,

1991) and elsewhere (Intriligator & Cavanagh, 1992; Yantis, 1992; as well as personal communications from A. Treisman and B. Julesz, 1995) have replicated these results, confirming that subjects can successfully track independently moving objects in parallel. Some of these studies carefully controlled for guessing strategies and also demonstrated qualitatively different patterns of performance than would be predicted by any reasonable serial-scanning algorithms we have considered. The results also showed that a zoom-lens model of attention (Eriksen & St. James, 1986; Eriksen & Yeh, 1985) would not account for the data. Performance in detecting changes to elements located inside the convex hull outline of the set of targets was no better than performance on elements outside this region, as would be expected if the area of attention were simply widened or shaped to conform to an appropriate outline (Sears & Pylyshyn, in press). Intriligator and Cavanagh (1992) also reported no spread of attention in their tracking study.

## Subitizing

Other studies have shown the power of this framework to account for a large class of empirical phenomena in which simple visual objects are rapidly and preattentively individuated. One of these is subitizing, a phenomenon whereby the cardinality of sets of less than about four visual features can be ascertained very rapidly (about 60 ms per feature). We have shown (Trick, 1990, 1991; Trick & Pylyshyn, 1993, 1994a, 1994b) that subitizing does not occur when preattentive individuation is prevented (e.g., targets defined by conjunctions of features, or other properties that require focal attention, cannot be subitized). We have also shown that in determining the number of objects in a display, the spatial distribution of the objects is unimportant in the subitizing range but critical in the counting ($n > 4$) range, and that precuing the locations of objects (with either valid or invalid location cues) makes little difference to subitizing performance (Trick & Pylyshyn, 1993, 1994b). According to the indexing hypothesis, small numbers of salient, locally distinct points are indexed preattentively and in parallel. Hence, their cardinality can be determined by counting the number of active indexes without having to spatially scan focal attention over the display. In any case, these studies show that a preattentive stage of item individuation is critical for subitizing. Such a stage is postulated for entirely independent reasons by the theory. Moreover, Simon and Vaishnavi (1996) used an afterimage display to show that even when indefinite time is available for counting, the subitizing limit remains. They claim that this supports the contention that it is not the time available for counting that is the source of limitation, but the availability of resources for individuating items.

## *Attention-Dependent Line-Motion Illusion*

Another interesting phenomenon, apparently dependent on focal attention, was demonstrated by Hikosaka, Miyauchi, and Shimojo (1993). They showed that when attention is focused on a particular point in the visual field, a line displayed between that point and another (unattended) point appears to grow away from the point of focal attention. This phenomenon provides another way to test the hypothesis of a preattentive multiple-locus indexing mechanism. In a series of studies, Schmidt, Fisher, and Pylyshyn (in press) showed that the illusion could be induced by the late onset of up to six to seven noncontiguous items among a set of 12. A line displayed between any of the other pairs of points, or between a point and an unfilled location, does not show the illusion. So once again we have an attention-like phenomenon occurring simultaneously at several places in a visual scene. Whether this means that the line-motion illusion requires only preattentive indexing, or whether it means that attention can be rapidly shifted to each of the points in turn, is unknown. However, the result is consistent with our earlier reported subset-selection phenomenon. In the present case, the onset objects are preselected, and this in itself appears to be enough to cause the line-motion illusion to occur at any of the preselected objects.

## Mental Images, Indexes, and Visual Stability

The phenomenologies of both mental imagery and of vision are extremely misleading from the perspective of constructing an information-processing theory of the underlying representation and process. I have already commented extensively on the problems raised by the intuitive assumption that mental imagery involves the examination of a two-dimensional (2-D) display projected on some rigid internal surface (or at least on a surface that ensures that the display obeys local Euclidean properties). I will not rehearse this argument here. But I do want to make two comments. One is that studies in which mental images are projected onto visual perception involve a special case of the use of imagery, inasmuch as the physical stimulus can provide, in this case, some of the properties attributed to the image medium itself. So long as we have a way to link objects in our imaginal representation to objects in the visual field, the mental representations can inherit some of the properties of real rigid surfaces. The other comment is that, though it may not always be recognized, some of the very same issues that arise in understanding the nature of mental images actually arise in vision itself. This is particularly true when vision is thought to involve the construction of an iconic representation whose extent goes beyond the fovea and which is constructed by superimposing information from individual fixations as the eye moves about.

## Superposition of Mental Images and Perception

Many studies have purported to show that mental images involve information that is displayed in a 2-D format (I do not pretend that "two-dimensional" is even close to being a well-defined notion – indeed this is part of the problem with the so-called imagery debate; see Pylyshyn, 1994b – I simply use the term roughly the way it is used by its proponents). Some of the more robust findings come from experiments involving superimposing images onto visual perception. For example, Hayes (1973) has shown that anticipating a figure by projecting an image of the correct one enhances its detection. Shepard and Podgorny (1978) have shown that if a spot is displayed on a grid on which a subject imagines a figure, the response times for detecting whether the spot is on or off the figure shows exactly the same pattern that it does when the figure is actually displayed (e.g., faster times for on-figure versus off-figure detection, faster times when the spot is at a corner or vertex of the figure, etc.). Farah (1989) has shown that detection sensitivity for light flashes is greater for locations *on* an imagined figure than for those *off* that figure. I have argued that all these results can be explained more simply by assuming that indexes can be assigned to relevant objects in the display, including regions such as columns and rows of the grid. This assignment would serve to indicate where various "imagined" objects would fall on the scene, and hence where to direct focal attention. Thus, if we can think that this column (where the locative *this* refers to a particular indexed column) is where the vertical stroke of the imagined letter will be placed, then we can assign focal attention to those parts of the pattern. Indeed, in one condition of her experiment, Farah (1989) simply asked subjects to focus their attention on the appropriate parts of the grid rather than imagine a figure projected on them, and she obtained exactly the same results.

Another well-known result is also easily understood in terms of indexes assigned to objects in an actual display. This is the "mental scanning" result of Kosslyn, Ball, and Reiser (1978), in which it was found that the time it takes to switch attention from one point in an image to another is a linear function of the physical distance in the imagined situation (typically a memorized map). We have shown that this phenomenon disappears when the experimental demands are changed (e.g., when subjects are not asked to imagine that they are in a real situation of looking at a display in which they have to scan from place to place) (Pylyshyn, 1981). But the scanning result appears to be robust when done in image-projection mode (i.e., when the experiment is done in the light, and subjects have to imagine the map while looking at some visual display). But in this case, I have argued, if subjects have the capability to index a number of objects (or even bits of text on features) in the real scene, and to link their representations of the recalled objects to those locations, then they can of course scan their attention, and even their eyes, from place to place on the display (Pylyshyn, 1989). Having a real display with objects to which mental representations can be bound ensures that all relative distance and pattern properties entailed by the recalled information hold – including some inferred or previously unnoticed properties – because of the physical and geometric properties of the display. For example, suppose we imagine that three places lie on a line (call them $A$, $B$, and $C$). Suppose, further, that we do this while looking at some scene, and that we choose three collinear objects in the scene, and associate or bind the imagined places to the scene objects. In that case, when we scan from imagined object $A$ to imagined object $C$, we are bound to pass over the real location of imagined object $B$ – because of geometrical properties of the physical scene in which $A$, $B$, and $C$ are bound. In the real scene, $B$ does lie on the path from $A$ to $C$. In a purely mental representation, we would have to make use of knowledge that might be stated as the constraint, "If three points $A$, $B$, and $C$ are collinear, in that order, then in travelling from $A$ to $C$ we must pass by $B$." The only alternative is the assumption that there is a brain property that realizes this constraint, and that it is used when we imagine collinear points. Although this is a logical possibility, the facts of cognitive penetrability of geometrical reasoning argue against it in general (but for more on this argument see Pylyshyn, 1981).

Finally, there are a number of other results that are equally amenable to being explained in terms of the indexing mechanisms, including the adaptation of perceptual-motor coordination to imagined locations (Finke, 1979). So long as we can think of an object being located at an indexed point, we can act towards it in ways that may resemble our actions towards real objects located at those places.

## Saccadic Integration and Visual Stability

The phenomenology of visual perception suggests that we have access to a large vista of a spatially stable scene, extending far beyond the foveal region. It seems as though the percept fills in blind spots and other scotomas, corrects for the rapid drop in resolution and color sensitivity with retinal eccentricity, and combines pictorial information from successive glances into a single, extended, internal image. Yet none of this is objectively true. It can easily been shown that the visual system does not have access to nearly the kind of information we feel is there. Consider just two brief relevant examples to illustrate this point.

First, there is good evidence to suggest that far less information is extracted from individual glances than we feel is the case, based on our phenomenal experience, unless the information is relevant to some task at hand. Several researchers have shown that surprisingly little qualitative information is retained between saccades (e.g., Irvin, 1993; Irwin, McConkie, Carlson-Radvansky, & Currie, 1994; McKonkie & Currie, 1995). Moreover, the idea that pictorial information from successive glances is superimposed onto a master-image has been pretty generally discredited (Bridgeman, van der Heijden, & Velichkovsky, 1994; Intraub, Mangels, & Bender, 1992; Irwin, 1993; O'Regan, 1992).

Second, there is good reason to believe that information that is currently not on the fovea is stored in a different form from foveal information. Many of the signature properties of early vision, such as spontaneous perception of line drawings as three-dimensional and spontaneous reversal of figures, do not arise when part of the figure is off the fovea (Hochberg, 1968). Indeed, the nonfoveal portion of the display differs in many ways from the foveal information and is much more like an abstract visual memory than a continuation of the foveal display. For example, the ability to construct a phenomenal percept from sequentially presented information, such as occurs in an orthoscope (Rock, 1983) or in the sequential presentation of segments taken from different parts of a picture, depends on the memory load of the information not foveally present (Hochberg, 1968).

Many people have recognized the similarity between theories of mental imagery and theories of visual stability. Indeed, Kosslyn (1994) has explicitly argued that one reason for positing a pictorial display for mental imagery is that it is also required in order to explain the stability and temporal continuity of vision. Thus, it is not surprising that the same issues arise. We have already suggested ways in which indexes may play a role in endowing representations underlying mental images with geometrical and metrical properties. Under certain conditions, indexes can also play a crucial role in explaining visual stability and saccadic integration without requiring that we posit an extended pictorial representation. Before discussing how indexes might play a role, consider what the functional requirements are for realizing what we call visual stability. At the very minimum, we need the following.

(1) The visual system must be able to keep track of the individuality of objects independent of their location in the visual field. There are several ways in which this could be done:

(a) The correspondence of items from one fixation to another might be computed by locating distinctive properties or distinctive objects in the successive views and establishing a mapping between them.

(b) The correspondence might arise from a global recalibration that makes use of efferent information. This is the "corollary discharge" view. Although the idea that some sort of extraretinal signals are involved in visual stability is usually associated with the global image assumption, it is in fact independent of this assumption, and it is premature to dismiss it.

(c) Correspondence maintenance for a small number of objects may simply be a result of a primitive preattentive mechanism of the visual system, such as the FINST indexing mechanism. For this to be possible, the indexing mechanism must be capable of operating at very high speed, since saccades are very fast. We shall return to this issue below.

(2) The visual system must be able to connect seen properties with recalled properties in order to integrate them into some sort of global representation. As we have already noted, however, this global representation will not just be an image consisting of superimposed glances. Indeed, the representation will contain abstract visual and also nonvisual information.

(3) The visual system must be able to establish that an object is the same object that was previously viewed, even when eye movements cause the object to leave the visual field briefly and then return. This is one of the most challenging requirements. It is the reason why we have had to posit another type of index, called an *anchor*, which operates in the proprioceptive and motor modalities but which can be crosslinked to visual indexes. Studies of this mechanism are in their infancy, and the properties of this type of index are still unknown (see, however, Pylyshyn, 1989, Table lb).

As mentioned earlier, the amount of information that is carried over from one glance to another is extremely limited. Irwin (1995) has shown that the position of only three to four objects is retained from one fixation to another, and this is most likely to include the position to which the eye is about to saccade. Based on such observations, Irwin, McConkie, Carlson-Radvansky, and Currie (1994) and McKonkie and Currie (1995) have argued that on each fixation, only one significant benchmark is encoded, and on the next fixation a fast parallel search attempts to identify that benchmark, which is then used to calibrate the location in space of other items in that fixation. However, the relocation-by-features idea seems implausible, even if it could be accomplished in the short time available, since it ought to lead to frequent and significant errors when the scene is uniformly textured or otherwise free of unique features. Furthermore, it is not clear how the information from a pair of benchmark objects could be used to calibrate locations of the other items in the scene unless it does so by establishing a mapping between two 2-D displays – a proposal which the authors themselves eschew. The process of transsaccadic integration would be simpler and more reliable if the visual system could keep track of a small number of significant features through the saccade. These tracked features would provide the anchors by which the visual system could integrate schematically encoded perceptual information from fixation to fixation, in a manner suggested by Pylyshyn (1989) and others (e.g., Intraub, Mangels, & Bender, 1992).

This proposal, however, raises the important question of whether indexes can remain assigned during a saccadic eye movement. If index maintenance were based on purely local retinal processes, such as those proposed in the network models of Koch and Ullman (1985) or Acton (1993), it seems implausible that an index could keep tracking an object moving across the retina at up to about 800 deg / sec – even putting aside the problem of saccadic suppression and smearing. The fastest covert attention movement reported in the literature – and even this has been questioned as being too high – is 250 deg / sec (Posner, Nissen, & Ogden, 1978). However, if index maintenance were able to make use of predictive information, such rapid tracking might be possible. There are two main sources of such predictive information. One is extrapolation from portions of the current trajectory, using some sort of adaptive filtering with local data support, as proposed by Eagleson and Pylyshyn (1991). The other is extraretinal information such as efferent and afferent signals associated with the eye movement. The appeal to extraretinal signals has usually been associated with metrical superposition theories of visual stability. As we have already noted, the superposition view has been discredited in recent years. Yet the role of extraretinal information in some aspect of transsaccadic integration has continued to be accepted.

If it can be shown that indexing survives saccadic shifts, it would provide an important mechanism for transsaccadic integration that would be compatible with current evidence on the subject. This question continues to be an open empirical issue that we are currently planning to examine in our laboratory. In particular, we are planning to ask whether the phenomena that we believe demonstrate indexing – such as subset search, multiple object tracking, and subitizing – survive a saccadic eye movement during the part of the process when indexes are keeping track of the critical visual elements.

## Acknowledgments

This research was supported by grants from the Institute for Robotics and Intelligent Systems (Project HMI-1 through the University of Western Ontario) and the Natural Sciences and Engineering Research Council of Canada. It was carried out over the past several years by members of the University of Western Washington research group:

B. Acton, J. Burkell, M. Dawson, R. Eagleson, B. Fisher, P. McKeever, W. Schmidt, C. Sears, R. Storm, L. Trick, and R. Wright. Zenon Pylyshyn can be contacted via e-mail at zenon@ruccs.rutgers.edu.

# References

Acton, B. (1993). *A network model of indexing and attention.* Unpublished Master's Thesis, Department of Electrical Engineering, University of Western Ontario, London, Canada.

Acton, B., & Eagleson, R. (1993). A neural network model of spatial indexing. *Investigative Ophthalmology and Visual Science, 34,* 413.

Ballard, D.H., Hayhoe, M.M., Pook, P.K., & Rao, R.P.N. (in press). Deictic codes for the embodiment of cognition. *Behavioral and Brain Sciences.*

Bridgeman, B., van der Heijden, A.H.C., & Velichkovsky, B.M. (1994). A theory of visual stability across saccadic eye movements. *Behavioral & Brain Sciences, 17,* 247–292.

Burkell, J.A., & Pylyshyn, Z. (in press). Searching through selected subsets of visual displays: A test of the FINST indexing hypothesis. Submitted for publication. *Spatial Vision.*

Cavanagh, P. (1990). Pursuing moving objects with attention. In the *Proceedings of the 12th Annual Meeting of the Cognitive Science Society* (pp. 1046–1047). Hillsdale, NJ: Erlbaum.

Dawson, M.R.W., & Pylyshyn, Z. (1989). Natural constraints in apparent motion. In Z.W. Pylyshyn (Ed.), *Computational processes in human vision: An interdisciplinary perspective.* Norwood, NJ: Ablex.

Eagleson, R., & Pylyshyn, Z. (1991). *The role of indexing and tracking in visual motion perception.* Paper presented at the Conference on Spatial Vision in Humans and Robots, York University, Toronto, Canada.

Eriksen, C.W., & St. James, J.D. (1986). Visual attention within and around the field of focal attention: A zoom lens model. *Perception & Psychophysics, 40,* 225–240.

Eriksen, C.W., & Yeh, Y. (1985). Allocation of attention in the visual field. *Journal of Experimental Psychology: Human Perception & Performance, 11,* 583–597.

Farah, M.J. (1989). Mechanisms of imagery-perception interaction. *Journal of Experimental Psychology: Human Perception & Performance, 15,* 203–211.

Finke, R.A. (1979). The functional equivalence of mental images and errors of movement. *Cognitive Psychology, 11,* 235–264.

Hayes, J.R. (1973). On the function of visual imagery in elementary mathematics. In W.G. Chase (Ed), *Visual information processing.* New York: Academic Press.

Hikosaka, O., Miyauchi, S., & Shimojo, S. (1993). Focal visual attention produces illusory temporal order and motion sensation. *Vision Research, 33,* 1219–1240.

Hochberg, J. (1968). In the mind's eye. In R.N. Haber (Ed.), *Contemporary theory and research in visual perception.* New York: Holt, Rinehart & Winston.

Intraub, H., Mangels, J., & Bender, R. (1992). Looking at pictures but remembering scenes. *Journal of Experimental Psychology: Learning, Memory, & Cognition, 18,* 180–191.

Intriligator, J., & Cavanagh, P. (1992). An object-specific spatial attentional facilitation that does not travel to adjacent spatial locations. *Investigative Ophthalmology and Visual Science, 33,* 2849.

Irwin, D.E. (1993). Perceiving an integrated visual world. In D.E. Meyer & S. Komblum (Eds.), *Attention & Performance, Vol. 14* (pp. 121–143). Cambridge, MA: MIT Press.

Irwin, D.E. (1995). Properties of transsaccadic memory: Implications for scene perception. Paper presented at the Cambridge Basic Research Conference.

Irwin, D.E., McConkie, G.W., Carlson-Radvansky, L.A., & Currie, C. (1994). A localist evaluation solution for visual stability across saccades. *Behavioral & Brain Sciences, 17,* 265–266.

Koch, C., & Ullman, S. (1985). Shifts in selective visual attention: Toward underlying neural circuitry. *Human Neurobiology, 4,* 219–227.

Kosslyn, S.M., Ball, T.M., & Reiser, B.J. (1978). Visual images preserve metrical spatial information: Evidence from studies of image scanning. *Journal of Experimental Psychology: Human Perception & Performance, 4,* 46–60.

Kosslyn, S.M. (1994). *Image and brain.* Cambridge, MA: MIT Press.

McConkie, G.W., & Currie, C. (1995). *Coordinating perception across saccades: The saccade target theory of visual stability.* Paper presented at the Cambridge Basic Research Conference.

McKeever, P. (1991). *Nontarget numerosity and identity maintenance with FINSTs: A two component account of multiple target tracking.* Unpublished Master's Thesis, Department of Psychology, University of Western Ontario, Canada.

Merton, P.A. (1961). The accuracy of directing the eyes and the hand in the dark. *Journal of Physiology, 156,* 555–577.

Minsky, M.L., & Papert, S. (1969). *Perceptrons.* Cambridge, MA: MIT Press.

O'Regan, J.K. (1992). Solving the "real" mysteries of visual perception: The world as an outside memory. *Canadian Journal of Psychology, 46,* 461–488.

Posner, M.I., Nissen, M.J., & Ogden, W.C. (1978). Attended and unattended processing modes: The role of set for spatial location. In H.L. Pick & I.J. Saltzman (Eds.), *Modes of perceiving and processing information.* Hillsdale, NJ: Erlbaum.

Posner, M.I. (1980). Orienting of attention. *Quarterly Journal of Experimental Psychology, 32,* 3–25.

Pylyshyn, Z. (1981). The imagery debate: Analogue media versus tacit knowledge. *Psychological Review, 88,* 16–45.

Pylyshyn, Z. (1989). The role of location indexes in spatial perception: A sketch of the FINST spatial-index model. *Cognition, 32,* 65–97.

Pylyshyn, Z. (1994a). Some primitive mechanisms of spatial attention. *Cognition, 50,* 363–384.

Pylyshyn, Z. (1994b). Mental Pictures on the brain: Review of "Image and Brain" by S. Kosslyn. *Nature, 372,* 289–290.

Pylyshyn, Z., Burkell, J., Fisher, B., Sears, C., Schmidt, W., & Trick, L. (1994). Multiple parallel access in visual attention. *Canadian Journal of Experimental Psychology, 48,* 260–283.

Pylyshyn, Z., & Storm, R.W. (1988). Tracking multiple independent targets: Evidence for a parallel tracking mechanism. *Spatial Vision, 3,* 1–19.

Rock, I. (1983). *The logic of perception.* Cambridge, MA: MIT Press.

Schmidt, W.C., Fisher, B.D., & Pylyshyn, Z. (in press). Multiple location access in vision: Evidence from illusory line-motion. *Journal of Experimental Psychology: Human Perception & Performance.*

Sears, C. (1991). *Spatial indexing and information processing at multiple locations in the visual field.* Unpublished Master's Thesis, Department of Psychology, University of Western Ontario, London, Canada.

Sears, C. (1995). *Inhibition of return of visual attention and visual indexing.* Unpublished Doctoral Dissertation, Department of Psychology, University of Western Ontario, London, Canada.

Sears, C., & Pylyshyn, Z. (in press). Multiple object tracking and attentional processing. *Canadian Journal of Experimental Psychology.*

Shepard, R.N., & Podgorny, P. (1978). Cognitive processes that resemble perceptual processes. In W.K. Estes (Ed.), *Handbook of learning and cognitive processes (Vol 5).* Hillsdale, NJ: Erlbaum.

Simon, T., & Vaishnavi, S. (1996). Subitizing and counting depend on different attentional mechanisms: Evidence from visual ennumeration in afterimages. *Perception & Psychophysics, 58,* 915–926.

Treisman, A. (1988). Features and objects. *Quarterly Journal of Experimental Psychology, 40A,* 201–237.

Trick, L. (1990). *Subitizing and counting.* Paper presented at the annual meeting of the Canadian Psychological Association, Ottawa.

Trick, L. (1991). Three theories of enumeration that won't work and why, and then one that will: Subitizing, counting and spatial attention. In J. Campbell (Ed.), *Nature and origins of mathematical abilities.* New York: Elsevier Press.

Trick, L., & Pylyshyn, Z. (1993). What enumeration studies can show us about spatial attention: Evidence for limited capacity preattentive processing. *Journal of Experimental Psychology: Human Perception & Performance, 19,* 331–351.

Trick, L., & Pylyshyn, Z. (1994a). Why are small and large numbers enumerated differently? A limited capacity preattentive stage in vision. *Psychological Review, 101,* 1–23.

Trick, L., & Pylyshyn, Z. (1994b). Cueing and counting: Does the position of the attentional focus affect enumeration? *Visual Cognition, 1,* 67–100.

Tsotsos, J.K., Culhane, S., Wai, W., Lai, Y., Davis, N., & Nuflo, F. (1995). Modeling visual attention via selective tuning. *Artificial Intelligence, 78,* 507–547.

Ullman, S. (1984). Visual routines. *Cognition, 18,* 97–159.

Wright, R.D. (1994). Shifts of visual attention to multiple simultaneous location cues. *Canadian Journal of Experimental Psychology, 48,* 205–217.

Wright, R.D., & Richard, C.M. (in press). Inhibition-of-return at multiple locations in visual space. *Canadian Journal of Experimental Psychology.*

Yantis, S., & Jonides, J. (1984). Abrupt visual onsets and selective attention: Evidence from visual search. *Journal of Experimental Psychology: Human Perception & Performance, 10,* 601–621.

Yantis, S. (1992). Multielement visual tracking: Attention and perceptual organization. *Cognitive Psychology, 24,* 295–340.

# 9

## Cross-Modal Control of
## Attention Shifts

Lawrence M. Ward, John J. McDonald,
and Narly Golestani

The study of the control of visual attention in space is one of the most exciting and rewarding directions of modern cognitive science research, as the other chapters in this book amply demonstrate. However, the modern study of attention began in the auditory domain, and for many years much of what we learned about attention phenomena was learned in the context of processing of simple and complex auditory stimuli. Indeed, the early studies in the control of visual attention made frequent reference to comparable, or noncomparable, phenomena in other modalities, especially audition and touch (e.g., Posner, 1978). Yet by the mid-1980s, researchers' attention had shifted to the visual domain, with dramatic results. These new understandings beg the question of whether similar systems exist in other modalities, and whether the other-modality systems share common operating principles, perhaps even common brain areas, with those involved in the control of visual attention. This chapter summarizes much of what we know about the interaction of auditory and visual attention systems, including quite a bit of previously unpublished research. We conclude that there is indeed deep interaction between the mechanisms that control visual and auditory attention, and argue that a cross-modal approach promises a different and more generally useful view of attention mechanisms than does study of attention within any single modality.

### Control of Visual Attention Shifts

The chapter of this book by Wright and Ward ("The Control of Visual Attention") summarizes most of the behavioural results on visual attention relevant to this chapter. Here we will mention only a few important facts and briefly describe one model of how these phenomena might arise.

Visual attention is under both stimulus-driven (often called "exogenous") and goal-driven (often called "engodenous") control. An uninformative (only signals the target's location by chance) abrupt-onset visual stimulus (a "cue") appears to cause a momentary, involuntary, stimulus-driven orienting of attention to its location in space. If a subsequent target stimulus appears at or near that location, detection, localization, and discrimination responses regarding that target are facilitated relative to those to a target appearing at a different location in space. Both speed and accuracy of responding are affected. Theoretically, responding is facilitated when attention is aligned with the location of the target in advance because attention is required for the relevant perceptual and cognitive processing (e.g., forming a perceptual object – see Treisman & Gormican, 1988; Wright & Ward, this volume). The facilitative effect of such a cue builds up to a maximum over a time period (cue-target onset asynchrony or CTOA) of about 100 to 150 ms, and then declines rapidly. Under many conditions, a complementary effect, termed "inhibition of return," is seen at longer CTOAs (up to 1 sec or more) such that responding to targets at the cued location is inhibited relative to that at uncued locations.

Humans are also able to use a symbolic cue (a stimulus that indicates where a target stimulus is likely to occur) to implement goal-driven shifts of attention to a visual locus. When such a symbolic cue, such as an arrow, is followed by a target at or near the indicated location, processing of that target is facilitated relative to that of a target at an uncued location, both in speed and in accuracy. Since the observer must first interpret the symbolic cue, and then shift attention to the cued location, the time course of goal-driven attention shifts is somewhat different than it is for stimulus-driven covert orienting. Full effectiveness of the cue is not attained until about 300 ms after cue onset, and the effects of the cue can be seen for longer than 1 sec after cue presentation. Abrupt-onset stimulus cues that predict target location better than chance (informative cues) also can be used to inform goal-driven attention shifts. Under these conditions, the early time course is similar to that of stimulus-driven shifts, but instead of declining, cue effects are observed to remain near maximum for up to 1 sec, as with goal-driven shifts. Inhibition of return does not occur as a result of goal-driven attention shifts unless a saccadic eye movement was prepared or made (Rafal, Calabresi, Brennan, & Sciolto, 1989). Goal-driven control sometimes may dominate stimulus-driven control, since abrupt-onset stimulus cues can fail to capture attention while a higher priority, symbolically cued location is being processed (Yantis & Jonides, 1990).

Many chapters in this book deal with the neural mechanisms thought to be responsible for the behavioural phenomena described above. Here we briefly describe a model that is broadly consistent with others in this book but resembles most closely that outlined by Wright and Ward (this volume). The attention network we illustrate is, like many others, derived in part from neurophysiological studies of overt orienting. Our goal is not to provide a definitive model of visual attention, but rather to show that a model of this type can aid in the interpretation of the results of cross-modal attention research.

Figure 1 is a diagram of some of the important connections between relevant bran areas involved in the control of visual attention. The superior colliculus (SC), pulvinar nucleus of the thalamus (PN), and posterior parietal cortex (PPC) all contain visually responsive neurons that discharge prior to saccadic eye movements. Converging evidence that these areas are also involved in directing covert visual attention comes from a number of sources. Single-cell recordings from awake monkeys show that visual responses of some PPC neurons vary depending on whether a stimulus in the cell's receptive field is the target of a goal-driven attention shift (or a saccade; see Bushnell, Goldberg, & Robinson, 1981). Stimulus-driven, covert orienting studies with neurologic patients reveal that damage to each of these three brain areas incurs specific attention deficits. Such studies implicate the PPC in the disengagement of attention, the PN in engagement, and the SC in attention shifting (Posner, Peterson, Fox & Raichle, 1988). Further studies with neurologically normal subjects support the SC's involvement in the control of visual attention. The superficial layers of this midbrain structure receive heavy projections from the contralateral retina. Most, but not all, of this input comes from the nasal side of the retina, resulting in a temporal hemifield (nasal hemiretina) bias. Under monocular viewing conditions, both the facilitation provided by a stimulus-cue and the later inhibitory component (inhibition of return) are greater in the temporal hemifield (Rafal, Calabresi, Brennan, & Sciolto, 1989; Rafal, Henik, & Smith, 1991), thus implicating the retinotectal pathway in covert orienting.

Neurophysiological studies with monkeys (e.g., Hikosaka & Wurtz, 1985) have shown that, when gaze is fixated (and attention presumably engaged) on a visual stimulus, the substantia nigra pars reticulata (SNr) tonically inhibits the SC everywhere except for certain fixation cells, thus suppressing saccadic eye movements. This SC suppression may come indirectly from the PPC (Hikosaka, 1991), and may suppress attention shifts in addition to eye movements. In fact, since microstimulation of the SNr fails to elicit eye movements in monkeys, it has already been proposed that the efferent pathway from SNr to SC is involved in the engagement and disengagement of attention rather than in the conveying of saccadic parameters (Jackson & Lees, 1993).

In the model presented in Figure 1, the PPC tonically suppresses activity in the various visual feature maps of V4 (and possibly other

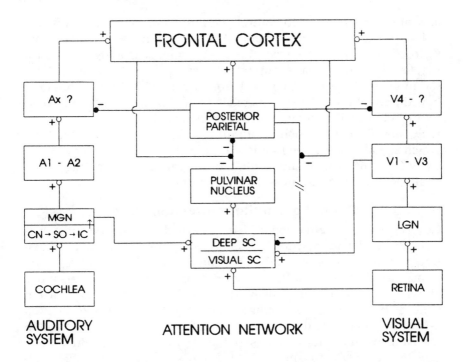

*Figure 1:* Functional interactions between visual and auditory systems and the attention network. Positive (+) and negative (−) connections imply excitatory and inhibitory effects respectively. Note that only a few functionally important connections are shown. SC = superior colliculus, LGN = lateral geniculate nucleus, V1, etc. = areas of visual cortex, CN = cochlear nucleus, SO = superior olive, IC = inferior colliculus, MGN = medial geniculate nucleus, A1, etc. = areas of auditory cortex. The broken connection between posterior parietal and SC indicates other areas (e.g., SNr) possibly mediating the pathway.

visual cortical areas). The PN, a site at which various cortical and subcortical influences on attention may converge (most not shown in Figure 1 but see LaBerge, this volume), suppresses this tonic PPC activity at the currently attended location. This disinhibits all of the visual feature maps at that location, allowing the features at these locations to stand out from those that are not attended, and to be bound together into a single perceptual object. Thus, the PN keeps attention engaged by controlling from which part of the spatiotopic map in the PPC the tonic inhibition of visual processing is suppressed. When an abrupt-onset stimulus cue is presented, the temporary PN suppression of the currently attended location in PPC and the tonic suppression of the SC (by the PPC via the SNr) are both removed (perhaps by the frontal cortex). The former action disengages attention, while the latter disinhibits the SC, allowing a new centre of SC activity (at the location of the abrupt-onset stimulus) to control the output of the PN. Finally, the PN's suppression of PPC and the PPC's suppression of the SC are both restored, the former at the recently cued location, engaging attention at that location, and the latter suppressing any further attention shifts for the moment. It seems likely that frontal cortical areas can influence how the attention network depicted in Figure 1 is deployed in response to an individual's overall and situation-specific goals in interaction with specific environmental stimuli, perhaps through influencing which signals control the location of the PN's suppression of PPC activity. Such influence could result in both goal-driven orienting and in strategic control of stimulus-driven orienting.

## Control of Auditory Attention Shifts

Covert orienting of attention was first clearly demonstrated and extensively studied in the auditory domain. Perhaps its most evocative illustration is in Cherry's "cocktail party phenomenon," in which a person is imagined to be able to attend to various of the ongoing conversations at will without looking away from their conversational partner (Cherry, 1957). Dichotic listening studies of auditory selective attention established many of the most important early facts about attention mechanisms, and informed most of the early theories (e.g., Broadbent, 1958; Moray, 1970; Treisman, 1964). The dissociability of auditory attention from visual fixation, and head and body orientation, are obvious facts. Not so obvious is the fact that localization of sound sources aids attending to one of many voices heard in babble. This is called the "masking level difference" when it refers to differences in speech intelligibility threshold between monophonic (no location cues) and stereophonic (location cues) presentation of stimuli and noise. Thus, localization of a sound source is intimately related to attentional orientation to that source, even though there is really no such thing as a "point of auditory fixation."

### Some Relevant Properties of the Auditory System

Unlike the visual system, spatial location of sound sources is not coded directly in the spatial layout of receptors or peripheral neurons. The spatial dimensions of neuron organization are used in audition to encode frequency: the auditory system is said to be "tonotopic" everywhere, from the cochlea to the auditory cortex. This implies that the frequency domain is very important in audition, and indeed moment-to-moment changes in sound frequency, and frequency spectrum, carry most pattern information in audition (e.g., in speech, music). Location of sound sources is computed by specialized neurons in several auditory centres that receive input from both ears. Azimuth (i.e., the horizontal direction of a sound source) is computed using interaural intensity differences for relatively high-frequency sounds and interaural time, or phase, differences for relatively low-frequency sounds. Noises with broad spectra can be located by using either type of information or both. Elevation is computed from spectral differences between the two ears, mostly created by reflections of the sound from the pinnae. Such information is available only for sounds of frequencies higher than about 6 kHz; elevation localization for lower frequency sounds is very poor. In fact, auditory localization is relatively poor in general; the minimum audible angle for pure tones of about 2° at 0° azimuth represents maximum performance (Mills, 1960), as compared to typical resolution acuity in the fovea of the eye of about 1 min of arc. As Figure 2 illustrates, each sound appears to emanate from a somewhat broad and fuzzy area in auditory space called the "cone of confusion." Thus, although sounds can be detected more quickly than can visual stimuli (e.g., Posner, 1978), the relatively poor localization of auditory stimuli usually causes slower and more error-prone auditory localization responses (e.g., Ward, 1994). Interestingly, there is evidence that auditory location information is available very quickly in some brain areas in some animals (e.g., SC; see Stein & Meredith, 1993). The implications of these results for human localization and orienting responses are not clear, but some possible ones are explored later in this chapter.

The neurons that perform sound-location computations are located in the superior olives, inferior colliculi, and medial geniculate nuclei of the auditory system (see Figure 1). Surprisingly, in some animals, neurons in several non-auditory areas respond to sound location as well, the most dramatic ones being located in the deep layers of the SC (Stein & Meredith, 1993) and in parts of the PPC. Localization responses in the SC are particularly fast and best to moving, novel, complex sounds. Habituation to such sounds in the SC is also very fast.

Again, unlike the visual system, the auditory system has no "focusing" system; sounds from all parts of the auditory environment are physically mixed into the complex signal arriving at the ear. This leads to a unique problem for the auditory system: the "auditory scene" must be analyzed into a set of sound sources that provide information about unique events in the environment (see Bregman, 1990). Auditory scene analysis is accomplished by two sets of mechanisms: a fast, involuntary mechanism that uses basic auditory system mechanisms to group sounds by location and frequency, and a slower, voluntary mechanism that uses learned schemata to further associate sounds, thus forming a coherent pattern, an auditory "perceptual object." These mechanisms solve one kind of "binding problem," that of associating sound in

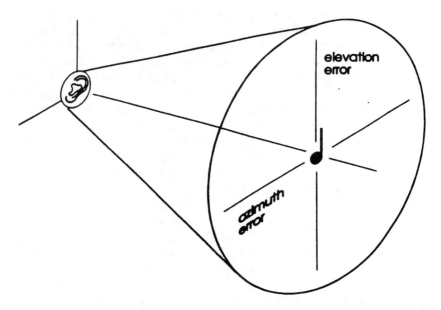

*Figure 2:* The cone of confusion as to the location of a sound source (represented by the musical quarter-note).

various frequency bands with particular spatial locations in space. An additional binding problem, that of associating sound sources with visual patterns that are causally related to them, also must be solved before the environment can be coherently perceived. In aid of this, the highly precise and direct visual localization dominates the imprecise and indirect auditory localization ("visual capture"), such that sounds localized to be "near" a moving visual object (in the sense of the cone of confusion) are heard to be emanating from that object. Thus, there must be a functionally important interaction between auditory and visual systems involved with location and pattern processing in order that the auditory and visual signatures of environmental events be correctly associated. This necessary connection is one indication that cross-modal interactions can be expected in localization tasks. The model outlined in Figure 1 makes this explicit in the inhibitory effects of the PPC on the higher cortical areas of the visual and auditory systems. When paying attention to a particular spatial location, the relevant sensory cortical areas in both systems can be simultaneously disinhibited by suppressing PPC activity at that location in its spatiotopic map, thus possibly effecting, or at least aiding, the binding of auditory and visual aspects of perceptual objects. Similar mechanisms may be available for other intermodal binding problems (e.g., visual-tactile).

## Attention Orienting in Audition

In typical auditory detection experiments, pure tones are presented at a single frequency and at various intensities over many trials. Observers come to expect the tone to occur at that frequency. Then, if a tone occurs at an intensity that would typically be detected but at an "unexpected" frequency, it usually will not be detected at all (the "uncertain frequency effect"; Greenberg & Larkin, 1968; Tanner & Norman, 1954). Providing a cue tone prior to the target tone at the frequency at which the target will occur improves performance to about the level obtained when there is no uncertainty (Johnson & Hafter; 1980; Scharf, Quigley, Aoki, Peachey, & Reeves, 1987), even when the target tone's frequency varies randomly from trial to trial. Such cues also aid detection when the stimuli are more complex (e.g., Leek, 1987; Leek, Brown, & Dorman, 1991). Moreover, both stimulus cues and symbolic cues (such as a diagram of the musical note that has the same frequency as the target) aid detection (Hafter & Schlauch, 1991). Most such data have been modelled in terms of an attentionally controlled band of enhanced processing at either expected or cued frequencies, possibly mediated by innervation of the cochlea by the crossed olivo-cochlear bundle of efferent nerve fibers (e.g., Dai, Scharf, & Buus, 1991; Leek et al., 1991; Schlauch & Hafter, 1991; Scharf, 1989). Hubner and Hafter (1995) recently argued that multiple-band listening is used in uncertain-frequency detection situations, while informative auditory cues (pure tones at the target frequency presented prior to the targets) induce single-band listening under the same conditions.

Similar mechanisms to control the frequency focus of auditory attention appear to operate for processing of suprathreshold auditory stimuli. There is an analogous uncertain frequency effect for discrimination of the intensity of pure tones, and observers can use both stimulus and symbolic cues to improve intensity resolution performance under uncertain frequency conditions (Mori & Ward, 1991, 1992; Ward & Mori, 1996). A similar effect exists for duration discrimination (Mondor & Bregman, 1994). Even uninformative auditory stimulus cues appear to orient auditory attention to their frequency region, improving intensity resolution for subsequent targets at the same frequency but impairing performance for targets at other frequencies (Ward, 1997).

There is also evidence that appropriate alignment of auditory attention with the spatial location of auditory events aids processing of those events. Table 1 summarizes most of the studies conducted on this problem. Symbolic cues appear to aid detection performance but only under certain conditions, such as when a go-nogo frequency discrimination must be made before responding (Bédard, Massioui, Pillon, &

Nandrino, 1993; Posner, Davidson & Nissen, 1976; Scharf, Canevet, Possamai, & Bonnel, 1986). Uninformative stimulus cues (sounds that do not predict target location) do not appear to affect detection at all (Spence & Driver, 1994). One reason may be that the auditory localization process required for covert orienting in space is too slow and/or imprecise to affect auditory detection. However, in localization tasks, both informative and uninformative cues affect performance (Bédard et al., 1993; Rhodes, 1987; Spence & Driver, 1994; Ward, 1994). This is understandable, since the mechanisms involved in performing the localization task may also be involved in mediating the effects of the attention cues. These findings also indicate that it would be best to study cross-modal, attention-orienting phenomena using localization tasks, since auditory detection is only faintly susceptible (if at all) to the effects of attention cues.

| Study | Task | Cue | CTOA | Cue Effect |
|-------|------|-----|------|------------|
| **Informative Cues** | | | | |
| Posner et al. (1976) | A SRT | symbolic | 1,000 | no |
| | A Disc | symbolic | 1,000 | no |
| Scharf et al. (1986) | A SRT go-nogo | A + V stimulus | 1,000 | yes |
| Rhodes (1987) | A loc | A stimulus | 2,000 | yes |
| Bédard et al. (1993) | A SRT | symbolic | 350–750 | yes |
| | A Loc | symbolic | 350–750 | yes |
| Mondor & Zatorre (1995) | A Disc | A stimulus | 150 | yes |
| **Uninformative Cues** | | | | |
| Ward (1994) | A Loc | A stimulus | 100–1,000 | yes |
| Spence & Driver (1994) | A SRT | A stimulus | 100–700 | no |
| | A U/D | A stimulus | 100–700 | yes |

*Table 1:* Auditory Spatial Attention Orienting Studies
CTOA = cue-target onset asynchrony; A = auditory; V = visual; SRT = simple reaction time; Loc = localization response time; Disc= discrimination response time; U/D = up/down localization task

# Cross-Modal Control of Attention Shifts

Although the study of cross-modal control of attention alignment is still in its early stages, several suggestive results have been reported. Table 2 summarizes many of these results, several of which are still unpublished. The remainder of this chapter will be devoted to a detailed discussion of a few of these results that seem particularly important in resolving what we now know and in directing future research. In addition, several new experiments will be reported. These experiments both fill in the parts of the evolving tapestry and also resolve some of the uncertainties connected with the earlier results.

| Study | Task | Cue | CTOA | Cue Effect |
|---|---|---|---|---|
| **Informative Cues** | | | | |
| Butchel & Butter (1988) | V SRT | A/V stimulus | 50–1,000 | A & V |
| | A SRT | A/V stimulus | 50–1,000 | no |
| Butter et al. (1989) | V SRT | V/T stimulus | 50–1,000 | T & V |
| | T SRT | V/T stimulus | 50–1,000 | T & V |
| **Uninformative Cues** | | | | |
| Klein et al. (1987) | A SRT | V stimulus | 0–500 | no |
| | V SRT | A stimulus | 0–500 | yes |
| Farah et al. (1989) | V SRT (right parietal patients) | A/V stimulus | 50–1,000 | $Vc > Vi$ $Ac > Ai = 0$ |
| Ward (1994) | ALoc | A/V stimulus | 100–1,000 | A & V |
| | V Loc | V/A stimulus | 100–1,000 | V no A |
| Spence & Driver (1997) | A/V U/D | V stimulus | 100–700 | V no A |
| | A/V U/D | A stimulus | 100–700 | A & V |

*Table 2:* Cross-Modal Attention Orienting Studies
CTOA = cue-target onset asynchrony; A = auditory; V = visual; T = tactile; SRT = simple reaction time; Loc = localization response time; U/D = up/down localization task; c = contralesional; i = ipsilesional

Consistent with earlier findings, neither informative nor uninformative visual cues appear to affect auditory detection (as measured by simple reaction time; Buchtel & Butter, 1988; Klein et al., 1987).

However, there are reports of both informative (Buchtel & Butter, 1988) and uninformative (Farah et al., 1989; Klein, Brenner, & Gilani, 1987) auditory cues affecting visual simple reaction time. Although the latter two results, in particular, are provocative, there is reason to believe they are not representative (see Spence & Driver, 1997; Ward, 1994). For this reason, both Ward (1994) and Spence and Driver (1997) carried out a series of experiments that attempted to determine whether uninformative cues in one modality would elicit attention shifts to their spatial location that would affect performance on targets presented in the other modality. Intriguingly, the two series of studies obtained exactly opposite results, as shown in Table 2: Ward (1994) found reliable effects of a visual cue on auditory localization but no effects of an auditory cue on visual localization, while Spence and Driver (1997) found just the opposite. The remainder of this chapter is devoted to a discussion of these experiments and to a presentation of new data that suggest that both results are valid. Taken together, these cross-modal asymmetries do not support the existence of independent modality-specific visual and auditory attentional mechanisms. Instead, they suggest a supra-modal mechanism such as the attention network outlined in Figure 1. The asymmetries also reveal, however, that covert orienting in one modality does not always produce orienting in the other modality, as a supramodal mechanism might suggest. We explore the possibility that situational factors, such as cue and task environments, invoke strategic control of the supramodal attention mechanism, thus producing different cross-modal asymmetries in different experimental situations.

## Ward's Experimental Paradigm

Ward (1994) adapted a paradigm used by several researchers for cross-modal simple reaction time studies (Butter & Buchtel, 1988; Farah et al., 1989). This paradigm, with variations to be described as they are relevant, was used in most of the new studies reported in this chapter, and it will be described in some detail here. Figure 3 shows the experimental setup. The subject faced a computer monitor with a speaker mounted on either side. Small boxes appeared on the monitor at the level of the speakers and in the centre and at the extreme left and right of it. An "×" appeared in the centre box, and subjects were instructed to fixate this stimulus throughout each run of the experiment. Visual cues were 50 ms brightenings of one of the three boxes, and auditory cues were 50 ms, 964 Hz, 86 dB pure tones from either the left, right, or both speakers (the latter localized centrally). Visual targets were the 50 ms appearance of an "×" in either the left or right box. Auditory targets were 50 ms, 3000 Hz, 76 dB pure tones from either left or right speakers. The subjects' task was to press one key of a response box if a

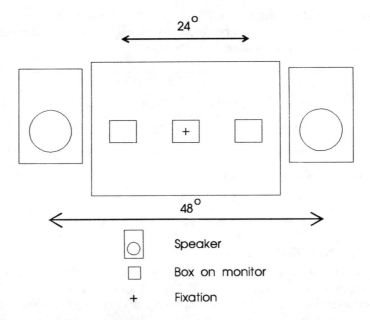

*Figure 3*: Stimulus conditions for the experiments of Ward (1994) and for Experiments 1 through 6 and Experiment 9 that are reported in the present article.

target appeared on the left side of the display and a different key if a target appeared on the right side. Accuracy was maintained at (or above) 92% correct in all runs. Median response times for each subject in each condition were based on 30 correct responses.

Ward (1994) created a very complex cue environment. Table 3 summarizes the various possible cues that occurred during each run of trials. On any given trial, there could be an auditory cue alone, a visual cue alone, both auditory and visual cues, or no cues. Each cue could come from the left side, the right side, or the centre, and when both cue types occurred, they could come from the same or different locations. Moreover, cues could precede targets by 100 ms, 200 ms, 550 ms, or 1050 ms at random, and one or both cues could be at the same location or at different locations vis-à-vis the target. All cues were completely uninformative: their location was randomly associated with that of the target. Finally, only one type of target appeared over many runs of the experiment: either visual or auditory. Thus, there was a great incentive for subjects to ignore the cues (if they could). The model displayed in Figure 1 is consistent with the idea that the influence of stimuli occurring in any modality on the attention network can be modulated by the frontal cortex. Given that target modality was fixed throughout Ward's (1994) experiments, it could be expected that the influence of cues presented in the nontask modality would be more easily suppressed than those from the task modality, even though cues in each modality were equally uninformative.

|  |  | Auditory Cue Location | | | |
|---|---|---|---|---|---|
|  |  | Left | Right | Centre | None |
|  | Left | LL | LR | LC | LN |
| Visual Cue Location | Right | RL | RR | RC | RN |
|  | Centre | CL | CR | CC | CN |
|  | None | NL | NR | NC | NN |

*Table 3:* Design of the Cue Conditions in Ward's (1994) Experiments

## Localization Task Results

Figure 4 illustrates the kind of results obtained by Ward (1994) in the crucial cross-modal and intramodal conditions in which only a single directional cue or an appropriate neutral cue occurred (for a more complete presentation of the data, see Ward, 1994). Response time to localize the auditory targets decreased as a function of CTOA (an alerting effect), and was shorter at 100-ms and 200-ms CTOAs for the Valid (cue and target at same location) than for the Invalid (cue and target at different locations) trials for both auditory and visual cues. This relationship disappeared or reversed at longer CTOAs. Both costs of an Invalid cue (Invalid RT − Neutral RT > 0) and benefits of a Valid cue (Neutral RT − Valid RT > 0) were found. This pattern of response times is typical of that interpreted in previous studies, especially of visual attention orienting, as being indicative of stimulus-driven orienting of attention caused by the uninformative cues (see Wright & Ward, this volume, for a summary). Apparently both auditory and visual cues caused this stimulus-driven attention orienting in audition. For the visual localization task, however, the results differed. Only visual cues caused stimulus-driven orienting; auditory cues had no effect whatsoever on visual localization. Ward (1994) interpreted this asymmetry of cross-modal cueing effects to be the result of the dominance of auditory localization by visual localization discussed above. Since the visual cue gave rapid and precise location information, it facilitated localization of an auditory target that occurred nearby shortly thereafter. However, since the auditory cue was localized more slowly (auditory localization responses were about 150 ms slower than visual localization responses) and much less precisely, it was unable to influence the faster and more precise visual localization. Ward (1994) considered the possibility that these results might be caused by response priming (e.g., Simon, Acosta, Mewaldt, & Speidel, 1976) but dismissed it for several reasons discussed in detail later in the "Response Priming" section. In particular, the fact that no auditory cue effects occurred for the visual task seemed to argue against a priming explanation.

## Simple Reaction Time Task

We ran two new experiments (Experiment 1: visual targets and Experiment 2: auditory targets) using a simple reaction time task in place of the localization task but with a cueing situation identical to that of Ward (1994). Although we felt that cross-modal cueing effects were unlikely to be found using simple reaction time (cf. Spence & Driver, 1994), others had found such effects (e.g., Klein, Brennen, & Gilani, 1987). It was necessary to establish whether they would occur with the cue and task environments used by Ward (1994) in order to make more general statements about cross-modal control of attention.

In each of these studies, 15 subjects each gave 1,920 responses after about 100 practice trials. We calculated the median response time for each condition/CTOA/validity combination for each subject based on 30 acceptable (reaction time between 100 ms and 1500 ms) responses per combination. The studies were identical to those of Ward (1994) in every detail except two. (1) Here we used CTOAs of 50 ms, 100 ms, 200 ms, and 500 ms, since previous studies had found cueing effects at very short CTOAs; and (2) subjects were not required to localize the visual or auditory targets, and responded by pressing the same key to the onset of each target. Although the complete analysis of these data was done (see Table 4 for the mean response times in all conditions), discussion will generally be limited to the cue effects (Invalid RT − Valid RT) at the 100-ms CTOA, since the interest is in stimulus-driven attention shifts. Evidence for such effects when uninformative cues are used is available only around a CTOA of about 100 ms. Furthermore, such effects cannot be influenced by eye movements, since these typically take at least 200 ms to initiate under these conditions.

Figure 5 summarizes the cue effects observed in the single-cue conditions of the visual and auditory simple reaction time experiments at the 100-ms CTOA.[11] Only the effect of visual cues on reaction to the visual target was significant (Visual Target : Visual Cue, or VT:VC). There was no cross-modal effect of auditory cues on visual simple reaction time (VT:AC) at the 100-ms CTOA (nor at the 50-ms CTOA), nor any effect of either type of cue on auditory simple reaction time (including, again, the 50-ms CTOA). Results in all other, more complicated, cue conditions were consistent with these statements as well. Since the visual cues were effective in orienting visual attention, and also gave the

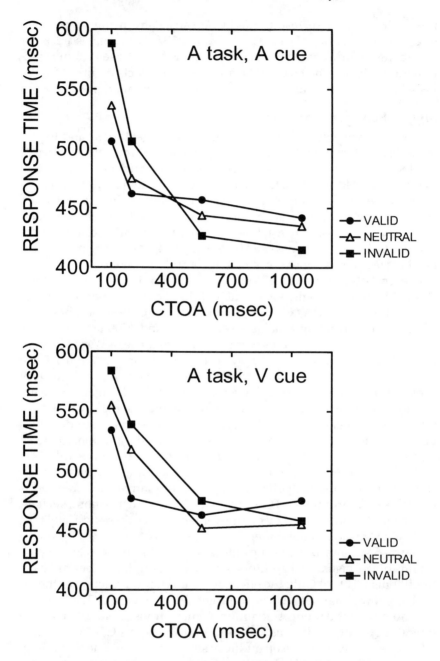

*Figure 4a:* Response times to localize auditory targets as a function of cue-target onset asynchrony (CTOA) and cue condition for the single-cue conditions in Ward's (1994) experiments.

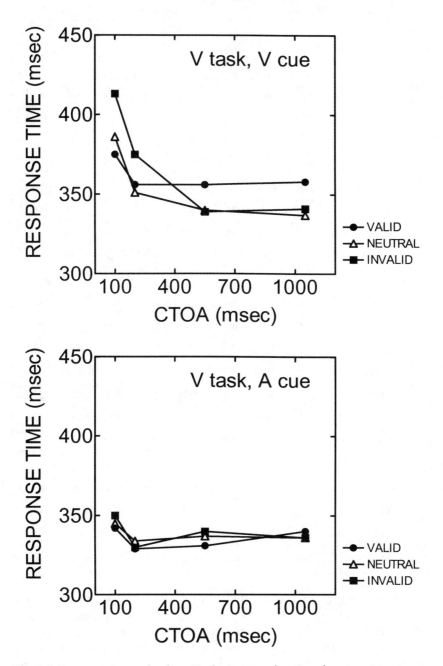

*Figure 4b:* Response times to localize visual targets as a function of cue-target onset asynchrony (CTOA) and cue condition for the single-cue conditions in Ward's (1994) experiments.

| Exp. | Target | Cue | CTOA | | | | | | | |
|---|---|---|---|---|---|---|---|---|---|---|
| | | | 50 | | 100 | | 200 | | 500 | |
| | | | Valid | Inv'd | Valid | Inv'd | Valid | Inv'd | Valid | Inv'd |
| 1 | Vis | Vis | 353 | 372 | 339 | 365 | 330 | 315 | 326 | 385 |
| | Vis | Aud | 348 | 357 | 326 | 326 | 296 | 305 | 283 | 287 |
| 2 | Aud | Vis | 407 | 419 | 382 | 394 | 350 | 362 | 303 | 312 |
| | Aud | Aud | 344 | 348 | 318 | 330 | 295 | 312 | 290 | 287 |
| 3 | Vis | Vis | 568 | 603 | 564 | 596 | 559 | 595 | 568 | 569 |
| | Vis | Aud | 577 | 580 | 560 | 561 | 549 | 556 | 551 | 550 |
| 4 | Aud | Vis | 555 | 537 | 534 | 534 | 502 | 500 | 496 | 499 |
| | Aud | Aud | 535 | 534 | 515 | 521 | 508 | 518 | 498 | 506 |
| | | | 100 | | 200 | | 550 | | 1,050 | |
| | | | Valid | Inv'd | Valid | Inv'd | Valid | Inv'd | Valid | Inv'd |
| 5 | Vis | Vis | 398 | 451 | 399 | 434 | 390 | 409 | 389 | 370 |
| | Vis | Aud | 386 | 396 | 365 | 376 | 339 | 353 | 343 | 349 |
| 6 | Vis | Vis | 459 | 521 | 459 | 513 | 452 | 482 | 454 | 447 |
| | Vis | Aud | 467 | 470 | 440 | 439 | 420 | 429 | 426 | 427 |
| 7 | Vis | Vis | 451 | 491 | 446 | 442 | 439 | 396 | 439 | 404 |
| | Vis | Aud | 418 | 407 | 404 | 390 | 396 | 396 | 400 | 408 |
| | | | 100 | | 200 | | 700 | | | |
| | | | Valid | Inv'd | Valid | Inv'd | Valid | Inv'd | | |
| 8 | Vis | Vis | 487 | 494 | 438 | 459 | 434 | 432 | | |
| | Vis | Aud | 455 | 434 | 428 | 410 | 423 | 419 | | |

*Table 4:* Mean Response Times for Individual Conditions in Experiments 1 to 8
CTOA = cue-target- onset asynchrony; Aud = auditory; Vis = visual; Inv'd = Invalid

cue effect reversal at 500 ms (−41 ms) that is often taken as evidence of inhibition of return in such data (see Posner & Cohen, 1984), the lack of other effects does not indicate an experiment failure. Rather, consistent with previous studies (e.g., Spence & Driver, 1994), it appears to be very difficult to produce significant cue effects for auditory simple reaction time. Moreover, auditory cues also do not appear to affect responses to visual targets. Thus, at the level of simple detection, there is

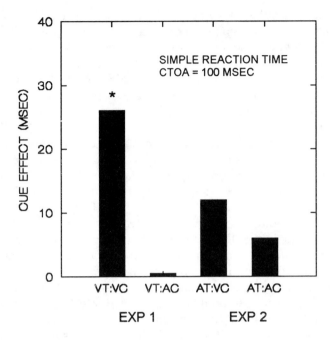

*Figure 5:* Cue effects (Invalid response time − Valid response time) as a function of condition in Experiment 1 (VT:VC and VT:AC) and Experiment 2 (AT:VC and AT:AC) for the 100 ms cue-target onset asynchrony (CTOA). The asterix (*) indicates that the cue effect is statistically significant. (VT = visual target; VC = visual cue; AT = auditory target; AC = auditory cue)

little evidence for cross-modal cueing effects. If such effects exist, they must be very small. These results are consistent with the idea that auditory location information becomes available too late in the stream of information processing to affect simple detection. On this view, the direct nature of visual location coding is responsible for the effects of visual cues on visual detection.

## Discrimination Task

We ran two new studies (Experiment 3: visual targets, and Experiment 4: auditory targets) using a stimulus discrimination task in place of the localization task but with a cueing situation identical to that of Ward (1994). In the visual discrimination study, 15 subjects each gave 1,920 responses after about 100 practice trials; in the auditory discrimination study, each of 12 subjects did the same. We calculated the median response time for each condition-CTOA-validity combination for each subject, based on 30 correct responses per combination. These studies were identical to the simple reaction time studies reported above, except that here subjects responded by pressing the leftmost of two response keys if one of two possible targets appeared, and they pressed the rightmost key if the other target appeared. For the visual task, the two possible targets were an "×" or a "+"; for the auditory task the two targets were pure tones of either 3000 Hz or 4000 Hz at an intensity of 86 dB. Again, although a complete analysis of these experiments was done (as in Ward, 1994; see Table 4 for the mean response times), only the cue effects (Invalid RT − Valid RT) at the 100 ms CTOA will be discussed here, since the interest is in stimulus-driven cueing effects.

Figure 6 summarizes the cue effects observed in the single-cue conditions of the discrimination experiments at the 100 ms CTOA.[2] Only the effect of visual cues was significant for the visual task (VT:VC), and that effect was similar to earlier results (e.g., Downing, 1988). There was no cross-modal effect of auditory cues on visual discrimination response time, nor were there any effects of any cues on auditory discrimination response time. Similar to the simple reaction time results, cue effects in all other, more complex, cue conditions were consistent with the above statements. Thus, under these conditions, there seem to be no reliable cross-modal cueing effects for a discrimination task, nor any such effects within audition. Again, the inability of auditory spatial cues to affect auditory discrimination seems to arise from the late availability of location information in the auditory system. Like simple detection, then, at least some auditory discrimination responses may be too quick to be influenced by auditory location information. Although Mondor and Zatorre (1995) reported an auditory discrimination task that was affected by spatial cueing, they used auditory cues that were highly predictive of target location. Thus, although cueing effects were observed in their studies, it is difficult to rule out the contribution of goal-driven orienting. Nevertheless, it remains to be seen whether all discrimination responses are too rapid to be influenced by spatial cueing or whether it depends on the type of discrimination required.

## Spence & Driver's Cross-Modal Experiments

Spence and Driver (1997) examined cross-modal links in attention using a paradigm that differed from Ward's (1994) in several critical ways. Foremost among these, Spence and Driver designed a modified localization task that, unlike left-right localization tasks, was not subject to response priming criticisms. Targets were located above or below the horizontal meridian, either ipsilateral (valid cue condition) or contralateral (invalid cue condition) to the cue. Subjects made up-down localization responses for auditory and visual targets that were preceded by visual cues in one experiment and auditory cues in an-

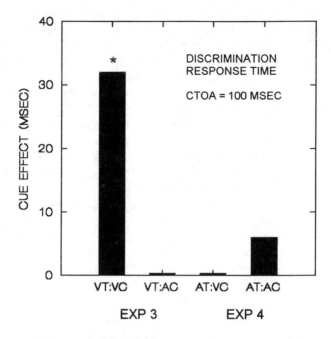

*Figure 6:* Cue effects (Invalid response time − Valid response time) as a function of condition in Experiment 3 (VT:VC and VT:AC) and Experiment 4 (AT:VC and AT:AC) for the 100 ms CTOA. An asterix (*) indicates that the cue effect is statistically significant. (VT = visual target; VC = visual cue; AT = auditory target; AC = auditory cue)

other. Thus, in both experiments, cues from a single modality were followed by targets from either modality. Under these conditions, Spence and Driver (1997) found that while auditory cues facilitated both auditory and visual localization, visual cues failed to influence auditory localization. In comparison to Ward (1994), then, precisely the opposite asymmetry was found.

Spence and Driver accounted for this apparent asymmetry on neurophysiological grounds. The superior colliculus (SC) has been implicated in the control of both overt orienting (e.g., Sparks & Hartwich-Young, 1989; Wurtz & Munoz, 1995) and attention shifting (e.g., Posner, Rafal, Choate, & Vaughan, 1985; Wurtz, Goldberg, & Robinson, 1982). This midbrain structure can be broadly divided into two functionally separate layers: superficial and deep. Based on its afferents from the retina and visual cortices, the superficial SC is primarily a visual region. Much anatomical and neurophysiological evidence reveals the existence of a separate spatiotopic visual representation, or "map," within these superficial layers (e.g., Robinson & McClurkin, 1989). In contrast, the deep layers of the SC receive input from both visual and auditory (as well as tactile) modalities, and contain spatiotopic maps for each. Each map overlaps and is in general alignment with the others and with the saccadic motor map. Spence and Driver (1997) proposed that the existence of a separate visual map and absence of an independent auditory map might account for the cross-modal asymmetry they found in covert orienting. They hypothesized that the visual map in the superficial layers of the SC is the neural substrate of stimulus-driven visual attention. Consequently, because this map is independent of auditory input, shifts in visual attention may occur independent of auditory attention. In contrast, since the auditory map is located in the multimodal layers of the SC, auditory attention shifts cannot be made independent of visual (and presumably tactile) attention.

Thus, we seem to have a consistent picture of spatial cueing effects in vision and audition, except for the crucial cross-modal conditions. Table 5 summarizes these results and the critical disagreement. Clearly it is very important to determine whether or not the two different patterns of cross-modal effects are reliable. If they are, then situational factors must be modulating the cross-modal stimulus-driven cue effects.

| | | Task | | |
| Cue | Target | Detection | Localization | Discrimination |
|---|---|---|---|---|
| Vis | Vis | Yes | Yes | Yes |
| Aud | Aud | No | Yes | No |
| Vis | Aud | No (WMG) | Yes (W); No (S&D) | No (WMG) |
| Aud | Vis | No (WMG) | No (W); Yes (S&D) | No (WMG) |

*Table 5:* Visual, Auditory, and Cross-Modal Cue Effects.
Vis = visual; Aud = auditory; W = Ward (1994); S&D = Spence & Driver (1997): WMG = Ward, McDonald & Golestami

## Response Priming?

All cue effects so far described are vulnerable to several different classes of explanations other than those based on attention orientation. Broadly, they fall into two groups: perceptual system effects (such as apparent movement) and response system effects (such as response priming). In all cases, it is necessary to counter the argument that responses to validly cued targets are faster or more accurate (or both) than responses to invalidly cued targets, because the task was made easier by some perceptual or response advantage that was present in the valid case but not in the invalid case. Spence and Driver's (1997) up-down spatial localization task is subject to such alternative explanations, and in their paper they experimentally discounted one such explanation involving relative location or perceived motion judgments based on perceived elevation of the cue. In the same paper, they argued cleverly that the pattern of cue effects with left-right localization tasks reported by Ward (1994) could have arisen from response priming. If correct, this would rule out cross-modal cue effects such as those found by Ward (1994), and would suggest that audition is, in fact, dominant in all cross-modal conditions. If this were the case, a single supramodal mechanism of attention would seem highly unlikely. However, we argue here that response priming did not seriously affect Ward's (1994) pattern of cue effects, and that both results are valid examples of attention-orienting effects.

There are several arguments against a response-priming explanation of Ward's (1994) results. First, the situation was really not very similar to those in which response priming occurs (e.g., Simon & Craft, 1970). In response-priming studies, although the priming stimuli are irrelevant to the task, they occur on every trial, and are simple and clear. In Ward's (1994) studies, the cues sometimes occurred and sometimes did not, and sometimes were consistent with each other and sometimes were in conflict. In each run, the probability of a visual cue only [$p$(V only)] was 0.125, $p$(A only) = 0.125, $p$(V&A same location) = 0.125, $p$(V&A different locations) = 0.375, $p$(Central cue only) = 0.1875, and $p$(no cue) = 0.0625. Also, it would be expected that response priming effects would be only benefits (relative to no priming), since priming activates the primed response but does not affect the unprimed response (Posner, 1978). Thus, on trials when the wrong response is primed, the (unprimed) correct response is activated no less than on "neutral" trials where no response is primed. In contrast, attention effects typically yield both costs and benefits, since the cue helps on valid trials by orienting attention correctly before the target occurs, and hinders on invalid trials by guaranteeing that attention will be oriented incorrectly (Posner, 1978). Ward (1994) reported both costs and benefits of cross-modal and intramodal cues. Moreover, Simon and Craft (1970) found an effect of the irrelevant auditory cues on responses to a visual task, and Ward (1994) did not.

However, Spence and Driver (1997) argued that response priming could explain even Ward's (1994) null result because of the relative locations of auditory and visual stimuli in his experiments. As Figure 3 shows, the auditory stimuli were presented from speakers located outside the locations of visual stimuli on the computer monitor. Spence and Driver (1997) argued that, for example, an auditory cue on the left side would prime the "left" response while the visual target on the left side, since it appeared to the right of the auditory cue, would prime the "right" response. The two response primings would cancel out and yield a null result in this condition. Unfortunately, this explanation appears to allow the attention effect of the auditory cue found by Spence and Driver (1997) to emerge, but none was found. It also appears to predict a strong response-priming effect when a central visual cue and a directional auditory cue both occur: since the visual target is presented between two cues, it should not prime either (left or right) response, leaving only the response priming produced by the directional auditory cue. However, Ward (1994) found no cue effect in that condition either. Nonetheless, because of the importance of the null results, and the difficulty of "proving" the null hypothesis, we thought it necessary to further establish the reliability of the asymmetry found by Ward (1994).

We conducted four new experiments (Experiments 5 to 8) aimed at demonstrating that auditory directional cues have no effect on localization of visual targets under Ward's (1994) conditions. All four experiments used the identical cue environment to that of Ward (1994), and varied the environment's parameters in such a way that we would be more likely to obtain a cross-modal auditory cue effect if it existed. One change made in all experiments was to substitute a more easily localizable broadband noise (60 Hz to 10000 Hz) for the 964 Hz cue tone. In Experiment 5 this was the only change. All other details were the same as Ward's (1994) visual localization task. In Experiment 6 we also changed the response mapping, requiring subjects to press a button located on top of the response box if the target appeared on one side and a button located on the bottom of the box if the target appeared on the other side. All other details were the same as Ward (1994).

Figure 7 displays the cue effects (Invalid RT − Valid RT) for only the 100 ms CTOA for Experiments 5 and 6. Again full analyses were conducted on the results of both experiments,[3] and were highly similar to those reported by Ward (1994) for tonal cues (Table 4 shows the mean responses at all CTOAs). The usual effects of uninformative visual cues on responses to visual targets were found in both experiments (including the reversal of the effect at longer CTOAs not shown in Figure 7). However, as found by Ward (1994), there were no significant effects of the broadband noise cues on localization of visual targets in either experiment. Thus, even stronger auditory cues than the ones used by Ward (1994) failed to produce significant stimulus-driven attention orienting in a visual localization task. Moreover, changing the definition of responses also failed to affect the null cueing result. If response priming indeed is responsible for the null result observed in these experiments, only an exotic mechanism like that suggested by Spence and Driver (1997) could be responsible.

We ran two additional experiments (Experiments 7 and 8) to more directly test the possibility that Spence and Driver's (1995) argument

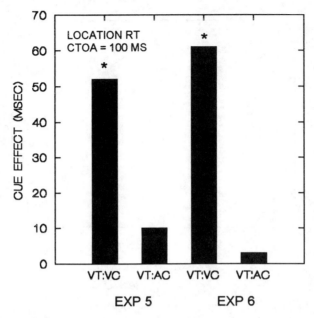

*Figure 7:* Cue effects (Invalid response time − Valid response time) as a function of condition in Experiment 5 (VT:VC and VT:AC) and Experiment 6 (VT:VC and VT:AC) for the 100 ms CTOA. The asterix (*) indicates that the cue effect is statistically significant. (VT = visual target; VC = visual cue; AT = auditory target; AC = auditory cue)

might be correct for our conditions. In Experiment 7, we again replicated all of Ward's (1994) conditions, except that in this case we attached light-emitting diodes (LEDs) to the speakers from which sounds came so that visual and auditory stimuli would emanate from precisely the same locations. In addition, we fixed a speaker in the centre of the visual field, and neutral auditory cues were presented from that speaker instead of from the two peripheral speakers. Figure 8 shows the stimulus conditions for this experiment (ignore the speakers above and below the middle row for present purposes). Visual cues consisted of a 50-ms flash of two green LEDs arranged horizontally, and visual targets consisted of a 50-ms flash of two red LEDs arranged vertically, all on the relevant speaker housing. Again auditory cues were 50-ms broadband noise bursts. In this experiment subjects were run in a darkened sound attenuation chamber with low ambient noise. Thus, this experiment created conditions under which Spence and Driver's (1997) explanation of cancelling response primings would not apply. Instead, according to Spence and Driver's (1997) argument, only the directional auditory cue should prime the response, leading to an auditory cue effect similar to the one they found (but arising from a different source).

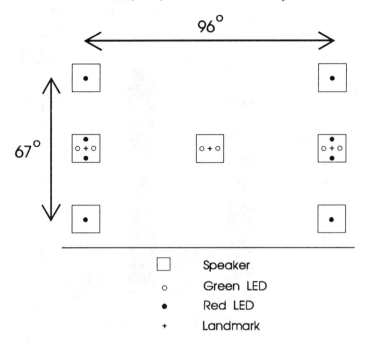

*Figure 8*: Stimulus conditions for Experiments 7 and 8. For Experiment 7, only the middle row of speakers was used for both cues and targets. In Experiment 8, cues emanated from the middle row of speakers, and targets occurred from the light-emitting diodes (LEDs) above and below the cue locations.

Figure 9 summarizes the cue effects at 100 ms for the single visual (VT:VC) and single auditory (VT:AC) cue conditions (Table 4 shows the mean responses at all CTOAs).[4] Again, the usual effect of visual cues on visual localization was found (including inhibition of return at longer CTOAs, see Table 4). However, there was no effect of auditory cues on visual localization; if anything, there was a trend toward a negative cue effect (smaller RTs in the invalid cue condition, see Table 4). Thus, eliminating the possibility of cancelling response priming effects from cues and targets did not create an effect of auditory cues on visual localization, as it should have if the auditory cues were priming responses.

Experiment 8 was a final attempt to deal with the possibility of response priming in the context of Ward's (1994) experiments. In this experiment, we used the task suggested by Spence and Driver (1994, 1997) to eliminate response priming while still engaging the spatial localization mechanisms of the auditory system. Figure 8 also shows the stimulus display for this task. In this experiment, cues were either broadband noises or green LED flashes from the central speaker and LED complex or from the speaker and LED complexes immediately to

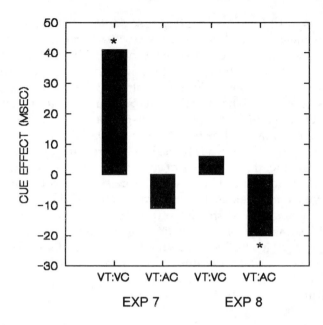

*Figure 9*: Cue effects (Invalid response time − Valid response time) as a function of condition in Experiments 7 and 8 for the 100 ms CTOA. The asterix (*) indicates that the cue effect is statistically significant. (VT = visual target; VC = visual cue; AT = auditory target; AC = auditory cue)

its left or right and in the same plane. Visual targets were red LED flashes from the top or bottom speaker and LED complexes. The subjects' task was to press a key labelled "up" if the red LED flash came from either of the top two speaker and LED complexes, and to press a button labelled "down" if the flash came from either of the bottom two speaker and LED complexes. Thus, the cues (occurring left, right, or centre) could not prime the responses to the up-down task. Also in this task, only three CTOAs were used: 100 ms, 200 ms, and 700 ms, as in Spence and Driver's (1997) experiments. All other details, especially including the complex cue environment, were identical to Experiment 7.

Figure 9 also displays the cue effects obtained at the 100 ms CTOA for the single visual and auditory cue conditions in Experiment 8 (Table 4 shows the mean responses for all CTOAs).[5] The data are somewhat unusual, in that the typical visual cue effect was not found at 100 ms (however, it was significant at the 200-ms CTOA, see Table 4). Interestingly, Spence and Driver (1997) also reported an experiment in which the visual cue effect was observed only at the 200-ms CTOA. Moreover, rather than the null effect of the auditory cue found in previous experiments, here there is a significant negative cue effect (which lasts until the 200-ms CTOA, see Table 4). This difference between cue effects for auditory and visual cues is reflected in a significant interaction between Cue Condition and Validity in the analysis of variance (ANOVA). In both conditions in which auditory direction cues occurred without visual directional cues, there was a significant negative cue effect. We believe this effect is unrelated to the inhibition of return effect commonly found in visual orienting, since it was a transient effect, maximal at the shortest CTOA interval (100 ms). In contrast, inhibition of return is typically observed at longer CTOAs, replacing earlier facilitatory effects of covert orienting. We postulate that the present negative cue effect resulted from sensory rather than attentional factors. For instance, many neurons in the SC show response depression for spatially disparate multisensory stimuli: neuronal responses to stimuli in one modality may be depressed by spatially disparate stimuli in another modality (Stein & Merideth, 1993). In the valid cue conditions of Experiment 8, cues and targets were separated by a 33.5° vertical angle. It seems plausible that the negative cue effect observed at short CTOA intervals resulted from this sort of multisensory integration.

Regardless of the source of the negative auditory cue effect, it is clear that even with the up-down task, in which response priming could not mimic an attention-orienting effect, the positive auditory cue effect on visual localization obtained by Spence and Driver (1997) was not produced by simply adopting their task. Thus, we must look elsewhere for an explanation of the conflicting asymmetries found in these two groups of studies.

### Cue Environment and Task Effects

If we assume that both sets of results are valid indications of attention orienting for different experimental conditions, it is appropriate to examine those conditions for clues as to how the conflict can be resolved. There are two striking differences in the conditions under which the conflicting results were obtained (in addition to the actual tasks used). These are the cue and task environments used. Ward (1994) established a highly complex cue environment, with one or both of two cue modalities and a variety of cue types occurring at random in every run. However, his subjects responded in a very simple task environment, with only a single modality involved. Ward's reasoning was that if subjects could ignore the irrelevant cues they would, especially the cross-modal ones, since they did not need to keep the nontask-related-modality channel open for targets. This seemed to provide a strong test of stimulus-driven cueing. In contrast, Spence and Driver (1997) used a very simple cue environment, with a single directional cue in a single, unvarying modality presented on every trial, but with a more complex task environment, (either a visual or an auditory target occurring at random on each trial). This would provide a reason to keep both modality channels open for targets, possibly making it impossible to ignore auditory cues. The lack of effect of visual cues on auditory targets found by Spence and Driver (1997) is problematic for this explanation, since the same incentive to keep both channels open existed in this condition. However, visual cues are easier to ignore than auditory cues, since it is possible to blur vision by squinting or to move the eyes. It seems reasonable to conclude that the conditions imposed by the two experimental situations could be responsible for the divergence in cross-modal cueing results obtained by differentially affecting strategic control of stimulus-driven orienting.

That goal-driven control of attention (i.e., strategy) can modulate the effects of abrupt-onset stimulus cues has already been observed in vision (e.g., Yantis & Jonides, 1990). The "open-channel" hypothesis described above can be viewed as a specific example of the more general hypothesis that situational factors can induce strategic control of cross-modal, stimulus-driven covert orienting. This hypothesis is readily falsifiable: if changes in experimental conditions that should cause a change in strategy do not modify the obtained cross-modal results, then cross-modal, stimulus-driven covert orienting is not influenced by strategic control, at least as implemented in the experimental condition changes carried out. More specifically, if changes in cue and task environments do not produce predictable results (outlined below), then the open-channel hypothesis cannot account for the opposing cross-modal asymmetries.

We ran Experiments 9a and 9b to test both the specific open-channel hypothesis and the more general hypothesis that strategic factors can modulate stimulus-driven, cross-modal cue effects. In Experiment 9a we created a paradigm comparable to Spence and Driver's (1997) in that only auditory cues were presented but both visual and auditory targets occurred at random (i.e., single cue modality; both target modalities). Experiment 9b created a situation comparable to Ward's (1994), featuring both cue modalities and a single target modality but with a somewhat simpler cue environment. Either auditory or visual directional cues (but *not* both or neither or neutral) occurred at random on each trial, but only visual targets appeared. Both experiments were run using Ward's (1994) paradigm as diagrammed in Figure 3, except that for the visual task we added boxes above and below the leftmost and rightmost boxes on the monitor, and targets appeared in one of those boxes at random. In both Experiments 9a and 9b, subjects responded "up" or "down" as in Spence and Driver's (1997) task. With

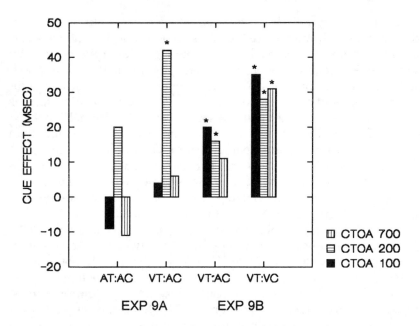

*Figure 10:* Cue effects (Invalid response time − Valid response time) as a function of condition and CTOA in Experiment 9a (AT:AC and VT:AC) and Experiment 9b (VT:AC and VT:VC). The asterix (*) indicates that the cue effect is statistically significant. (VT = visual target; VC = visual cue; AT = auditory target; AC = auditory cue)

only a single speaker on each side, we could not mimic Spence and Driver's auditory up-down task for Experiment 9a, so we used a frequency discrimination task instead. Auditory targets consisted of one of two frequencies of pure tone (3000 Hz or 4000 Hz), and subjects responded "up" for the higher and "down" for the lower. A single auditory cue (50-ms broadband noise) was presented from either the left or right speaker at random on each trial. Experiment 9a provides a strong test of the open-channel hypothesis, since the auditory task was not a spatial one but subjects should still have had to keep the auditory channel open for an auditory target. On each trial of Experiment 9b, only a single directional cue appeared, but it was either auditory (50-ms broadband noise) or visual (50-ms filling of the middle box on either left or right of the screen) at random. Only visual targets appeared in this experiment. We expected to find Spence and Driver's (1997) result in Experiment 9a and Ward's (1994) result in Experiment 9b if the simplest version of the open-channel hypothesis was correct.

The same 15 subjects performed in both Experiments 9a and 9b; 7 subjects did 9a first and 8 subjects did 9b first. Figure 10 displays the cue effects (Invalid RT − Valid RT) found in the two experiments.[6] Experiment 9a replicates the Spence and Driver (1997) finding of a significant auditory cue effect on a visual localization task, although the effect is found only at the 200-ms CTOA, which is at the outer limit for stimulus-driven orienting. The overall pattern of cue effects in this experiment, however, with null effects at both shorter and longer CTOAs, is consistent with a stimulus-driven interpretation. Interestingly there is a trend for an effect on the auditory task as well (20-ms effect) also at the 200-ms CTOA, although the auditory task was not a spatial one. Perhaps under some conditions auditory spatial cueing can affect non-spatial auditory processing (cf. Mondor & Zatorre, 1995). Regardless of whether such effects can be found, however, they are not necessary for the auditory cue to be effective in a visual spatial task. It appears to be sufficient that there be a reason to keep the auditory channel open.

The interpretation of the results of Experiment 9b is a little less straightforward. There appear to be significant cue effects of both auditory and visual cues in this experiment. The visual cue effects do not show a typical stimulus-driven pattern, but rather appear at all CTOAs. The auditory cue effects are significant only at the 100-ms and 200-ms CTOAs, consistent with a stimulus-driven interpretation. This is the first time we have seen significant auditory cue effects under multiple-cue-modality, single-task conditions. Apparently the salience of the auditory cues was sufficient to lead to a significant cue effect even when the cues were uninformative and there was no need to keep the auditory channel open (only visual targets appeared). The significant interaction of order of experiments by cue type by validity helps to interpret this result. Those subjects who completed Experiment 9a before they did Experiment 9b showed no auditory cue effects in Experiment 9b at the 100-ms and 200-ms CTOAs (7 ms and −1 ms, respectively). Only the effect at the 700-ms CTOA (21 ms) was significant, consistent with a goal-driven orienting interpretation. In contrast, the subjects who completed Experiment 9b first showed large auditory cue effects in Experiment 9b at the 100-ms and 200-ms CTOAs (32 ms and 31 ms, respectively) and no effect at the 700-ms CTOA (2 ms), consistent with stimulus-driven orienting. Both groups showed the same pattern of visual cue effects as that in Figure 10. Apparently the simplification of the cue environment (remember that only a single, directional cue appeared on each trial) in Experiment 9b was sufficient to induce auditory cue effects for the group who experienced that situation first. However, the group who first experienced only auditory cues and both auditory and visual tasks in Experiment 9a, perhaps were induced to disregard the auditory cues in Experiment 9b, since the task simplification made it apparent that this would be an effective strategy. The lack of an auditory cue effect at the 700-ms CTOA for the former group implies that such a strategy only affected stimulus-driven orienting at short CTOAs.

## Summary and Conclusions

Recent covert orienting studies strongly indicate that the alignment of auditory attention with a particular spatial location can facilitate processing there. Unlike visual attention, though, not all auditory processing is strongly affected by auditory spatial cues: simple detection and many discrimination tasks do not seem to be affected by auditory cues. Given that the locations of auditory stimuli are computed rather than being directly coded in the receptor array, it seems likely that only auditory processing that requires localization will be affected strongly by auditory spatial cues. In accord with this notion, auditory localization tasks produce cue effects comparable to those found in visual localization tasks. The fact that visual detection and discrimination are also facilitated by the alignment of visual attention suggests that location information can, when available in the proper time course, affect non-location-based processing.

The similarity between visual and auditory spatial cueing effects (for localization tasks) begs the question of whether a supramodal attention mechanism exists or whether such effects are entirely independent. Neurophysiological studies have demonstrated that different modalities do, in fact, converge in various brain areas involved in orienting (e.g., SC: Stein & Merideth, 1993), suggesting the possibility of a supramodal mechanism. Indeed, the existence of completely independent mechanisms has been ruled out by many recent cross-modal studies of attention (e.g., Spence & Driver, 1997; Ward, 1994) that show that covert orienting in one modality is often accompanied by covert orienting in another. But while the alignment of attention by visual cues facilitated localization of both visual and auditory targets, Ward (1994) found that visual processing was unaffected by auditory cues. We have shown here that this cross-modal asymmetry is not due to response priming (Experiments 5 to 8). We have also shown, however, that the "open-channel" hypothesis, in its simplest form, is not sufficient to account for the discrepancies between Ward's (1994) results and the opposite asymmetry reported by Spence and Driver (1997).

In Experiment 9, we attempted to produce results consistent with both asymmetries by manipulating the cue and task environments. In Experiment 9a, only auditory cues were presented, but both auditory and visual targets occurred. As predicted by the open-channel hypothesis (since both channels were monitored), auditory cues did significantly affect visual localization. Surprisingly, however, this effect was only observed at the 200-ms CTOA and not at the 100-ms CTOA. A similar pattern was seen for the auditory discrimination task, although the cue effect at 200 ms did not quite reach significance. In Experiment 9b, only visual targets occurred, but these were preceded by both auditory and visual cues. In this situation, the open-channel hypothesis would not predict any effect of auditory cues on visual targets, since the auditory channel did not have to be monitored. Nevertheless, significant cue effects were obtained: RTs to localize visual targets were faster when preceded by valid auditory cues. This result seems to disconfirm the open-channel hypothesis. However, the significant interaction between order of running the two experiments and cue effects in Experiment 9b tempers this conclusion. Those subjects who ran in Experiment 9a and then in Experiment 9b showed no auditory cue effects at short CTOAs, consistent with the open-channel hypothesis, while those who ran Experiment 9b first showed significant auditory cue effects at the short CTOAs, disconfirming the open-channel hypothesis. Thus, even subtle factors, such as the order in which conditions are run, seem to be able to influence the strategy with which subjects approach these tasks.

Whatever the interpretation of the details of Experiments 9a and 9b, the overall finding that changes in cue and task environment changed the obtained cue effects provides confirmation of the hypothesis that strategic factors can influence stimulus-driven cross-modal orienting. Examination of Figure 1 reveals that the connections between visual and auditory systems and the attention network provide multiple ways in which events occurring in one sensory system can affect processing of events in the other, including something resembling the mechanism suggested by Spence and Driver (1997) for their results, as well as other mechanisms involving the PN or the PPC in various combinations. Moreover, modulation of the attention network by frontal cortical areas allows strategic control of these cross-modal influences similar to that already demonstrated in vision (e.g., Yantis & Jonides, 1990). Further research in this area will focus on determining the precise conditions under which different types of cross-modal orienting occur, and on linking these conditions to specific interactions between the attention network and sensory-perceptual systems.

## Acknowledgments

This work was supported by a grant from the Natural Sciences and Engineering Research Council of Canada to Lawrence M. Ward. The authors thank David Sewell, Paul Smith, Dominic Baba, Lisa Deguchi, and Ali Nassar for laboratory assistance, and Robert West for useful discussions. Correspondence should be addressed to Lawrence M. Ward, Department of Psychology, University of British Columbia, 2136 West Mall, Vancouver, B.C., Canada V6T 1Z4. E-mail: lward@cortex.psych.ubc.ca.

# Notes

1  A repeated-measures ANOVA (6 Cue Conditions × 4 CTOAs × 2 Validities) of the median reaction times in the visual task revealed a significant effect of Cue Condition [$F(5,70) = 10.00, p < .001$], and CTOA [$F(3,42) = 52.52, < .001$] but not of Validity, and significant interactions of Cue Condition × CTOA [$F(15,210) = 3.12, p = .006$], CTOA × Validity [$F(3,42) = 11.49, p < .001$], and Cue Condition × CTOA × Validity [$F(15,210) = 12.28, p < .001$]. In these and all ANOVAs reported here, Huynh-Feldt corrected degrees of freedom were used to calculate $p$-values. Overall, $\alpha = .05$ was used for statistical significance. For purposes of determining significance of planned comparisons a Bonferroni procedure was used in which each Cue Condition was considered to be the experimental unit (since these are usually run as separate experiments) and EW was set at .10. With 4 comparisons planned (Invalid versus Valid at each CTOA) in each Cue Condition, $\alpha$ was set to .025 for each comparison. For the visual simple reaction times the critical difference between Invalid and Valid trials was 15 ms. Thus, differences in visual simple reaction time greater than 15 ms are said to be reliable under these conditions, and differences exceeding this value are indicated by an asterisk (*) in Figure 5. Similarly, a repeated-measures ANOVA (6 Cue Conditions × 4 CTOAs × 2 Validities) of the median reaction times in the auditory task revealed a significant effect of Cue Condition [$F(5,70) = 41.46, p < .001$], and CTOA [$F(3,42) = 38.17, p < .001$] but not of Validity, and a significant interaction of Cue Condition × CTOA [$F(15,210) = 7.88, p < .001$]. The critical difference for the auditory simple reaction time planned comparisons was 14 ms; there were no differences exceeding that value.

2  A repeated-measures ANOVA (6 Cue Conditions × 4 CTOAs × 2 Validities) of the median reaction times in the visual discrimination task revealed a significant effect of Cue Condition [$F(5,70) = 4.63, p = .002$], CTOA [$F(3,42) = 14.30, p < .001$], and Validity [$F(1,14) = 34.73, p < .001$], and significant interactions of Cue Condition × CTOA [$F(15,210) = 3.90, p < .001$], and Cue Condition × Validity [$F(5,70) = 17.10, p < .001$]. The critical difference for the visual discrimination response time planned comparisons was 20 ms, and differences exceeding that value are indicated by an asterisk (*) in Figure 6. A similar repeated-measures ANOVA (6 Cue Conditions × 4 CTOAs × 2 Validities) of the median reaction times in the auditory discrimination task revealed a significant effect of CTOA [$F(3,42) = 12.75, p = .001$] but no other significant effects. The critical difference for the auditory discrimination response time planned comparisons was 23 ms, and there were no differences exceeding that value.

3  A repeated-measures ANOVA (6 Cue Conditions × 4 CTOAs × 2 Validities) of the median reaction times in Experiment 5 revealed a significant effect of Cue Condition [$F(5,70) = 39.07, p < .001$], CTOA [$F(3,42) = 72.36, p < .001$], and Validity [$F(1,14) = 26.22, p < .001$], and significant interactions of Cue Condition × CTOA [$F(15,210) = 4.59, p < .001$], Cue Condition × Validity [$F(5,70) = 7.19, p = .001$], CTOA × Validity [$F(3,42) = 30.06, p < .001$], and Cue Condition × CTOA × Validity [$F(15,210) = 14.53, p < .001$]. The critical difference for the planned comparisons was 15 ms, and single differences exceed-

ing that value in Experiment 5 are indicated by an asterisk (*) in Figure 7. A similar repeated-measures ANOVA (6 Cue Conditions × 4 CTOAs × 2 Validities) of the median reaction times in Experiment 6 revealed a significant effect of Cue Condition [$F(5,70) = 21.48, p < .001$], CTOA [$F(3,42) = 73.43, p < .001$], and Validity [$F(1,14) = 44.48, p < .001$], and significant interactions of Cue Condition × CTOA [$F(15,210) = 5.70, p < .001$], Cue Condition × Validity [$F(5,70) = 30.09, p = .001$], CTOA × Validity [$F(3,42) = 6.05, p = .004$], and Cue Condition × CTOA × Validity [$F(15,210) = 10.36, p < .001$]. The critical difference for the planned comparisons was 19 ms, and single differences exceeding that value in Experiment 6 are indicated by an asterisk (*) in Figure 7.

4  A repeated-measures ANOVA (6 Cue Conditions × 4 CTOAs × 2 Validities) of the median reaction times in Experiment 7 revealed a significant effect of Cue Condition [$F(5,75) = 12.84, p < .001$], CTOA [$F(3,45) = 8.68, p = .002$], and Validity [$F(1,15) = 5.74, p = .03$], and significant interactions of Cue Condition × CTOA [$F(15,225) = 4.52, p < .001$], CTOA × Validity [$F(3,45) = 4.12, p = .015$], and Cue Condition × CTOA × Validity [$F(15,225) = 11.79, p < .001$]. The critical difference for the planned comparisons was 20 ms, and single differences exceeding that value in Experiment 7 are indicated by an asterisk (*) in Figure 9.

5  A repeated-measures ANOVA (6 Cue conditions × 3 CTOAs × 2 Validities) of the median reaction times in Experiment 8 revealed a significant effect of Cue Condition [$F(5,70) = 13.22, p < .001$], CTOA [$F(2,28) = 34.49, p < .001$], but not Validity, and significant interactions of Cue Condition × CTOA [$F(10,140) = 3.18, p = .005$], and Cue Condition × Validity [$F(5,70) = 7.83, p < .001$]. The critical difference for the planned comparisons was 14 ms, and single differences exceeding that value in Experiment 8 are indicated by an asterisk (*) in Figure 9.

6  Separate between (Order of experiments)-within (Target Type x CTOA x Validity for 9a or Cue Type x CTOA x Validity for 9b) ANOVAs were performed for Experiments 9a and 9b. For Experiment 9a, there was no significant main effect of the Order of completing the experiments, nor did Order interact with any other factor. There was a significant main effect of Target Type [Auditory or Visual, $F(1,13) = 146.59, p < .001$], CTOA [$F(2,26) = 14.45, p < .001$], and Validity [$F(1,13) = 5.42, p = .037$], and significant interactions of Target Type × CTOA [$F(2,26) = 9.24, p = .002$], Target Type × Validity [$F(1,13) = 7.47, p = .017$], and CTOA × Validity [$F(2,26) = 9.56, p = .002$]. The critical difference for 6 planned comparisons (Bonferroni EW = .12) was 22 ms, and differences exceeding that value in Experiment 9a are indicated by an asterisk (*) in Figure 10. For Experiment 9b, the main effect of Order was also not significant, but there was a significant Order × Cue Type × Validity interaction [$F(1,13) = 5.25, p = .039$]. There were also significant main effects of Cue Type [Auditory or Visual, $F(1,13) = 57.70, p < .001$], CTOA [$F(2, 26) = 7.04, p = .007$], and Validity [$F(1,13) = 43.20, p < .001$], and significant interactions of Cue Type × CTOA [$F(2, 26) = 4.87, p = .028$], and Cue Type × Validity [$F(1, 13) = 24.42, p < .001$]. The critical difference for 6 planned comparisons (Bonferroni EW = .12) was 16 ms, and differences exceeding that value for Experiment 9b are indicated by an asterisk (*) in Figure 10.

# References

Bédard, M.A., El Massioui, F., Pillon, B., & Nandrino, J.L. (1993). Time for reorienting of attention: A premotor hypothesis of the underlying mechanism. *Neuropsychologia, 31*, 241–249.

Bregman, A.S. (1990). *Auditory scene analysis.* Cambridge, MA: MIT Press.

Broadbent, D. (1958). *Perception and communication.* London: Pergamon.

Buchtel, H.A., & Butter, C.M. (1988). Spatial attention shifts: Implications for the role of polysensory mechanisms. *Neuropsychologia, 26*, 499–509.

Bushnell, M.C., Goldberg, M.E., & Robinson, D.L. (1981). Behavioral enhancement of visual responses in monkey cerebral cortex: I. Modulation in posterior parietal cortex related to selective visual attention. *Journal of Neurophysiology, 46*, 755–772.

Cherry, C. (1957). *On human communication.* London: Wiley.

Dai, H., Scharf, B., & Buus, S. (1991). Effective attenuation of signals in noise under focused attention. *Journal of the Acoustical Society of America, 89*, 2837–2842.

Downing, C. (1988). Expectancy and visual-spatial attention: Effects on perceptual quality. *Journal of Experimental Psychology: Human Perception & Performance, 14*, 188–202.

Farah, M.J., Wong, A.B., Monheit, M.A., & Morrow, L.A. (1989). Parietal lobe mechanisms of spatial attention: Modality specific or supramodal? *Neuropsychologia, 27*, 461–470.

Greenberg, G., & Larkin, W. (1968). Frequency-response characteristic of auditory observers detecting signals of a single frequency in noise: The probe-signal method. *Journal of the Acoustical Society of America, 44*, 1513–1523.

Hafter, E.R., & Schlauch, R.S. (1991). Cognitive factors and selection of auditory listening bands. In A.L. Dancer, D. Henderson, R.J. Salvi, & R.P. Hammernik (Eds.), *Noise induced hearing loss.* Philadelphia: B.C. Decker.

Hikosaka, O. (1991). Basil ganglia: Possible role in motor coordination and learning. *Current Opinion in Neurobiology, 1*, 638–643.

Hikosaka, O., & Wurtz, R.H. (1985). Modification of saccadic eye movements by GABA-related substances. II. Effects of muscimol in monkey substantia nigra pars reticulata. *Journal of Neurophysiology, 53*, 292–308.

Hubner, R., & Hafter, E.R. (1995). Cueing mechanisms in auditory signal detection. *Perception & Psychophysics, 57*, 197–202.

Jackson, S., & Lees, M. (1993). The significance of the basal ganglia in suppressing hyper-reflexive orienting. *Behavioral & Brain Sciences, 16*, 581–582.

Johnson, D.M., & Hafter, E.R. (1980). Uncertain-frequency detection: Cueing and condition of observation. *Perception & Psychophysics, 28*, 143–149.

Klein, R., Brennan, M., & Gilani, A. (1987). *Covert cross-modality orienting of attention in space.* Paper presented at the annual meeting of the Psychonomic Society, Seattle, Washington.

Leek, M.R. (1987). Directed attention in complex sound perception. In W.A. Yost & C.S. Watson (Eds.), *Auditory processing of complex sounds* (pp. 278–289). Hillsdale, NJ: Erlbaum.

Leek, M.R., Brown, M.E., & Dorman, M.F. (1991). Informational masking and auditory attention. *Perception & Psychophysics, 50*, 205–214.

Mills, A.W. (1960). Lateralization of high-frequency tones. *Journal of the Acoustical Society of America, 32*, 132–134.

Mondor, T.A., & Bregman, A.S. (1994). Allocating attention to frequency regions. *Perception & Psychophysics, 56*, 268–276.

Mondor, T.A., & Zatorre, R.J. (1995). Shifting and focusing auditory spatial attention. *Journal of Experimental Psychology: Human Perception & Performance, 21*, 387–409.

Moray, N. (1970). *Attention: Selective processes in vision and hearing.* New York: Academic Press.

Mori, S., & Ward, L.M. (1991). Listening versus hearing: Attentional effects on intensity discrimination. *Technical Report on Hearing: The Acoustical Society of Japan, No. H-91–36.*

—————— (1992). Listening versus hearing II: Attentional effects on intensity discrimination by musicians. *Technical Report on Hearing: The Acoustical Society of Japan, No. H-92–48.*

Posner, M.I. (1978). *Chronometric explorations of mind.* New York: Oxford University Press.

Posner, M.I., Davidson, B.J., & Nissen, M.J. (1976). The process of stimulus detection. Paper presented at the annual meeting of the Psychonomic Society, St. Louis. Cited in Posner, M.I. (1978). *Chronometric explorations of mind.* New York: Oxford University Press.

Posner, M.I., & Cohen, Y. (1984). Components of visual orienting. In H. Bouma & D.G. Bouwhuis (Eds.), *Attention & Performance, Vol. 10*, (pp. 531–556). Hillsdale, NJ: Erlbaum.

Posner, M.I., Rafal, R.D., Choate, L.S., & Vaughan, J. (1985). Inhibition of return: Neural basis and function. *Cognitive Neuropsychology, 2*, 211–228.

Posner, M.I., Peterson, S.E., Fox, P.T., & Raichle, M.E. (1988). Localization of cognitive operations in the human brain. *Science, 240*, 1627–1631.

Rafal, R.D., Calabresi, P., Brennan, C., & Sciolto, T. (1989). Saccadic preparation inhibits reorienting to recently attended locations. *Journal of Experimental Psychology: Human Perception & Performance, 15*, 673–685.

Rafal, R.D., Henik, A., & Smith, J. (1991). Extrageniculate contributions to reflexive visual orienting in normal humans: A temporal hemifield advantage. *Journal of Cognitive Neuroscience, 3*, 322–328.

Rhodes, G. (1987). Auditory attention and the representation of spatial information. *Perception & Psychophysics, 42*, 1–14.

Robinson, D.L., & McClurkin, J.W. (1989). The visual superior colliculus and pulvinar. In R. Wurtz & M.E. Goldberg (Eds.), *The neurobiology of saccadic eye movements* (pp. 213–255). Amsterdam: Elsevier.

Scharf, B. (1989). Spectral specificity in auditory detection: The effect of listening on hearing. *Journal of the Acoustical Society of Japan, 10*, 309–317.

Scharf, B., Canevet, G., Possamai, C-A., & Bonnel, A-M. (1986). Some effects of attention in hearing. Cited in Scharf, B. (1988). The role of listening in the measurement of hearing. *Advances in Audiology, 5*, 13–26.

Scharf, B., Quigley, S., Aoki, C., Peachey, N., & Reeves, A. (1987). Focused auditory attention and frequency selectivity. *Perception & Psychophysics, 42*, 215–223.

Schlauch, R.S., & Hafter, E.R. (1991). Listening bandwidths and frequency uncertainty in pure-tone signal detection. *Journal of the Acoustical Society of America, 90*, 1332–1339.

Simon, J.R., & Craft, J.L. (1970). Effects of an irrelevant auditory stimulus on visual choice reaction time. *Journal of Experimental Psychology, 86*, 272–274.

Simon, J.R., Acosta, E., Mewaldt, S.P., & Speidel, C.R. (1976). The effect of an irrelevant directional cue on choice reaction time: Duration of the phenomenon and its relation to stages of processing. *Perception & Psychophysics, 19*, 16–22.

Sparks, D.L., & Hartwich-Young, R. (1989). The deep layers of the superior colliculus. In R. Wurtz & M.E. Goldberg (Eds.), *The neurobiology of saccadic eye movements* (pp. 213–255). Amsterdam: Elsevier.

Spence, C.J., & Driver, J. (1994). Covert spatial orienting in audition: Exogenous and endogenous mechanisms. *Journal of Experimental Psychology: Human Perception & Performance, 20*, 555–574.

Spence, C.J., & Driver, J. (1997). Audio-visual links in exogenous covert spatial orienting. *Perception & Psychophysics, 59*, 1–220.

Stein, B.E., & Meredith, M.A. (1993). *The merging of the senses.* Cambridge, MA: MIT Press.

Tanner, W., & Norman, R. (1954). The human use of information: II. Signal detection for the case of an unknown signal parameter. Cited in Scharf (1989).

Treisman, A. (1964). Selective attention in man. *British Medical Journal, 20*, 12–16.

Treisman, A., & Gormican, S. (1988). Feature analysis in early vision: Evidence from search asymmetries. *Psychological Review, 95*, 15–48.

Ward, L.M. (1994). Supramodal and modality-specific mechanisms for stimulus-driven shifts of auditory and visual attention. *Canadian Journal of Experimental Psychology, 48*, 242–259.

Ward, L.M. (1997). Involuntary listening aids hearing. *Psychological Science, 8*, 112–118.

Ward, L.M., & Mori, S. (1996). Attention cueing aids auditory intensity resolution. *Journal of the Acoustical Society of America, 100*, 1722–1727.

Wright, R.D., & Ward, L.M. (this volume). The control of visual attention. In R. D. Wright (Ed.), *Visual attention.* New York: Oxford University Press.

Wurtz, R.H., Goldberg, M.E., & Robinson, D.L. (1982). Brain mechanisms of visual attention. *Scientific American, 246*, 100–107.

Wurtz, R.H., & Munoz, D.P. (1995). Role of monkey superior colliculus in control of saccades and fixation. In M. Gazzaniga (Ed.), *The cognitive neurosciences.* Cambridge, MA: MIT Press.

Yantis, S., & Jonides, J. . (1990). Abrupt visual onsets and selective attention: Voluntary versus automatic allocation. *Journal of Experimental Psychology: Human Perception & Performance, 16*, 121–134.

# 10

# The Development of Orienting
# to Locations and Objects

## Michael I. Posner, Mary K. Rothbart,
## Lisa Thomas-Thrapp and Gina Gerardi

In recent years, many issues in cognition have been illuminated by the study of their origin in early life. In the first year of life, infants show signs of language (Mehler & Christophe, 1995), appreciation of number (Starkey, Spelke, & Gelman, 1990), and preliminary understanding of physical objects (Baillargeon, 1995). There has been a similar effort to study the early development of the mechanisms of infant visual attention (Johnson, 1995).

A primary purpose of these studies of infant visual attention is to help us understand what capacities in the natural behaviour of infants are influenced by changes in underlying attentional networks. Knowledge of attention can illuminate developmental questions such as the relation of orienting to emotion, differences between infants in temperament, and the role of socialization in infant behaviour (Posner & Rothbart, 1994; Posner, Rothbart, Gerardi, & Thomas-Thrapp, in press; Rothbart, Derryberry, & Posner, 1994).

Cognitive studies of attention have uniformly involved adult subjects whose nervous systems and skills of orienting are highly developed. In this chapter, we have tried to specifically relate our infant studies to issues currently debated by cognitive psychologists. We believe that, in some cases, the infant data can provide evidence that supports one or another view of the mechanisms of adult attention. Below we discuss a number of such cognitive issues, and examine infant data that seems to us to be related to them.

## Cognitive Issues

Many adult studies concern the presence of internal mechanisms of covert attention. Although studies have consistently shown that adults can give priority to a spatial location without an eye movement (Posner, 1988), there still remains the question of how closely covert shifts and eye movements are related. This problem is somewhat more complex in infants for whom it is often necessary to substitute an eye movement for a key press as a performance indicant. In general, as recent summary articles indicate, it has proven possible to use the eye movement system in infants as a marker of covert attention shifts (Hood, 1994; Johnson & Tucker, 1996). However, we will discuss some complexities in comparing infant studies with adult studies in the sections below on covert orienting in infants.

A related issue in cognition concerns the separation of mechanisms involved in exogenous and endogenous forms of covert orienting. Exogenous orienting involves cues that occur at the location to which attention is summoned. Endogenous orienting is based upon a symbol that indicates the attended location. A number of findings in cognitive psychology have suggested that the two forms of orienting are separate (see Klein, Kingstone, & Pontefract, 1993), but lesion and Position Emission Tomography (PET) data indicates that the same parietal based system is involved whether attention is shifted by a peripheral stimulus or a central cue (Corbetta, Meizen, Shulman, & Petersen, 1993; Posner & Raichle, 1994).

Recently, Egly, Driver, and Rafal (1994) have proposed that the mechanisms for orienting to locations are separate from the mechanisms for orienting to objects. Their idea is that left parietal mechanisms shift attention between objects, while right parietal mechanisms shift attention to spatial locations. Infants show novelty preferences for both locations and objects, so it is possible to ask when each preference develops and how they relate to each other and to activity of the two cerebral hemispheres.

An issue less discussed in the cognitive literature but important in neuropsychology involves the role of subcortical mechanisms in selective attention. Several investigators in cognitive neuroscience have proposed that thalamic and midbrain areas are involved in aspects of selective attention (LaBerge, 1995; Posner, 1988). Infants in the early months of life appear to rely more prominently on the subcortical visual system than do adult subjects (Haith, 1980). Thus, infant studies could be critical in providing evidence about subcortical systems.

One of the most important questions in modern studies of cognition is how attention is related to the constructs of explicit and implicit memory. Explicit memory is thought to involve conscious processes of recollection, and thus is considered to be closely related to attention (Curran & Keele, 1993). Implicit memories, however, need not depend on attention. Infants begin learning well before higher level cognitive operations, such as those involved in voluntary control, are fully developed. Thus, it may be possible to relate attention systems of orienting and higher executive control to aspects of memory; we devote a major section of the chapter to this issue.

# Orienting by Infants

## Covert Orienting

Attention to visual stimuli in adults can be either overt or covert. The key to separation of the two requires the adult to remain fixated, assessing covert attention by improvement in reaction time (RT), reduction in threshold, or increases in electrical activity at the cued location (Posner, 1988). It is impossible to instruct infants either to remain fixated or to press a key. Thus, head and eye movements are often used as the behavioural index of attention.

If eye movements are the response, how can we know if the attention shift is covert? Several methods have been used. First, a cue can be presented too briefly to elicit an eye movement, followed by a target of longer duration, which is presented at the cued location or on the opposite side (Clohessy, Posner, Rothbart, & Vecera, 1991; Hood, 1994; Johnson & Tucker, 1996). In general, there is an early speeding of eye movements to targets appearing at the cued location and a later inhibition in response speed if attention is drawn back to fixation. This result was also found with key presses for adults (Posner, 1988). However, it is possible that the briefly presented cue programs the eyes to move in the direction of the subsequent target, even if no actual eye movement is involved.

Another effort to examine the relation of eye movements to covert attention in infants involves teaching the infants to perform a countersaccade (Johnson, Posner, & Rothbart, 1994). Infants learn that a cue presented briefly in one location is followed by a target on the opposite side of the visual field. The infants learn to move their eyes in the direction opposite the cue. Then on a test trial a target is presented on the same side as the cue. Our idea was that infants first switched attention to the cue and then to the target. If a target were presented shortly after the cue, attention would still be on the cued side, and thus a fast eye movement would result. We did find that infant eye movements to the target on the cued side were very fast. This finding is consistent with what had been found in adults. If adults are given a cue indicating a following target will likely occur on the side opposite the cue, at short cue-to-target intervals, they make a key-press response faster to targets at the cued location than to those on the more probable side opposite the cue. For longer cue-to-target intervals, reaction times are faster to targets occurring on the more probable side opposite the cue.

Thus, infants, having learned to make a countersaccade, seem able to prepare to move the eyes in one direction while attending covertly in the opposite direction. This finding seemed to the authors a remarkable dissociation between the direction of attention and eye-movement preparation, but the idea that the attention shifts are covert may not be completely convincing (Klein, personal communication, 1995). Klein suggests, instead, that there are two separate mechanisms of eye movement preparation, one endogenous and one exogenous. Evidence that the eyes are being prepared to execute the countersaccade by moving in a direction opposite the cue would still allow the cue to influence eye preparation via an exogenous mechanism operating opposite to the learned program. Thus, it is still not certain that our infant studies are investigating covert mechanisms that have the same independence from eye movements observed in adults. It does seem likely to us that the mechanisms we are studying in infants are those that develop into what in adults is responsible for covert attention to locations.

## Development of Orienting

Orienting to locations appears to undergo a very rapid development in the infant between two and four months. First, we found that the probability of disengaging from a central attractor to process a peripheral target increased very dramatically during this time (Johnson, Posner, & Rothbart, 1991). While this finding might reflect the improvement in acuity that is also found during this period (Gwiazda, Bauer, & Held, 1989), studies equating acuity still find evidence for the development of disengagement (Hood, in press). Moreover, when we associated one central attractor with a subsequent movement to the right and another with a movement to the left, infants of four but not two months learned to anticipate the direction of the cue. The common development of peripheral and central cue use supports the view of common mechanisms involved in both exogenous and endogenous orienting. Lesion (Posner, 1988) and PET (Corbetta et al., 1993) data also suggest that parietal mechanisms are involved in both central and peripheral cue use. We now suggest that both mechanisms develop between two and four months, just at the time PET studies suggest a strong increase in metabolic processes in the parietal lobe (Chugani, Phelps, & Mazziotta, 1987). Thus, our infant data is consistent with the maturation of a single internal parietal system that supports orienting of attention to both peripheral and central cues.

## Inhibition of Return

One principle of development in infancy is that subcortical visual mechanisms tend to develop prior to cortical mechanisms. Inhibition of return (IOR) is a bias against returning attention to a just-examined location. Its function appears to be to produce a bias toward the examination of novel locations. Since we believe that inhibition of return (Posner, 1988; Rafal, Posner, Friedman, Inhoff, & Bernstein, 1988) depends upon a collicular mechanism, we expected it to be present at the

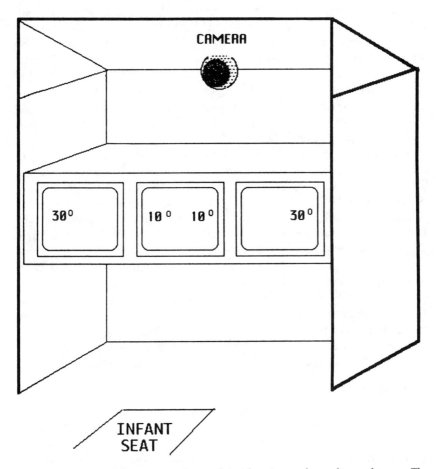

*Figure* 1: Experimental apparatus for studying location and novelty preference. The Central Attractor is placed in the middle of the central monitor. Objects are presented 10° or 30° from fixation in the various studies described in this chapter.

youngest ages we studied. We were surprised to find that inhibition of return was not present at three months but developed between four and six months at a time generally overlapping with the cortical covert attention mechanisms we have been describing. Our studies employed three cathode ray tubes organized as in Figure 1.

The first set of studies used targets displayed 30° from fixation (Clohessy et al., 1991). We observed that three- and four-month-olds, but not older infants, tended to reach the target by making a series of small saccades rather than a single integrated eye movement. They usually took more than a second to reach the 30°. Adult studies have indicated that the necessary and sufficient conditions for observing IOR in adults was the programming of an eye movement (Rafal, Calabresi, Brennan, & Scioloto, 1989). We reasoned that if IOR requires the programming of eye movements, the infants with hypometric saccades might not be showing IOR because, rather than programming their eye movements to the target, they were searching for it. Since most three-month-olds moved their eyes directly to 10° targets, they should, by this logic, also show IOR. Harman, Posner, Rothbart, and Thomas-Thrapp (1994) studied IOR for stimuli presented at 10° from fixation, and found it to be fully present at three months.

Recently, IOR has been shown for newborn infants, presumably reflecting the midbrain mechanisms that are dominant at birth (Valenza, Simion, & Umilta, 1994). When infants in the Valenza et al. (1994) study oriented directly to 30° targets, they showed clear evidence of IOR. This finding, taken with our results for 10° targets in three-month-old infants, suggests that the basic computations for IOR are present at birth. Their implementation appears to depend upon whether a stimulus evokes a programmed eye movement or not. We are not sure of the factors that produce so many hypometric eye movements in infants of three months. However, these may relate to maturation of the cortical systems (e.g., parietal lobe, frontal eye fields) that appear to occur about this time (Johnson et al., 1991). These data generally support the idea that the subcortical computations involved in IOR are present earlier than the parietally based ability to disengage from a visual stimulus.

## Objects and Locations

The ability to study eye movements to targets at 10° at three months allowed us to begin to compare the development of preference for novel locations with preference for novel objects. In adults, there appear to be separate mechanisms involved in orienting to objects and to locations (Egly, Driver, & Rafal, 1994). IOR clearly is a kind of preference for a novel location over a just-attended location. We have argued that this computation depends upon midbrain structures that are strongly dominant at birth. However, preference for novel objects must depend in part upon maturation of cortical systems involved in object recognition.

In recent studies, we have directly compared novelty preference for location and for objects. In our first studies (Harman et al., 1994), we found that the two forms of novelty produced a very strong preference in infants of three and six months. When a novel object appeared at a novel location, infants showed an overall novelty preference on 73% of the trials at three months and 77% at six months. When the two forms of preference were put in competition, three-month-olds no longer showed an object novelty preference, but by six months they oriented toward the novel object 63% of the time, even though it occurred at a

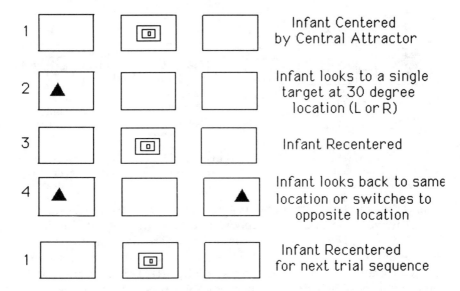

1   Infant Centered
    by Central Attractor

2   Infant looks to a single
    target at 30 degree
    location (L or R)

3   Infant Recentered

4   Infant looks back to same
    location or switches to
    opposite location

1   Infant Recentered
    for next trial sequence

*Figure* 2: Sequence of events used to study inhibition of return (IOR) in infants. Infants' eyes are drawn to a target 10° or 30° from fixation (depending on the study) and, after being returned to centre, the infant is presented with the same object at the same location on both sides. Eye movements were recorded and superimposed on the stimuli for ease of coding.

repeated location. Since object novelty seemed to be stronger at six months than at three months, we interpreted our results as indicating that object novelty preference develops at a somewhat slower pace than does preference based upon location.

Recently, we have been able to extend these studies to show the relative independence of the two forms of novelty preference at six months. We (Thomas-Thrapp, Posner, & Rothbart, 1995) compared the same six-month-old infants in single trial paradigms involving either exposure to a single object or to a single location, followed by forced choice between two objects or two locations (see Figures 2 and 3).

On trials to assess preference for novel objects, the infants were presented with a single object at fixation (see Figure 3). After an interval, they were presented with that object and a novel one, each at 10° from fixation. In the location condition, the infant's eyes were drawn to a single object 30° from fixation, and their eyes were then returned to fixation. The choice involved identical stimuli presented either at the position to which they had been oriented or on the opposite side of fixation.

When infants had sufficient exposure time to the single object, they showed a preference for the novel object and for the novel location. We

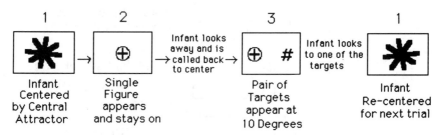

*Figure 3*: Sequence of events for novel-object trials (infant-controlled presentation interval). Only 10° locations on monitor (see Figure 1) are used. Infant receives a single object at fixation and is then given a choice between that object and another object both at 10°.

found the object novelty preference when the infant examined the first object for three seconds or more, but not when they oriented to it for only 1 second. The time of exposure necessary to show an object preference in our six-month-old infants was similar to that previously reported for infant monkeys (Gunderson & Swartz, 1986). Location preference was established even when orienting was as brief as we could make it. Thus, we were able to replicate both forms of novelty preference in these infants. Because of the large number of infants involved, it was possible to ask if the two forms of novelty preference were correlated. The data were clear in showing that they were not. This finding is congruent with the interpretation that we are studying two independent forms of novelty preference.

In our previous work on orienting to locations, we often found a bias for turning toward the left when the infant had a choice between two lateral locations. However, these effects were not significant within any study, and showed extremely high variability. In the current data, we again found that during the novel location trials, infants were more likely to orient to their left, but the bias was not significant. However, during our experiments involving orienting to an old or new object, we found that infants were more likely to orient to the object on the right than they were to the object on the left, and we found that this effect was independent of which object was novel. Thus, the trend is for the occurrence of opposite biases in orienting direction in the location novelty and object novelty studies. Infants seem more likely to turn left during location novelty trials and more likely to turn right during object novelty trials. Although these lateralized turning preferences are not strong enough to form the basis of any firm interpretation, their overall direction is in accord with findings of adult studies suggesting a right-hemisphere bias for orienting to locations and a left-hemisphere bias for orienting to objects (Egly et al., 1994).

## Summary

In this section, we have briefly reviewed a number of infant studies designed to examine the development of orienting in the first year of life. We have found that orienting arises in close correspondence with the eye movement system, and that elements of orienting are present from birth. The course of development appears to reflect the general maturation of cortical visual systems during the first year of life (Johnson et al., 1991). Thus, IOR is present at birth, but only later does the ability to voluntarily disengage from a fixation show strong development. The development we have seen between two to four months is probably a consequence of maturation of parietal systems. The novelty preference for objects appears to develop strongly from four to six months, and is probably driven by maturation of the ventral prestriate structures involved in object identification. The independence of novelty preference for objects and locations fits well with the view, emerging from adult data, that these involve different mechanisms (Egly et al., 1994). Orienting from exogenous and orienting from endogenous cues appear to develop together, supporting the lesion and PET evidence of strong involvement of the parietal lobe in both forms of orienting. The ability of four-month-old infants to use central cues to direct anticipation toward an upcoming target suggests that learning is exhibited by the eye movement system at this age. In the next section we examine the development of this form of implicit learning.

## Learning

In the previous sections, we emphasized the act of orienting toward visual events. In this section, we consider the ability of infants to learn where to orient their attention. Two forms of learning are under active examination in current cognitive studies (Schacter, 1995). They differ primarily in their relation to the ability to reinstate the trace by attention. Explicit memory in adults is marked by the ability to report what has been previously learned as a new fact. One can consciously bring the prior learning to mind and recall it as an experience. Of course, infants cannot tell us about their learning, and so we often do not know if they have learned in an explicit manner. A second form of learning is implicit. This form of learning is thought to occur even without the ability to engage in conscious recall of the learned material, but performance is altered by previous experience. Normally the two forms of learning go together. If we have learned a new skill, we can describe the experience of learning it, the place it was learned, and so forth, even if we cannot describe the skill itself in detail. However, in amnesic patients, these forms of learning can be dissociated. Persons who cannot recall or recognize even having had an experience, or who cannot place a person with whom it occurred, may show by their performance that they have learned the skill, often in a completely normal way. These forms of learning can often be dissociated in normal subjects by distracting their attention when they learn the task.

One task widely used to explore the distinction between implicit and explicit learning had subjects press a key corresponding to the spatial location of a visual target (Nissen & Bullemer, 1987). Without the subject's knowledge, a repeating sequence of locations was embedded in the test trials. Subjects exhibited that they had learned the sequence by pressing the appropriate key more rapidly than for non-sequence lights. Amnesic patients, although a bit slower, learned the skill normally, but could not remember having practised it as well as could the normal subjects (Nissen & Bullemer, 1987). Some lists, in which each of the repeating associations is unique (e.g. 2431), can be learned easily by normal subjects, even when distracted. After having learned the list, they may be totally unable to recall or recognize any of the associations (Curran & Keele, 1993). Thus, when light 2 follows light 1, they are fast because they have learned the association implicitly, but they do not recognize that association when asked whether 2 or 3 follows 1. One part of their information processing system knows the association, but another does not. When subjects have learned implicitly in this way, they do not usually press the key in anticipation of the light being presented. While they are faster in responding to a light in sequence, they do not seem to have the information to anticipate its occurrence. When an unexpected item is presented during the course of an implicitly learned sequence, however, they are abnormally slow, as though they had somehow already oriented to the expected event and had to reorient to the new location (Bullemer & Nissen, 1990). Although some of these findings have been disputed in adults (Perruchet & Amorim, 1993), it seems important to investigate the origins of these forms of learning in preverbal infants.

## Simple sequences

The basis of sequence learning is an arbitrary association between two spatial locations. Haith, Hazen, and Goodman (1988) showed that infants' ability to learn this type of association was developed at about three and one-half months. In this work, improvements in reaction time were the primary dependent measures. In our laboratory, four-month-old infants were taught such associations (Clohessy, 1994; Johnson et al., 1991). If two different central attractors are presented, one of which means "look right" and the other, "look left," four-month-old infants learn to move their head and eyes in the indicated

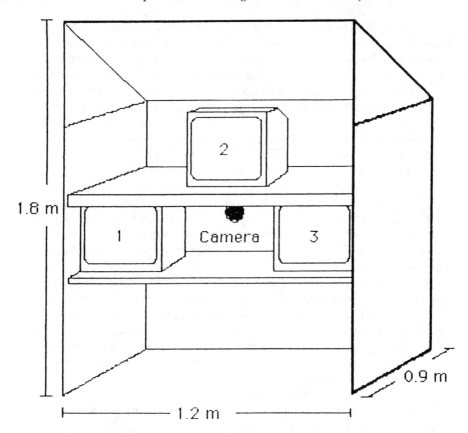

*Figure* 4: Organization of 3 monitors to study simple and complex sequences of locations. The numbers on the monitors are for illustration only. In the actual experiment, the starting location was counterbalanced across infants.

directions in the sense that they show increasing speed over trials and often anticipate the target location. Moreover, for the four-month-olds, the percentage of correct anticipation was significantly above chance. We did not find evidence of such learning in infants younger than four months, nor in subsequent work did we see any improvement in this learning ability between four and 10 months.

Our initial studies involved learning an association between the identity of a central attractor and the location of a subsequent target. In sequence learning, associations are between successive locations. To explore the development of sequence learning, we studied the ability of four and 10-month-old infants and adults to anticipate sequences of locations. Since infants could not press keys, we used a measure of the percent correct anticipatory eye movements for all groups (Clohessy, 1994). We presented infants with a display of three monitors as shown in Figure 4. We used either random orderings of targets on the three monitors or fixed target sequences. One such sequence we called the simple sequence. The simple sequence involved consistent, unambiguous associations so that each location was always followed by a single, associated location (e.g. $1 \rightarrow 2, 2 \rightarrow 3, 3 \rightarrow 1$; the monitor assigned to each number was counterbalanced over infants). Under these circumstances infants often move their eyes in anticipation of the target, and four-month-old infants learned the simple sequence in the sense that their anticipations were correct more than would be expected by chance. There seemed little improvement between four and 10 months of age.

One problem with sequences of this type is that each new association required orienting to the one location that had not been examined recently. Moving from $1 \rightarrow 2 \rightarrow 3 \rightarrow 1$ never requires infants to return attention to a position to which they had just looked. The learning of these infants could then be limited to sequences that follow the bias against returning attention to a previously examined location (IOR). To see if the learning was more general, Gerardi (1994) used a display in which there were four positions arranged in a square. Target stimuli moved around the periphery of the square in either a clockwise or counterclockwise direction. When infants moved their eyes from position $1 \rightarrow 2$, both positions three and four were novel in the sense that the stimuli were emanating not simply from the just previously attended location. We could then test if the infant could learn to anticipate the correct association even when both were equally novel. Results showed that infants at four months could learn these associations.

It seems reasonable to suppose that the form of learning exhibited by our four-month-old infants is implicit. As we mentioned, this form of learning arises by three and one-half months of age (Haith et al., 1988), and does not seem to show very much improvement between about four and 10 months. While our studies of adults performing this task suggest that they do better than the infants, even when we try to separate out those who have explicit knowledge, there are striking similarities between the purely implicit learning of adults and the infant behaviour (Clohessy, 1994). It appears that the ability to learn this kind of task implicitly arises at about three to four months. It occurs at about the same time as the development of cortical computations involved in orienting and it may not show a great deal of change after that. Although the evidence that orienting and the learning of sequences emerge at about the same time is not a very strong argument for a common mechanism, there is evidence from adults that implicit learning of locations involves basal ganglia structures (Grafton, Hazelton, & Ivry, 1995) that have strong links to parietal systems involved in covert shifts of attention (Jackson, Marrocco, & Posner, 1994).

## Context-Sensitive Sequences

So far, we have been examining orienting to simple sequences in which a single, unambiguous association has to be learned. We have found that infants can learn to anticipate the occurrence of such events even when they are formed into sequences that must be carried in memory. In our studies of attention in adults, we have argued that the mechanisms related to orienting to visual locations constitute a special brain network involving areas of the parietal lobe, pulvinar, and colliculus (Posner & Petersen, 1990). However, there is also evidence that frontal structures have input into the visual object recognition pathways during attention to visual objects (Posner & Dehaene, 1994). When people attend selectively to the color, form, and motion of targets, there is evidence that frontal cortical areas and the basal ganglia become active (Corbetta, Miezen, Dobmeyer, Shulman, & Petersen, 1991). These frontal areas act as a source of attentional effects, for example, when people have to locate a particular form or color of target in a visual array (Posner et al., 1994). The anterior cingulate is active not only in orienting to visual objects, but in orienting to words, in creating visual images, and other high-level mental activity. Studying the development of these areas in infancy is an important means of understanding how higher level cognitions can guide the voluntary control of orienting.

Studies of adults have distinguished between unambiguous associations, in which each stimulus always implies a single next location, and context-dependent associations, in which the nature of the association depends upon context (Curran & Keele, 1993). These adult studies indicate that unambiguous associations can be learned, presumably implicitly, even when attention is diverted by a secondary task, but context-dependent associations cannot be learned without focal attention (Curran & Keele, 1993).

We reasoned that, if the sequence learning we have observed in our infants depends upon orienting to stimuli and not upon the higher forms of attention involved in explicit learning, then four- and 10-month-olds should learn unambiguous associations but not ambiguous ones. The ability to learn ambiguous associations could then serve as a marker task for the development of more complex forms of attention related to executive control by anterior structures.

In our studies of four- and 10-month-old infants, we also employed a complex sequence in which one of the associations was context-dependent or ambiguous (Clohessy, 1994). In this sequence, infants were shown a sequence where the target moved from monitor 1 to 2, and then after returning to 1, moved to 3 (i.e., $1 \rightarrow 2 \rightarrow 1 \rightarrow 3$). Thus, the association of the location that followed monitor 1 was dependent upon where in the sequence they were. We found that infants of four and 10 months learned to anticipate correctly the unambiguous returns to position 1, but showed no evidence of learning the context-dependent associations.

By 18 months, infants are showing many signs of higher level attentional control. This includes the "language explosion," the emergence of multiple word utterances, the ability to sort and classify objects, and evidence of self-recognition (Meltzoff, 1990). For this reason, we examined sequence learning in 18-month-old infants. We studied each infant in two sessions. In recent studies (reported in Clohessy, A.B., Rundman, D., Gerardi, G., Posner, M.I., & Rothbart, M.K., 1995) in our laboratory, we found clear evidence that 18-month-olds had learned both unambiguous and ambiguous associations by the second session. The simple sequence made up of unambiguous associations appeared to be learned within the first block of 15 trials. This is more rapid than the learning of these sequences by four and 10-month-olds, who do not show clear evidence of learning until the second block. In the complex sequence, the return to 1 appears to be learned more slowly by 18-month-olds than their learning of the simple sequence, but there is evidence of above chance learning of this association during the second session.

There is also clear evidence that the 18-month-olds learn the context-dependent association by the second session, and we have been able to replicate this finding in three different experiments. While there was no evidence of such learning in the four- and 10-month-olds, we cannot say with certainty that the skill could not be acquired earlier than 18 months with more extensive practice. However, there is some internal evidence that the ability to learn the context was developing at about 18 months. Some infants showed by their correct anticipations that they had learned this skill very well, and others showed little evidence of learning. This finding suggests that infants of this age are only beginning to acquire the ability to learn this skill, and that it might be worthwhile observing how this form of learning develops in somewhat older infants.

We were also able to show some links between the learning by infants at this age and aspects of their language performance in daily life. We found a significant correlation between their laboratory performance in sequence learning and parental reports of the number of words the infant used. Although this link needs to be replicated and extended, it does provide tentative support for the idea of the development of an attention system involved both in learning complex sequences and in the control of language.

Indeed, several very general cognitive skills, including the ability to exhibit simple grammars in multiword language (Dore, Franklin,

Miller, & Ramer, 1976), the development of spontaneous alternation (Vecera, Rothbart, & Posner, 1991), and the ability to hold representations in mind while operating upon them (Meltzoff, 1990; Ruff & Rothbart, 1995) seem to undergo important development at or near this age. This is also the same age at which self-recognition is first exhibited in the form of operating on one's own image in a mirror is first exhibited (Gallup, 1979; Lewis & Brooks-Gunn, 1979). The evidence of a relation between the context-sensitive learning and aspects of language skill present in our data would also fit with this idea. In our future efforts, we hope to try to relate the development of context-dependent associations to a number of linguistic and conceptual skills that might mark important developments in this central attention system.

The ability to learn context-dependent associations is only one sign of the development of executive attentional systems during the period around 18 months. Curran and Keele (1993) suggest that context dependent associations require attention because the learning of these associations is reduced by distraction from a concurrent tone-counting task. There is evidence that distraction, of the type Curran and Keele used to influence learning, involves the form of attention shown in brain imaging studies that involves midline frontal structures (Posner et al., 1990; Posner et al., 1994).

The frontal mechanisms involved with higher order attention go well beyond the concept of visual attention that is the theme of this volume. The developments at 18 months appear more closely related to senses of executive function that are popular within cognitive psychology (Posner & Rothbart, 1990). However, there are clear relations between these frontal networks and networks we have discussed for visual orienting (Jackson et al., 1994).

In her thesis, Clohessy (1994) presented data from adult subjects who participated in the same sequence-learning experiments we have been describing for infants. In order to obtain enough anticipatory movements, these subjects had to be instructed to move to the targets as quickly as possible. With adults, dual task conditions were studied, as had been done in previous sequence-learning experiments involving key presses (Curran & Keele, 1993; Nissen & Bullemer, 1987). Eye movements were coded from a TV record, and in all other respects the experiments were conducted and scored just as they had been for the infants. The adults learned both the simple and complex sequences, and were successful in doing so both with and without distraction.

In the complex sequence under dual task conditions, many of the adults were unaware of there having been a sequence. However, with these "unaware" adults, anticipatory eye movements were correct much more often than would be expected by chance. It was interesting that, in these conditions, anticipatory eye movements were more common under distraction conditions than under undistracted conditions. This suggested that the movement of the eyes to an anticipated location is rather automatic. The fact that even in implicit learning there were anticipations contradicts what had been found when key presses are used as the response. In key-press conditions, implicit learning improves reaction time, but generally does not produce anticipations. The eyes seemed to move to the targets in a much more automatic fashion than key presses could be generated. Another feature of special interest to us in adult learning was adults' strong bias against returning to location 1 following orienting to locations 2 or 3. Early in learning they were well below chance in correct anticipations of these "return" movements. Thus, under these conditions, IOR was even stronger in our adult subjects than in the infants. However, the adults did learn the context-dependent association more rapidly and completely than did the 18-month-old infants.

With infants, we found that orienting to objects and to locations arises independently in early development, and adult studies also suggest separate mechanisms for the two forms of orienting (Egly et al., 1994). Recently, a striking independence was shown in adult learning of sequences of objects and locations (Mayr, 1996). Mayr taught adult subjects two independent sequences, one involving locations and one involving object identity. Both the location and the order of the objects were repeated, but the two were uncorrelated. In this situation, Mayr showed that subjects could learn the two sequences at the same time without apparent interference between them, as long as they were learned implicitly. However, when learning was explicit, there was clear evidence of interference when learning the two sequences. The clear evidence of interference between sequences when explicit learning occurs supports the idea that explicit learning is more likely to involve the frontal executive attention network we discussed above in connection with our 18-month-old studies.

We believe that the implicit learning of spatial locations involves mechanisms more related to the visual orienting network we have been describing in this chapter. When new learning is involved, this network might also include connections between the basal ganglia, thought to be involved in various forms of procedural learning, and the posterior parietal lobe (Grafton et al., 1995). It seems likely that the learning of unambiguous location sequences we have observed in four-month-olds is based upon the same pathways. The evidence for the continued presence of implicit learning of locations in adults illustrates the continuity between infant and adult mechanisms that has been the central theme of this chapter. As in the case of IOR, we find, in sequence learning, evidence that mechanisms found in early infancy are modified and supplemented by later systems, but that these mechanisms remain present and continue to operate in adults. We hope that a fuller picture of the emergence of these mechanisms in early life will help explicate the continuing role of attention throughout development.

## Summary

In this chapter, we have attempted to illustrate how studies of infants can help illuminate issues of importance for cognitive psychologists. We have examined two of the major issues in the current cognitive literature. First, we considered the debate about orienting based on spatial location versus orienting based on object identity. We traced the origins of the mechanisms of orienting to locations and objects by examining preference for novel locations and objects in young infants. We found that although both forms of novelty preference appear to be present at birth, there are major developmental changes in them that occur between three and six months. Preference for locations seems to develop earlier than preference for object novelty, and is independent of it. Second, we discussed the effort of cognitive psychologists to understand implicit learning and its relation to our ability to consciously recall what we have learned. We also showed that infants as young as four months learn sequences of visual events, provided the associations are unambiguous. This form of sequence learning occurs implicitly in adults without attention. We believe that implicit learning of location sequences takes place within the brain mechanisms related to covert visual orienting. At 18 months, infants also learn the type of ambiguous associations that require attention in adults. We speculate that this form of learning is a marker of a period of rapid development of the frontal executive attention network. These two areas, orienting and learning, provide support for the use of infant studies to further our understanding of the mechanisms of attention.

## Acknowledgments

This work was supported in part by a grant from the National Institute of Mental Health (grant MH 43361–06) to M.K. Rothbart, and by grants from the W.M. Keck, J.S. McDonnell Foundations and Pew Memorial Trusts to the Center for the Cognitive Neuroscience of Attention. We appreciate the help of Kendra Gilds and Lena Ontai.

# References

Baillargeon, R. (1995). Physical reasoning in infancy. In M.S. Gazzaniga (Ed.), *The cognitive neurosciences* (pp. 181–204). Cambridge, MA: MIT Press.

Bullemer, P., & Nissen, M.J. (1990). *Attentional orienting in the expression of procedural knowledge.* Paper presented at the annual meeting of the Psychonomics Society, New Orleans.

Chugani, H.T., Phelps, M.E., & Mazziotta, J.C. (1987). Positron emission tomography study of human brain functional development. *Annals of Neurology, 22,* 487–497.

Clohessy, A.B. (1994). *Visual anticipation and sequence learning in four- and ten-month-old infants and adults.* Unpublished doctoral dissertation. University of Oregon.

Clohessy, A.B., Posner, M.I., Rothbart, M.K., & Vecera, S.P. (1991). The development of inhibition of return in early infancy. *Journal of Cognitive Neuroscience, 3/4,* 345–350.

Clohessy, A.B., rundman;, D., Gerardi, G., Posner, M.I., & Rothbart, M.K. (1995). Development of visual anticipation in sequence learning. Unpublished manuscript.

Corbetta, M., Miezen, F.M., Dobmeyer, S., Shulman, F., & Petersen, S.E. (1991). Selective and divided attention during visual discrimination of shape, color, and speed. *Journal of Neuroscience, 11,* 1283–1302.

Corbetta, M., Meizin, F.M., Shulman, G.L., & Petersen, S.E. (1993). A PET study of visual spatial attention. *Journal of Neuroscience, 13,* 1202–1226.

Curran, T., & Keele, S.W. (1993). Attentional and nonattentional forms of sequence learning. *Journal of Experimental Psychology: Learning, Memory, & Cognition, 19,* 189–202.

Dore, J., Franklin, M.M., Miller, R.T., & Ramer, A.L.H. (1976). Transitional phenomena in early language development. *Journal of Child Language, 3,* 13–27.

Egly, R., Driver, J., & Rafal, R.D. (1994). Shifting visual attention between objects and locations. *Journal of Experimental Psychology: General, 123,* 161–177.

Gallup, G.G. (1979). Self awareness in primates. *American Scientist, 67,* 417–421.

Gerardi, G. (1994). *Looking behavior as a measure of sequence learning in infancy* Unpublished studies, University of Oregon.

Grafton, S.T., Hazelton, E., & Ivry, R. (1995). Functional mapping of sequence learning in normal humans. *Journal of Cognitive Neuroscience, 7,* 497–510.

Gunderson, V.M., & Swartz, K.B. (1986). Effects of familiarization time on visual recognition memory in infant pigtailed macaques. *Developmental Psychology, 22,* 477–480.

Gwiazda, J., Bauer, J., & Held, R. (1989). From visual acuity to hyperacuity: Ten year update. *Canadian Journal of Psychology, 43,* 109–120.

Haith, M.M. (1980). *Rules that babies look by.* Hillsdale, NJ: Erlbaum.

Haith, M.M., Hazan, C., & Goodman, G.S. (1988). Expectations and anticipation of dynamic visual events by 3.5 month old babies. *Child Development, 59,* 467–479.

Harman, C., Posner, M.I., Rothbart, M.K., & Thomas-Thrapp, L. (1994). Development of orienting to objects and locations in human infants. *Canadian Journal of Experimental Psychology, 48,* 301–318.

Hood, B. M. (1994). Visual selective attention in infants: A neuroscientific approach. In L. Lipsitt and C. Rouce-Collier (Eds.), *Advances in Infancy Research.*

Jackson, S., Marrocco, R., & Posner, M.I. (1994). Networks of anatomical areas controlling visual spatial attention. *Neural Networks, 7*, 925–944.

Johnson, M.H. (1995). The development of visual attention: A cognitive neuroscience approach. In M.S. Gazzaniga (Ed.), *The cognitive neurosciences* (pp. 735–750). Cambridge, MA: MIT Press.

Johnson, M.H., Posner, M.I., & Rothbart, M.K. (1991). Components of visual orienting in early infancy: Contingency learning, anticipatory looking and disengaging. *Journal of Cognitive Neuroscience, 3/4*, 335–344.

Johnson, M.H., Posner, M.I., & Rothbart, M.K. (1994). Facilitation of saccades toward a covertly attended location in early infancy. *Psychological Science, 5*, 90–93.

Johnson, M.H., & Tucker, L.A. (1996). The development and temporal dynamics of spatial orienting in infants. *Journal of Experimental Child Psychology, 63*, 171–188.

Klein, R.M., Kingstone, A., & Pontefract, A. (1993). Orienting of visual attention. In K. Rayner (Ed.), *Eye movements and visual cognition: Scene perception and reading* (pp. 46–65). New York: Springer Verlag.

LaBerge, D. (1995). Computational and anatomical models of selective attention in object identification. In M.S. Gazzaniga (Ed.), *The cognitive neurosciences* (pp. 649–664). Cambridge, MA: MIT Press.

Lewis, M., & Brooks-Gunn, J. (1979). *Social cognition and the acquisition of self.* New York: Plenum Press.

Mayr, U. (1996). Spatial attention and implicit sequence learning: Evidence for independent learning of spatial and nonspatial sequences. *Journal of Experimental Psychology: Learning, Memory, & Cognition, 22*, 350–364.

Mehler, J., & Christophe, A. (1995). Maturation and the learning of language in the first year of life. In M.S. Gazzaniga (Ed.), *The cognitive neurosciences* (pp. 943–958). Cambridge, MA: MIT Press.

Meltzoff, A.N. (1990). Towards a developmental cognitive science. In A. Diamond (Ed.), *The development and neural bases of higher cognitive functions.* (pp. 1–37). New York: New York Academy of Sciences.

Nissen, M.J., & Bullemer, P. (1987). Attentional requirements of learning: Evidence from performance measures. *Cognitive Psychology, 19*, 1–32.

Perruchet, P., & Amorim, M.A. (1993). Conscious knowledge and changes in performance in sequence learning: Evidence against dissociation. *Journal of Experimental Psychology: Human Perception & Performance, 18*, 785–800.

Posner, M.I. (1988). Structures and functions of selective attention. In T. Boll & B. Bryant (Eds.), *Master lectures in clinical neuropsychology and brain function: Research, measurement, and practice* (pp. 171–202). American Psychological Association.

Posner, M.I., & Dehaene, S. (1994). Attentional networks. *Trends in Neurosciences, 17*, 75–79.

Posner, M.I., & Petersen, S.E. (1990). The attention system of the human brain. *Annual Review of Neuroscience, 13*, 25–42.

Posner, M.I., & Raichle, M.E. (1994). *Images of mind*. New York: Scientific American Library.

Posner, M.I., & Rothbart, M.K. (1994). Constructing neuronal theories of mind. In C. Koch & J. Davis (Eds.), *High level neuronal theories of the brain* (pp. 183–199). Cambridge, MA: MIT Press.

Posner, M.I., Rothbart, M.K., Gerardi, G., & Thomas-Thrapp, L. (in press). Functions of orienting in early infancy. To appear in P. Lang, M. Balaban, & R.F. Simmons (Eds.), *The study of attention: Cognitive perspectives from psychophysiology, reflexology and neuroscience*. Hillsdale, NJ: Erlbaum.

Rafal, R.D., Calabresi, P., Brennan, C., & Scioloto, T. (1989). Saccadic preparation inhibits reorienting to recently attended locations. *Journal of Experimental Psychology: Human Perception & Performance, 15*, 673–685.

Rafal, R.D., Posner, M.I., Friedman, J.H., Inhoff, A.W., & Bernstein, E. (1988). Orienting of visual attention in progressive supranuclear palsy. *Brain, 111*, 267–280.

Rothbart, M.K., Derryberry, D., & Posner, M.I. (1994). A psychobiological approach to the development of temperament. In J.E. Bates & T.D. Wachs (Eds.), *Temperament: Individual differences at the interface of biology and behavior* (pp. 83–116). Washington, DC: American Psychological Association.

Ruff, H.A., & Rothbart, M.K. (1996). *Attention in early development: Themes and variations*. New York: Oxford University Press.

Schacter, D.L. (1995). Implicit memory: A new frontier in cognitive neuroscience. In M.S. Gazzaniga (Ed.), *The cognitive neurosciences* (pp. 815–824). Cambridge, MA: MIT Press.

Starkey, P., Spelke, E.S., & Gelman, R. (1990). Numerical abstraction by human infants. *Cognition, 36*, 97–127.

Thomas-Thrapp, L.J., Posner, M.I., & Rothbart, M.K. (1995). *Development of orienting to objects and locations*. Poster presented at the second meeting of the Cognitive Neuroscience Society. San Francisco.

Valenza, E., Simion, F., & Umilta, C. (1994). Inhibition of return in newborn infants. *Infant Behavior & Development, 17*, 293–302.

Vecera, S.P., Rothbart, M.K., & Posner, M.I. (1991). Development of spontaneous alternation in infancy. *Journal of Cognitive Neuroscience, 3/4*, 351–354.

# 11

## *Attention in Saccades*

### Burkhart Fischer

During the last 30 years, neurophysiologists and psychologists have shown close interest in visual functions related to brain processes that contribute to visually guided saccades accompanying natural vision. While work with human observers allows only indirect conclusions, recording from single cells in the visuomotor structures of monkeys performing several fixation and saccade tasks gives more direct insight into processes preceding the beginning of a saccade. One of these pre-saccadic processes is attention de-allocation and/or attention allocation. Because the experimental results reported in this chapter are closely related to the early findings in trained monkeys, and because the *express saccade* was first discovered in the monkey (Fischer & Boch, 1983), the relevant main results of this earlier research are briefly described and discussed in this chapter.

Cells have been found in the monkey that were particularly activated by visual stimuli that, at the time of their presentation, became targets for saccades. These cells would give a moderate visual response when stimulated during active fixation. And this response was then enhanced if the same stimulus was a target of a saccade. These enhancement effects were observed in several cortical and subcortical brain structures (see Fischer, 1987). If, for whatever reason, the animal did not make a saccade as requested but rather maintained fixation at the middle of the screen even though the fixation point was turned off, some cells in visual cortical area V4 were still activated (Fischer & Boch, 1981). In this situation, the animal was suddenly left with only one stimulus in the periphery (within the receptive field of the cell under study). It was the dimming of this stimulus that the animal had to detect out of "the corner of its eye" in order to get a reward.

An example of the discharge pattern of such a cell is depicted in Figure 1 (adapted from Fischer & Boch, 1985). In B, the weak visual response of the cell can be seen. The enhancement effect due to a stimulus-directed saccade becomes clear from the records in A, as compared to those in B, where the visual response is stronger. In C, trials are selected in which the animal did not make a saccade at all.

The cell remains active in a sustained way (compare this with B, where a strong decay of the response can be seen after 100 ms). In D, the stimulus was presented while the fixation point remained visible for a second and was then turned off. Note that when the fixation point disappeared and the monkey did not make a saccade, the cell became active again. It is likely that this kind of discharge is related to the animal paying attention to the stimulus without foveating it. In any case, the observation shows that the presence or absence of a fixation point influences the behaviour of such cells in the presence or absence of a saccade.

We decided to study the circumstances of this extraretinal discharge by manipulating the timing of the stimulus presentation in the receptive field and the fixation point offset. In order to dissociate in time the enhancement effect from fixation offset activation, the fixation point was turned off before the stimulus was presented and before the animal made a saccade. This resulted in a "gap" condition in which the animal was left for a short period of time with no stimulus. Surprisingly, the reaction times of saccades in this condition were extremely short and stable (Fischer & Boch, 1983). Because of their shorter latencies, these saccades were called *express saccades*. They often form an extra peak at about 70 to 80 ms in a multimodal distribution.

These short latency saccades were also found in human observers (Fischer & Ramsperger, 1984). But, unlike in monkeys, they form a peak at about 100 ms. The original idea of attentional processes playing a role in the generation of express saccades (Mayfrank, Mobashery, Kimmig, & Fischer, 1986) was proposed for human observers because humans can easily use instructions to manipulate the direction of their attention. Before we consider the corresponding human experimental results, we briefly describe some basic observations about saccadic reaction times and especially about express saccades, because the latter appear to be related to visual fixation and attention. Here, as in the rest of this chapter, the data are presented without much statistical evaluation. Where necessary, the reader is referred to the literature.

## Basic Observations

The fundamental task in which the express saccades are found in both monkeys and man is the *gap task*. The fixation point is turned off some time (the gap) before the target is presented. For comparison, the *overlap task* is used. In this case, the fixation point remains on throughout the trial. The temporal aspects of both tasks are shown in Figure 2.

In all experiments reported in this chapter, the targets were presented at (at least) two different locations – 4° to the right or left of the fixation point and in random order. The targets were generated on a

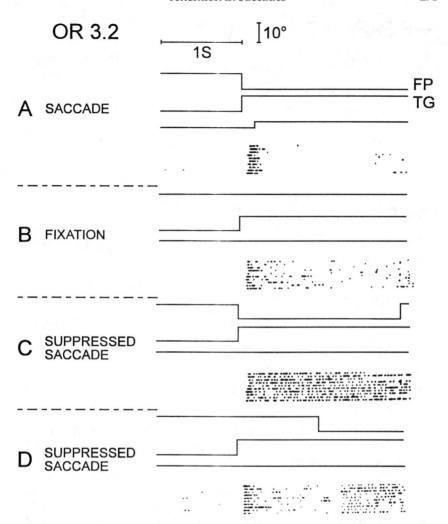

*Figure* 1: Recordings from a single cell in cortical visual area V4 from a behaving monkey performing different fixation and saccade tasks (adapted from Fischer & Boch, 1981). FP indicates fixation point; TG indicates target; the eye-position trace may be seen below. The cells exhibit a moderate visual response to a receptive field stimulus presented during fixation (B). This response is enhanced when the fixation point is extinguished simultaneously with stimulus onset such that the animal makes a saccade to the stimulus (A). The cell is also activated after fixation point offset when the animal suppresses the saccade (C and D).

computer screen, and the time of their presentation was synchronized with the frame impulse such that target onset could be determined with an accuracy of 1 ms. Eye movements were recorded by an infrared

# GAP PARADIGM

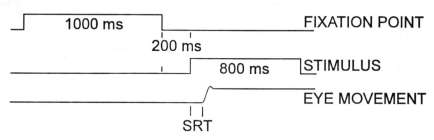

# OVERLAP PARADIGM

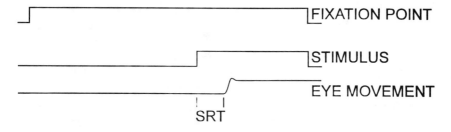

*Figure* 2: The temporal course of fixation point offset and target onset in the gap and overlap tasks.

light reflection technique involving one eye. The beginning and the end of a saccade were detected by a velocity threshold criterion (15% of the maximum velocity).

Figure 3 presents the results of a single subject. The data in the left panel were obtained when the subject was instructed to attend to the fixation point. Those in the right panel were obtained when the instruction was to attend to a peripheral location. This subject produced express saccades almost exclusively, and made very few fast regular saccades in the region of 150 to 200 ms. In the overlap task, no express saccades were made and even fast regular saccades were almost completely absent. Instead, in this task, there was a broad peak of slow regular saccades.

The instruction to attend to a peripheral location changed the distribution in a characteristic way: in the gap task, the express mode was reduced in favour of fast regular saccades. This difference cannot be attributed to the fact that 100 trials as opposed to 200 trials were used, because the blocks were obtained in pseudo-random order. Moreover, fatigue or general alertness never played a major role in the production

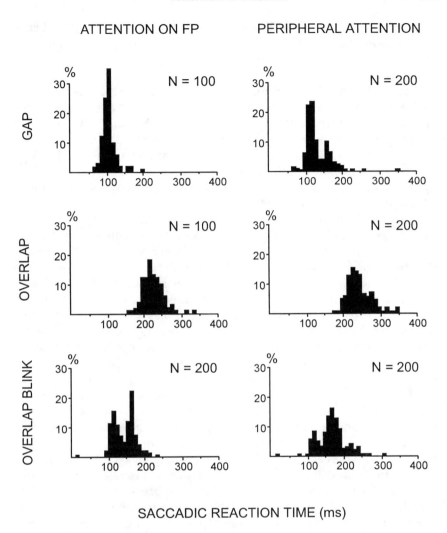

ATTENTION ON FP          PERIPHERAL ATTENTION

SACCADIC REACTION TIME (ms)

*Figure* 3: Distributions of saccadic reaction times of a single human subject under different conditions. Note the occurrence of two or three modes in the distributions and the reduction of the first mode (around 100 ms) in the right as compared to the left panels.

of express saccades. Interestingly, when subjects were instructed to attend to the peripheral location, only slight changes occurred to the pattern of saccadic response times in the overlap task.

If the fixation point was only blinked for a short (40 ms) period of time 200 ms before target onset instead of being removed for the rest of the trial, the number of express saccades was reduced in comparison to the gap task but was increased in comparison to the overlap task (Figure 3, lower left). The instruction to attend to the periphery also reduced the express mode in favour of fast and slow regular saccades. Note that the corresponding lower right distribution exhibits three peaks.

One has to consider all of these distributions to see that the main effect of the introduction of the gap was not so much an overall decrease of reaction times as described earlier (Saslow, 1967) but rather the occurrence of one peak at 100 ms and another (very small) peak at 150 ms. The overlap task yields still another peak just above 200 ms. The up and down modulation of the different peaks may also be accompanied by small shifts of the peak positions as has been observed by others (Wenban-Smith & Findlay, 1991).

There has been much discussion about whether the first peak constitutes an extra class of visually guided saccades or whether the saccades it represents are anticipatory in nature (Fischer & Weber, 1993; Kingstone & Klein, 1993; Reuter-Lorenz, Hughes, & Fendrich, 1991; Wenban-Smith & Findlay, 1991). When the variety of conditions under which express saccades have been obtained with increasing degrees of randomization are considered, it is clear that the express saccade is a real phenomenon. The arguments and the corresponding experimental facts have been summarized earlier (Fischer & Weber, 1993). Furthermore, most naïve subjects show express saccades in the gap task (Fischer, Weber, Biscaldi, Aiple, Otto, & Stuhr, 1993b) and some naive subjects make express saccades almost exclusively, even in the overlap task in which these saccades are usually absent (see below). Moreover, the express saccade phenomenon has now been replicated by several laboratories.

Age and experience also affect the frequency of express saccades. In particular, it has been demonstrated that teenagers and children make more express saccades than most naive adults (Fischer et al., 1993b). Naïve subjects can increase the number of express saccades by daily practice (Fischer & Ramsperger, 1986). And even in the overlap task in which express saccades are usually absent, training can facilitate the occurrence of express saccades.

Despite the fact that a generally accepted definition of attention does not exist, the instruction to "pay attention" is often used, and it leads to corresponding changes in the subjects' performance. In order to determine the conditions under which express saccades are possible, the attentional context of the experiment was manipulated because it was already demonstrated that attentional processing modulates the different modes in the reaction-time distribution.

The most natural spatial location towards which attention may be directed is the foveal stimulus we are looking at. Therefore, we considered what happens when subjects are instructed to attend to the fixation point as a visual stimulus or to the location of that fixation point.

## Fixation

When talking about eye movements, we almost automatically think of the generation of the movement but we often forget to think about how unwanted movements are prevented. In fact, preventing saccades must be a major optomotor function because thousands of potential targets become available after each shift of the retinal image by each saccade. The most straightforward answer to the challenge of preventing unwanted saccades could be that fixation is an active process that prevents the eye from moving.

Figure 4 shows the results of a rather simple experiment. The saccadic reaction-time distribution of the upper panel was obtained using the gap task, with the instruction to attend to the fixation point. The lower distribution was obtained when the experiment was repeated with the instruction to attend to the location of the fixation point (i.e., the middle of the screen). One clearly sees the difference. In the upper panel, there is a small population of anticipatory saccades with reaction times below 80 ms that is followed by a large peak of express saccades (Fischer et al., 1993b; Wenban-Smith & Findlay, 1991). Attending to the location (which of course does not disappear with the offset of the fixation point) decreased the number of anticipations and also the number of express saccades in favour of a large peak of fast regular saccades and a small peak of slow regular saccades. Thus, the effect of fixation point offset, which leads to anticipations and express saccades, is reduced when attention is no longer directed to the physical stimulus in the fovea.

This observation led to the idea of a fixation system that is activated both by visual stimuli close to the fovea and also by the intention to fixate (or by focusing attention at the spatial location of the fovea; see below). This, in turn, inhibits saccade generation. It is proposed that for a saccade to be generated, the attentional or fixational system has to be disengaged. Other processes in saccade preparation that eventually follow attentional or fixational disengagement, such as decision making (Jüttner & Wolf, 1991), are accordingly delayed.

Consider the effect of foveal or parafoveal stimuli that are targets for saccades. One may expect that targets presented close to the fovea would require only small saccades. There targets cannot be reached by express saccades because they will activate the fixation system. In fact, a parafoveal deadzone for express saccades has been found in monkeys and in man (Weber, Aiple, Fischer, & Latanov, 1992).

The deadzone comes into play whenever small saccades to visual stimuli are required. This happens after primary saccades are made that slightly undershoot or overshoot the target. Secondary (corrective) saccades are then necessary. Because of the deadzone, these secondary saccades can be initiated rapidly, only when the error to be corrected is large. An analysis of secondary saccades following small undershoots

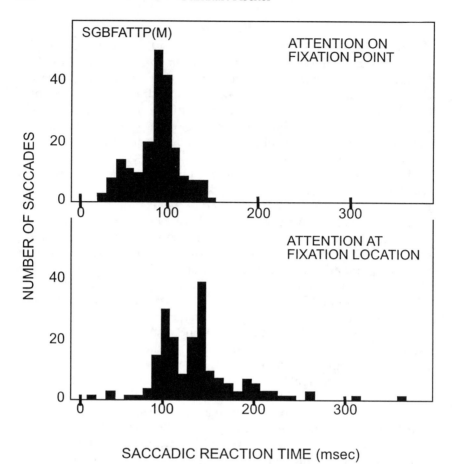

*Figure* 4: Effect of attending to the fixation point as a visual stimulus presented at the fovea versus attending to the location of the fixation point (i.e., to the middle of the screen).

and overshoots or following direction errors (which leave very large errors) indicated the existence of secondary express saccades (Fischer et al., 1993a). These are corrective saccades initiated 100 ms after target onset despite the fact that another (anticipatory) saccade in the wrong direction preceded them. In these cases, the intersaccadic interval may even be decreased to 0 ms. Small undershoots and overshoots, on the other hand, were corrected after the usual intersaccadic interval of 100 to 180 ms depending on the size of the error.

These results favour the idea that there exists a fixation system that can be activated voluntarily on the one hand, but is also under automatic reflex-like control due to the onset of visual input. The saccade generating system seems to share this dual control with the fixation system. While saccades are certainly under voluntary control, they can also be generated involuntarily, or even counter to a subject's conscious decision. This clearly happens in an antisaccade task in which subjects are instructed to look to the side opposite to where the stimulus is presented. If the target is randomly presented to the right or left, subjects will, in a few trials, make direction errors by looking at the target. The reaction time analysis of these saccades has shown that they are of the express and/or fast regular type, while correct antisaccades are usually not of the express type (Fischer & Weber, 1992).

The reflex character of express saccades becomes clearly evident in special naïve subjects who, for some reason, make almost exclusively express saccades. Even in the overlap task in which express saccades are normally virtually absent, subjects make large numbers of express saccades. And when tested with the antisaccade gap task, it turns out that these subjects, called *express saccade makers*, can hardly follow the instructions. Instead of looking to the opposite side as required by the instruction, they involuntarily look to the target. In addition to this failure to consistently produce antisaccades, their erratic prosaccades are mostly of the express type (Biscaldi, Fischer, & Stuhr, 1996). Morevoever, in a memory-guided saccade task in which subjects are instructed to maintain fixation until the offset of the fixation point, express saccade makers look reflexively to the shortly presented stimulus with express saccades. Most but not all of these subjects also have difficulties in reading and writing (dyslexia). Their optomotor behaviour during text reading is not known at present.

These observations suggest that in humans there exists a separate neural subsystem that serves to prevent unwanted saccades. We can call it a fixation system. This notion should not come as a surprise, because abnormalities in fixation (low fixation activity) and deficits in initiating saccades (hyperactive fixation system) have long been reported in patients with parietal lesions (Balint, 1909). Moreover, there is convincing evidence for a separate fixation system in the monkey. During active fixation, thresholds for eliciting saccades by electrical microstimulation are elevated in the parietal cortex (Shibutani, Sakata, & Hyvarinen, 1984) and frontal cortex (Goldberg, Bushnell, & Bruce, 1986). The superior colliculus also contains in its rostral part a system of fixation cells (Munoz & Wurtz, 1992). When these cells are chemically deactivated, the animal makes many unwanted saccades of the express type (Munoz & Wurtz, 1993), and thus its saccades are very reminiscent of a human express saccade maker (Biscaldi et al., 1996).

At this point, it remains an open question whether patients with frontal lobe lesions (Guitton, Buchtel, & Douglas, 1985) and schizophrenics (Matsue et al., 1994b) who are impaired on an antisaccade task and who produce excessive numbers of express saccades (Matsue et al., 1994a) have a deficit in their fixation system, or in the voluntary control of saccade generation, or both.

## Attention

Throughout the literature on attention, one often finds the claim that attention, once allocated at a certain location, will decrease the reaction time to stimuli presented at this location, as compared to stimuli presented elsewhere (e.g., Posner & Driver, 1992). It has been proposed, however, that this may not be true if one considers express saccades (Fischer & Weber, 1993; Mayfrank et al., 1986). Allocating attention voluntarily and in a sustained manner to a specified location actually decreases the frequency of express saccades to targets presented at that location, and therefore increases the overall saccadic reaction time (Mayfrank et al., 1986) even in a spatially selective way (Weber & Fischer, 1995). At first glance, this sounds like a contradiction. On the other hand, a dual concept of attention has been developed during recent years (Nakayama & Mackeben, 1989). According to this concept, features of attentional processing can be subdivided into two components: involuntary/voluntary; exogenous/endogenous; bottom up/top down; transient/sustained

If one assumes that the first component facilitates the saccade system allowing more express saccades while the second component inhibits the saccade system thus reducing the chances of express saccades, the contradiction may no longer exist. In the following sections, a few experiments are considered that were attempts to pin down these different effects of voluntary versus involuntary attention allocation on the distribution saccadic reaction times.

We already know that sustained voluntary attention allocation tends to abolish express saccades and favour regular saccades. Following up on this, we examined the spatial selectivity of this effect in a gap task. It turns out that the number of express saccades returns to the control value (obtained with attention being directed to the fixation point) when the sustained attention target is no longer in spatial register with the saccade target. Moreover, the strength of this inhibitory effect on express saccades is strongly dependent on the gap duration and is largely absent in overlap tasks (Weber & Fischer, 1995). An issue that remains open in this context is the nature of decision processes and their relation to voluntary attention allocation (Jüttner & Wolf, 1992).

## Valid and Invalid Cueing of Prosaccades

The use of location cueing is a well-known technique for initiating the involuntary allocation of attention to one position and withdrawing it from another. The effect on saccadic reaction times in a gap task with 100% valid peripheral cues (cue lead time 100 ms, gap duration 200 ms) is shown in the upper panel of Figure 5 for a single subject. Reaction time distributions for left and right directed saccades (elicited in random order) are presented separately in the left and right panels, respectively. The uppermost pair shows the control data obtained with no cue. The second pair presents the test data with the valid cues (a slight and short luminance increase of one of two line boxes surrounding the location of target presentation). It is clear that the cues not only allowed the occurrence of express saccades but even increased their number and decreased their reaction time in accordance with the findings of Cavegn & Biscaldi (1996). This is the opposite effect to that obtained when attention is allocated in a sustained and voluntary manner by instruction.

If, in a subsequent experiment, the attentional cue and the saccade target are dissociated in space (the cue always being presented at 4° to the right, and the targets at 8° to the right or left in random order such that the cue provides no information about the saccade direction), the facilitation of express saccades is obtained for the right-directed saccades (despite the dissociation of 4° between target and cue), while express saccades to the left are almost completely abolished. If, finally, the cue is presented at 4° to the right or to the left in random order such that they are 100% valid with respect to the direction of the saccade but 100% invalid with respect to the location of the target, the facilitation occurs for saccades to both sides. This indicates that a spatial selectivity of the cueing effect, if it exists at all, must be relatively weak, while the specificity for the direction (the hemifield of cue presentation) is rather strong. These aspects of spatial specificity of cueing on saccades need, however, more quantitative experimental evaluation before final conclusions can be drawn.

For endogenous cueing, one often uses foveally presented stimuli that indicate to the subject where the target stimulus is going to be presented (valid trials). These cues, however, sometimes carry visual spatial information (e.g., an arrow being asymmetric) as well as temporal information about the impending target's onset. Therefore, they cannot be considered completely endogenous, and they may very well have additional reflexive effects on reaction time (Müller & Rabbitt, 1989).

## Anticues and Prosaccades

To demonstrate the coexistence of two different components of attention, an anticue-prosaccade task was designed. The experiment was physically identical to the cueing experiment described above, but the cue was always presented (100% valid) at the side opposite to the

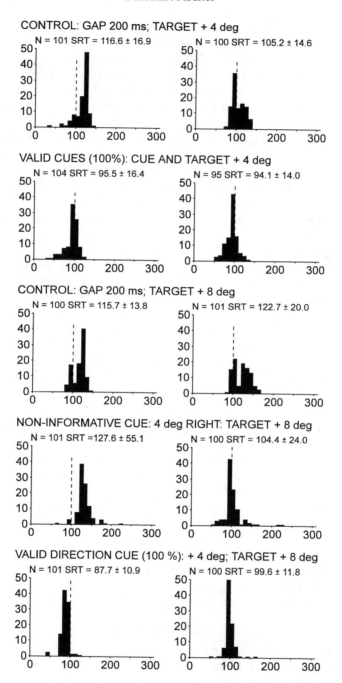

*Figure* 5: Effect of valid and invalid cues presented with a cue lead time of 100 ms before target presentation on the saccadic reaction times of a single subject.

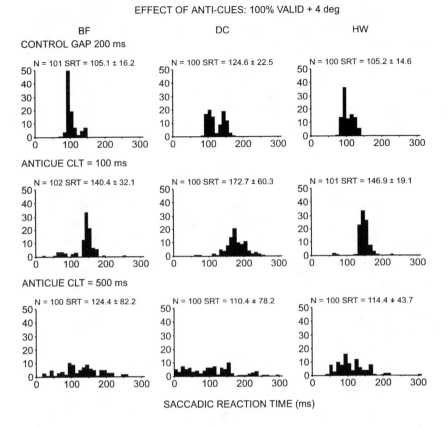

EFFECT OF ANTI-CUES: 100% VALID + 4 deg

Figure 6: Effect of anticues presented with two different cue lead times (100 and 500 ms) before target presentation on the saccadic reaction times of three subjects. Note that the maximum of express saccades (first peak) is obtained in the control condition with no cue.

target. The subjects' instruction was to use this anticue to attend to the side opposite to the cue. In this situation, the locations for exogenous and endogenous attention allocation are in opposite fields, and the task for the attentional system, if there is only one, is in a way contradictory. This experiment allowed us to determine which of the two components would have a stronger effect on express saccade generation.

Figure 6 shows the results for three subjects and for two cue lead times (100 and 500 ms). The upper triplet shows the control data: all three subjects exhibited express saccades in bimodal distributions. The second triplet shows the results for an anticue lead time of 100 ms: the anticue, even though 100% valid, abolished almost all express saccades. A few anticipations can be seen, while the rest of saccades formed prominent peaks of fast regular saccades. And even some slow regular saccades were obtained in subject DC.

When the anticue lead time was increased to 500 ms, such that subjects had enough time to overcome the automatic effects of cueing and to voluntarily shift their attention to the opposite side, the lowermost triplet was obtained: the number of anticipations was increased (because the situation was completely predictive trial by trial) and a few express saccades can be seen but, for all three subjects, fast and slow regular saccades also occurred. The latter result does not come as a surprise, given our knowledge that voluntary attention allocation can inhibit express saccade generation.

## Procues and Antisaccades

To further study the effect of valid cueing on saccade generation, the anticue-prosaccade experiment described in the previous section was repeated with a different instruction. While the physical arrangements of the experiment were exactly the same, the instruction was now to generate antisaccades in response to the stimulus. Since the preceding cue was always presented at the side opposite to the stimulus, it was again 100% valid. Thus, it indicated correctly the direction of the antisaccade to be generated on each trial. Subjects had to make a saccade to the location of the cue after onset of the go-stimulus, and they could program the antisaccade during the cue lead time. In this situation, one might expect very short antisaccade reaction times and a reduction of the error rate (percentage of erratic prosaccades). The result, however, was completely opposite and counterintuitive. With a cue lead time of 100 ms, subjects produced more errors and longer reaction times as in the control condition with no cue (Fischer & Weber, 1996). When the cue lead time was increased to 300 ms, these effects were reduced. But with a still longer cue lead time (700 ms), the effects became stronger again (Weber & Fischer, 1996). These observations indicate that automatic preallocation of attention due to spatially valid cueing facilitates saccade generation only when the cue and the saccade stimulus are presented on the same side. If the cue and the stimulus are presented on opposite sides, saccadic reaction times are prolonged (i.e., the chances for express saccades are reduced). Why the error rate increases remains a matter for speculation. Perhaps the subject trying to produce antisaccades falls into a mode of operation that also involves treating the cue in an antimode.

## Conclusions

When considering the role of attention in saccade generation, it is very important to differentiate between the methods used to manipulate attention. We now have evidence that voluntarily attending to a peripheral location in a sustained manner (for a second or two) according to instructions has an effect on saccade latencies opposite to the one that occurs when visual cues are presented shortly before target presentation. Not only are the effects opposite in sign, but they also seem to have different temporal and spatial properties. While voluntary allocation is slow and long-lasting, the cueing effects are fast and transient; the location of voluntary attention allocation seems to be quite spatially selective, while cueing seems to be selective for a hemifield.

In experiments in which express saccades were not specifically examined, it has also been found that the facilitation effect of location cueing at short cue lead times can turn into inhibition at longer cue lead times (Posner & Cohen, 1984). The distinction between transient and sustained visual attention has also been made by other researchers (Nakayama & Mackeben, 1989)

Findings like these raise a question about why one should use the same term "attention" for phenomena that are so different in nature? The verbal description of the interaction between oculomotor control and higher brain functions such as attention and decision processes becomes or remains confusing or even contradictory. And, because of this conflict, the understanding of the real neural mechanism underlying these functional aspects of sensorimotor coordination may be impeded rather than promoted.

The three-loop model for the generation of saccade latencies (Fischer, Gezeck, & Huber, 1995) is one possible account of the effects of spatial cues and voluntary attentional focusing: a valid visual cue will activate the visual and visuomotor cells, and therefore saccades (especially express saccades) to the corresponding location will be facilitated. If, on the other hand, attention is disengaged from the fixation point and engaged again voluntarily, activity in the saccade generating system is lower, and so are the chances for express saccades. The latter effect is spatially selective, as we have seen above. Since all saccade-related cells may have an inhibitory effect on the fixation cells (e.g., the fixation cells in the superior colliculus, Munoz & Wurtz, 1992), it seems plausible that lower fixation activity is obtained by any cue irrespective of its location in the same hemifield. This would imply that the cueing effects are mediated by the mutually inhibitory interaction between saccade and fixation cells at a relatively low level (perhaps the tectum?) while the voluntary attentional effects are mediated by a spatially selective inhibitory control of the saccade system at a relatively high level (parietal & frontal systems).

It may be suggested that the term *attention* be reserved for the voluntary aspect of saccade control and that we use the term *reflexive orienting* for the effects introduced automatically by the visual spatial cues (Müller & Rabbitt, 1989).

## Acknowledgments

This work was supported by grants from the Deutsche Forschungs-gemeinschaft (DFG), SFB325 - Tp C5/C7 and Fi 227. Burkhart Fischer may be reached via e-mail at bfischer@uni-freiburg.de

## References

Balint, R. (1909). Seelenlähmung des schauens, optische ataxie, räumliche störung der aufmerksamkeit. *Monatsschrift für Psychiatrie und Neurologie, 25*, 51–81.

Biscaldi, M., Fischer, B., & Stuhr, V. (1996). Human express-saccade makers are impaired at suppressing visually-evoked saccades. *Journal of Neurophysiology*

Cavegn, D., & Biscaldi, M. (1996). Fixation and saccade control in an express-saccade maker. *Experimental Brain Research, 109*, 101–116

Fischer, B. (1987). The preparation of visually guided saccades. *Reviews in Physiology, Biochemistry & Pharmacology, 106*, 1–35.

Fischer, B., Weber, H., & Biscaldi, M. (1993a). The time of secondary saccades to primary targets. *Experimental Brain Research, 97*, 356–360.

Fischer, B., Weber, H., Biscaldi, M., Aiple, F., Otto, P., & Stuhr, V. (1993b). Separate populations of visually guided saccades in humans: Reaction times and amplitudes. *Experimental Brain Research, 92*, 528–541.

Fischer, B., Gezeck, S., & Huber, W. (1995). The three-loop-model: A neural network for the generation of saccadic reaction times. *Biological Cybernetics, 72*, 185–196.

Fischer, B., & Boch, R. (1981). Selection of visual targets activates prelunate cortical cells in trained rhesus monkey. *Experimental Brain Research, 41*, 431–433.

Fischer, B., & Boch, R. (1983). Saccadic eye movements after extremely short reaction times in the monkey. *Brain Research, 260*, 21–26.

Fischer, B., & Boch, R. (1985). Peripheral attention versus central fixation: Modulation of the visual activity of prelunate cortical cells of the rhesus monkey. *Brain Research, 345*, 111–123.

Fischer, B., & Ramsperger, E. (1984). Human express saccades: Extremely short reaction times of goal directed eye movements. *Experimental Brain Research, 57*, 191–195.

Fischer, B., & Ramsperger, E. (1986) Human express saccades: Effects of randomization and daily practice. *Experimental Brain Research, 64*, 569–578.

Fischer, B., & Weber, H. (1992). Characteristics of "anti" saccades in man. *Experimental Brain Research, 89*, 415–424.

Fischer, B., & Weber, H. (1993). Express saccades and visual attention. *Behavioral & Brain Sciences, 16*, 553–567.

Fischer, B., & Weber, H. (1996). Research note: Effects of procues on error rate and reaction times of antisaccades in human subjects. *Experimental Brain Research, 109*, 507–512.

Goldberg, M.E., Bushnell, M.C., & Bruce, C.J. (1986). The effect of attentive fixation on eye movements evoked by electrical stimulation of the frontal eye fields. *Experimental Brain Research, 61*, 579–584.

Guitton, D., Buchtel, H.A., & Douglas, R.M. (1985). Frontal lobe lesions in man cause difficulties in suppressing reflexive glances and in generating goal-directed saccades. *Experimental Brain Research, 58*, 455–472.

Jüttner, M., & Wolf, W. (1992). Occurrence of human express saccades depends on stimulus uncertainty and stimulus sequence. *Experimental Brain Research, 89,* 678–681.

Kingstone, A., & Klein, R.M. (1993). What are human express saccades? *Perception & Psychophysics, 54,* 260–273.

Matsue, Y., Osakabe, K., Saito, H., Goto, Y., Ueno, T., Matsuoka, H., Chiba, H., Fuse, Y., & Sato, M. (1994a). Smooth pursuit eye movements and express saccades in schizophrenic patients. *Schizophrenia Research, 12,* 121–130.

Matsue, Y., Saito, H., Osakabe, K., Awata, S., Ueno, T., Matsuoka, H., Chiba, H., Fuse, Y., & Sato, M. (1994b). Smooth pursuit eye movements and voluntary control of saccades in the antisaccade task in schizophrenic patients. *Japanese Journal of Psychiatry & Neurology, 48,* 13–22.

Mayfrank, L., Mobashery, M., Kimmig, H., & Fischer, B. (1986). The role of fixation and visual attention in the occurrence of express saccades in man. *European Archives of Psychiatry & Neurological Science, 235,* 269–275.

Müller, H.J., & Rabbitt, P.M. (1989). Reflexive and voluntary orienting of visual attention: Time course of activation and resistance to interruption. *Journal of Experimental Psychology: Human Perception & Performance, 15,* 315–330.

Munoz, D.P., & Wurtz, R.H. (1992). Role of the rostral superior colliculus in active visual fixation and execution of express saccades. *Journal of Neurophysiology, 67,* 1000–1002.

Munoz, D.P., & Wurtz, R.H. (1993). Fixation cells in monkey superior colliculus. II. Reversible activation and deactivation. *Journal of Neurophysiology, 70,* 576–589.

Nakayama, K., & Mackeben, M. (1989). Sustained and transient components of focal visual attention. *Vision Research, 29,* 1631–1647.

Posner, M.I., & Cohen, Y. (1984). Components of visual orienting. In H. Bouma & D.G. Bouwhuis (Eds.), *Attention & Performance, Volume 10,* pp 531–556. Hillsdale, NJ: Erlbaum.

Posner, M.I., & Driver, J. (1992). The neurobiology of selective attention. *Current Opinions in Neurobiology, 2,* 165–169.

Reuter-Lorenz, P., Hughes, H.C., & Fendrich, R. (1991). The reduction of saccadic latency by prior offset of the fixation point: An analysis of the gap effect. *Perception & Psychophysics, 49,* 167–175.

Saslow, M.G. (1967). Latency for saccadic eye movement. *Journal of the Optic Society of America, 57,* 1030–1033.

Shibutani, H., Sakata, H., & Hyvarinen, J. (1984). Saccade and blinking evoked by microstimulation of the posterior parietal association cortex of the monkey. *Experimental Brain Research, 55,* 1–8.

Weber, H., Aiple, F., Fischer, B., & Latanov, A. (1992). Dead zone for express saccades. *Experimental Brain Research, 89,* 214–222.

Weber, H., & Fischer, B. (1995). Gap duration and location of attention focus modulate the occurrence of left/right asymmetries in the saccadic reaction times of human subjects. *Vision Research, 35,* 987–998.

Weber, H., & Fischer, B. (1997). Voluntary versus automatic attention allocation. II. Effects of procues on the execution of antisaccades. Submitted.

Wenban-Smith, M.G., & Findlay, J.M. (1991). Express saccades: Is there a separate population in humans? *Experimental Brain Research, 87,* 218–222.

# 12

## *The Attentional Blink: The Eyes Have It (But So Does the Brain)*[†]

### Kimron Shapiro and Kathleen Terry

Attention is a highly functional property of the brain, whereby limited cognitive resources can be directed to facilitate the processing of briefly presented sensory information by limiting processing of other information competing for the same resources. For example, attentional mechanisms can facilitate rapid detection of a target by allowing the brain to monitor a particular region of visual space (Posner, Snyder, & Davidson, 1980). In a second example, pointing to a different functional property of attention, attentional mechanisms can be required to decide if a specified target is present among a number of nontarget distractors (Treisman & Gormican, 1988).

A different but highly related purpose for which attention appears useful is processing information over time, rather than over space.[1] In this regard, attention has been found to assist in processing a target stimulus by limiting the subsequent processing of information for a significant period of time, such that a second target maintains a relatively low probability of detection (Broadbent & Broadbent, 1987; Raymond, Shapiro, & Arnell, 1992; Reeves & Sperling, 1986; Weichselgartner & Sperling, 1987). Various inhibitory mechanisms have been postulated to account for this outcome, facilitating the access of target-relevant information by permitting uninterrupted processing of the first stimulus.

In recent years there has been a lively interest in inhibitory mechanisms and in the role they play in perception and action. The importance of the role of inhibition as a companion process to the more commonly studied mechanism of excitation (facilitation) is not a recent idea: Pavlov (1927) and subsequently Konorski (1967) researched and

---

[†] Please note that this chapter was written in the Fall of 1995. Due to unforeseen delays in publication, some of the work reported here does not reflect the first author's current thinking in all aspects. Readers are requested to read more recent papers as cited in the present chapter if they wish to become more familiar with current views on the Attentional Blink phenomenon.

wrote extensively on the topic, and described the two processes as working in synchrony to facilitate adaptive performance. Recently, the interaction between these two mechanisms as they relate to attention has come into focus (e.g., Posner & Cohen, 1984; Hatfield, this volume). Following Posner and Cohen (1984), the interaction between facilitation and inhibition in attention has grown to encompass several recently termed phenomena – for example, repetition blindness, the attentional blink, and negative priming.

The phenomenon of negative priming (Tipper, 1996, this volume) has been interpreted as an example of the interaction between facilitation and inhibition. In the typical negative priming paradigm outcome, humans are slower to respond to an "ignored" stimulus that occurred on a previous trial in the presence of a target selected for action, when the ignored stimulus becomes the target on a subsequent trial. An explanation that has been offered for this outcome is that a stimulus which has been selected *against* during the act of selecting *for* another, becomes inhibitory (Tipper, 1991). In the learning literature, it has been known for some time and even formulated into a law (Wagner & Rescorla, 1972; Williams, Overmier, & LoLordo, 1992) that an inhibitory stimulus takes longer to become excitatory than one that was not previously made so. An examination of what is known from the learning literature regarding the relationship between excitation and inhibition would likely prove highly informative for the study of these same processes as regards attention, but is beyond the scope of the present effort.

Another theme concerning information processing, and one receiving considerable discussion in recent years, is the notion of the organization of attention surrounding the perception of objects (e.g., Duncan, 1984; Kahneman, Treisman, & Gibbs, 1992). A landmark study in this regard by Duncan (1984) reveals that, when attention is directed to a particular object, all of the properties of that object potentially are available for retrieval. The alternative situation, in which attending the same properties that are drawn from more than one object, results in divided-attention costs. Similar findings by Treisman and her colleagues (Kahneman, Treisman, & Gibbs, 1992) have led to a view that the percept of an object matching a predefined template initiates an object file, where information about that object is then stored. Subsequently occurring, related stimuli then cause the object file to be updated, rather than a new one initiated. It will be argued later in this chapter that object file updating may not yield divided attention costs, as does the formation of a new object file, but may nevertheless yield awareness of the new object. Treisman's example of such an object file's initiation and updating has become a classic: when an observer's percept of what is first believed to be a distant airplane suddenly becomes that of a bird, as the object becomes nearer then flaps its wings and lands in a tree, the observer does not interpret this as the sudden disappearance of the airplane and equally sudden occurrence of the bird, but instead understands it as a single object (bird) erroneously first perceived (Kahneman, Treisman, & Gibbs, 1992).

The central theme of this chapter is that inhibitory and excitatory connections developing over time form the working mechanism underlying the notion of object files. The object files in turn produce a stable and sensible world percept. The study of attention over time has received considerable interest in recent years. Time-based, or temporal, attention stands in contrast to the study of attention at a brief moment in time using popular procedures such as visual search (see Treisman, this volume). The purpose of this chapter is to present and discuss various findings in support of these themes. The studies to be discussed in the present chapter have in common the use of the method of rapid serial visual presentation (RSVP) and a phenomenon that has received some consideration as of late, the attentional blink (AB).

## Single-Target versus Dual-Target RSVP Tasks

In this section, we will briefly review the RSVP procedure and summarize findings from experiments preceding studies on the AB. The reader is referred to an earlier chapter by Shapiro and Raymond (1994) for a more complete description of these studies. The RSVP method presents a series, or stream, of items such as letters, digits, pictures, words and even sentences in rapid succession on a computer screen. Rates of item presentation vary from about 6 items/sec up to nearly 30 items/sec. In experiments on visual attention, RSVP procedures usually consist of a sequence of between 15 and 20 items. In most cases, except studies of repetition blindness (e.g., Kanwisher, 1987), all items in the sequence are different.

Single-target RSVP studies require one target to be detected or identified from among the stream of nontarget or distractor items. The target is differentiated in some way (e.g., luminance) from other stream items. By detection, we refer to the requirement to determine whether or not a fully specified target is present. An example of such a task would be to decide if the white letter O was present from among a black letter stream. In identification tasks, the target is partially specified and the participant is given the key (i.e., target-defining) feature and asked to supply the response feature. An example would be when a participant is asked to view a sequence of black stream letters and to report the letter name (response feature) of the white (key feature) item. On each trial, the target is randomly assigned (with some constraints, see section to follow) a serial position approximately midway through the sequence. This target's serial position is designated a value of 0, items preceding the target are labelled as $-n$ items, and items succeeding the target are referred to as $+n$ items.

In multiple-target RSVP studies, typically one additional target is presented following the first, and the participant's task is to detect or identify both, in the order in which they were presented. As in research reports from our laboratory, we will use the term *target* to refer to the first target in the stimulus stream and the term *probe* to refer to the second. The serial position of the probe relative to the target is manipulated systematically so that the effect of the target-probe interval on performance can be investigated. We and others before us view the purpose of multiple-task RSVP experiments as a means for tracking the time course of events succeeding selection of a single target.

D.E. Broadbent and M. H. P. Broadbent (1987; Experiment 3), using words in one of the first RSVP studies similar to those later arising from Shapiro's laboratory, suggest that successful target identification produces a lengthy temporal deficit in correct probe detection. They concluded that the factor responsible for poor probe detection was the demanding task initiated by the target identification requirement (but see the description of Shapiro, Raymond, & Arnell, 1994 to follow). Using a variant on the multiple-task RSVP procedure that is described more fully in Shapiro Raymond (1994), Reeves and Sperling (1986) and later Weichselgartner and Sperling (1987) observed large deficits in the accurate processing of second targets. Weichselgartner and Sperling used a reporting requirement that could be construed to overly tax memory but Raymond, Shapiro, and Arnell (1992) eliminated this as a possible explanation for the probe deficit prior to accepting an attentional account of this phenomenon (see below).

Weichselgartner and Sperling (1987) proposed a dual-process attentional account to explain this effect. The first process was reputed to be a short-lived, automatic, effortless one enabling target detection. The second, sustained component was purported to be a more controlled process, initiated by the target identification task but necessitating time to reach viability. Thus, according to this account, deficits in probe report are due to a period of temporal nonoverlap between these two processes. Nakayama and Mackeben (1989) proposed a similar dual-process model of attention to account for cueing effects and, more recently, argued for a similar two-stage account to explain AB deficits in their experiments. (Chun & Potter's 1995 theory will be described more fully later).

## The Attentional Blink

The dual-task studies described above have in common the finding of a significant deficit in reporting items following successful target detection/identification for approximately 100 to 500 ms. The similarity of the time course of this deficit suggested to Raymond, Shapiro, and

Arnell (1992) that a common mechanism operates to inhibit visual processing following completion of the target task. Such a mechanism seemed analogous to that of an eyeblink, which acts to limit perceptual information reaching the retina for a brief period of time. This analogy prompted us to name the phenomenon the "attentional blink" and to initiate a series of experiments designed to uncover some of its properties. Little did we know that we were uncovering the proverbial Pandora's box. The scope of the present chapter does not provide the opportunity to describe in detail the methods used to investigate the AB in all the studies to which we wish to refer. Thus, we will begin with a brief overview of the basic method, and refer the reader to a more complete description of the methods and stimulus parameters that can be found in Shapiro and Raymond (1994).

A schematic of a typical RSVP experiment appears in Figure 1. The top panel of this figure reveals an example of the critical items in a given trial, as well as the temporal parameters. The bottom panel of this same figure schematizes the total sequence of events in a given RSVP trial. In a typical AB experiment, on half of all trials, participants are required to identify the white target letter and to report whether or not the probe letter X occurred in the subsequent eight-item stimulus stream. The other half of trials contain no target, and provide a control condition in which only the probe must be detected, when it occurs. As far as the probe task is concerned, half of all trials contain a probe and half do not, the latter allowing us to calculate a false alarm rate for the probe.

A representative outcome (see Figure 2, from Raymond, Shapiro, & Arnell, 1992) shows the typical AB effect. The percent correct report of the probe is plotted on the $y$-axis for only those trials when the target was identified correctly. As can be seen in this figure, controls are able to correctly report the probe on approximately 90% of trials regardless of the probe's relative position, whereas experimental participants experience a marked deficit in correct probe report between 100 to 400 ms post target. This deficit is the AB.

The first series of experiments performed by Raymond, Shapiro, and Arnell (1992) revealed a number of important properties of the AB. First, they showed that the time course of the effect was very similar to that found by Broadbent and Broadbent (1987). Second, these experiments reveal that the AB effect is not due to sensory masking, but is instead due to attentional factors. And third, they show that the effect is attenuated when the stimulus item immediately following the target is omitted, but the effect is left intact when any other item in the post-target stimulus stream is omitted instead. Raymond et al. (1992) drew an important conclusion from this initial set of studies, a conclusion that is relevant to the issue of inhibition, as described in the introduction above. Raymond et al. (1992) suggested that the function of

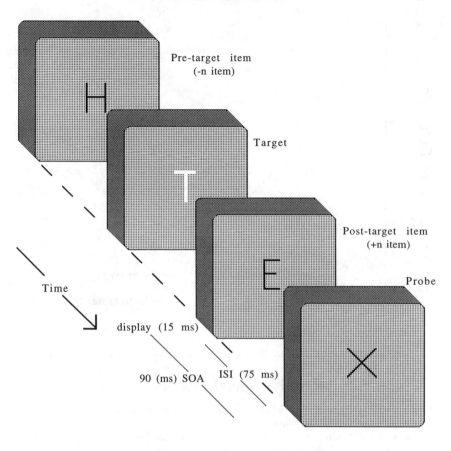

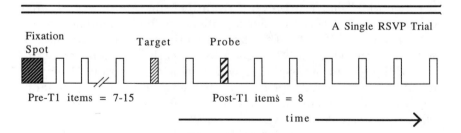

*Figure* 1: The top panel illustrates the critical stimuli employed by Raymond, Shapiro, and Arnell (1992; Experiment 2). The target, embedded in the stimulus stream, is denoted by a key feature, in this example the colour white, with participants required to report its identity. The probe is the fully specified item, in this example the letter "X," and must be detected (i.e., present vs. absent). The bottom panel shows a diagram of a single RSVP trial schematically showing all the stimuli.

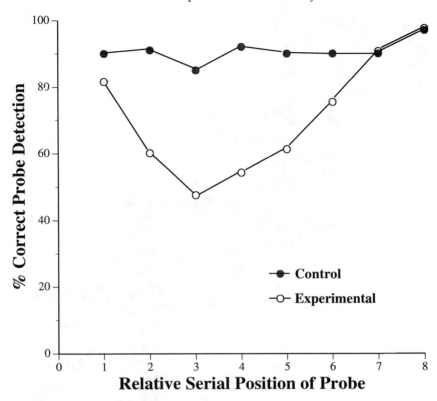

*Figure* 2: The group mean percentage of trials in which the probe was correctly detected plotted as a function of the relative serial position of the probe in Experiment 2 of Raymond et al. (1992). Closed symbols represent data obtained in the control condition in which subjects were told to ignore the target letter. Open symbols represent data obtained in the experimental condition in which subjects were told identify the target letter.

the attentional blink is to prevent any further stimulus processing after the target's occurrence in order to mitigate potential confusion stemming from the difficulty of the target identification task. For this reason, Raymond et al. (1992) argued for an early-selection, inhibitory role of the AB. In hindsight, as will be elucidated below, it may be noted that perhaps Raymond et al. extended their reasoning too far in suggesting that no stimuli following the AB were processed – but in other respects that may have been correct.[2]

A second series of experiments (Shapiro, Raymond, & Arnell, 1994) argued for a different mechanism to account for the AB, while still attempting to preserve the general notion of an inhibitory function of this effect. Shapiro et al. (1994) found evidence against an early-selection, target difficulty-based account in a series of studies demonstrating that the AB was not susceptible to any difficulty manipulations of the target task itself. Target tasks were created yielding d' values from easy to hard, with the resultant magnitude of the AB effect remaining unchanged.[3] Shapiro et al. (1994) suggested a late-selection, interference-based account in place of the early-selection account offered by Raymond et al. (1992), on the basis of the outcome of the difficulty manipulation just described and on the basis of another finding from this same set of experiments: we found that target tasks not possessing pattern information did not yield an AB. The nonpatterned target task was created by removing a letter from the RSVP stream on 50% of trials and having participants judge if there was a "gap" in the stimulus stream. Participants were able to do so quite well, revealing nearly a full attenuation of the AB effect.

Before leaving this discussion of experiments illustrating the AB, it is important to point out that a recent paper by Duncan, Ward, and Shapiro (1994; see also Ward, Duncan, & Shapiro, 1996) demonstrated that the interference revealed in the AB phenomenon is not limited to items appearing in the same location in visual space. In an adaptation of the RSVP procedure described previously, Duncan et al. (1994) presented participants with a target followed by a pattern mask in one spatial location separated, from trial to trial by a variable, stimulus-onset asynchrony (SOA), from an identically masked probe appearing in a different location. The variable SOA allowed the time-course of the interference to be probed. An effect that Duncan et al. termed "dwell time" was obtained with this modified RSVP procedure, and recent research has demonstrated that both the dwell time and AB effects are tapping similar attentional interference (Ward, Duncan, & Shapiro, 1996).

## A Model of the Attentional Blink

To accommodate these new findings, Shapiro and his colleagues suggested that the target, the probe, and likely the stimulus item following each were placed in a visual short-term memory (VSTM) buffer. From this buffer, stimuli were later selected for report. A first-in, first-out scheme was suggested to account for better target than probe report. The AB was held to occur when the target and probe were perceptually similar and interfered with each other for access to or retrieval (we prefer retrieval) from VSTM in a manner similar to that described by Duncan and Humphreys (1989). A more thorough treatment of this theory may be found in Shapiro and Raymond (1994) and in Shapiro, Caldwell, and Sorensen (in press). Though referred to as an interference account, the notion of the AB as an inhibitory-like process nevertheless remains preserved: we argue that the inhibition, in this case, is against selecting a probe when it matches the selected target too closely. It remained for later experiments (see following section) to find direct evidence that: (1) stimuli during the AB interval are indeed being processed, as would be required by a late-selection account, and (2) interference can directly be shown to be the cause of the AB outcome. Each of these will be discussed in turn.

## Late Selection and the Attentional Blink

Two recently conducted experiments provide support for a late-selection account of the AB. Late-selection accounts generally hold that all superthreshold stimulus information is processed to a later stage of analysis, though not necessarily accessible to conscious awareness. This view stands in contrast to a class of early-selection theories, in which such stimulus information may be shunted from further analysis at a very preliminary stage.

The first bit of recent evidence in support of a late-selection account of the AB comes from a study by Shapiro, Caldwell, and Sorensen (in press). In this experiment, we adapted a well-known effect from the auditory domain, the "cocktail party" phenomenon, to enable us to support our preferred theoretical view in the visual domain. The cocktail party phenomenon has been experienced by nearly everyone, and occurs when a person is engaged in a conversation with another, successfully ignoring other surrounding conversations, only to find that they have heard their own name uttered from a conversation to which they were previously not attending. This phenomenon, so named by Moray (1959), is usually interpreted as evidence in support of a late-selection view, in that a person must have been processing information from the supposedly unattended conversation to have been able to detect their name.

In keeping with the spirit of the "cocktail party" phenomenon, we constructed an experimental situation in which participants were asked in three separate conditions to search for their own name as probe, another name as probe, or a noun as probe in RSVP streams composed of nouns (Experiment 1) or names (Experiment 2). The results of this study suggest that own names as probes survive the AB fate, regardless of the type of distractor stream from which they are chosen. Other name and noun probes evidenced the typical AB effect, as did own names when they occurred as the target, rather than as the probe. The data enable us to argue strongly that stimulus processing can and does occur during the AB period.

A recent experiment (Shapiro, Driver, Ward, & Sorensen, in press) provides a second source of evidence that the probe is being processed during the AB and is thus consistent with a late-selection account. We created an experimental situation in which not two, but three targets were required to be analyzed for report. We will refer to these as T, $P_1$, and $P_2$ to denote the first target, the first probe, and the second probe, respectively. The basic notion was that if the probe occurring in the normally blinked region is being processed to some extent, then we can arrange this stimulus to have a potential effect on another stimulus subsequently occurring outside the blinked region.

Based on two well-established effects, the outcome for which we were searching could take one of two forms. Either $P_1$ could positively prime $P_2$ (Monsell, 1978) or the first could cause repetition blindness for the second (Kanwisher, 1987). Both positive and negative priming effects require close temporal proximity between the two targets (probes, by our naming scheme) which was accomplished by placing them 270 ms (three stimulus positions) apart in the RSVP stream. Positive priming takes the form where, for example, in our particular circumstance, an uppercase D ($P_1$) speeds responding to the occurrence of a lowercase d ($P_2$), whereas repetition blindness takes the opposite form where $P_1$ reveals slower responding to identical $P_2$.[4] Only those trials in which T was reported correctly were included in the analyses to ensure that we were looking at an appropriate occasion in which the AB could occur. Participants were required to identify from among a distractor stream of black digits: $T_1$, which was a white digit, $P_1$, which was an uppercase letter in a particular colour, and $P_2$, which was a lowercase letter in a different colour. $P_1$ and $P_2$ could either match in identity (e.g., D/d) or not match (e.g., D/e).

The outcome of this experiment, as shown in Figure 3, suggests the occurrence of positive priming (as revealed by percent correct responses to $P_2$) when participants were unable to correctly report $P_1$ but repetition blindness when participants were able to report $P_1$.[5] Without our going into a discussion of the significance of the particular conditions under which positive priming as opposed to repetition blindness were obtained, we can state that both results provide clear evidence of processing during the AB and in turn support a late-selection account.

It is worth mentioning here that Maki, Frigen, and Paulson (in press) have used a priming technique to arrive at the same conclusion as did Shapiro, Driver, Ward, and Sorensen (in press). Maki and his colleagues found evidence that $T_1$ is able to prime a semantically related $T_2$ that occurs in the AB interval. Such evidence is consistent with the late-selection account that we are favouring.

## Interference as the Source of the Attentional Blink

We turn our attention now to various sources of evidence supporting the second of the two notions mentioned above, that interference in VSTM is responsible for the deficit in probe report. First, Isaak, Shapiro, and Martin (1997) created a modification of the typical AB

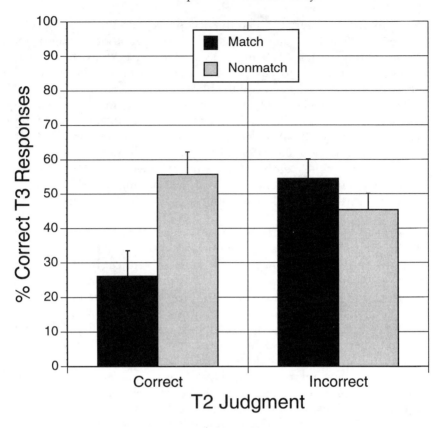

*Figure* 3: Overall percent of correct P2 responses, as a function of correct versus incorrect P1 judgments (distinguished along the abscissa), on match versus mismatch trials (light vs. dark bars respectively). P1 correct judgments show repetition blindness (match worse than mismatch), whereas P1 incorrect judgments reveal positive priming (match better than mismatch).

paradigm to enable us to load VSTM with specific stimuli and assess the types of errors committed on those trials when the probe was reported incorrectly. In Experiment 2, participants were required not only to detect the target but also to identify the probe. The target (T), the item immediately following the target (T+1), the probe (P), and the item immediately following the probe (P+1) were each drawn from a restricted set of letters. Distractors were letters drawn at random from the set of letters not set aside as possible T, T+1, P, or P+1 items. The probe letter was distinguished from other letters in the distractor stream by its size (smaller). Probe identification errors in this second task were useful in probing the contents of VSTM. The results of this experiment reveal that, when probe errors are made in the typical AB interval, participants are most likely to choose the P+1 item instead of the probe. In a distant second place, the target was the item most likely to be chosen. Finally, there were few importations – that is, letters selected as the probe that were not part of any restricted set.

In Experiment 2, the distractor stream was removed from the RSVP sequence in order to assess its contribution to the errors in probe report. Participants were presented with only the target and probe, each of which was masked and separated by an interval corresponding to those occurring in Experiments 1 and 2 when the distractor stream was present. Setting the outcome of this experiment apart from the previous two, probe errors were represented equally by the T, T+1, and P+1 items.

The results of these experiments show that, when the probe cannot be identified, there is a significant likelihood that a letter presumed to be in VSTM will be chosen instead. Such results suggest that target decay is not a viable explanation for the pattern of results in Experiment 2, given that the temporal relationship between the target and probe did not change in Experiment 2, yet an equal proportion of errors came from the target in the latter case. Thus, it appears that VSTM acts as a repository for potential target and probe candidates, and that the likelihood of an item occupying a slot in this buffer is a function of the number of items competing for entry. It must be pointed out, however, that these data support equally well an alternative account. The data could be interpreted as supporting an inhibitory account, assuming such an account does not presume (as has been presumed above) that no processing can occur during the AB. Such an inhibitory account would need to posit that the inhibition produced by the target is not complete, but rather acts to suppress the signal strength of stimuli following the target for the duration of the AB. A period of reduced signal strength might in turn leave no one stimulus as a clear contender for probe report, yielding the same pattern of results as just described in Isaak, Shapiro, & Martin (submitted). It remains for subsequent experiments to provide additional support for one over the other of these two accounts. A further treatment of the inhibitory account will be provided near the conclusion of this chapter.

A second study and one lending specific support to an interference account as the basis for the AB comes from another experiment by Isaak, Shapiro, & Martin (submitted). The hypothesis for this study was that an interference account for the AB would have to argue that the magnitude of the effect should reflect: (1) the number of items competing for report, and (2) the degree of similarity among the competing items. For this series of experiments, we employed the no-distractor stream version of the RSVP paradigm, as described above

(Experiment 2; Isaak, Shapiro, & Martin, submitted). To reiterate, on each trial a target was followed immediately by a T+1 item, followed with a variable SOA by the probe, which was followed immediately by the P+1 item.

The target task was to identify which of two possible white target letters ("E" or "O") was presented. The probe task was to identify the probe letter from a second set of two alternative letters ("T" or "H"). The T+1 and P+1 items were a third and fourth set of two-item alternatives, in each case a letter and the same pattern mask, the latter being composed of letter-like features ("F" and mask, and "L" and mask, respectively). Each possible combination of T, P, T+1, and P+1 items was presented randomly on an equal number of trials. We discovered that the magnitude of the AB was a direct function of the number of *categorically similar competitors*. In other words, there was a direct relationship between the number of letters and the amount of interference, but this relationship held only for letters and not for the nonletter (pattern mask) stimuli. A subsequent experiment employed the identical design but used false-font masks, instead of pattern masks, to further test the notion that only categorically similar items are considered competitors. The results of this experiment showed the same outcome as the previous one: letters compete with each other but false-font stimuli, in spite of their greater similarity to letters than to pattern masks, do not.

The results of an experiment by Maki, Frigen, Couture, and Lien (in press) support the above contention that only categorically similar items compete for retrieval in RSVP. Words, nonwords, consonant strings, and false-font words at two display durations were used as distractors in their experiment. The first two distractor conditions revealed an AB, the third showed an attenuated effect, but the two false-font distractor conditions both revealed the absence of an AB.

In a final experiment in this series, we investigated the level at which the categorical similarity operates to yield or restrict competition by placing digits in competition with letters. If the semantic information in VSTM is sufficiently elaborated only to specify that items have meaning, but not that they are members of a particular conceptual category, then all the items should compete equally with each other, regardless of how many are letters and how many are digits. Furthermore, through the design of this experiment, we were able to assess the operation that determines the "definition" of the category into which stimulus items are placed. This experiment used perceptually similar letters and digits to define each of the stream items. The target could be a "G" or a "6," the T+1 either an "A" or a "4," the T+2 either a "Z" or a "2," the probe either an "S" or a "5," and the P+1 either a "B" or a "3." All participants were required to identify the target, half were required to determine whether or not a *letter* probe (S) occurred, and the other half were required to determine whether or not a *digit* probe (5) occurred. The logic was that, if the probe task specifies the definition of the category, then digits should not be effective probe competitors when the probe task is to detect a letter and letters should not be effective probe competitors when the probe task is to detect a digit. The results of this experiment revealed that the probe task does set the categorical definition for a trial, and that letters and digits are seen as categorically different by whatever mechanism is involved in producing the AB.

## Competing Hypotheses

Chun and Potter (1995) proposed a two-stage model to account for AB findings, similar to that proposed by Broadbent and Broadbent (1987). Stage 1 involves the rapid detection of relevant features (e.g., colour, case) of each item in an RSVP stream. By Chun and Potter's account, every item in the RSVP sequence is processed through Stage 1, at which point possible targets are detected for subsequent processing. Items that are detected as possible targets are then identified for report in Stage 2. Stage 2 involves serial, capacity-limited processing. According to this theory, the AB is the direct result of a bottleneck at Stage 2, when a second possible target is identified in Stage 1 prior to the completion of the processing of the first target by Stage 2. This in turn delays Stage 2 processing of the second target.

In a series of experiments, Chun and Potter (1995) presented participants with letter target and probe tasks embedded among digits and/or symbols as distractors. They found the largest AB magnitude when digits followed both the target and the probe, as compared to the experimental situation when symbols alone or a mixture of symbols and digits, served as distractors. One of their principal claims – one that distinguishes their account from that proposed by Shapiro, Raymond, and Arnell (1994) – is that the target processing difficulty modulates the magnitude of the AB.[6] As described above, Shapiro et al. (1994) found no correlation between blink magnitude and d' measures resulting from various target difficulty manipulations. It is the opinion of the present authors that this issue can be resolved if one takes into account the way in which target difficulty was manipulated between Chun and Potter's (1995) experiments and those by Shapiro et al. (in preparation) but a discussion of this issue will be postponed until the present review of Chun and Potter (1995) is completed.

To compare Chun and Potter's theory with that of Shapiro et al., we believe that Chun and Potter's results can be explained equally well by an interference account. Interference theory purports that the magnitude of the AB is a function of the degree of similarity between items in VSTM. It stands to reason that digits, and in turn symbols, would be expected to yield less interference with letter targets than would letters as distractors. Moreover, this account is consistent with data discussed previously from experiments by Isaak, Shapiro, & Martin (submitted).

According to Chun and Potter (1995), Stage 2 processing cannot commence analyzing the probe until after it has finished analyzing the target. Thus it seems to follow that the probe should only be processed to a featural level (i.e., not a conceptual level) until after the AB interval.[7] Evidence from Chun and Potter's (1995) own data would seem to contradict this, as letters are interfered with less by digits than by other letters. A further challenge to Chun and Potter's theory comes from the previously described study by Shapiro, Driver, Ward, & Sorenson (in press). In this experiment, we found that a probe occurring during the AB that went undetected could nevertheless semantically prime a second probe (third target) occurring outside the "blinked" region. If the first probe went undetected (was "blinked"), then it caused repetition blindness for the second probe. Semantic priming is certainly considered to be evidence of a high level of processing, and thus the outcome of this study appears to be at odds with the claim made by Chun and Potter (1995).

Before going on to describe an inhibitory model of the AB, a series of experiments by Seiffert and Di Lollo (in press) are deserving of mention for two reasons. First, their findings were interpreted by the authors as support for the recently described two-stage model of Chun and Potter (1995). Second, Seiffert and Di Lollo (in press) present an interesting addition to our knowledge of the effect of the target+1 item on the AB. The purpose of the Seiffert and Di Lollo experiments was to examine the contribution of various forms of masking to the blink. In a clever novel condition, they presented the target+1 stimulus in the *same* temporal frame as the target. In one condition, the target+1 item overlapped spatially with the target, and in another, the target+1 item was spatially adjacent, but nonoverlapping. Both conditions yielded an AB, but the spatially overlapping condition caused more of an AB than the nonoverlapping condition. In the general discussion of this paper, they suggest that their data support Chun and Potter's model, in that masking acts to affect the target processing which in turn acts to delay the probe processing.

Seiffert and Di Lollo (in press) then used their data, that of Chun and Potter's (1995), and that reported by Shapiro and his colleagues (Raymond et al., 1992, 1995; Shapiro et al., 1994) to evaluate a proposition that stems directly from their belief concerning the relationship between the target and the probe just stated – that is, target difficulty affects the magnitude of the AB. They conclude that it does, after finding a significant correlation. In recent reports, others have recently come to a similar conclusion.[8] It appears now that there may be two different ways of affecting the target that have a different effect on the probe, though a full discussion of this is beyond the scope of this chapter. It has been suggested that manipulations directly affecting the difficulty of the target selection, for example, making it easier by requiring participants to detect a target defined by a contrast change (Shapiro, Raymond, & Arnell, 1994) have no effect on the probe. On the other hand, manipulations designed to limit the time during which a selected target has to be processed (e.g.,masking) may have an effect on the probe.

Before leaving this topic, we must point out that a VSTM interference model can account for the data of Seiffert and Di Lollo (in press). Based on well-established findings by Duncan (1980), it has been shown that all attributes of a single object may be attended to without cost, whereas attending to the same attributes of two objects engenders costs. With this in mind, it may be argued that the overlapping condition used by Seiffert and Di Lollo (in press) caused participants to process more of the attributes of both targets than in the condition in which the two targets were adjacent but nonoverlapping. According to our VSTM model, more attributes processed would be expected to yield more interference and, hence, a greater AB.

The VSTM-based interference account offered by Shapiro and his colleagues offers a viable way of explaining the results of the diverse experiments revealing a deficit in performance on a second target when that target is separated from the first by less than 500 ms (the AB effect). There are, however, other equally viable accounts of our and others' data. One such account is based on the notion of inhibition. As discussed in the introduction to this chapter, inhibition, along with its companion, process facilitation, plays a major role in stimulus selection. To explain the attentional blink, an inhibitory account must be able to account for the recent findings (e.g., Luck, Vogel, & Shapiro 1996; Shapiro, Caldwell, & Sorensen, in press; Shapiro, Driver, Ward, & Sorensen, in press) showing that a high level of processing does occur during the AB period. The inhibitory account offered by Raymond, Shapiro, and Amell (1992) did not really have a provision for continued processing, but could be modified to do so.

Such an inhibitory account of the AB might suggest that the target processing causes a reduction in the energy available from stimuli occurring during the interval that we call the attentional blink. Such a reduction could be thought of as a general dampening function arising from some process initiated by the target detection task.[9] A general dampening function could be modeled easily enough, and some preliminary attempts at doing so show functions similar to those found empirically. The reduction in posttarget processing subsequently causes a deficit in probe detectability, rendering the probe detectable on the approximately 50% of trials that characterize the AB. Recovery to baseline levels of performance would be accounted for, depending on the process believed to initiate the inhibition to the target in the first place, by postulating a recovery of the inhibition brought about either by neural decay or as a result of the demands of the target task being completed successfully.

Inhibitory accounts of the AB must, however, bring into line certain empirical findings from recent studies, a few of which have been discussed previously in this chapter. First, such an account must deal with the finding that when the probe is unable to be identified correctly from among a full set of distractor stimuli, the item just after the probe (P+1) is most likely to be selected (see the description of the experiment by Isaak, Shapiro, & Martin, submitted, above) but when probe identification fails in the presence of *only* the target, the probe and their respective masks, both the T+1 as well as the P+1 items are highly likely to be selected. A general account of inhibition has no problem explaining the occurrence of the AB effect but has a more difficult time accounting for the pattern of errors just described.

A second problem faced by an inhibition account of the AB concerns the finding that "interference" arising from the RSVP stream is more acute when the nontarget stream is composed of items categorically dissimilar to the target and probe (see Isaak, Shapiro, & Martin, submitted, above). To explain such an outcome, one has to postulate a "smart" inhibitory mechanism, one able to selectively inhibit semantically specific stimulus items. It must be pointed out, however, that on the basis of the Isaak et al. data, the interference hypothesis suggested by Shapiro and Raymond (1994) must be refined to go beyond perceptual similarity as the basis of the interference underlying the AB.

We do not want to leave the reader with the belief that an inhibitory account for the AB should be dismissed. On the contrary, inhibition is a powerful neural mechanism, and may have an important role to play even at the level of attention under consideration here. As an example, Tipper and his colleagues have strong support for an inhibitory-based account of a well researched attentional phenomenon, negative priming, and such an account may serve to explain the AB effect, as well (Tipper, Weaver, Cameron, Brehaut, & Bastedo, 1991; see also this volume). The interference model as we have described it in this chapter is an example of a strong late-selection account in which the selection of an item for probe report reflects competition among fully identified items in VSTM. Inhibition models on the other hand, at least in an extreme form, represent the counterpoint of late selection, in that they argue that selection is early in the stimulus processing stream. In a recent paper by Martin, Isaak, and Shapiro (submitted), we suggest that an item may "win" the competition for probe report at any of the levels implicated in object processing, from feature detection (i.e., early) to full identification (i.e., late). Further, Martin et al. (in preparation) argue that items are rejected as probe candidates as early as possible within the joint constraints of the particular stimuli and the specific task. For example, under some circumstances, it may be necessary to identify all four critical items (T, T+1, P, and P+1) before it is possible to select a probe, whereas in other circumstances, it may be possible to select a probe solely on the basis of a unique perceptual feature. Our most recent claim that the locus of attentional selection is flexible is called the *smart selection hypothesis* to distinguish it both from the early selection view that items are always selected at a relatively low perceptual level and from the contrasting late selection notion that items are always selected only after they have been fully identified. The term *smart selection* also reflects our contention that when the attentional system is approaching a capacity limitation, it expends computational resources with maximal efficiency, processing items only until they can be eliminated as probe candidates. These views are similar to those expressed by Wolfe and his colleagues (Wolfe, Cave, & Franzel, 1989) in their choice of the "guided search" metaphor to explain an analogous smart selection mechanism purported to guide visual search in the spatial domain.

## An Alternative Hypothesis

Concluding this chapter, we would like to propose another way in which the data presented here may be viewed. The notion of VSTM interference and the mechanisms producing protection from interference elaborated in this paper are compatible with more recent theories of visual attention. This alternative view of the basis of the AB results from incorporating the notion of interference with the hypothesis that objects constitute units of attentional analysis. This hypothesis has been elaborated recently by Kahneman, Treisman, and Gibbs (1992) in their theory of "object files." According to these investigators, the presentation of a second target initiates a reviewing process to determine if the second target is consistent with the first. If the two targets (such as the target and probe in an RSVP stream) can be linked as one object, then the opening of a new object file is hypothesized to be unnecessary. A single object file prevents an excessive demand on the attentional system. This notion is very similar to that suggested by Duncan (1984), in which he proposed that multiple attributes of a single object can be processed effectively, whereas the same attributes of different objects yield attentional cost.

To present this idea in a way consistent with our notions of interference, we propose the following account. The target task demands attentional processing, and establishes an object file. Items of importance occurring within approximately 500 ms after the target (i.e., the first posttarget item, the probe, and possibly the item immediately following the probe) have the potential to interfere with the target task and force one of two outcomes. On some occasions these items are assimilated with the object file created by the target, and no new object file is necessitated, though the observer is aware of the update. Under this circumstance no AB is predicted, as no interference is experienced. On other occasions, one or more of these critical posttarget items is unable to be assimilated with the target. On these occasions, an AB effect is hypothesized to occur, as the second object file is established, and yields a divided attention deficit. In such cases, the proposed mechanisms that determine the amount of interference, such as item similarity or semantic salience of the probe, would still operate. The idea of a target object necessitating time to be fully processed is elaborated as the dwell-time hypothesis proposed by Duncan, Ward, and Shapiro (1994) and is consistent with the Integrated Competition Hypothesis recently proposed by Duncan (1996).

Evidence in support of the object-file hypothesis as it relates to the AB may be found in an experiment by Raymond and Sorensen (1994). In their experiment, apparent motion in the RSVP stream was produced by the random rotation of a "trident" stimulus from one RSVP stream item to the next. In a critical condition, the target and probe were the same trident objects as constituted distractor stream stimuli, but were distinguished by an added feature. In a corresponding control condition the probe was a different "object." An attenuated AB was observed in the experimental condition, which the authors explained by arguing that a single object file was opened and updated throughout the RSVP sequence.

The model just described, involving object-based notions as well as elements of interference theory, adequately accounts for the results of recent pilot experiments from our laboratory showing that grouping of certain key elements in the RSVP stream attenuates the AB effect (Raymond, Caldwell, & Shapiro, 1993; Shapiro, Moroz, & Raymond, 1993). In an attempt to provide subjects with a means by which a single object file could be formed, we examined four factors designed to facilitate such grouping. The factors were luminance (i.e., contrast), 2-D cues, 3-D cues, and colour. We were correct in hypothesizing that some but not all of these grouping factors would reveal an attenuated AB.

In summary, the attentional blink phenomenon represents a tool for examining the limits of human attentional capability. Our experiments have shown that the AB effect occurs whenever two successive, patterned visual targets must be detected or identified (but cannot be "linked" by an object file) and whenever they are separated by less than approximately 500 ms. We propose a "smart" selection mechanism that incorporates elements of both VSTM-based interference and target-generated inhibition to account for the findings from the various laboratories working on this problem. Considerable investigation is required before a full account of this phenomenon can be derived.

Before concluding, it should be pointed out that, very recently, reports of both failures (Duncan, Martens, & Ward, in press; Potter, Chun, & Muckenhoupt, 1995; Shulman & Hsieh, 1995) and successes (Arnell & Jolicoeur, 1995) to obtain cross modality (vision and audition) attentional blinks have surfaced. Various procedural differences between the experiments claiming success and failure might account for the different outcomes, but it is too early at this time to tell. For example, while Potter et al. (1995) failed to find definitive support for crossmodal AB, they did find a deficit of an auditory target on an auditory probe but one that failed to recover to baseline performance within the 500 ms period typically defining the AB. Needless to say, if crossmodality AB is real, a visually based interference account would have to be seriously revised! However, before abandoning our account altogether, it should be noted that the studies claiming to get good crossmodal AB have used compressed speech as the auditory stimulus, and it is possible that the formation of an iconic representation of a compressed speech cue might still preserve the visual interference account argued by the present authors.

## Acknowledgments

The authors wish to thank Richard D. Wright for his patient efforts in organizing this book and for inviting us to contribute a chapter. We also wish to thank Jesse Martin and Jane Raymond for carefully reading the manuscript and providing us with help at various points along the way.

## Notes

1 It is very likely that processing information over space, even though in an apparent single "moment in time," actually involves processing over time. In addition to highlighting one of the most useful aspects of employing rapid serial visual presentation techniques (RSVP) to study attention as described subsequently in this chapter, it also presents an interesting paradox that is discussed in Duncan, Ward, and Shapiro (1994).

2 To be completely accurate, Raymond et al.(1992) did suggest that the item immediately following the target was processed along with the target, but an explanation for this one particular stimulus having to do with temporal imprecision was offered.

3 This outcome will be qualified in a section to follow later in this chapter.

4 Both positive priming and negative priming effects described here are evaluated relative to a control condition in which, for example, a "D" was followed by an "e."

5 It should be noted here that the interpretation of this study was somewhat confounded by a methodological issue, and prompted a second experiment. Moreover, the appropriate interpretation of these experiments requires more discussion than can be entertained here, and the reader is advised to consult Shapiro, Driver, Ward, and Sorensen (in press) for a more thorough treatment.

6 Note that, as stated previously in the chapter, Shapiro, Raymond, and Arnell (1994) claim that the magnitude of the AB is *not* related to the difficulty of the target task; rather, the AB is the result of "all or nothing" demands imposed by any patterned target. Seiffert and Di Lollo (in press) refute this claim and state that the AB *is* determined by target task difficulty. More will be said about Seiffert and Di Lollo's study in a later section.

7 Chun and Potter (1995) do suggest that Stage 1 processes information to a categorical level, but this statement seems inconsistent with other statements of theirs concerning the limitations of Stage 1 processing. If it is true that Stage 2 processing occurs at the level of meaning, then Chun and Potter's view and that of Shapiro and his colleagues are not so far apart.

8 These findings are consistent with those recently reported by Moore, Egeth, Berglan, and Luck (in press), where they reduced the effectiveness of the mask and, in this case, predictably found an attenuation of the AB.

9 We will not speculate here on what the nature of that target process is, but various plausible accounts have been proposed by Raymond et al. (1992) and more recently by Chun and Potter (1995).

# References

Arnell, K.M., & Jolicoeur, P. (1995). *Allocating attention across stimulus modality: Evidence from the attentional blink phenomenon.* Paper presented at the annual meeting of the Psychonomic Society, Los Angeles, CA.

Broadbent, D.E., & Broadbent, M.H.P. (1987). From detection to identification: Response to multiple targets in rapid serial visual presentation. *Perception & Psychophysics, 42*, 105–113.

Chun, M.M., & Potter, M.C. (1995). A two-stage model for multiple target detection in rapid serial visual presentation. *Journal of Experimental Psychology: Human Perception & Performance, 21*, 109–127.

Duncan, J. (1980). The locus of interference in the perception of simultaneous stimuli. *Psychological Review, 87*, 272–300.

Duncan, J. (1984). Selective attention and the organization of visual information. *Journal of Experimental Psychology: General, 113*, 501–517.

Duncan, J. (1996). Co-ordinated brain systems in selective perception and action. In T. Inui and J.L. McClelland (Eds.), Attention and Performance XVI (Cambridge, MA: MIT Press).

Duncan, J., & Humphreys, G. (1989). Visual search and stimulus similarity. *Psychological Review, 96*, 433–458.

Duncan, J., Martens, S., & Ward, R. (in press). Restricted attentional capacity within but not between sensory modalities. *Nature*.

Duncan, J., Ward, R., & Shapiro, K.L. (1994). Direct measurement of attentional dwell time in human vision. *Nature, 369*, 313–315.

Isaak, M.I., Shapiro, K.L., & Martin, J. (1995). Visual short term memory load effects in RSVP: The attentional blink reflects competition among probe candidates. Manuscript under review.

Kahneman, D., Treisman, A., & Gibbs, B.J. (1992). The reviewing of object files: object-specific integration of information. *Cognitive Psychology, 28*, 195–217.

Kanwisher, N.G. (1987). Repetition blindness: Type recognition without token individuation. *Cognition, 27*, 117–143.

Konorski, J. (1967). *Integrative activity of the brain*. Chicago: University of Chicago Press.

Luck, S.J., Vogel, E.R., & Shapiro, K.L. (1996). Word meanings can be accessed but not reported during the attentional blink. *Nature, 383*, 616–618.

Maki, W.S., Frigen K., & Paulson, K. (in press). Associative priming by targets and distractors during rapid serial visual presentation: Does word meaning survive the attentional blink? *Journal of Experimental Psychology: Human Perception & Performance*.

Maki, W.S., Couture, T., Frigen K., & Lien, D. (in press). Sources of the attentional blink during rapid serial visual presentation: Perceptual interference and retrieval competition. *Journal of Experimental Psychology: Human Perception & Performance*.

Martin, J., Isaak, M.I., & Shapiro, K.L. (1995). Temporal attentional selection: Sometimes early, sometimes late, always smart. Manuscript in preparation.

Monsell, S. (1978). Recency, immediate recognition memory, and reaction time. *Cognitive Psychology, 10*, 465–501.

Moore, C.M., Egeth, H., Berglan, L.R., & Luck, S.J. (in press). Are attentional dwell times inconsistent with serial visual search? *Psychonomic Bulletin and Review*.

Moray, N. (1959). Attention in dichotic listening: Affective cues and the influence of instruction. *Quarterly Journal of Experimental Psychology, 11*, 56–60.

Nakayama, K., & Mackeben, M. (1989). Sustained and transient components of focal visual attention. *Vision Research, 29*, 1631–1647.

Pavlov, I.P. (1927). *Conditioned reflexes*. Oxford University Press.

Posner, M.I. & Cohen, Y. (1984). Components of visual orienting. In H. Bouma & D.G. Bouwhuis (Eds.), *Attention & Performance, Volume 10*, (pp. 531–556). Hillsdale, NJ: Erlbaum.

Posner, M.I., Snyder, C.R.R., & Davidson, B.J. (1980). Attention and the detection of signals. *Journal of Experimental Psychology: General, 109*, 160–174.

Potter, M.C., Chun, M.M., & Muckenhoupt, M. (1995). *Auditory attention does not blink*. Paper presented at the annual meeting of the Psychonomic Society, Los Angeles, CA.

Raymond, J.E., & Sorensen, R. (1994). *Motion, object selection, and the attentional blink.* Paper presented at the annual meeting of the Psychonomics Society, St. Louis, MO.

Raymond, J.E., Caldwell, J.I., & Shapiro, K.L. (1993). *Perceptual grouping in RSVP.* Paper presented at the annual meeting of the Psychonomic Society, Washington, DC.

Raymond, J.E., Shapiro, K.S., & Arnell, K.M. (1992). Temporary suppression of visual processing in an RSVP task: An attentional blink? *Journal of Experimental Psychology: Human Perception & Performance, 18,* 849–860.

Raymond, J.E., Shapiro, K.S., & Arnell, K.M. (1995). Similarity determines the attentional blink. *Journal of Experimental Psychology: Human Perception & Performance, 21,* 653–662.

Reeves, A., & Sperling, G. (1986). Attention gating in short term visual memory. *Psychological Review, 93,* 180–206.

Seiffert, A.E., & Di Lollo, V. (1995). *Low-level masking in the attentional blink.* Manuscript under review.

Shapiro, K.L., & Raymond, J.E. (1994). Temporal allocation of visual attention: Inhibition or interference? In D. Dagenbach & T. Carr (Eds.), *Inhibitory processes in attention, memory, and language,* (pp. 151–188). New York: Academic Press.

Shapiro, K.L., Caldwell, J.I., & Sorensen, R.E. (in press). Personal names and the attentional blink: The "cocktail party" effect revisited. *Journal of Experimental Psychology: Human Perception & Performance.*

Shapiro, K.L., Driver, J., Ward, R., & Sorensen, R.E. (in press). The attentional blink and repetition blindness are failures to extract visual tokens, not visual types. *Psychological Science.*

Shapiro, K.L., Raymond, J.E., & Arnell, K.M. (1994). Attention to visual pattern information produces the attentional blink in RSVP. *Journal of Experimental Psychology: Human Perception & Performance, 20,* 357–371.

Shapiro, K.L., Moroz, T., & Raymond, J.E. (1993). *Probe manipulations in the attentional blink paradigm.* Paper presented at the annual meeting of the Psychonomic Society, Washington, DC.

Shulman, H., & Hsieh, V. (1995). *The attention blink in mixed modality streams.* Paper presented at the annual meeting of the Psychonomic Society, Los Angeles, CA.

Tipper, S.P., Weaver, B., Cameron, S., Brehaut, J.C., & Bastedo, J. (1991). Inhibitory mechanisms of attention in identification and localization tasks: Timecourse and disruption. *Journal of Experimental Psychology: Learning, Memory, & Cognition, 17,* 681–692.

Treisman, A., & Gormican, S. (1988). Feature analysis in early vision: Evidence from search asymmetries. *Psychological Review, 95,* 15–48.

Wagner, A.R., & Rescorla, R.A. (1972). Inhibition in Pavlovian conditioning: Application of a theory. In R.A. Boakes & S.M. Halliday (Eds.), *Inhibition and learning,* (pp. 301–336). San Diego, CA: Academic Press.

Ward, R., Duncan, J., & Shapiro, K.L. (1996). The slow time-course of visual attention. *Cognitive Psychology, 30,* 79–109.

Ward, R., Duncan, J., & Shapiro, K.L. (in press). Effects of presentation, similarity, and difficulty on the time-course of visual attention. *Perception & Psychophysics*.

Weichselgartner, E., & Sperling, G. (1987). Dynamics of automatic and controlled visual attention. *Science, 238*, 778–780.

Williams, D.A., Overmier, J.B., & LoLordo, V.M. (1992). A reevaluation of Rescorla's early dictums about Pavlovian conditioned inhibition. *Psychological Bulletin, 111*, 275–290.

Wolfe, J.M., Cave, K.R., & Franzel, S.E. (1989). Guided Search: An alternative to the feature integration model for visual search. *Journal of Experimental Psychology: Human Perception & Performance, 15*, 419–433.

# 13

## Inhibition of Return Is Not Reflexive

### Richard D. Wright and Christian M. Richard

Searching for objects is perhaps the most common visual task we perform. Whenever we look for a face in a crowd, or an item in a container, or a street name on a map, we are carrying out a serial search routine. And search is usually so rapid that researchers have only recently begun to appreciate the complexity of the operations involved. The discovery of the *inhibition-of-return* effect (Posner & Cohen, 1984) has provided some important clues about serial search. Inhibition of return (IOR) appears to be associated with a procedure that many researchers believe allows us to keep track of objects when looking through a large collection of them. More specifically, some type of marking operation seems to occur in order to make the performance of tasks involving serial inspection more efficient, and the IOR effect may be caused by this marking.

If you were asked about the number of dots in Figure 1, your strategy might be to count them by beginning on the left and moving to the right. As you did this, you would adjust your tally while somehow keeping track of the dots once they have been inspected. Without some means of keeping counted and uncounted dots distinct, the task would be difficult to perform efficiently and accurately. Counting therefore involves a serial analysis that maintains the locations of previously inspected objects in some way.

Higher-level vision is, for the most part, serial in nature (Ullman, 1997). The eye movements we make to foveate and analyze an object of interest are physically constrained to a single location at a time, and there is also compelling evidence that the focus of visual attention is unitary and constrained to a single location (see, e.g., Wright & Ward, this volume). The frequency and speed of this serial analysis (we can move our eyes and attentional focal point several times in less than one second) requires that an associated marking mechanism operate rapidly and automatically without the need for a conscious decision to keep track of each inspected location. Such a mechanism would operate at an early stage of visual processing, and maintain location information independently of the attentive analysis of the currently in-

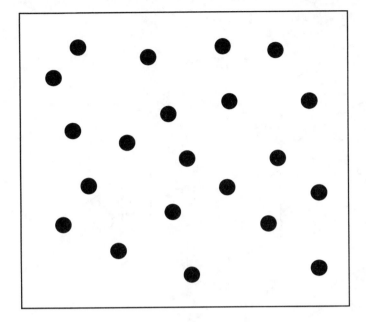

*Figure* 1: When counting a cluster of dots, we seem to keep track of those that have already been tallied with some form of marking operation.

spected object. The IOR effect we describe in this chapter appears to be associated with this type of marking mechanism.

Researchers generally agree that IOR is somehow involved in the selection of locations to be searched. Posner and his colleagues (e.g., Clohessy, Posner, Rothbart, & Vecera, 1991; Harman, Posner, Rothbart, & Thomas-Thrapp, 1994; Posner & Cohen, 1984; Posner, Rafal, Choate, & Vaughan, 1985) proposed that it biases saccadic eye movements away from recently sampled locations and toward novel locations, thereby making visual search more efficient. Eye movement biasing proposals make good sense from an efficiency standpoint because saccades are relatively time consuming – saccade execution can last up to 50 ms and this is followed by a refractory period of up to 200 ms during which another saccade cannot be made (Abrams & Dobkin, 1994).

The IOR effect is typically obtained in the laboratory in one of two ways. *Saccade-induced IOR* occurs when observers make a saccadic eye movement to one location and then to another. When a target is presented at the first fixated location, detection response times are slower than would be the case if it was presented elsewhere (e.g., Posner et al., 1985). The increase in response time is usually attributed to some form of inhibition related to eye movement programming (e.g., Harman et

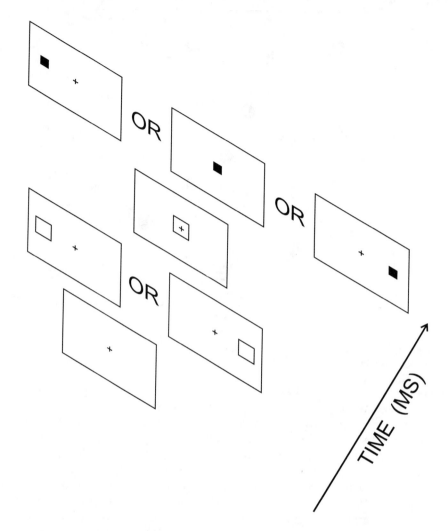

*Figure* 2: Typical display used for generating stimulus-induced inhibition of return (IOR). Outline boxes serve as location cues at the peripheral and central locations.

al., 1994; Rafal, Egly, & Rhodes, 1994). Stimulus-induced IOR can be obtained by presenting two successive abrupt-onset stimuli; one at a peripheral location followed 200 ms later by one at the central location. And 200 ms after the presentation of the second cue, a target is either presented at the first cued location, the second cued location, or an un-cued location (see Figure 2). As with saccade-induced IOR, detection response times are significantly slower for targets presented at the first cued location than for those presented elsewhere.

There are several proposals about how the visual system produces IOR. Maylor (1985; Maylor & Hockey, 1987) claimed that in order for IOR to occur, a channel of focused attention must first be directed to the location in question. On the other hand, Posner and Cohen (1984) claimed that it occurs as the result of sensory events (e.g., the onset of a direct location cue) that trigger the activation of a facilitative and an inhibitory component. The facilitative effect initially masks the inhibitory effect, and IOR occurs when the former attenuates and the inhibitory effect then becomes dominant. Rafal, Calabresi, Brennan, and Sciolto (1989) and Tassinari, Biscaldi, Marzi, and Berlucchi (1989) claimed that IOR is caused by some aspect of oculomotor system activation. Abrams and Dobkin (1994) proposed that saccade-induced IOR is due to inhibition of oculomotor processes, whereas stimulus-induced IOR is due to inhibition of both oculomotor and stimulus-detection processes. Thus, there is currently some disagreement about the roles that attention and saccadic eye movement programming play when IOR occurs.

## Spatial Indexing and Inhibition of Return

In this chapter, we suggest an account of IOR that is not purely attentional and not purely oculomotor. It is based on the idea of multiple spatial indexing. One motivation for this account is a finding that IOR can occur at more than one location at the same time. Posner and Cohen (1984) were among the first to report *multiple-location IOR*. They conducted an experiment in which direct cues were presented simultaneously at two peripheral locations and then, 200 ms later, a distractor stimulus was presented in the centre of the display. IOR occurred when a target was presented at either peripherally cued location. And, more important, the magnitude of IOR on double-cue trials was not significantly different than that on single-cue trials. It is difficult to explain this multiple-location IOR effect purely in terms of attentional processing because, as mentioned previously, there is a general consensus that the focus of visual attention cannot be divided between two or more locations. Therefore, Posner and Cohen (1984) claimed that multiple-location IOR is not the result of attending to the direct cued locations in sequence with a single channel of focused attention but instead is the result of the onsets of the cues themselves or, in their terms, "the energy change present at the cued positions" (p. 539).

This claim was challenged when a replication study yielded different results (Maylor, 1985). In particular, IOR magnitude on simultaneous double-cue trials was roughly 50% of that on single-cue trials. This suggested that, on any given double-cue trial, only one of the two simultaneously cued locations was actually inhibited. It was concluded that IOR is the result of a serial attentive analysis of the cued

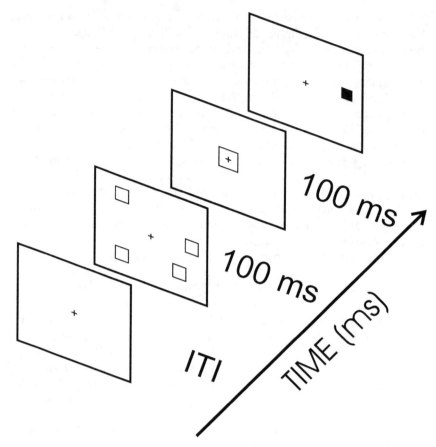

*Figure* 3: Simultaneous location cueing display used for generating the multiple-location inhibition-of-return (IOR) effect.

locations. This is quite a different claim than Posner and Cohen's (1984) idea that IOR is the result of a sensory analysis of the cued locations that is triggered by cue onsets.

In the early 1990s, we conducted several studies to determine the extent to which IOR is due to sensory or attentional processes (Wright & Richard, 1993, 1994, 1996a). Like Posner and Cohen (1984), we compared the IOR magnitude associated with single-cue and multiple-cue conditions (see Figure 3). We found that IOR occurred with roughly equal magnitude following simultaneous single, double, triple, and quadruple cues (see Figure 4). IOR at four locations is particularly difficult to account for in terms of a serial attentive analysis of cued locations and its occurrence suggests that IOR is mediated by parallel sensory analysis.

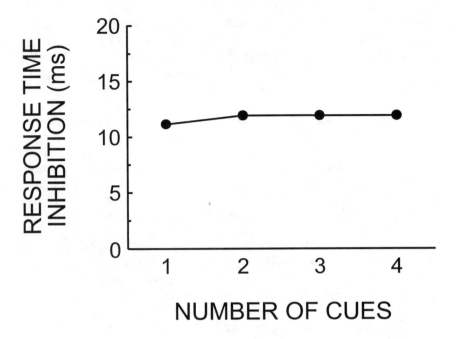

*Figure* 4: Mean inhibition-of-return (IOR) magnitudes for single, double, triple, and quadruple simultaneous cue presentations.

We conducted another study in which cues were presented sequentially at 100 ms intervals rather than simultaneously (Wright & Richard, 1994). The results indicated that fewer locations were inhibited at the same time following multiple sequential cue presentation than following simultaneous cue presentation. To elaborate, when four peripheral direct cues were presented in sequence before a central distractor, there was strong IOR (24 ms) at the most recently cued location, less but still significant IOR (12 ms) at the second most recently cued location, and no inhibition at the other cued locations. Interestingly, when another sequential-cue study was conducted with a longer delay between the presentation of the central distractor and the second most recently cued location (1560 ms as opposed to 400 ms in our experiment), no IOR occurred at that cued location (Pratt & Abrams, 1995). Instead, IOR occurred at only the most recently cued location. Thus, IOR produced by sequential multiple cueing appears to depend on the delay between cue onsets. When this delay is shorter, IOR may occur at two or more sequentially cued locations, but with a magnitude that decreases as the time between the cue's onset at that location and the onset of the central distractor is increased. A similar finding has since been reported (Tipper, Weaver, & Watson, 1996). We suggested that, when multiple cues are presented sequentially, some form of serial processing is carried out at each cued location in turn that diminishes IOR magnitude at the previously inspected cue location (Wright & Richard, 1994, 1996a). And, combined with a long delay between sequential cues, this can be sufficient to diminish IOR at all but the most recently cued location.

IOR can be produced if goal-driven attention shifts are accompanied by goal-driven saccades (Posner et al., 1985) and even if subjects merely prepare to make an accompanying goal-driven saccade without actually making it (Rafal et al., 1989). Therefore, a relationship exists between IOR and eye movement programming. Some researchers have argued that IOR is the direct result of a saccadic eye movement program being inhibited. And, because of this oculomotor inhibition, a target appearing at that saccade destination will take longer to respond to (e.g., Tassinari et al., 1989). The multiple location IOR finding is inconsistent with oculomotor accounts of IOR, however, because eye movements cannot be programmed and executed to more than one location at a time. What might be simultaneously inhibited are the locations *not* to be favoured as eye movement destinations. Therefore, we argue that the relationship between eye movement programming and IOR is indirect. IOR may occur at a saccade destination because saccade preparation involves preliminary spatial indexing of that destination; and it is this indexing that occurs prior to oculomotor programming (and also as a result of abrupt stimulus onsets) that could mediate IOR.

If, as we claim, indexing mediates IOR, then IOR should conform to one of the general properties of indexes. As pointed out in other chapters (e.g., Pylyshyn, this volume; Wright & Ward, this volume), a spatial index can remain dynamically bound to an object while it moves. This leads to the following prediction. If IOR is mediated by indexing and an indexed object moves during the course of an experimental trial, then the inhibition associated with that object should move along with it. And this, in fact, is what occurs (Tipper, Driver, & Weaver, 1991). To elaborate, if the first of two successive direct cues is presented and then changes location prior to target onset as in Figure 5, IOR occurs at the cue's new location. IOR is said to *object-based* because it is dynamically bound to the moving cue just as spatial indexes remain bound to moving objects.

The discovery of object-based IOR raised questions about a continued inhibitory effect at the cue's old location after that cue was moved elsewhere. Recent studies indicate that IOR occurs at both the original and the new cue locations on the same trial (Tipper, Weaver, Jerreat, & Burak, 1994). The former is referred to as *location-based* IOR. The occur-

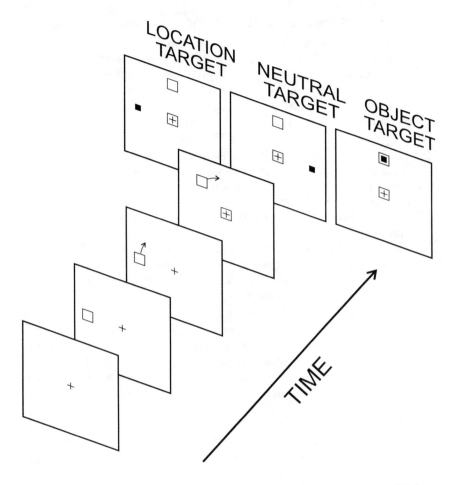

*Figure* 5: Typical display used for generating object-based inhibition of return (IOR).

rence of simultaneous location-based and object-based IOR is further evidence of multiple-location IOR. But, rather than presenting two cues in sequence, the same cue is simply moved from one position to another to produce IOR at both locations.

In summary, the multiple-location IOR effect is difficult to explain purely in terms of attentional processes or purely in terms of oculomotor inhibition. We suggest that IOR is mediated by a location encoding procedure called spatial indexing. In the next section, we examine data indicating that spatial indexing is the only the first stage of operations mediating IOR. Those that follow are not reflexive and may be the result of intermediate-level vision.

## Automatic and Reflexive Effects of Location Cueing

Direct location cues (e.g., a bar marker or outline box) trigger saccades or attention shifts by appearing at or near a probable target location. Symbolic cues (e.g., an arrow or digit) provide information about where to voluntarily aim saccades or attention shifts. Saccades and attention shifts triggered by direct cues are under stimulus-driven control and those initiated by symbolic cues are under goal-driven control (Wright & Ward, this volume). Valid cues correctly indicate the impending target's location, and can facilitate the speed and accuracy of responses associated with that target. On the other hand, invalid cues incorrectly indicate the impending target's location, and can inhibit response speed and accuracy.

When IOR occurs, direct location cues first facilitate and then inhibit target-detection response times as the cue-target-onset-asynchrony (CTOA) is increased from 100 to 300 ms (Maylor, 1985; Maylor & Hockey, 1987; Posner & Cohen, 1984; Possamai, 1985; Wright, Richard, & McDonald, 1994; Wright & Richard, 1996b; see Figure 6). It has been suggested that when the CTOA is 100 ms or less, a facilitative component is active and dominant; and when the CTOA is 300 ms or more, an inhibitory component is active and dominant (Maylor, 1985; Posner & Cohen, 1984). This is sometimes referred to as the "biphasic" effect of location cueing. In this section, we argue that activation of the inhibitory component is not mandatory. There are some situations, for example, in which a direct cue will continue to facilitate rather than inhibit response times when the CTOA is 300 ms or more (e.g., Cheal & Lyon, 1991). Furthermore, IOR does not appear to be elicited by direct location cueing if attention is actively engaged while the cues are presented (Richard & Wright, 1995). Therefore, the time-course of direct location cue effects as a function of CTOA should be described as follows. Direct cues facilitate detection response times for targets presented within 100 ms of cue onset and, in some but not all cases, inhibit response times for targets presented 300 ms or more after cue onset.

The commonly held view that IOR occurs as a reflexive consequence of direct location cueing is consistent with Posner and Cohen's (1984) proposal that it is due to sensory rather than attentional processing. We agree that the inhibitory effects of location cueing may be automatic but, as the title of this chapter states, they are not in our opinion reflexive (cf. Tipper, Weaver, & Houghton, 1994). Instead, IOR may be due, in part, to nonreflexive processes that occur after low-level sensory operations but prior to high-level serial operations associated with alignments of attention.

Automatic and reflexive processing are both thought to be carried out independently of attention (e.g., Anderson, 1982; Kahneman &

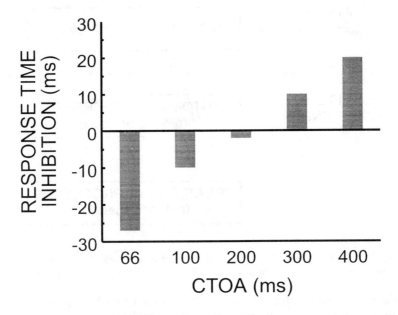

*Figure* 6: Time course of facilitative and inhibitory direct location cue effects on target-detection latencies as a function of CTOA (cue-target-onset-asynchrony).

Treisman, 1984; LaBerge & Samuels, 1974; Logan, 1988, 1992; Logan & Compton, this volume; Schneider, Dumais, & Shiffrin, 1984). Because of this similarity, a distinction between them is not always made. In general, automaticity develops with practice, presumably to enable skilled performance to be autonomous from attention. On the other hand, reflexive processing is mediated by low-level mechanisms that are unaffected by practice and operate independently of attention.

Visual search for a target object positioned among an array of distractor objects can be rapid and effortless in some cases, or slow and effortful in others. Usually, rapid detection or "pop out" of a target is the result of reflexive, preattentive processing; and slower detection is the result of serial attentive analysis of the visual array. In the latter case, however, visual search can become rapid if practice leads to automatization of responses to the target (e.g., Czerwinski, Lightfoot, & Shiffrin, 1992; Schneider et al., 1984; Treisman, Vieira, & Hayes, 1992). A series of experiments was carried out to determine whether or not automatized search processes are the same as (unpracticed) rapid preattentive search processes (Treisman et al., 1992). Automatized search was found to be more task-specific and target-location-specific than search mediated by preattentive analysis. This suggests that preattentive target popout is mediated by fundamentally lower-level processes than automatized target popout (see Figure 7).

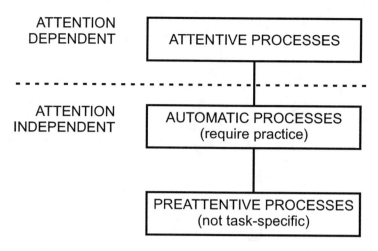

*Figure* 7: Attention dependent and independent processing. The latter includes automatic and reflexive operations.

Reflexive processing should not be affected by observers' expectations and cognitive strategies. For example, it should not be affected by changes in location cue validity. As observers progress through an experimental session, the usefulness of a location cue for performing the task becomes apparent to them. But if processing is reflexive, then this information should make no difference because reflexes are not strategic. As seen in Figure 3, when targets are likely to appear at cued or uncued locations with roughly equal probability, response-time facilitation usually occurs when the CTOA is 100 ms or less and inhibition can occur when the CTOA is 300 ms or more (e.g., Abrams & Dobkin, 1994; Maylor & Hockey, 1987; Posner & Cohen, 1984). We conducted a set of experiments in which cue validity was manipulated to determine how it would affect this pattern of facilitation and inhibition (Wright & Richard, 1996b; Wright, Richard, & McDonald, 1994). We found, as expected, that with both low-validity cues (10% probability that the target would appear at the cued location) and high-validity cues (90% target probability), response-time facilitation still occurred at shorter CTOAs (100 ms). On the other hand, IOR did not occur at the longer CTOAs (400 ms) with low-validity or high-validity cues. Thus, changes in cue validity affected the inhibitory but not the facilitative effects of location cueing. This suggests that the former is less reflexive than the latter.

We concluded that IOR will not occur at a direct cued location unless there is a reasonable degree of uncertainty (more than 10%) about the target appearing there. The occurrence of inhibition appears to depend on whether it will make target search more efficient. That is, given the choice, why use processing resources to inspect and keep track of a location where the target probably will not occur? IOR may depend instead on whether the perceiver needs to keep track of inspected locations in order to bias the search to other novel locations.

We were intrigued by the finding that IOR is not invoked reflexively and yet occurs rapidly and without our conscious awareness. Processes like this are often the result of automatization. Therefore, we reasoned that if IOR is an automatized phenomenon, then it should become more efficient with practice. We tested this prediction by comparing the performance of experienced observers who had participated in several IOR experiments in our laboratory with the performance of inexperienced subjects. Prior to the study, we had observed informally that experienced observers showed IOR even at quite short CTOAs. The results of the first experiment verified that with a 200 ms CTOA, experienced observers showed a significant IOR effect whereas inexperienced observers did not (Richard, Wright, & McDonald, 1994). This suggests that practice increases the efficiency of IOR by decreasing the delay required for it to occur. Practice effects on IOR have since been found in other laboratories (e.g., Tipper & Weaver, this volume).

We also asked inexperienced subjects to perform the same task but with a 100 ms CTOA. This delay was chosen because, initially, the effect of location cueing on target-detection responses was expected to be facilitative. We examined the effect of practice over the course of successive testing sessions on different days and found that the facilitation magnitude of direct cueing decreased significantly from the first block (13 ms) to the fourth (-6 ms), and this change from facilitation to inhibition across sessions showed a significant linear trend. Increases in IOR efficiency that occurred as inexperienced observers became more practiced is another indication that IOR is not a completely reflexive phenomenon and that some aspect of the processing is becoming more automatic even though the perceiver may not be consciously aware of it.

IOR magnitude appears to change not only over the course of a target detection experiment but sometimes even over successive trials. In one study, targets were sometimes presented at the same location on two or more successive trials, and response times on the second of these trials were still inhibited when a target was presented at the same location as that of the previous target (Maylor & Hockey, 1987). This inhibition decreased slightly, however, when a target was presented at the same location as the previous two targets, and continued to decrease with further increases in the number of target location repetitions (see also, Posner, Cohen, Choate, Hockey, & Maylor, 1984). Maylor and Hockey (1987, p. 53) claimed that this "location-repetition effect" on IOR can be attributed to the observer's subjective expectancy about the target's location, and speculated that, in order for IOR to occur, the locations of successive events may need to be random. Notice the consistency of their claim with our finding that IOR is more likely to occur following uninformative location cues and less likely to occur when there is a reduction in the uncertainty about the impending target's location (Wright & Richard, 1996b; Wright et al., 1994).

Unlike reflexive processes, higher-level visual processes appear to require attentional resources. This was tested with a target-detection task involving direct and symbolic location cues (Jonides, 1981). In one condition, when observers also performed a concurrent memory-load task, the response-time facilitation caused by direct cueing was virtually unaffected by the concurrent task but the facilitation caused by symbolic cueing was significantly attenuated. It was concluded that the symbolic cue task competed for attentional resources with the memory load task, but that the direct cue task did not. In other words, the facilitative effects of direct location cueing were more reflexive. When another concurrent task experiment was conducted under conditions in which direct cueing produced response-time inhibition, the magnitude of cue effectiveness decreased (Posner et al., 1984). This suggests that the inhibitory effects of direct cueing are less reflexive than the facilitative effects.

Table 1 summarizes the facilitative and inhibitory effects of direct location cueing. In general, facilitation appears to be reflexive and inhibition appears to be nonreflexive.

|  | Facilitation | Inhibition |
| --- | --- | --- |
| CTOA (cue-target-onset-asynchrony) | Active within 200 ms of cue onset | Occurs from 300 ms to as long as 3000 ms after cue onset |
| Cue Validity | Little or no effect | Occurs if cues are uninformative |
| Practice | Little or no effect | Reduces minimum CTOA at which inhibition occurs |
| Location Repetition | Little or no effect | Reduces inhibition magnitude |
| Concurrent Tasks | Little or no effect | Reduces inhibition magnitude |

*Table* 1: Factors that interact with the facilitative and inhibitory effects of direct-location cueing

## Intermediate-Level Visual Processing

If IOR is an automatic process, why does it only occur in some cases and how do we control its initiation? Answers to these questions can be framed by a discussion of three levels of visual processing. There is a consensus among researchers studying different aspects of vision that the underlying operations occur in stages (e.g., Dawson, 1991; La-Berge, 1995; Marr, 1982; Neisser, 1967; Posner, Petersen, Fox, & Raichle, 1988; Pylyshyn, 1989; Rock, 1983; Treisman & Gormican, 1988; Ullman, 1979, 1984). One way in which processing stages have been distinguished is the extent to which they are under bottom-up control versus top-down control. Another is the extent to which parallel versus serial processing is involved. The initial stage, often referred to as low-level vision, is characterized by parallel processes that are triggered in a stimulus-driven manner (e.g., edge detection & motion correspondence matching). They are not consciously available to the perceiver and seem immediate and effortless. In contrast, high-level visual processes are usually serial and under voluntary control. The perceiver is also usually aware of their execution (e.g., when visually searching a collection of objects for a target). Between low- and high-level vision there appears to be another stage involving rapid but serial operations such as those required for determining spatial relations among objects (Ullman, 1984). Like low-level processes, they seem immediate and effortless (e.g., determining whether X is inside Y) but, like higher level processes, are under voluntary control. This stage has been called *intermediate-level visual processing* because it can be rapid and not fully available to conscious awareness without, at the same time, being purely reflexive, like low-level processing.

Processing at the intermediate level has been described in terms of *visual routines* of primitive or basic operations (Ullman, 1984). A routine is said to be "tailored" to carry out the perceptual task at hand by putting together some of these basic operations in a particular sequence. And there are some indications that spatial indexing is a basic operation (Jolicoeur, Ullman, & MacKay, 1986; Pylyshyn & Storm, 1988; Yantis, 1992). Routine assembly and execution begins with the formulation of a *computational goal* (hence the term *goal-driven*, commonly used to describe voluntary attention shifts and eye movements). The perceiver decides what task to perform, and then a specialized routine composed of basic visual operations (e.g., marking a location) is assembled and triggered. We propose that this is the level of processing at which IOR occurs.

The occurrence of IOR that is modifiable with practice may seem contradictory. We suggest that it can occur because the IOR routine involves two separate processing stages. The first is a *spatial indexing* stage that encodes locations of stimuli. The second is an *inhibitory designation* stage that receives input about indexed locations and invokes an inhibition routine that designates certain encoded positions as low-probability target locations. If a target appears at a location with this designation, more time will be required to respond to it because it is no longer part of the high priority search set. The efficiency of the second stage can be modified with practice, perhaps because the speed of inhibitory designation becomes more streamlined with repeated execution (cf. Anderson, 1982; Ullman, 1984). To summarize, we propose that activation of the indexing stage operates in combination with an automatized inhibitory designation stage to enable IOR to be visually triggered by direct location cueing or voluntarily initiated by saccade initiation, but modifiable with learning.

## Concluding Remarks

The IOR findings described in this chapter have several ramifications. Regarding the debate between Posner and Cohen (1984) and Maylor (1985) about whether or not attention must be focused at a particular location before it can be inhibited, it seems clear that Posner and Cohen (1984) were correct – attentive analysis of a location is not a necessary condition for IOR. Multiple-location IOR is indicative of parallel sensory analysis. The multiple location IOR effect also raises doubts about a purely oculomotor account of IOR because it is unlikely that multiple saccade programs can be initiated at the same time. By process of elimination, this leaves us with a mechanism that must be neither purely attentional nor purely oculomotor, and must account for the dynamic binding of IOR with objects that move from one location to another. We suggest that when IOR occurs, spatial indexes serve as location pointers that an intermediate-level routine uses to guide serial analysis by constraining the search set.

## Acknowledgments

This project was supported by Natural Sciences and Engineering Research Council of Canada Grant 133551 awarded to RDW. We appreciate many insightful discussions about IOR with Lawrence Ward and John McDonald. Richard Wright may be contacted via e-mail at rwright@arts.sfu.ca.

## References

Abrams, R.A., & Dobkin, R.S. (1994). Inhibition of return: Effects of attentional cueing on eye movement latencies. *Journal of Experimental Psychology: Human Perception & Performance, 20,* 467–477.

Anderson, J.R. (1982). Acquisition of cognitive skill. *Psychological Review, 89,* 369–406.

Cheal, M., & Lyon, D.R. (1991). Central and peripheral precueing of forced-choice discrimination. *Quarterly Journal of Experimental Psychology, 43A*, 859–880.

Clohessy, A., Posner, M.I., Rothbart, M.K., & Vecera, S.P. (1991). The development of inhibition of return in early infancy. *Journal of Cognitive Neuroscience, 3*, 346–357.

Czerwinski, M., Lightfoot, N., & Shiffrin, R.M. (1992). Automatization and training in visual search. *American Journal of Psychology, 105*, 271–315.

Dawson, M.R.W. (1991). The how and why of what went where in apparent motion: Modeling solutions to the motion correspondence problem. *Psychological Review, 98*, 569–603.

Harman, C., Posner, M.I., Rothbart, M.K., & Thomas-Thrapp, L. (1994). Development of orienting to locations and objects in human infants. *Canadian Journal of Experimental Psychology, 48*, 301–318.

Jolicoeur, P., Ullman, S., & MacKay, M. (1986). Curve tracing: A possible basic operation in the perception of spatial relations. *Memory & Cognition, 14*, 129–140.

Jonides, J. (1981). Voluntary versus automatic control over the mind's eye's movement. In J.B. Long & A.D. Baddeley (Eds.), *Attention & Performance, Vol. 9*. Hillsdale, NJ: Erlbaum.

Kahneman, D., & Treisman, A. (1984). Changing views of attention and automaticity. In R. Parasuraman & R. Davies (Eds.), *Varieties of attention*. New York, NY: Academic Press.

LaBerge, D. (1995). *Attentional processing*. Cambridge, MA: Harvard University Press.

LaBerge, D., & Samuels, S.J. (1974). Toward a theory of automatic information processing in reading. *Cognitive Psychology, 6*, 293–323.

Logan, G.D. (1988). Toward an instance theory of automatization. *Psychological Review, 95*, 492–527.

Logan, G.D. (1992). Attention and preattention in theories of automaticity. *American Journal of Psychology, 105*, 317–339.

Marr, D. (1982). *Vision*. New York, NY: Freeman.

Maylor, E.A. (1985). Facilitory and inhibitory components of orienting in visual space. In M.I. Posner & O.S.M. Marin (Eds.), *Attention & Performance, Vol. 11*. Hillsdale, NJ: Erlbaum.

Maylor, E.A., & Hockey, R. (1985). Inhibitory component of externally controlled covert orienting in space. *Journal of Experimental Psychology: Human Perception & Performance, 11*, 777–787.

Maylor, E.A., & Hockey, R. (1987). Effects of repetition on the facilitory and inhibitory components of orienting in visual space. *Neuropsychologia, 25*, 41–54.

Neisser, U. (1967). *Cognitive psychology*. New York: Appleton, Century, Crofts.

Posner, M.I., & Cohen, Y. (1984). Components of visual attention. In H. Bouma & D.G. Bouwhuis (Eds.), *Attention & Performance, Vol. 10*. Hillsdale, NJ: Erlbaum.

Posner, M.I., Cohen, Y., Choate, L.S., Hockey, R., & Maylor, E.A. (1984). Sustained concentration: Passive filtering or active orienting? In S. Kornblum & J. Requin (Eds.), *Preparatory states and processes*. Hillsdale, NJ: Erlbaum.

Posner, M.I., Petersen, S.E., Fox, P.T., & Raichle, M.E. (1988). Localization of cognitive operations in the human brain. *Science, 240,* 1627–1631.

Posner, M.I., Rafal, R.D., Choate, L., & Vaughan, J. (1985). Inhibition of return: Neural basis and function. *Cognitive Neuropsychology, 2,* 211–218.

Possamai, C. (1985). Relationship between inhibition and facilitation following a visual cue. *Acta Psychologica, 61,* 243–258.

Pratt, J., & Abrams, R.A. (1995). Inhibition of return to successively cued spatial locations. *Journal of Experimental Psychology: Human Perception & Performance, 2,* 1343–1353.

Pylyshyn, Z. (1989). The role of location indexes in spatial perception: A sketch of the FINST spatial-index model. *Cognition, 32,* 65–97.

Pylyshyn, Z., & Storm, R.W. (1988). Tracking multiple independent targets: Evidence for a parallel tracking mechanism. *Spatial Vision, 3,* 179–197.

Rafal, R.D., Calabresi, P.A., Brennan, C.W., & Sciolto, T.K. (1989). Saccade preparation inhibits reorienting to recently attended locations. *Journal of Experimental Psychology: Human Perception & Performance, 15,* 673–685.

Rafal, R.D., Egly, R., & Rhodes, D. (1994). Effects of inhibition of return on voluntary and visually guided saccades. *Canadian Journal of Experimental Psychology, 48,* 284–300.

Richard, C.M., & Wright, R.D. (1995). *Attentional engagement and inhibition-of-return of visual processing.* Paper presented at the annual meeting of the Canadian Society for Brain, Behaviour, and Cognitive Science, Halifax, Nova Scotia.

Richard, C.M., Wright, R.D., & McDonald, J.J. (1994). *Practice effects and inhibition-of-return of visual processing.* Paper presented at the annual meeting of the Canadian Psychological Association, Penticton, British Columbia.

Rock, I. (1983). *The logic of perception.* Cambridge, MA: MIT Press.

Schneider, W., Dumais, S.T., & Shiffrin, R.M. (1984). Automatic and controlled processing and attention. In R. Parasuraman & D.R. Davies (Eds.), *Varieties of attention.* Orlando, FL: Academic Press.

Tassinari, G., Biscaldi, M., Marzi, C.A., & Berlucchi, G. (1989). Ipsilateral inhibition and contralateral facilitation of simple reaction time to non-foveal visual targets from non-informative visual cues. *Acta Psychologica, 70,* 267–291.

Tipper, S.P., Driver, J., & Weaver, B. (1991). Object-centred inhibition of return of visual attention. *Quarterly Journal of Experimental Psychology, 43*(A), 289–298.

Tipper, S.P., Weaver, B., & Houghton, G. (1994). Behavioural goals determine inhibitory mechanisms of selective attention. *Quarterly Journal of Experimental Psychology, 47A,* 809–840.

Tipper, S.P., Weaver, B., Jerreat, L.M., & Burak, A.L. (1994). Object- based and environment-based inhibition of return of visual attention. *Journal of Experimental Psychology: Human Perception & Performance, 20,* 478–499.

Tipper, S.P., Weaver, B., & Watson, F.L. (1996). Inhibition of return to successively cued spatial locations: A commentary on Pratt and Abrams (1995). *Journal of Experimental Psychology: Human Perception & Performance, 22,* 1284–1293.

Treisman, A., & Gormican, S. (1988). Feature analysis in early vision: Evidence from search asymmetries. *Psychological Review, 95,* 15–48.

Treisman, A., Vieira, A., & Hayes, A. (1992). Automaticity and preattentive processing. *American Journal of Psychology, 105,* 341– 362.

Ullman, S. (1979). *The interpretation of visual motion.* Cambridge, MA: MIT Press.

Ullman, S. (1984). Visual routines. *Cognition, 18,* 97–159.

Ullman, S. (1997). *High-level visual processing.* Cambridge, MA: MIT Press.

Wright, R.D., & Richard, C.M. (1993). *Inhibition-of-return of visual processing and multiple location cues.* Paper presented at the annual meeting of the Psychonomic Society, Washington, D.C.

Wright, R.D., & Richard, C.M. (1994). *Inhibition-of-return to successively and sequentially cued locations.* Paper presented at the annual meeting of the Psychonomic Society, St. Louis, Missouri.

Wright, R.D., & Richard, C.M. (1996a). Inhibition-of-return at multiple locations in visual space. *Canadian Journal of Experimental Psychology, 50.*

Wright, R.D., & Richard, C.M. (1996b). *Location cue validity affects inhibition-of-return of visual processing.* Manuscript submitted for publication.

Wright, R.D., Richard, C.M., & McDonald, J.J. (1994). *Cue validity effects on inhibition-of-return.* Paper presented at the annual meeting of the Canadian Psychological Association, Penticton, B.C.

Wright, R.D., & Ward, L.M. (this volume). The control of visual attention. In R.D. Wright (Ed.), *Visual attention.* New York: Oxford University Press.

Yantis, S. (1992). Multielement visual tracking: Attention and perceptual organization. *Cognitive Psychology, 24,* 295–340.

# 14

## Attentional Effects in Visual Search: Relating Search Accuracy and Search Time

### John Palmer

In this article, I will describe a program of research that distinguishes among the leading theories of divided attention. Divided attention has often been studied using set-size effects in visual search. A typical search task is illustrated in Figure 1. In both panels the task is to search for the target disk which has a higher luminance than the distractor disks. The subject is to respond "yes" when the higher luminance disk is present and "no" when it is absent. The target is present in both of the panels of Figure 1. The panels differ in the number of disks present: the panel on the left has a set size of 2, and the panel on the right has a larger set size. Increasing set size usually decreases performance. These set-size effects have been measured both in accuracy paradigms that use brief displays to prevent multiple eye fixations and in response time paradigms that allow extended inspection of the display with multiple eye fixations. Such set-size effects are of interest because different theories of attention predict set-size effects of different magnitudes.

### Two Contrasting Hypotheses

I will focus on two classes of hypotheses, unlimited-capacity perception versus limited-capacity perception. Both predict set-size effects, but for different reasons. According to the *unlimited-capacity perception hypothesis*, the internal representations that arise from each of the individual stimuli are independent of the number of stimuli presented. Despite this independence in perception, there will still be set-size effects on behaviour due to other phenomena such as decision and memory. In particular, if the individual representations are noisy, then there will be a set-size effect in search due to the need to integrate the multiple noisy inputs. In contrast, the *limited-capacity perception hypothesis* presumes that the internal representations of the individual stimuli are interdependent because they require some kind of attentional processing. For example, there may be a processing resource that must be distributed across the stimuli. This resource might be in the form of a sampling process or perhaps even eye movements. Thus, the more

348

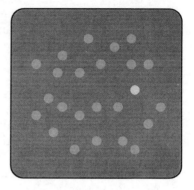

*Figure* 1: An illustration of the set-size manipulation for a contrast increment search task. Set Size 2 is shown in the left panel, and a large set size is shown in the right panel.

stimuli, the less processing each individual stimulus receives per unit time, and hence performance decreases with set size.

Each of these hypotheses has a history. Models incorporating independent processing of separate stimulus features go back at least to Helmholtz's (1896; see Wyszecki & Stiles, 1982, for a review in English) theory of colour discrimination. More relevant to visual search, Tanner (1961) was the first to point out that tasks such as visual search introduce the necessity of integrating multiple sources of information. From Tanner's findings, one can infer that set-size effects are not inconsistent with unlimited-capacity perception. His work was largely in auditory frequency detection. Since then, one of the best known examples of an unlimited-capacity model is Shiffrin and Gardner's (1972) "independent channels model" which was applied largely to letter perception. There has also been a considerable body of work in psychophysics. Particularly productive is the analysis of uncertainty effects on near-threshold visual patterns using the independent spatial-frequency-channels model. This is summarized by Graham (1989); for an introduction, see Davis, Kramer, and Graham (1983). In addition, Shaw (1980, 1984) extended this model to several search accuracy tasks.

The development of models of limited-capacity perception also goes back over 40 years. Perhaps the earliest quantitative model was the single-channel theory proposed by Welford (1952). According to the single-channel theory, only one source of information can receive processing at a time – hence, it is also known as an all-or-none model – and it focuses on attention switching rather than attention sharing. Broadbent (1958) generalized the concept by allowing multiple, simultaneous processes with the restriction that the processing of the total system is limited. The limit was defined as the processing of a constant amount of information per unit time. This allowed one to consider the strategies of attention switching or attention sharing. Since then there have been several efforts to generalize the idea of capacity (e.g., Kahneman, 1973; Navon & Gopher, 1979). For more empirical studies, the limited-capacity perception hypothesis has provided an interpretation of response time experiments in both cueing and visual search (e.g., Posner, Snyder, & Davidson, 1980; Hoffman, 1978). Also relevant is Townsend's theoretical analysis of these response time models (Townsend, 1974; Townsend & Ashby, 1978, 1983; Townsend & Nozawa, 1995). In particular, Townsend relates capacity to other issues such as parallel versus serial processing.

In addition to work which focuses on either unlimited- or limited-capacity perception, there is a large body of work that embraces both. In visual search, these theories are often called *two-stage theories* (Hoffman, 1979). Such theories presume that some kinds of visual search can be accomplished by unlimited-capacity perceptual processing of the individual stimuli and other kinds of search require limited-capacity perceptual processing (Hoffman, 1979; Treisman & Gelade, 1980; Wolfe, Cave, & Franzel, 1989). For example, identifying a letter may require capacity even though detecting a luminance increment does not.

Two preliminary comments are in order about this distinction between unlimited- and limited-capacity perception. First of all, I am using the term *limited capacity* in the sense of non-independence rather than with a particular view of capacity. When Broadbent described his limited-capacity model, he had a very specific view of capacity in terms of information theory. Here I am going to follow later researchers and use limited capacity as a general term for any reduction in capacity relative to capacity being independent of the number of stimuli (i.e., unlimited capacity, Townsend, 1974). To refer to more specific theories such as Broadbent's, I will use more specific labels, such as the *fixed-in-formation-capacity hypothesis*. This hypothesis predicts a specific reduction in capacity with each additional stimulus.

The second comment has to do with the question: to what does capacity refer? There are at least three usages of the term. In the beginning, Broadbent defined capacity with respect to the entire behaviour. The organism was treated as a single, unitary communication channel. I will refer to this molar use of the term as *system capacity*. As the theories became more detailed, there was interest in specifying limits on performance due to distinct component processes. Some of the more refined theories involving network models of separate processes focus on the capacity of individual component processes (e.g. Townsend, 1974). In this work, the term *capacity* could be applied to different "levels" of the system. One could refer to the capacity of components or to any particular subsystem of components. Here, I will refer to *component capacity* as the capacity of the most elemental components of a theory. It is quite possible that the components have unlimited capacity but that they are arranged in such a way that a subsystem of the same components has limited capacity. For example, serial scanning with unlimited-capacity components results in a limited-capacity system. The performance of each component is independent of set size, but the processing time of the subsystem does depend on set size. Finally, there is a third usage of capacity which is the focus of this article. In terms of level, it is somewhere between the component and the system. The idea is to identify a subsystem of components such as perception, memory, or decision (e.g., Broadbent, 1971; Shaw, 1980). Then one can specify the capacity of the perceptual subsystem. To determine this, one must distinguish performance limits due to perception from other limits due to decision-making, memory, and early sensory processing such as limits on peripheral vision. For unlimited-capacity perceptual processing, the perception of individual stimuli must be independent of the number of stimuli (the set size). I will refer to this usage as *perceptual capacity*. In this article, my focus will be on this last usage.

## Critical Experiments

I now turn to the central concern of this chapter: what kinds of experiments will distinguish unlimited-capacity perception from limited-capacity perception? These hypotheses have been investigated in several domains (for a review, see Sperling & Dosher, 1986). The two that I review in detail are search accuracy (Palmer, Ames, & Lindsey, 1993; Palmer, 1994) and search time. I will not review here, but do recommend, the related work on how duration affects search accuracy (Bergen & Julesz, 1983a; 1983b; Verghese & Nakayama, 1994). The temporal phenomena of these duration effects may be related to temporal phenomena of search time. Other relevant domains not reviewed here include comparisons between sequential and simultaneous displays (Shiffrin & Gardner, 1972; Hung, Wilder, Curry, & Julesz, 1995) and dual tasks performed simultaneously (Duncan, 1980; Kantowitz, 1974; Pashler, 1989).

To begin, consider the measurement of search time as a function of set size. A typical search task is illustrated in Figure 2. In this example, an initial fixation display indicates to a subject where to direct his or her gaze. Then, a stimulus display is presented. In the figure, the display is a set of disks which may or may not vary in luminance. Half the time the display contains the target, a high luminance disk (Target Present); and the other half of the time the target is absent (Target Absent). The subject indicates the presence or absence of the target using

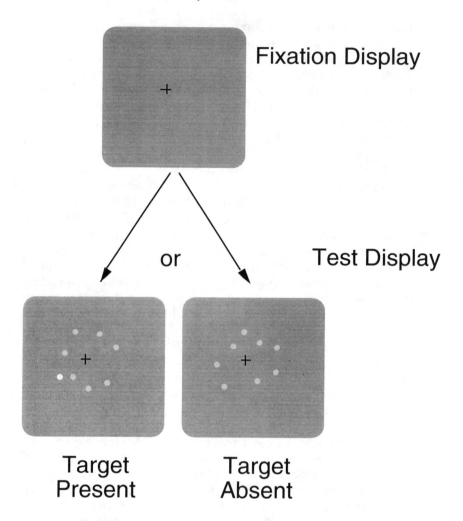

*Figure* 2:  An illustration of the procedure for a Yes-No search task.

one of two key presses. One special feature was that subjects were instructed to maintain an error percentage of 10%. To make this possible, conditions were blocked and extensive error feedback and training were used. As shown at the bottom of the forthcoming graphs, subjects were nearly always successful at staying within 1% or 2% of the intended 10% error percentage.

The results of the experiment depend strongly on the contrast difference between targets and distractors (the contrast increment). In the left panel of Figure 3, the target had a contrast of 52% and the distractors had a contrast of 20%, resulting in a large contrast increment of

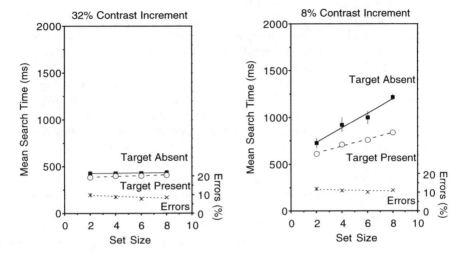

*Figure* 3: In the left panel, search time as a function of set size for a large contrast increment; in the right panel, search time as a function of set size for a small contrast increment. Error bars here and in all figures represent standard errors.

32%. The mean search time for four subjects is plotted as a function of set size. There was very little effect of set size on search time. Thus, search behaviour was essentially independent of set size for this large contrast increment.

In the right panel of Figure 3, the target had a contrast of 28% and the distractors had a contrast of 20%, resulting in a small contrast increment of 8%. Mean search times for the same four subjects increased from around 750 ms to 1300 ms. Thus, behaviour was definitely not independent of set size for this small contrast increment.

Does such a set-size effect rule out the unlimited-capacity perception hypothesis? Some interpret this result in terms of serial processing. Some go much further and conclude that such large set-size effects are inconsistent with unlimited-capacity perception of the individual stimuli. This conclusion is premature if not wrong. I show here that such set-size effects in themselves are not a critical test of the unlimited-capacity perception hypothesis.

## Search Accuracy, Search Time, and Their Relation

I can now introduce the three specific topics addressed within the body of this article. First, I will review briefly whether or not set-size effects for search accuracy are consistent with unlimited- or limited-capacity perception. Second, I would like undertake exactly the same analysis for search time. However, this analysis is too broad a step, and instead I will discuss two narrower subtopics. The second topic becomes: how can one compare set-size effects for accuracy and time? Specifically, how can one conduct a search-time experiment that is modeled after the search-accuracy experiments that have previously distinguished the two hypotheses. This leads to a third topic on the relation between the search-time data and the search-accuracy data: is there a common process mediating the set-size effects for accuracy and time? My analysis does not resolve contradictions between hypotheses about the unlimited-capacity and limited-capacity perception. However, this approach helps to clarify what will be necessary to resolve them.

## Search Accuracy

Search accuracy experiments from my lab have distinguished between prominent special cases of the unlimited- and limited-capacity perception hypotheses (reviewed in Palmer, 1995). In particular, they illustrate how even the simplest unlimited-capacity perception model is consistent with set-size effects.

### Methods

*Overview for Search Accuracy and Time*    The principal innovation is to exploit the effect of the stimulus difference between the target and the distractors (cf. Bergen & Julesz, 1983a; Duncan & Humphreys, 1989; Pashler, 1987; Verghese & Nakayama, 1994). In particular, we measure the interaction between set size and the stimulus difference (i.e., the contrast increment). It is this interaction that is crucial to distinguishing the alternative hypotheses.

A measure of the effects of the stimulus difference and set size is developed in four steps. First, a psychometric function describes performance as a function of the stimulus difference; second, this function is summarized by a difference threshold; third, the threshold is measured for each set size to obtain a threshold-versus-set-size function; fourth, the effect of set size on threshold is summarized by the slope of a linear regression on a log-log graph.

*Search Accuracy Methods*    Stimuli were briefly displayed for 100 ms to minimize eye movements. The accuracy of search was measured as a function of the contrast increment and the set size. Then, for each set size, I estimated the contrast increment that yields 75% correct discrimination – the *contrast increment threshold* (for a review of these psychophysical methods see Gescheider, 1985). Examples of the displays are shown in Figure 4. The four panels represent Set Sizes of 2, 4, 6, and 8 and in all cases a target is shown. In these displays, a number of sensory phenomena were controlled that might affect performance if

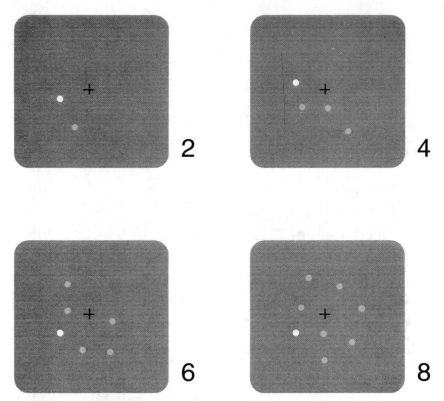

*Figure* 4: An illustration of the displays for Set Sizes 2, 4, 6, and 8. A target stimulus is shown in each display.

they were allowed to covary with set-size: The stimuli fell in a limited range of eccentricities and had a limited distribution of interstimulus spacing. A complete description of these experiments can be found in Palmer (1994).

### Results

*Psychometric Functions and Thresholds*    A sample of the results of this experiment is shown in Figure 5. This is a psychometric function that shows the probability correct as a function of the contrast increment for one subject. The curve parameter is set size; circles and squares indicate the Target Absent and Target Present conditions, respectively. The contrast increment produces a large effect on performance. As the contrast increment increases, performance rises from near chance to over 90 percent correct. In addition, there was an effect of set size that is fairly large for the smaller increments and smaller with large

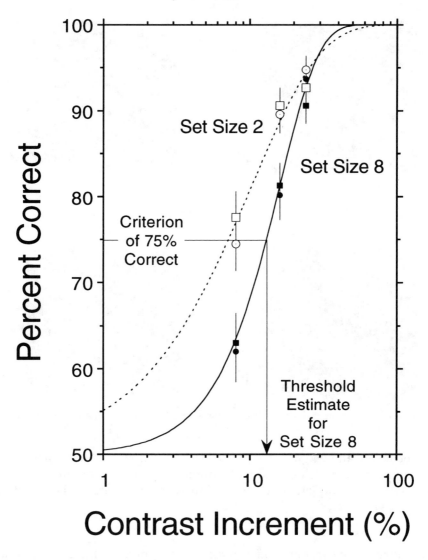

*Figure* 5: Psychometric Functions: percent correct for a single subject as a function of the contrast increment. Threshold estimation is illustrated using the best fitting Weibull function and a criterion of 75% correct. The circles represent Target Absent conditions (correct rejections) and the squares represent Target Present conditions (hits).

increments. The results for each set size were fit with a Weibull function with parameters for threshold and slope (Watson, 1979). In Figure 5, the estimation of the threshold parameter is graphically illustrated for Set Size 8. A contrast increment of around 13% yields 75% correct discrimination.

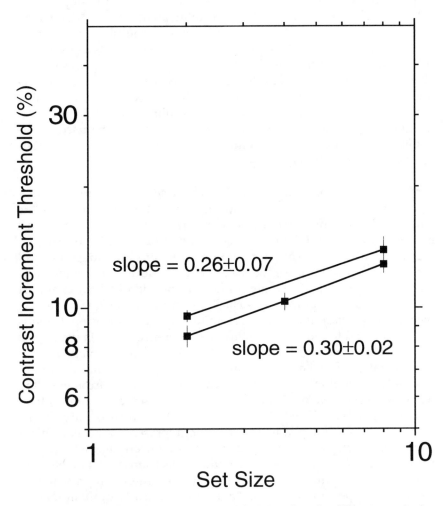

*Figure* 6: Mean threshold for four subjects as a function of set size; 75% correct criterion was used. Two separate experiments are shown and summarized using the slope on log-log coordinates.

*Threshold-versus-Set-Size Functions*   The results can be further summarized by plotting the contrast increment thresholds as a function of set size, as in Figure 6. This figure has both axes scaled logarithmically. The results from two experiments are shown: one with Set Sizes 2 and 8 and another with Set Sizes 2, 4, and 8 (Palmer, 1994; Experiments 2 and 1 (less Set Size 1)). The data are the mean thresholds for four subjects.

*Log-Log Slope*  These results are further summarized in terms of the slope on these log-log axes. For the two experiments, the slopes were 0.26 and 0.30. This measure was used to make the slope independent of the units of the stimulus (percent increment contrast). In addition, the log-log slope is independent of the response units because the thresholds are for a constant level of accuracy. It also measures the set-size effect for a fixed level of discriminability. Thus, the use of the log-log slope provides a built-in control for the degree of discriminability across stimuli and tasks (cf. Duncan & Humphreys, 1989). The slope of threshold versus set size on log-log coordinates will be used as the summary measure of the magnitude of the set-size effect, and will be referred to as simply the *log-log slope*.

*Predictions Based on Unlimited-Capacity Perception*  Perhaps the simplest version of the unlimited-capacity perception hypothesis is the "independent channels model" (summarized in Graham, 1989). This model includes the defining characteristic of unlimited-capacity perception, that the relevant internal representations are independent of set size. In addition, this model adopts five additional assumptions. First, for judgments of a single stimulus dimension such as a contrast increment, the model uses the usual assumptions of signal detection theory: the relevant internal representation is one-dimensional, and is linearly related to the relevant stimulus difference between the targets and the distractors (Green & Swets, 1966). Second, the relevant internal representation is noisy. This is in contrast to a deterministic "high-threshold" model in which false alarms can only arise from guessing (Green & Swets, 1966). Third, these noisy representations are statistically independent. In other words, the trial-to-trial variability on one representation is independent of the other representations. Fourth, independent decisions (Shaw, 1982) are made concerning each individual stimuli. For a yes-no task, independent decisions result in the stimulus with the maximum value of the relevant internal representation determining the response. This "max rule" is nearly optimal for this situation. Fifth, to make numerical predictions, I assume a constant-variance normal distribution for the noise. However, the results can be derived for any distribution (Palmer et al., 1993).

The consequences of these assumptions are presented graphically in Figure 7. The top panel of Figure 7 is the typical situation in signal detection theory in which there is a single stimulus and it is either a distractor or a target. Shown in the figure is the probability density of two random variables, one that corresponds to the distribution of the internal representations of a single distractor and the other that corresponds to the distribution of the internal representations of a single target.

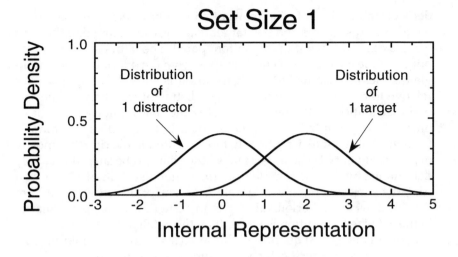

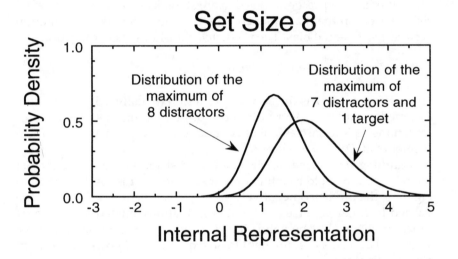

*Figure 7*: An illustration of the independent channels version of the unlimited-capacity perception hypothesis. Probability distributions for the relevant internal representations are shown for Set Sizes 1 and 8.

Here the probability distributions are assumed to be constant-variance normal. To make a judgment, the subject picks a criterion value somewhere along the internal representation axis and responds "yes" if the representation on a particular trial is higher than the criterion value.

Now consider what happens when set size increases (Graham, 1989; Pelli, 1985; Tanner, 1961). Each distractor adds noise and makes the decision more difficult. The relevant stimuli have eight distractors or have seven distractors and one target. The corresponding distributions for this case are shown in the bottom panel. The leftmost is the distribution of the maximum of eight samples from the distribution for a single distractor. This maximum distribution is shifted to higher values relative to the distribution for a single distractor (top panel). The second distribution in the bottom panel is the distribution of the maximum of one sample from the target distribution and seven samples from the distractor distribution. It, too, is shifted to the right but mostly in just its lower tail. The upper tail is little changed because it is largely determined by the one sample from the target distribution. On a given trial, the subject compares a sample from one of these two maximum distributions to a criterion value. For any criterion value, performance in the Set Size 8 condition is worse than the Set Size 1 condition.

Palmer et al. (1993) quantified this analysis of the threshold-versus-set-size function. Specifically, we assumed target distributions identical to the distractor distributions with a shift proportional to the stimulus difference, representations that are statistically independent, a decision based on the max rule, and the threshold defined at a criterion accuracy with equal bias. The predicted threshold was proportional to

$$F^{-1}(k^{1/n}) - F^{-1}[(1-k)/(k^{((n-1)/n)})], \tag{1}$$

where $n$ is set size, $k$ is the accuracy criterion (usually .75) and, $F$ is the assumed cumulative distribution of both target and distractor representations. A special case of this equation was given for $k = .75$ in Palmer et al. (1993, Equation A14).

Assuming the normal as the relevant distribution, one can predict the relative threshold as a function of set size. On the log-log graph in Figure 8, the predicted negatively accelerated function is shown by the dashed line. For Set Sizes 2 to 8, it is well approximated by the linear function shown by the solid line. The linear function has a log-log slope of 0.22. (This is equivalent to an exponent of a power law on linear coordinates.)

Equation 1 also captures the effect of the accuracy criterion. For most common distributions, the increasing set size will steepen the predicted psychometric function. Thus, the predicted set-size effect on a threshold will be smaller if the threshold is defined by a higher accuracy criterion. For these set sizes and the normal distribution, the predicted log-log slope decreases from 0.42 to 0.14 as the accuracy criterion increases from .6 to .9.

Assuming an analytic cumulative distribution with an analytic form allows for an analytic prediction. For example, the logistic

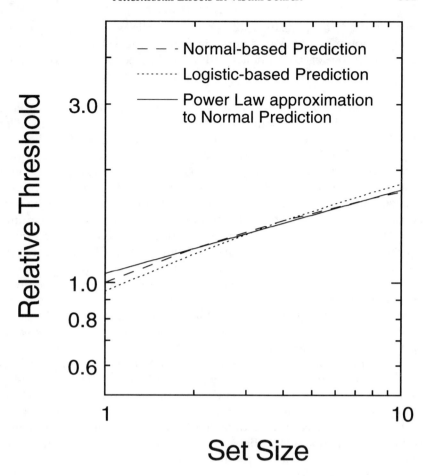

*Figure* 8: Relative thresholds are predicted as a function of set size for alternative versions of the unlimited-capacity perception hypothesis. Exact predictions are shown for normal (dashed curve) and logistic (dotted curve) distributions. In addition, the normal prediction is approximated from Set Size 2 to 8 by a linear function on log-log coordinates (solid line).

distribution, which is very similar to the normal, has an analytic cumulative distribution function,

$$1/(1+e^{-x}). \tag{2}$$

With this distribution, the threshold is proportional to:

$$\text{Log}(k^{1/n}) - \text{Log}[(1-k)/k^{(n-1)/n}] - \text{Log}(1-k^{1/n}) + \tag{3}$$
$$\text{Log}[1-(1-k)/k^{(n-1)/n}].$$

For Set Sizes 2 to 8, this function is also nearly linear on a log-log graph, and is shown by the dotted curve in Figure 8. It has a linear approximation on log-log coordinates with a log-log slope of approximately 0.28 for Set Sizes 2 to 8 (this approximation is not shown).

*The Prediction of the Limited-Capacity Hypothesis*    In contrast, consider a similar model with the same decision process and with the addition of limited-capacity perceptual processes along the lines described by Broadbent (1958) using information theory. In this model, perception can be considered a sampling process (see the sample size model, Lindsay, Taylor, & Forbes, 1968; Shaw, 1980; Taylor, Lindsay, & Forbes, 1967). When only one stimulus is relevant, then all of the samples can be concentrated on the single relevant stimulus. This results in the maximum possible precision for judgments of that one stimulus. When $n$ stimuli are relevant, then the samples are distributed across the relevant stimuli. If they are equally allocated, the number of samples per stimuli will be reduced by a factor of $1/n$. This can be shown to result in the precision of the representation dropping by a factor of $1/\sqrt{n}$. Such a model can be formalized by making similar assumptions as made above for the independent channels model. This *fixed-information-capacity model* predicts a log-log slope of 0.72 (for details see Palmer et al., 1993).

These predictions can be compared to the observed set-size effects which had log-log slopes that ranged from 0.26 to 0.30. The 0.22 log-log slope predicted by the independent channels model falls near this range, while the 0.72 log-log slope predicted by the fixed-information-capacity model clearly falls outside of this range. Thus, the independent channels model is sufficient to describe the observed results, and the fixed-information-capacity model can be rejected.

*Generality*    The above analysis has been repeated using a second procedure and several other stimuli. Of particular interest is the use of a procedure that eliminates any non-attentional account of these effects. This can be done using the cueing procedure shown in Figure 9. The stimulus sequence ends in the same way as the previous visual search experiments, a display of eight stimuli. What differs is the cue. In the case shown in the top right panel, the cue display contains a central fixation point and dark crosses at the location of all eight stimuli. This display indicates that all eight stimuli may be the target, and this condition is referred to as having a *relevant set size* of 8. In contrast, the display in the top left panel is a central fixation cross surrounded by two dark crosses that indicate the two locations where the target will appear, if it appears anywhere. In addition, the white crosses indicate locations where distractor disks will appear and that one can safely

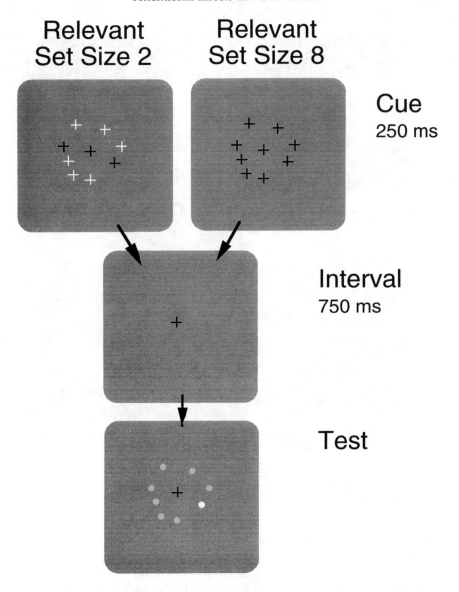

*Figure* 9: An illustration of the cueing procedure. The final test display is constant, and cues specify relevant set sizes of 2 and 8.

ignore. This condition reduces the relevant set size to 2. Because of the use of identical test stimuli, any effect of the cues must be due to some sort of selective attention phenomenon.

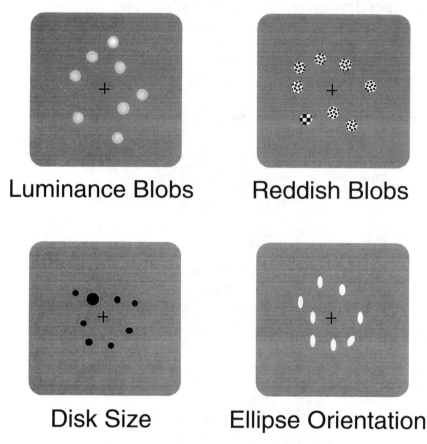

*Figure* 10: An illustration of the displays used in four additional search tasks. For the reddish blob condition, the coarser texture is intended to represent increasing saturation. The stimuli themselves contained no such texture.

The display-set-size and cueing procedures were combined with four new stimulus judgments which are depicted in Figure 10 (see Palmer, 1994 for details) and summarized as follows: (a) another contrast increment task using luminance "blob" stimuli which were varied in space and in time according to a normal probability distribution profile (eliminating any sharp edges or abrupt onsets); (b) a colour task using reddish blobs in which the target was a more saturated blob then the distractors; (c) a size task in which the target was larger in size than the distractors; (d) an orientation task with small ellipses in which the target differed in orientation from the distractors.

Results of the new cueing procedure and new stimulus judgments are shown in Figure 11 along with the original set-size procedure and

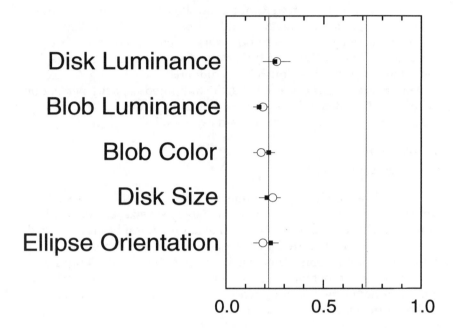

## Set-Size Effect (slope measure)

*Figure* 11: The set-size effect measured by the mean log-log slope for five tasks, using both the display-set-size and cueing procedures. The vertical line on the left indicates the prediction of the independent channels model (unlimited capacity), and the line on the right indicates the prediction of the fixed-information-capacity model (limited capacity).

contrast increment task. This figure plots the mean value of the log-log slope for each task conducted both as a display-set-size experiment and as a cueing (relevant-set-size) experiment. For both measures and for all five tasks, performance ranged from 0.20 to 0.25. This range is consistent with the 0.22 log-log slope predicted by the independent channels model that is shown by the vertical line on the left of the graph. For comparison, the 0.72 log-log slope predicted by the fixed-in-formation-capacity model is shown by the vertical line at the right of the graph. Thus, the results of all of these search accuracy experiments are consistent across a variety of stimulus judgments and with both cueing and traditional visual search paradigms. Similar results have been reported for motion by Verghese and Stone (1995, Experiment 2) and for letters by Bennett and Jaye (1995).

Key to obtaining this consistency is the use of a fixed level of discriminability and a summary measure independent of the stimulus units. If discriminability were not controlled (as is common current practice) then this consistency would be absent. Consider, as an example, the wide range of response-time-versus-set-size slopes reported by Treisman and Gormican (1988). The analysis presented here reveals a consistency that has previously been hidden.

In summary, for observed results, the unlimited-capacity perception hypothesis is sufficient; the proposed version of the limited-capacity perception hypothesis can be rejected.

## Search Time
### Prototype Experiment

*Methods*    The search time experiments were identical to the search accuracy experiments that manipulated display set size, except for three differences. (a) The stimuli were displayed until the subject responded. (b) Subjects were required to respond as quickly as possible while maintaining 10% errors. This was made possible by blocking the set size and contrast increment conditions and giving feedback about errors. (c) Search time rather than accuracy was measured as a function of the contrast increment and set size.

*Results*    The results are shown in Figure 12. The mean search time is graphed as a function of the contrast increment, with both axes scaled logarithmically. The curve parameters are set size and the presence or absence of the target. In addition, the curves at the bottom of the graph show the error percentage for Set Sizes 2 and 8. The mean errors were within 2% of the 10% goal for all set size and contrast increment conditions.

There were large effects of both manipulations on search time. As the contrast increment was increased, the search time dropped dramatically until it approached 400 ms. There were also large set-size effects for the smaller contrast increments. For the Target Absent conditions, the mean search time increased from less than 800 for Set Size 2, to around 1,500 ms for Set Size 8. The set-size effects were reduced for larger contrast increments, and approached very small values for very large increments.

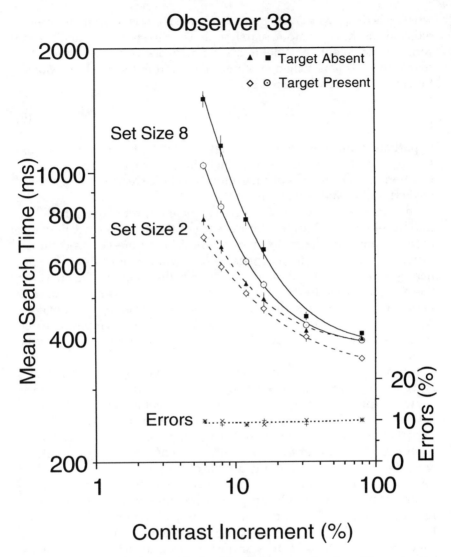

*Figure* 12: Mean search time for a single subject is shown as a function of the contrast increment. The curve parameters are Set Size 2 versus Set Size 8, and Target Absent versus Target Present.

The smooth curves are the best fitting *modified power functions* (Mansfield, 1973). They represent search time, *y*, as a function of contrast increment, *x*, for each condition, by

$$y = c\,(x/d)^b + t_0, \tag{4}$$

where $b$ is the power law exponent, $d$ is the contrast increment threshold, and $t_0$ is the asymptotic search time. The threshold is defined as the contrast increment that yields a $c$ ms increase over the asymptotic search time. This is a change of parameters from the modified power function defined by Mansfield (1973):

$$y = a\, x^b + t_0. \tag{5}$$

In particular, the $d$ parameter is equal to $(c/a)^{(1/b)}$. For a further discussion of stimulus intensity effects including alternatives to the power function, see the analysis of such effects on choice reaction time by Schweikert, Dahn, and McGuigan (1988).

The three parameters, $b$, $d$, and $t_0$, can be interpreted using the illustrations of Figure 13. In this figure, each of the panels shows how one of the parameters affects the shape of the search-time-versus-contrast-increment function. The top panel shows what happens as the exponent $b$ is varied. The exponent determines the shape of the curve on these log-log axes. In the middle panel, the threshold parameter $d$ is varied. On log-log axes, the threshold parameter determines the horizontal position of the curve. In the bottom panel, the asymptotic search time $t_0$ is varied. On log-log axes, the asymptotic time determines the vertical position.

This modified power-law model fits the data very well for all set sizes and conditions that have been examined. An illustration of these fits is shown in Figure 14. This figure shows the Target Absent condition for Set Sizes 2 and 8 for four subjects. Each subject has reasonable fits, and in particular the subject in the upper-left panel showed an excellent fit in which most of the error bars were the size of the points or smaller.

Similar results were found using the cueing procedure as described previously for search accuracy. The results of both the cueing experiment that manipulated relevant set size and the display-set-size experiment are given in Figure 15. The open symbols and dotted curves are the results and fits, respectively, for the cueing conditions, and the solid symbols and solid lines are for the display-set-size conditions. For the sake of simplicity, only the Target Absent condition is shown. Results for the cueing conditions were similar to the corresponding display-set-size conditions. There were large set-size effects at small contrast increments, which diminished with larger contrast increments. Particularly striking is the fact that the relevant-set-size manipulation has large effects despite the use of identical stimulus displays for Relevant Set Sizes 2 and 8. For small contrast increments, the cue manipulation increased search time by a full second, even though the stimulus displays were unchanged.

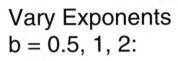

## Vary Exponents
## b = 0.5, 1, 2:

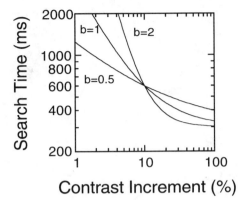

## Vary Threshold
## d = 3, 10, 30:

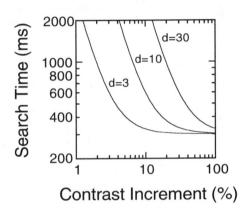

## Vary Asymptotic
## Time $t_0$ =
## 250, 400, 600:

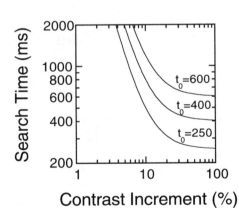

*Figure* 13: Each panel illustrates the effect of one parameter of the modified power-law model. In the top panel, the slope of the curve is specified by the exponent. In the middle panel, the horizontal position of the curve is specified by the threshold parameter. In the bottom panel, the vertical position of the curve is specified by the asymptotic search time parameter.

John Palmer

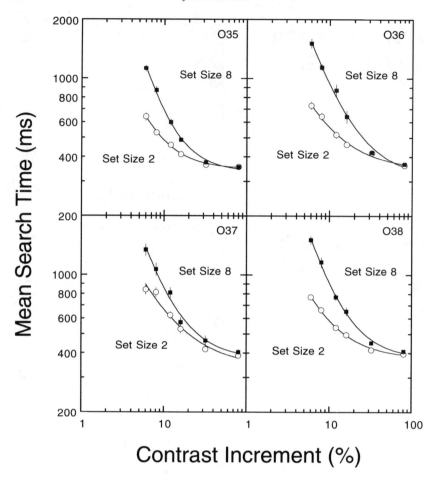

*Figure* 14: The mean search time for four subjects is shown as a function of the contrast increment for Set Sizes 2 and 8. Functions are shown for Target Absent only.

### Estimating Thresholds for Search Time

The next step of this analysis was to estimate a threshold value for search time that is analogous to the threshold value estimated for search accuracy. Similar estimates have been made before for certain colour search tasks by Nagy and Sanchez (1990). Here, the search time data were fit with the modified power-law model, and were used to estimate the contrast increment that yields a search time of a particular criterion value above the asymptotic search time. I assumed a criterion value of +100 ms. This value is essentially arbitrary, although 100 ms is well under the time needed for a second eye movement. The impact of this choice will be considered in detail in the last part of this article.

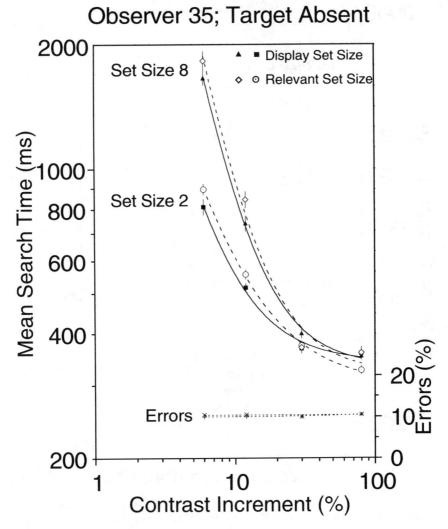

*Figure* 15: The mean search time is shown as a function of the contrast increment for variations of both display-set-size and relevant-set-size. The two manipulations produce similar results. For simplicity, data are shown for Target Absent only.

The analysis also focused on the Target Absent condition, which has the largest effects and the simplest theory.

An illustration of the threshold analysis is given in Figure 16, which is a plot of the Target Absent data from Figure 12. In particular, the asymptotic search time for the Set Size 2 condition is shown by the bottom horizontal line and a +100 ms additional criterion time is marked by the upper horizontal line. The intersection of the upper line and the

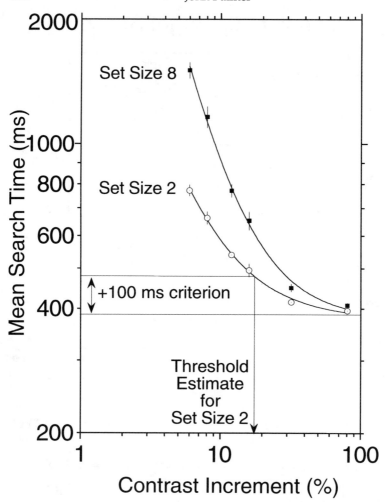

*Figure* 16: An illustration of the estimation of a time threshold. The curve is the best-fit modified power law, and a +100 ms criterion is used to define the threshold contrast increment.

curve fit for Set Size 2 is the contrast increment threshold estimate for Set Size 2, approximately a 17% contrast increment.

In Figure 17, the results of the search time experiment are plotted in the same format used for the search accuracy experiments. The axes are the same as before: log contrast increment threshold versus log set size. The accuracy data shown before in Figure 6 appear again at the bottom of this graph. The results of two search time experiments appear near the top of the graph. All of the points represent the means of four subjects. There was a consistent set-size effect and the log-log slope was around 0.3 for the 100 ms time criterion. Thus, threshold performance can now be defined by either a time criterion or by an accuracy criterion.

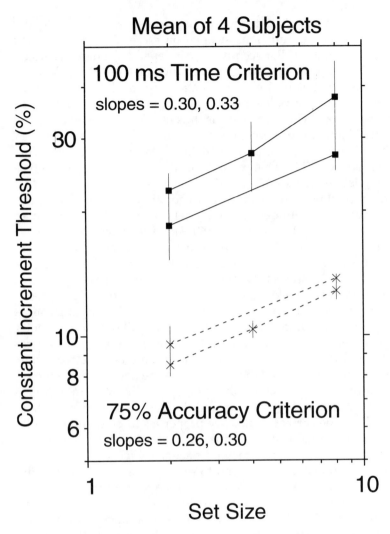

*Figure* 17: Mean threshold for four subjects as a function of set size. At the bottom are previously shown results for search accuracy; at the top are the new results for two search time experiments.

### Criterion Effects

The analysis thus far is successful in allowing one to summarize the results of the accuracy and time experiments in a common fashion. This approach, however, leads to a final problem: there is no justification for comparing the 75% accuracy criterion to the particular 100 ms time criterion. These criteria would not matter if the functions describing probability correct as a function of contrast increment and search time as a function of contrast increment had constant shapes for all set sizes.

Unfortunately, these functions do not have consistent shapes. As the set size increases, the functions steepen on these log-log graphs for both accuracy and time. For accuracy, the independent channels model predicts this change in the psychometric function (e.g., the effect of $k$ in Equation 1, see also Pelli, 1985). But for search time, I do not yet have an unlimited-capacity perception model that is detailed enough to make a prediction. While the analysis thus far showed the two experimental paradigms to be similar, it remains unclear what time criterion can be justified as being comparable to the 75% accuracy criterion. This problem is addressed in the next section, which considers general theories that relate search accuracy and search time.

Before proceeding, I will make a brief aside about the possible nature of an unlimited-capacity perception model for search time (see Pavel, 1990; Pavel, Econopouly, & Landy, 1992). There are at least two general approaches. Geisler and Chow (1995) focus on the fact that in many search time experiments, the stimuli are presented until the subjects respond, and thus the subjects have the opportunity to make eye movements. Indeed, for some kinds of stimuli, the limitations of peripheral vision require that an eye movement be made to each individual stimulus to allow an accurate judgment. Geisler and Chow use the limits due to peripheral vision to estimate how many eye movements are required for a given level of accuracy. As the stimuli become more confusable to peripheral vision, there must be more and more eye movements. Moreover, for confusable stimuli, an increase in set size increases the noise, and thus requires additional eye movements. Thus, this model has the correct qualitative properties to predict the results shown here. It highlights the potential importance of limitations of peripheral vision as a mediating factor for set-size effects.

The second approach is to extend to search time the analysis of the integration of noisy information. This was the heart of the unlimited-capacity perception hypothesis discussed above. The key is to consider models that describe the response time as a function of the confusability of the targets and distractors. Begin by recalling the analysis of search accuracy. For confusable stimuli, increasing the set size increases the noise affecting the decision. In most stochastic models of response time, an increase in noise will result in a slower accumulation of information. Thus, increasing the set size must increase the search time. Such models have not yet been detailed for visual search, but a starting point can be found in Palmer and McLean (1995). See also the related models of similar response time phenomena (the memory search model of Ratcliff, 1978; alternative stochastic processes are developed by Link, 1975; or Rudd, 1996). For a general review, see Luce (1986).

The strategy that I pursue here is to set aside the question of developing a specific model for search time, and instead to turn to more general models of the relation between search accuracy and search time. These models will provide a context in which one can compare accuracy and time experiments.

## Relating Search Accuracy and Search Time

Here I will introduce a more general theoretical question: Is there a common bottleneck that determines the set-size effects for both search accuracy and search time? I begin by describing what I mean by a common bottleneck, and then describe a method to test the predictions of such a hypothesis. In addition, this analysis reveals the effects of criterion that bedevilled the previous comparison between search accuracy and search time.

### The Common Bottleneck Hypothesis

I focus my analysis again on the interaction between the stimulus difference and set-size manipulations. In particular, assume that both dependent variables depend on a *common bottleneck* that accounts for the interaction between the stimulus difference and set size. By a common bottleneck, I mean that a common, single-valued representation mediates the set-size effect for both dependent measures. To my knowledge, this idea was first formalized by Bamber's (1979) "state-trace analysis." His analysis is an example of a decomposable representation (Krantz, Luce, Suppes, & Tversky, 1971). Such decomposable representations have been used in similar applications including light adaptation (Stiles & Crawford, 1932) and identifying visual features (Palmer, 1986).

For a formal definition, denote the set size by $n$ and the stimulus difference by $d$. In addition, let $S$ denote a single-valued function of $n$ and $d$, and let $F$ and $G$ denote monotonic real-valued functions. The common single-variable representation corresponds to the value of the function $S$ within the following system of two equations:

Probability correct $\quad = \quad F[S(n, d)]$, and $\qquad\qquad$ (6)

Mean response time $\quad = \quad G[S(n, d)]$.

The function $S$ corresponds to the internal representation that combines the effects of the stimulus difference and set size for both dependent variables. One can think of $S$ as describing the signal-to-noise ratio that results from the two manipulations. This single representation is then related to the two different response measures by two different monotonic functions. Thus, this is also an example of a decomposable representation.

While this theory is very general, it does predict a particular property on equivalence relations. To define that property, denote the equivalence relation by ~ and the different set size and stimulus difference conditions by subscripting $n$ and $d$. In addition, the response to the condition with set size $n_i$ and stimulus difference $d_i$ is denoted by the ordered pair $(n_i, d_i)$. With this notation, the predicted equivalence property is:

$$(n_1, d_1) \sim (n_2, d_2) \text{ for search accuracy, if and only if} \qquad (7)$$

$$(n_1, d_1) \sim (n_2, d_2) \text{ for search time.}$$

This equivalence property is very similar to the threshold measures mentioned earlier. For example, the stimulus difference thresholds for 75% correct at two different set sizes defines an example of estimating one of the equivalence conditions for accuracy. The new aspect is that the same pairing of stimulus difference and set size conditions will be equivalent for search time. It does not, however, predict for what response time they will be equivalent. The two conditions that match for 75% correct in search accuracy must match for some search time, but one does not know if they will match for a search time of 500 ms, or 600 ms, or what have you. The prediction only specifies that there does exist a search time that will always match.

The nature of this equivalence property is shown by the graphs in Figure 18. The top panel of Figure 18 is a small reproduction of the threshold-versus-set-size functions already shown. In that graph, the set-size effect is the difference in threshold for the two set sizes. The same information is plotted in a single point in the scatterplot in the bottom panel (this analysis builds on that of Bamber, 1979). The axes are the increment contrast threshold for Set Size 8 plotted against the increment contrast threshold for Set Size 2. The results for one equivalence relation is summarized by a single point in this graph. The $x$ value on the scatterplot is taken from one of the points of the upper panel and the $y$ value is taken from the other point in the upper panel. With this new scatterplot, the magnitude of the set-size effect is the vertical shift above the diagonal line that marks identical thresholds for the two set sizes. The point shown is for an accuracy criterion of 75% correct.

The next step is to plot the thresholds for a variety of criteria. This offers the additional benefit of showing off the effect of the accuracy criterion. These results are shown in Figure 19. This scatterplot has the same point for the 75% criterion along with results for 60%, 90%, and 95%. There are set-size effects for all criteria, but the effect is reduced for higher criteria. This effect was also shown in Figure 5 in the psychometric functions.

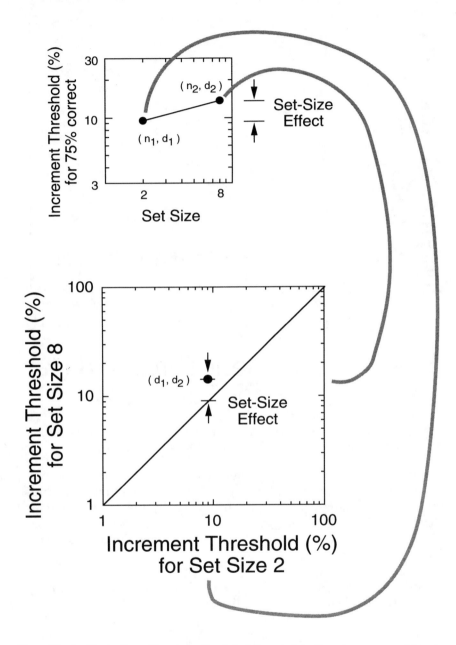

*Figure* 18: An illustration of how a scatterplot of the set-size effects is constructed from a threshold-versus-set-size function.

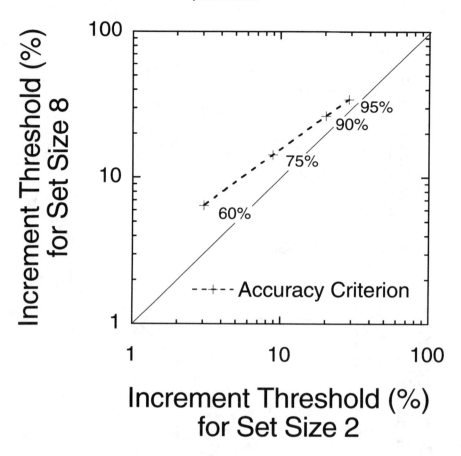

*Figure* 19: A scatterplot of the threshold for Set Size 8 versus the threshold for Set Size
Estimated thresholds are shown for four different accuracy criteria.

With this machinery, one can state again the prediction of the common bottleneck hypothesis. It requires that the search time thresholds fall along the same contour as that defined by the search accuracy thresholds. There is no prediction about where the particular 100 ms criterion will fall, but it must fall somewhere along the contour made by the accuracy criteria.

*Testing the Common Bottleneck Hypothesis*   The results are shown in Figure 20. The solid curve and open diamonds indicate the results for the search time, and the dashed curve and pluses indicate the results of search accuracy. They coincide quite closely. Thus, the common bottleneck hypothesis is sufficient to account for both search accuracy and search time.

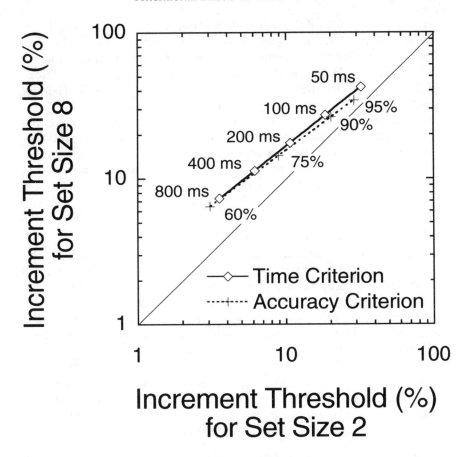

*Figure* 20: A scatterplot of the threshold for Set Size 8 versus the threshold for Set Size 2. Estimated thresholds are shown for both search accuracy and search time.

To complete this analysis, I consider a measure of the reliability of these estimated equivalences. This is particularly important in the current situation because the graphs presented thus far can be misleading in one respect. The points on the contours shown in Figures 19 and 20 do not represent independent data points. Rather, they are a series of estimates for different performance criteria based on the same data. Thus, their consistency need not indicate consistent data. Consequently, one needs another way to represent the variability of these data. This was accomplished by estimating these contours independently for each subject. The individual subject contours were described by straight lines in these log-log scatterplots and summarized in terms of the two parameters of a line, a slope and a particular *y*-intercept. The first parameter is the usual slope as defined on a log-log scatterplot. It

represents the effect of the criterion. No effect of the criterion would result in a slope of 1, and the observed slope was around 0.8, which reflects the smaller set-size effects for more accurate or more rapid response criteria. The second parameter is the $y$-value (vertical position)
of these lines above the identity line at a particular $x$-value (horizontal
position). This $y$-intercept is specified by the set-size effect at a 10% increment contrast. This set-size effect was expressed in terms of the
equivalent log-log slope on the threshold-versus-set-size functions that
were used previously. Specifically, let $T_8$ be the estimated threshold for
Set Size 8 at the criterion that yielded a contrast increment threshold of
10 for Set Size 2. Then, the set-size effect is defined by the log-log slope,

$$(\text{Log } T_8 - \text{Log } 10) / (\text{Log } 8 - \text{Log } 2). \tag{8}$$

With this definition, the log-log slopes were around 0.35.

Using these two summary measures for each individual subject, the
means and standard errors are plotted in Figure 21. The figure shows
the criterion effect plotted against the set-size effect. One point represents the search accuracy experiment and the other point represents
the search time experiment. The two points fall close enough that their
error bars overlap. Thus, the differences between accuracy and time
measure are not reliably different.

*Summary*   I defined a model that specifies a common bottleneck for
the interaction between the stimulus difference and set size, and then
showed that this common bottleneck was sufficient to describe these
effects for search accuracy and search time.

## Discussion

### Relations among Theories

Consider the relations among the various hypotheses using the implication diagram of Figure 22. Such an implication diagram shows the
relations among more specific versus more general hypotheses. Any
specific hypothesis that implies a more general hypothesis is shown by
an arrow that points to the more general hypothesis. The resulting diagram can be thought of as the family tree of related hypotheses.

In Figure 22, one can begin at the middle left side with the contrasting unlimited- and limited-capacity perception hypotheses. This is the
contrast at the heart of this article. In the analysis of the search accuracy experiments, I derived specific predictions for special cases of
each of these hypotheses. For the unlimited-capacity perception hypothesis, the special case was the independent channels model; for the
limited-capacity perception hypothesis, the special case was the fixed-

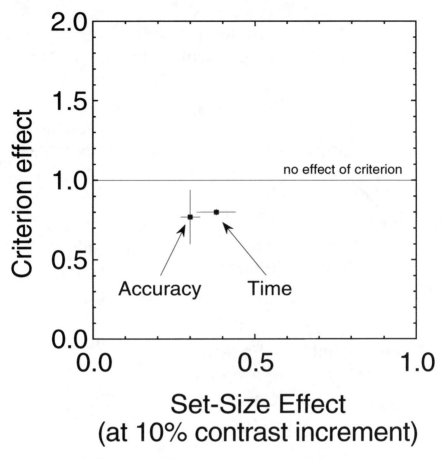

*Figure* 21: A scatterplot of the summary statistics estimated for both the search accuracy and search time paradigms.

information-capacity model. The independent channels model was sufficient to account for all the search accuracy results, and the fixed-information-capacity model was rejected.

In the last part of the article, I addressed the more general issue of whether or not set-size effects in search accuracy and in search time were accounted for by a common single-valued representation. I referred to this as the common bottleneck hypothesis. One possibility is that regardless of whether there is unlimited or limited-capacity perception, there is a common representation on which the two dependent measures are based. In the implication diagram, this is illustrated by the common bottleneck hypothesis implied by either the unlimited- or limited-capacity perception. In contrast to the common bottleneck hypothesis is a hypothesis that allows multiple bottlenecks. One example

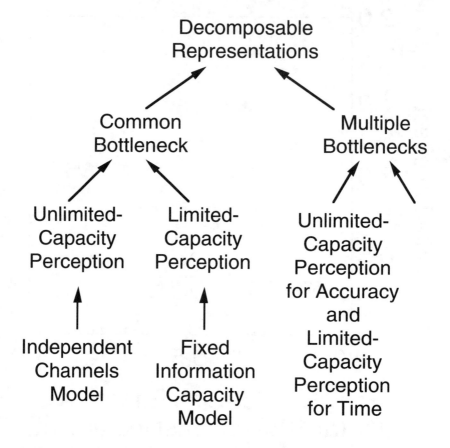

*Figure* 22: An implication diagram illustrating the relations among the hypotheses discussed in this article. The arrows indicate the special case hypotheses that imply more general hypotheses.

is to have unlimited-capacity perception for accuracy and a limited-capacity perception for time. This could result from a serial scanning that introduces a capacity effect on response time but has accuracy independent of the number of component processes. More stimuli take longer but do not affect the precision of the representation of any individual stimulus.

A prediction was derived for the common bottleneck hypothesis and the test of that prediction showed that this hypothesis was sufficient to account for the interaction between stimulus difference and set-size manipulations. Something that I did not do was to reject a specific version of the multiple bottleneck hypothesis. Indeed, an initial step for the future is to work out predictions for some of the special cases of the multiple bottleneck hypothesis. It is unknown at present whether or not the interesting special cases make a distinctive prediction from the common bottleneck hypothesis. Resolving that issue and coming up with more detailed predictions for the unlimited-capacity perception model for search time will answer the questions raised at the beginning of this article.

### Applications to More Complex Search Tasks

The analysis presented here can be applied to a variety of search tasks. Figure 23 shows a schematic illustration of some of the more complex search tasks in the visual search literature. The top panel illustrates an orientation and contrast conjunction task in which a subject has to find a target of a particular orientation and contrast (Treisman & Gelade, 1980). The middle panel shows an illustration of a task in which one has to find a target that consists of a rotated T-like character among rotated L-like characters (Beck & Ambler, 1973; Egeth & Dagenbach, 1991). The bottom panel shows a spatial relations task in which one has to judge the orientation of a pair of opposite polarity points (O'Connell & Treisman, 1990). Key to this last example is that the task involves a relation among distinct objects rather than an attribute of a single grouped object. Grouping is minimized by the use of widely spaced dots of opposite contrast (Zucker & Davis, 1988). The existing literature on each of these tasks has shown relatively large set-size effects, and they have been interpreted as demonstrating some kind of limited-capacity perception.

I have begun to analyze each of these tasks using the methods of the search accuracy experiments described here. An initial analysis of the conjunction tasks suggests that once one controls for discriminability using threshold measures, the differences between conjunction tasks and feature tasks are much reduced (Aiken & Palmer, 1992). The remaining differences may well be accounted for by the differences in the decision models necessary for integrating information across multiple attributes as well as across multiple objects. Thus, I question whether large set-size effects are inherent in the conjunction task.

For the rotated T's and L's experiment, controlling discriminability only modestly reduces the set-size effects. On the other hand, the comparison between the cueing paradigm and the display-set-size paradigm indicates that under conventional conditions there are probably large sensory interactions among the stimuli. The experiments were repeated with very large separations among the stimuli to eliminate differences between the cueing paradigm and the display-set-size paradigm. Under these conditions, the set-size effects were reduced to be within the range of those predicted by an unlimited-capacity perception

- # Conjunctions

- # Rotated Ts and Ls

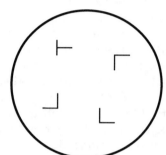

- # Spatial relations

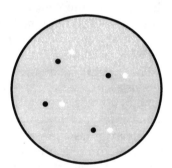

*Figure* 23: Illustrations of three search tasks that have been claimed to result in inherently large set-size effects.

model (Palmer, 1994). Thus, I suspect that the previously reported large set-size effects for the rotated T's and L's stimuli may not be fundamentally due to attentional phenomena, but rather may have more to do with configural or textural phenomena. In addition, a recent study by Bennett and Jaye (1995) has measured set-size effects for a variety of letter search tasks, and has shown many of them to be consistent with unlimited-capacity perception.

Only for the spatial-relations task do I find consistently larger set-size effects than with simple stimuli. For a typical experiment, the log-log slopes are around 0.5, which is about twice that found for simple tasks (Palmer, 1994). This is still not as large as predicted by the information-theory special case of the limited-capacity model described earlier. Curiously, however, this is exactly what one would predict from an infor-mation-theory, limited-capacity hypothesis that considers the whole behaviour as a communication channel rather than considering merely the perceptual stage as a communication channel (system capacity rather than perceptual capacity). Thus, this task does satisfy the defini-tion of limited capacity as originally proposed by Broadbent (1958).

## Conclusion

There are several novel aspects to this work: (a) the isolation of atten-tional phenomena with the cueing paradigm; (b) the control of discrim-inability using threshold measures; (c) the comparison of set-size ef-fects for both accuracy and time; and (d) the test of the common bottleneck hypothesis for accuracy and time. The focus, nevertheless, must remain on the contrast between unlimited-capacity perception and limited-capacity perception. The analysis of the search accuracy experiments has provided one critical test distinguishing these hypoth-eses. This analysis will soon be generalized to search time. Together, these two analyses revise the foundation for theories of visual search.

## Acknowledgments

I thank my colleagues Cynthia Ames, Jennifer McLean, Misha Pavel, and Davida Teller for many contributions to this research. In addition, I thank Karen Dobkins, David Peterzell, James Townsend, and Preeti Verghese for comments on previous versions of this article. This work was supported by the generous donations of Verda Churchill and Joe and Helen Zabinsky. John Palmer may be reached via e-mail at jpalmer@u.washington.edu

## References

Aiken, D., & Palmer, J. (1992). *Pursuing an alternative theory of the difference be-tween conjunctions and disjunctions in visual search.* Unpublished manu-script, University of Washington, WA.

Bamber, D. (1979). State-trace analysis: A method of testing simple theories of causation. *Journal of Mathematical Psychology, 19,* 137–181.

Beck, J., & Ambler, B. (1973). The effects of concentrated and distributed atten-tion on peripheral acuity. *Perception & Psychophysics, 14,* 225–230.

Bennett, P.J., & Jaye, P.D. (1995). Letter localization, not discrimination, is con-strained by attention. *Canadian Journal of Experimental Psychology 49,* 460–504.

Bergen, J.R., & Julesz, B. (1983a). Parallel versus serial processing in rapid pattern discrimination. *Nature, 303,* 696–698.

Bergen, J.R., & Julesz, B. (1983b). Rapid discrimination of visual patterns. *IEEE Transactions on Systems, Man, and Cybernetics, 13,* 857–863.

Broadbent, D.E. (1958). *Perception and communication.* London: Pergamon.

Broadbent, D.E. (1971). *Decision and stress.* NY: Academic Press.

Duncan, J. (1980). The locus of interference in the perception of simultaneous stimuli. *Psychological Review, 87,* 272–300.

Davis, E.T., Kramer, P., & Graham, N. (1983). Uncertainty about spatial frequency, spatial position, or contrast of visual patterns. *Perception & Psychophysics, 33,* 20–28.

Duncan, J., & Humphreys, G. (1989). Visual search and stimulus similarity. *Psychological Review, 96,* 433–458.

Egeth, H., & Dagenbach, D. (1991). Parallel versus serial processing of visual search: Further evidence from subadditive effects of visual quality. *Journal of Experimental Psychology: Human Perception & Performance, 17,* 551–560.

Gescheider, G.A. (1985). *Psychophysics: Method, theory, and application.* Hillsdale, NJ: Erlbaum.

Geisler, W.S., & Chou, K.L. (1995). Separation of low-level and high-level factors in complex tasks: Visual search. *Psychological Review, 102,* 356–378.

Graham, N. (1989). *Visual pattern analyzers.* New York: Oxford University Press.

Green, D.M., & Swets, J.A. (1966). *Signal detection theory and psychophysics.* New York: Krieger.

Helmholtz, H. von (1896). Handbuch der Physiologischen Optik. 2nd ed. Hamburg: Vos.

Hoffman, J.E. (1979). A two-stage model of visual search. *Perception & Psychophysics, 25,* 319–327.

Hung, G.K., Wilder, J., Curry, R., & Julesz, B. (1995). Simultaneous better than sequential for brief presentations. *Journal of the Optical Society of America, 12,* 441–449.

Kahneman, D. (1973). *Attention and effort.* Englewood Cliffs, NJ: Prentice Hall.

Kantowitz, B.H. (1974). Double stimulation. In B.H. Kantowitz (Ed.), *Human information processing: Tutorials in performance and cognition,* (pp. 83–132). Hillsdale, NJ: Erlbaum.

Krantz, D.H., Luce, R.D., Suppes, P., & Tversky, A. (1971). *Foundations of measurement, Vol. 1: Additive and Polynomial Representations.* New York: Academic Press.

Lindsay, P.H., Taylor, M.M., & Forbes, S.M. (1968). Attention and multidimensional discrimination. *Perception & Psychophysics, 4,* 113–117.

Link, S.W. (1975). The relative judgment theory of two-choice response time. *Journal of Mathematical Psychology, 12,* 114–135.

Luce, R.D. (1986). *Response times.* New York: Oxford University Press.

Mansfield, R.J.W. (1973). Latency functions in human vision. *Vision Research, 13,* 2219–2234.

Nagy, A.L., & Sanchez, R.R. (1990). Critical color differences determined with a visual search task. *Journal of the Optical Society of America, 7,* 1209–1225.

Navon, D., & Gopher, D. (1979). On the economy of the human processing systems. *Psychological Review, 86,* 254–255.

O'Connell, K.M., & Treisman, A.M. (1990). *Is all orientation created equal?* Paper presented at the annual meeting of the Association for Research in Vision and Ophthalmology, Sarasota, FL.

Palmer, J. (1986). Mechanisms of displacement discrimination with and without perceived movement. *Journal of Experimental Psychology: Human Perception & Performance, 12,* 411–421.

Palmer, J. (1994). Set-size effects in visual search: The effect of attention is independent of the stimulus for simple tasks. *Vision Research, 34,* 1703–1721.

Palmer, J. (1995). Attention in visual search: Distinguishing four causes of set-size effects. *Current Directions in Psychological Science, 4,* 118–123.

Palmer, J., Ames, C.T., & Lindsey, D.T. (1993). Measuring the effect of attention on simple visual search. *Journal of Experimental Psychology: Human Perception & Performance, 19,* 108–130.

Palmer, J., & McLean, J. (1995). Imperfect, unlimited-capacity, parallel search yields large set-size effects. Paper presented at the annual meeting of the Society of Mathematical Psychology, Irvine, CA (transcript available from the authors).

Pashler, H. (1987). Target-distractor discriminability in visual search. *Perception & Psychophysics, 41,* 285–292.

Pashler, H. (1989). Dissociations and dependencies between speed and accuracy: Evidence for a two-component theory of divided attention in simple tasks. *Cognitive Psychology, 21,* 469–514.

Pavel, M. (1990). *A statistical model of preattentive visual search.* Paper presented at the annual meeting of the Psychonomic Society, New Orleans, LA.

Pavel, M., Econopouly, J., & Landy, M. S. (1992). *Psychophysics of rapid visual search.* Paper presented at the annual meeting of the Association for Research in Vision and Ophthalmology, Sarasota, FL.

Pelli, D.G. (1985). Uncertainty explains many aspects of visual contrast detection and discrimination. *Journal of the Optical Society of America, 2,* 1508–1532.

Posner, M.I., Snyder, C.R.R., & Davidson, B.J. (1980). Attention and the detection of signals. *Journal of Experimental Psychology: General, 109,* 160–174.

Ratcliff, R. (1978). A theory of memory retrieval. *Psychological Review, 85,* 59–108.

Rudd, M.E. (1996). A neural timing model of visual threshold. *Journal of Mathematical Psychology, 40,* 1–29.

Schweickert, R., Dahn, C., & McGuigan, K. (1988). Intensity and number of alternatives in hue identification: Piéron's law and choice reaction time. *Perception & Psychophysics, 44,* 383–389.

Shaw, M.L. (1980). Identifying attentional and decision-making components in information processing. In R.S. Nickerson (Ed.), *Attention & Performance, Vol. 8* (pp. 106–121). Hillsdale, NJ: Erlbaum.

Shaw, M.L. (1982). Attending to multiple sources of information. *Cognitive Psychology, 14,* 353–409.

Shaw, M.L. (1984). Division of attention among spatial locations: A fundamental difference between detection of letters and detection of luminance increments. In H. Bouma & D.G. Bouwhuis (Eds.), *Attention & performance, Vol. 10: Control of language processes.* Hillsdale, NJ: Erlbaum.

Shiffrin, R.M., & Gardner, G.T. (1972). Visual processing capacity and attentional control. *Journal of Experimental Psychology, 93,* 72–82.

Sperling, G., & Dosher, B.A. (1986). Strategy and optimization in human information processing. In K.R. Boff, L. Kaufman, & J.P. Thomas (Eds.), *Handbook of perception and human performance* (pp. 2.1–2.65). New York: Wiley.

Stiles, W.S. (1978). *Mechanisms of color vision.* New York: Academic Press.

Stiles, W.S., & Crawford, B. (1932). Equivalent adaptation levels in localized retinal areas. In *The Physical and Optical Societies Report, Joint Discussion on Vision* (pp. 194–211). London: The Physical Society. Reprinted in Stiles, 1978.

Tanner, W.P., Jr. (1961). Physiological implications of psychophysical data. *Annals of the New York Academy of Science, 89,* 752–765.

Taylor, M.M., Lindsay, P.H., & Forbes, S.M. (1967). Quantification of shared capacity processing in auditory and visual discrimination. *Acta Psychologica, 27,* 223–229.

Townsend, J.T. (1974). Issues and models concerning the processing of a finite number of inputs. In B.H. Kantowitz (Ed.), *Human information processing: Tutorials in performance and cognition* (pp. 133–185). Hillsdale, NJ: Erlbaum.

Townsend, J.T., & Ashby, F.G. (1978). Methods of modeling capacity in simple processing systems. In N.J. Castellan, Jr. & F. Restle (Eds.), *Cognitive theory,* Vol. 3 (pp. 199–239). Hillsdale, NJ: Erlbaum.

Townsend, J.T., & Ashby, F.G. (1983). *Stochastic modeling of elementary psychological processes.* New York: Cambridge University Press.

Townsend, J.T., & Nozawa, G. (1995). Spatio-temporal properties of elementary perception: An investigation of parallel, serial, and coactive theories. *Journal of Mathematical Psychology, 39,* 321–359.

Treisman, A., & Gelade, G. (1980). A feature-integration theory of attention. *Cognitive Psychology, 12,* 97–136.

Treisman, A., & Gormican, S. (1988). Feature analysis in early vision: Evidence from search asymmetries. *Psychological Review, 95,* 15–48.

Verghese, P., & Nakayama, K. (1994). Stimulus discriminability in visual search. *Vision Research, 34,* 2453–2467.

Verghese, P., & Stone, L.S. (1995). Combining speed information across space. *Vision Research, 35,* 2811–2823.

Watson, A.B. (1979). Probability summation over time. *Vision Research, 19,* 515–522.

Welford, A.T. (1952). The "psychological refractory period" and the timing of high-speed performance: A review and a theory. *British Journal of Psychology, 43,* 2–19.

Wolfe, J.M., Cave, K.R., & Franzel, S.L. (1989). Guided search: An alternative to the feature integration model for visual search. *Journal of Experimental Psychology: Human Perception & Performance, 15,* 419–433.

Wyszecki, G. & Stiles, W.S. (1982). *Color science: Concepts and methods, quantitative data and formulae.* 2nd ed. New York: Wiley.

Zucker, S.W., & Davis, S. (1988). Points and endpoints: A size/spacing constraint for dot grouping. *Perception, 17,* 229–247.

# 15

## Search via Recursive Rejection (SRR): Evidence with Normal and Neurological Subjects

Hermann J. Müller, Glyn W. Humphreys
and Andrew C. Olson

## Introduction to SRR

### Image Segmentation and Visual Grouping

Visual processing in the human brain takes place in massively parallel operations, generating a detailed and (relatively) accurate representation of our surroundings, including information about the shape, colour, size, (relative) position, distance (depth), orientation and motion of surfaces and objects within the scene (e.g., Marr, 1982). One of the most important problems to be solved in deriving this representation is the delineating of object boundaries from background, thereby segmenting the image into entities that can form the basis of an action. There is a great deal of evidence supporting the idea that, initially (i.e., prior to the segmentation of objects), the retinal image is coded with primitive descriptors or simple features along a set of feature dimensions at each location simultaneously (e.g., Felleman & Van Essen, 1991; Treisman, Cavanagh, Fischer, Ramachandran, & von der Heydt, 1990; Van Essen, 1985; Zeki, 1993). For instance, colour (the dimension) is coded for all image locations in terms of features such as red, blue, and so forth. From these primitive features, the visual system reconstructs coherent percepts of complex objects.

An important process in object segmentation and reconstruction is the grouping of primitive elements that are components of the same object. Segmentation based on grouping between image features of the same dimension has been widely studied (e.g., the emergence of boundaries based on form discontinuities between regions of field in texture segregation; Julesz, 1975, 1986). However, objects in real-world scenes are composed of many different features in different dimensions. Thus, the coherent percept of an object segmented from its back-

389

ground necessarily involves the grouping not only of features within a given dimension, but also of sets of features across different dimensions. The grouping of primitive features both within and across dimensions introduces the additional problem of representing these groupings. If special processing units had to be devoted to coding every possible combination of simple features for all image locations, the number of such complex units would increase exponentially with the number of relationships between features requiring representation. The problem of representing grouped sets of features is formally stated as the binding problem (Feldman & Ballard, 1982).

## Feature Binding and Visual Search

One influential account of how primitive features extracted in early visual processing are combined is provided by Feature Integration Theory (FIT) (e.g., Treisman, 1988; Treisman & Gelade, 1980). FIT was formulated on the basis of evidence from visual search experiments. The search reaction time (RT) functions, which relate the RTs taken to decide Target Present or Target Absent to the number of elements in the display (the "display size"), were considered to fall into two classes: linearly increasing functions and flat functions. FIT proposed that flat functions, indicating spatially parallel search, occur when the search involves a target object that differs from the nontargets ("distractors") in a single simple feature (e.g., a vertical line amongst horizontal lines). Linearly increasing functions occur when the target is defined by a conjunction of simple features, each of which is separately present among the nontarget items (e.g., a red vertical line among red horizontal lines and green vertical lines). Linear functions with 1:2 Present:Absent slope ratios have been taken as indicative of a spatially serial (item-by-item) search process, where search is exhaustive on absent trials and self-terminates upon detecting a target on present trials (the "serial, self-terminating search" (SSTS) model). FIT holds that search for conjunction targets is dependent upon display size because their unique combination of features can only be detected by a capacity-limited process (involving focal attention) that serially conjoins (binds) simple features at one location at a time. The features present at a location sampled by focal attention are assembled and passed to later stages of processing (object recognition and response). The important point is that features are bound together, and bound objects are selected, on the basis of common location.

However, there is no simple dichotomy between search RT functions; rather, the functions form a continuum ranging from flat to linearly increasing with various slopes (search rates). To account for this continuum, some theorists have proposed that the range over which attentional processing operates in parallel is variable, encompassing only one item in the extreme (e.g., Pashler, 1987; Treisman & Gormican, 1988). Others have proposed two-stage models in which a rapid but error-prone, spatially parallel analysis stage is followed by an accurate serial stage (involving attention), where the parallel stage serves to compute the selection priorities for the subsequent stage by indexing the locations of likely targets (e.g., "Guided Search": Cave & Wolfe, 1990; Wolfe, 1994; and "Revised FIT": Treisman & Sato, 1990). These models present a significant advance on the earlier accounts, because they allow for the possibility of (top-down) mechanisms that suppress items not sharing a target feature (or that enhance items sharing target features) in parallel. However, these mechanisms operate on individual features prior to their binding, and so do not involve "grouping." Binding (and selection) are still strictly serial, the implicit assumption being that all relevant features of an object are present in a spatially contiguous image region. While this may be the case with the items used in visual search experiments, it is hardly true for everyday scenes in which objects are frequently occluding (or entirely overlapping).

An alternative to these space-based accounts is provided by the connectionist SRR[1] model of Humphreys and Müller (1993; Müller & Humphreys, 1993). The SRR network is a spatially parallel visual pattern recognizer that implements several aspects of Duncan and Humphreys's (1989, 1992) "similarity" account of the continuum of empirical search RT functions. According to Duncan and Humphreys, and as implemented in SRR, there is no qualitative distinction between the processes that produce parallel and serial search functions. Rather, (at least) simple conjunctions of form features are encoded (i.e., features are bound) independently and in parallel across the functional visual field, and search rates vary as a function of two orthogonal factors: (i) the similarity in appearance of the target and the distractors and (ii) the similarity in appearance of the distractors (e.g., where similarity is measured in terms of the number of shared features). The higher the target-distractor similarity and the lower the distractor-distractor similarity, the longer the search will take. Similarity governs the probability that the visual elements will group, the members of a group being selected together. In SRR, simple form features are conjoined (assembled) locally to form feature conjunctions, using principles such as collinearity of line segments constrained by line terminations, and feature conjunctions are grouped globally on the basis of their whole-item similarity (though similarity grouping is scaled by item proximity). Selected groups of items are recursively rejected until either no items are left (Respond Absent) or the target is detected (Respond Present).

In this chapter, we (i) provide an overview of SRR's basic architecture and operation, (ii) review empirical tests of SRR that demonstrate its power in simulating both normal and abnormal human performance across a range of visual search and object selection tasks, and (iii) discuss SRR's relations to other computational models of visual search, its limitations as a general account of human search performance, and how these limitations are addressed in current modeling work.

## SRR's Basic Architecture and Operation

SRR consists of a hierarchy of topographic maps, corresponding to increasingly complex aspects of visual form. Displays are presented to the network by clamping "On" the units in the retinal array that receive input (see Figure 1). At the second level, units respond to simple line segments at a particular orientation (horizontal or vertical) in the retinal image. Units at this single-feature level feed into combined-feature units at the third level, corresponding to simple conjunctions of line segments. The most important combined-feature units code L-junctions, by integrating the output from single-feature units from different second-level maps. Other units code line terminations, combining the output from single-feature units from the same second-level map. Terminator units are important for forming local whole-item conjunctions, but play no direct role in the global similarity grouping among whole items, in contrast to the junction units. Therefore, the term *combined-feature units* is meant to refer, primarily, to the junction units. Grouping between form conjunctions is implemented by a process of facilitatory activation ("crosstalk") within a map – more precisely, between the match map units that draw different feature combinations together to form maps for the particular target and distractor items used in the simulation (see below).

The network operates stochastically, using the "Boltzmann machine" activation function (Hinton & Sejnowski, 1986). This allows visual similarity between form conjunctions to be captured by the likelihood that a conjunction present in the field will switch "On" a unit that corresponds to another conjunction containing some of the same features. The probability that this occurs depends on the number of features shared between conjunctions (and on the network temperature). One side effect of the stochastic operation of the network is that grouping based on crosstalk within a combined-feature, L-junction map would be unstable, as combined-feature units could come "On" incorrectly, representing hallucinated conjunctions. To prevent this, in the implemented version of the network, grouping amongst like conjunctions is modulated by location units that code whether stimuli are present at particular locations. Crosstalk from conjunction unit A to

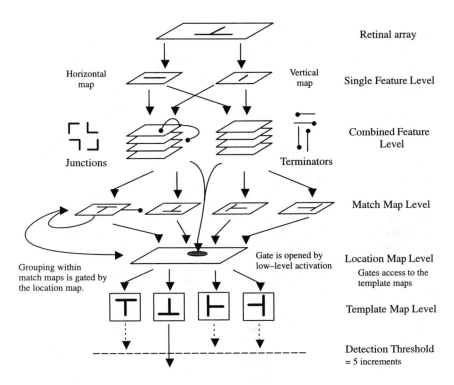

*Figure* 1:  The architecture of Search via Recursive Rejection (SRR).

conjunction unit B is enabled only if the location (gating) unit corresponding to B is activated. The locational gating is implemented by replicating the combined-feature maps into a second set of maps, termed *match maps* (see above). Match map units are placed in an On state only when there is input from both the combined-feature units and the location units.

Decisions as to whether a target is present or absent in a display can be made in either of two ways. Activation within the match maps is summed and given as input to temporary template units, representing the targets and distractors being used in the simulation. On each network iteration, there is competition amongst the templates, with only the winner being incremented. Targets are selected as soon as their template reaches threshold, when a Target Present response can be made. This is the first procedure. The second procedure involves the recursive rejection of distractor groups. The template unit receiving the most activation on any iteration will be that whose match map exhibits the strongest grouping, which is likely to be a distractor template. When a distractor template reaches threshold, the grouped distractors are removed from the search. This is done by inhibiting the match map corresponding to the suprathreshold distractor template and by disabling the location units supported by the inhibited match map. Location units are excluded from the search by instantaneous template-based inhibition of the corresponding match map and of all location units. Only location units supported by other still active match map units will survive the top-down inhibition. The search then proceeds over a reduced set of items and over a reduced region of field, provided some stimuli remain. This process operates recursively either until the target is detected (via activation of its template: Respond Present) or until no items are left (Respond Absent).

The first run of SRR can be likened to a first glance at a display. Processing during this first run is noisy and error-prone, with target misses far exceeding those exhibited by human subjects instructed to minimize errors. Misses arise when two or more distractor types attempt to group at the target's location (i.e., attempt to place into an On state distractor units at the target's location), inhibiting the target unit below threshold. If the search then runs quickly to completion, the target is missed (i.e., the target location is rejected from the search). With human subjects, under normal viewing conditions, the search may continue until the error rate reaches an acceptable level (i.e., there may be checking). With SRR, this is analogous to rerunning the simulation. Since misses are stochastically independent of each other, rerunning the network on absent decisions will reduce the likelihood that a target is missed. In all simulations reported below, the results are based on SRR's error-checked responses. Checking was carried out by modeling the effects of rerunning the network on a proportion of Target Absent decision runs – in order to have a growth in miss rates across the display sizes matched to that exhibited by human subjects.

SRR's performance measures correspond to the usual measures obtained in visual search experiments with human subjects: RT, clocked in terms of iterations (one iteration is the time it takes to update all the units in the network), and error rates (after checking). For a detailed description of SRR's architecture and operation, see Humphreys & Müller (1993, pp. 51–57.

## Empirical Tests of SRR

### Search with Homogeneous and Heterogeneous Distractors

The basic data to be simulated by SRR were the differential search RT functions obtained with homogeneous and heterogeneous distractors. Humphreys, Quinlan and Riddoch (1989) found that, when human subjects searched for an inverted T among homogeneous upright T dis-

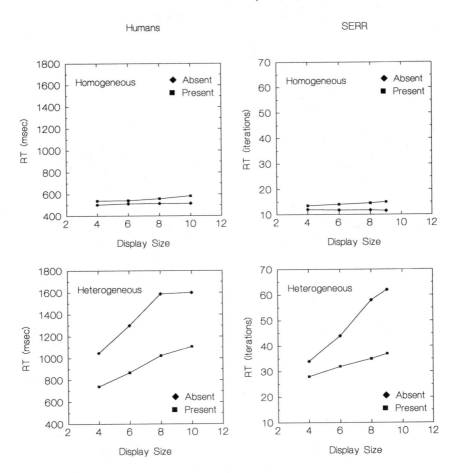

*Figure* 2: Human subjects' (left) and SRR's (right) search for form conjunctions amongst homogeneous (top) and heterogeneous (bottom) distractors. Each panel shows the present and absent response times (RTs) (in msec or iterations) as a function of display size.

tractors, their RT functions were relatively flat, and Absent Responses could be faster than Present Responses (arguing against the possibility that parallel search was based on some local feature that emerged when the target was present). When the distractors were heterogeneous, sharing some of the target features (e.g., search for an inverted T amongst upright, left- and right-oriented T's), the RTs increased linearly with the number of distractors, and the Present:Absent slope ratio approximated 1:2. See Figure 2.

Humphreys and Müller (1993) showed that SRR, by employing recursive rejection of grouped distractors and error checking, successfully simulated the effects of distractor similarity exhibited by human

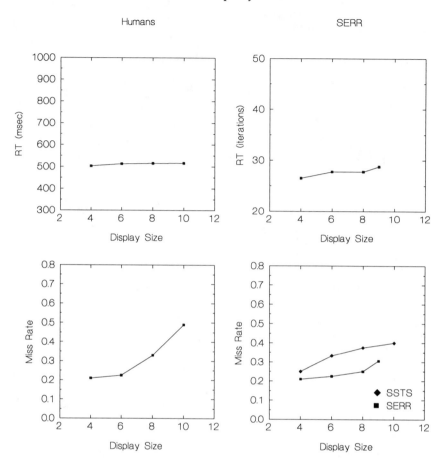

*Figure* 3: Human subjects' (left) and SRR's (right) search for form conjunctions amongst heterogeneous distractors under response deadline conditions. The top panels show the human subjects' positive (go) response times (RTs) (in msec) and SRR's first-pass positive RTs (in iterations) as a function of display size. The bottom panels show the corresponding miss rate data; also shown are the miss rates generated by a serial self-terminating search (SSTS) model with unbiased present and absent guessing.

subjects. SRR's search functions were flat with homogeneous distractors (with faster absent than present responses), and linear with heterogeneous distractors (with a present:absent slope ratio of approximately 1:2). See Figure 2. Thus, with SRR, the particular search functions produced depend only on the similarity of the distractors, not on qualitatively different processes that need to come into play under appropriate conditions (e.g., an spatially serial, self-terminating scanning process).

SRR's ability to produce linear search functions depends on the checking for errors (in particular, misses). The validity of the check process needs to be justified. With heterogeneous distractors, SRR's first-pass miss rates showed a strong, positively accelerating increase with display size, which was 25 times greater than that produced by human subjects instructed to minimize errors (Humphreys et al., 1989). Thus, SRR predicts that, when checking is prevented with human subjects (e.g., by imposing a response deadline), there should be a similar, positively accelerating increase in miss rates. In contrast, SSTS models predict a negatively accelerating increase, approaching an asymptotic level which depends on a subject's bias to Respond Absent. For example, assume that subjects are set a response deadline such that only two items can be inspected serially within the time available. If none of the inspected items matches the target, subjects make an unbiased Target Present or Target Absent guess. The probability, $p$, of the target location being inspected on Target-Present trials is then $1/(n/2)$, with $n$ being the number of display items ($\geq 2$). Hence, the probability of a guess is $1-p$, and the probability of a miss $(1-p)/2$. This would produce a negatively accelerating, asymptotic increase in miss rate up to a 50% level. However, Humphreys and Müller (1993; Experiment 1) found that, under response deadline conditions (with deadlines adjusted individually to allow 75% accuracy with display size 4), human subjects produced positively accelerating miss rates – consistent with SRR, but at variance with the SSTS model. See Figure 3 for the RT and miss rate functions. This provides some justification for the use of the check process in modeling linear search RT functions under non-deadline conditions.

One further assumption of SRR is that vertical and horizontal line features transferred onto higher order conjunction units according to whether the features fell in specific locations within the receptive field of a conjunction unit. In other words, similarity between display items is coded not just in terms of the presence of shared features, but also in terms of their location relative to the whole shape of the items. For example, inverted and upright T's (which have line features in corresponding locations), will be more similar than, say, inverted and left-oriented T's (which do not have line features in corresponding locations). Two predictions follow from this way of coding interitem similarity. With homogeneous displays, faster Absent than Present responses should arise predominantly with target-similar distractors – due to the high likelihood that distractor units are activated at the target location, slowing the activation of the target template and hence Present responses. With heterogeneous distractors, the (detrimental) effect of heterogeneity should be most marked when one type of distractor is more similar to the target than it is to the other distractors – because of the tendency to group the target with the similar distractors. These predictions were borne out in experiments with human subjects (Experiment 2 of Humphreys & Müller, 1993). See Table 2 for a summary of the experimental and simulation results. With homogeneous distractors, fast Absent responses were manifest only with target-similar, not with target-dissimilar, distractors. With heterogeneous distractors, search for an inverted T target was less efficient in the presence of upright and left-oriented T distractors than in the presence of left- and right-oriented T distractors. This indicates that human subjects perceive form conjunctions as more similar if their features fall in the same relative location, defined in terms of each shape's orientation, consistent with SRR.

| | Human Subjects | | SRR | |
|---|---|---|---|---|
| | Search rates[a] | Mean RT[b] | Search rates[c] | Mean RT[d] |
| **Homogeneous distractors** | | | | |
| Similar distractors | | | | |
| Absent | 2.5 | 492 | −0.3 | 12.0 |
| Present | 8.0 | 502 | 0.0 | 13.5 |
| Dissimilar distractors | | | | |
| Absent | 1.2 | 517 | −0.3 | 12.0 |
| Present | 9.0 | 513 | 0.0 | 12.5 |
| **Heterogeneous distractors** | | | | |
| Similar distractors | | | | |
| Absent | 50.5 | 806 | 1.3 | 27.7 |
| Present | 28.0 | 634 | 0.4 | 21.3 |
| Dissimilar distractors | | | | |
| Absent | 13.5 | 606 | 0.3 | 24.8 |
| Present | 11.5 | 529 | 0.1 | 21.5 |
| [a]in msec/item; [b]in msec; [c]in iterations/item; [d]in iterations. | | | | |

Table 1: Human subjects' and SRR's search for form conjunctions among target similar and dissimilar distractors. The table presents the search rates and mean response times (RTs) for search with homogeneous and heterogeneous distractors. [Note 1][1]

## Search for Single and Dual Targets

Search for dual conjunction targets provides another empirical test for distinguishing between serial and parallel models of visual search. SSTS models fail to account for the slopes of the Target Absent RT functions, both when the Target Present response requires the detection of only 1 of the 2 targets (0T, i.e. 0 targets, on Absent trials) and when it requires the detection of both targets (1T on Absent trials; Ward & McClelland, 1989). Further, under redundant (i.e., dual) target conditions, the probability of fast Present RTs is greater than that expected from the independent (serial) processing of the target stimuli (Mordkoff, Yantis, & Egeth, 1990). Müller, Humphreys, and Donnelly (1994) tested how well SRR could account for human search performance under dual conjunction target conditions. SRR, at present, operates only within the form dimension, so that the human data simulated necessarily involved search for dual *form conjunctions*.

Displays consisted of varying numbers of heterogeneous T stimuli. There were two tasks: (i) 1-target positive response (1TPR) and (ii) 2-target positive response (2TPR). In the 1TPR task, subjects and SRR had to detect the presence of at least one inverted T. Displays contained either 1 or 2 inverted T targets (equally probable) on Present trials and no target on Absent trials. Thus, subjects could respond positively as soon as they found 1 target. In the 2TPR condition, displays contained 2 targets on Present trials and either 1 target or no target (equally probable) on Absent trials. Thus, subjects and SRR could respond positively *only* upon finding 2 targets. The slopes of the search functions are given in Table 2.

In task 1 (1TPR), the slopes of the human search RT functions were 29, 35 and 134 msec/item with 2T (Present), 1T (Present), and 0T (Absent) in the display, respectively. The corresponding slope ratios were 1.0 : 1.2 : 4.6. In task 2 (2TPR), the slopes were 104, 221 and 147 msec/item with 2T (Present), 1T (Absent) and 0T (Absent) in the display, respectively. The slope difference between the 0T and 1T Absent conditions was not predicted by SSTS models, according to which Absent responses should always involve exhaustive search of the displays. Using as a reference slope the 1TPR 1T Present RT slope, the human subjects' slope ratios were 3.6 (2T Present): 7.6 (1T Absent) : 5.1 (0T Absent); SSTS models predict 2.0 : 3.0 : 3.0 ratios. In contrast to SSTS models, SRR provides a reasonable fit with human performance (see Table 2). Steeper slopes with SRR correspond to steeper slopes with humans ($r = .97$), accounting for approximately 95% of the variance.

SSTS models can be assessed further by equating the different conditions for the number of serial searches predicted (i.e., by plotting the RTs for each condition against the number of serial searches predicted).

|  | Humans[a] | SRR[b] |  | Humans[a] | SRR[b] |
|---|---|---|---|---|---|
| Task 1 (1TPR) | | | Task 2 (2TPR) | | |
| Present 2T | 29 | 2.1 | Present 2T | 104 | 3.4 |
| Present 1T | 35 | 2.1 | Absent 1T | 221 | 5.9 |
| Absent 0T | 134 | 4.6 | Absent 0T | 147 | 4.0 |
| [a]in msec/item; [b]in iterations/item. | | | | | |

Table 2: Human subjects' and SRR's search for single and dual form conjunctions. The table presents the search rates in task 1 (1-target positive response, 1TPR) and task 2 (2-target positive response, 2TPR) as a function of the number of targets in the display (OT, 1T, 2T).

Assuming that the time to execute a single search is constant across the different tasks and display compositions, SSTS models predict that the data from all conditions fall along a single line, the slope of which gives the time required per search. With human subjects, two conditions in task 1TPR fell along a single line with an average slope of 79 msec/search, and two conditions in task 2TPR fell along a line with an average slope of 152 msec/search. But task 2 slopes tended to be greater than task 1 slopes. This was predicted by SRR. With SRR, two of the conditions in task 1 fell along a single line with an average slope of 4.4 iterations per search; two of the conditions in task 2 fell along a line, but with an average slope of 5.5 iterations/search. Thus, SRR closely matches the pattern found with human subjects, which itself violates the SSTS model assumption that the time per search is constant.

A further test distinguishing serial from parallel search models involves the presentation of redundant targets (e.g., Mordkoff, Yantis, & Egeth, 1990). On Present trials, there can be either 1 or 2 targets; on Absent trials, there is no target. Various models, including the SSTS model, predict a redundancy gain on mean RTs when there are two targets rather than just one. In SSTS models, this redundancy gain occurs simply because 1 of 2 targets has a higher chance of being encountered early during the serial search than a single target in the display. However, there is a specific form of redundancy gain that is inconsistent with any strictly serial model. Testing for this gain requires an analysis of the entire distribution of RTs. Miller (1982) showed that all models which assume that each target produces an independent, separate activation must satisfy the following *race-model inequality*:

$$P(RT > t/T_1 \ \& \ T_2) \leq P(RT < t/T_1) + P(RT < t/T_2),$$

where RT is response time, $t$ is the time since stimulus onset, and $T_1$ and $T_2$ are targets at locations 1 and 2. Thus, the cumulative distribution function $P(RT < t/T_1 \& T_2)$ gives the cumulative probability that a response has occurred before time $t$, given that there is a target at both display locations. Violation of this inequality constitutes evidence against serial processing.

Müller et al. (1994; Experiment 3) examined whether both SRR and human subjects would show violations of the redundant target inequality. The display size was kept constant at 4 items. Figures 4a and 4b show the dual-target cumulative distribution function (CDF) and the sum of two single-target CDFs, separately for the human subjects (Figure 4a)and for SRR (Figure 4b). (Note that with SRR, the CDFs are based on first- pass data, with 1 or 2 targets present in the display.) For fast responses, the CDFs for the dual-target conditions (continuous lines) lie above and to the left of the CDFs representing the sum of two single-target conditions (dashed lines). That is, both SRR and the human subjects violate the redundant-target inequality. The finding of any violations argues against models that posit a spatially serial search process. According to SRR, the redundant target benefits (over and above those expected from a race of two independent targets for the detection response) are produced by the spatially parallel grouping of simple form conjunctions.

## Lesioning SRR: Visual Agnosia

Humphreys, Freeman, and Müller (1992) investigated whether pathological visual search performance of the type observed in visual agnosia (e.g., Humphreys & Riddoch, 1987; Humphreys, Riddoch, Quinlan, Price, & Donnelly, 1992) could be generated by SRR when lesioned. Detailed testing of an agnosic patient, HJA (who suffered bilateral occipital lobe lesions following a stroke), showed a normal search pattern with heterogeneous distractors, but an abnormal pattern when the task required detection of a simple form conjunction amongst homogeneous distractors. In the latter condition, RTs were slow, there were substantial display size effects, and Absent RTs were slower than Present RTs – unlike young and age-matched control subjects who show fast Absent responses (see Figure 5 for the performance of HJA and age-matched control subjects, and Figure 2 for the performance of young control subjects).

Humphreys et al. (1992) simulated the effects of brain damage by running the SRR network with increased noise (i.e., temperature) in its activation functions. Figure 5 gives sample search functions generated by SRR when run under low and high temperature conditions. Interestingly, increasing the temperature in the network selectively affected performance with homogeneous distractors: search RTs were slowed overall; Absent RTs were slower than Present RTs; and RTs increased

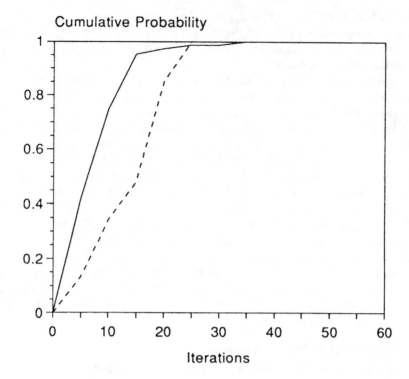

*Figure* 4a: Human subjects' search for single and dual form conjunction targets. The panel present the dual target (solid line) and sum of single target (dashed line) cumulative distribution functions.

with display size. In contrast, search with heterogeneous distractors was relatively unaffected. Increasing the noise in the activation functions made it more likely that junction stimuli in the input (e.g., an L junction) activated inappropriate junction units (e.g., a mirror-image L junction). With heterogeneous distractors, this did not impair performance because the chance of the target junction activating an inappropriate junction unit, harming performance, was offset by this occurring between distractors. In contrast, since search with homogeneous displays depends on grouping between distractors, inappropriate coding of distractors generated competition within what should have been stable distractor groups, impeding performance.

Thus, the effect of increasing the noise in SRR's activation functions is to produce a selective impairment on search with homogeneous (relative to heterogeneous) distractor junctions. This is the same pattern of disturbance observed in HJA, suggesting that HJA has a fundamental impairment due to increased noise in the processes that normally

Cumulative Probability

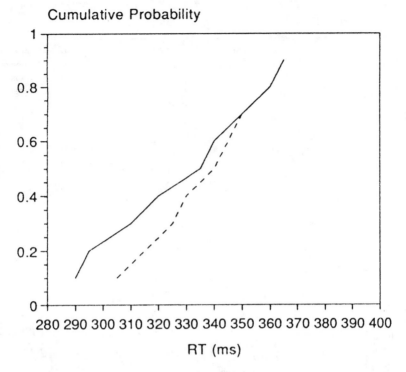

*Figure* 4b: SRR's search for single and dual form conjunction targets. The panel presents the dual target (solid line) and sum of single target (dashed line) cumulative distribution functions (SRR data based on first-pass positive RTs).

group together computationally important properties of forms, such as corner junctions. This impairs image segmentation via parallel grouping; elements in the field that ought to group instead form competing subgroups, leading to inappropriate segmentation of images, and, consequently, to impaired object identification.

Note that, with heterogeneous displays, the lesioned (high-temperature) SRR model performed less efficiently on Absent trials than the unlesioned (low-temperature) model, while HJA showed no such difference relative to the control subjects. This discrepancy does not pose a serious problem for SRR. A good fit can be obtained by fine-tuning the simulation parameters, in particular: by lowering the network temperature (e.g., to 0.075) and/or by relaxing the permitted growth in error rates across display size (error checking criteria). It should be borne in mind that, while SRR's speed-accuracy trade-off functions could be precisely matched between the lesioned and unlesioned simulations, this was not possible for HJA and the control subjects. Thus, although

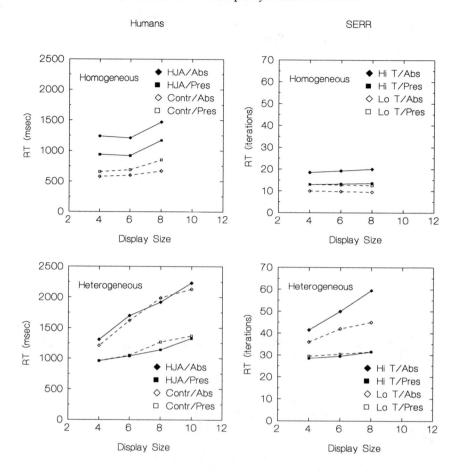

*Figure* 5: Human subjects' (left) and SRR's (right) search for form conjunction targets amongst homogeneous (top) and heterogeneous (bottom) distractors. Each panel shows the present and absent response times (RTs) (in msec or iterations) as a function of display size, separately for HJA and age-matched controls (left) and SRR with high (Hi T: 0.10) and low (Lo T: 0.05) network temperatures (right).

discrepancies between the simulations and the human data are potentially revealing about shortcomings of SRR, what is important in the present context is the qualitative similarity between the simulations and the human data, rather than their quantitative similarity.

## *Lesioning SRR: Spatial Neglect and Extinction*

Two recent studies have reported that, in patients with spatial extinction following unilateral parietal brain damage, the degree of the deficit – namely, extinction of a stimulus presented contralateral to the lesion in the presence of an ipsilateral stimulus – can be modulated by the similarity relationship between the two stimuli. Baylis, Driver, and Rafal (1993) observed that, when presented with one coloured letter stimulus on each side of the display, their patients tended to miss the stimulus contralateral to their lesion. The miss rate was increased when the two stimuli were the same on the to-be-reported dimension (colour or shape), but similarity on the irrelevant dimension had no effect. Ward, Goodrich, and Driver (1994) reported that Gestalt-based grouping between two items in the ipsilesional and contralesional fields reduced extinction.

Olson and Humphreys (1995) recently demonstrated these apparently contradictory, negative and positive, effects of similarity in a single patient, GK, who had suffered bilateral parietal lesions (a right occipito-parietal lesion and a left temporal-parietal lesion). GK took part in two experiments. In the first, he had to identify a red target letter presented at fixation, which could be flanked by a green distractor letter either to the right or left (stimuli were shown for 200 msec). The target letter was either curved (C, G, O) or angular (A, E, T), and the flanking distractor letter had either similar features or different features. GK identified over 80% of single (unflanked) target letters correctly and 80% with a left distractor. With a right distractor, his accuracy averaged only 40% and exhibited a negative effect of target-distractor similarity: it was less than 30% with a similar right distractor and more than 50% with a dissimilar right distractor. See top half of Table 3 for the results. In the second experiment, GK had to discriminate a central red target letter – C or A – which could be flanked by a green distractor symbol – Ɔ or ∩ – presented to the right. The distractors were chosen so that the Ɔ, but not the ∩, grouped with the C target, while neither distractor grouped with the A target (which served as a control). GK identified about 80% of single C targets correctly, but performance was markedly better with a Ɔ distractor (approximately 80%) than with a ∩ distractor (50%). This positive effect of target-distractor similarity was not simply due to guessing the identity of the target, C, from the distractor, Ɔ, since performance for the A target was equally reduced (by about 30%) with both types of distractor. See bottom half of Table 3.

Olson and Humphreys (1995) reasoned that the crucial factor for these differential effects of target-distractor similarity was the strength of the distractor (in the privileged, right, location) relative to that of the emergent target-distractor object. In Experiment 2, strong grouping between target and distractor – that is, C Ɔ – facilitated the emergence of one object, benefiting performance; but when grouping – that is, C ∩ – was weak, the representation of the distractor was dominant, impairing performance. In Experiment 1, the representation of the distractor,

|  | GK | SRR |
|---|---|---|
| **Experiment/Simulation 1** | | |
| **Target alone** | 82 | 74 |
| **Distractor left (control)** | | |
| **Similar distractor** | 77 | — |
| **Dissimilar distractor** | 84 | — |
| **Distractor right** | | |
| **Similar distractor** | 28 | 34 |
| **Dissimilar distractor** | 51 | 56 |
| **Experiment/Simulation 2** | | |
| **Control target** | | |
| **Target alone** | 90 A | — |
| **Similar distractor** | 56 Ɔ | — |
| **Dissimilar distractor** | 59 ∩ | — |
| **Critical target** | | |
| **Target alone** | 80 C | 76 ⊥ |
| **Similar distractor** | 76 Ɔ | 70 ⊥ |
| **Dissimilar distractor** | 51 ∩ | 56 ⅃ |

*Table* 3: Negative (Experiment/Simulation 1) and positive effects (Experiment/Simulation 2) of target-distractor similarity in a patient with spatial extinction, GK, and SRR. The table presents the percentages of correct target identifications. Also shown are the target and distractor stimuli used in Experiment/Simulation 2.

a familiar letter that did not cohere with the target to form a single object, was also dominant, and high target-distractor similarity may simply have reinforced the distractor as the dominant object for selection.

Olson and Humphreys (1995) went on to examine whether positive and negative similarity effects could be simulated by a version of SRR with selective lesions to the outputs from the match map to the template units, reducing (by some random amount) the likelihood that a template unit would be activated even if there were appropriate input from connected match map units. The lesion was spatially specific – that is, the (range of the random) reduction was larger on the left than in the middle of the field, and larger in the middle than in the right of the field. Performance was examined in two simulations which both required detection of an inverted-T target ($\perp$) presented in the lesioned part of the field (with the number of network cycles limited to fix the accuracy for single targets at about 80%). In Simulation 1, the target had to be identified either alone or in the presence of a target-similar upright-T distractor (⊤), sharing the vertical line feature in the same relative location within the shape, or a target-dissimilar right-oriented T distractor (⊣). Performance was reduced by the presence of a distractor relative to a single target, but more markedly so with a target-similar than a target- dissimilar distractor; see top half of Table 3 (negative similarity effect). In Simulation 2, the target was paired with one of two distractors, either a ⌐ or a ⌐, that were nonobjects to the model in the sense that corresponding representations did not exist at match map or template levels. The ⌐ distractor was similar to the target (sharing a vertical line feature at the same relative location), similar to the ⊤ distractor in Simulation 1. Performance was higher when the target was paired with a similar nonobject distractor than with a dissimilar nonobject distractor; see bottom half of Table 3 (positive similarity effect).

In the model, these differential effects of target-distractor similarity arise as follows. In Simulation 1, the ⊥ target tended to activate the match map unit for a (similar) ⊤ distractor at the target's location, producing competition at the match map level. Activation of the ⊤ unit at the target location was supported by the presence of a ⊤ distractor in the unlesioned part of the field. There was also competition at the level of the template units, with the ⊤ distractor template being supported by activation of the ⊤ match map unit at the target location. As a result of these competitive interactions, the ⊥ target in the lesioned area of the field tended to lose against the distractor, in particular when the distractor was target-similar. In Simulation 2, the unfamiliar ⌐ distractor tended to activate both the ⊥ (target) and ⊤ (nontarget) match map units at the distractor location. However, the presence of a ⊥ target favoured the activation of the ⊥ match map unit at the distractor location, and the (grouped) target and distractor match map units in turn supported the activation of the ⊥ target template. (In contrast, the dissimilar ⌐ distractor, rather than grouping with the target, tended to produce competition by activating the ⊣ and ⊤ nontargets.)

Thus, in SRR, positive effects of similarity arise when targets, but not distractors, have stored representations, while negative effects emerge when both targets and distractors have stored representations. Distractors with stored representations shift the critical level of competition from that at which stimuli are bound into perceptual objects to that at which they activate response-relevant templates. However, what is likely to be critical is not the presence or absence of stored representations (as simulated), but the relative strength of the representations for individual targets and distractors and for target-distractor groups. If the combined target and distractor form a more familiar or better object than the distractor alone, the emergent target-distractor object may sometimes win the competition for selection over a distractor presented in a spatially advantaged position (e.g., in the right visual field of a patient with left neglect).

A different way of conceptualizing the human performance and model dynamics in Experiments 1 and 2 and, respectively, Simulations 1 and 2, is in terms of *response level interference* produced by the distractors (we are grateful to R. Ward for suggesting this to us): in Experiment 1, "nontargets [which are reportable letters] ... can produce interference with the response associated with the target ... By increasing similarity, and therefore grouping, the probability of selecting the distractor is increased, and so then is the response level interference from the distractor" (R. Ward, personal communication, October 24, 1995). However, in Experiment 2, the nontarget is a nonletter which would not be expected to produce response level interference. "Grouping/similarity between target and nontarget ... might even produce a benefit if selection of the distractor pulls out the grouped target letter" (ibid.). In SRR, response level interference is equivalent to mutual inhibition between templates. In Simulation 1, response level (template) interference is increased by similarity, since the distractor's template is partially reinforced by the target and the target is too weak (on the lesioned side) to overcome competition from the distractor. In Simulation 2, response level (template) competition is eliminated because there is no template corresponding to the distractor. The only effect of the distractor can then be at the match map (grouping) level, where it tends to reinforce the representation of the target.

Thus, SRR, by incorporating multiple loci of competition for selection, can simulate both positive and negative effects of target-distractor similarity of the type observed in patients with extinction. The simulations can, of course, never prove that SRR's account is correct. But they do show that the performance of a model that was developed on the basis of data from a different (visual search) paradigm is consistent with the data. In summary, positive and negative effects of target-distractor similarity emerge out of SRR as it stands. It is difficult to see how negative as well as positive effects might emerge in alternative models designed to simulate spatial neglect and extinction (e.g., Cohen, Romero, Servan-Schreiber, & Farah, 1994; Mozer & Behrmann, 1990) unless they are suitably extended.

## Discussion

We have shown that SRR can account for a large range of human search data, including: the effects of target-distractor and distractor-distractor similarity; error functions under response deadline conditions; RT functions and distributions under dual target conditions; abnormal search patterns in a visual agnosic patient; and positive and negative effects of target-distractor similarity in patients with spatial extinction. Other human search data accounted for by SRR include: the relation between target detection and localization; and the contrast between search for a known target and a target defined by being an "odd one out" (see Humphreys & Müller, 1993).

### Relations to Other Models

In most of these cases, alternative, SSTS-based models make incorrect predictions or cannot coherently account for apparently contradictory effects. One computationally (though not neuronally) implemented SSTS-based model is Guided Search (GS) developed by Wolfe and his colleagues (e.g., Cave & Wolfe, 1990; Wolfe, 1994; Wolfe, Cave, & Franzel, 1989). GS assumes that the visual field is initially represented, in parallel, as a set of basic stimulus attributes in separate modules (such as colour, orientation, etc.). Each dimension-specific module computes a saliency signal for each item, indicating how dissimilar it is in comparison with the other items represented in the module (the more dissimilar it is, the greater its saliency). Dimension-specific saliency values are computed in parallel for all stimulus locations, and these signals are then summed across dimensions by units in an overall map of activations / locations. The activity on this master map is used to guide focal attention, the most active locations being sampled in priority. Focal attention gates the passage of visual information to the higher stages of processing (i.e., object recognition and response systems). GS also incorporates top-down control of attention, which can be used to make the search more efficient when the target identity is known in advance. Top-down control is dimension-specific, and involves parallel comparisons of the feature values at each location, with the desired feature value defining the target. The better the match between the desired and actual feature values, the larger the top-down enhancement. Top-down knowledge provides a useful means of guiding search, in particular for targets defined by a conjunction of features. Together, the bottom-up (feature contrast) and top-down mechanisms implemented in GS go a long way in explaining similarity effects in both single-feature and feature-conjunction search. For example, in conjunction search, the discriminability of the target-defining features will influence the relative master map activations achieved by the target and distractors, and hence will affect the likelihood that the target is selected first (when noise is added to the output of the parallel processing stage). However, GS maintains that conjunctions are focally attended to and coded in a spatially serial manner. It thus fails to explain, for example, how there can be overadditive effects in search situations with dual conjunction targets in the display, violating Miller's (1982) race model inequality (see above).

One other recent (but not fully implemented) model that can account for such redundant target benefits is the Spatial and Object Search algorithm (SOS) proposed by Grossberg, Mingolla, and Ross (1994). See Ross, Mejia-Monasterio, and Mingolla (1995) for a demonstration of overadditive effects due to grouping between dual conjunction targets in human subjects and SOS. According to SOS, the search runs through a series of dimension-specific (similarity-based) grouping processes, homing in on the target. For example, colour-based grouping may be used to isolate a candidate target region that may comprise a number of items sharing the target colour. This region may then be further segmented into subregions on the basis of a new dimension (e.g., orientation), and so forth, until a target is detected. That SOS, like SRR, is capable of simulating overadditive redundant target benefits is not surprising, given that it embodies two of SRR's central tenets: preattentive grouping and recursive rejection (the serial, recursive, operation of dimension-specific grouping processes in SOS is analogous to Humphreys and Müller's, 1993, Search via Recursive Rejection, SRR, principle). However, unlike SRR, SOS is not fully implemented. Consequently, it is difficult to assess whether SOS would be as successful as SRR in simulating the temporal dynamics of human performance and patterns of performance breakdown after brain lesions.

## Limitations of SRR

Although the SRR model can account for a large range of human performance data, it is limited as a general account of visual search and selection. Particular limitations are that: (i) it deals with fixed-domain, two-dimensional form junctions; (ii) it is not sensitive to nonaccidental properties of shape (such as [long-range] collinearity, parallelism, closure); (iii) grouping involves interactions between junction units that are retinotopically coded. Concerning point (iii), it is clear that the model encounters the binding problem (see Introduction). To provide a more general solution to the question of image segmentation between multiple objects, the binding problem must be addressed.

The crucial question is whether SRR's basic architecture and operation could naturally be extended to deal with search for targets defined across separable dimensions. It should be noted in this context that the within-domain data of Müller et al.'s (1994) dual-target experiments show good agreement with the cross-dimension data of Mordkoff et al. (1990) and Ward and McClelland (1989). This suggests that: (i) the processes involved in intradimensional and transdimensional conjunction search are not fundamentally different; and, (ii) since SRR provides a reasonable account of the human form-domain data, its basic operation (recursive rejection of grouped display items and error checking) should also, in principle, extend to search for transdimensional conjunctions.

Grouping within the form domain may be plausibly explained by within-map crosstalk between units coding single form conjunctions. However, it is unlikely that this approach is feasible for explaining grouping across separate dimensions. One possible alternative, which we are currently exploring further, is given by temporal binding (synchronization) of single-feature units across dimension-specific maps.

## Temporal Image Binding and Segmentation

The idea of using temporal synchrony in the firing of processing units in order to bind features dynamically was first introduced by von der Malsburg (1975, 1987). More recently, evidence for synchronous firing of neurons linked to global properties of patterns has been reported by Singer and colleagues (e.g., Eckhorn, Frien, Bauer, Kerr & Woelbern, 1993a; Eckhorn, Frien, Bauer, Woelbern & Kerr, 1993b; Engel, König, Kreiter, Schillen & Singer, 1992; Gray, König, Engle & Singer, 1989; Gray & Singer, 1989). For instance, visual cortical neurons in the cat and monkey (e.g., Eckhorn et al., 1993a, 1993b), exhibit oscillatory responses that are synchronized over relatively large distances of the cortex (within and across visual areas) in a stimulus-specific manner. Further, these synchronized oscillations can be established very rapidly, within 100–200 msec (Gray et al., 1989). This last point is of some importance if synchronized firing is to play a role for object coding in the brain, where there is rapid activation of higher order neurons (in temporal cortex) within similar time periods (e.g., see Thorpe & Imbert, 1989, for a review).

Temporal binding could provide an efficient and elegant means of representing the grouped features of complex objects. For example, Feldman and Ballard (1982) consider the presence of a red square and blue circle in the visual field which activate feature units for red, blue, square and circle. Without temporal binding, it is difficult to link the features appropriately without representing each possible combination across the field. With temporal binding, the two objects would be represented by the synchronized firing of the red and square units and the blue and circle units, respectively (where the two assemblies would fire on different slices of time). There would thus be no need to replicate units for specific combinations of features across the field. Temporal binding of features across separate dimensions could be achieved by Re-entrant Cortical Integration (RCI) (Finkel & Edelman, 1989; Finkel,

Reeke, & Edelman, 1992; see also Zeki, 1993), where re-entry is a "dynamic, temporally ongoing, parallel, and recursive process" of signalling along feedforward and feedback connections between visual areas.

In a system with temporal image binding and segmentation, recognition may involve higher order units responding to combinations of image features that are relatively abstracted from the absolute position of the features on the retina. However, actions (e.g., picking up the blue circle) need to be directed to specific locations (e.g., Allport, 1987). This may be accomplished by having a set of location units, activated by the presence of items in the field rather than their identity, whose firing oscillates in phase with the identity units (which represent blue and circle). Considerable neurophysiological and neuropsychological evidence supports the separation of pattern recognition ("what") from location coding ("where") units in the brain (e.g., Desimone & Ungerleider, 1989; Ungerleider & Mishkin, 1982), and rudimentary ideas along these lines were incorporated into SRR's simulations of visual search.

The neurophysiological evidence for phase-locked temporal oscillations is not uncontroversial, but the idea is of such importance as to merit further exploration. There are already models of visual processing incorporating principles along this line – for example, see Hummel and Biederman's (1992) object (shape) recognition network. Yet to date, no psychophysical evidence has been found (to our knowledge) demonstrating that temporal image binding and segmentation is utilized in human vision (e.g., see Fahle, 1993; Fahle & Koch, 1995; in fact, the latter concluded that "spatial displacement, but not temporal asynchrony, destroys figural binding"). We are currently approaching this issue by using displays with multiple elements that either group or fail to group (the displays were developed by Donnelly, Humphreys & Riddoch, 1991, for which independent evidence of grouping was provided). We are looking for evidence that grouping occurs more strongly when elements are presented within the same time slice. Placing elements in a separate slice along with distractor stimuli ought to disrupt grouping. The experimental paradigm we are developing will form the basis of a series of experiments that will be linked to computational studies of image segmentation using processing units with oscillatory patterns of activation.

## Acknowledgments

The work reported in this chapter was supported by grants from the Joint Research Council Initiative in Cognitive Science and Human Computer Interaction (UK), the Medical Research Council (UK), the Science and Engineering Research Council (UK) and the Human Frontier Science Programme (School of Psychology, University of Birmingham, UK). The authors would like to thank Kyle Cave, Robert Ward, and Richard Wright for their extremely helpful comments on an earlier version of this chapter. Hermann Müller can be contacted via e-mail at h.muller@psyc.bbk.ac.uk.

## Note

1 "SRR" refers to "Search via RecursiveRejection," the same phenomenon described earlier as "SERR" (SEarch via Recursive Rejection) in Müller, Humphreys, & Donnelley (1994).

2 The miss rate used in the simulations do not exactly match those produced by human subjects. For this reason, search rates and mean RTs cannot be directly compared. The emphasis is on qualitative similarities.

## References

Allport, D.A. (1987). Selection for action: Some behavioral and neurophysiological considerations of attention and action. In H. Heuer & A.F. Sanders (Eds.), *Perspectives on perception and action.* Hillsdale, NJ: Erlbaum.

Baylis, G.C., Driver, J., & Rafal, R.D. (1993). Visual extinction and stimulus repetition. *Journal of Cognitive Neuroscience, 5,* 453–466.

Cave, K.R., & Wolfe, J.M. (1990). Modeling the role of parallel processing in visual search. *Cognitive Psychology, 22,* 225–271.

Cohen, J.D., Romero, R.D., Servan-Schreiber, D., & Farah, M.J. (1994). Mechanisms of spatial attention: The relation of macrostructure to microstructure in parietal attentional deficits. *Journal of Cognitive Neuroscience, 6,* 337–387.

Desimone, R., & Ungerleider, L.G. (1989). Neural mechanisms of visual processing in monkeys. In F. Boller & J. Grafman (Eds.), *Handbook of neuropsychology,* Vol. 2 (pp. 267–299). Elsevier: Amsterdam.

Donnelly, N., Humphreys, G.W., & Riddoch, J.M. (1991). Parallel computation of primitive shape descriptions. *Journal of Experimental Psychology: Human Perception & Performance, 17,* 561–570.

Duncan, J., & Humphreys, G.W. (1989). Visual search and stimulus similarity. *Psychological Review, 96,* 433–458.

Duncan, J., & Humphreys, G.W. (1992) Beyond the search surface: Visual search and attentional engagement. *Journal of Experimental Psychology: Human Perception & Performance, 18,* 578–588.

Eckhorn, R., Frien, A., Bauer, R., Kehr, H., & Woelbern, T. (1993a). Phase-locked high frequency oscillations between visual cortical areas V1 and V2 of an awake monkey. In N. Elsner & M. Heisenberg (Eds.), *Gene, brain, behaviour.* Stuttgart: Thieme.

Eckhorn, R., Frien, A., Bauer, R., Woelbern, T., & Kehr, H. (1993b). High-frequency (60–90 Hz) oscillations in primary visual cortex of awake monkey. *NeuroReport, 4,* 243–246.

Engel, A.K., König, P., Kreiter, A.K., Schillen, T.B., & Singer, W. (1992). Temporal coding in the visual cortex: new vistas on integration in the nervous system. *Trends in Neuroscience, 15,* 218–226.

Fahle, M. (1993). Figure-ground discrimination from temporal information. *Proceedings of the Royal Society of London B, 254*, 199–203.

Fahle, M., & Koch, C. (1995). Spatial displacement, but not temporal asynchrony, destroys figural binding. *Vision Research, 55*, 491–494.

Feldman, J.A., & Ballard, D.H. (1982). Connectionist models and their properties. *Cognitive Science, 6*, 205–254.

Felleman, D.J., & Van Essen, D.C. (1991). Distributed hierarchical processing in the primate cerebral cortex. *Cerebral Cortex, 1*, 1–47.

Finkel, L.H., & Edelman, G.M. (1989). The integration of distributed cortical systems by reentry: A computer simulation of interactive functionally segregated visual areas. *Journal of Neuroscience, 9*, 3188–3208.

Finkel, L.H., Reeke, G.N., & Edelman, G.M. (1992). A cortically based model for integration in visual perception. In H. Wechsler, (Ed.), *Neural networks for perception*, Vol. 1. Boston, MA: Academic Press.

Gray, C.M., König, P., Engel, A.E., & Singer, W. (1989). Oscillatory responses in cat visual cortex exhibit inter-column synchronisation which reflects stimulus properties. *Nature, 338*, 334–337.

Gray, C.M., & Singer, W. (1989). Stimulus specific neuronal oscillations in orientation columns of cat visual cortex. *Proceedings of the National Academy of Science, 86*, 1698–1702.

Grossberg, S., Mingolla, E., & Ross, W.D. (1994). A neural theory of attentive visual search: Interaction of boundary, surface, spatial, and object representations. *Psychological Review, 101*, 470–489.

Hinton, G.E., & Sejnowski, T.J. (1986). Learning and relearning in Boltzmann machines. In D.E. Rumelhart & J.L. McClelland (Eds.), *Parallel distributed processing*, Vol. 1, (pp. 282–317). Cambridge, MA: MIT Press.

Hummel, J.E., & Biederman, I. (1992). Dynamic binding in a neural network for shape recognition. *Psychological Review, 99*, 480–517.

Humphreys, G.W., Freeman, T.A.C., & Müller, H.J. (1992). Lesioning a connectionist model of visual search: Selective effects on distractor grouping. *Canadian Journal of Psychology, 46*, 417–460.

Humphreys, G.W., & Müller, H.J. (1993). SEarch via Recursive Rejection (SERR): A connectionist model of visual search. *Cognitive Psychology, 25*, 43–110.

Humphreys, G.W., Quinlan, P.T., & Riddoch, M.J. (1989). Grouping processes in visual search: Effects with single- and combined-feature targets. *Journal of Experimental Psychology: General, 118*, 258–279.

Humphreys, G.W., & Riddoch, M.J. (1987). *To see but not to see: A case study of visual agnosia*. London: Erlbaum.

Humphreys, G.W., Riddoch, M.J., Donnelly, N., Freeman, T., Boucart, M., & Müller, H.J. (1994). Intermediate visual processing and visual agnosia. In M.J. Farah & G. Ratcliff (Eds.), *The neuropsychology of high-level vision* (pp. 63–101). Hillsdale, NJ: Erlbaum.

Humphreys, G.W, Riddoch, M.J., Quinlan, P.T., Price, C.N., & Donnelly, N. (1992). Parallel pattern processing and visual agnosia. *Canadia Journal of Psychology, 46*, 377–416.

Julesz, B. (1975). Experiments in the visual perception of texture. *Scientific American, 232,* 34–43.

Julesz, B. (1986). Texton gradient: The texton theory revisited. *Biological Cybernetics, 54,* 245–251.

Marr, D. (1982). *Vision.* Freeman: New York.

Miller, J. (1982). Divided attention: Evidence for coactivation with redundant signals, *Cognitive Psychology, 14,* 247–279.

Mozer, M.C., & Behrmann, M. (1990). On the interaction of selective attention and lexical knowledge: A connectionist account of neglect dyslexia. *Journal of Cognitive Neuroscience, 2,* 96–123.

Mordkoff, T.J., Yantis, S., & Egeth, H.E. (1990). Detecting conjunctions of color and form in parallel. *Perception & Psychophysics, 48,* 157–168.

Müller, H.J., & Humphreys, G.W. (1993). A connectionist model of visual search for simple form conjunctions. In D. Brogan, A. Gale & K. Carr (Eds.), *Visual Search 2* (pp. 61–71). London: Taylor & Francis.

Müller, H.J., Humphreys, G.W., & Donnelly, N. (1994). SEarch via Recursive Rejections (SERR): Visual search for single and dual form conjunction targets. *Journal of Experimental Psychology: Human Perception & Performance, 20,* 235–258.

Olson, A.C., & Humphreys, G.W. (1995). Similarity effects and visual extinction: Neuropsychological and computational evidence. *Cognitive Neuropsychology,* in press.

Pashler, H. (1987). Detecting conjunctions of color and form. *Perception & Psychophysics, 41,* 191–201.

Ross, W.D., Mejia-Monasterio, N., & Mingolla, E. (1995). Grouping effects in double target visual search. Unpublished manuscript.

Thorpe, S.J., & Imbert, M. (1989). In R. Pfeifer, Z. Schreter & F. Fogelman-Soulie (Eds.), *Connectionism in perspective* (pp. 63–92). Amsterdam: Elsevier.

Treisman, A. (1988). Features and objects: The fourteenth Bartlett memorial lecture. *Quarterly Journal of Experimental Psychology, 40A,* 201–237.

Treisman, A., & Gelade, G. (1980). A feature integration theory of attention. *Cognitive Psychology, 12,* 97–136.

Treisman, A., & Gormican, S. (1988). Feature analysis in early vision. *Psychological Review, 95,* 15–48.

Treisman, A., & Sato, S. (1990). Conjunction search revisited. *Journal of Experimental Psychology: Human Perception & Performance, 16,* 459–478.

Treisman, A.M., Cavanagh, P., Fischer, B., Ramachandran, V.S., & von der Heydt, R. (1990). Form perception and attention: Striate cortex and beyond. In L. Spillman & J.S. Werner (Eds.), *Visual perception: The neurophysiological foundations.* San Diego: Academic Press.

Ungerleider, L.G., & Mishkin, M. (1982). Two cortical visual systems. In D.J. Ingle, M.A. Goodale & R.J.W. Mansfield (Eds.), *Analysis of visual behavior* (pp. 549–586). Cambridge, MA: MIT Press.

Van Essen, D.C. (1985). Functional organisation of the primate visual cortex. In A.A. Peters & E.G. Jones (Eds.), *Cerebral Cortex* Vol. 3. New York: Plenum Press.

Von der Malsburg, C. (1975). Nervous structures with dynamical links. *Berichte der Bunsen-Gesellschaft für Physikalische Chemie, 89,* 703–709.

Von der Malsburg, C. (1987). Synaptic plasticity as a basis of brain organisation. In J.P. Chaneaux & M. Konishi (Eds.), *The neural and molecular basis of learning.* New York: Wiley.

Ward, R., Goodrich, S., & Driver, J. (1994). Grouping reduces visual extinction: Neuropsychological weight-linkage in visual selection. *Visual Cognition, 1,* 101–129.

Ward, R., & McClelland, J.L. (1989). Conjunctive search for one and two identical targets, *Journal of Experimental Psychology: Human Perception & Performance, 15,* 664–672.

Wolfe, J.M. (1994). Guided Search 2.0: A revised model of visual search. *Psychonomic Bulletin & Review, 1,* 202–238.

Wolfe, J.M., Cave, K.R., & Franzel, S.L. (1989). Guided Search: An alternative to the feature integration model for visual search. *Journal of Experimental Psychology: Human Perception & Performance, 15,* 419–433.

Zeki, S. (1993). *A vision of the brain.* London: Blackwell Scientific Publications.

# 16

## Attentional Emphasis in Visual Orienting and Resolving

### David LaBerge

This chapter examines the role of attention in the perception of an object, particularly when an object is displayed with other objects. Attention is typically directed to a particular object (termed the target object) by a cue which, through training or instructions, indicates the location of that object in the visual field. Other objects that appear with the target object are typically referred to as distractors, and subjects may or may not be explicitly instructed to ignore them. Despite the label, distractors may not always exert an observable distracting effect on the processing of the target. A major purpose of this essay is to describe some general task conditions together with two neuroanatomical mechanisms that seem to influence how a distractor may or may not affect the processing of a target.

Recent research has given us a relatively clear picture of the major effects of distractors at the time of the onset of a display (Folk, Remington, & Johnston, 1992; Koshino, Warner, & Juola, 1992; Theeuwes, 1991; Wright, 1994; Wright & Ward, 1997; for a review see Yantis, 1993). Onsets of distractors can interrupt ongoing attention to a target and typically induce a shift of attention to the distractor. Two potent ways to vary the magnitude of the distractor effect on target processing are to change the luminance associated with the distractor onset and to change the intensity of attention directed at the target prior to the onset of the display.

Experiments conducted to investigate the effect of abrupt distractor onsets on the interruption of target-directed attention typically position the distractor sufficiently far from the target to define clearly two separate objects. When a distractor is placed as close to a target object as two adjacent letters on a page of text, the ensemble of objects may initially be perceived as one object, particularly when it is located away from a centre fixation point (see Figure 1). In this case, the entire cluster may produce the onset effect as a single object. Nevertheless, the presence of close distractors is known to exert a profound effect on the attentional processing of the target (e.g., Eriksen & Eriksen, 1974; LaBerge, Carter, & Brown, 1992).

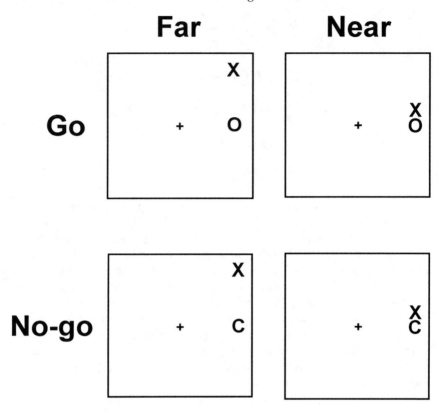

*Figure* 1: Idealized displays in which orienting may be contrasted with resolving. Subjects are first shown a central cross followed by two objects. The instructions are to identify the target shape, a letter which appears to the right (shown here) or to the left of the cross (not shown here). A letter (or letters) in other locations are regarded as a distractor(s). When the distance between the target and distractor is sufficiently large (Far), the display is presumed to induce orienting only; when the distance between the target and distractor is small (Near), the display is presumed to induce resolving after orienting to the cluster of two objects.

## Orienting versus Resolving

It has been proposed that different mechanisms of attention dominate the processing of a target when a distractor is positioned near to rather than far from the target (LaBerge, 1995a, 1995b). The proposal specifies that when the target and distractor are sufficiently separated to induce different eye movements (although an overt eye movement itself may not be executed), the oculomotor circuits corresponding to a saccade to each object's location mutually inhibit each other, and the circuit that receives the larger input activation becomes dominant in a winner-take-all type of competition. When the target and distractor are sufficiently close to each other to induce only one eye movement, then the proposal specifies that circuits in the thalamus that correspond to each object's location mutually inhibit each other, and the circuit having the greater input activation becomes dominant, again in a winner-take-all type of competition. The reasoning leading up to this two-mechanism proposal for spatial attention involves several considerations that will be described in the paragraphs which follow.

Although tasks whose displays exhibit near or far target-distractor separations appear to have the same general computational goal of selecting or partitioning the information arising from the target and distractor locations, their specific computational goals appear to differ. When objects are well separated, the specific goal is simply to orient the sensory receptors of the fovea to the target's location, and when objects are in such close proximity that they stimulate many of the same sensory receptors, the specific goal is to resolve the overlapping information arising from the target and distractor locations. For example, when the word *cat* is displayed, the observer first orients to the whole word and then can report the middle letter of the word without changing the orientation of the eye, either overtly or covertly. Attending to the word as a whole is relatively straightforward, since no distractor is present in the display, but attending to the centre letter involves a competition between the centre target letter and the distractor letters on each side of it. More specifically, the competition is between sources of information whose registrations in cortical neurons (e.g., neurons in area V1) overlap considerably. The problem for the visual system, then, is to separate or resolve the information of the target source from overlapping information arising from the distractors.

The general problem of how input information is selected by orienting, by resolution, or by both confronts the engineer engaged in designing a robot that must quickly identify a target object in a cluttered visual scene. Although theoretically there are many different algorithms that can be constructed to compute orienting operations and resolution operations, an informal comparison of the problems to be solved in orienting and resolution suggests that the class of algorithms that produces resolution is probably more complex than the class that produces orienting. However, it is well to keep in mind that it is possible to design complicated computations to perform simple operations (as in a Rube Goldberg device), and that circuits of the nervous system apparently have been selected phylogenically on the basis of factors other than their engineering optimality.

It may be helpful to consider the computational question of whether or not one algorithm could perform both orienting and resolving, and whether or not such an algorithm would be more effective in some sense than two separate algorithms. For such an algorithm, the distance between target and distractor is represented by a parameter that can increase continuously from zero to the limiting case in which the distractor moves out of the visual field and the target is displayed alone. A clear answer to this question requires a more formal computational description of orienting and resolving than is presented here, but when considering how the brain selects target information in a visual scene, one might look for two different mechanisms rather than one. Physiological research has suggested that the superior colliculus contains a mechanism for orienting to spatially separated objects (Rafal, Posner, Friedman, Inhoff, & Bernstein, 1988; Rizzolatti, Riggio, Dascola, & Umilta, 1987; Sheliga, Riggio, & Rizzolatti, 1994; Wurtz, Goldberg, & Robinson, 1980), although the orienting operations in the superior colliculus may be more typically involved with the stimulus-driven (exogenous) type, while the parietal areas may be more involved with the voluntarily driven (endogenous) type of orienting (Bowman, Brown, Kertzman, Schwartz, & Robinson, 1993; Kingstone & Klein, 1993; Klein 1994; Rafal & Robertson, 1995; Robinson, Bowman, & Kertzman, 1995; Robinson & Kertzman, 1995). Physiological research also suggests that the thalamus contains a mechanism that selectively resolves information arising from closely spaced objects (LaBerge, 1990; Liotti, Fox, & LaBerge, 1994). These considerations lead to the hypothesis that the brain may employ two separate mechanisms rather than one mechanism to solve the problem of target-distractor competition, when the distance that separates a target from a distractor can vary along a continuum ranging from the very small to the very large. In an attempt to clarify the operations believed to be involved in orienting and resolving, this chapter describes a neural-based model of spatial attention for the solving of target-distractor competitions, in which the relative contributions of superior collicular and thalamic circuits may vary according to the spatial separation of the target and its distractor(s).

## The Expression of Attention

In describing the mechanisms by which orienting and resolving may be accomplished in the brain, it is helpful to consider what the output of these mechanisms are assumed to accomplish in terms of attentional processing. In other words, we ask how attention is expressed in the flow of neural information in brain pathways. An illustrative example may serve to introduce the assumption of attentional expression as it is employed in this chapter.

If the word *stone* were displayed and an observer is asked to identify the middle letter of the word, somewhere in the observer's system the information arising from the location of the centre letter must be segregated from the information arising from the surrounding (distracting) letters; otherwise the observer will simply identify the whole word *stone*, or, while the width of attention is being narrowed to the target size of one letter, the observer may briefly identify the nested words *tone*, *ton*, *one*, *to* or *on*. The operation of attention in selecting information from the location of the centre letter (or from that of the nested words) is assumed to correspond to a higher firing rate in neural pathways corresponding to the location of the centre letter than in pathways corresponding to the locations of the surrounding letters. This difference between activity at target and distractor sites in the brain may be accomplished in three general ways: by enhancing the activity at the target site, by suppressing the activity at the distractor sites, or by doing both. These three operations, or algorithms, by which attention is expressed may be regarded as instances of modulatory emphasis. Consider how one might induce an observer to attend to the middle letter of the word *stone*: one could vary the sensory input by increasing the intensity or thickness of the ink in which the letter O is printed, or by decreasing the ink intensity or thickness of the surrounding letters, or one could do both. However, in the absence of such emphasis in the sensory input, there is still the need for an emphasis of the information in the letter O, somewhere else in the observer's system in order to select information arising from the target location away from the information arising from the distractor locations. And that emphasis is assumed to be produced by one of the three algorithms.

All three algorithms of attentional expression may be regarded as modulatory changes in the neural signal, as opposed to informational changes, and therefore are grouped under the term *emphasis*, whose meaning appears to reach across the cognitive science disciplines of cognitive psychology, computational science, neuroscience, and philosophy of mind.

Three main descriptive questions are to be asked of attentional expression: When does it begin, how long does it last, and how intense is it (more specifically, what is the time course of its intensity while it lasts)? For example, in the case of attending to unexpected abrupt stimulus onsets, the expression of attention may be very brief but highly intense; when attending to singletons (a red apple seen among many green apples), the expression may be brief but less intense; but in both cases, the cortical activity corresponding to these stimulus events may at times be prolonged and/or intensified beyond its initial registration, presumably by operations arising from areas of executive control residing either in the anterior cingulate cortex (Posner & Petersen, 1990) or in the prefrontal cortex (LaBerge, 1995a, 1995b).

The expression of attention is manifest also during periods of preparation for an upcoming stimulus. A typical laboratory task that involves preparatory attention is the match-to-sample task. The observer is first shown a stimulus (the sample object), for example, an oriented bar, and after a delay a second stimulus appears (the test object), and the observer is instructed to make one response if the test item matches the sample stimulus, and to make another response (or withhold responding) if the test item does not match the sample stimulus. The match-to-sample task may be varied to test spatial location rather than object attribute or shape by presenting a stimulus in a particular location (the sample location), and after a delay a second stimulus in some location (the test location), and the observer is instructed to respond according to whether the sample and test locations match. Preparations to perceive the test object or location are presumed to undergo intensification during the course of the delay between the sample onset and the test onset, and the level of intensity of preparatory attentional expression is presumed to be regulated by the executive control in prefrontal cortex according to the difficulty of the test-to-sample match. The smaller the distance between target and distractor, the greater the difficulty of the task and therefore the greater the attentional demand.

The expression of attention, as described here, is presumed to take place in areas of the cerebral cortex, and several physiological measures have been used to identify specific areas of monkey and human cortex that are active during attention tasks: these include single-cell recordings, event-related potentials (ERPs), event-related fields (ERFs), positron emission tomography (PET), functional magnetic resonance imagery (fMRI), and, more indirectly, lesion studies. Some experiments that use these measures have attempted to determine whether the underlying neural signals expressing attention in specific areas are being enhanced, suppressed, or both. A review of a sample of these neurophysiological studies follows.

### Single-cell Recordings

In the 1970s, several investigators discovered cells in the parietal cortex and superior colliculus that showed enhanced firing when a monkey attended to a particular location in space (Robinson et al., 1978; Wurtz & Goldberg, 1972; Yin & Mountcastle, 1977). In the 1980s, Spitzer, Desimone, and Moran (1988) presented coloured and oriented bars to monkeys in a match-to-sample task, and found that cells in V4 increased their firing as the colour or orientation of the sample and test bars were made more similar. These findings strongly suggest that attention to object location and attributes such as colour and orientation is expressed by the enhancement of activity in particular neurons at the corresponding target site in the brain.

Other studies have shown that attention to the location of a target object when distracting objects are present produces enhancement of some cortical cells and suppression in others. In the early and influential study by Moran and Desimone (1985), a target and distractor presented in the receptive field of a V4 cell produced a suppression of firing, compared to the condition in which the distractor was presented outside the receptive field. Chelazzi, Miller, Duncan, and Desimone (1993) found the same pattern of results for cells in the inferotemporal (IT) area. In both of these studies the distance separating the target from the distractor appeared to be at least 1° or more of visual angle, enough to stimulate separate eye movements (although overt eye movements were prevented in their study).

In a related study of visual attention in the monkey, Motter (1993) used displays of oriented bars with two to seven distractors, and recorded from neurons in V1, V2, and V4. Although information about visual angles was not reported in this study, it appeared that the target-distractor distance was decreased as the number of distractors in the display increased. Motter found that the firing of neurons was modulated even when attention was directed to a stimulus outside the neuron's receptive field when large numbers of distractors were shown with the target. The majority of the responsive neurons in V1, V2, and V4 exhibited higher firing rates when attention was directed toward the neuron's receptive field than when attention was directed away from the neuron's receptive field. In each of these cortical areas, attention affected about one-third of the cells, and, of those cells, about two-thirds showed attentional modulatory effects only when at least one distractor was present with the target. To determine whether the modulatory differences in firing rates were produced by a relative increase or decrease in firing rates, the attend-toward and attend-away conditions were compared with a baseline condition. For the cells that showed an increase in firing when attention was directed toward the receptive field, half of the cells showed this increase due to a rise above baseline firing rate; the other half showed a decrease from baseline firing rate when attention was directed away from the receptive field. Therefore, modulatory emphasis in these 88% of cells was produced about equally often as enhancement at the target site and as suppression at the distractor sites. However, in the data reported, there was no clear trend favouring enhancement over suppression as the number of distractors increased (and the target-distractor distances decreased). For the 12% of cells that showed decreases in activity when attention was directed toward the receptive field, approximately 80% showed a decrease in activity below baseline level in the attend-toward condition.

In another related study, Maunsell (1995) reported single-cell recordings in V4 and in the motion-sensitive medial superior temporal area (MST) while the monkey directed attention to a target object that either fell in the receptive field of the cell or did not. In contrast to the findings of Moran and Desimone (1985), Maunsell found an enhancement of firing when the distractor was either inside or outside the receptive field of the cell.

For all of the foregoing studies of single-cell recordings in cortical areas, the vast majority of neurons that show modulatory changes during attention tasks produce higher firing rates when attention is directed toward their receptive fields than when attention is directed away from their receptive fields, regardless of whether the changes in firing rate come about by target enhancement or distractor suppression. These data therefore support the assumption that the expression of attention in the cortical substrate takes the form of a relative enhancement of neuronal activity at the target site compared to the activity at the distractor site. As to whether the algorithm that produces this relative enhancement is (a) enhancement of neural firing at the attended site, (b) suppression of neural firing at the distractor sites, or (c) both, the evidence for attention to object location appears to suggest that some cells show (a), and others (b), with no clear evidence of cells that show (c). On the other hand, the cellular recording evidence for attention to object attributes (Spitzer, Desimone, & Moran, 1988; Haenny & Schiller, 1988) so far seems to support (a).

### Event-related Potentials

Many studies in the literature show increased amplitudes of wave components of the ERP waveform while humans attend to visual locations (for a review, see Näätänen, 1990). However, most of these studies do not include the kind of control condition that indicates whether the observed ERPs produced this attentional effect by an enhancement of neuronal activity during the attend-toward condition or by a suppression of neuronal activity during the attend-away condition.

Luck et al. (1994) did include such a control condition in a luminance detection task that was compared with attend-toward and attend-away conditions, so that suppression or enhancement effects of attention could be distinguished. Displays consisted of four boxes placed at equal distances from a central fixation cross, and a central arrow cued the box that was most likely to display a small dot within it (valid condition). Occasionally a dot occurred in a box that was not cued on that trial (invalid condition). On other trials, all four boxes were cued (neutral condition). The early waveform components, P1 (at 100 ms following onset) and N1 (150 ms following onset), were compared across cued, uncued and neutral conditions. The ERP results showed that both the P1 and N1 waves showed greater amplitudes on cued trials than on uncued trials, thus indicating expressions of attention at these times. Determining whether these expressions of attention are produced by enhancements of activity at the attended target area or by suppressions of activity at the unattended distractor areas requires a comparison of the cued and uncued trials with the neutral trials. These comparisons showed that the P1 wave was reduced on uncued trials and not enhanced on cued trials, while the N1 component was enhanced on cued trials and not suppressed on uncued trials. The implications of these data for the present proposal concerning mechanisms of orienting and resolving will be discussed at the end of the next section on a neural model.

## Positron Emission Tomography

The current literature contains several PET studies of a subject's brain activity while attending to attributes and locations of objects. Many of these studies used the match-to-sample task to study attention to attributes or shape of an object, and many employed some form of location-cueing to study attention to the location of an object. Almost all of these studies compared attend-toward conditions with some form of neutral condition and found that attention to visual location or to various visual attributes such as shape, colour, and motion velocity produced increases in blood flow in particular areas of the cortex. Areas of the anterior cortex are particularly responsive to attentional planning of actions; for example, moving the fingers in a particular sequence (Roland, 1985), selecting what object attribute to attend to (Corbetta, Miezin, Dabmeyer, Shulman, & Petersen, 1991), and the generating of words (Petersen, Fox, Posner, Minton, & Raichle, 1988; Petersen, Fox, Snyder, & Raichle, 1990). Figure 2 shows the cortical areas that have been most consistently responsive to visual attention tasks in a sample of recent studies.

When humans attend to the shape or colour of an object, PET enhancements are found in cortical regions near the occipito-temporal border, which probably include areas V4 and IT in the monkey (face identification areas in the human brain appear to lie more anterior in the temporal lobe than face matching; Haxby et al., 1994; Sergent, Ohta, & MacDonald, 1992). Tasks involving attention to location produce increased blood flow in parietal areas (Corbetta, Miezin, Shulman, & Petersen, 1993; Haxby et al., 1994), although there is some controversy as to whether the parietal area activity arises only from

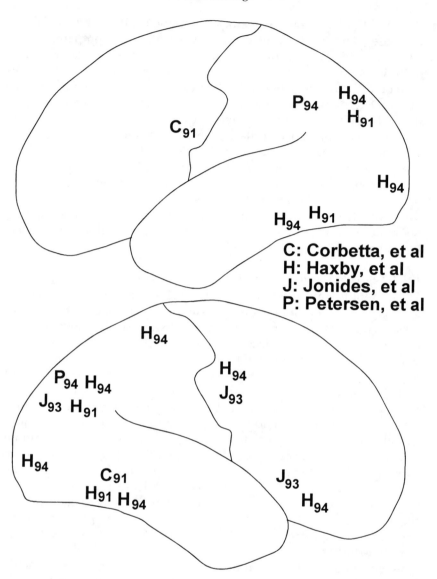

*Figure* 2: Cortical locations of increased blood flow in location and shape tasks indicated by positron emission tomography (PET) studies. Letter refers to the initial letter of the first author's name, and subscript refers to the year of the study.

attention shift operations (Posner, Walker, Friedrich, & Rafal, 1984), or from sustained attention to a location as well (LaBerge, 1995b). Sustained attention to an object typically involves storing in working memory some representation of its location and attributes between the time of the onset of the sample (or cue) and the onset of the test stimulus (Goldman-Rakic, 1988). In the anterior cortical areas, single-cell firings presumed to correspond to working memory have been found in the dorsolateral prefrontal cortex (DLPFC) for location and the ventrolateral prefrontal cortex (VLPFC) for shape and colour attributes (Wilson, O'Scalaidhe, & Goldman-Rakic, 1993). Storage of information relevant to the preparation of actions appears to enhance activity in the anterior cingulate cortex (ACC) and the supplemental motor area (SMA) as well as in parietal areas.

While a human is attending to an attribute of an object (e.g., its shape), brain activity as measured by PET in a particular cortical area is generally enhanced (over control conditions), but at the same time brain activity as measured by PET is not noticeably suppressed in areas that serve location (Haxby et al., 1994). However, while attending to visual aspects of an object, brain activity as measured by PET in tactual and auditory areas show significant suppression, and vice versa. Crossmodal suppression of neural activity was also observed by Hackley, Woldorff, and Hillyard (1990). Hence, these studies suggest that attention to one modality involves a diffuse suppression effect in other modalities, while focused attending within a modality involves a relatively precise enhancement effect within the region serving that modality. Thus, the between-versus-within modality hypothesis of attentional expression by suppression may hold only between relatively large cortical regions that are devoted to particular sensory modalities, while attentional expression by enhancement holds for smaller sectors of cortex within a given sensory subarea. Even though a particular sensory subarea shows both enhancement and suppression effects at the cellular level (as described in the foregoing section on single-cell recordings), the net activity of circuit clusters (in cortical columns) in that sensory area, measured by PET and ERPs, still appears to be produced by enhancement of those circuit clusters, and not simply by suppression of surrounding circuit clusters from a base rate of activity.

When PET data indicate an increase in activity (indicated by increased blood flow or metabolic uptake of glucose) in a particular brain area while subjects are engaged in a task (e.g., attending to a visual shape), it is generally concluded that increased neural activity is occurring in that brain area. But neural activity is expressed by both excitatory and inhibitory cells, so that activity increases as measured by PET could conceivably be indicating increased inhibitory activity in the region of interest. However, a general principle of neuroanatomy suggests that this interpretation is not likely, especially for cortical areas. It is known that a given cortical region (i.e., a cluster of cortical columns) contains about 75 to 80% excitatory cells (Hendry, Schwark, Jones, &

Yan, 1987) so that the average activity level of a sector of cortex measured by PET is almost always dominated by activity in the excitatory cells. Another principle relevant here is that long-range axons, particularly those that interconnect cortical areas, are almost always excitatory (Douglas & Martin, 1990). The notable exceptions to the long-range excitatory axon rule are the axons projected by the basal ganglia to the superior colliculus and to the thalamic nuclei that serve the anterior cortex. Hence, it appears that activity in one cortical area almost always excites rather than inhibits cells in other cortical areas.

In view of these considerations, increased activations as measured by PET in cortical areas during attention tasks appear to be generally interpretable as indicating enhanced activity in excitatory cells and circuits of that area and therefore as enhanced processing of neural information. Thus, the several cortical areas in Figure 1 that show activations as measured by PET while an observer is attending to some aspect of visual processing could be said to be sites of attentional expression – that is, sites showing modulatory emphasis of neural activity.

## A Neural Model of Two Mechanisms of Visual Attention

While the expression of attention, defined as enhanced activity at the target site relative to the activity at the distractor site, is assumed here to take place in cortical areas, the circuit mechanisms that produce these activity differences are assumed to be located in subcortical structures (LaBerge, 1995a, 1995b). The relationship of the expression of a process to its generating mechanism can be clarified by the example of breathing, a process that is expressed as the movement of air in and out of the lungs (and respiratory passages), and whose mechanisms are the diaphragm in the abdomen and the intercostal muscles in the rib cage that change the lung volume like a bellows. Thus, in breathing, the muscular mechanisms that produce the movements of air in respiratory passages are structurally distinguishable from the passages through which air moves.

A mechanism of breathing, like a mechanism of attention, may generate a variety of expressions. Varieties of breathing include the transient breathing observed in coughing, sneezing, hiccupping, as well as the sustained breathing observed in normal speaking, singing, and in sedentary activities such as writing a paper. But underlying these diverse manifestations of breathing are the same expression (flow of air through respiratory passages) and mechanisms (respiratory muscles). Many years ago when physiologists already had in hand a clear understanding of how breathing is expressed and produced, the tasks of giving satisfactory accounts for each variety of breathing became relatively easy and straightforward.

Attention also is manifest in a variety of ways (Parasuraman & Davies, 1984): transient attentional operations are believed to take place in abrupt onsets of stimuli and in rapid selective operations of search and reading; sustained attentional operations are presumed to take place during periods of preparation, as typically occurs in the delay between a cue and a target stimulus. Does each manifestation of attention necessarily imply a different underlying neural process by which it is expressed and a different neural mechanism that produces the expression? Or, do many of the varieties of attention share expressive processes and underlying mechanisms?

This section of the paper is a description of a model of two mechanisms that operate separately or together in generating many of the varieties of visual spatial attention. Each mechanism codes the target and distractor locations, and provides the interactions between these location codes that eventually lead to the dominance of one or the other code for the generation of attention in an appropriate cortical pathway. Computationally speaking, one mechanism serves the goal of orienting to a new stimulus, and the other mechanism serves the goal of resolving closely spaced stimuli. Figure 1 shows examples of simple stimulus displays that contrast the processing involved during alignment of attention to well separated objects and concentration of attention to clustered objects.

For the present model, the guiding source of information concerning the structure and functions of these two structures is the primate brain; specifically, it is conjectured that the superior colliculus serves as the mechanism that mediates the competitive component of the process of orienting (following, e.g., Kingstone & Klein, 1993; Rafal et al., 1988; Rizzolatti et al., 1987), and the thalamus serves as the mechanism that mediates the process of resolving (LaBerge, 1995a, 1995b; LaBerge & Brown, 1989; LaBerge & Buchsbaum, 1990; Liotti et al., 1994).

Both the superior colliculus and the thalamus are closely connected to the cortex (see Figure 3). The relay cells in many thalamic nuclei project to and receive projections from virtually every area of the cortex (Jones, 1985). In particular, the pulvinar nucleus of the thalamus is directly connected with visual areas of the posterior cortex (Dick, Kaske, & Creutzfeldt, 1991; for a review, see Robinson & Petersen, 1992). The several layers of the superior colliculus receive fibers from a wide variety of cortical areas, but all fibers that it sends to the cortex synapse first in a thalamic nucleus (Abramson & Chalupa, 1988; Harting, Huerta, Frankfurter, Strominger, & Royce, 1980). Therefore, the outputs of the circuit mechanism of the superior colliculus undergo additional processing by the circuit mechanism of the thalamus before they reach the cortical area in which attention is assumed to be expressed (see Figure 4). Other

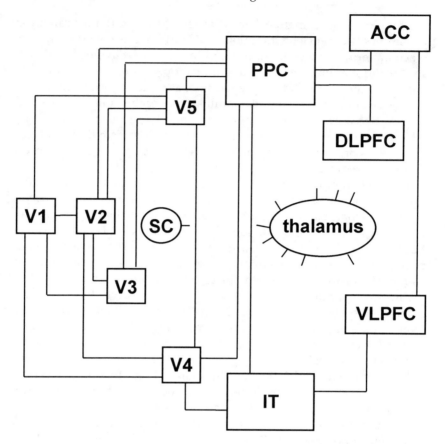

*Figure* 3: Posterior and anterior cortical areas serving visual attention, together with the subcortical areas of the superior colliculus and thalamus. The superior colliculus receives fibers from a wide variety of cortical areas but sends fibers to cortical areas via synapses in the thalamus. The thalamus sends and receives fibers directly from cortical areas. SC: superior colliculus; PPC: posterior parietal cortex; ACC: anterior cingulate cortex; VLPFC: ventrolateral prefrontal cortex; IT: inferotemporal area

direct projections to the superior colliculus include many anterior and posterior cortical areas as well as the principal external source of inhibition, the basal ganglia (Hikosaka & Wurtz, 1983).

The circuit architecture of the present two-mechanism model is shown in Figures 4 and 5 along with the conjectured time course of attentional expression in areas V4 and/or IT following the onset of the stimulus display. Figure 4 depicts the stimulus task in which target and distractors are well-separated, and Figure 5 depicts the stimulus task in which target and distractors are clustered.

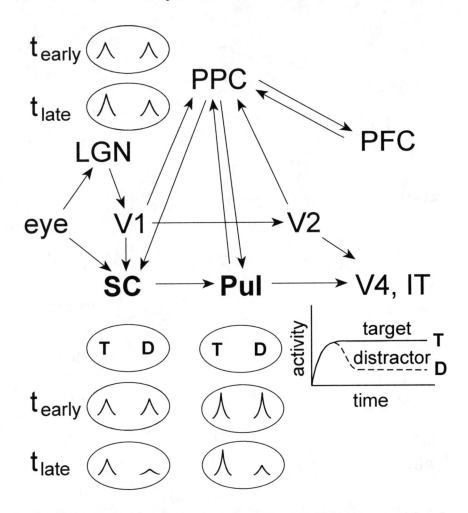

*Figure* 4: Model: Attentional expression in areas V4 and/or IT when target and distractors are spatially well separated (i.e., evoke more than one eye movement). Activations at target and distractor location sites in superior colliculus (SC), pulvinar (Pul), and posterior parietal cortex (PPC) are shown for two points in time following the display onset (Early and Late). No object location is cued. LGN: lateral geniculate nucleus.

When target and distractor objects are sufficiently separated to evoke different eye movement programs, the circuitry of the superior colliculus is presumed to provide the computations that decide which object location site will eventually show the dominant activity level. The locations of objects are apparently coded in collicular cells as movement fields, which are large and coarsely tuned (Glimcher &

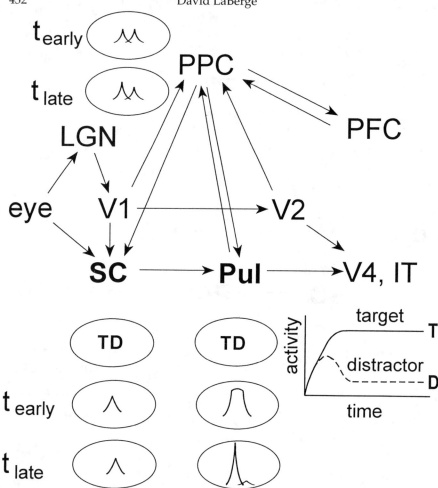

*Figure* 5: Model: Attentional expression in areas V4 and/or IT when target and distractors are spatially close (i.e., evoke one eye movement). No object location is cued.

Sparks, 1992). The influence of the pulvinar circuitry on the outputs of the superior colliculus is assumed simply to provide a moderate gain in their respective activity levels; no further interactions occur in the pulvinar between the target and distractor locations because their widely separated sites in the pulvinar do not interconnect through the limited-range cells of the reticular nucleus (see Figure 6).

When target and distractor are clustered sufficiently close to evoke one eye movement, then the coarse location code in the superior colliculus circuitry presumably registers them initially as one object/location, which precludes any spatial interactions between the target and

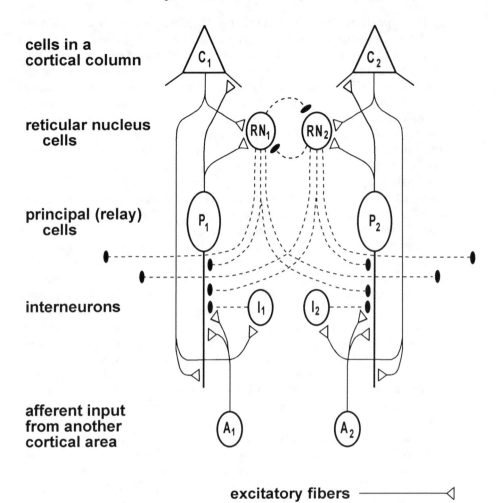

**cells in a cortical column**

**reticular nucleus cells**

**principal (relay) cells**

**interneurons**

**afferent input from another cortical area**

excitatory fibers ──────◁

inhibitory fibers ┄┄┄┄┄┄┄●

*Figure* 6: The standard thalamocortical circuit. Inhibitory fibers from the reticular nucleus (RN) cells project to cells in the same and neighbouring columns, but apparently not to cells in remote columns (Jones, 1985). Thus, competitive interactions between columns are limited to columns coding relatively closely spaced object locations.

distractor location codes in the superior colliculus. An abrupt onset of a stimulus cluster is presumed to be registered in the superior colliculus, and evokes the eye movement mechanism to orient toward the stimulus cluster. However, the perception of one of the component stimuli of the cluster requires a subsequent resolution process whose initiation is delayed beyond the dynamics of onset processing.

The type of mechanism that is conjectured to perform resolution operations on components of a stimulus cluster is the thalamus – in particular, the pulvinar nucleus, which occupies about two-fifths of the human thalamus volume, and is directly connected to extrastriate areas (Jones, 1985). Some cells of the pulvinar have very small receptive fields (Petersen, Robinson, & Keys, 1985) so that spatial locations can be relatively precisely coded. When location sites of objects are sufficiently close, the sites interact through inhibitory interconnections in the reticular nucleus, and thereby determine which object's location will eventually achieve the dominant activity level (see Figure 6). Thus, the spatial separation of a target and distractor determine in a straightforward manner whether the interactive processing of the object locations takes place in the superior colliculus or the pulvinar (or both, when separation distance is intermediate).

Attentional processing of displays with widely separated objects is not immune to thalamic effects, even though the competitive interactions between coded target sites may take place in the superior colliculus (for the case of exogenous orienting), or in the prefrontal/parietal areas (for the case of endogenous orienting). Output fibers from the superior colliculus synapse on pulvinar relay cells, which then project to extrastriate cortical areas (as do fibers from the prefrontal and parietal areas), and pulvinar-to-extrastriate circuits are presumed to enhance these outputs. Therefore, impairments of pulvinar circuit function by lesion (Rafal & Posner, 1987) or by an inhibitory drug (Petersen, Robinson, & Morris, 1987) are expected to affect performance of attention tasks, even when target and distractor objects are located in opposite hemifields. But the effect on pulvinar function in such cases is assumed here to be on the relaying of outputs from attentional competitive circuits located elsewhere, and not on competitive processing within the pulvinar itself. Competitive circuits within the pulvinar are assumed to be invoked only when coded object locations are sufficiently close to mutually inhibit each other though the limited-diameter arborization of reticular nucleus dendrites.

The controlling inputs to the superior colliculus are retinal ganglion cells and axon fibers from cells in all of the cortex. Of particular interest here are the inputs to the superior colliculus from the posterior parietal cortex (PPC), where object locations are coded (Blatt, Andersen, & Stoner, 1990; Goldberg et al., 1990). As shown in Figures 4 and 5, the pair of activation distributions registered in the PPC representing the target and distractor locations serve as inputs to both superior colliculus and pulvinar circuits. The inputs that the PPC provides to both mechanisms is influenced by fibers from the prefrontal cortex (Goldman-Rakic, Chafee, & Friedman, 1993), by which voluntary processes in the anterior cortex are believed to influence rather closely the height of one or the other activity distribution shown in PPC. Many object locations may be registered by activity distributions in the PPC simultaneously, but this does not imply that all or any of them express attention. For attention to a location to be expressed in the PPC, it is assumed that the peak of an activity distribution at that particular location site is increased to a high level and sustained for a time. The enhancement of firing rate in PPC presumably requires additional input from the location maps of voluntary areas of the prefrontal cortex (PFC). An abrupt onset of sufficient magnitude would also produce a high level of activity at a location site in PPC, but this effect may be too brief to qualify as an expression of attention. Therefore, the registration of many object locations in the PPC as activity distributions does not imply that there are many loci of attention; rather it implies that many active sites exist as preattentive registrations or indexings of locations (Pylyshyn, 1997; Pylyshyn et al., 1994; Wright, 1994; Wright & Ward, 1997), any of which may be subsequently enhanced to an attentional expression of location by the one-at-a-time activation from PFC voluntary areas.

When voluntary processes residing in the PFC project to the PPC a sufficiently strong activation to the target location prior to the onset of a target-distractor display, the PPC, in turn, is assumed to project a sufficiently large difference in target and distractor inputs to the pulvinar, which projects an enhanced target-distractor difference to V4 or IT, thereby providing the basis of selecting featural information from the target location for subsequent identification of the target. In this manner, voluntary attention to location can provide the basis for the selection of the featural information that is needed to identify a target object among distractors. Expressions of attention within this sequence of events are presumed to be taking place not only in V4 and IT, but also in the PPC. For this scenario (sometimes called endogenous cueing, but also regarded here as preparatory attention), the curves in the lower part of Figure 4 depicting the trajectories of target and distractor activities in V4 or IT should show initial values that are close to their asymptotic values. Thus, when the target location is strongly cued, the early sectors of the target and distractor curves should not show a divergence in activity levels (produced by competitive processing in superior colliculus), but instead should reflect the large target-distractor differences already established in PPC prior to the onset of the display. The case of strong cueing will be discussed further in the later section on control of spatial attention.

In view of the range of possible differences in activation levels at target and distractor locations that can be established in the PPC by cueing events prior to display onset, it is expected that the superior colliculus competitive computations will be revealed only in tasks in which location cueing is relatively weak. In such cases, the dominant information about target location is contained in the stimulus display.

One way that a task can shift the location information of the target from a cue to the stimulus display is to cue the shape property of the target instead of its location. This was done in the task used by Chelazzi et al. (1993) in which a shape is shown to the monkey as a cue (or sample) followed by a test display containing two shapes, one that matched the sample and one that did not. Since the locations of the target and distractor were not known prior to onset of the test display, the PPC presumably registered no difference in the activity distributions of the two objects until the shape was identified and its location information directed to the PPC (e.g., from IT to V2 to PPC). Therefore, during this initial period of time, the target and distractor location information from both the PPC and superior colliculus were presumed to be equal in modulatory strength, and then began to diverge as the location information from the target shape accumulated in PPC. Recordings from cortical cells representing the target and distractor objects in the Chelazzi et al. (1993) shape cueing study show trajectory patterns similar to the one shown at the bottom of Figure 4.

Although the conjectured time course of interactive location processing in the superior colliculus which is subsequently projected to cortical V4 and IT (shown in Figure 4) appears to match the time course of cortical single-cell recordings (Chelazzi et al., 1993), no comparable data is apparently available for the case of interactive processing of location codes in the pulvinar. However, because the circuitry of the pulvinar and the thalamus in general is relatively well-known (Jones, 1985; Steriade et al., 1990), and is relatively simple in structure, a neural network model of the circuit was easily constructed and this network served as a basis for simulations of target-distractor interactions in a visual attention task (LaBerge et al., 1992). The results of this simulation showed that the trajectories of activities at the target and distractor sites exhibit the pattern shown in Figure 7, which is similar to the pattern shown by the target and distractor firing rate projectories in Figure 5. These simulations specifically show that the pulvinar circuit can function in a competitive mode to enhance activity at the target site and suppress activity at the distractor site.

The consistent finding that the simulated pulvinar circuit can generate enhancements of activity at the target location is not surprising, given the many recurrent excitatory connections between cells in a cortical column and the thalamic relay (principal cell) that serves that cortical column (Jones, 1985). When the enhancement component is combined with the lateral inhibitory component (via the reticular nucleus cells)

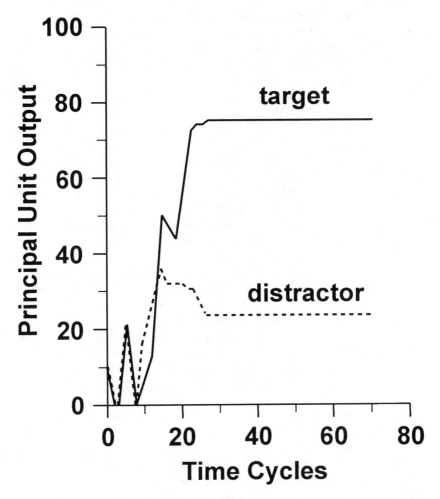

*Figure* 7: Simulated trajectories of principal (relay) cell outputs to the cortex, based on the circuit shown in Figure 6 (LaBerge, Carter, & Brown, 1992). Initial firing rates of the cells are 10 spikes/sec, and the afferent target-distractor inputs are 38 and 37 spikes/sec, respectively.

within the thalamocortical circuit, the size of the activity difference between target and distractor sites is potentially much higher than produced in a circuit whose interactions are based only on lateral inhibitory components. This is particularly the case when the target site in the thalamocortical circuit receives prolonged activation from sources of voluntary control.

One of the first proposals for a cortical circuit (serving attention) that contained these two types of components was proposed by Walley and

Weiden (1973). Later studies by Ojemann and his colleagues (1975, 1983) and Crick (1984) suggested that the thalamus could enhance cortical activity, and the enhancement properties of the thalamocortical circuit were detailed in a more recent study (LaBerge, 1990). This latter study led to the simulation of the thalamocortical circuit operations, described in the foregoing paragraph, and illustrated in Figure 7, which showed that the thalamocortical circuit is able to generate enhancements in cortical activity not only from small input differences arising from a sensory receptor or a remote cortical area but also from the cortical area to which the thalamic nucleus projects. A recent study by de Carvalho (1994) simulated cell activity within the thalamocortical loop and also showed that cortical activity can influence its own level of attention by means of the corticothalamic loop.

Having described the way in which thalamic enhancement effects, driven from top-down, voluntary sources of control, may follow initial superior colliculus suppressive effects, we return to the description, earlier in this chapter, of attentional enhancement and suppression effects measured by ERP in the experiment by Luck et al. (1994). In this experiment, subjects attended toward or away from one of four boxes, or attended to all four boxes in a neutral attention mode. One may interpret these results as indicating that the suppressive effect of the earlier P1 component reflects the cortical expression of attention driven by the superior colliculus and enhancement effect of the later N1 component reflects a cortical expression of attention driven by the pulvinar. The implication for the trajectory patterns of cells corresponding to the target box and distractor boxes is that the first divergence between the target and distractor firing rates is one of suppression of activity at the distractor site (the pattern shown at the bottom of Figure 4), followed by a further divergence produced by enhancement of the activity at the target site (the pattern shown in Figure 5). One interpretation of this implication is that the mechanism that produced the P1 component was largely controlled by onset of the target stimulus, while the subsequent N1 component was controlled largely by voluntary (top-down) processes.

In summary, the attentional competition between a target and distractors in the orienting mechanism is assumed to operate by suppression of activity at distractor sites; the attentional competition between a target and distractors in the resolution mechanism is assumed to operate mainly by enhancement of activity at the target site together with some suppression of activity at the distractor site. The orienting mechanism is presumed to be embodied in superior colliculus circuits, and is evoked when objects in a display are sufficiently separated to generate potential competing eye movements; the resolving mechanism is presumed to be embodied in thalamic circuits, and is evoked when objects in a display are clustered sufficiently close to produce considerable overlap in foveal receptor stimulation. At intermediate object spacings, both mechanisms may be called into operation. Outputs of the two mechanisms generate expressions of attention in the cortical areas to which they (eventually) project. Since superior colliculus output fibers synapse on thalamic relay cells *en route* to the cortex, the final common path of outputs from both attentional mechanisms is the thalamic relay cell axon. Since this axon is excitatory (Jones, 1985), the direct effect of output fibers from the two attention mechanisms appears to be that of enhancing the cortical neurons that receive these fibers. Therefore, in order to determine whether the expression of attention takes place by enhancement or suppression of cortical cells, it is important to examine the time course of the outputs from the two mechanisms, which are presumed to reflect the ongoing competition within the mechanisms, as shown in Figures 4, 5 and 7. Figure 4 shows a pure suppressive effect on the mechanism output cells, following the initial registration of sensory input; both Figures 5 and 7 show both a suppressive and an enhancement effect following initial registration of sensory input, but the suppressive effect in Figure 7 is small.

## Converging Evidence for the Thalamic Enhancement Hypothesis

The results from simulation studies of thalamocortical circuits do not prove that the thalamus functions to produce attentional enhancement and selection of visual location sites in cortical pathways. Rather, these simulations show that the thalamocortical circuit has the capability of performing these functions, and these results could be considered as one part of the converging evidence supporting the hypothesis that the thalamocortical circuit provides selective enhancements in activity of cortical areas.

Physiological studies of the pulvinar suggest that it has a role in visual processing. Single-cell recordings in pulvinar by Bender (1981) and Petersen, Robinson, and Keys (1987) identified cells that were sensitive to visual stimuli and had receptive fields that approached the small sizes of cells of the striate cortex. In another study, Petersen et al. (1986) injected an inhibitory drug into the pulvinar of one hemisphere of a monkey and showed impairments in attending to the contralateral visual field. Human patients with lesions in the left thalamus showed deficits on a location-cueing task (Rafal & Posner, 1987). However, studies described here that implicate the pulvinar in attention may only be addressing the gain function of the pulvinar, not the interactive competitive function of the pulvinar (as pointed out in the previous

section of this chapter), since the target and distractor objects in the behavioral tasks were always well-separated. The amount of the pulvinar
amplification is presumed to be relatively small when target and distractor objects are well-separated compared to when they are clustered
together, because clustering is believed to induce relatively intense and
prolonged activity directed to the pulvinar circuits from voluntary processes in the PFC, in order to achieve resolution of the objects.

Visual attention tasks that displayed targets in close proximity with
distractors were given to humans while their brain activity was measured by PET. In one study (LaBerge & Buchsbaum, 1990), a nine-item
cluster of letters having O at the centre, and surrounded by G's and
Q's, was presented on one side of a central fixation point, and a single
large O (the size of the 3 × 3 cluster) was presented on the other side.
Subjects were instructed to respond with a button press when the O
was present, but to withhold their response when a C or zero (with a
slash) was substituted for the O. The results of the PET measures
showed significantly more glucose uptake in the pulvinar opposite to
the side of the nine-letter cluster than in the pulvinar opposite to the
side of the single letter.

While these results suggested that the pulvinar is involved in visual
attention to a target clustered with distractors more than a target alone,
the lack of a neutral control condition precluded a determination of
whether the obtained increase for the cluster display was produced by
an enhancement of activity on cluster display trials or by a suppression
of activity during single-letter display trials. Furthermore, since the
thalamic area received the bulk of scans, no measurements were taken
of concurrent attentional activity in extrastriate and anterior cortices so
that the activity of the pulvinar mechanism could be correlated with
the activity of the cortical expressions.

A recent PET study (Liotti et al., 1994) attempted to remedy these two
problems by adding a neutral condition to the Hard and Easy attention
conditions, and by scanning all cortical areas along with the subcortical
areas, including the thalamus. The Hard condition used the same 3 × 3
letter cluster that surrounded an O with G's and Q's, and an Easy condition, in which the central O was surrounded by eight slashes (\). 
Prior to the onset of the letter displays, for 1,600 ms a cue was presented
that indicated the side (left or right) of the central fixation cross where
the letter display would appear. For the Neutral condition, no letter
displays appeared, and subjects responded randomly when the cue
went off. A block of trials was devoted to only one type of condition.
Subjects' brains were scanned as they performed the tasks.

The results showed strongly significant differences in blood flow
across the Hard, Easy, and Neutral conditions in the pulvinar, confirm-

ing the results of the earlier related study (LaBerge & Buchsbaum, 1990). In addition, significant blood flow differences were found in the second largest human thalamic nucleus, the mediodorsal nucleus, which serves the anterior cortical areas. Also, highly significant differences in blood flow in some or all of these pairwise comparisons of conditions were found in extrastriate areas that apparently correspond to PPC, V4, and IT, and in prefrontal area VLPFC. All of these cortical areas have been implicated in other PET studies and in single-cell recording studies that use visual tasks in which attention to location and shape are involved (see the review in the earlier part of this chapter). The general pattern of coincident blood flow increases observed in this study offers converging evidence that attention to closely spaced objects produces increased activity in both pulvinar and extrastriate areas in the posterior cortex, and in the mediodorsal nucleus and visually related areas in the anterior cortex. It is assumed that, in general, posterior cortical areas express attention to perceptual processing while anterior areas control the durations and intensities of these expressions by driving the thalamic mechanisms that serve them.

Additional converging data for the thalamocortical enhancement hypothesis is given by neuroanatomical studies of the thalamus and cortex. The output axons from the thalamus to the cortex are virtually all excitatory, as are the output axons from the cortex to the thalamus (Jones, 1985). Thus, when a thalamic nucleus, such as the pulvinar or mediodorsal nucleus, shows increased activation, it can be confidently concluded that it is projecting activity to the columns of the particular cortical area that it serves. Furthermore, as indicated earlier in this chapter, the majority of cortical cells in a column are excitatory, and the cortical cells that receive thalamic axons appear to be almost entirely (97%) excitatory for cortical areas outside the primary projection areas (Johnson & Burkhalter, 1994).

In conclusion, the physiological and neuroanatomical data reviewed in this section provide converging support for the hypothesis that cortical and thalamic neurons interconnect in loops that produce enhancements of firing rates, and that physiological indicators such as PET reveal high levels of neural activity in thalamic nuclei (especially the pulvinar and mediodorsal nuclei) during attention tasks in which visual objects are closely clustered.

## The Control of Spatial Attention

For the process of breathing, the question of control asks what commands the rib-cage muscles and diaphragm muscle (the bellows-like mechanism) to modulate the flow of air in respiratory pathways (the expression of breathing). The answer to this question involves two sources of control: a midbrain circuit that computes the involuntary commands, and a cortical circuit that computes the voluntary commands. Cortical commands are relayed through the midbrain circuit where they can override involuntary commands to the respiratory muscles under certain conditions.

For the process of spatial attention, the commands to the superior colliculus and pulvinar mechanisms (which compute the interactive processing between target and distractor sites) also arise from two general sources, one involuntary and the other voluntary. These sources of control are, respectively, external visual information and the internal circuits of anterior cortex, particularly the prefrontal cortex. It is tempting to assume at the outset that the superior colliculus mechanism is controlled only by external information and that the pulvinar mechanism is controlled only by internal information. However, this simple scheme is immediately rejected in view of the anatomical fact that the pulvinar is activated indirectly by external information sources because the superior colliculus output to cortical areas of attentional expression is relayed through the pulvinar circuit mechanism. Furthermore, eye movement plans computed in the superior colliculus can be evoked by internal voluntary commands (e.g., by projections from PFC to the superior colliculus directly or via the PPC), and information from external visual objects can reach pulvinar circuits through extrastriate areas (V1, V2, PPC, etc.) without first passing through anterior cortical areas of voluntary control. In view of these considerations, it appears that the orienting operations of the superior colliculus mechanisms and the resolving operations of the pulvinar mechanism each receive a mix of controlling commands from external and internal sources, as shown in the schematic descriptions of the present model in Figures 4 and 5.

Several investigators (Kingstone & Klein, 1993; Klein, 1994; Rafal & Robertson, 1995) have proposed that stimulus-controlled orienting (exogenous orienting) and voluntary-controlled orienting (endogenous or cued orienting) are governed by different mechanisms. According to Kingstone and Klein (1993) and Klein (1994), exogenous orienting is mediated by oculomotor readiness involving the superior colliculus, but the endogenous orienting mechanism is left unspecified. Rafal and Robertson (1995) also propose that exogenous orienting is mediated by a superior colliculus mechanism, and propose that endogenous orienting is mediated by cortical mechanisms at or near the posterior parietal cortex PPC). Posner, Rothbart, Thomas-Thrapp, and Gerardi (this volume) remind us that shifting attention by either exogenous or endogenous cues involves the parietal area, according to lesion and PET data. The present view, which shares features with all of these proposals, specifically assumes that parietal areas are part of the controlling circuitry of attention which can influence both the superior colliculus and the pulvinar mechanisms of attention. This influence can occur prior to stimulus onset via preparatory attention induced by a cue, and after stimulus onset, by activation from PFC areas that control the sustaining of attention (see Figures 4 and 5).

## Weak Cueing of the Target

It is also assumed here that the superior colliculus interactive processing (of stimulus-evoked activities at target and distractor sites) will dominate the production of attentional expressions when PPC activity at the target location is relatively weak prior to display onset. An example of weak target activity in parietal areas prior to the display onset occurs in the frequently used detection task in which targets appear to the left or right of a central warning signal cross (Posner, Snyder, & Davidson, 1980). Although a central fixation cross gives no information concerning the location of the upcoming object, the cumulative effects of object displays at the right and left locations produces a relatively enduring, low-level, enhancement at those coded locations in PPC (LaBerge, 1995b; LaBerge & Brown, 1986). Thus, even though subjects do not prepare explicitly for one or both of the target locations during the warning signal, the residual enhancement at the target locations, relative to other locations, should operate as a weak cueing effect, presumably registered in PPC as a kind of working memory for location (LaBerge, 1995b). Weak cueing effects in PPC areas can also be explicitly produced by presenting a location cue just prior to the target-distractor display (e.g., Klein & Hansen, 1991; Yantis & Gibson, 1994), so that insufficient time is provided for the buildup of activity to a high level at the cued location before the onset of the target-distractor display.

## Strong Cueing of the Target

On the other hand, when the cue is presented well in advance of the target-distractor display *and* if the subject opts to prepare intensely for the cued location (by voluntarily projecting high levels of activity from PFC to the target location site in PPC), then the output from PPC to the superior colliculus will strongly favour the target location over the distractor location(s) prior to onset of the display, so that there is no need for the superior colliculus circuits to provide further interactive processing between these sites (see Figure 8).

While the PPC is activating the superior colliculus, it is assumed that the output from PPC to pulvinar begins to induce an expression of attention in V4/IT areas. However, because the target and distractors are well-separated, the pulvinar circuitry does not engage in interactive

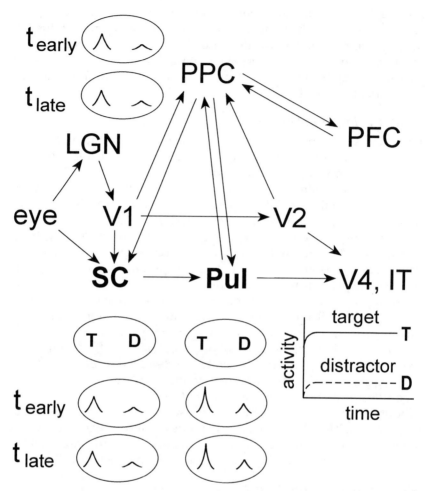

*Figure* 8: Model for Orienting: Expression of attention in V4 and/or IT when target and distractors are spatially well-separated (i.e., evoke more than one eye movement). Target object location is strongly cued prior to display onset.

processing; rather it merely performs a gain function on the activities already existing in PPC. Thus, neither the superior colliculus mechanism nor the pulvinar mechanism provides interactive attentional processing following the onset of the display, owing to the large difference in activity level at the target and distractor sites that are projected to these mechanisms. Hence, under strong precueing conditions of the target, the trajectories of target and distractor activities (e.g., as shown at the bottom of Figure 8) should show no divergence, but should be virtually at asymptote at display onset.

In the foregoing strong cueing case, the superior collicular and pulvinar mechanisms are assumed not to perform appreciable interactive operations between the coded target and distractor sites at display onset or following the display onset, since the activity at the coded target site already dominates the activity at distractor sites prior to display onset (i.e., the target is declared the winner before the game begins). Prior to display onset, the cue induces preparatory attentional activity in one or both of the attention mechanisms. If the cue induces preparatory attentional activity over a broad area of the visual field, the voluntary controls in PFC may activate oculomotor orienting in the superior colliculus mechanism and send copies of this activation to the PPC. If the cue induces the subject to prepare for a narrow area of the visual field, the problem becomes one of spatial resolution (the cued area is selected against nearby surrounding areas), and requires the finer-grained maps of the pulvinar (Marracco & Li, 1977; Meredith & Stein, 1990; Petersen et al., 1985).

Given the present assumption that the interactive processing algorithm of the pulvinar circuit is carried out mainly by enhancement while that of the superior colliculus is carried out mainly by suppression, it would be predicted that a cue could establish stronger levels of preparatory activity in the PPC corresponding to the target location when a relatively small area is cued rather than when a relatively large area is cued. This prediction is based on the fact that typical base rates of cortical cell firings (e.g., less than 50 Hz) are nearer to zero than to the 1000 Hz maximum, so that the range of (SC) suppressive effects on cell firings is limited to 50 Hz or less, while the range of pulvinar enhancement effects on cell firings in principle is at least as high as 950 Hz.

Implicit in the foregoing analysis of superior collicular and pulvinar contributions to spatial attention is the assumption that strong precueing of a particular object location sets up an immunity to displays of objects at other locations (Folk et al., 1992; Koshino et al., 1992; Theeuwes, 1991; Yantis & Jonides, 1990). For example, if a distractor is unexpectedly made more salient (by increasing its luminance contrast and displaying it with an abrupt onset), its registered activity in either the superior colliculus or in PPC (via V1) may not reach a magnitude that will compete with the existing high level of activity already existing at the cued coded target location in the superior colliculus and PPC. In consequence, the salient distractor will show little or no effect on the expression of attention to the target in V4/IT, and therefore little or no effect on related behavioural measures. However, if the distractor is made sufficiently salient (e.g., by a large luminance contrast and presented with an abrupt onset), then the registered activity at the distractor site may be greater than the activity existing at the cued locations in superior colliculus and PPC, and therefore it will interfere with the formation of the expression of attention to the target location in V4/IT. The trajectories of target and distractor activity levels for this case of strong abrupt distractor onset combined with strong target precueing is expected to show the trajectory pattern of attentional expression depicted in Figure 9.

The trajectories in Figure 9 describe two phases in the development of attentional expression in V4/IT. The first phase shows higher activity (in V4/IT) for the distractor object after a period of rapid divergent interaction, and the second phase shows higher activity for the target object after a second period of somewhat slower divergent interactive processing. The duration of the first phase, in which the distractor site shows the higher activity, is assumed to be brief (Figure 9, Case A), unless voluntary processes (of the PFC) activate the distractor location and sustain the high level of processing (Figure 9, Case B). Some researchers, myself included, prefer to regard brief surges of activity brought about by abrupt onsets as instances of attentional expressions only when they are subsequently sustained by top-down, voluntary activations (e.g., Figure 9, Case B), and to regard unsustained brief surges of activity as "preattentive location indexing" (Pylyshyn, this volume; Pylyshyn et al., 1994; Wright, 1994; Wright & Ward, this volume), which serve as "gateways" to attention, not as attentional states.

Because the target and distractor objects that exhibit the two trajectories of Figure 9 are well-separated, the locus of the competitive interactive processing is presumed to take place within superior colliculus circuitry. At some point, as the separation between the target and distract is decreased, the pulvinar circuitry presumably would become involved.

The foregoing descriptions of the roles of the superior colliculus and PPC in mediating attention effects to well-separated objects may imply that the PPC should also be regarded as a mechanism of attention. However, this claim seems inappropriate, given the assumption that the PPC circuits themselves do not produce interactive processing of coded object locations, as do the superior colliculus and pulvinar. Instead of interacting, the different activity distributions in the PPC area that code locations are assumed simply to combine additively (LaBerge, 1995a; LaBerge, 1995b, LaBerge, Bunney, Carlson, & Williams, 1997). For example, the distributions corresponding to the range of recently displayed target locations adds with the momentary activity distribution induced by a cue. Thus, the PPC circuits are viewed here as a *control* on the mechanisms of attention, where top-down PFC and bottom-up stimulus input combine their influences into a common representation of object locations, which in turn influences the mechanisms of attention in the superior colliculus and pulvinar.

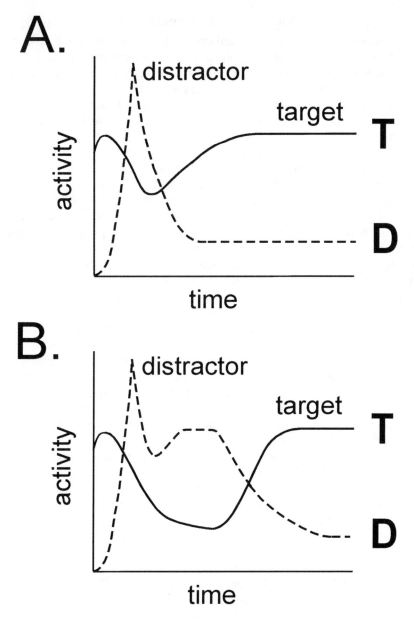

*Figure* 9: Model for Orienting: Expression of attention in V4 and/or IT when target and distractors are spatially well-separated, the target object is strongly cued, and a high-luminance distractor is displayed abruptly. (A) Abrupt onset of the distractor delays the attentional expression of the target, which is sustained from the prefrontal cortex (PFC), but the distractor itself is not sustained by PFC. (B) Abrupt onset of the distractor delays the attentional expression of the target which is sustained from PFC, but not until the distractor itself is first sustained by PFC.

## Summary and Conclusion

In an attempt to clarify the attentional interactions of targets and distractors in a visual display, this chapter treats separately the expression, mechanisms, and controls of attention. Computational considerations suggest that orienting to a target when the distance between the target and distractor is large represents a different computational goal than resolving a target when the distance between the target and distractor is small; hence it is proposed that different mechanisms may carry out the operations of orienting and resolving.

Attention is presumed to be expressed in cortical pathways in this way: greater activity takes place in neurons corresponding to the target location than in neurons corresponding to distractor locations. This relative enhancement or emphasis of activity in neural sites representing the target is assumed to involve modulatory (as opposed to informational) changes in information flow. This expression of attention, shown by physiological measures to occur in many different cortical areas, can be generated by three classes of algorithms. One algorithm class, the suppression of activity at distractor sites, is assumed to be generated mainly in circuits of the superior colliculus; the other two classes, the enhancement of activity at distractor sites with or without suppression at the distractor sites, are assumed to be generated mainly in circuits of the thalamus. These assumptions about the mechanisms of attention are integrated within a single model of spatial attention, and predictions are derived for the attentional processing target-distractor displays under conditions in which target-distractor separations are large versus small, and under conditions in which the location is cued weakly or strongly.

While the two-mechanism model of spatial attention may be somewhat oversimplified as described here, it appears to predict the general patterns of results in the some of the literature of spatial cueing and abrupt onsets. Clearly, more detailed tests of these and other results are required for evaluating the suitability of the model, and for suggesting changes in its assumptions to make it more suitable.

## Acknowledgments

The author is grateful to Robert Carlson and John Williams for discussions and criticisms of the ideas described in this chapter. David LaBerge may be contacted via e-mail at dlaberge@vmsa.oac.uci.edu

## References

Abramson, B.P., & Chalupa, L.M. (1988). Multiple pathways from the superior colliculus to the extrageniculate visual thalamus of the cat. *Journal of Comparative Neurology, 271,* 397–418.

Bender, D.B. (1981). Retinotopic organization of macaque pulvinar. *Journal of Neurophysiology, 46*, 672–693.

Blatt, G.J., Andersen, R.A., & Stoner, G.R. (1990). Visual receptive field organization and cortico-cortical connections of the lateral intraparietal area (Area LIP) in the macaque. *Journal of Comparative Neurology, 299*, 421–445.

Bowman, E.M., Brown, V.J., Kertzman, C., Schwarz, U., & Robinson, D.L. (1993). Covert orienting of attention in macaques. I. Effects of behavioral context. *Journal of Neurophysiology, 70*, 431–443.

de Carvalho, L.A.V. (1994). Modeling the thalamocortical loop. *International Journal of Bio-Medical Computing, 35*, 267–296.

Chelazzi, L., Miller, E.K., Duncan, J., & Desimone, R. (1993). A neural basis for visual search in inferior temporal cortex. *Nature, 363*, 345–347.

Corbetta, M., Miezin, F.M., Dobmeyer, S., Shulman, G.L., & Petersen, S.E. (1991). Selective and divided attention during visual discrimination of shape, color, and speed: Functional anatomy by positron emission tomography. *Journal of Neuroscience, 11*, 2383–2402.

Corbetta, M., Miezin, F.M., Shulman, G.L., & Petersen, S.E. (1993). A PET study of visuospatial attention. *Journal of Neuroscience, 13*, 1202–1226.

Crick, F. (1984). The function of the thalamic reticular complex: The searchlight hypothesis. *Proceedings of the National Academy of Sciences (USA), 81*, 4586–4590.

Dick, A., Kaske, A., & Creutzfeldt, O.D. (1991). Topographical and topological organization of the thalamocortical projection to the striate and prestriate cortex in the marmoset. *Experimental Brain Research, 84*, 233–253.

Douglas, R.J., & Martin, K.A.C. (1990). Neocortex. In G.M. Shepherd (Ed.), *The synaptic organization of the brain*. New York: Oxford University Press.

Eriksen, B.A., & Eriksen, C.W. (1974). Effects of noise letters upon the identification of a target letter in a nonsearch task. *Perception & Psychophysics, 16*, 143–149.

Folk, C.L., Remington, R., & Johnston, J.C. (1992). Involuntary covert orienting is contingent on attentional control settings. *Journal of Experimental Psychology: Human Perception & Performance, 18*, 1030–1044.

Glimcher, P., & Sparks, D.L. (1992). Movement selection in advance of action: Saccade-related bursters of the superior colliculus. *Nature, 355*, 542–545.

Goldberg, M.E., Colby, C.L., & Duhamel, J.-R. (1990) Representation of visuomotor space in the parietal lobe of the monkey. *Cold Spring Harbor Symposia on Quantitative Biology, 55*, 729–739.

Goldman-Rakic, P.S. (1988). Topography of cognition: Parallel-distributed networks in primate association cortex. *Annual Review of Neuroscience, 11*, 137–156.

Goldman-Rakic, P.S., Chafee, M., & Friedman, H. (1993). Allocation of function in distributed circuits. In T. Ono, L.R. Squire, M.E. Raichle, D.I. Perrett, & M. Fukuda (Eds.), *Brain mechanisms of perception and memory: From neuron to behavior*, pp. 445–456. New York: Oxford University Press.

Hackley, S.A., Woldorff, M., & Hillyard, S.A. (1990). Cross-modal selective attention effects on retinal, myogenic, brainstem, and cerebral evoked potentials. *Psychophysiology, 27*, 195–208.

Haenny, P.E., & Schiller, P.H. (1988). State dependent activity in monkey visual cortex: I. Single cell activity in V1 and V4 on visual tasks. *Experimental Brain Research, 69*, 225–244.

Harting, J.K., Huerta, M.F., Frankfurter, A.J., Strominger, N.L., & Royce, G.J. (1980). Ascending pathways from the monkey superior colliculus: An autoradiographic analysis. *Journal of Comparative Neurology, 192*, 853–882.

Haxby, J.V., Grady, C.L., Horwitz, B., Ungerleider, L.G., Mishkin, M., Carson, R.E., Herscovitch, P., Schapiro, M.B., & Rapoport, S.I. (1991). Dissociation of spatial and object visual processing pathways in human extrastriate cortex. *Proceedings of the National Academy of Sciences (USA), 88*, 1621–1625.

Haxby, J.V., Horwitz, B., Ungerleider, L.G., Maisog, J.M., Pietrini, P., & Grady, C.L. (1994). The functional organization of human extrastriate cortex: A PET-rCBF study of selective attention to faces and locations. *Journal of Neuroscience, 14*, 6336–6353.

Hendry, S.H.C., Schwark, H.D., Jones, E.G., & Yan, J. (1987). Similarity in numbers and proportions of GABA immunoreactive neurons in different areas of monkey cerebral cortex. *Journal of Neuroscience, 7*, 1503–1068.

Hikosaka, O., & Wurtz, R.H. (1983). Visual and oculomotor functions of the monkey substantia nigra pars reticulata IV: Relation of substantia nigra to superior colliculus. *Journal of Neurophysiology, 49*, 1285–1301.

Hillyard, S.A., Mangun, G.R., Woldorff, M.G., & Luck, S.J. (1994). Neural systems mediating selective attention. In M. Gazzaniga (Ed.), *The cognitive neurosciences*, pp. 665–681. Cambridge, MA: MIT Press.

Hillyard, S.A., Luck, S.J., & Mangun, G.R. (1994). The cueing of attention to visual field locations: Analysis with ERP recordings. In H.J. Heinze, T.F. Munte, & G.R. Mangun, (Eds.), *Cognitive electrophysiology: Event-related brain potentials in basic and clinical research*, pp 1–25. Boston: Birkhauser.

Johnson, R.R., & Burkhalter, A. (1994). Different microcircuits for forward corticocortical and LP (pulvinar) projections in rat extrastriate visual cortex. *Society for Neuroscience Abstracts, 20*, 427.

Jones, E.G. (1985). *The thalamus*. New York: Plenum Press.

Jonides, J., Smith, E.E., Koeppe, R.A., Awh, E., Minoshima, S., & Mintun, M.A. (1993). Spatial working memory in humans as revealed by PET. *Nature, 363*, 623–625.

Kahneman, D., & Chajczyk, D. (1983). Tests of the automaticity of reading: Dilution of Stroop effects by color-irrelevant stimuli. *Journal of Experimental Psychology: Human Perception & Performance, 9*, 497–509.

Kingstone, A., & Klein, R.M. (1993). On the relationship between overt and covert orienting: The effect of attended and unattended offsets on saccadic latencies. *Journal of Experimental Psychology: Human Perception & Performance, 19*: 1251–1265.

Klein, R.M. (1994). Perceptual-motor expectancies interact with covert visual orienting under conditions of endogenous but not exogenous control. *Canadian Journal of Experimental Psychology, 48*, 167–181.

Klein, R.M., & Hansen, E. (1990). Chronometric analysis of spotlight failure in endogenous visual orienting. *Journal of Experimental Psychology: Human Perception & Performance, 16*, 790–801.

Klein, R.M., & Pontefract, A. (1994). Does oculomotor readiness mediate cognitive control of visual attention? Revisited. In C. Umilta & M. Moscovitch (Eds.), *Attention & Performance, Vol. XV: Conscious and unconscious processing.* Cambridge, MA: MIT Press.

Koshino, H., Warner, C.B., & Juola, J.F. (1992). Relative effectiveness of central, peripheral, and abrupt-onset cues in visual attention. *Quarterly Journal of Experimental Psychology, 45A,* 609–631.

LaBerge, D. (1990). Thalamic and cortical mechanisms of attention suggested by recent positron emission tomographic experiments. *Journal of Cognitive Neuroscience, 2,* 358–372.

LaBerge, D. (1995a). Computational and anatomical models of selective attention in object identification. In M. Gazzaniga (Ed.), *The cognitive neurosciences.* Cambridge, MA: MIT Press.

LaBerge, D. (1995b). *Attentional processing: The brain's art of mindfulness.* Cambridge, MA: Harvard University Press.

LaBerge, D., & Brown, V. (1986). Variations in size of the visual field in which targets are presented: An attentional range effect. *Perception & Psychophysics, 40,* 188–200.

LaBerge, D., & Brown, V. (1989). Theory of attentional operations in shape identification. *Psychological Review, 96,* 101–124.

LaBerge, D., Brown, V., Carter, M., Bash, D., & Hartley, A. (1992). Reducing the effects of adjacent distractors by narrowing attention. *Journal of Experimental Psychology: Human Perception & Performance, 17,* 65–76.

LaBerge, D., & Buchsbaum, M.S. (1990). Positron emission tomographic measurements of pulvinar activity during an attention task. *Journal of Neuroscience, 10,* 613–619.

LaBerge, D., Carter, M., & Brown, V. (1992). A network simulation of thalamic circuit operations in selective attention. *Neural Computation, 4,* 318–331.

LaBerge, D., Bunney, B., Carlson, R., & Williams, J.K. (1997). Shifting attention in space: Tests of a spotlight model versus a preparation/selection model. *Journal of Experimental Psychology: Human Perception and Performance.*

Liotti, M., Fox, P.T., & LaBerge, D. (1994). PET measurements of attention to closely spaced visual shapes. *Society for Neurosciences Abstracts, 20,* 354.

Luck, S.J., Hillyard, S.A., Mouloua, M., Woldorff, M.G., Clark, V.P., & Hawkins, H.L. (1994). Effects of spatial cueing on luminance detectability: Psychophysical and electrophysiological evidence for early selection. *Journal of Experimental Psychology: Human Perception & Performance, 20,* 887–904.

Marracco, R.T., & Li, R.H. (1977). Monkey superior colliculus: Properties of single cells and their afferent inputs. *Journal of Neurophysiology, 40,* 844–860.

Maunsell, J.H.R. (1995). The brain's visual world: Representation of visual targets in cerebral cortex. *Science, 270,* 764–768.

Meredith, M.A., & Stein, B.E. (1990). The visuotopic component of the multisensory map in the deep laminae of the cat superior colliculus. *Journal of Neuroscience, 10,* 3727–3742.

Moran, J., & Desimone, R. (1985). Selective attention gates visual processing in the extrastriate cortex. *Science, 229,* 782–784.

Motter, B.C. (1993). Focal attention produces spatially selective processing in visual cortical areas V1, V2, and V4 in the presence of competing stimuli. *Journal of Neurophysiology, 70,* 909–919.

Mountcastle, V.B. (1978). Brain mechanisms of directed attention. *Journal of the Royal Society of Medicine, 71,* 14–27.

Näätänen, R. (1990). The role of attention in auditory information processing as revealed by event-related potentials and other brain measure of cognitive function. *Behavioral and Brain Sciences, 13,* 201–288.

Näätänen, R. (1992). *Attention and brain function.* Hillsdale, NJ: Erlbaum.

Ojemann, G.A. (1975). Language and the thalamus: Object naming and recall during and after thalamic stimulation. *Brain & Language, 2,* 101–120.

Ojemann, G.A. (1983). Brain organization for language from the perspective of electrical stimuluation mapping. *Behavioral & Brain Sciences, 2,* 189–206.

Parasuraman, R., & Davies, D.R. (1984). *Varieties of attention.* New York: Academic Press.

Petersen, S.E., Fox, P.T., Posner, M.I., Minton, M., & Raichle, M.E. (1988). Positron emission tomographic studies of the cortical anatomy of single word processing. *Nature, 331,* 585–589.

Petersen, S.E., Fox, P.T., Snyder, A.Z., & Raichle, M.E. (1990). Activation of extrastriate and frontal cortical areas by visual words and word-like stimuli. *Science, 249,* 1041–1044.

Petersen, S.E., Robinson, D.L., & Keys, W. (1985). Pulvinar nuclei of the behaving rhesus monkey: Visual responses and their modulation. *Journal of Neurophysiology, 54,* 867–886.

Petersen, S.E., Robinson, D.L., & Morris, J.D. (1987). Contributions of the pulvinar to visual spatial attention. *Neuropsychologia, 25,* 97– 105.

Petersen, S.E., Corbetta, M., Miezin, F.M., & Shulman, G.L. (1994). PET studies of parietal involvement in spatial attention: Comparison of different task types. *Canadian Journal of Experimental Psychology, 48,* 319–338.

Posner, M.I., & Petersen, S.E. (1990). The attention system of the human brain. *Annual Review of Neuroscience, 13,* 25–41.

Posner, M.I., Rothbart, M.K., Thomas-Thrapp, L., & Gerardi, G. (this volume). Development of orienting to locations and objects. In R.D. Wright (Ed.), *Visual attention.* New York, NY: Oxford University Press.

Posner, M.I., Snyder, C.R.R., & Davidson, B.J. (1980). Attention and the detection of signals. *Journal of Experimental Psychology: General, 109,* 160–174.

Posner, M.I., Walker, J.A., Friedrich, F.J., & Rafal, R.D. (1984). Effects of parietal injury on covert orienting of attention. *Journal of Neuroscience, 4,* 1863–1874.

Pylyshyn, Z., Burkell, J., Fisher, B., Sears, C., Schmidt, W., & Trick, L. (1994). Multiple parallel access in visual attention. *Canadian Journal of Experimental Psychology, 48,* 260–282.

Pylyshyn, Z. (this volume). Visual indexes in spatial vision and imagery. In R.D. Wright (Ed.), *Visual attention.* New York: Oxford University Press.

Rafal, R.D., & Posner, M.I. (1987). Deficits in human visual spatial attention following thalamic lesions. *Proceedings of the National Academy of Sciences (USA), 84,* 7349–7353.

Rafal, R.D., Posner, M.I., Friedman, J.H., Inhoff, A.W., & Berstein, E. (1988). Orienting of visual attention in progressive supranuclear palsy. *Brain, 111,* 267–280.

Rafal, R., & Robertson, L. (1995). The neurology of visual attention. In M. Gazzaniga (Ed.), *The cognitive neurosciences.* Cambridge, MA: MIT Press.

Rizzolatti, G.L., Riggio, L., Dascola, I., & Umilta, C. (1987). Reorienting attention across the horizontal and vertical meridians: Evidence in favor of a premotor theory of attention. *Neuropsychologia, 25,* 31–40.

Robinson, D.L., Goldberg, M.E., & Stanton, G.B. (1978). Parietal association cortex in the primate: Sensory mechanisms and behavioral modulations. *Journal of Neurophysiology, 41,* 910–932.

Robinson, D.L., Bowman, E.M., & Kertzman, C. (1995). Covert orienting of attention in macaques. II. Contributions of parietal cortex. *Journal of Neurophysiology, 74,* 698–712.

Robinson, D.L., & Kertzman, C. (1995). Covert orienting of attention in macaques. III. Contributions of the superior colliculus. *Journal of Neurophysiology, 74,* 713–721.

Robinson, D.L., & Petersen, S.E. (1992). The pulvinar and visual salience.*Trends in Neurosciences, 15,* 127–132.

Roland, P.E. (1985). Cortical organization of voluntary behavior in man.*Human Neurobiology, 4,* 155–167.

Sergent, J., Ohta, S., & MacDonald, B. (1992). Functional neuroanatomy of face and object processing: A positron emission tomography study.*Brain, 115,* 15–36.

Sheliga, B.M., Riggio, L., & Rizzolatti, G. (1994). Orienting of attention and eye movements. *Experimental Brain Research, 98,* 507–522.

Spitzer, H., Desimone, R., & Moran, J. (1988). Increased attention enhances both behavioral and neuronal performance. *Science, 240,* 338–340.

Steriade, M., Jones, E.G., & Llinas, R.R. (1990). *Thalamic oscillations and signaling.* New York: Wiley.

Theeuwes, J. (1991). Exogenous and endogenous control of attention: The effect of visual onsets and offsets. *Perception & Psychophysics, 49,* 83–90.

Walley, R.E., & Weiden, T.D. (1973). Lateral inhibition and cognitive masking: A neuropsychological theory of attention. *Psychological Review, 80,* 284–302.

Wilson, F.A.W., O'Scalaidhe, S.P., & Goldman-Rakic, P.S. (1993). Dissociation of object and spatial processing domains in primate prefrontal cortex. *Science, 260,* 1955–1958.

Wright, R.D. (1994). Shifts of visual attention to multiple simultaneous location cues. *Canadian Journal of Experimental Psychology, 48,* 205–217.

Wright, R.D., & Ward, L.M. (this volume). The control of visual attention. In R.D. Wright (Ed.), *Visual attention.* New York, NY: Oxford University Press.

Wurtz, R.H., & Goldberg, M.E. (1972). Activity of superior colliculus in behaving monkey. III. Cells discharging before eye movements. *Journal of Neurophysiology, 35,* 575–586.

Wurtz, R.H., Goldberg, M.E., & Robinson, D.L. (1980). Behavioral modulation of visual responses in the monkey: Stimulus selection for attention and movement. *Progress in Psychobiology & Physiological Psychology, 9,* 43–83.

Yantis, S. (1993). Stimulus-driven attentional capture. *Current Directions in Psychological Science, 2,* 156–161.

Yantis, S., & Gibson, B.S. (1994). Object continuity in apparent motion and attention. *Canadian Journal of Experimental Psychology, 48,* 182–204.

Yantis, S., & Jonides, J. (1990). Abrupt visual onsets and selective attention: Voluntary versus automatic allocation. *Journal of Experimental Psychology: Human Perception and Performance, 16,* 121–134.

Yin, T.C.T., & Mountcastle, V.B. (1977). Visual input to the visuomotor mechanisms of the monkey's parietal lobe. *Science, 197,* 1381–1383.

# 17

# *Visual Attention and the Binding Problem: A Neurophysiological Perspective*

Steven J. Luck and Nancy J. Beach

A great deal of effort has been devoted to understanding the processes by which the primate visual system can identify objects, and, for reasons of simplicity and control, most studies of object perception have used stimuli presented in isolation on a blank screen. However, natural visual scenes typically contain large, complex arrays of objects, and object identification under these conditions poses special computational problems that are absent or minimized when objects are presented in isolation. This chapter will focus on one of these computational problems, namely the "binding problem," that arises when the visual system must combine the separately coded features of an object and must avoid miscombining features that arise from different objects. This problem appears to be solved, in part, by attentional processes. Recent neurophysiological studies of attention have begun to identify the specific mechanisms by which these attentional processes bind together the features of an object.

## Psychological and Neural Views of the Binding Problem

The problem of correctly binding the features of an object was brought to the forefront of attention research by the Feature Integration Theory (FIT) of Treisman and colleagues (Treisman, 1988; Treisman & Gelade, 1980; Treisman & Gormican, 1988). According to this theory, visual scenes are initially decomposed into several independent maps of primitive features, and attention is then focused onto a single location in order to bind together the features from different maps that are present at that location. Without focused attention, this theory proposes, there are no direct links between the features from different maps, and features arising from different objects may be combined together by accident. As a result, attention is necessary to prevent "illusory conjunctions" of features that belong to different objects. In contrast, this theory also proposes that the presence of activity within a feature map can be detected without attention, although the location of a feature cannot be determined without attention. Attention is therefore primarily important for tasks in which features must be localized or conjoined.

Although this theory was based on psychological considerations, many of its predictions can essentially be derived from an analysis of the response properties of neurons in visual cortex and from the transformations that occur as information about an object travels from early visual areas (such as primary visual cortex [area V1]) to the high-level object processing areas in the inferior temporal lobe (such as area TE). At the early stages, neurons typically respond to any stimulus with an appropriately oriented and coloured contour, as long as that contour is placed in a very specific location. In contrast, neurons at late stages typically respond to a relatively narrow set of more complex shapes, and will produce approximately the same response even if the low-level features that comprise the shape are changed or if the entire shape is moved to a different location (Gross & Mishkin, 1977; Ito, Tamura, Fujita, & Tanaka, 1995; Sáry, Vogels, & Orban, 1993). In other words, the representation is transformed from a set of units that code simple features at precise locations to a set of units that code more complex configurations and are relatively insensitive to small changes in low-level features and object location. This transformation is important for two reasons. First, it is important to be able to recognize an object as independent of its location, and the higher-level stages of the visual system appear to achieve this translation invariance by means of large receptive fields that lead to similar responses over a wide range of spatial locations. In addition, these large receptive fields provide an economical representation, because a separate neuron is not needed for every possible feature at every possible location.

Despite the advantages of a progressive increase in receptive field size, however, this aspect of the visual system's organization becomes problematic when multiple objects are presented concurrently, because there is no simple way to determine which of the many objects is responsible for activating a given neuron. An example of this is shown in Figure 1, which shows a set of colour-selective and orientation-selective neurons with large, overlapping receptive fields, similar to the neurons at intermediate stages of the object recognition pathway (e.g., area V4). The red-selective and vertical-selective neurons respond when a red vertical bar is presented alone, whereas the blue-selective and horizontal-selective neurons respond when a blue horizontal bar is presented alone. When both bars are presented simultaneously, all four of the neurons respond, and this output pattern could be interpreted as either a red vertical bar and a blue horizontal bar or a blue vertical bar and a red horizontal bar. Without an attentional mechanism that can bind together the features that comprise a given object, incorrect combinations of features are likely to be perceived. Thus, just as in FIT, this analysis suggests that illusory conjunctions are likely to occur in the absence of attention. In addition, attention should not be necessary when subjects are simply asked to detect the presence of a simple feature, because the feature-sensitive units give an unambiguous response about feature presence, and this parallels FIT's proposal that attention is unnecessary for feature detection. Attention should be necessary, however, in any task in which the location of a feature is relevant, such as a conjunction search task or a feature localization task.

A different solution to the binding problem would be to add a set of units that are selective for both the colour and the orientation of a given stimulus (e.g., red-vertical and green-horizontal neurons), and to use these units to code conjunctions explicitly. Indeed, the visual system contains neurons that are selective along more than one dimension (Kobatake & Tanaka, 1994), and these units could in theory be used to code conjunctions. However, Feldman (1985) has shown that the number of neurons required to implement a full-scale combinatorial system is implausibly high, even with a relatively limited set of possible feature dimensions and values on each dimension. There simply are not enough neurons in the brain to provide individual neurons for every possible combination of features. Instead, the brain appears to represent an object by the pattern of activation over a set of units that code object features (although the features may be relatively complex). As the colour-and-orientation example described above shows, however, this sort of population coding scheme is prone to errors when multiple objects must be represented simultaneously.

## The Temporal Tagging Hypothesis

There are two main classes of neural mechanisms that have been proposed for solving the binding problem. The first of these classes is, at essence, serial processing. Before discussing serial processing however, we would like to discuss briefly the second and newer proposal, which has been called the "temporal tagging" hypothesis (Niebur, Koch, & Rosin, 1993). According to this hypothesis, the units that code the features of an object are given a specific tag, and the features of different objects can then be segregated on the basis of these tags (Eckhorn, Bauer, Jordan, Brosch, Kruse, Munk, & Reitboek, 1988; Mozer, Zemel, Behrmann, & Williams, 1992; Singer & Gray, 1995). Each processing unit therefore has two values: an activation level that reflects the presence or absence of a specific feature, and a tag that indicates the object to which that feature belongs. In most models of this nature, the

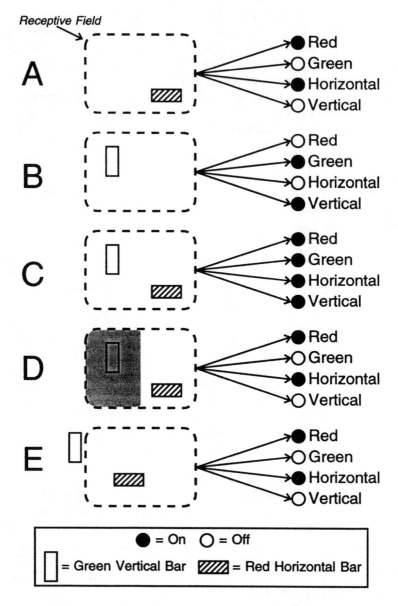

*Figure* 1: Example of how the binding problem can result from the presence of multiple stimuli within a receptive field. Each panel shows the responses of four neurons, which are assumed to have identical receptive fields (represented by the region outlined by a broken line). Each neuron codes a different feature and is represented by a circle; the circle is black if the feature is present within the receptive field and neuron is active or white if the feature is absent within the receptive field. The left half of the receptive field is shaded in panel D to represent an attention-induced suppression of information arising from that part of the receptive field.

activation level and the tag are multiplexed together in the neuron's output. That is, the mean firing rate of the neuron is taken to represent the activation level, and the temporal microstructure of the firing is used to code the tag. There are several possible ways in which the temporal microstructure could represent the tag, but recent electrophysiological studies have suggested that there may be temporal correlations between the outputs of neurons that code the same object (e.g., Eckhorn et al., 1988; Engel, König, Kreiter, & Singer, 1991; Gray, König, Engel, & Singer, 1989), and these correlations may comprise the tag. More specifically, neurons that code the same object may tend to fire at the same time, whereas neurons that code different objects would fire in an uncorrelated manner. There are several variations on this general theme, but most recent tag-based models use coincident firing to link the different units that code a given object.

The temporal tagging hypothesis has several advantages. First, it is consistent with the known neurophysiology of the visual system: there is growing evidence that neural outputs may become correlated under certain conditions, even if those neurons are in different areas of the visual cortex (Eckhorn, Schanze, Brosch, Salem, & Bauer, 1992; Nelson, Salin, Munk, Arzi, & Bullier, 1992), and there is also significant evidence that correlated activity can dynamically modulate the connections between neurons (see review by Cotman, Monaghan, & Ganong, 1988). Second, some of these models require only a modest level of correlation between any two units to achieve accurate feature binding, and a given unit may therefore be correlated with two units that are not correlated with each other, making possible a multidimensional correlation matrix. This could be useful in the processing of hierarchically organized objects, in which two subparts must be treated separately (i.e., no correlation between subparts and high correlation within each subpart), and in which the subparts must nevertheless also be treated as part of the same object (i.e., some correlation between each subpart and the representation of the whole object). A third advantage of the temporal tagging hypothesis is that it allows feature binding to operate accurately in parallel, with all the advantages that parallel processing entails. In spite of these advantages, however, temporal tagging alone is probably insufficient to solve the binding problem under realistic conditions of complex, multiple-object stimulus arrays. As the number of objects increases, the number of active units increases, and there is a dramatic increase in the probability of accidental simultaneity in the outputs of neurons that represent different objects. Determining which features belong together under such conditions would simply require too much time (see Hummel & Biederman, 1992). Thus, it seems unlikely that temporal tagging alone could solve the binding problem during the parallel processing of large, complex stimulus arrays. It should be noted, however, that temporal tagging could be combined with some additional mechanism to aid in solving the binding problem (see, e.g., Niebur et al., 1993).

Although temporal correlations probably cannot solve the binding problem at the level of object recognition, they may be important for solving a somewhat different binding problem that arises at a lower level of visual processing, as illustrated in Figure 2. At the early stages of the visual system, receptive fields are so small that a given neuron may code only a small portion of an object, and as information travels forward toward areas with larger receptive fields, it is necessary for the higher-level neurons to link inputs that correspond to different portions of an object. As shown in Figure 2A, for example, the edge of a bar might pass through several V1 receptive fields, and a neuron in area V2 might interpret the outputs of these neurons correctly as the edge of a single object. However, the overall pattern of activity across the V1 neurons would be only slightly different if two bars were present, as shown in Figure 2B, and this could lead to an incorrect interpretation in area V2. This problem could be solved by a mechanism that causes the V1 neurons that are coding the same object to fire synchronously, such that all the V1 neurons in Figure 2A would fire synchronously whereas the neurons that code the left and right objects in Figure 2B would form two groups, with synchronized firing within each group but no correlation between groups. Synchronous inputs are typically much more effective in driving a neuron, and the V2 neuron would therefore be much more likely to fire with the configuration shown in Figure 2A than with the configuration shown in Figure 2B. It should be noted that this temporal tagging mechanism would have to be fairly sophisticated to operate properly when occluding objects cause breaks in a contour, as shown in Figure 2C; in this case, the V2 neurons should respond as if the V1 neurons are being stimulated by a single object, as in Figure 2A, and not by two objects, as in Figure 2B. V2 neurons have been shown to respond to illusory contours (Peterhans & von der Heydt, 1989), which is presumably closely related to the amodal completion that is required in Figure 2C, and this level of sophistication therefore appears to be plausible even at early stages of the visual system.

What about the problem of accidental synchronizations, which makes synchronization-based binding implausible at higher levels of the visual system? Because receptive fields are relatively small in early areas such as V1 and V2, neurons in these areas rarely receive inputs from more than a few objects at one time, and the probability of an accidental synchronization is therefore relatively low. Thus, although temporal tagging appears to be unable to solve the binding problem at

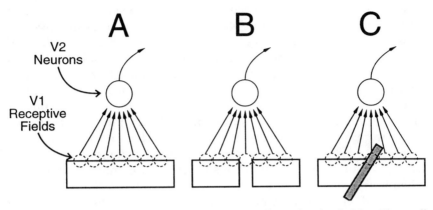

*Figure* 2: Example of the necessity of appropriate binding in low-level vision. The small broken circles represent the receptive fields of a set of V1 neurons that are selective for horizontal bars, and the large unbroken circles represent neurons in area V2 that receive inputs from the V1 neurons and code the presence or absence of a long, horizontal contour.

high levels of the visual system, this mechanism may play an important role in binding the microfeatures of objects at early stages of processing. This low-level, synchronization-based binding would then be followed by a higher-level binding process that employs some other mechanism. Consistent with this general view, Rensink and Enns (1995) have recently provided evidence indicating that low-level grouping effects occur prior to the stage at which visual search operates (see also Aks & Enns, 1992; He & Nakayama, 1992; Kleffner & Ramachandran, 1992; Treisman & Paterson, 1984).

## Selective Attention and the Suppression of Neural Responses

The most commonly proposed mechanism for solving the binding problem is to select a single object for processing at any given moment, such that the features of only the selected object can influence object recognition processes at any one time. In FIT, for example, the binding problem is solved by means of the serial application of a "focal attention" process, which is hypothesized to join together the features of the attended object. Mozer (1991) has shown that this conjunction process can be achieved by simply suppressing information arising from unattended locations and assuming that all units that remain active reflect features of a single object. This approach is shown in Figure 1D, which shows the effects of filtering out information arising from part of the receptive field. Because the outputs of the neurons reflect only one object, any active neurons must be coding the features of the same object, and the binding problem has therefore been solved. A similar hypothesis concerning the specific mechanism of attention has been described by Treisman and her colleagues (e.g., Treisman & Gormican, 1988).

According to this analysis of the binding problem, attentional suppression is necessary because neural responses are ambiguous when multiple objects are presented concurrently within the receptive field. Specifically, when multiple stimuli are present inside the receptive field of a neuron that codes a particular feature, that neuron's output indicates only the presence of the feature and not which object contains that feature. When neurons that code different features are active concurrently, it is therefore unclear which features belong together as attributes of the same object. This ambiguity is eliminated, however, when only a single stimulus is present inside the receptive field, as shown in Figure 1E. When the neuron is stimulated by only a single stimulus, the neuron's output unambiguously codes the features of that stimulus, which may completely eliminate the need for attentional suppression in that particular neuron. As will be discussed next, this surprising prediction has been verified in recordings obtained from individual neurons.

In their now-classic study of the operation of attention in macaque visual cortex, Moran and Desimone (1985) found that information arising from an ignored location was suppressed under exactly the conditions that would lead to the binding problem. Specifically, suppression of ignored information was observed in areas V4 and IT, where receptive fields are large and the potential for mislocalizing a feature is great, but was absent in areas V1 and V2, where receptive fields are small and the locations of features are coded implicitly by means of the topographic organization of these areas (see also Desimone, Wessinger, Thomas, & Schneider, 1990). Moreover, suppression was found only when both the attended and ignored locations were inside the receptive field of the neuron being studied. No suppression was observed when one stimulus was inside the receptive field and the other was outside, presumably because this minimized the opportunity for information from the two locations to be miscombined. We recently conducted a follow-up study in which these results were confirmed and extended (Luck, Chelazzi, Hillyard, & Desimone, 1997). Specifically, single-unit responses in area V4 were found to be smaller for ignored stimuli than for attended stimuli, but such effects occurred primarily when the attended and ignored stimuli were both inside the receptive field of the neuron being recorded. These effects were eliminated when the stimuli were shifted so that one stimulus remained inside the excitatory receptive field and the other was just outside (often in the neuron's inhibitory surround area). In addition, the suppression of the ignored stimulus was substantially larger when the attended and ignored stimuli were presented simultaneously rather than sequentially; the potential for miscombining features would be greater under conditions of simultaneous presentation, and so this result also supports the proposal that attentional suppression is used to mitigate the binding problem. We were also able to demonstrate attentional modulation in area V2, but only in the small subset of neurons whose receptive fields were large enough to include both the attended and ignored stimuli.

The general relationship between attentional modulation and the positions of the stimuli with respect to the receptive field is illustrated in Figure 3. This figure shows two groups of neurons with receptive fields that are slightly different, such that both of the stimuli are inside the receptive fields of one set of neurons, but only one of the stimuli is inside the receptive fields of the other set of neurons. The neurons whose receptive fields contain only one stimulus can unambiguously code the features of that stimulus, and these neurons are unaffected by attention. In contrast, the neurons whose receptive fields contain two stimuli would have ambiguous outputs in the absence of attention, which can allow their outputs to reflect primarily the features of the attended stimuli.[1]

The present analysis of the binding problem makes it seem unsurprising that large attention effects are obtained primarily when attended and ignored stimuli are presented simultaneously inside the receptive field. In some respects, however, this pattern of results is indeed quite surprising, because it implies that the visual system somehow "knows" the locations of the stimuli with respect to the receptive field borders of every cell. However, this knowledge is almost certainly implicit rather than explicit, and probably reflects competitive interactions between stimuli (see Desimone et al., 1990). For example, the parietal lobes may send a signal to area V4 indicating which location is to be attended, but this signal may have no effect on a given V4 neuron unless that neuron is receiving inputs from multiple sources, which can presumably be determined locally.

The pattern of results observed by Moran and Desimone (1985) and Luck et al. (1997) has an additional implication that should be noted. When we are identifying an object within a complex scene, we do not usually have the subjective impression that we are filtering out everything except for the object being identified, as serial processing theories would seem to imply. This may be due, in part, to the fact that only a subset of neurons within the visual system have receptive fields that include both the object being identified and other objects at the same time. For example, because receptive fields are so small in area V1, this area may be completely insensitive to the effects of attention, leading

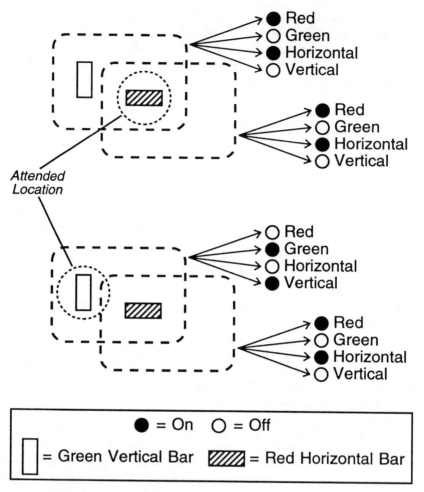

*Figure* 3: Summary of the effects of attention on single-unit responses in area V4 of extrastriate visual cortex (based on results reported by Luck et al., 1997; Moran & Desimone, 1985). When only a single stimulus is inside the receptive field, the neurons are equally responsive whether that stimulus is attended or ignored. In contrast, when two stimuli are present inside the receptive field, the outputs of the neurons primarily reflect the features of the attended stimulus.

to a complete low-level representation of the visual input no matter where attention is focused. Similarly, although attention effects have been observed in area V2 (Luck et al., 1997), very few receptive fields in this area are large enough to contain both attended and ignored stimuli, and very few V2 neurons would therefore be affected by the direction of attention at any given moment. Moreover, although most receptive fields in area V4 are large enough that they could contain both attended and ignored objects, an attended object of moderate size will generally fall within the receptive fields of only a relatively small subset of the entire population of V4 neurons. Consequently, widespread attentional suppression should typically be observed only in inferotemporal cortex where the receptive fields are so large that they almost always contain both attended and ignored objects. Thus, to the extent that our phenomenological impressions arise from multiple areas within the ventral object recognition pathway, the absence of widespread filtering in subjective experience may be explained by the finding that attention effects are limited to the subset of neurons that receive inputs from both attended and ignored stimuli. It should also be noted that attention does not completely suppress the response to ignored stimuli, even when both attended and ignored stimuli fall inside a single receptive field. This incomplete suppression of ignored objects may also contribute to our subjective impression of an unfiltered visual world.[2]

In the discussion thus far, we have stressed the importance of attention in mitigating the problems that arise when multiple stimuli are present inside a neuron's receptive field, but it should be noted that there may be conditions under which attentional filtering is necessary even when only a single stimulus falls inside the receptive field. For example, when large numbers of stimuli are presented simultaneously, ambiguities in neural coding may arise even if no two stimuli fall within the same receptive field in a given area of cortex. Evidence in support of this proposal was provided by Motter (1993), who found that attention effects could be observed in areas V1, V2, and V4 when many stimuli were presented simultaneously, even though only one stimulus fell inside the receptive field of the neuron being recorded (see also Connor, Gallant, Preddie, & Van Essen, 1996). Motter's results are somewhat difficult to interpret, however, because many cells actually showed a significantly smaller response when the stimulus inside the receptive field was attended. Additional work in this area is therefore necessary to determine the role of attention when a single stimulus falls within the receptive field.

## Attentional Suppression and Feature Coding

In the previous discussion, we assumed that visual neurons operate as linear feature detectors that simply code the presence of a particular feature and are unaffected by nonpreferred features. However, this is not a realistic assumption for the majority of neurons, especially in higher-level areas. In area TE, for example, Miller, Gochin, and Gross (1993) found that the response of a neuron to an optimal stimulus was reduced when another stimulus was presented concurrently with the optimal stimulus. We have found similar results in area V4, where a typical neuron might show a large response to a red vertical bar, little or no response to a blue horizontal bar, and an intermediate response when both bars are presented simultaneously (Luck et al., 1997). An intermediate response can also be obtained from these neurons by using stimulus features that are somewhat different from the neuron's preferred features, and the neuron's output is therefore ambiguous, being the same for an effective-ineffective pair and for a single stimulus that is not quite optimal. Attentional suppression could also be useful in eliminating this ambiguity, because presumably it would allow the neuron to respond as if only one stimulus were present.

An example of this may be found in Figure 4, which shows the response of a V4 neuron to a blue vertical bar presented alone, to a green horizontal bar presented alone, and to both stimuli presented simultaneously. This neuron gave a much larger response to the blue vertical bar than to the green horizontal bar when they were presented individually, and these responses were not strongly influenced by whether the stimulus was attended or ignored (presumably because there was little ambiguity about which features belonged to which stimulus when they were presented at different times). When these stimuli were presented simultaneously, however, the neuron's response was strongly modulated by attention. Specifically, a large response was obtained when the blue vertical bar was attended and a small response was obtained when the green horizontal bar was attended, paralleling the responses obtained when the blue and green bars were presented alone. Thus, a suppression of inputs from an ignored item may allow a neuron's output to code the features of the attended item in an unambiguous manner. In this manner, attention may influence the accuracy of feature perception in addition to aiding in the perception of conjunctions (although this would probably be important primarily for feature discriminations that are relatively subtle; see Treisman & Gormican, 1988).

## Attentional Suppression in Humans

Electrophysiological evidence for attentional suppression has also been obtained from human subjects by means of the event-related potential (ERP) technique. ERPs are electrical potentials that arise in specific brain areas during sensory, cognitive, and motor processing and are volume-conducted through the brain and skull to the scalp, where they can be recorded noninvasively from normal volunteers (see reviews by Donchin, Karis, Bashore, Coles, & Gratton, 1986; Hillyard & Picton, 1987; Näätänen, 1992). Although these potentials are less neuroanatomically precise than single-unit recordings, they can provide useful information about the effects of attention on neural and cogni-

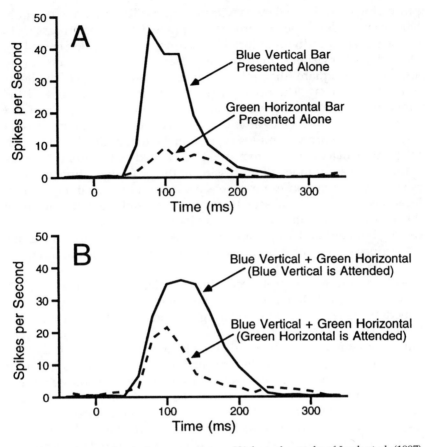

*Figure* 4: Responses of a single neuron in area V4 from the study of Luck et al. (1997). Panel A shows that this neuron gave a large response to a blue vertical bar when presented alone, but gave a small response to a green horizontal bar when presented alone. Panel B shows that the response obtained for the simultaneous presentation of both stimuli depended on which stimulus was attended. Specifically, the neuron's output to the simultaneous pair became more similar to the response to the blue vertical bar alone when attention was directed to the blue vertical bar and became more similar to the response to the green horizontal bar alone when attention was directed to the green horizontal bar

tive processes in normal human subjects without the use of expensive and potentially dangerous invasive techniques. We have conducted several ERP studies to examine sensory processing during the perception of multiple-element stimulus arrays (e.g., Luck, Fan, & Hillyard, 1993; Luck & Hillyard, 1990, 1994a, 1994b), and have found results that are generally compatible with the single-unit results described above.

In general, the ERP waveform elicited by an array reflects the processing of all items in the array, which makes it difficult to measure the processing of individual items within an array. To overcome this problem, we have developed a "probe" technique that allows processing to be measured at individual locations within an array (see Figure 5A). On each trial, a visual search array is presented, and after a short delay a small white square (the probe) is presented around one of the items in the search array. The brief delay between the array onset and the probe allows the visual system time to find a potential target item and focus attention on it. Once attention has been focused on the potential target item, the probe stimulus is presented either at that location or at the location of a distractor item. The ERP elicited by the probe stimulus is then used as an index of processing at the probed location. By comparing sensory responses for probes presented at target and nontarget locations within a visual search array, it is possible to determine how the focusing of attention onto a target location influences sensory processing both at that location and at ignored locations within the array. This approach has also been used in single-unit studies of attention (e.g., Connor et al., 1996).

An example of the probe technique is diagrammed in Figure 5A (Luck & Hillyard, 1995). In this experiment, each search array contained 16 items, 14 of which were grey and two of which were coloured. The two coloured items were selected at random from a set of four colours (red, green, blue, and purple) with the constraints that the two coloured items in a single array had to be different in colour from each other and located on opposite sides of the array. At the beginning of each trial block, subjects were told that one of the four colours would be the target colour for that block. They were then required to make a response for each array to indicate the shape of the target item (i.e., the item presented in the target colour), which could be either an upright T or an inverted T; no response was made when the target colour was absent from the array. Previous research suggested that subjects would localize and focus attention onto the target within approximately 200 ms of array onset (Luck & Hillyard, 1994b), and we therefore presented the probe stimulus 250 ms after the onset of the search array.

The probe was always presented at the location of one of the two coloured items, and the probed item was one of the following: (a) the target on half of the target-present trials; (b) the nontarget coloured item on the other half of the target-present trials; or (c) one of the two nontarget coloured items on target-absent trials. These three classes of probe trials allowed us to measure sensory processing inside the focus of attention (when the probe was at the target location), outside of the focus of attention (when the probe was on the opposite side of the array from the target), and in the absence of focused attention (when the array did not contain a target). By comparing sensory responses on these three classes of trials, we were able to make a distinction between enhanced processing within the focus of attention – which would lead to increased sensory responses at the location of the target item compared to target-absent trials – and suppressed processing outside the focus of attention – which would lead to decreased sensory responses at a location on the opposite side of the array from the relevant item compared to relevant-absent trials.

The results of this experiment are displayed in Figure 5A, which shows the amplitude of the probe-elicited P1 and N1 waves as a function of probe location. The P1 and N1 waves are stimulus-driven, exogenous visual responses that are automatically evoked by an appropriate stimulus independent of any task requirements. The P1 wave appears to be generated in lateral extrastriate cortex (Heinze et al., 1994; Mangun, Hillyard, & Luck, 1993) and typically peaks around 100 ms poststimulus. The neural origins of the N1 wave are poorly understood at present, but the N1 wave appears to arise from either the lateral extrastriate cortex or the parietal cortex, and typically peaks around 180 ms poststimulus. Both of these waves have previously been shown to be sensitive to attentional manipulations, and Figure 5A shows that they were influenced in the present experiment by the position of the probe stimulus with respect to the direction of attention. Specifically, the P1 wave was suppressed for probes presented at the location of a nontarget item when it was on the opposite side of the array from the target. Compare this to when no target was present, and attention was presumably diffusely distributed. Interestingly, there was no additional enhancement at the target location (compared to target-absent trials), which indicates that the mechanism reflected by this wave serves simply to suppress processing at ignored locations.

The N1 wave showed exactly the opposite pattern. The N1 was enhanced when the probe was presented at the location of the target compared to target-absent trials, but was not suppressed at the location of the nontarget item on the opposite side of the array from the target. Thus, the initial P1 attention effect appears to consist of a suppression of the irrelevant items, just like the single-unit attention effects observed in monkey extrastriate cortex, whereas the N1 effect appears to consist of an enhancement of the relevant item (for additional discussion of this issue, see Luck, 1995; Luck, Hillyard, Mouloua, Woldorff, Clark, & Hawkins, 1994).

In this experiment, subjects were required to discriminate the form of the relevantly coloured item, and any mislocalization of the features of the surrounding distractor items would have made accurate performance impossible. This is exactly the type of situation in which the binding problem is relevant and attentional suppression is particularly

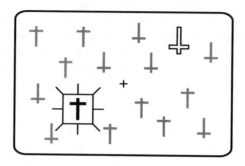

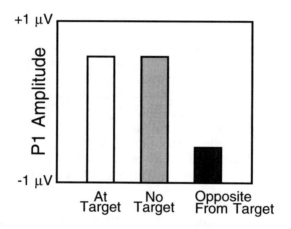

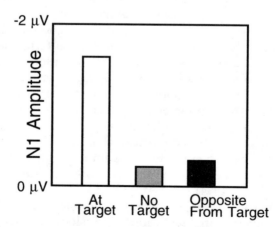

*Figure* 5A: Stimuli and results from the study of Luck and Hillyard (1995). This figure represents an experiment in which subjects were required to attend to one of four colours and press a button to indicate whether the item presented in the attended colour was an upright T or an inverted T. The probe stimulus is represented by the outline square around the black item, and was presented 250 ms after the onset of the search array.

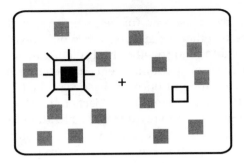

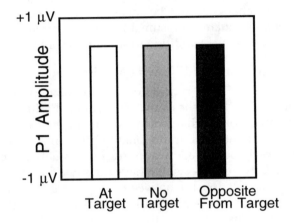

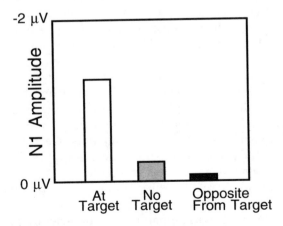

*Figure* 5B: Stimuli and results from the study of Luck and Hillyard (1995). This figure represents an experiment in which subjects were simply required to indicate whether or not the attended colour was present in each array. The probe stimulus is represented by the outline square around the black item, and was presented 250 ms after the onset of the search array.

useful. To extend this reasoning further, we conducted an additional experiment to see whether the suppression would be eliminated if we eliminated the need to bind together multiple features. To accomplish this, we used the same shape for all items in the array, and asked subjects simply to report the presence or absence of the target colour (see Figure 5B). This task did not require subjects to localize or conjoin the features of the target item, and feature mislocalizations would not have affected performance, so we predicted that the P1 suppression effect would be eliminated. As shown in Figure 2B, this prediction was confirmed. Although the P1 suppression effect was eliminated in this experiment, however, the N1 facilitation effect remained, suggesting that some attentional mechanisms may be engaged even when the binding problem has been eliminated, presumably because attentional selection serves other functions in addition to solving the binding problem.

## Limitations of Filtering Mechanisms

The single-unit and ERP experiments described above provide compelling evidence for the hypothesis that the primate brain uses a relatively simple suppression mechanism to mitigate the binding problem. However, there is a related computational problem in visual perception that cannot easily be solved by suppression; namely the problem of discriminating between objects that have the same features and differ only in the spatial relationship between the features. We call this the "relationships problem." Like the binding problem, the relationships problem arises as a consequence of the large receptive fields and feature-based coding that appear to characterize the higher levels of the primate visual system. An example of this problem is diagrammed in Figure 6, which shows the responses of a set of hypothetical neurons when a horizontal bar and a vertical bar are presented in various spatial configurations. As long as these two bars are present, the horizontal- and vertical-selective neurons will be active and it will be impossible to determine the relative positions of the bars from these neurons alone. This is a simplified example, of course, and additional low-level feature information about T-junctions, L-junctions, and terminators might allow the visual system to discriminate between these simple shapes. However, the principle illustrated here is applicable whenever the presence or absence of a set of features is not alone sufficient for object identification and the relationships among the features of an object must be perceived.

With simple stimuli such as alphanumeric characters, a suppressive process could be used to filter various parts of the receptive field, thereby allowing the visual system to determine the positions of the individual line segments (see Figure 6D). It would be very time consuming to determine the exact positions of the features in this manner,

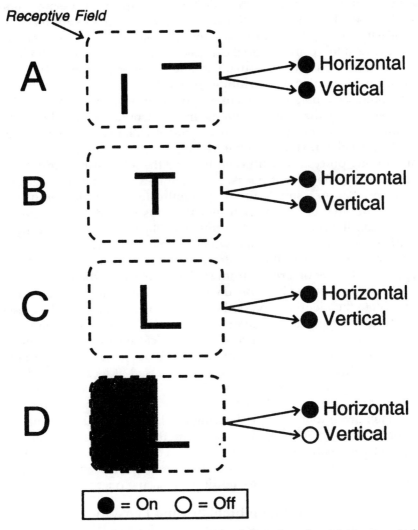

*Figure* 6: Example of the "relationships problem" that arises when it is necessary to determine the relative positions of the elements of an object. As shown in panels A, B, and C, the horizontal-selective and vertical-selective neurons are active whenever horizontal and vertical bars are present, independently of the relative positions of the bars. Figure D shows that this problem could be solved by a filtering process that allows only one line segment to be processed at a given time; note, however, that this solution does not readily "scale up" to allow the identification of more complex objects.

however, and such a mechanism could not account for the speed with which complex objects are identified. Another solution would be to use higher order processing units that code combinations of features: Indeed, it seems very likely that simple and highly familiar stimuli such as alphanumeric characters are coded by specialized processing units (see Petersen, Fox, Snyder, & Raichle, 1990). However, this approach is not feasible for a general-purpose, object recognition system, because it would lead to a combinatorial explosion in the number of processing units required to code the virtually infinite number of combinations of line segments that might constitute an object.

It would seem parsimonious to propose that the relationships problem is solved by the same attentional mechanism that solves the binding problem. According to the present analysis, however, the binding problem is solved, at least in part, by a passive filtering process, and this filtering process is insufficient to solve the relationships problem. We therefore propose that at least two separate attentional mechanisms exist, one that uses simple filtering to mitigate the binding problem, and another that uses a mechanism as yet unspecified that computes the relationships between the features of an object. One primary difference between these mechanisms would be that the filtering mechanism would be applied to locations outside the focus of attention in order to suppress information arising from irrelevant objects, whereas the second mechanism would be applied within the focus of attention in order to facilitate the identification of the attended item. Interestingly, these proposed mechanisms of unattended-location suppression and attended-location facilitation correspond quite closely to the characteristics of the P1 and N1 components in the ERP experiments described above. Specifically, the P1 wave was suppressed at locations outside the focus of attention, whereas the N1 wave was facilitated inside the focus of attention. In addition, the sequence of these waves seems appropriate, given that a simple filtering mechanism could presumably be applied more quickly than a mechanism that computes the relationships between features. Thus, there are both computational and neurophysiological reasons to believe that two separate mechanisms of spatial selective attention exist (for additional discussion, see Luck, 1995).

## The Binding Problem beyond Perception

Although much of the computational and neurophysiological work on the issue of the binding problem has been confined to visual processing, similar issues arise at all levels of the nervous system, from sensory input systems to motor output systems. For example, neurons in the frontal eye fields (FEFs) that control voluntary eye movements have "response fields" that are analogous to the receptive fields of sensory neurons, and Schall and Hanes (1993) have shown that these neurons exhibit attention effects that are analogous to the effects that have been observed in area V4. Specifically, FEF neurons respond vigorously when a to-be-fixated visual search target is within the response field, but this response is suppressed when the item inside the response field is a nontarget and the to-be-fixated item is just outside the response field. However, this suppression is not observed when the to-be-fixated target is distant from the receptive field. Thus, suppression of motor activity appears to depend on the positions of potential movement targets with respect to the response field, just as attentional suppression of sensory activity depends on the positions of stimuli with respect to the receptive field.

Similar limitations may also apply to higher level cognitive processes. For example, the limited span of short-term memory (traditionally considered to be $7 \pm 2$ items) might be a consequence of errors in binding together the various components of a representation in the presence of a large number of concurrently active representations. Indeed, Virzi and Egeth (1984) have shown that illusory conjunctions may sometimes arise at an abstract, presumably polymodal level: subjects may report having seen the word "big" presented in green ink following the presentation of the word "big" in red ink and the word "green" in blue ink. Interestingly, the parallel nature and limited span of short-term memory mirror the characteristics of correlation-based binding discussed above, suggesting that temporal tagging may play a role in short-term memory.

The binding problem may also be evident in high-level processes when subjects attempt to perform multiple tasks simultaneously, even if the individual tasks are not perceptually demanding. Specifically, it appears that some high-level processes cannot be conducted for two tasks at the same time, and these processes may be postponed for one task if another task has already engaged them (De Jong, 1993; McCann & Johnston, 1992; Osman & Moore, 1993; Pashler, 1993). This may reflect a need to separate the representations involved in each task, just as it is necessary to separate the representations of different objects during visual perception. Thus, the binding problem may not be confined to visual perception, but may be a fundamental issue throughout all levels of cognitive processing.

## Acknowledgments

We would like to thank Steve Hillyard, Bob Desimone, and Leonardo Chelazzi, who played a major role in shaping the ideas discussed in this chapter. We would also like to thank Anne Treisman, Maritta Maltio-Laine, and Steve Hillyard for providing useful comments on the manuscript. Preparation of this chapter was supported by a grant from the McDonnell-Pew Program in Cognitive Neuroscience.

## Notes

1  From results such as this, it might be tempting to suppose that there is a sudden change in the effects of attention at the border of the receptive field.

However, receptive fields do not usually have discrete edges: the response to a stimulus tends to fade away gradually as it is moved away from the center of the receptive field. As a result, a stimulus placed just inside the border of a receptive field does not have a very strong influence on the neuron and may not need to be suppressed when a location near the center of the receptive field is attended. Further research is necessary to test this prediction.

2 It should be noted that attentional suppression need not be complete in order to solve the binding problem As long as the "correct" solution has a stronger activation than the "incorrect" solution, a recognition network can usually settle on the correct solution and suppress the incorrect solutions.

# References

Aks, D.J., & Enns, J.T. (1992). Visual search for direction of shading is influenced by apparent depth. *Perception & Psychophysics, 52,* 63–74.

Connor, C.E., Gallant, J.L., Preddie, D.C., & Van Essen, D.C. (1996). Responses in area V4 depend on the spatial relationship between stimulus and attention. *Journal of Neurophysiology, 75,* 1306–1308.

Cotman, C.W., Monaghan, D.T., & Ganong, A.H. (1988). Excitatory amino acid neurotransmission: NMDA receptors and Hebb-type synaptic plasticity. *Annual Review of Neuroscience, 11,* 61–80.

De Jong, R. (1993). Multiple bottlenecks in overlapping task performance. *Journal of Experimental Psychology: Human Perception & Performance, 19,* 965–980.

Desimone, R., Wessinger, M., Thomas, L., & Schneider, W. (1990). Attentional control of visual perception: Cortical and subcortical mechanisms. *Cold Spring Harbor Symposium on Quantitative Biology, 55,* 963–971.

Donchin, E., Karis, D., Bashore, T.R., Coles, M.G.H., & Gratton, G. (1986). Cognitive psychophysiology and human information processing. In M.G.H. Coles, E. Donchin, & S.W. Porges (Eds.), *Psychophysiology: Systems, processes and applications* (pp. 244–267). New York: Guilford Press.

Eckhorn, R., Bauer, R., Jordan, W., Brosch, M., Kruse, W., Munk, M., & Reitboeck, H.J. (1988). Coherent oscillations: A mechanism of feature linking in the visual cortex. *Biological Cybernetics, 60,* 121–130.

Eckhorn, R., Schanze, T., Brosch, M., Salem, W., & Bauer, R. (1992). Stimulus-specific synchronizations in cat visual cortex: Multiple microelectrode and correlation studies from several cortical areas. In E. Basar & T.H. Bullock (Eds.), *Induced rhythms in the brain* (pp. 47– 82). Boston: Birkhauser.

Engel, A.K., König, P., Kreiter, A.K., & Singer, W. (1991). Interhemispheric synchronization of oscillatory neuronal responses in cat visual cortex. *Science, 252,* 1177–1179.

Feldman, J. (1985). Connectionist models and parallelism in high level vision. *Computer Vision, Graphics, & Image Processing, 31,* 178–200.

Gray, C.M., König, P., Engel, A.K., & Singer, W. (1989). Oscillatory responses in cat visual cortex exhibit inter-columnar synchronization which reflects global stimulus properties. *Nature, 338,* 334–337.

Gross, C.G., & Mishkin, M. (1977). The neural basis of stimulus equivalence across retinal translation. In S. Harnad, R.W. Doty, L. Goldstein, J. Jaynes, & G. Krauthamer (Eds.), *Lateralization in the nervous system* (pp. 109–122). New York: Academic Press.

He, Z.J., & Nakayama, K. (1992). Surfaces versus features in visual search. *Nature, 359*, 231–233.

Heinze, H.J., Mangun, G.R., Burchert, W., Hinrichs, H., Scholz, M., Münte, T.F., Gös, A., Scherg, M., Johannes, S., Hundeshagen, H., Gazzaniga, M.S., & Hillyard, S.A. (1994). Combined spatial and temporal imaging of brain activity during visual selective attention in humans. *Nature, 372*, 543–546.

Hillyard, S.A., & Picton, T.W. (1987). Electrophysiology of cognition. In F. Plum (Ed.), *Handbook of physiology, Section 1: The nervous system: Volume 5. Higher functions of the brain, Part 2* (pp. 519–584). Bethesda, MD: Waverly Press.

Hummel, J.E., & Biederman, I. (1992). Dynamic binding in a neural network for shape recognition. *Psychological Review, 99*, 480–517.

Ito, M., Tamura, J., Fujita, I., & Tanaka, K. (1995). Size and position invariance of neuronal responses in monkey inferotemporal cortex. *Journal of Neurophysiology, 73*, 218–226.

Kleffner, D.A., & Ramachandran, V.S. (1992). On the perception of shape from shading. *Perception & Psychophysics, 52*, 18–36.

Kobatake, E., & Tanaka, K. (1994). Neuronal selectivities to complex object features in the ventral visual pathway of the macaque cerebral cortex. *Journal of Neurophysiology, 71*, 856–867.

Luck, S.J. (1995). Multiple mechanisms of visual-spatial attention: Recent evidence from human electrophysiology. *Behavioural Brain Research, 71*, 113–123.

Luck, S.J., Chelazzi, L., Hillyard, S.A., & Desimone, R. (1997). Mechanisms of spatial selective attention in areas V1, V2, and V4 of macaque visual cortex. *Journal of Neurophysiology, 77*, 24–42.

Luck, S.J., Fan, S., & Hillyard, S.A. (1993). Attention-related modulation of sensory-evoked brain activity in a visual search task. *Journal of Cognitive Neuroscience, 5*, 188–195.

Luck, S.J., & Hillyard, S.A. (1990). Electrophysiological evidence for parallel and serial processing during visual search. *Perception & Psychophysics, 48*, 603–617.

Luck, S.J., & Hillyard, S.A. (1994a). Electrophysiological correlates of feature analysis during visual search. *Psychophysiology, 31*, 291–308.

Luck, S.J., & Hillyard, S.A. (1994b). Spatial filtering during visual search: Evidence from human electrophysiology. *Journal of Experimental Psychology: Human Perception & Performance, 20*, 1000–1014.

Luck, S.J., & Hillyard, S.A. (1995). The role of attention in feature detection and conjunction discrimination: An electrophysiological analysis. *International Journal of Neuroscience, 80*, 281–297.

Luck, S.J., Hillyard, S.A., Mouloua, M., Woldorff, M.G., Clark, V.P., & Hawkins, H.L. (1994). Effects of spatial cuing on luminance detectability: Psychophysical and electrophysiological evidence for early selection. *Journal of Experimental Psychology: Human Perception & Performance, 20*, 887–904.

Mangun, G.R., Hillyard, S.A., & Luck, S.J. (1993). Electrocortical substrates of visual selective attention. In D. Meyer & S. Kornblum (Eds.), *Attention and Performance, Vol. 14* (pp. 219–243). Cambridge, MA: MIT Press.

McCann, R.S., & Johnston, J.C. (1992). Locus of the single-channel bottleneck in dual-task interference. *Journal of Experimental Psychology: Human Perception & Performance, 18*, 471–484.

Miller, E.K., Gochin, P.M., & Gross, C.G. (1993). Suppression of visual responses of neurons in inferior temporal cortex of the awake macaque monkey by addition of a second stimulus. *Brain Research, 616,* 25–29.

Moran, J., & Desimone, R. (1985). Selective attention gates visual processing in the extrastriate cortex. *Science, 229,* 782–784.

Motter, B.C. (1993). Focal attention produces spatially selective processing in visual cortical areas V1, V2 and V4 in the presence of competing stimuli. *Journal of Neurophysiology, 70,* 909–919.

Mozer, M.C. (1991). *The perception of multiple objects.* Cambridge, MA: MIT Press.

Mozer, M.C., Zemel, R.S., Behrmann, M., & Williams, C.K. (1992). Learning to segment images using dynamic feature binding. *Neural Computation, 4,* 650–665.

Näätänen, R. (1992). *Attention and brain function.* Hillsdale, NJ: Erlbaum.

Nelson, J.I., Salin, P.A., Munk, M.H.J., Arzi, M., & Bullier, J. (1992). Spatial and temporal coherence in cortico-cortical connections: A cross-correlation study in areas 17 and 18 in the cat. *Visual Neuroscience, 9,* 21–38.

Niebur, E., Koch, C., & Rosin, C. (1993). An oscillation-based model for the neuronal basis of attention. *Vision Research, 18,* 2789–2802.

Osman, A., & Moore, C.M. (1993). The locus of dual-task interference: Psychological refractory effects on movement-related brain potentials. *Journal of Experimental Psychology: Human Perception & Performance, 19,* 1292–1312.

Pashler, H. (1993). Dual-task interference and elementary mental mechanisms. In D.E. Meyer & S. Kornblum (Eds.), *Attention and Performance Vol. 14* (pp. 245–264). Cambridge, MA: MIT Press.

Peterhans, E., & von der Heydt, R. (1989). Mechanisms of contour perception in monkey visual cortex. II. Contours bridging gaps. *Journal of Neuroscience, 9,* 1749–1763.

Petersen, S.E., Fox, P.T., Snyder, A., & Raichle, M.E. (1990). Activation of extrastriate and frontal cortical areas by visual words and word-like stimuli. *Science, 249,* 1041–1044.

Rensink, R.A., & Enns, J.T. (1995). Preemption effects in visual search: Evidence for low-level grouping. *Psychological Review, 102,* 101–130.

Sáry, G., Vogels, R., & Orban, G.A. (1993). Cue-invariant shape selectivity of macaque inferior temporal neurons. *Science, 260,* 995– 997.

Schall, J.D., & Hanes, D.P. (1993). Neural basis of saccade target selection in frontal eye field during visual search. *Nature, 366,* 467– 469.

Singer, W., & Gray, C.M. (1995). Visual feature integration and the temporal correlation hypothesis. *Annual Review of Neuroscience, 18,* 555–586.

Treisman, A. (1988). Features and objects: The Fourteenth Bartlett Memorial Lecture. *Quarterly Journal of Experimental Psychology, 40,* 201–237.

Treisman, A., & Gelade, G. (1980). A feature-integration theory of attention. *Cognitive Psychology, 12,* 97–136.

Treisman, A., & Gormican, S. (1988). Feature analysis in early vision: Evidence from search asymmetries. *Psychological Review, 95,* 15–48.

Treisman, A., & Paterson, R. (1984). Emergent features, attention, and object perception. *Journal of Experimental Psychology: Human Perception & Performance, 10,* 12–31.

Virzi, R.A., & Egeth, H.E. (1984). Is meaning implicated in illusory conjunctions? *Journal of Experimental Psychology: Human Perception & Performance, 10,* 573–580.